OXFORD STUDIES IN MODERN LEGAL HISTORY

GENERAL EDITOR

A. W. Brian Simpson
Professor of Law, University of Michigan

OXFORD STUDIES IN MODERN LEGAL HISTORY

The series aims to publish monographs of high quality and originality on legal history covering the period 1750 onwards.

FREDERICK POLLOCK AND THE ENGLISH JURISTIC TRADITION

NEIL DUXBURY

OXFORD
UNIVERSITY PRESS

This book has been printed digitally and produced in a standard specification in order to ensure its continuing availability

OXFORD
UNIVERSITY PRESS

Great Clarendon Street, Oxford OX2 6DP

Oxford University Press is a department of the University of Oxford.
It furthers the University's objective of excellence in research, scholarship, and education by publishing worldwide in

Oxford New York

Auckland Cape Town Dar es Salaam Hong Kong Karachi
Kuala Lumpur Madrid Melbourne Mexico City Nairobi
New Delhi Shanghai Taipei Toronto

With offices in

Argentina Austria Brazil Chile Czech Republic France Greece
Guatemala Hungary Italy Japan South Korea Poland Portugal
Singapore Switzerland Thailand Turkey Ukraine Vietnam

Oxford is a registered trade mark of Oxford University Press in the UK and in certain other countries

Published in the United States by Oxford University Press Inc., New York

Reprinted 2011

ISBN 978-0-19-927022-4

Printed and bound in Great Britain by CPI Antony Rowe, Chippenham and Eastbourne

For Alice, Rebecca, Martin, and Simon

I was more interested in the stories of the solitary chemistry, unarmed and on foot, at the measure of man, which with few exceptions has been mine: but it has also been the chemistry of the founders, who did not work in teams but alone, surrounded by the indifference of their time, generally without profit, and who confronted matter without aids, with their brains and hands, reason and imagination.

Primo Levi

GENERAL EDITOR'S PREFACE

Every educated lawyer in the common law world, and many outside it, knows something about Frederick Pollock, as a correspondent with Holmes, as a treatise writer, as a somewhat second rate collaborator with Maitland, and as the long time editor both of the *Law Quarterly Review* and of the Law Reports. When I was working in Oxford Pollock remained present as a ghostly figure, being listed in the University Statutes as late as the 1960s as one of the electors for the Chair of Legal History, which had by then been converted into a Chair of Jurisprudence; a footnote helpfully explained that he had died in 1937. One could only suppose that he remained available for consultation from the other side. There is a consensus that he was an important and significant jurist, whatever that means, but perhaps someone who was not quite in the same class as such great figures as Maine or Maitland or Dicey. And since his career was spent partly in the academy, and partly at the Inns of Court, he seemed, somehow, to be neither fish nor fowl.

Precisely what Pollock's significance was, and in what way he bridged the gulf between the world of the legal practitioners and the world of scholarship, have remained obscure. What we have lacked is a study of his work which locates him in the history of the common law tradition. In this book, which represents a new departure for the *Oxford Studies in Modern Legal History*, Neil Duxbury has set out to fill this serious gap in the literature.

The book is not in a conventional sense a biography, though it does relate Pollock's work and writings to his curious career. Instead it is a study in the history of legal thought, in which Pollock's writings, and somewhat elusive theoretical ideas, are analysed and related to wider themes. It is a pleasure to welcome it into this series.

A. W. Brian Simpson
June 2004

ACKNOWLEDGEMENTS

This book is not a biography. While it obviously has a biographical element, it is first and foremost an exercise in intellectual history. It is also a compromise. Around a decade ago I wrote another book, about American jurisprudence from the late nineteenth century to the late twentieth. The project was fuelled by chutzpah—half of it was written before I had ever set foot in the United States—and was great fun to write because I never really appreciated the scale of the task. Once the project was completed I tried to begin work on a book about English legal thought throughout roughly the same period. In this instance, however, I did appreciate the scale of the task. It seemed bigger, more difficult to outline, far more labyrinthine, than the American project had been; and there was no similarly vast body of readily accessible collected literature akin to the American law reviews that could be easily called upon over and again for information and inspiration. I started to chip away at the project, but soon realized that there would be no grand book, that the work would have to be done in instalments.

This book is the main instalment to date. It has at its heart the life and work of Frederick Pollock, one of the most important—although also one of the more neglected—jurists of the modern common law tradition. Initially I was disinclined to accord Pollock much attention: there seemed to be a fairly obvious message in the fact that legal historians had not bothered all that much with him. Yet the more I encountered Pollock the more he puzzled me. In particular, it seemed odd that there should be so many statements about the greatness of the man and yet so little effort to tackle his work at length. After a while, however, this absence of effort started to make sense. Pollock's writing is—just as, in life, Pollock reputedly was—difficult to engage with: one usually has to dig deep to find his opinions, which will often come with a string of provisos attached; he never set out his stall in a key text; his preoccupations can seem archaic; perhaps most significantly, he was not a juristic pioneer in the mould of, say, Holmes, Maitland, or Dicey. Increasingly it became clear that Pollock was an intriguing juristic figure because his failures could prove significant—this seemed especially to be the case in the realm of jurisprudence—and because his successes were often complicated and unconventional. Some rudimentary questions started to emerge. What did Pollock contribute to the development of law as a university subject? Was he, at heart, an academic lawyer? Did he have an identifiable perspective on law? What does it mean to say—as so many commentators do say—that his treatises on contract and torts mark the move to a modern, principle-oriented tradition of juristic inquiry? Is there anything significant about the fact that he did a great deal of editing?

If readers consider that I have made a hash of addressing these questions, I can hardly complain that nobody tried to advise me on how to tackle them properly. Papers based on chapters of this book have been presented at the American Bar Foundation, Chicago; the Benjamin N. Cardozo School of Law, New York; the Institute of United States Studies, London; Northwestern University Law School, Chicago; University College London; Vanderbilt University Law School, Nashville; Wayne State University Law School, Detroit; and at the law schools of the universities of Manchester, Michigan, and Virginia. The benefit from these occasions has tended to come not on the day of the talk but two or three days later—this being how long it usually takes me to formulate the answer I should have given to most research-related questions. That difficult questions were asked in the first place is what matters most, and so I wish to express my thanks to all those scholars who attended these events and took my work so seriously.

I am also grateful to the following people for providing feedback on draft chapters and, in certain instances, for help with specific research queries: Paul Baker, Brian Bix, Rodney Brazier, Roger Brownsword, Hazel Carty, John Cobbett, Hugh Collins, Robert Cryer, Barry Cushman, Richard Francks, John Goldberg, Andrew Griffiths, Andrew Halpin, Stephen Hardy, Guy Holborn, John Hostler, David Ibbetson, Bruce Kimball, Nicola Lacey, Martin Loughlin, William Lucy, John Murphy, Jeffrey O'Connell, Sallyanne Payton, Richard Posner, Alan Rodger, John Henry Schlegel, Philip Schofield, Nigel Simmonds, Aviam Soifer, David Sugarman, Michael Taggart, Stephen Waddams, Jules Winterton, and Christian Witting. I owe especial thanks to Matthew Kramer, Anthony Ogus, Mike Redmayne, and Ted White—each of whom commented on virtually all of the manuscript—and also to Brian Simpson for the same and for accepting the book within the *Oxford Studies in Modern Legal History* series.

During the writing of this project I have benefited from the help of four first-rate law librarians: Janet Hirt at Vanderbilt, Cathy Palombi and Micheal Klepper at Virginia, and, last but certainly not least, Sue Bate at Manchester. More generally, I am grateful for help to the staff of the following archives and libraries: the Alderman Library and the Law School Library, University of Virginia; the Alpine Club Library, London; the American Jewish Archives, Cincinnati, Ohio; the British Library; the British Library of Political and Economic Science; the Department of Special Collections and Western Manuscripts, Bodleian Library, Oxford; the Brymnor Jones Library, University of Hull; Cambridge University Library; the Charles E. Young Research Library, University of California; Churchill College Library, Cambridge; the Special Collections Department, Glasgow University Library; the Harvard

Law School Library; the Harvard University Archives; the House of Lords Record Office; the library of the Institute of Advanced Legal Studies, London; Lincoln's Inn Library; the Macmillan Archive, Basingstoke; the Alyce Queener Massey Law Library, Vanderbilt University; the University of Michigan Law School Library; the John Murray Archive, London; the Pritzker Legal Research Center, Northwestern University School of Law; the John Rylands Library, University of Manchester; University College London Library; the library of the School of Oriental and African Studies, London; the Squire Law Library, Cambridge; the West Yorkshire Archive Service, Bradford; and the Wren Library, Cambridge. The British Academy generously awarded me a small research grant which covered costs for most of the archival work. The School of Law at the University of Manchester and Institute of Advanced Legal Studies—where I was a non-residential Visiting Senior Research Fellow from May 2000 to May 2003—were also kind enough to help with research expenses.

Completing this book was made easier by virtue of a year-long sabbatical: leave for one semester was awarded by the University of Manchester and for the other by the Arts and Humanities Research Board. I am grateful both to my colleagues and to the AHRB for this privilege. Having so much time to write can, of course, be a mixed blessing—one thinks of Jack Nicholson's character in *The Shining*—but I was fortunate to be able to interrupt my period of leave with two short teaching stints, one at Vanderbilt University Law School and the other at the School of Law at the University of Virginia. I have been lucky enough to receive numerous invitations to the latter institution since the first time I presented a paper there in April 1994. This book, more than any other project I have worked on, owes a great deal to my occasional colleagues and the wonderful research environment at Virginia. Among the staff there, I should like to express particular thanks to Barry Cushman and Ted White—not only for their hospitality, but also for providing me with some insight into how historians think and work.

An earlier version of chapter 3—with bits taken out and parts of chapter 2 mixed in—appears in (2005) 57 *Current Legal Problems*. Chapters 2, 4, and 6 contain modified excerpts from my 'When We Were Young: Notes in the *Law Quarterly Review*, 1885–1925' (2000) 106 *Law Quarterly Review* 474–503. I am grateful to Michael Freeman and the Oxford University Press in the first instance and to Francis Reynolds in the second for permissions to republish.

Neil Duxbury
Manchester
January 2004

CONTENTS

List of Illustrations xvii
Manuscript Sources xix
Abbreviated Works xxi

1. INTRODUCTION 1

2. 'F. P.' 13
   i. Formative years 13
   ii. The talkative profession 30
   iii. Candour and character 37
   iv. University law 41
   v. After Oxford 64
   vi. Concluding reflections 79

3. WHY ENGLISH JURISPRUDENCE IS ANALYTICAL 85
   i. Cul-de-sac 91
   ii. *Rechtswissenschaft*, English-style 97
      a. The utility of analysis 106
      b. The centrality of comparison 110
      c. The reliance on science 116
   iii. The path of modern jurisprudence 127
   iv. Conclusion 137

4. THE SANCTIFICATION OF THE COMMON LAW 139
   i. Authority and reason 142
   ii. The qualities of the common law 147
   iii. Reason, common sense, and principle 156
   iv. The lady's servants 167
   v. Legislation 169
   vi. Politics 174
   vii. Conclusion 180

5. JURISTS' LAW 184
i. Contract 189
a. Conceptualizing contract 191
b. Offer, acceptance, and consideration 201
c. Mutual promises 208
d. Good faith 215
ii. Torts 224
a. The natural law backdrop 227
b. The forms of action 232
c. A law of torts 235
1. Compartmentalization 236
2. A family of principles 248
3. At the head of the family 262
d. Torts of intention 270
iii. Conclusion 279

6. EDITORSHIPS 284
i. Money 289
ii. The Law Reports 294
iii. The *Law Quarterly Review* 309
iv. Concluding observations 322

7. EPILOGUE 324

Index 329

LIST OF ILLUSTRATIONS

Plate section between pp. 160–161.

1. Sir Frederick Pollock, by Harry Furniss. (*National Portrait Gallery, London*)
2. Great Court, Trinity College Cambridge, 1860s. (Adv. Alb. 23, p. 8, *courtesy of the Masters and Fellows of Trinity College Cambridge*)
3. Bronze bust of F. W. Maitland. (*Courtesy of Professor Sir John Baker*)
4. Interior of Lincoln's Inn Library, 1917. (*Courtesy of the Treasurer and Masters of the Bench of Lincoln's Inn*)
5. James Shaw Willes. (*Courtesy of the Treasurer and Masters of the Bench of Lincoln's Inn*)
6. Nathaniel Lindley. (*Courtesy of the Treasurer and Masters of the Bench of Lincoln's Inn*)
7. Oliver Wendell Holmes, Jr, 1909. (*Courtesy of Art and Visual Materials, Special Collections Department, Harvard Law School Library*)
8. Sir Courtenay Peregrine Ilbert, by Sydney Prior Hall. (*National Portrait Gallery, London*)
9. Corpus Christi College, Oxford, *c.*1900. (GA Oxon. 6. 18. p. 19, *Bodleian Library, University of Oxford*)
10. Frederick Pollock at work. (*Courtesy of the Treasurer and Masters of the Bench of Lincoln's Inn*)

MANUSCRIPT SOURCES

In preparing this study, I have made use of the following collections (citatory details are provided at appropriate points in the footnotes):

James Barr Ames correspondence (1872–1910), Special Collections, Harvard Law School Library, Langdell Hall, Cambridge, Mass.

W. Paley Baildon papers, West Yorkshire Archive Service, Bradford.

Robert Seymour Bridges correspondence, Department of Special Collections and Western Manuscripts (Modern Papers), Bodleian Library, Oxford.

British Museum Reading Room papers, Manuscript Collections, British Library.

James Bryce papers, Department of Special Collections and Western Manuscripts (Modern Papers), Bodleian Library, Oxford.

J. R. M. Butler papers, Trinity College Library, Cambridge.

Albert Venn Dicey correspondence and papers, Special Collections Department, Glasgow University Library.

Charles W. Eliot papers, Harvard University Archives.

Esher papers—William Johnson letters, Churchill College Library, Cambridge.

E. A. Freeman papers, John Rylands Library, Special Collections, University of Manchester.

Arthur Lehman Goodhart papers, Department of Special Collections and Western Manuscripts (Modern Papers), Bodleian Library, Oxford.

Oliver Wendell Holmes papers, Special Collections, Harvard Law School Library, Langdell Hall, Cambridge, Mass.

John Knox papers, Special Collections Department, Alderman Library, University of Virginia, Charlottesville, Va.

Macmillan Archive (vol. ccxcviii), Manuscript Collections, British Library.

Frederic William Maitland papers, Department of Manuscripts and University Archives, Cambridge University Library.

Adolph S. Oko papers, American Jewish Archives, Cincinnati, Ohio.

Frederick Pollock correspondence, Special Collections, Harvard Law School Library, Langdell Hall, Cambridge, Mass.

Frederick Pollock correspondence (Appointments. 1882: Jurisprudence), Special Collections, University College London Library.

Frederick Pollock correspondence (Murray), John Murray Archive, 50 Albemarle Street, London, W1S 4BD.

Frederick Pollock correspondence (Wren), Trinity College Library, Cambridge.

Sir Frederick Pollock manuscripts (1883–*c.*1936), Department of Special Collections and Western Manuscripts (Modern Papers), Bodleian Library, Oxford.

Frederick Pollock notebooks, Lincoln's Inn Library, London.

Roscoe Pound papers, Special Collections, Harvard Law School Library, Langdell Hall, Cambridge, Mass.

President's papers: Charles William Eliot, Harvard University Archives, Cambridge, Mass.

Herbert Samuel papers, Parliamentary Archives, House of Lords Record Office, London.

Ferdinand Canning Scott Schiller papers, Department of Special Collections, Charles E. Young Research Library, University of California, Los Angeles.

G. L. Strachey papers (20th Century Series, vol. xxxvii), Manuscript Collections, British Library.

John Tyndall papers (vol. i), Manuscript Collections, British Library.

Material from the Public Record Office of the National Archives is referred to by class—which, in all instances in this study, is T (indicating that the Treasury Board was the department of origin)—followed by item number.

ABBREVIATED WORKS

In this study, the following works by Pollock are abbreviated thus:

DLP	*A Digest of the Law of Partnership*, 1st edn. (London: Stevens & Sons, 1877).
DLP(2)	*A Digest of the Law of Partnership*, 2nd edn. (London: Stevens & Sons, 1880).
DLP(4)	*A Digest of the Law of Partnership*, 4th edn. (London: Stevens & Sons, 1888).
DLP(5)	*A Digest of the Law of Partnership, Incorporating the Partnership Act, 1890*, 5th edn. (London: Stevens & Sons, 1890).
ECL	*The Expansion of the Common Law* (London: Stevens & Sons, 1904).
EIL	*Essays in the Law* (London: Macmillan, 1922).
EJE	*Essays in Jurisprudence and Ethics* (London: Macmillan, 1882).
EL	(with Ella Fuller Maitland) *The Etchingham Letters* (New York: Dodd, Mead, & Co., 1899).
EOD	*English Opportunities and Duties in the Historical and Comparative Study of Law* (London: Macmillan, 1883).
FBJ	*A First Book of Jurisprudence for Students of the Common Law* (London: Macmillan, 1896).
FL	*The Fishery Laws* (London: Clowes, 1883).
FMG	*For My Grandson: Remembrances of an Ancient Victorian* (London: Murray, 1933).
GCL	*The Genius of the Common Law* (New York: Columbia UP, 1912).
HEL	(with Frederic William Maitland) *The History of English Law Before the Time of Edward I*, 2 vols., 2nd edn. S. F. C. Milsom (Cambridge: Cambridge UP, 1968 [1898]).
ICA	(with Dinshah Mulla) *Indian Contract Act and Specific Relief Act*, 1st edn. (London: Sweet & Maxwell, 1905).
IHSP	*An Introduction to the History of the Science of Politics*, 2nd edn. (London: Macmillan, 1911).
JLE	*Jurisprudence and Legal Essays* (London: Macmillan, 1961).
LCDE	*Leading Cases Done into English, and Other Diversions* (London: Macmillan, 1892. An earlier edition, without the 'other diversions', first appeared in 1876).
LFM	*The Law of Fraud, Misrepresentation and Mistake in British India* (London: Thacker, 1894).
LL	*The Land Laws* (London: Macmillan, 1883).
LL(3)	*The Land Laws*, 3rd edn. (London: Macmillan, 1896).
LN	*The League of Nations* (London: Stevens & Sons, 1920).
LN(2)	*The League of Nations*, 2nd edn. (London: Stevens & Sons, 1922).

LNCR	*The League of Nations and the Coming Rule of Law* (London: Oxford UP, 1918).
OL	*Outside the Law: Diversions Partly Serious* (Kensington: Cayme Press, 1927).
OLOD	*Oxford Lectures and Other Discourses* (London: Macmillan, 1890).
PCL	(with R. S. Wright) *An Essay on Possession in the Common Law* (Oxford: Clarendon Press, 1888).
PCLE	*Principles of Contract at Law and in Equity: Being a Treatise on the General Principles Concerning the Validity of Agreements, With a Special View to the Comparison of Law and Equity, and With References to the Indian Contract Act, and Occasionally to Roman, American, and Continental Law* (London: Stevens & Sons, 1876).
PCLE(2)	*Principles of Contract*, 2nd edn. (London: Stevens & Sons, 1878).
PCLE(3)	*Principles of Contract*, 3rd edn. (London: Stevens & Sons, 1881).
PCLE(4)	*Principles of Contract*, 4th edn. (London: Stevens & Sons, 1885).
PCLE(5)	*Principles of Contract*, 5th edn. (London: Stevens & Sons, 1889).
PCLE(6)	*Principles of Contract*, 6th edn. (London: Stevens & Sons, 1894).
PCLE(7)	*Principles of Contract*, 7th edn. (London: Stevens & Sons, 1902).
PCLE(8)	*Principles of Contract*, 8th edn. (London: Stevens & Sons, 1911).
PCLE(9)	*Principles of Contract*, 9th edn. (London: Stevens & Sons, 1921).
PHL	*The Pollock–Holmes Letters: Correspondence of Sir Frederick Pollock and Mr Justice Holmes 1874–1932*, 2 vols., ed. M. DeWolfe Howe (Cambridge: Cambridge UP, 1942).
S	*Spinoza* (London: Duckworth, 1935).
SHLP	*Spinoza: His Life and Philosophy*, 2nd edn. (London: Duckworth, 1899).
TLT	*The Law of Torts: A Treatise on the Principles of Obligations Arising from Civil Wrongs in the Common Law* (London: Stevens & Sons, 1887).
TLT(2)	*The Law of Torts: A Treatise on the Principles of Obligations Arising from Civil Wrongs in the Common Law, to which is added the Draft of a Code of Civil Wrongs Prepared for the Government of India*, 2nd edn. (London: Stevens & Sons, 1890).
TLT(3)	*The Law of Torts*, 3rd edn. (London: Stevens & Sons, 1892).
TLT(5)	*The Law of Torts*, 5th edn. (London: Stevens & Sons, 1897).
TLT(6)	*The Law of Torts*, 6th edn. (London: Stevens & Sons, 1901).
TLT(7)	*The Law of Torts*, 7th edn. (London: Stevens & Sons, 1904).
TLT(8)	*The Law of Torts*, 8th edn. (London: Stevens & Sons, 1908).
TLT(10)	*The Law of Torts*, 10th edn. (London: Stevens & Sons, 1916).
TLT(11)	*The Law of Torts*, 11th edn. (London: Stevens & Sons, 1920).
TLT(12)	*The Law of Torts*, 12th edn. (London: Stevens & Sons, 1923).
TLT(13)	*The Law of Torts*, 13th edn. (London: Stevens & Sons, 1929).
TLT(14)	*Pollock's Law of Torts: A Treatise on the Principles of Obligations Arising from Civil Wrongs in the Common Law*, 14th edn. P. A. Landon (London: Stevens & Sons, 1939).

Where I have cited unsigned notes in the *Law Quarterly Review*, it should be assumed in the absence of contrary indication that Pollock is the author; likewise with the citation of letters to *The Times*.

1

INTRODUCTION

> Ever since the Renaissance, until quite recent days, all Englishmen who received a humanist education were brought up to be familiar with Horace's poems and think of him almost as one of themselves. The fashion is gone or going out; I am old enough to regret it. . . .[1]

Most of Frederick Pollock's public expressions of regret concern failures of law. As the Editor of the *Law Quarterly Review* from 1884 to 1919, Pollock turned regret—as in: 'It is to be regretted that the learned judge did not produce a more thoughtful opinion'—into a form of art.[2] But in the quotation above, taken from his final book, we find him regretting not some species of legal slovenliness but the passing of an era. Pollock was, as various commentators have noted and he himself admitted, a Victorian to the tips of his fingers.[3] While he was neither narrow-minded nor prone to nostalgia, the world upon which he looked in 1935, two years before his death, would probably have caused him considerable sadness. Away from the law Pollock had numerous interests and hobby horses (as sundry letters to *The Times* attest),[4] but it was only during the latter decades of his life that he became dedicated to a cause that suggested he was in any way a public moralist.[5]

[1] Pollock, *S* 140.

[2] See Neil Duxbury, 'When We Were Young: Notes in the *Law Quarterly Review*, 1885–1925' (2000) 116 *LQR* 474–503 at 500–2.

[3] See, e.g., *FMG* vi; Sir John Pollock, *Time's Chariot* (London: Murray, 1950), 49–50; and cf. A. L. Goodhart, 'Introduction', in *JLE* ix–xlviii at xlviii. When the portraitist Walter Tittle visited Pollock's home in the mid-1920s he found both the house and his host to be throwbacks to the late-Victorian period: see Walter Tittle, 'Portraits in Pencil and Pen' (May–October 1924) 108 *Century Magazine* 497–512, 641–56, 785–800 at 796.

[4] Many of Pollock's extra-legal activities and interests are noted in Lord Wright, 'Pollock, Sir Frederick, Third Baronet 1845–1937', in *DNB (1931–1940)*, 711–13. For illustrations of Pollock's efforts at literary criticism, prose, and verse, see Frederick Pollock, 'John Milton' (1890) n.s. 48 *Fortnightly Rev.* 510–19; 'The Choice of Churches' (1882) n.s. 31 *Fortnightly Rev.* 651–4 (verse); *LCDE* (also 'The Six Carpenters' Case' (1895) 18 *New Jersey L. J.* 287 (verse)); 'Sir Michael: A Fantasy on an Altar-Piece of Perugino' (1891–2) 65 *Macmillan's Magazine* 302–11 (short story); also the majority of the pieces that make up *OL*; and his epistolary novel, co-authored with Ella Fuller (no relation to F. W.) Maitland, *EL* (on which see *FMG* 83 and Pollock to Holmes, 22 February 1899, in *PHL* i. 91–2).

[5] It is worth noting that Stefan Collini's *Public Moralists: Political Thought and Public Life in Britain 1850–1930* (Oxford: Clarendon Press, 1991), although it contains a chapter on the Victorian jurist as

Resisting Germany had been one of Pollock's favourite public subjects during the First World War.[6] Between 1915 and 1917 he was a strident (though not always the most welcome) supporter of Sir Francis Younghusband's anti-pacifist, anti-German, and fiercely patriotic 'Fight for Right' movement[7]; and as a member of James Bryce's commission (established in September 1914) investigating alleged German atrocities in Belgium, he acquired a reputation as 'a "fire eater"' who was 'ready to read the evidence [concerning the alleged atrocities] in a manner most damaging to the reputation of the German army.'[8] After the War, Pollock became an optimistic supporter of the idea that long-term peace could be secured through the work of the League of Nations.[9] But he saw that initiative fail. With the advantage of hindsight, his earnest efforts to explain how the Covenant of the League of Nations could be implemented 'make melancholy reading'.[10] 'When the Protocol of Geneva was rejected in 1924,' Hazeltine remarks, 'he considered that the usefulness of the League in major matters was ended.'[11] Even Pollock's son—who offers a rosy portrait of his father's 'unshakable optimism'—confesses to being happy that his father should not have lived to see the outbreak of the Second World War.[12]

public moralist, features Pollock only peripherally. Unlike, say, Henry Maine, James Fitzjames Stephen, or A. V. Dicey, Pollock did not attempt to address his work to the fundamental cultural and political issues of the day; as with Maitland and Austin, 'his professional "voice"'—to use Collini's words about the former—'did not easily lend itself to direct participation in political debate' (ibid. 303–4). This is not to claim that Pollock's voice failed entirely to lend itself to such debate, only that, generally speaking, his writings do not conform to the style of those which Collini associates with public moralism.

6 See, e.g., Sir Frederick Pollock, *German 'Truth' and European Facts about the War* (London: The Central Committee for National Patriotic Organizations, 1915); (1916) 32 *LQR* 351; *The Times* (letter), 7 March 1917, 7, col. C.

7 For Pollock's anti-pacifism, see W. C. Lubenow, *The Cambridge Apostles, 1820–1914: Liberalism, Imagination, and Friendship in British Intellectual and Professional Life* (Cambridge: Cambridge UP, 1998), 194; and for his ill-starred involvement in the Fight for Right movement, see Patrick French, *Younghusband: The Last Great Imperial Adventurer* (London: HarperCollins, 1994), 299, 307–8, and A. W. Brian Simpson, *Human Rights and the End of Empire: Britain and the Genesis of the European Convention* (Oxford: Oxford UP, 2001), 161–7. Pollock looked more fondly upon the movement than perhaps many of its members did upon him: see, e.g., Frederick Pollock to R. Bridges, 26 November 1918, in Bridges correspondence, Dep. Bridges 113 ff.136–7 ('I was sorry for the rather abrupt end of the Fight for Right movement last winter, but it was quite inevitable, indeed the War Aims Committee was almost a deus ex machina to get us decently off the stage').

8 Stuart Wallace, *War and the Image of Germany: British Academics 1914–1918* (Edinburgh: Donald, 1988), 180. On the founding and composition of the Bryce Commission, see ibid. 176–7; also H. A. L. Fisher, *James Bryce*, 2 vols. (New York: Macmillan, 1927), ii. 132–3.

9 See *LNCR*; *LN*; *LN(2)*; (1918) 34 *LQR* 113–14; 'The Permanent Court of International Justice' (1926) 7 *British Yearbook of International Law* 135–40; Pollock to Holmes, 11 April 1920, in *PHL* ii. 40; *The Times* (letters), 1 January 1917, 9, col. C; 2 April 1918, 4, col. C. *LN* is a remarkably optimistic essay (see, e.g., 83) which concludes on a distinctly upbeat note (175–6) about which Pollock seems rather self-conscious at *LN(2)* 193.

10 See Goodhart, above n.3, xx; and cf. *LN* 112–60; *LN(2)* 117–70.

11 H. D. Hazeltine, 'Sir Frederick Pollock, Bart., 1845–1937' (1949) 35 *Proc. Brit. Acad.* 233–56 at 249.

12 John Pollock, *Time's Chariot*, above n.3, 249, 126; and cf. *The Times* (letters), 17 October 1933, 15, col. E; 15 May 1935, 15, col. E; 18 May 1936, 15, col. E; *FMG*, 124–5, 202.

Building upon this last paragraph, we could conveniently and quite easily concoct an image of Pollock as a man who strove in vain, whose hopes and visions were consigned to a bygone age. Transforming that image into a juristic assessment would probably not be all that difficult. After all, who reads Pollock nowadays? His juristic longevity fails so much as to compare with that of his friend, Oliver Wendell Holmes, and various other Victorian jurists have enjoyed considerably more staying-power: Dicey, Maine, Maitland, Austin, and Fitzjames Stephen have all been subjected to the type of detailed academic scrutiny that has not been accorded to Pollock. By no means is it surprising to find one legal historian describing Pollock as 'a fossil from an earlier legal era', whose work 'has been consigned to jurisprudential oblivion.'[13] As a legal writer, he appeared hardly interested in trying to demonstrate flair or evoke charisma. Occasionally we see a wonderfully dry humour at work, but so too we find dry pedantry.[14] Dryness in its least appealing sense seems to have been, for him, a fair price to pay in the effort to ensure analytical precision, to uncover nuance, to question easy conclusions and winner's history, and to promote general scholarly good sense. Pollock's epithets rarely have that collar-grabbing, fortune-cookie quality so often associated with many of Holmes's,[15] and it is noticeable in the correspondence between the two men that Pollock's letters, while generally the more learned and less self-absorbed, contain no sound-bites provoking reaction as has, say, 'all I mean by truth is what I can't help thinking'[16] or, 'I look on man as a cosmic ganglion.'[17] The thesis that classic texts often become so because they are ambiguous in a manner that elicits exegesis rather than exasperation may go some way to explaining both the popularity of Holmes and the relative insignificance of Pollock.[18] For Pollock always endeavoured to be clear. In so far as he was ever unclear, it was usually qualification and circumlocution that got the better of him. Indeed, like his fellow Cambridge Apostle, Henry Sidgwick, Pollock

[13] Richard A. Cosgrove, *Our Lady the Common Law: An Anglo-American Legal Community, 1870–1930* (New York: New York UP, 1987), 156, 134.

[14] For illustrations of the humour, see, e.g., *EJE* 199; *OLOD* 106; *SHLP* 13, 302 (on 'that unhappy would-be philosophical phrase of Ulpian's "ius quod natura omnia animalia docuit" which Justinian's commissioners preserved for the confusion of many generations'). For pedantry, see, e.g., *EJE* 11, 16–17, 50; F[rederick] P[ollock], review of T. Baty, *Polarized Law* (1915) 31 *LQR* 106–7 at 106; and cf. *FMG* 189.

[15] See, e.g., *EJE* 377 ('History is fertilized by analysis, and analysis is guided by history, but each works in its own way').

[16] Holmes to Pollock, 27 October 1901, 23 June 1906, 17 June 1908, in *PHL* i. 100, 126, 139, 182. For reaction to which see, e.g., Francis E. Lucey, 'Holmes—Liberal—Humanitarian—Believer in Democracy?' (1951) 39 *Georgetown L. J.* 523–62 at 531–3.

[17] Holmes to Pollock, 28 July 1911, in *PHL* i. 182. For reaction to which see, e.g., Paul L. Gregg, 'The Pragmatism of Mr Justice Holmes' (1943) 31 *Georgetown L. J.* 262–95 at 268–74; also cf. John C. Ford, 'The Fundamentals of Holmes' Juristic Philosophy' (1942) 11 *Fordham L. Rev.* 255–78 at 268–9.

[18] For the general thesis, see Conal Condren, *The Status and Appraisal of Classic Texts: An Essay on Political Theory, Its Inheritance, and the History of Ideas* (Princeton, NJ: Princeton UP, 1985), 171–252.

was a dab hand at qualifying an argument.[19] Not that he would have considered this a fault. Simple truths, Pollock insisted, often require complex articulation.[20]

Throughout Pollock's work there runs the image of the scholar as labourer, toiling to produce something fruitful (like many others, Pollock was keen on the image of good scholarship 'bearing fruits').[21] At times, he seemed to value the toil as much as the fruits: our ancestors may have provided accounts of the law which were often wrong, he was fond of noting, but they ought to be commended at least for trying and for leaving us with something to endeavour to rectify.[22] Fulfilment in scholarship comes from this endeavour, from the effort to get it—whatever 'it' happens to be—right.[23] Juristic inquiry has no need for fashions, partisanship, or any other contrivance; for what we ultimately value is the open-minded pursuit of truth.[24] 'Disinterested searching after truth has, in one way or another, given us a large proportion of the benefits we enjoy; while indifference and hostility to free inquiry have produced infinite mischief of all sorts.'[25] There is a 'difference . . . between performance . . . that you guess . . . will have to do, and a performance that counts', and although '[t]he true craftsman may wait long for his opportunity, . . . when it comes he will never be taken for a journeyman again.'[26] The notion of 'selling one's ideas' seemed insignificant to Pollock. '[T]he world's final judgement is certain in the long run': good ideas find their market.[27]

Perhaps this conviction that good scholarship will out explains what Goodhart calls Pollock's 'lack of emphasis' when presenting arguments.[28] The failure of Pollock's work to age well might be attributable in part to the fact that his prose often seems reticent to a modern readership ('I make no claim to novelty', or similar, is a regular Pollockian refrain).[29] But the failure seems

[19] See, e.g., *EJE* 43 ('By laws we can, more or less, make men behave in particular ways . . .'); also Goodhart, above n.3, xxii ([H]e never seemed to make a statement or express an opinion on any matter, even if of only slight importance, without carefully considering its accuracy'). On the Apostles, see chapter 2, 14–15. On Sidgwick, cf. Collini, above n.5, 199–202.

[20] See Frederick Pollock, 'The Nature and Meaning of Law' (1894) 10 *LQR* 228–39 at 228; *FBJ* 3 ('We find in all human sciences that those ideas which seem to be most simple are really the most difficult to grasp with certainty and express with accuracy'); and, in a similar vein, *GCL* 14.

[21] See, e.g., *EIL* dedication, vii, 112; *EJE* 286; *FBJ* 336; *OLOD* 50; *SHLP* 79.

[22] See, e.g., *OLOD* 26; *ECL* vi; *GCL* 121; *HEL*, i. 28. The last citation refers to one of the few portions of *HEL* that was written by Pollock.

[23] See *OLOD* 108–10, 140.

[24] For Pollock's aversion to juristic fashions, see, e.g., *GCL* 108, 116; in praise of truth-seeking, see *SHLP* 282–3; and cf. *EIL* 275–6.

[25] *EJE* 298. [26] *GCL* 112.

[27] Frederick Pollock, 'Frederic William Maitland, 1850–1906' (1906) 2 *Proc. Brit. Acad.* 455–60 at 460.

[28] Goodhart, above n.3, xxiii.

[29] See, e.g., *OLOD* 233; *EIL* 111; *FBJ* v; also Goodhart, above n.3, xlviii ('[H]is classical style is perfectly balanced and without sharpness of contour. The reader may find this lack of stress disconcerting for he may be more accustomed to the emphatic statements made by others, who are less concerned with precision of thought and accuracy of expression'). In a similar vein, see Arthur L. Goodhart,

ascribable also to the fact that he never tried to set out anything approaching a systematic jurisprudence. Pollock resisted being identified clearly with any particular school or 'ism'. While there are plenty of local arguments there is no grand project and, voluminous *oeuvre* notwithstanding, no classic text in the mould of *Ancient Law*, *The Common Law*, *The Law of the Constitution*, or *The Province of Jurisprudence Determined.*[30] Diligence defines him.[31] Not that we should underestimate his talents and achievements: Pollock produced important textbooks, particularly on contract, torts, and the law of partnership; he wrote a detailed, readable, and highly regarded account of a notably abstruse philosopher; and he had a remarkable talent for condensing formidable amounts of learning into short studies without being superficial. In particular, his collections of lectures on the science of politics and the evolution of the common law display the air of authority of someone drawing upon knowledge and thoughts which have been sedimenting in his mind for a considerable period of time. But on the page as, reputedly, in life, connecting with him is often hard work. His frequently antiquated, laborious, and cautious style seems almost to invite neglect. In the modern academic world, of course, such invitations rarely need suggesting more than once.

All of which raises the question of what this book is supposed to achieve. There are in essence, three objectives to this study. The most straightforward of these is to examine the career, achievements, and principal ideas of a comparatively unsung Victorian jurist—to introduce Pollock and, as it were, try to bring him out of his shell. But one might fairly ask why we should bother. If

English Contributions to the Philosophy of Law: The Seventh Annual Benjamin N. Cardozo Lecture Delivered before the Association of the Bar of the City of New York, 25 May 1948 (New York: Oxford UP, 1948), 42–3 ('Sir Frederick Pollock proved that philosophy "is able to descend to earth". . . . It is, perhaps, due to the clarity of his style that we tend to forget how profound are his ideas').

30 *HEL* is, of course, such a text, but it is hardly Pollock's. Milsom's introduction to the 1968 reissue treats the work as if Maitland were the sole author. Both Cecil Fifoot, *Pollock and Maitland* (Glasgow: University of Glasgow (Murray Foundation lecture no. 31), 1971), 16–17 and H. E. Bell, *Maitland: A Critical Examination and Assessment* (London: Black, 1965), 62–4 suggest that Pollock's influence on *HEL* was in some ways adverse. Even if this assessment is correct, it would be wrong to conclude that Pollock was not a serious legal historian. For his main solo forays into English legal history, see Frederick Pollock, 'The Oath of Allegiance' (1880) 42 *Macmillan's Magazine* 312–20 (repr. *EJE* 176–97); 'Anglo-Saxon Law' (1893) 8 *English Historical Rev.* 239–71; 'The Pope Who Deposed Himself' (1895) 10 *English Historical Rev.* 293–4; 'The Pope Who Sentenced Himself' (1895) 10 *English Historical Rev.* 536; 'English Law Before the Norman Conquest' (1898) 14 *LQR* 291–306 (slightly different version in *Alfred the Great*, ed. A. Bowker (London: Black, 1899), 209–39); 'The King's Justice in the Early Middle Ages' (1898) 12 *Harvard L. Rev.* 227–42; 'The King's Peace in the Middle Ages' (1899) 13 *Harvard L. Rev.* 177–89; 'The King's Peace' (1885) 1 *LQR* 37–50 (repr. *OLOD* 65–90); and 'A Brief Survey of Domesday' (1896) 11 *English Historical Rev.* 209–30 (also his correspondence, ibid. 813). According to his son, Pollock was not much interested in seventeenth-century history—a claim which seems suspect not least because it was made as part of an attempt to assert originality: see Sir John Pollock, *The Popish Plot: A Study in the History of the Reign of Charles II*, rev. edn. (Cambridge: Cambridge UP, 1944), xiii; and cf. Frederick Pollock's comments on 'Sir Matthew Hale on Hobbes: An Unpublished MS.' (1921) 37 *LQR* 274–303 at 274–5.

31 See, e.g., Fifoot, above n.30, 25 ('Pollock . . . was a man of great and varied gifts which he faithfully cultivated. Maitland was a genius').

good ideas find their market, and Pollock's works are fated to remain on the shelves, has he not been judged? Do we not do best to move on?

The second objective of this book is to argue that it is not entirely clear that we have moved on. Many of the legal issues that concerned Pollock continue to trouble us, and it would be wrong to assume that the ways in which he grappled with those issues have become irrelevant. Indeed, as will become apparent in the later stages of this study, certain of his juristic perspectives and mannerisms have survived and his imprint upon English legal thought is more significant than many modern academic lawyers might suspect. This is not to deny that Pollock relied on a number of arguments which were neither novel nor influential, and this study will not try to put those arguments in a flattering light. Yet even some of those arguments and positions which he advanced and which were rejected are worth studying, for in the accounts of these rejections we sometimes find important insights into why English academic law evolved as it did: in the illustrations of failure, that is, we occasionally find explanations for what succeeded.

The final basic objective of this book is to suggest that although Pollock wrote in the period before academic law had developed much of a professional identity—or, indeed, any sort of identity—his initiatives proved important because, rather than in spite, of this. As a jurist, Pollock worked for the best part of his life among senior lawyers and judges rather than academics. He was very much aware of the needs and the failings of the legal profession, and usually, in his legal writings, his main objective was to meet those needs and suggest remedies for those failings. He was a lawyer's jurist. Of course, many others since Pollock have sought to be lawyers' jurists. But from most of these others Pollock seemed to differ. First of all, he 'was born in the purple of the law'.[32] As a member of an eminent legal family, he naturally found himself in the company of many of the most powerful lawyers of his era: these were not connections that needed to be sought out. Secondly, his juristic initiatives were diverse: not only did he teach and write about law but he performed legal committee work and other forms of public service. Furthermore he was, as chief editor of the semi-official Law Reports, largely responsible for determining which judgments were and which were not reported. This broad range of pursuits meant that he enjoyed a degree of legal power which few if any academic lawyers hold nowadays. Modern legal academics may be more readily identifiable as part of a profession than was Pollock, but it is unlikely that the accomplishments of any of them extend into the legal world as far as his did.

Pollock's impact on English law receives some attention in chapter 2—though this chapter is for the most part biographical. The primary purpose of the chapter is to identify and locate Pollock within his social, legal, and

[32] C. H. S. Fifoot, *Judge and Jurist in the Reign of Victoria* (London: Stevens & Sons, 1959), 27 n.64.

intellectual milieu. An appreciation of Pollock as a jurist, we will see, requires more than just an appreciation of him as a university lawyer. As intimated above, most of his juristic projects evolved outside the university environment—indeed, as Corpus Professor of Jurisprudence at the University of Oxford, he was non-resident and appears never to have been especially involved in university affairs. As an academic he was nevertheless well suited to his era, since his commitment to scholarship complemented the emphasis placed within the great universities of the late-Victorian period upon the professionalization of academic life and the development of research ideals.

A secondary purpose of chapter 2 is to try to make sense of Pollock's apparently contradictory persona. By all accounts, he was taciturn often to the point of rudeness, and a disaster on the handful of occasions that he appeared as counsel. Yet the judiciary and the Bar clearly held him in high regard, often allowing citation of his works in the courtroom notwithstanding that there existed at this time a convention which forbade counsel from citing the works of living jurists in support of courtroom arguments. How could someone as difficult as Pollock be so highly regarded? First-hand accounts of the man suggest that his rather forbidding nature may in fact be crucial to understanding just why he was held in such high regard. With Pollock one knew, even if one did not like, where one stood. Those senior lawyers who wanted to determine whether particular ideas or proposals might be worth pursuing knew that his opinion was worth seeking out: if a proposition was dead in the water, he would say so within a matter of seconds; if he did not declare a proposition foolish, it was probably a stroke of genius. Besides suggesting that commentators have sometimes made too much of and been too disparaging about the peculiarity of Pollock's manner, this chapter also shows that he shared with many other Victorian men of letters a preoccupation with the virtue of good character. Not only did he share this preoccupation, it is argued, but he also epitomized the virtue as he described it—which may explain further his ability to win the respect and trust (if not always the affection) of the barristers and judges with whom he came into more or less daily contact.

Chapter 3 is dedicated to Pollock's jurisprudence. At this point we are most definitely not emphasizing his enduring legacy. The history of English jurisprudential thought shows that Pollock's project—and it is hard to say exactly what that project amounted to—was sidelined. He produced rigorous and well-received philosophical work, yet seemed suspicious of philosophy as applied to law. In particular, he was suspicious of analytical jurisprudence. He was more favourably disposed to historical and comparative jurisprudence as developed by Sir Henry Maine. Yet he was not an out-and-out supporter of that perspective, just as he was not wholly opposed to the analytical project. Pollock's jurisprudential perspective is nuanced and resists categorization.

Although he was unequivocally in favour of the development of legal science, his own conception of legal science is difficult to identify. At the heart of this chapter lies the thesis that analytical jurisprudence, for all its shortcomings, has thrived as an academic project because it embodies an identifiable method. Historical and comparative jurisprudence lacked such a method—indeed, it generally lacked the intellectual rigour that was being sought after in the late-Victorian universities. Whether Pollock could have brought fresh life to the historical and comparative project is debatable—perhaps, in anybody's hands, it would have been destined for general redundancy. But there is no doubt that he did little to prevent such an outcome. Although Pollock was well placed, both historically and institutionally, to advance the cause of comparative legal science, he achieved nothing of lasting jurisprudential significance. He was simply one of the more recognizable late nineteenth- and early twentieth-century names associated with a jurisprudential project that, after Maine, needed clear thematization and methodological explication. Rather than rescue and revive Maine's legacy, he tended to confirm the suspicion of many twentieth-century legal theorists that comparative jurisprudence is essentially soft-centred and old-fashioned.

Chapter 4 considers in detail Pollock's attitude towards the common law. Pollock lauded what he called the genius of the common law: for him, it represents a cautious, organic, incremental accretion of judicial wisdom which, as compared with statute law, tends to deal more sensitively and flexibly with novel problems. He contrasted the modest, ad hoc nature of the common law with the tendency of legislators to overestimate the capacity for statutory intervention to remedy problems and to fail to see that legislation sometimes creates more difficulties than it solves. When writing about the common law, Pollock often returned to the idea of character, claiming that the English possess a peculiar talent for appreciating liberty, integrity, and noble conduct. The common law mind, he argued, is but an instantiation of this special talent. Examination of this argument requires that Pollock be placed within a broader English politico-juridical tradition which connects national temperament with jurisdictional character. To conceive of the common law mind as representative of a distinct political perspective would be, he believed, a mistake. The common law shares with socialism a distrust of, and a desire for, the public control of monopolies; but it also shares with conservatism a general preference for private ordering and wariness about ambitious legislative schemes. Common law philosophy—indeed, Pollock's philosophy, for he was nothing if not a common lawyer—turns out to be oriented far more to the right than to the left of the political spectrum; nevertheless, with Pollock as with the common law, identifying him in political terms is no straightforward matter.

Chapter 5 examines the arguments underlying, and the influence of, Pollock's treatise writing. Pollock, like Lord Mansfield, believed that the law does not consist of particular cases, but of the general principles illustrated and explained in those cases. As other commentators have noted, Pollock's many editions of his two great treatises, *Principles of Contract* and *The Law of Torts*, are very much exercises in capturing the principles latent in what are often fragmentary bodies of doctrine. The purpose of this chapter is not to question this common assessment of Pollock's treatises. Neither, however, is its purpose simply to reiterate the assessment. In essence, this chapter examines just how Pollock shone the spotlight of principle on contract and torts.

Having originally been inspired by the great continental will theorists, particularly Savigny, Pollock gradually became less enthusiastic about the idea of contractual validity stemming from a meeting of minds. However, he never completely renounced that idea. Throughout his editions of *Principles of Contract*, Pollock is to be found developing an account of contractual validity which, to some degree, keeps faith with the will theory, though it seems he would generally have preferred questions of contractual enforcement to be resolved by reference to reasonable expectations rather than to what the parties apparently agreed. Although Pollock argued that the central purpose of contract law ought to be the enforcement of good faith between the parties to a bargain, his version of this argument basically fell on deaf ears. His account of consideration, by contrast, was well received by the English courts—his explanation of the mutual promise as a form of consideration, furthermore, was accorded a good deal of significance by early twentieth-century American contracts scholars. Ironically, however, Pollock had little time for the doctrine of consideration and seemed to regard the debate over mutual promises as essentially trivial. With the law of contracts, to put the matter crudely, he was most influential where he was least committed.

The law of contract was very much a theorized subject by the time that Pollock came to write about it. But the same cannot be said of torts. In *The Law of Torts*, Pollock had to undertake much of the theoretical groundwork for himself—which probably explains why this treatise proves a more interesting proposition than *Principles of Contract.* In dealing with Pollock's work on torts, we begin with an examination of the natural law backdrop to nineteenth-century torts scholarship. In the seventeenth and eighteenth centuries, English jurists resorted to a mixture of Roman law and natural law ideas in their efforts to impose a degree of structure on the mish-mash of actionable injuries that pre-dated the modern law of torts. The best known of these jurists was no doubt Blackstone, and it is to Blackstone that Pollock initially turned when he embarked on his own attempt to demonstrate that there exists a genuinely unified law of torts which can be systematized in terms of general principles. Simply to describe Pollock's effort at systematization as Blackstonian would, however, be wrong: he also adopted a modified form of Holmes's classification of torts under the headings of strict liability, negligence, and intentional wrongs in his effort to fix the boundaries of the subject. Although there was no distinctive theoretical backdrop to Pollock's torts scholarship, in other words, he was able to devise a framework by fusing together elements of Blackstonian and Holmesian thinking. Having considered how Pollock developed and applied a method of compartmentalization to the law of torts, we then examine how he advanced and defended certain arguments about tort in preference to others. Indeed, we will see that Pollock was generally a more prescriptive writer when dealing with torts as compared with contract—though determining his personal opinions with respect to either subject often proves very difficult. Various of Pollock's normative positions are examined, and particular attention is accorded to his views regarding the establishment of a general principle of negligence liability and the extent to which liability should be imposed for intentional wrongdoing. Not only did Pollock adopt a more normative approach to torts as compared with contract, we will see, but the arguments which he advanced as a torts lawyer were generally better received and more influential than was his argument in support of a contractual principle of good faith.

As we noted above, Pollock did more than just research and write about the law. Chapter 6 is principally devoted to his major initiatives as an editor. It begins with an examination of Pollock's earnings from his numerous professional pursuits—including certain of his editorial earnings. Editing appears to have been, for Pollock, one of his more lucrative sources of income—though it has to be said that a good deal of information relating to his general earnings is simply not available, and so comparisons and conclusions are often difficult to draw. Enough information survives, nevertheless, to make possible a sketch of Pollock's various income sources. Pollock was not wealthy to the extent that he could be completely indifferent to money—there is evidence, indeed, that money mattered considerably to him. It is also clear that his salary as an Oxford professor would not have matched his earnings as an editor. While it is important not to make too much of this, it is interesting nevertheless that there was no great financial incentive for Pollock, who spent only twenty-one years of his long professional life working within the university system, to remain committed to a career as a university lawyer.

The remainder of chapter 6 focuses specifically on Pollock's achievements as a legal editor. Pollock acted in a number of editorial capacities, two of which deserve careful examination. As Editor-in-Chief of the Law Reports, he influenced significantly the reporting of judge-made law. He was known to be a ruthless editor of court transcripts who worked hard to ensure that judicial language would never appear inelegant in print. He adopted a fairly strict policy, furthermore, of reporting only select decisions of the appeal courts. Pollock took pride in what he considered to be the informal manner in which the Law Reports operated. Yet although he liked to present the activity of law reporting as if it were essentially an exercise in easy-going teamwork, it is clear that he endeavoured to control operations and that he would scarcely tolerate attempts at interference. Certainly he consulted with judges and counsel regarding the inclusion and the wording of decisions in the Law Reports. Determinations of what should and should not be reported were, nevertheless, ultimately his alone. This chapter shows that although he was generally an energetic and clear-minded editor of the Law Reports, mid-twentieth-century concerns about the state of law reporting—particularly the danger of important cases sometimes going unreported—were hardly eased by his editorial approach. There is no doubt that he could, on occasions, be reluctant or slow to report important cases.

As the first Editor of the *Law Quarterly Review*, Pollock did a great deal to define law as an academic discipline in England. Before the establishment of this journal in 1884, no English legal periodical had taken scholarship very seriously. The latter part of chapter 6 shows that Pollock brought a certain Victorian polymath perspective to the *LQR*, so ensuring that scholarship of the black-letter variety actually featured very little throughout its pages during its first three-and-a-half decades. Pollock himself contributed more to the journal than did anyone else—it is probably fair to say that he contributed too much, given that some of his essays in the *LQR* are short on inspiration. The contributions which may well be of the most historical significance are his case notes. During the years of Pollock's editorship, he wrote the Notes section almost single-handedly from one quarter to the next. He would use this section to pursue specific campaigns—against bad law reporting, misguided legislative initiatives, unfortunate legal decisions, and so on—but, perhaps most importantly, he used it to emphasize the importance of academic legal critique to the development of the law. Such critique, Pollock believed, could be dedicated to teasing out the general principles that courts might sometimes miss or misunderstand in particular cases. It could also be dedicated to determining what else, in reaching this or that decision, a court might usefully have done. Pollock's case notes would occasionally influence the thinking of the courts, though their more enduring legacy was probably in contributing to the tone and manner of twentieth-century English juristic inquiry.

Between the founding of the first professorship of English law in 1758 and the later decades of the twentieth century, law generally remained moribund within the universities. The one exception to this general state of affairs was the mid- to late nineteenth century, during which period law faculties were established at Oxford, Cambridge, and London. Out of this environment there emerged a number of jurists—Maine, Austin, Maitland, and Dicey being the most recognizable names—whose projects were to influence significantly the growth of English legal scholarship. Although Pollock is commonly regarded as an important figure within the late-Victorian juristic tradition, he has rarely been considered central to it. We can only speculate as to why this should be the case—his failure to produce either a celebrated, agenda-defining text or a distinctive jurisprudential perspective may be contributory factors. The basic purpose of this study is to show that, in not entirely obvious ways, Pollock's legacy has in fact been crucial to the development of modern English legal thought. Indeed, while the impact of his endeavours has not always been especially visible, an examination of his initiatives in context reveals that he made a deep impression on the development of law and juristic inquiry.

2

'F. P.'

Among the anecdotes that make up the remembrances of William Frederick Pollock we catch glimpses of a nine-year-old boy with 'precise habits', a young teenager elected as a King's Scholar at Eton, a Cambridge undergraduate who enjoyed life and flourished at Trinity College and who 'delighted' his father by demonstrating 'not mere book work, but that mental power, capacity to think, and to think hard and well', and a man in his early twenties who, while holidaying in France, was 'too proud' to be piggy-backed across a pool of water which obstructed access to his carriage.[1] Beyond this, however, we learn little from the father about his eldest son.

Almost half a century later, the son was to publish his own remembrances. Yet these reveal less about his inner character than did his father's. While many personal memoirs tend towards detailed self-aggrandizement, Pollock eschews even modest introspection. *For My Grandson*, he informs us, offers but 'grandfatherly chatter' and 'memories of professional wanderings'.[2] Do not expect autobiography, he warns: '[w]hat I now proceed to tell you is not a story of my life; I have not been directly concerned in great events, nor had any surprising adventures.'[3] The purpose of the book is to offer some observations on the world in which he lived. But Pollock makes little effort to locate himself within that world, and at all times he looks outwards.

i. Formative years

Not that Pollock's aversion to self-reflection proves too much of a hindrance. Numerous profiles of the man exist, from which we can build a general picture.[4] He was born on 10 December 1845 and he died, at the age of 91, on

[1] *Personal Remembrances of Sir Frederick Pollock, Second Baronet, Sometime Queen's Remembrancer*, 2 vols. (London: Macmillan, 1887), ii. 23, 76, 119–20, 148–9, 163, 212–14.

[2] *FMG* 225, 200.

[3] *FMG* xii.

[4] See the obituary notices by Lord Wright, Lord Maugham, Herbert Samuel, William Holdsworth, H. D. Hazeltine, E. S. P. Haynes, Edward Potton, and A. L. Goodhart at (1937) 53 *LQR* 151–206; Lord

18 January 1937. His marriage of over sixty years to Georgina Pollock (d.1935) produced a daughter, Alice, and a son, the historian and dramatist Sir John Pollock (1878–1963). He was educated at Eton and at Trinity College, Cambridge, where he won the Pitt Scholarship for Classics in 1865, came second in the Classical Tripos of 1867 and sixth among the senior optimes of the Mathematical Tripos of that same year. He was awarded the first Chancellor's medal in 1867 and elected a Fellow of Trinity College in 1868. For all that his juristic career was Oxonian, his 'chief academic allegiance' was always to Trinity, not least because certain of those who taught him classics and antiquity there instilled in him a love of scholarship.[5]

Possibly it is at Cambridge that he developed a fondness for clubs. Of all the fraternities to which Pollock belonged, he refers to none more regularly or affectionately than he does to the Cambridge Conversazione Society or 'Apostles'.[6] Founded in 1820, the Apostles were an important influence on English intellectual life throughout the nineteenth century, and it was largely out of

Wright, 'Pollock, Sir Frederick, Third Baronet 1845–1937', in *DNB (1931–1940)*, 711–13; Anon., 'Sir Frederick Pollock, K.C.: The "Old Broad Culture"', in *The Times*, 19 January 1937, 14, col. B; Sir John Pollock, *Time's Chariot* (London: Murray, 1950), 47–75; A. L. Goodhart, 'Introduction', in *JLE* ix–xlviii; H. A. Hollond, 'The Late Sir Frederick Pollock' [1937] *Jnl. of the Society of Public Teachers of Law* 49–50; Gareth H. Jones, 'Pollock, Sir Frederick', in *Biographical Dictionary of the Common Law*, ed. A. W. B. Simpson (London: Butterworths, 1984), 421–3; H. D. Hazeltine, 'Sir Frederick Pollock, Bart., 1845–1937' (1949) 35 *Proc. Brit. Acad.* 233–56; Anon., 'Sir F. Pollock, 91, Legal Expert, Dies', in *New York Times*, 19 January 1937, 23; Anon., 'Sir Frederick Pollock: A Distinguished Jurist', in *Manchester Guardian*, 19 January 1937, 5; Francis R. Jones, 'Sir Frederick Pollock' (1904) 16 *Green Bag* 1–3; Sir William Holdsworth, *Some Makers of English Law: The Tagore Lectures, 1937–38* (Cambridge: Cambridge UP, 1938), 279–90; Richard A. Cosgrove, *Our Lady the Common Law: An Anglo-American Legal Community, 1870–1930* (New York: New York UP, 1987), 134–60; Steve Hedley, 'Sir Frederick Pollock and the Teaching of English Law', in *Learning the Law: Teaching and the Transmission of Law in England 1150–1900*, eds. J. A. Bush and A. Wijffels (London: Hambledon Press, 1999), 407–17; Joseph Foster, *Men-at-the-Bar: A Biographical Hand-List of the Members of the Various Inns of Court, Including Her Majesty's Judges, etc.* (London: Reeves and Turner, 1885), 370–1; Mario Sarfatti, 'Frederick Pollock (1845–1937)' (1937) 17 *Rivista Internazionale di Filosofia del Diritto* 3–7; and Christiane Köckler-Beuser, 'Pollock, Sir Frederick (1845–1937)' in *Juristen. Ein biographisches Lexikon Von der Antike bis zum 20. Jahrhundert*, ed. M. Stolleis (Munich: Beck, 1995), 493–4. I have also made use of [Adolph S. Oko], 'Sir Frederick Pollock, Bt. (1845–1937)', paper presented to the Quarto Club, 24 October [1943?], in Oko papers, MS 14, box 9, file 23. 'We really ought to have a Pollock bibliography', Lord Macmillan wrote to Arthur Goodhart in 1934, 'and he ought to compile it himself!' Macmillan to A. L. Goodhart, 11 February 1934, in Pollock correspondence, box 1, folder 53; see also Macmillan, review of *FMG* in (1934) 50 *LQR* 275–7 at 277. Pollock never did compile a bibliography, though a very much incomplete one (by Adrienne C. deVergie), along with a short profile of Pollock (by Roy M. Mersky), can be found in the modern reprint of *OLOD* (Buffalo, NY: Hein, 1970), i–viii.

[5] *FMG* 20; and see more generally ibid. 20–30 (at Eton and Trinity College); Hazeltine, above n.4, 235–6; and, on the award of the Pitt scholarship, H. W. Cookson to Lord Chief Baron [Sir Jonathan Frederick Pollock], 9 March 1865, and [Sir Jonathan] Fred[erick] Pollock to Frederick Pollock, 11 March 1865, in Lord Hanworth, *Lord Chief Baron Pollock: A Memoir* (London: Murray, 1929), 169–70.

[6] See, in particular, *FMG* 29–33 (repr. (1933) 74 *Cornhill Magazine* 1–15 at 2–5); and, generally, Peter Allen, *The Cambridge Apostles: The Early Years* (Cambridge: Cambridge UP, 1978); Paul Levy, *Moore: G. E. Moore and the Cambridge Apostles* (Oxford: Oxford UP, 1981); Richard Deacon, *The Cambridge Apostles: A History of Cambridge University's Élite Intellectual Secret Society* (London: Royce, 1985); and W. C. Lubenow, *The Cambridge Apostles, 1820–1914: Liberalism, Imagination, and Friendship in British Intellectual and Professional Life* (Cambridge: Cambridge UP, 1998). Lubenow reports (ibid. 64) that Pollock missed the annual dinner of the Apostles on only three occasions over sixty years. See also Deacon, above, 90.

their number that another of Pollock's clubs, the Metaphysical Society (see below), was formed in the late 1860s.[7] Pollock was elected to the Conversazione Society in 1865—he was Apostle Number 160[8]—and he clearly regarded apostolic fellowship as a special kind of belonging. 'It is a body to which I owe much', he wrote to Holmes in 1926.[9] 'Without the bond of the Society', he noted in his memoirs, 'I could not have known Sir Henry Maine and Fitzjames Stephen. . . . Later there was F. W. Maitland: our common devotion to the history of English law would have made us friends in any case, but the apostolic fellowship set a specially delightful seal on our intimacy.'[10]

There were other clubs, too: at various points in his life Pollock was active in the Rabelais Club, the Alpine Club (of which he became an honorary librarian), the London Fencing Club, and the Freemasons.[11] These memberships are largely indicative of his lust for life. Like Holmes, he was blessed with an angular physique and remarkable physical as well mental stamina (while Pollock never endured anything akin to Holmes's Civil War wounds, he did, in later life, recover remarkably from serious setbacks).[12] Very much a believer

[7] See Lubenow, above n.6, 227–8; and Alan Willard Brown, *The Metaphysical Society: Victorian Minds in Crisis, 1869–1880* (New York: Columbia UP, 1947), 1–9.

[8] See Levy, above n.6, 252, 307.

[9] Pollock to Holmes, 21 January 1926, in *PHL* ii. 174.

[10] *FMG* 31–2; see also, Frederick Pollock, 'Frederic William Maitland' (April 1907) 411 *Quarterly Rev.* 401–19 at 406 ('this bond made friendship with Maitland quicker and easier').

[11] On the various memberships, see John Pollock, *Time's Chariot*, above n.4, 49; *FMG* 209–25; 'Sir Frederick Pollock, K.C.: The "Old Broad Culture"', above n.4; and David Williams, *George Meredith: His Life and Lost Love* (London: Hamish Hamilton, 1977), 174. The Alpine Club, founded in 1857, apparently had a fairly close bond with Pollock's college at Cambridge. According to Hansen, the *Alpine Club Register* shows that throughout the period 1857–90 'Trinity College, Cambridge, was the most heavily represented of the Oxbridge colleges, with almost one in seven Alpine Club members calling it their alma mater.' Peter H. Hansen, 'Albert Smith, the Alpine Club, and the Invention of Mountaineering in Mid-Victorian Britain' (1995) 34 *Jnl. of British Studies* 300–24 at 311. In the late 1880s, Pollock updated the library catalogue of the Club: Frederick Pollock, *Catalogue of Books in the Library of the Alpine Club* (London: Spottiswoode, 1888); see also Frederick Pollock, 'The Library of the Alpine Club' (1886) 3 *Library Chronicle* 136–40 (repr. *OLOD* 250–9). Holmes clearly viewed Pollock's 'Masonic hobby' with a degree of amusement (see Holmes to Pollock, 24 January 1918, in *PHL* i. 257), though Pollock took his involvement seriously and believed that the movement helped to promote Anglo-American legal relations (see Pollock to Holmes, 11 February 1924, in *PHL* ii. 126–7). The first appearance of his *Principles of Contract* in an American edition may have been due to his Masonic connections: see the American edition of *PCLE(2)*, adapted with notes by Gustavus H. Wald (Cincinnati: Clarke & Co., 1881), vii.

[12] In May 1923, at the age of 78, Pollock suffered a fractured skull when he was struck by a bicyclist in Hyde Park. (During his own cycling days he had, perhaps ironically, been keen to defend the safety of bicycle riding: see Frederick Pollock, '"Hidden Dangers": A Reply' (March 1897) 29 *National Rev.* 113–17.) In September the following year, he slipped and damaged the tendons in his left knee (see Pollock to Holmes, 3 September 1924, in *PHL* ii. 146). In July 1927, he underwent surgery for a strangulated hernia. John Pollock's account of just how well his father recovered from these setbacks (see *Time's Chariot*, above n.4, 54) may well be overblown. The fact is that *Time's Chariot* is at times rather romanticized (e.g., '[i]t is a certain fact that summers were summers when I was a boy. . . . You really could count on the weather' [86–7]) and it is sometimes hard not to suspect embellishment. It is clear from Frederick Pollock's progress in the years following these problems, none the less, that he did recover—notwithstanding that the recoveries might not always have been as swift as his son would have us believe. Holmes's war wounds are the stuff of legend: for a matter-of-fact account, see G. Edward White, *Justice Oliver Wendell Holmes: Law and the Inner Self* (New York: Oxford UP, 1993), 52–60.

in the link between healthy body and healthy mind, Pollock epitomized the late-Victorian incarnation of the 'godliness and good learning' ideal.[13] Indeed, he wrote about physical fitness as if it were integral to good character—'the exercise of arms', he believed, 'is the most admirable of regular correctives for the ill habits of a sedentary life', and he advised law students to 'learn to bear arms for the defence of the realm, a wholesome discipline and service of citizenship for which the Inns of Court offer every encouragement.'[14] Occasionally, his prose invokes the image of a martinet: thus we find him insisting to the readers of the *Law Quarterly Review* that '[s]everity may be unkind—even unjust—but it is bracing', that '[t]he law is a track which must be followed, and not an open plain which can be galloped over at pleasure', and that there is often much value to be had from harsh lessons.[15] Pollock was a great walker—his centrality to the Sunday Tramps (see below) is testimony to this—and even more, until age put him beyond the pastime, he enjoyed mountaineering.[16] Most of all, he loved fencing.[17] When one of his obituarists remarked that Pollock had not been a good fencer, certain of those who had been close to him reacted much as they might have done had he been declared a bad lawyer.[18] He travelled widely, and was well versed—indeed, he wrote verse—in Latin, Greek, French, German, and Italian, besides having a fair knowledge of Persian, Russian, and Sanskrit. He was interested in public house reform, in the preservation of rights of way (signs stating that 'Trespassers will be prosecuted', he was apparently fond of telling landowners, are but mendacious bluff, since trespass is not a criminal offence but a tort), and he supported the introduction and extension of various rights for women.[19]

[13] On which see David Newsome, *Godliness and Good Learning: Four Studies on A Victorian Ideal* (London: Murray, 1961). Very much associated with early Victorian Cambridge, 'the ideal of godliness and good learning' originally 'assumed that education and religion were essentially allied' (ibid. 25). Over time, the ideal evolved so as to incorporate the notion of 'manliness' (an idea which in this context embraces qualities such as athleticism, strenuousness, stoicism, and self-denial). It was in the context of Victorian walking and mountaineering clubs of the type to which Pollock belonged, Newsome claims, that this evolution was most evident (see ibid. 215–16, 228–9).

[14] *OLOD* 298, 108.

[15] (1899) 15 *LQR* 4; (1911) 27 *LQR* 146–7; (1907) 23 *LQR* 256.

[16] For Pollock on mountaineering, see Sir Frederick Pollock, 'The Early History of Mountaineering', in *Mountaineering*, ed. C. T. Dent (London: Longman's, Green & Co. (Badminton Library series), 1892), 1–38; also *FMG* 211–16; and 'The Last Evening in the Alps. A Dialogue' (January 1868) 17 *Macmillan's Magazine* 248–54. Pollock liked to compare juristic endeavour to mountaineering: see, e.g., *GCL* 122.

[17] See *FMG* 216–25; and also, for his scholarship on the history of the sword, Frederick Pollock, 'Sword', in *Encyclopaedia Britannica*, 9th edn. (1875–99), xxii. 800; *OLOD* 260–98; 'The Forms and History of the Sword' (July 1883) 48 *Macmillan's Magazine* 195–207.

[18] See Lord Maugham (1937) 53 *LQR* 168; and cf. John Pollock, *Time's Chariot*, above n.4, 58.

[19] That Pollock was '[d]eeply interested in public-house reform' is noted under his entry in J. A. Venn, *Alumni Cantabrigienses: A Biographical List of All Known Students, Graduates and Holders of Office at the University of Cambridge, from the Earliest Times to 1900. Part II (from 1752 to 1900), volume v: Pace—Spyers* (Cambridge: Cambridge UP, 1953), 149. On his interest in common rights to use land, see John Pollock, *Time's Chariot*, above n.4, 57; and Cecil Fifoot, *Pollock and Maitland* (Glasgow: University of Glasgow (Murray Foundation Lecture no. 31), 1971), 11. Regarding common rights over the Forest of Dartmoor, Pollock wrote that 'abuses have crept in; . . . rights meant for the common good have been bartered

'You do so many things' Holmes wrote to him in 1883, 'that I never know next whether to expect a drama, a lawbook, a symphony or a system of philosophy.'[20] We might also note, adopting the style of a newspaper 'personals' column, that Pollock was particularly fond of Milton, Shakespeare, Dartmoor, Surrey, Blake, Wagner, fine wines, great architecture, the Monarchy, and the United States of America. More than anything—though there is more to be done before we can tackle this subject—he was attached to the law.

Pollock connected with, even if he was not central to, that vast Victorian intellectual aristocracy classically described by Noel Annan.[21] Among his friends he could count Lytton Strachey, Leslie Stephen, William Kingdon Clifford, and various other members of the higher intellectual stratum of late-Victorian London.[22] With Stephen he not only edited Clifford's lectures and

into private hands, oftentimes beyond recall; wholesome customs have been disused, or the better part of them foregone and the worst part kept. . . . [T]he law, as our law stands, has been weighted against the popular side.' Frederick Pollock, 'Introduction', in Percival Birkett, *A Short History of the Rights of Common upon the Forests of Dartmoor and the Commons of Devon* (Plymouth, Devon: Brendon (Dartmoor Preservation Association), 1890), vii–x at vii–viii. (Pollock seems to have been especially interested in Devon: see Sir Frederick Pollock, 'The Devonshire Domesday' (1893) 25 *Report and Transactions of the Devonshire Association for the Advancement of Science, Literature, and Art* 286–98; 'Dartmoor and the Walkham' (January 1884) 1 *English Illustrated Magazine* 203–14.) On women's rights, see *OL* 92–8 (in support of women's fencing); Pollock to Holmes, 27 October 1921, in *PHL* ii. 84 (supporting admission of women to Cambridge); (1917) 33 *LQR* 114 (on admission of women to the Bar); *The Deceased Wife's Sister's Bill: Letters From W. Holman Hunt, Sir Frederick Pollock, and others* (London: Marriage Law Reform Association, 1901), 26–8 (supporting, in a characteristically pedantic fashion, the proposal that a woman should be permitted to marry her deceased sister's husband); also Neil Duxbury, 'When We Were Young: Notes in the *Law Quarterly Review*, 1885–1925' (2000) 116 *LQR* 474–503 at 496–7; and E. S. P. Haynes (1937) 53 *LQR* 195. On the matter of women's suffrage, Pollock provided a number of legalistic interventions regarding the Franchise Bill: see, e.g., *The Times* (letters), 12 July 1910, 11, col. E; and cf. *The Times* (letters), 20 January 1913, 8, col. E.

[20] Holmes to Pollock, 27 August 1883, in *PHL* i. 22.

[21] N. G. Annan, 'The Intellectual Aristocracy', in *Studies in Social History: A Tribute to G. M. Trevelyan*, ed. J. H. Plumb (London: Longmans, Green & Co., 1955), 241–87.

[22] For some of Pollock's friendships, see Hazeltine, 'Sir Frederick Pollock, Bart., 1845–1937', above n.4, 255–6. For Pollock on Strachey, see *FMG* 32; on Stephen, see 'Leslie Stephen' (June 1904) 3 *Independent Rev.* 48–60; and on Clifford, see 'William Kingdon Clifford' (May 1879) n.s. 25 *Fortnightly Rev.* 667–87; *FMG* 32, 105; E. S. P. Haynes (1937) 53 *LQR* 194 ('W. K. Clifford . . . was Sir Frederick's *alter ego* in their Cambridge period'); and Pollock's 'Introduction' to *Lectures and Essays by the Late William Kingdon Clifford*, 2 vols., eds. L. Stephen and F. Pollock (London: Macmillan, 1879), i. 1–72. Pollock clearly held Henry Sidgwick's reputation in high regard—see F. W. Maitland to Henry Jackson, 30 June 1906, in *The Letters of Frederic William Maitland*, ed. C. H. S. Fifoot (London: Selden Society, 1965), 478—and it seems correct to suggest, as does Oko (above n.4, 7–10), that Pollock was an especially close friend of Sidgwick and that Sidgwick inspired Pollock's interest in philosophy while both men were at Cambridge. That Sidgwick was at least partially responsible for bringing out the philosopher in Pollock can certainly be ascertained: the first volume of *Mind* contains an article by Sidgwick on practical applications of evolutionary theory, and a response by Pollock in which he challenges Sidgwick's view that evolutionary theory cannot advance our inquiries into practical matters of ethics. See Henry Sidgwick, 'The Theory of Evolution in its Application to Practice' (1876) 1 *Mind* 52–67; Frederick Pollock, 'Evolution and Ethics' (1876) 1 *Mind* 334–45; also Frederick Pollock, 'Happiness or Welfare' (1877) 2 *Mind* 269–72. In his brief but affectionate obituary for Sidgwick, Pollock notes that although Sidgwick 'had no legal training', he 'was much interested in general questions of legal principle. The law school of [Cambridge] University owes much to him, not only in encouragement, but in the actual supply of pecuniary means when they were much needed, and could scarcely be obtained except by private munificence.' Frederick Pollock, 'Henry Sidgwick', *The Pilot*, 15 September 1900,

essays but also, in 1879, founded a walking fraternity, the Sunday Tramps, which for around fifteen years was something of a meeting-post for many Victorian men of letters.[23] Also in that year, Pollock was elected as the Secretary of another great Victorian intellectual institution, the Metaphysical Society—'that distinguished body,' as Strachey described it, 'which met once a month during the palmy years of the seventies to discuss, in strict privacy, the fundamental problems of the destiny of man.'[24] Unlike most applicants for a permit to use the Reading Room of the British Museum (even in the 1870s), Pollock was not obliged to have his suitability for admission confirmed by a third party: it went without saying that he was 'a fit and proper person' to be allowed entry.[25] He dabbled in Victorian higher journalism, and for a time contributed regularly to some of the leading periodicals, particularly the *Saturday Review* (which was for many years edited by his brother, Walter Herries Pollock).[26] Like his Oxford precursor, Sir Henry Maine, he delighted in the

325–6 at 326. See further Frederick Pollock to Mrs Sidgwick (A. S. F. Gow), 30 August 1900, in Pollock correspondence (Wren), Add. MS c. 104, 77 ('I have never known any one who had, either as teacher or companion, the same power of leading others to bring out and develop whatever was best of their own'); and Frederick Pollock to Mrs Sidgwick, 17 September 1900, in Pollock correspondence (Wren), Add. MS c. 104, 78(1).

[23] On Pollock and the Sunday Tramps, see John Pollock, *Time's Chariot*, above n.4, 56–7; Hazeltine (1937) 53 *LQR* 191; Frederic William Maitland, *The Life and Letters of Leslie Stephen* (London: Duckworth, 1906), 357–8, 363; Noel Annan, *Leslie Stephen: The Godless Victorian* (London: Weidenfeld & Nicolson, 1984), 97–8. 'Stephen', according to Pollock ('Leslie Stephen', above n.22, 53), 'ruled . . . the "Sunday Tramps" with an absolute and beneficent patriarchal government.' George Croom Robertson, the first editor of *Mind*, was also involved in the founding of the Tramps.

[24] Lytton Strachey, *Eminent Victorians* (London: Penguin, 1948 [1918]), 97. The Metaphysical Society was founded in 1869. Pollock read one paper to the Society (in March 1880, on the subject of 'Generic and Symbolic Images') and made numerous contributions to a journal which was fairly closely associated with the Society, the *Nineteenth Century*. In December 1880, the Society was dissolved. In his memoirs, Pollock writes about certain of the Society's philosophical pretensions with detached bemusement (see *FMG* 93–6). 'You know of course that the Society was intended to satisfy Tennyson concerning the immortality of the soul', he wrote to Sidgwick's widow in 1904. 'I believe he attended one meeting.' Frederick Pollock to Mrs Sidgwick, 4 April 1904 in Pollock correspondence (Wren), Add. MS c. 104, 50. Brown suggests that Pollock, like Tennyson, was an unenthusiastic member. So why was he willing to be elected? Possibly he could not resist the badge of honour, though it seems equally possible that the Society—which had, by 1879, lost much of its direction and support—delivered less than Pollock had hoped for. See Brown, above n.7, 29, 91, 103–4, 157–8.

[25] Frederick Pollock to the Principal Librarian of the British Museum [E. A. Bond], 31 October 1879, in British Museum Reading Room papers, Add. 48341 f.228.

[26] See *FMG* 89–93. For examples, see [Frederick Pollock], 'Nasmith's Institutes of English Private Law' (8 January 1876) 41 *Saturday Rev.* 54–5; 'Sir Travers Twiss's Bracton' (1 February 1879) 47 *Saturday Rev.* 153–4; 'Bigelow's Placita Anglo-Normannica' (13 September 1879) 48 *Saturday Rev.* 327–8; and 'Holmes on the Common Law' (11 June 1881) 51 *Saturday Rev.* 758–9. For Pollock on his brother as editor of the *Saturday Review*, see Pollock to Holmes, 1 March 1926, in *PHL* ii. 176. Certainly between the 1860s and 1870s the *Saturday Review*, according to one historian, 'was far above all other political-literary Reviews of the time, both in terms of quality of writing, and importance as an organ of opinion. Readers were middle to upper class, highly educated, of both liberal and conservative opinions, though apparently, as in the paper, with some preponderance of the latter.' Alvar Ellegård, 'The Readership of the Periodical Press in Mid-Victorian Britain' (1957) 63 *Göteborgs Universitets Årsskrift* 1–41 at 24. On the significant quantity of journalism produced by the Victorian intelligentsia, see Stefan Collini, *Public Moralists: Political Thought and Public Life in Britain 1850–1930* (Oxford: Clarendon Press,

surroundings of the Athenaeum Club.[27] In 1902 he was appointed as one of the first Fellows of the British Academy.[28] As an undergraduate he knew Tennyson, and at Hind Head Copse—Pollock's Surrey retreat, the address for which prefaces so many of his early letters to Holmes—he and his wife entertained Rudyard Kipling, George Bernard Shaw, and many other figures of Victorian art and literature.[29] There is no doubt at all that Pollock was well acquainted with the late-Victorian cultural elite.

From his work there sometimes emanates that tone of collusive self-assuredness so often evident among this elite.[30] 'If the reader wants impartial criticism, he is warned that he must seek it elsewhere; but I shall be surprised if the judgment of impartial critics differs greatly from mine.'[31] Thus it is that Pollock opened his review of a book about his friend, Leslie Stephen, written by another friend, F. W. Maitland (it almost goes without saying that Stephen and Maitland were also friends). In correspondence with Holmes, Pollock noted of the book that Maitland 'has had much trouble with it and professes not to be satisfied with his work'.[32] Maitland's own assessment may have been characteristically self-deprecating, but it is possible also that he was being sincere: he had written his biography of Stephen largely out of duty, often without access to research libraries (from 1898, respiratory problems led Maitland to winter in the Canary Islands), and in an increasingly poor state of health. What matters for our purposes is not Maitland's judgement of the

1991), 53–7; and on the concept of higher journalism in Victorian culture, see John Gross, *The Rise and Fall of the Man of Letters: Aspects of English Literary Life Since 1800* (London: Weidenfeld & Nicolson, 1969), 62–97; also Edwin Mallard Everett, *The Party of Humanity: The Fortnightly Review and Its Contributors 1865–1874* (Chapel Hill: University of North Carolina Press, 1939), 1–27.

[27] See *FMG* 4, 75–6; also John Pollock, *Time's Chariot*, above n.4, 56; and cf. George Feaver, *From Status to Contract: A Biography of Sir Henry Maine 1822–1888* (London: Longmans, 1969), 131, 134, 246. As compared with other London clubs, the Athenaeum has tended to admit to its membership a high number of writers, bishops, judges, and senior public servants. Other members of this period included Henry Sidgwick, Leslie Stephen, James Bryce, William Stubbs, and Walter Bagehot. See generally [Frank Richard Cowell], *The Athenaeum: Club and Social Life in London 1824–1974* (London: Heinemann, 1975). Pollock appears never to have been central to the affairs of the Athenaeum, though he did serve on the Library Committee of the Club in the early 1890s: see Humphry Ward, *History of the Athenaeum 1824–1925* (London: privately printed for the Club, 1926), 84. Pollock was also elected (in 1869) as a member of the Savile Club, which, although less distinguished than the Athenaeum, boasted a similarly eclectic membership along with a strong apostolic tradition. See Anon., *The Savile Club 1868 to 1923* (London: privately printed for the Committee of the Club, 1923), 76, 105; and also Lubenow, above n.6, 233.

[28] See 'The British Academy for the Promotion of Historical, Philosophical and Philological Studies: Charter of Incorporation' (1903) 1 *Proc. Brit Acad.* x–xiii at x; Frederic G. Kenyon, *The British Academy: The First Fifty Years* (London: Cumberlege, 1952), 8–12. '[T]he original Fellows of the British Academy in 1902 were', Collini notes, 'the first generation among whom an academic career was at all common' (above n.26, 22). The founding of the Academy, furthermore, 'reveals just how much a certain familiarity between members of the intellectual élite still prevailed, since the first steps depended upon a chain of acquaintance and even friendship' (ibid. 24–5).

[29] See *FMG* 87, John Pollock, *Time's Chariot*, above n.4, 82, 91–100, 200–3.

[30] For an account of this particular predisposition among this particular group of people, see Collini, above n.26, 13–59.

[31] Frederick Pollock, 'Leslie Stephen: A Review' (December 1906) 11 *Independent Rev.* 349–56 at 349.

[32] Pollock to Holmes, 19 October 1906, in *PHL* i. 135; see also F. W. Maitland to H. A. L. Fisher, 21 September 1906, in *The Letters of Frederic William Maitland*, above n.22, 378.

work, but Pollock's. His knowledge of how Maitland regarded the book was not appropriate for general disclosure—that, it seemed, was the sort of information that should only be conveyed from one Brahmin to another. To a general readership it was sufficient simply to declare the book a success, the work of 'a true scholar commemorating a true scholar'.[33]

Whereas Pollock occupied an outer circle of the general Victorian intellectual aristocracy, he was centrally placed among the legal aristocracy. 'As conspicuously in *you* as in myself, academic success has been the result of general *mental power*, and you can make yourself as good a Lawyer as Hardwicke was or Willes is', Pollock's grandfather wrote to him in 1868. His grandfather was Sir Jonathan Frederick Pollock, Lord Chief Baron of the Exchequer from 1844 to 1866. The letter quoted here appears in a short memoir of Pollock C. B. published in 1929, the work of the then Master of the Rolls, the first Lord Hanworth.[34] Formerly Sir Ernest Murray Pollock, Hanworth was Frederick Pollock's cousin. As compared with the careers of Pollock C. B. and Hanworth, that of Frederick's father was comparatively low-key: after several years practising at the Bar, he became a Master in the Court of Exchequer and later Queen's Remembrancer.[35] The family seemed as if genetically predisposed to legal achievement.

Yet for Pollock it almost did not work out that way. That he would practise appears to have been treated by his family as a given. He was called to the Bar by Lincoln's Inn in May 1871, having become a member there in January 1868 (he would be elected as a bencher of Lincoln's Inn in 1906). Lincoln's Inn was not the obvious choice for Pollock's legal career. Both his father and his grandfather were members of the Inner Temple. Since the early eighteenth century, however, Lincoln's Inn had been the lair of Chancery practitioners. '[W]hen it was determined or rather assumed that the Bar was the right profession for me,' Pollock recalls in his memoirs, 'my father considered (and I suppose my grandfather agreed) that the Chancery branch of it would suit better with my scholarly tastes.'[36] Whether this decision was the right one is not clear, for Pollock never fell in love with equity as he did with the common law. This is not to say that he neglected equity. His academic career began in the era of the Judicature Acts 1873–5—his first book, published in the wake of that legislation, is pointedly titled *Principles of Contract at Law and in Equity*—

[33] Pollock, above n.31, 356.

[34] [Sir Jonathan] F[rederick] Pollock to Frederick Pollock, in Hanworth, above n.5, 196.

[35] Pollock succeeded to his father's baronetcy—becoming Sir Frederick Pollock, third baronet—in December 1888. See *Burke's Peerage and Baronetage*, 105th edn. (London: Burke's Peerage (Genealogical Books), 1980), 2140. A Queen's (or King's) Remembrancer is an officer responsible for collecting debts due to the Crown.

[36] *FMG* 160. A study of the Bar during the last quarter of the nineteenth century shows that, during that period, 57 per cent of judges were members of Lincoln's Inn, this being the 'most fashionable' of the Inns of Court. 'However, only one quarter of the elite members of the bar were Lincoln's Inn men, while 44 per cent went to the Inner Temple.' Daniel Duman, 'The Late Victorian Bar: A Prosopographical Survey', in *Law, Litigants and the Legal Profession*, eds. E. Ives and A. H. Manchester (London: Royal Historical Society, 1983), 140–54 at 151.

and he never doubted that the common law and equity were mutually supportive.[37] He produced an excellent historical sketch of the development of the equity jurisdiction, furthermore, tracing equitable notions through Christopher St German back to Aristotle.[38] Generally, nevertheless, his pronunciations on equity tend to put one in mind of *Bleak House*. Throughout his thirty-five years as Editor of the *Law Quarterly Review*, he would regularly write anonymous notes—not that many barristers or judges could have failed to be aware of their provenance—variously disparaging slipshod Chancery judges, the 'cobwebs' of an equity jurisdiction which has 'hardened into a system as rigid as the common law', and 'equity practitioners who persistently ignore common law decisions' and who exhibit an 'immemorial talent for hair-splitting'.[39] In his *Essays in Jurisprudence and Ethics*, collected together in 1882, he complains of the 'cumbrous and uncertain' operation of equity in relation to land law: 'equity . . . tends to increase the perils of purchasers', leaving 'the law of property . . . so intricate and confused that not only no layman can understand it, but it is all but impossible even for the experts who do understand it to translate it as it stands into anything like plain English.'[40]

This last observation probably came from the heart. Conveyancing, it seems, nearly put an end to Pollock's legal career. Having forfeited his hard-won and highly cherished fellowship at Trinity in 1868 in order to enter Lincoln's Inn, he began pupillage in a conveyancer's chambers. The experience was anything but edifying. The conveyancer for whom he served 'was a master of forms and a very neat draftsman, but had no great interest in either the science or the history of law.' The idea of returning to Cambridge as a classics don became increasingly attractive. 'After a year of this disjointed learning I came away with a certain rule of thumb knowledge of the conveyancer's art, pretty confused notions of the laws of England and the foundations of legal science, and considerable doubt whether I had found my proper vocation. If at that moment any definite occasion had offered for returning to Cambridge and the classics, it might have been hard to resist.'[41]

Pollock was kept on course by a change of chambers. On the advice of another former Apostle, Howard Elphinstone, he became in 1870 the pupil of Nathaniel Lindley, one of the leading juniors in the Chancery Courts (Lindley was later to become Master of the Rolls and, ultimately, a Lord of Appeal). A decade earlier, Lindley had produced his two-volume *Treatise on the Law of Partnership*[42]—a work which would later be 'the guide and foundation'[43] of Pollock's own *Digest of the Law of Partnership*. Entering the chambers of Lindley

[37] See *GCL* 79–80; also Hazeltine, above n.4, 244. [38] See *EIL* 180–98.

[39] See (1908) 24 *LQR* 117–18; (1903) 19 *LQR* 258; (1899) 15 *LQR* 3; (1916) 32 *LQR* 16; (1897) 13 *LQR* 11; and cf. Hazeltine (1937) 53 *LQR* 161–2.

[40] *EJE* 73–4. See also Pollock to Holmes, 19 May 1927, in *PHL* ii. 199. [41] *FMG* 161–2.

[42] Nathaniel Lindley, *A Treatise on the Law of Partnership: Including its Application to Joint-Stock and other Companies*, 2 vols. (London: William Maxwell, 1860).

[43] *DLP* xxi.

marked the point at which the scales fell from Pollock's eyes. To his delight, Lindley took the trouble to teach, and would listen to, his pupils. Pollock dedicated his first book, *Principles of Contract*, to Lindley—'To my master in the law . . . I dedicate the first fruits of his teaching'. By his example, Pollock wrote, 'I learnt that the law is neither a trade nor a solemn jugglery, but a science.'[44] The *annus mirabilis* did not end with Lindley: in the summer of 1870, Pollock served as marshal on the Western Circuit for James Shaw Willes, a Justice of the Common Pleas and friend of the family. Pollock had the good fortune to find himself again in the company of a lawyer with scholarly sensibilities and a desire to impart knowledge. The first edition of Pollock's *The Law of Torts*—very much the companion to his *Principles of Contract*—is dedicated to the memory of Willes and contains a letter in which Pollock describes his qualities to Holmes: 'he was not only a man of profound learning in the law, joined with extraordinary and varied knowledge of other kinds, but one of those whose knowledge is radiant, and kindles answering fire.'[45] 'F[rederick] . . . learned a great deal of law from him,' Pollock's father noted, 'and conceived a deep regard and respect for him personally, which he has never failed to evince on all suitable occasions'.[46] 'I learnt more of the Common Law from him in a month', Pollock recalled in 1933, 'than I could have learnt in any other fashion in six months. . . . It was Willes, moreover, who sent me to the Year Books and started me on the path of discovering that modern English law cannot be properly understood without going back to its medieval origins and development.'[47]

Through Willes, Pollock became fascinated by English legal history, whereas Lindley's principal achievement had been to make him conceive of law as a science. Lindley affected Pollock's historical outlook also, having encouraged him to study Roman law. Unfortunately, the Roman law texts available to Pollock in 1870 were elementary and outdated.[48] Help, however, was at hand.

[44] *FMG* 163. Judge Paul Baker holds at 9 Old Square, Lincoln's Inn, a small collection of books from Pollock's personal library. Among these books is a copy of Francis Vaughan Hawkins, *A Concise Treatise on the Construction of Wills* (London: William Maxwell, 1863). The volume is signed by Pollock and dated 1870, and it seems likely that Pollock would have read it around the time that he was Lindley's pupil. The book is heavily annotated by Pollock, particularly with details of cases omitted from the book. What is interesting about the annotations is that they demonstrate Pollock's early talent for offering concise statements of legal principle—a talent which Pollock himself felt Lindley helped to nurture. Not that Pollock considered wills to be, in the long term, a suitable topic for developing this talent. Judge Baker also holds Pollock's copy of the second edition of Hawkins on *Wills*, ed. C. P. Sanger (London: Sweet & Maxwell, 1912). It is completely unmarked.

[45] *TLT* vii.

[46] *Personal Remembrances of Sir Frederick Pollock, Second Baronet*, above n.1, 191–2.

[47] *FMG* 166. See also Frederick Pollock, 'Learning the Law' (1924) 40 *LQR* 287–301 at 298; 'Introduction', in William Craddock Bolland, *The Year Books: Lectures Delivered in the University of London at the Request of the Faculty of Laws* (Cambridge: Cambridge UP, 1921), ix–xi at ix.

[48] See *FMG* 168–9. Half of one of Pollock's notebooks (Misc. 796, 15–123) contains his detailed notes on Theodor Marezoll's *Lehrbuch der Institutionen des römischen Rechtes*, probably the 7th edition (Leipzig: Barth, 1862). The notes on Marezoll are undated, but are preceded by Pollock's brief notes on a number of cases decided between February and March 1870. It seems most likely that this is the year in which Pollock produced his notes on Marezoll. The other half of the same notebook—Pollock was in the habit of writing inwards from both ends of his notebooks—contains notes (9–49) on Joseph

James Bryce had entered Lincoln's Inn in 1862—eight years later he would become the Regius Professor of Civil Law at Oxford. Bryce and Pollock were bonded by more than just membership of Lincoln's Inn. Bryce shared Pollock's love of mountaineering (Pollock became a member of the Alpine Club while at Trinity; Bryce would be elected to its circle in 1879, and would eventually become its President). In due course, both men would be appointed as founder members of the British Academy and, as already noted, would serve together—on the commission bearing Bryce's name—reporting on alleged German atrocities in Belgium. Both, furthermore, were associated with Francis Younghusband's 'Fight For Right' movement and were to become advocates for the establishment of a League of Nations.[49] But in the early 1870s, Bryce's principal achievement was to revive at Oxford the study of Roman law, and it was for his talents as promoter of the Roman law tradition that Pollock primarily accorded him credit. 'Bryce never applied himself directly to the history of English law,' Pollock wrote in his obituary for the man, 'but indirectly he did much to dispel the darkness by restoring contact between English and continental learning.'[50] According to Pollock, Bryce enabled him to remedy the shortcomings in his learning about Roman law by advising that he turn to the works of Friedrich Carl von Savigny.[51] Again, this marked a point from which Pollock never looked back: Savigny's adaptation of Roman law principles to the needs of modern European legal orders constituted, for him, a master-stroke.[52] The truth is probably that Pollock was impressed first and foremost by Savigny's learning and his ability to synthesize rather than by his argumentation. Whatever the case, Pollock, having discovered the founder of the historical school, rarely neglected an opportunity to laud him. 'Savigny,' he wrote in 1883, 'we do not yet know or honour enough'.[53] Even Maine—another of Pollock's juristic mentors—'began his work in the mighty and still present shadow of Savigny.'[54] The explanation of contract provided by Savigny captured the concept better—so Pollock would have it—than any definition to be found within the common law tradition.[55] Savigny was, quite simply, 'the greatest master of jurisprudence in modern times'.[56]

Story's *Commentaries on Equity Jurisprudence*, the 10th edition of which appeared (edited by Isaac Redfield) in 1870, though it could well be that the notes are based on an earlier edition.

[49] See Viscount Bryce, 'The Defence of Right', in *For the Right: Essays and Addresses by Members of the 'Fight for Right Movement'* (London: T. Fisher Unwin, 1916), 1–4; and Sir Frederick Pollock, 'A League of Peace', ibid. 125–34.

[50] Sir Frederick Pollock, 'James Bryce' (April 1922) 471 *Quarterly Rev.* 400–14 at 404. See also Pollock to Holmes, 13 February 1922, in *PHL* ii. 88–9; and 9 March 1922, ibid. 91.

[51] See *FMG* 168–9.

[52] The relevant work here is Savigny's *System des heutigen römischen Rechts* [*System of present-day Roman law*], 9 vols. (Berlin: Veit, 1840–51). See generally Hermann Kantorowicz, 'Savigny and the Historical School' (1937) 53 *LQR* 326–43; and Friedrich Engel-Janosi, 'The Intellectual Background of Savigny' (1947) 5 *Seminar* 39–61.

[53] *OLOD* 41.

[54] *OLOD* 153.

[55] See *SHLP* 139. The point is taken up in chapter 5.

[56] *IHSP* 126.

There are other influences to be noted from Pollock's early years at the Bar. Frederic William Maitland joined Lincoln's Inn as a student in June 1872, was called to the Bar in November 1876, and spent the next eight years succeeding where Pollock had struggled—as a conveyancer and equity draftsman. In 1879, Maitland had published in the *Westminster Review* an article on the reform of English property law which impressed Pollock greatly: '[w]hat I do remember is the impression made on me by the brilliance of the writing and the extraordinary range of learning shown by so young a man—he was of three years' standing at the bar.'[57] It was at Lincoln's Inn, according to Pollock, that the two men first met,[58] and we have noted already that—certainly in Pollock's eyes—their shared apostolic roots effectively sealed their friendship. Maitland and Pollock not only shared the Apostles: both had studied at Eton and at Trinity College, both would become Sunday Tramps (Maitland being admitted to the fraternity in 1880) and members of the Athenaeum Club, and Maitland would be another founder member of the British Academy. Most of all, Maitland and Pollock shared a scholarly apparatus. Maitland tended to carry his learning lightly, and could be erudite without ever being overbearing or intimidating.[59] Although Pollock lacked Maitland's lightness of touch, he recognized it to be a gift.[60] Throughout his obituary for Maitland in the *Proceedings of the British Academy*, Pollock emphasizes Maitland's humour as much as his erudition. Maitland had been 'a lifelong friend and fellow worker', 'a genius equipped with sound professional training', able to combine 'the rigorous method of a specialist with profound insight, sure judgement, and constructive imagination', blessed with 'the practical sense of affairs that teaches generalities to know their place, and the saving sense of humour that chokes off paradox.'[61] In Maitland, Pollock found someone who could appeal to his lighter side but also match his own learning and scholarly standards.

Similar could be said of Oliver Wendell Holmes, Jr., whom Pollock appears first to have met in 1874.[62] While immensely learned, Holmes, unlike Maitland, could not always reach Pollock's heights. Perhaps even Holmes

57 Pollock, 'Frederic William Maitland', above n.10, 406.

58 Pollock to Maitland, 9 November 1887, Maitland papers, Add. 7006.

59 For an illustration, see DeLloyd J. Guth and M. H. Hoeflich, 'F. W. Maitland and Roman Law: An Uncollected Letter, with Notes and Comments' [1982] *Univ. Illinois L. Rev.* 441–8.

60 See, e.g., *EIL* dedication, 88; *GCL* 41.

61 Frederick Pollock, 'Frederic William Maitland, 1850–1906' (1906) 2 *Proc. Brit. Acad.* 455–60 at 460, 456–7.

62 Pollock's *DNB* entry claims that Pollock first met Holmes in 1874, as does David H. Burton, 'The Intellectual Kinship of Oliver Wendell Holmes, Jr., Frederick E. [*sic*] Pollock, and Harold J. Laski' (1975) 119 *Proceedings of the American Philosophical Society* 133–42 at 135, where it is also claimed that Leslie Stephen introduced the two men. That this would necessarily have been their first meeting is questioned by Pollock's son in his introduction to *PHL* i. xiii–xxiii at xv. Pollock himself suggests that 1874 is about correct but denies that Stephen made the introduction: Frederick Pollock to Adolph S. Oko, n.d. [1934] (no. 2–234), in Oko papers, MS 14, box 5, file 13 ('The date was not 1867 but four or five years later, after I was called to the Bar: the place my parents' house where I was still living, and I think the introduction was to my father not to me—nor from L. Stephen whom I did not yet know very well').

himself was of this view: 'You abase and amaze me by your ever present and available learning', he wrote to Pollock in 1916. 'I . . . wonder helplessly at your collateral knowledge.'[63] As between the two men, however, Holmes was the more original thinker. Pollock eulogized him, as he did Maitland, for putting life into the 'dry bones' of legal history.[64] Holmes impressed Pollock also with his jurisprudence of external standards: the 'scientific importance' of the notion of an 'external standard of reasonableness, which enables the law to keep in close touch with the moral and practical sense of mankind in the affairs of life,' Pollock claimed in 1904, 'was demonstrated once and for all, more than twenty years ago, by my friend Mr Justice Holmes; and if my own endeavours to pursue its application in detail have any value, it is largely due to his example.'[65] Pollock's indebtedness to Holmesian jurisprudence is a theme to which we will return in due course.

That Maitland and Holmes were inspirational figures for Pollock is much to be expected and probably fairly well known. Less well documented is the influence upon Pollock of Sir Courtenay Ilbert. By no means the most significant influence on Pollock's career, Ilbert is nevertheless noteworthy because the mark that he made was distinct. Another Lincoln's Inn Chancery barrister, Ilbert was called to the Bar two years before Pollock, and it seems that the two men met through James Bryce.[66] Like Pollock, Ilbert would go on to write books about law, but his main talent would be as a parliamentary draftsman. In 1882, he left practice in order to become a legal member of the Governor-General's council in India, in which role he was vested with responsibility for advancing the codification of Indian law (a project which had been set in motion by Thomas Babbington Macaulay some fifty years earlier).

The general project, as Pollock was to note, did not run altogether smoothly.[67] From Pollock's own point of view, however, it 'bore good fruit': Ilbert had been keen to impress upon Pollock the importance attaching to the Anglo-Indian codes and in 1882 asked Pollock to draft a Bill codifying the Indian law of civil wrongs.[68] Although the draft code was never brought forward, the work that Pollock undertook resulted—as was the case with most things that he did—in scholarly output. He included his Civil Wrongs Bill, along with commentary, as an appendix to the second edition of *The Law of Torts*. Further work on Indian law was to follow: in 1894 Pollock produced a

[63] Holmes to Pollock, 24 March 1916, in *PHL* i. 234; and 16 October 1916, ibid. 238.

[64] See *EOD* 10–13; *OLOD* 44–6; and cf. 'Frederic William Maitland, 1850–1906', above n.61, 456. Pollock also wrote a poem paying tribute to Holmes's father: see F[rederick] P[ollock], 'Paulo Post. To Dr O. W. Holmes, on His 75th Birthday' (30 September 1884), in *Recreations of the Rabelais Club* (London: privately printed, 1885), 3–4; repr. in Burton, above n.62, 135.

[65] *ECL* 108–9. For a more general tribute, see Frederick Pollock, 'Ad Multos Annos' (1931) 31 *Columbia L. Rev.* 349–51.

[66] See Frederick Pollock, 'Sir Courtenay Peregrine Ilbert, G.C.B.: 1841–1924' (1925) 11 *Proc. Brit. Acad.* 441–5 at 442.

[67] Ibid. 443.

[68] See ibid.; Hazeltine, above n.4, 238; John Pollock, *Time's Chariot*, above n.4, 62.

book, based in the main on his Tagore Lectures at the University of Calcutta, on the *Law of Fraud, Misrepresentation and Mistake in British India*; and in 1905 he co-authored an often critical commentary on the Indian Contract Act 1872.[69] Ilbert would not have been alone in fuelling Pollock's interest in Indian law: credit here must also be borne by Sir Henry Maine (whom we have yet properly to encounter) and the Anglo-Indian administrator and writer, Sir Alfred Comyn Lyall.[70] But Ilbert deserves to be singled out because it is owing to his initiatives in India that Pollock found himself grappling with codification.

On this subject Pollock proceeded with his customary caution. In an essay originally published in the *Pall Mall Gazette* in 1874, he questioned whether Parliament was sufficiently serious or competent to carry out a programme of codification.[71] When certain opponents of codification attempted to use Pollock's words as ammunition, he was alarmed. 'I had to explain that such was not my meaning', he wrote to Holmes in 1877.[72] And when his words were reprinted in his *Essays in Jurisprudence and Ethics*, he added that 'inasmuch as I found when this essay was first published that some of its expressions were liable to be perverted by enemies of codification to uses they were never meant for, it may be not amiss to say now that I am a strong believer in codification, and have given my reasons for it in some detail elsewhere.'

It may be profitable to detour briefly so as to consider where most of that detail can be found. In 1866, at the behest of the then Chancellor, Lord Westbury, a Royal Commission was established under the chairmanship of Lord Cranworth to enquire into the expediency of collecting together the statutes and cases relevant to particular areas of law with a view to producing legal 'digests.'[73] The Commission recommended the preparation of digests of particular branches of the law, and jurists were invited to produce specimen drafts.[74] Initially, no one appeared willing to rise to the challenge, but the lawyer who eventually found the courage to do so set about the task with remarkable energy. Sir James Fitzjames Stephen, elder brother of Sir Leslie Stephen, preceded Courtenay Ilbert (and succeeded Sir Henry Maine) as legal member of the Governor-General's council in India and, from December 1869 until April 1872, advanced with considerable success the project of codifying Indian law.[75]

[69] See *LFM*; *ICA*. [70] For Pollock on Lyall and India, see *FMG* 72–4; *OLOD* 56; *EOD* 23.

[71] See *EJE* 242–3. [72] Pollock to Holmes, 26 July 1877, in *PHL* i. 7.

[73] See [T. E. Holland], 'Codification' (1867) 27 *Edinburgh Rev.* 347–76 at 367–8.

[74] See J. H. Baker, *An Introduction to English Legal History*, 4th edn. (London: Butterworths, 2002), 219–20.

[75] On Fitzjames Stephen's successes and failures as legal member of the Governor-General's council, see James A. Colaiaco, *James Fitzjames Stephen and the Crisis of Victorian Thought* (London: Macmillan, 1983), 97–105; and also C. P. Ilbert, 'Sir James Stephen as a Legislator' (1894) 10 *LQR* 222–7. Ilbert wrote that '[p]robably no one ever believed more absolutely in the utility and in the practicability of codification than Fitzjames Stephen'; while he 'was a Cyclopean builder', however, '[h]e hurled together huge blocks of rough hewn law. It is undeniable that he left behind him some hasty work in the Indian Statute Book, some defective courses of masonry which his successors had to remove and replace' (ibid. 223–4). Pollock had anticipated much the same line of criticism almost twenty years

One of Stephen's most highly regarded achievements in India was The Evidence Act 1872, and, on his return to England, he set about trying to replicate that accomplishment on home soil.[76] Stephen's Evidence Bill, prepared in 1873 with the approval of Sir John Duke (later Lord) Coleridge, was never passed into law. But this was not the high-watermark of his initiative. In 1876, he in effect responded to the Cranworth Commission with the publication of his *Digest of the Law of Evidence*. In the following year there appeared his *Digest of the Criminal Law*, and in 1883 *A Digest of the Law of Criminal Procedure*.[77] A trend had been set in motion, which others were keen to follow.

In 1878 there appeared Chalmers's *Digest of the Law of Bills of Exchange*,[78] and in the previous year Pollock's *Digest of the Law of Partnership*. Both Chalmers's and Pollock's digests were to find their way to the statute-book—Chalmers's as the Bills of Exchange Act 1882, Pollock's as the Partnership Act 1890.[79] Both digests, furthermore, had been inspired by the efforts of Stephen. 'My desire', Pollock noted in the introduction to the first edition of *A Digest of the Law of Partnership*, 'has been to follow to the best of my power the example set by Sir James Stephen in his "Digest of the Law of Evidence," and now being repeated by him in the yet more weighty and difficult work of a "Digest of the Criminal Law." '[80] Stephen's Anglo-Indian codification initiative was, Pollock added, 'an example not to be merely copied, but to be followed and improved upon.'[81] Codification 'is an instrument of new constructive power, enabling the legislator to combine the good points of statute law and case-law . . . while avoiding almost all their respective drawbacks'[82]; and while the Anglo-Indian codes are not 'perfect in execution', they 'furnish us in their general method and design with a pattern which we should do well to follow'.[83] '[B]eing of modern growth, homogeneous, and for the most part well settled', the law of partnership, like the law of evidence, might be 'specially fit . . . for

earlier: see Frederick Pollock, 'Stephen's Digest of the Law of Evidence' (1876) n.s. 20 *Fortnightly Rev.* 383–94 at 387–90. It seems that Maine's legislative initiatives in India, while numerous, made little impact. See Carl Landauer, 'From Status to Treaty: Henry Sumner Maine's *International Law*' (2002) 15 *Canadian Jnl. of Law and Jurisprudence* 219–54 at 225–6. More generally, see Eric Stokes, *The English Utilitarians and India* (Oxford: Clarendon Press, 1959); also Benjamin Evans Lippincott, *Victorian Critics of Democracy: Carlyle, Ruskin, Arnold, Stephen, Maine, Lecky* (New York: Octagon, 1974), 134–206.

[76] See K. J. M. Smith, *James Fitzjames Stephen: Portrait of a Victorian Rationalist* (Cambridge: Cambridge UP, 1988), 84–8.

[77] See Smith, ibid. 53.

[78] M. D. Chalmers, *A Digest of the Law of Bills of Exchange, Promissory Notes and Cheques* (London: Macmillan & Co., 1877). As with Stephen and Ilbert, Chalmers served as legal member of the council in India. He produced a further digest, on the law of sale, which became the Sale of Goods Act 1893.

[79] 'Following the publication of his digest of the law of partnership, the young Mr Frederick Pollock was paid £100 to draft a Partnership Bill for the Associated Chambers of Commerce. By June 1879 the bill was ready and it was introduced later that session. Since it tried to do more than merely to restate the existing law, it ran into considerable difficulties and its progress was blocked for many years so that it did not reach the statute book until 1890. In its original form it did not apply to Scotland but in the final stages of its passage through Parliament this was changed.' Alan Rodger, 'The Codification of Commercial Law in Victorian Britain' (1992) 108 *LQR* 570–90 at 578.

[80] *DLP* iii. [81] *DLP* xii. [82] *DLP* iv. [83] *DLP* x.

an experiment of this kind.'[84] Of course, codes must not remain static—'successive revisions, as Sir James Stephen has pointed out, are indispensable to keep a Code in efficient working order.'[85] But so long as the project of regular revision is attended to, there is no reason for not considering 'the Indian Codes a desirable model for the exposition of English law'.[86]

Thus it was that Pollock, in the first edition of his *Digest of the Law of Partnership*, came out in support of codification. The support was reiterated in two further essays which, while not entirely uncritical of the Anglo-Indian codification initiative, were essentially tributes to Stephen's work.[87] Like others, Pollock was somewhat irked by the tendency of English lawyers to dither over adopting what they had been happy to see imposed on other jurisdictions. 'There can be little doubt that England must soon make up her mind to do what the rest of the world has done, and what she herself has sanctioned in the case of some of her remote dependencies', Thomas Erskine Holland had written in 1867.[88] In his *Essays in Jurisprudence and Ethics*, Pollock remarks in a similar vein that it seems odd, to say the least, to find English lawyers imposing codification upon India while declaring it impracticable for England. 'The Anglo-Indian codes are the work of Englishmen, and founded on English law. . . . We are told, however, that what Englishmen have done with success for British India they are incapable of doing for themselves.'[89] Almost two decades later, in his *First Book of Jurisprudence*, we find him more forthright: '[c]odification was forced upon British India by the necessities of Indian government, and the experiment has on the whole been remarkably successful. There is no reason why it should not succeed in England'.[90] As the principal case note writer for the *LQR*, however, he was not prepared to freewheel thus: '[t]he main reason for dreading codification is the fear that our judges should decline to treat a code as a body of principles'; '[t]he real, though unperceived difficulty in the way of codifying the law is the tendency of our judges to interpret statutory enactments with a narrowness which they do not display when

[84] *DLP* xx. See also Robert B. Ferguson, 'Legal Ideology and Commercial Interests: The Social Origins of Commercial Law Codes' (1977) 4 *British Jnl. of Law and Society* 18–38 at 27 ('Pollock . . . felt that the great bulk of commercial law wanted only putting "into shape" to be accepted as satisfactory. He regarded partnership law as "modern and rational in substance", and thus unusually favourable for the enterprise of codification').

[85] *DLP* viii. See also Frederick Pollock, 'Sir James Fitzjames Stephen' (1895) 25 *National Rev.* 817–23 at 820–1.

[86] *DLP* iii.

[87] Pollock, 'Sir James Fitzjames Stephen', above n.85; 'Stephen, Sir James Fitzjames' *Encyclopaedia Britannica*, 11th edn. (1911), xxv. 883–5. Pollock had earlier produced a review essay assessing Stephen's attack on the liberal vision of John Stuart Mill, in which he supported Stephen on certain points and defended Mill on others: see F[rederick] P[ollock], 'Liberty, Equality, Fraternity' (July 1873) n.s. 8 *Fraser's Magazine* 86–97.

[88] Holland, above n.73, 365.

[89] *EJE* 71, and see also ibid. 90.

[90] *FBJ* 341–2. See also F. Pollock, 'General Introduction', in *Encyclopaedia of the Laws of England, being a New Abridgement of the Most Eminent Legal Authorities*, ed. A. W. Renton, 12 vols. (London: Sweet & Maxwell, 1897), i. 1–13 at 13 ('codes may, and in some cases have been, as in India, valuable instruments of political and even moral education to the general public . . .').

called upon to interpret the principles of Common Law or of Equity.'[91] In India, such interpretive difficulties had not materialized.[92] Until fears over such difficulties could be allayed, however, many English lawyers would 'continue to deprecate the codification of the law.'[93]

By no means is this the last time that we will encounter Pollock working hard to add provisos to his arguments. Other instances, however, are for later. At this point, a good deal of biographical ground remains to be covered. From 1871, Pollock spent over a decade making Lincoln's Inn his primary place of work. But what did he do there? Two volumes of his notebooks show that he quite regularly wrote opinions on briefs.[94] In the main, however, he dedicated himself to establishing his reputation as a jurist with both nitty-gritty knowledge of black-letter technicalities and the ability carefully to explain law at the level of general principle. 'He is (probably) the only high philosopher that loves the real English Common Law', Pollock's former Eton tutor wrote of him in 1874.[95] Throughout the 1870s Pollock produced numerous reviews and essays (some of which would eventually form his *Essays in Jurisprudence and Ethics*), the first two editions of his *Principles of Contract*, and the first two editions of his *Digest of the Law of Partnership*. During this period he also produced a juristic *jeu d'esprit*, *Leading Cases Done into English*, completed the first edition of *The Land Laws*, and was probably also working on his short monograph, *The Fishery Laws*, which was published in 1883. In 1879, furthermore, he drafted a Bill for the Consolidation and Amendment of the Law of Partnership.[96] In letters from this period, Pollock can be found confessing to being busy.[97] But he was not busy practising. 'Make yourself a *good lawyer*', his grandfather had written to him in 1868, 'and you are sure not to want practice'.[98] Although there appears to be no evidence that Pollock actually heeded this advice, his career unfolded as if he did so. Sightings of him before the bench—only twice is he recorded as appearing in court[99]—were as rare as sightings of him in print were frequent.

[91] (1894) 10 *LQR* 291; (1892) 8 *LQR* 183. [92] (1904) 20 *LQR* 115.

[93] (1894) 10 *LQR* 110. For further reflections on Pollock's ambivalent attitude towards codification, see Hedley, above n.4, 414–17.

[94] The whole of one of Pollock's notebooks (Misc. 794) contains opinions which he wrote between December 1871 and July 1884, and half of another (Misc. 793) contains opinions written between June 1885 and November 1912. It seems clear that he wrote fewer opinions as the years passed.

[95] William Johnson (Cory) to Reginald Brett, 5 November 1874, in Esher Papers—William Johnson Letters, ESHR 9/4, ff.148–53 at 149. For Pollock on Johnson, see *FMG* 21.

[96] For Pollock's account of the preparation of which, see *DLP(2)* xxv; *DLP(4)* 161–2.

[97] See, e.g., Pollock to Holmes, 2 May 1876, in *PHL* i. 5–6.

[98] [Sir Jonathan] F[rederick] Pollock to Frederick Pollock, in Hanworth, above n.5, 196.

[99] See Fifoot, above n.19, 12. Certainly on one of these occasions it is highly unlikely that Pollock would have spoken. Although he prepared the written statement of the case for the appellants in *Martin v. Boulanger* (1883) 8 App. Cas. 296, P.C., he was not leading counsel and the appellants' case was presented by Arthur Cohen (see ibid. 297). Whereas Pollock hardly ever appeared in court, Cohen addressed the House of Lords and the Judicial Committee of the Privy Council more often than perhaps any other barrister of his generation. See Paul Baker, 'Lawyers Seen at the Athenaeum', in *Armchair Athenians: Essays from the Athenaeum*, ed. F. Férnandez-Armesto (London: The Athenaeum Club, 2001), 215–27 at 221–2.

ii. The talkative profession

Whether he would have wanted it this way we cannot determine. The courtroom clearly held some sort of appeal for him. In 1911, Pollock was admitted to the Privy Council: this was a significant honour for someone who was never a senior politician or public figure, though one imagines that he would have been happier had his admission to the Privy Council made him a member of its Judicial Committee.[100] In fact, the nearest Pollock would come to judicial office was his appointment in 1914 as Judge of the Admiralty Court of the Cinque Ports. He informed Holmes of the appointment with ironic humour: 'Behold I too am a judge—of a sort. . . . The work apparently consists of about one case in four years, and . . . I feel that there ought to be silver oars and three-cornered hats. . . . The fees are like nominal damages.'[101] The tone should not disguise the fact that the appointment was clearly a matter of great pride to Pollock. Within two months of being appointed, he addressed the Society of Public Teachers of Law about the history of the Cinque Ports jurisdiction.[102] As is evident from letters to Holmes subsequent to the appointment, furthermore, he was itching to decide a case.[103] The caseload turned out not to be sparse, however, but non-existent: to Pollock's regret, he was never called upon to adjudicate.[104] That he should have lamented so is not wholly surprising. Much of his work as a jurist—and particularly his initiatives as principal case note writer for the *Law Quarterly Review*—consisted of commenting on judicial performance. While it would be simplistic to declare Pollock a judge *manqué*, it ought at least to be noted at this point that he was possibly more responsible than was any other lawyer, practising or academic, for developing the appraisal and critique of judicial decision-making into a standard form of

[100] Another jurist, Sir William Anson, was also made a Privy Councillor in 1911. Although, like Pollock, Anson was for a considerable part of his career a university lawyer, he also spent many years active in politics as well as a few on the bench and in practice, and so his admission to the Privy Council was perhaps not as noteworthy as was Pollock's. Certainly many of Pollock's acquaintances were in no doubt about the honour bestowed upon him: see A. Ali to Frederick Pollock, 21 June 1911, in Pollock correspondence, box 1, folder 1; William R. Anson to Frederick Pollock, 23 June 1911, ibid. folder 3 ('What ceremonials await us I do not like to conjecture, nor what clothes: I already possess a uniform which is a splendid instrument of torture, and which casts a storm over tomorrow'); G. O. Trevelyan to Frederick Pollock, 29 June 1911, ibid. folder 73.

[101] Pollock to Holmes, 20 May 1914, in *PHL* i. 214. The appointment was noted in *The Times*, 19 May 1914, 8, col. C.

[102] See Frederick Pollock, 'Cinque Ports Jurisdiction: In the Matter of a Whale' (1925) 41 *LQR* 453–6. Although published in 1925, this paper was delivered to the SPTL in July 1914. Pollock's 'intention to pursue the subject was cut short by the war', and he eventually published his brief address 'in the hope that it may induce some younger scholar to go farther' with the topic (ibid. 453).

[103] See Pollock to Holmes, 19 August 1914, in *PHL* i. 218; and 15 September 1914, ibid. 220.

[104] 'I have never had an appeal . . . ; I have never had any suggestion that I ought to hold a sitting in full court, and I do not believe I ever shall. . . . [Y]ou may ask me why on earth does this go on. Well, the answer is simple: It does not cost a cent of public money. There is no salary.' Sir Frederick Pollock, 'The Admiralty Court of the Cinque Ports' (1930) 9 *Proc. Am. Foreign Law Assoc.* 5–13 at 11–12. See also *DNB*, above n.4, 712; Hazeltine, 'Sir Frederick Pollock, Bart.', above n.4, 241–2.

academic-legal activity. At least once in a while, we might presume, he would have liked to experience adjudication aside from writing about it.

Even if only in a fairly low-key setting, Pollock seemed to be eager to sit as a judge. But he never seemed keen to present a case before one. He was held in high regard by many judges—a sizeable number of the senior judiciary were present at his memorial service[105]—and it was Lord Birkenhead who in 1920 apparently insisted that he take silk. But without Birkenhead's insistence, it is almost inconceivable that he would ever have done so. Certainly Pollock made no pretence to being suited to advocacy.[106] 'I am rather busy the rest of this week with a rather curious and perplexed case coming on, my first appearance in Court for many years', he wrote to Roscoe Pound in 1922.[107] Possibly the case referred to is that recounted by the solicitor and divorce law reformer, E. S. P. Haynes, whose mother was Pollock's first cousin. 'I remember sending him a brief connected with private international law and his appearance in a particularly antediluvian wig', Haynes recalls. 'The judge expressed regret at not seeing him oftener in court.' Haynes also relates a story of how, many years earlier, Pollock assisted Haynes's father before the Judicial Committee of the Privy Council:

> His opponent sat down and there was dead silence. My father gently tapped him on the shoulder and indicated that a reply was expected. Sir Frederick turned round and said: 'There is nothing to answer. I never heard such nonsense.'[108]

Such, apparently, was Pollock's style. Among his friends, his son tells us, he liked to be known as 'Fred' or 'F. P.'[109] Yet the informality and intimacy of these appellations jar with his punctilious, aloof, occasionally rebarbative public image. 'No one can say that "grovelling servility" was one of Pollock's faults', wrote one particularly diplomatic observer.[110] Throughout the accounts of the man there recur the same motifs: Pollock was shy, terse, taciturn, stolid, inclined not to speak when speech was expected. It seems almost laughable

[105] See 'Memorial Service: Sir Frederick Pollock', in *The Times*, 29 January 1937, 17, col. B.

[106] See 'Sir Frederick Pollock, K.C.: The "Old Broad Culture"', above n.4 ('Sir Frederick knew his limitations, for he was not so well adapted as his kinsmen for the bear-garden of forensic strife'); Holdsworth (1937) 53 *LQR* 177 ('he was not so well fitted . . . to shine in the Courts'); also Hazeltine, 'Sir Frederick Pollock, Bart.', above n.4, 238 ('In 1920, at the suggestion of the Lord Chancellor (Lord Birkenhead), Pollock took silk. It seems clear, from the available evidence, that the Lord Chancellor regarded Pollock's attainment of this high rank in the profession as fitting recognition, not of his place in advocacy, but of his eminence in legal scholarship and of his distinguished work as General Editor of the current Law Reports ever since 1895').

[107] Pollock to Pound, 22 February 1922, in Pound papers.

[108] E. S. P. Haynes, *The Lawyer: A Conversation Piece, Selected from the Lawyer's Notebooks and Other Writings* (London: Eyre & Spottiswoode, 1951), xxxv.

[109] See Sir John Pollock, 'Introduction', in *PHL* i. xiii–xxiii at xiii.

[110] Goodhart (1937) 53 *LQR* 204.

that he should have highlighted talkativeness as the hallmark of any good lawyer.[111] Even his most charitable obituarists found themselves writing about 'his sovereign contempt for ignorance',[112] of how '[i]t is impossible to exaggerate his awkwardness of manner',[113] and of how '[h]e followed the principle, more suited to others than himself, of not speaking unless he was spoken to.'[114] Many an historian of English legal thought can recount a story about Pollock's anti-social behaviour. Lawson relates a particularly memorable one concerning how Pollock once invited a group of Oxford undergraduates to coffee, 'at which nothing was said for an hour until one of them timidly suggested that it was time to go home.'[115] Pollock once offended his cousin, Lord Hanworth, M. R., Harold Laski claims, when he chanced upon him at one end of Chancery Lane and accompanied him its entire length without uttering a word. 'The M. R. was rather angry and cherished a grudge; but four days later he met Leslie Scott who said to him "I met F. P. the other day, and he told me he had a delightful chat with you."'[116] The poet and novelist George Meredith was, according to Pollock's son, one of the closest friends of the family and greatly admired by his father.[117] Whatever Meredith made of Pollock generally, he knew only too well his demeanour. 'Whenever you say anything to Fred Pollock, whether he agrees with it or not,' G. M. Trevelyan recalls Meredith observing, 'he puts on a look as if he had just received the whole stench of the infernal pit into his nostrils.'[118]

These instances recount Pollock among his own; it almost goes without saying that in unfamiliar surroundings his manner was invariably interpreted as resting somewhere between eccentric and offensive. When Pollock's personal secretary remarked to Samuel Williston that in England Pollock was 'thought rather peculiar', Williston retorted 'that the thought was not insular but international.'[119] As a young assistant professor at the Harvard Law

[111] Sir Frederick Pollock, *The Talkative Profession* (Birmingham: The Holdsworth Club of the University of Birmingham, 1932), 4–5 ('Man is a social and an articulate animal; therefore it is necessary that men who live together should talk to one another. . . . [T]alking well is more important in our profession of the law than in any other').

[112] Edward Potton (1937) 53 *LQR* 203. See also 'Sir Frederick Pollock: A Distinguished Jurist', above n.4 ('He did not . . . suffer fools gladly, and the best-meant ignorance met from him unmerited contempt').

[113] Hollond, above n.4, 49. [114] Lord Maugham (1937) 53 *LQR* 169.

[115] F. H. Lawson, *The Oxford Law School, 1850–1965* (Oxford: Clarendon Press, 1968), 72. For more in the same vein, see Cosgrove, above n.4, 135–6.

[116] Harold J. Laski to O. W. Holmes, 1 March 1925, in *Holmes–Laski Letters: The Correspondence of Mr Justice Holmes and Harold J. Laski, 1916–1935*, 2 vols., ed. M. DeWolfe Howe (London: Cumberlege, 1953), i. 717.

[117] See John Pollock, *Time's Chariot*, above n.4, 101–6; and for his father's own words of appreciation regarding Meredith, see *FMG* 21–2, 77–8. In 1885, Meredith dedicated to Pollock senior a novel, *Diana of the Crossways*: see George Meredith to Arthur Doubleday, 17 June 1897, in *The Letters of George Meredith*, 3 vols., ed. C. L. Cline (Oxford: Clarendon Press, 1970), iii. 1269.

[118] G. M. Trevelyan, *An Autobiography and Other Essays* (London: Longmans, Green & Co., 1949), 22 n.1. Along with Pollock, Meredith and Trevelyan were fellow Tramps: see John Pollock, *Time's Chariot*, above n.4, 56.

[119] Samuel Williston, *Life and Law: An Autobiography* (Boston: Little, Brown & Co., 1941), 194.

School, Williston found being introduced to Pollock far from pleasurable: '[h]e looked upon me, as it seemed, without interest and said nothing. . . . I met him several times after that, but did not flatter myself that I had aroused his interest sufficiently to make him more than barely aware of my existence.'[120] Williston's dean at Harvard, James B. Thayer, received nothing better: 'he would have thought Sir Frederick's apparent indifference passed the bounds of courtesy if he had not known that he had crossed the Atlantic partly for the purpose' of meeting him.[121] Although Pollock was often an astute observer of mannerisms and manners when writing about others,[122] that astuteness seemed to melt away when he considered his own interpersonal conduct. Recalling his Lowell lectures at the Harvard Law School in 1903, he registered the inscrutability of the audience: '[f]or the first ten minutes of my first Lowell lecture I had no kind of indication of the impression I was making. One could only see that the hearers were not asleep but very much awake. Were they going to throw things at me, or what?'[123] Ultimately he concluded, and was impressed by the fact, that the audience was particularly attentive.[124] From the other side of the lectern, the Harvard Law Professor Edmund M. Morgan wondered whether Pollock realized that there was an audience present:

> The only spark of life in a dull lecture was when Pollock lifted his eyes from his manuscript and remarked that a judge in one of the western States had taken judicial notice that a five-cent drink of whiskey must be a small drink. It was only later, after I had read Pollock's lecture in its published form, that I realized how much I had missed owing to his dull and bored manner of delivery.[125]

One of Spinoza's teachers, Pollock claimed, 'had one power which may at times almost fill the place of genius', namely, 'that frank urbanity and polished conversation which is wont everywhere to draw confidence to it.'[126] Pollock manifestly lacked that power. Even his son acknowledged that there was about his father 'something . . . that made the average person find him odd', that 'shyness became an ingrained habit' so that 'a screen surround[ed] his qualities', that 'he could not abide the commonplace' and yet was inclined to regard all new acquaintances as part of the commonplace until they demonstrated

[120] Ibid. [121] Ibid.

[122] See, e.g., Pollock, 'Stephen, Sir James Fitzjames', above n.87, 883 ('Maine was subtle, swift and far-reaching; Stephen was massive, downright, indefatigable and sincere even to unnecessary frankness').

[123] *FMG* 197.

[124] See *FMG* 196–7; Pollock to Holmes, 10 August 1920, in *PHL* ii. 48.

[125] Edmund M. Morgan to Harold D. Hazeltine, n.d., cited in Hazeltine, above n.4, 239–40. Cf. the rather damning note—presumably the work of the editor—which appeared in *The Law Times* in December 1892: 'Sir Frederick Pollock has been discoursing in Glasgow upon "Archaism in Modern Law," before the Juridical Society of that city. As reported in the *North British Daily Mail*, the address does not seem to have been very brilliant. The most interesting features in the report are the misprints.' (1892–3) 94 *Law Times* 193.

[126] *SHLP* 7.

themselves to the contrary.[127] Both Pollock's son and Pollock himself attributed the shyness to short sightedness (a problem which was only diagnosed in Pollock's mid-twenties when he volunteered for the Inns of Court rifle corps!).[128] The picture of Pollock that emerges from the various available accounts, however, is not simply one of a man afflicted by shyness; his behaviour and manner often suggested snobbery and disdain. Maitland, Holmes, and a few others of their ilk may have penetrated the screen, but most did not. 'I *fear* Sir F. Pollock meditates a visit to us very soon', Maitland's wife wrote to the Boston University law professor, Melville Bigelow. 'I know you will sympathise with me for this.'[129] Pollock, to use the modern parlance, could be very hard work.

Those with a fondness for anecdotes could feast well on Pollock. While it would be easy and no doubt enjoyable to accumulate stories about his silences and inappropriate responses, however, to do so would be to risk missing something of the man. Good wines can come from struggling vines, and one senses that many of those who made the effort with Pollock ultimately felt rewarded for so doing. His friendship with Holmes provides the obvious example. In 1899, Holmes found himself reading *The Etchingham Letters*, Pollock's literary foray with Ella Fuller Maitland. 'They are good reading I think—pleasant and clear', Holmes remarked to Clare Castletown in May of that year. He continued:

> Pollock is an extraordinarily accomplished man. Not many goods in his shop window, but just when you think things are rather silent he spears out some shaft of wit or insight. He has written good law books—*Spinoza*, '*Leading Cases done in to English*' —admirable parodies of various poets and lord knows much more—learns all sorts of languages easily—has a mighty tough body—for a long pull at rowing or on the bicycle—likes fencing—has written about the sword—the kindest and most generous of hearts. Only defect a little too all round. But so much more interesting —so much more a living soul than most of the lawyers who have succeeded at the bar.[130]

The passage captures not only Holmes's admiration of Pollock's versatility—this being something we have already noted—but also his appreciation of Pollock's basic decency: never mind Pollock's essentially uncommunicative nature, Holmes appears to be saying; those who persevere with him are likely

[127] John Pollock, *Time's Chariot*, above n.4, 48. For glimpses of Pollock as an appreciative parent and grandparent, see Frederick Pollock, 'An Infant's Progress in Language' (1878) 3 *Mind* 392–401; Pollock to Holmes, 14 August 1928, in *PHL* ii. 226.

[128] See John Pollock, *Time's Chariot*, above n.4, 48; *FMG* 18, 179–83.

[129] Florence Maitland to Melville M. Bigelow, 16 September [1897?], in 'The Maitland–Bigelow Letters' (1957) 37 *Boston Univ. L. Rev.* 285–326 at 310. On Bigelow, see Brooks Adams, 'Melville M. Bigelow' (1921) 1 *Boston Univ. L. Rev.* 168–71.

[130] Oliver Wendell Holmes to Lady Clare Castletown, 12 May 1899, in Holmes papers, box 26 folder 13.

to discover someone who is kind-hearted, generous, and anything but dull. Other assessments corroborate what Holmes had to say. While 'F. P. (fireplug)' may have 'no manners', William Cory wrote in 1874, he ought not to be dismissed. 'Never mind what the Trin. Coll. say of him; he is worth many Jebbs. Thoroughbred, cool head, warm heart, high mind.'[131] 'His manners at first seemed odd and difficult', William Holdsworth wrote on Pollock's death, but 'on further acquaintance that impression vanished.'[132] Likewise the obituarist in *The Times* remarked on how Pollock's 'odd and curt manner of speaking yielded a most genial and benevolent disposition.'[133] The last two observations may simply be indicative of good form—obituaries being rarely an occasion for strafing. When the *Manchester Guardian* did run a moderately critical obituary—claiming that Pollock 'cast his net too widely' and so failed to establish 'a more enduring reputation', that his introduction to the 1906 edition of Maine's *Ancient Law* was 'neither apt nor profound', and that, 'as he grew older, a certain brusqueness made it difficult for younger men or strangers to approach him'[134]—E. S. P. Haynes responded that Pollock remained cordial in the company of others until the end of his life.[135] That Haynes had noted elsewhere Pollock's predilection for disdain and silence hardly rendered his claim credible. His closeness to Pollock, furthermore, made him a far from impartial witness.

Perhaps, however, this closeness is indicative of something. Haynes was no great scholar. His hobby horse was divorce law reform, but his writings on this subject (as on other subjects) suggested both that he was too lazy to engage in serious research and that he possessed a rather limited attention span.[136] In 1913, when Haynes was in his mid-thirties, Pollock produced a review of the then current literature on divorce reform,[137] noting that Haynes's contributions to the debate, 'addressed to the lay public', had been 'handy and vigorous' but 'not systematic'.[138] 'Many of the reformers' in this area, Pollock wrote to Holmes, 'give themselves away by lack of scholarship.'[139] It would not have

[131] William Johnson (Cory) to Reginald Brett, 5 November 1874, in Esher Papers—William Johnson Letters, ESHR 9/4, ff.148–53 at 149. 'Jebbs' = Sir Richard Claverhouse Jebb (1841–1905), fellow of Trinity College (1863–75) and Regius Professor of Greek (1889–1905) at Cambridge. See generally Caroline Jebb, *Life and Letters of Sir Richard Claverhouse Jebb, O.M., Litt.D.* (Cambridge: Cambridge UP, 1907).

[132] Holdsworth (1937) 53 *LQR* 180; also Holdsworth, *Some Makers of English Law*, above n.4, 280.

[133] 'Sir Frederick Pollock, K.C.: The "Old Broad Culture"', above n.4.

[134] 'Sir Frederick Pollock: A Distinguished Jurist', above n.4. The suggestion that Pollock tended to cast his net too widely is similarly made by F. R. Jones, above n.4, 2–3. The *Manchester Guardian* obituary also lauded Pollock: 'His most certain fame will be the fact that no man did more than he to revive the study of jurisprudence from the torpor into which it had fallen after the second Benthamite generation had passed away. When he began his work there were few serious legal scholars in the country; when he retired from his Oxford professorship both of the ancient universities had flourishing schools of law.'

[135] Haynes (1937) 53 *LQR* 197. For support for Haynes's response, see also Potton, (1937) 53 *LQR* 203.

[136] For representative Haynesian discussion of divorce law reform, see E. S. P. Haynes, *Life, Law and Letters* (London: Heinemann, 1936), 40–1, 141–8.

[137] See *EIL* 279–86. [138] *EIL* 285.

[139] Pollock to Holmes, 1 March 1913, in *PHL* i. 207.

been surprising had Pollock determined to scorn, or at least to ignore, Haynes's initiative; that he would, in private, have held distinct reservations about Haynes's approach to divorce law reform seems fairly obvious. Whether or not Pollock supported Haynes's reform campaign, however, what is clear is that he created in Haynes's mind the impression that he did. 'He sympathized with my campaign for divorce law reform' Haynes asserted in 1937.[140] He may have known only too well Pollock's foibles, but he clearly worshipped the man. 'Up until the end of his life he remained my hero.'[141] More or less all of Haynes's many books are peppered with deferential references to the great Pollock.[142] While this respect is largely attributable to Haynes's appreciation of Pollock as an intellectual, its roots in friendship are also clear.

Haynes was not the only young lawyer to appreciate the elderly Pollock's character. '[H]is reserve, which he never succeeded in overcoming except with his more intimate friends', Arthur Goodhart remarked, concealed 'a dry but pleasant sense of humour'.[143] Goodhart managed not only to penetrate the screen, but also to locate Pollock's supportive side: in 1926, on Pollock's recommendation, Goodhart, at the age of 34, became the editor of the *Law Quarterly Review*.[144] Cornelia Sorabji, the first Indian woman to become an English barrister, was a pupil of Pollock's at Oxford and regularly paid tribute to his supportiveness. 'I have . . . gone to him as to my *guru* in a thousand difficulties', she wrote in 1934, for '[t]here would seem to be no subject about which he cannot enrich one's knowledge'.[145] Even those who felt his iciness would often register subsequent thaws. Williston may have considered Pollock rather odious after early meetings with him; in later years, however, he found him to be a willing conversationalist and a reliable correspondent.[146] Laski, too, having regaled Holmes with his story of Pollock and Lord Hanworth, noted in subsequent letters how highly regarded and impressive a lawyer Pollock was.[147] According to Fifoot, Pollock, like Leslie Stephen, 'locked the door on

140 See Haynes (1937) 53 *LQR* 195; and cf. *The Times* (letters), 1 December 1922, 13, col. E.

141 Haynes, above n.108, xxxvi.

142 See, e.g., E. S. P. Haynes, *A Lawyer's Notebook* (London: Secker & Warburg, 1936), 16–17; *Fritto Misto* (Kensington: Cayme Press, 1924), 10, 24–9; *The Belief in Personal Immortality* (London: Watts & Co., 1913), 46, 151–2.

143 A. L. Goodhart, 'Introduction', in *JLE* ix–xlviii at xxii. Goodhart, Lawson remarks, knew Pollock not only professionally but, 'as far as humanly possible, as a person'. F. H. Lawson, 'A. L. G.: A Professor's View' (1975) 91 *LQR* 461–3 at 462.

144 See Anon., 'Professor A. L. Goodhart: Influence on Law in Britain', in *The Times*, 11 November 1978, 16, col. F; also (1925) 41 *LQR* 244.

145 Cornelia Sorabji, *India Calling* (London: Nisbett & Co., 1934), 127. See also Cornelia Sorabji, *India Recalled* (London: Nisbett & Co., 1936), 184. For Pollock on Sorabji, see F. Pollock to Roscoe Pound, 5 May 1922, in Pound papers ('there is nothing about Indian family quarrels & settlements she does not know'); and Pollock to Holmes, 14 August 1924, in *PHL* ii. 144. See further John Pollock, *Time's Chariot*, above n.4, 61–2.

146 See Williston, above n.119, 194.

147 See, e.g., Harold J. Laski to O. W. Holmes, 20 December 1925, in *Holmes–Laski Letters*, above n.116, i. 812 ('I went on Tuesday to hear Sir F. Pollock on the need for a philosophy of law. He was really admirable. . . . [F]or a man of 75 the freshness and vigour of his mind were really remarkable');

the outer world'; but whereas, with Stephen, 'those who were given the key found the warm heart which awaited them', with Pollock it 'is not easy to be sure that [his] few intimates reaped the same reward.'[148] The point of the foregoing discussion, however, has been to suggest that Pollock was not wholly cold-hearted, and that there were rewards to be reaped by those who did manage to pierce the veil.

iii. Candour and character

A basic problem with mildly revisionist analyses of the type attempted above is that they can very easily be pushed too far. It should be kept in mind that claims to the effect that Pollock often seemed to others to be detached and uncommunicative generally hold good. There was, none the less, something about the man that attracted the loyalty and affection of many whom he met. That Pollock did attract such loyalty and affection while remaining, by and large, difficult to befriend makes him all the more puzzling: to the extent that he was likeable, to frame the question crudely, what made him so? Certainly some of his acquaintances preferred tough mountains to easy terrains, and it seems not unrealistic to speculate that certain of those who took the trouble to crack his exterior preferred much the same in their friendships. There emerges out of correspondence with and recollections of Pollock, furthermore, the impression that others often admired him because he seemed largely indifferent to the matter of whether they did so. Possibly this apparent

30 November 1928, ibid. ii. 1117 ('[A]t Lincoln's Inn . . . I was pleased to discover that to all of them F. Pollock was a kind of hero, held in real awe and reverence'); 14 November 1931, ibid. ii. 1338–9 ('I went on Monday night to the University Law Society where F. Pollock read a paper. It was a remarkable performance. He never faltered for a word, and when the discussion was over he made a reply which did not miss a point and, in his dry Pollockian way was as incisive and direct as he must have been thirty years ago; and his familiarity with the recent literature I can only describe as astounding'). That Laski might have been saying what he thought Holmes would have wanted to hear about Pollock is not inconceivable. Certainly he was not averse to flattering Holmes: 'If I mistake not, it is now something like sixty-three years since you [and Pollock] first met one another—a wonderful record', he wrote (27 September 1930, ibid. ii. 1285). On Holmes's death, he wrote in similar terms to Pollock about Pollock's friendship with Holmes and 'the great happiness you gave him'. Harold J. Laski to Sir Frederick Pollock, 12 March 1935, uncollected letter inserted in Pollock's copy of Oliver Wendell Holmes, Jr., *Collected Legal Papers* (New York: Harcourt, Brace & Howe, 1920), Lincoln's Inn library (cellar). Whether Laski's praise for Pollock was sincere or strategic, it is questionable that Pollock would have felt moved to repay the compliment. Reviewing Laski's *Political Thought in England from Locke to Bentham,* he had nothing but praise to offer for what he described as 'a really admirable little book'. Sir Frederick Pollock, 'English Publicists', in *New York Evening Post (Literary Review)*, 6 November 1920, 4. Two years later, nevertheless, in his review of Laski's *The Foundations of Sovereignty and other Essays* (1922) 38 *LQR* 242–3, his tone was reserved and his assessment fairly critical. For further indications of the chill, see Pollock to Holmes, 27 August 1921, in *PHL* ii. 77; 10 April 1922, ibid. 93; 24 July 1924, ibid. 141; 24 March 1930, ibid. 260; and Tony Weir, 'Friendships in the Law' (1991–2) 6/7 *Tulane Civil Law Forum* 61–93 at 73–4; though cf. Holmes to Pollock, 21 May 1922, in *PHL* ii. 97; Pollock to Holmes, 19 September 1922, ibid. 103; and 15 November 1923, ibid. 125.

[148] Fifoot, above n.19, 15.

indifference made his judgement seem trustworthy. Pollock and Holmes corresponded on many issues and with great erudition, but when Holmes mentioned that he had been reading Thomas Malthus, Pollock's reply was blunt: 'I have never read Malthus.'[149] By the same token, when Pollock had read something that Holmes appeared to have only half-digested, he could be just as forthright: thus when, in 1918, Holmes sent Pollock a short essay on natural law—'suggested by reading volume two of Gény, on something or other I forget what'[150]—a friendship of almost forty-five years was not going to impede Pollock from candidly suggesting to Holmes that his piece demonstrated but the flimsiest grasp of Gény's ideas.[151] Neither was Holmes to be offended. He professed generally to enjoy seeing Pollock's 'fist in a letter'[152] and—probably because he knew that Pollock was not inclined to take issue with his claims unless confident of superior knowledge—would often accept his 'remarks in respectful silence'.[153]

There is something else about Pollock that explains why he earned the admiration, affection, and loyalty of many of those within his circle. Many a Victorian intellectual made a fuss over the idea of character. To offer but one example, the classics scholar Sir Richard Jebb—a man who shared not only many of Pollock's achievements, but also his intense reserve—insisted that force of character was the one quality above all others that made men socially influential.[154] Pollock argued in much the same manner. Perhaps not surprisingly, he stressed the correctness of *noblesse oblige*;[155] but his understanding of

[149] Pollock to Holmes, 15 September 1914, in *PHL* i. 221. Pollock married in 1873. His wife, Lady Georgina Pollock, appears to have been a more personally engaging—she can hardly have been a less personally engaging—figure than was he. See John Pollock, *Time's Chariot*, above n.4, 5–9; Hazeltine, above n.4, 238. Newspaper clippings which have surfaced occasionally in the archival sources also show that Lady Pollock was politically minded—she was certainly active among the women Liberal Unionists in the early years of the twentieth century—and by no means reluctant to air her own opinions. The openness and warmth of Holmes's letters to Lady Pollock in *PHL* provide some clue as to her personality—see, e.g., Holmes to Lady Pollock, 2 July 1895, in *PHL* i. 57–8; 10 January 1904, ibid. 115–16; also Sheldon M. Novick, *Honorable Justice: The Life of Oliver Wendell Holmes* (New York: Laurel, 1989), 209, 322—though it should be noted that Holmes was nearly always flirtatious with women in print. All in all, it seems reasonable to assume that some of Pollock's admirers would have found him less challenging in the company of his wife.

[150] Holmes to Pollock, 31 October 1918, in *PHL* i. 270, referring to O. W. Holmes, Jr., 'Natural Law' (1918) 32 *Harvard L. Rev.* 40–4, an article which, the opening (indeed, only) footnote tells us, is 'suggested by reading' the second volume (published October 1915) of François Gény, *Science et technique en droit privé positif. Nouvelle contribution à la critique de la méthode juridique*, 4 vols. (Paris: Tenin, 1914–24).

[151] Pollock to Holmes, 20 December 1918, in *PHL* i. 274–5.

[152] Holmes to Pollock, 12 October 1917, in *PHL* i. 247; also 10 June 1923, in *PHL* ii. 117.

[153] Holmes to Pollock, 9 June 1930, in *PHL* ii. 267; and see also 6 April 1899, in *PHL* i. 93 ('[y]our devilish readiness for any idea in any language, as well mathematical or metaphysical as Dutch or Persian, is the despair of other men'); 9 June 1930, in *PHL* ii. 267 ('[y]ou discourse with a learning that I do not attempt to emulate'); 15 May 1931, ibid. 286 ('you . . . flabbergasted me as usual with your critical knowledge').

[154] See Sheldon Rothblatt, *The Revolution of the Dons: Cambridge and Society in Victorian England* (London: Faber & Faber, 1968), 221. Even Maitland, according to Rothblatt (ibid. 219–20), could not pull back Jebb's screen.

[155] See *EJE* 316.

good character by no means concerned only the behaviour of the privileged. Character is not born of wealth, or rank, or intellect ('[n]o one would call Queen Victoria a woman of genius, but by her character she deserved and achieved greatness'[156]), but of right-mindedness and a proper sense of purpose.

A man of character, without any epithet, is a man who has set before himself a distinct conception of his own capacities and the conduct by which he can make the best use of them, and steadfastly follows it out, not to be driven off his path by fear of loss nor distracted from it by hope of gain or pleasure. For such men we in England have always had a special admiration and regard . . . You will find throughout English history that the men of character, in this sense, are those who most surely win the affection of their fellows and command the respect of their adversaries.[157]

For Pollock, as for many other late Victorians, good character entails an instinctive and unquestioning willingness to act selflessly. As Harris elaborates, '"character" in the later Victorian sense' was a feature 'of a much wider movement for the revival of public spirit, patriotism, and civic virtue . . . It rejected the ethic of egoism in favour of altruism; and—in marked contrast to early Victorian notions of virtue—it suggested that virtue was an essentially public characteristic, which consisted not simply of private rationality or piety but of promoting the best interests of society as a whole.'[158] She continues: 'social theorists of late Victorian and Edwardian Britain'—and, in this context, Pollock might reasonably be considered such a theorist—'believed that moral character, active citizenship and "public spirit" were the indispensable building blocks of a well-ordered society and a virtuous state.'[159] Although it would be a mistake to assume that, for these theorists, 'the concept of character was exclusively a "class" weapon, whereby the rich passed moral judgement upon the suppliant poor',[160] Victorian invocations of the virtues of character would, as Collini points out, invariably presuppose an agreed moral code.[161]

Within Pollock's writings, the appeals to consensus were none too subtle. It is hardly surprising that we in England should have always had an eye for good character, he believed, for 'there is a certain way of thinking on questions of morality which we expect to find in a reasonable civilized man or a reasonable Englishman taken at random'.[162] The general observation to be offered here is that Pollock can be counted alongside Edmund Burke, Ernest Barker, and other political theorists who have claimed that the English possess a peculiar talent for appreciating integrity and noble conduct.[163] For our purposes,

156 *S* 139. 157 *S* 138–9.

158 Jose Harris, *Private Lives, Public Spirit: A Social History of Britain 1870–1914* (Oxford: Oxford UP, 1993), 249. 159 Ibid. 250.

160 Ibid. 248. 161 See Collini, above n.26, 100, 273. 162 *EJE* 270.

163 See Julia Stapleton, 'The National Character of Ernest Barker's Political Science' (1989) 37 *Political Studies* 171–87; *Englishness and the Study of Politics: The Social and Political Thought of Ernest Barker*

however, there are two more specific observations that need to be made. The first is that Pollock was connecting a conception of good character not just with the English, but also with the English common law. Barker made the connection in the 1920s when he wrote about the character of the English nation being shaped by, among other things, 'the genius of the English common law.'[164] Burke, too, had made the connection—but in a significantly different manner. Having initially rejected Sir Matthew Hale's vision of English law as immemorial custom in perpetual adaptation, Burke gradually acceded to it, so that by 1782 he found himself writing in classic Whig fashion about how the English constitution 'is made by the peculiar circumstances, occasions, tempers, dispositions, and moral, civil and social habitudes of the people, which disclose themselves only in a long space of time.'[165] Burke's language here, Pocock argues, echoes very clearly the seventeenth-century common lawyers' preoccupation—epitomized by Hale—with the 'spirit' of the common law.[166] Whereas Barker believed that English law shapes English character, Burke appeared to believe that English character shapes English law. Pollock's sentiments were closer to Burke's than to Barker's. Indeed, throughout various of Pollock's writings there recurs the idea that the common law mind illustrates the English temperament, so that the legal system can be conceived as a reflection of national character. It almost goes without saying that the way in which Pollock makes the link between law and national character is an important element in his juristic reasoning, and that later in this study we will examine the link in some depth.[167]

We will also see later in this study that Pollock's influence upon both juristic inquiry and judicial decision-making in England was not insignificant. Arthur Goodhart—who, like Pollock, was a jurisprudence professor at Oxford for twenty years and Editor of the *Law Quarterly Review* for many more—was similarly influential upon the English courts, although not upon juristic thought. But with Goodhart the influence is to a significant degree attribut-

(Cambridge: Cambridge UP, 1994); 'Political Thought and National Identity in Britain, 1850–1950', in *History, Religion, and Culture: British Intellectual History 1750–1950*, eds. S. Collini et al. (Cambridge: Cambridge UP, 2000), 245–69.

164 Ernest Barker, *National Character and the Factors in its Formation* (London: Methuen, 1927), 136 ('The character of English feudalism, the genius of the English common law, the nature of the English parliament—none of them inevitable expressions of an English national spirit—all became moulds in which the English nation was set and in which it acquired its character'). See also Stapleton, 'The National Character of Ernest Barker's Political Science', above n.163, 181.

165 Edmund Burke, *On a Motion Made in the House of Commons . . . for a Committee to Enquire into the State of the Representation of the Commons in Parliament*, undelivered speech, cited after J. G. A. Pocock, 'Burke and the Ancient Constitution: A Problem in the History of Ideas' (1960) 1 *Historical Jnl.* 125–43 at 140. Cf. also J. W. Burrow, *A Liberal Descent: Victorian Historians and the English Past* (Cambridge: Cambridge UP, 1981), 105–6.

166 See Pocock, above n.165, 140–1.

167 See chapter 4, 147–56. Pollock's Burkean inclinations perhaps partly explain his admiration for Savigny, another admirer of Burke. For Savigny and Burke, see Peter Stein, *Legal Evolution: The Story of An Idea* (Cambridge: Cambridge UP, 1980), 56–65.

able to the fact that he connected well with others.[168] Pollock, of course, did not; and so we are drawn back to the question of what it was about Pollock—given that it was clearly not his personal manner—that led others to hold him in high regard. Our concluding reflection on this question takes us to the second observation to be made about Pollock and his notion of character. If his claim is correct—if the English have always tended to have a special admiration and regard for those who demonstrate good character as he describes it—then it would be surprising had he not won the affection of many of his acquaintances. For he was the epitome of what he described. There is no easy way to substantiate this assertion. Rather, we must wait to see Pollock's character unfold as this study progresses. Some of that unfolding will occur in later chapters. And some of it will occur presently, as we return to the details of Pollock's life.

iv. University law

For approximately the first twelve years of his juristic career, Pollock—like most legal writers of the late-Victorian era—held no university post. Biographical sketches of the man often create the impression that his first such post was at Oxford. But before Oxford there was London. With the founding of the University of London in 1826 came the establishment of a Chair in Jurisprudence and the Law of Nations, the first incumbent of which was to become its most famous. John Austin was appointed as Professor of Jurisprudence at the University of London in the summer of 1827, although his first course of lectures did not commence until the beginning of the 1829–30 session. It is part of jurisprudential lore that the lectures were poorly received and audiences dwindled quickly, leading Austin—a delicate plant at the very best of times—to cease lecturing at University College, London (as it had by now been renamed) some time between June 1832 and June 1833.[169] The post remained vacant for the next seven years, and throughout the middle part of the nineteenth century UCL endured a succession of jurisprudence professors who were basically part-time legal instructors, often with little interest in law,

[168] See Neil Duxbury, *Jurists and Judges: An Essay on Influence* (Oxford: Hart, 2001), 87–98.

[169] Anyone seeking the whole sad story should consult Lotte and Joseph Hamburger, *Troubled Lives: John and Sarah Austin* (Toronto: University of Toronto Press, 1985), 53–77; Wilfrid E. Rumble, *The Thought of John Austin: Jurisprudence, Colonial Reform, and the British Constitution* (London: The Athlone Press, 1985), 27–40; Wilfrid E. Rumble, 'Austin in the Classroom: Why Were his Courses on Jurisprudence Unpopular?' (1996) 17 *Jnl. Leg. Hist.* 17–40; W. L. Morison, *John Austin* (London: Arnold, 1982), 20–4; H. Hale Bellot, *University College London, 1826–1926* (London: University of London Press, 1929), 96–102; Raymond Cocks, *Foundations of the Modern Bar* (London: Sweet & Maxwell, 1983), 44–51; and R. C. van Caenegem, *Judges, Legislators and Professors: Chapters in European Legal History* (Cambridge: Cambridge UP, 1987), 99–100; along with Sarah Austin's candid yet defiant 'Preface', in John Austin, *Lectures on Jurisprudence or the Philosophy of Positive Law*, 2 vols., 5th edn. R. Campbell (London: Murray, 1885), i. 1–25. Austin did not formally resign from UCL until late 1834, taking effect early in 1835. In 1834, he began

let alone legal research.[170] That it should have been this way is not entirely surprising: the guaranteed remuneration for Austin and those who followed him in the UCL jurisprudence chair was modest, the idea being that basic pay would be supplemented in accordance with the number of students providing fees to attend the lectures.[171] Austin's successors were, in general, hardly any more successful than was he in securing enrolments, and so they tended to make up their income from other sources.[172] The only notable break from this pattern was Sheldon Amos, son of the first Professor of English Law and Austin's contemporary at UCL, Andrew Amos. Elected to the Chair of Jurisprudence in 1869, Amos the younger distinguished himself from his precursors by showing some commitment to a career as a jurist, producing books and essays on jurisprudence and a variety of other legal topics.[173] When ill health led him to vacate the Chair in 1878, UCL was faced again with the difficulty of finding someone both suited and willing to demonstrate commitment to the post. In May 1882, fifty years after Austin's resignation, the chalice passed to Pollock.[174]

but never completed a series of lectures at the Inner Temple, after which, it appears, he abandoned teaching for good. (Note that although it is a solecism to place a comma in 'University College London' nowadays, this was not the case in Austin's era.)

[170] See Philip Schofield, 'Jeremy Bentham and Nineteenth-Century English Jurisprudence' (1991) 12 *Jnl. Leg. Hist.* 58–88 at 68–9.

[171] See J. H. Baker, 'University College and Legal Education 1826–1976' (1977) 30 *Current Legal Problems* 1–13 at 4–5. '[I]n those harsh days,' Baker writes, 'the professor's living depended on the size of his class. After only four years of struggling, Austin felt obliged to resign, his hopes shattered, his efforts spurned. . . . The four men who followed him all resigned for the same reasons. Their fate exposed a serious weakness in the College establishment, in that it had failed to secure to its professors financial independence' (ibid. 5). According to Rumble (*The Thought of John Austin*, above n.169, 36), Austin was not wholly at the mercy of student numbers: 'private parties in 1831 raised sufficient funds to endow a salary of £200 per annum for him for the academic years 1831, 1832 and 1833. Nevertheless, this possibility apparently was not attractive enough to overcome his disenchantment with the low enrolment in his course.'

[172] See William Twining, '1836 and All That: Laws in the University of London 1836–1986' (1987) 40 *Current Legal Problems* 261–99 at 274–5; also Bellot, above n.169, 331.

[173] For representative works, see Sheldon Amos, *A Lecture on the Best Modes of Studying the Science of Jurisprudence. Being Introductory to a Course of Lectures on the Science of Jurisprudence, to be delivered in University College, London, during the session 1870–1871* (London: Ridgway, 1870); *Difference of Sex as a Topic of Jurisprudence and Legislation* (London: Longmans, Green & Co., 1870); *A Systematic View of the Science of Jurisprudence* (London: Longmans, Green & Co., 1872); *An English Code: its Difficulties and the Modes of Overcoming them; a Practical Application of the Science of Jurisprudence* (London: Strahan & Co., 1873); *Law as a Science and as an Art: An Introductory Lecture delivered at University College at the commencement of the session, 1874–75* (London: Stevens & Sons, 1874); *The Science of Law* (London: King, 1874); *The History and Principles of the Civil Law of Rome: An Aid to the Study of Scientific and Comparative Jurisprudence* (London: Paul, Trench, 1883). On Amos as Professor of Jurisprudence at UCL, see the brief account by R. K. Wilson in *Remembrances of Sheldon Amos. By a Few Friends* (Leeds: privately printed by Harrison and Waide, 1889), 60–9. On the Amos family and UCL, see Negley Harte and John North, *The World of UCL, 1828–1990* (London: University College London, 1991), 40–1.

[174] There were fifteen applicants for the Chair when Pollock was appointed. He apparently applied late, but was by far the strongest applicant: Report of Committee on applications for Professorship of Jurisprudence and of Constitutional Law, College Correspondence (AM/C/92), Special Collections, UCL Library. Having applied for the Chair on 3 May 1882, he had accepted an offer of the post five days later: Frederick Pollock to the Council of University College London, 3 May 1882; and

Amos had been a legal scientist more or less in the Austinian mould.[175] But Pollock, as we will see later in this study, generally found it difficult so much as to mention Austin without expressing antipathy towards his achievements. Austin's work began to attract the attention of many English lawyers after his death in 1859, largely because his widow became devoted to securing his inclusion in the juristic hall of fame.[176] In the early 1860s, numerous jurists—Austin's long-standing admirer, John Stuart Mill, the principal among them—wrote essays acknowledging his jurisprudential legacy.[177] 'The book is evidently taking root', 'my husband's influence grows', Austin's widow noted four years after she secured the reissue of his *The Province of Jurisprudence Determined*.[178] 'It is become [*sic*] an examination book at both Oxford and Cambridge, and I am assured by barristers that there is a perfect enthusiasm about it among *young* lawyers—men among whom it was unknown till since [*sic*] I published the second edition.'[179] The enthusiasm was not much shared by Pollock: he distanced himself from Austin's command theory soon after having been called to the Bar,[180] and, not long before taking the Chair in Jurisprudence at UCL, he wrote of how Austin's *Province* was 'a fragmentary publication' which was not suitable for those embarking upon the study of law.[181] T. E. Holland's *Elements of Jurisprudence*, he asserted, was far more congenial to an undergraduate readership.[182] No doubt there rested behind Pollock's election to the UCL chair the hope that he, too, would prove congenial to undergraduates.

From the beginning, the omens were not good. Pollock attracted a class the size of which would have sent Austin to his bed. The fact that Pollock's

Frederick Pollock to Mr [W. A.?] Hunter, 8 May [1882], in Pollock correspondence (Appointments. 1882: Jurisprudence). See also Bellot, above n.169, 386–7.

[175] However, determining precisely what Amos thought of analytical jurisprudence in the Austinian mould would be difficult. In *The Science of Law* (above n.173), published in 1874, he claimed that Austin—having separated law 'from the dead body of morality that still clung to it'—was 'the true founder of the Science of Law' (3). In his *A Systematic View of the Science of Jurisprudence* (above n.173), published two years earlier, he had asserted that modern legal science 'is essentially a German creation' (505). While complimentary about Austin's achievement, furthermore, he was not uncritical of it, arguing among other things that the analytical jurisprudential project might benefit were it to absorb some of the lessons of the historical school as represented by Maine and others: see Amos, *A Lecture on the Best Modes of Studying the Science of Jurisprudence*, above n.173, 4–6; *A Systematic View of the Science of Jurisprudence*, above n.173, 17–18; and the detailed discussion in Schofield, above n.170, 79–82.

[176] See Mrs Austin to M. Guizot, 31 December 1860, in Janet Ross, *Three Generations of Englishwomen. Memoirs and Correspondence of Mrs John Taylor, Mrs Sarah Austin, and Lady Duff Gordon*, 2 vols. (London: Murray, 1888), ii. 102 ('I must vindicate . . . him from the charge of indolence or indifference to truth'); and also Richard A. Cosgrove, *Scholars of the Law: English Jurisprudence from Blackstone to Hart* (New York: New York UP, 1996), 93–4.

[177] See [John Stuart Mill], 'Austin on Jurisprudence' (October 1863) 118 *Edinburgh Rev.* 439–82; and also chapter 3, 100–1.

[178] Mrs Austin to M. B. St Hilaire, 22 January 1865, in Ross, above n.176, ii. 151; Mrs Austin to M. Guizot, 20 December 1865, ibid. 158.

[179] Mrs Austin to M. Guizot, 2 March 1863, ibid. 138.

[180] See Frederick Pollock, 'Law and Command' (1872) n.s. 1 *Law Magazine & Rev.* 189–205.

[181] *EJE* 2. [182] See *EJE* 1–6.

predecessor enjoyed a larger class might have had something to do with Sheldon Amos—possibly the memory of him was still drawing in the students. This would not explain, however, why Pollock's successor attracted a still larger enrolment.[183] In October 1882, Pollock's lectures began.[184] 'The history of the modern scientific movement in our legal studies', he warned his audience, 'is written in books which all students who aim at real knowledge must have in their hands, and ought to be familiar with.'[185] His entire introductory lecture in fact proceeded on the assumption that the students had already read these books. Some books were, of course, most likely beyond their reach—'I am not aware that anything of Bluntschli's has been translated into English, though no modern writer on the philosophy of politics and law better deserves a good English translation.'[186] What would probably have perturbed many of Pollock's students was the ease with which he himself could move out of their reach. Jurisprudence, he told them, falls into three categories: 'Positive Jurisprudence (which sub-divides into practical, historical, comparative, and analytical)'; 'Final Jurisprudence, which has a practical side (theory of legislation) and a speculative one (ethical jurisprudence or *Naturrecht*)'; and 'International Jurisprudence, which again is diversely treated by different authors, and might be, like municipal jurisprudence, subdivided according to their several methods if we were examining it more closely.'[187] In taking his audience through this labyrinth, Pollock operated at a level of generality and assumed a degree of knowledge that would defeat many a trained jurist. During the

[183] For the 1882–3 session, thirteen students enrolled for Pollock's Jurisprudence lectures. The income for the course was £67.40, from which Pollock received a cheque for £57.12: *Professors' fees books, UCL Sessions [sic] 1882–83*, UCL Records Office, CA/UCL/Prof Fee Bks/2 f.123. Pollock's predecessor, W. A. Hunter, had eighteen students enrol for his course and was paid £92.16 (the overall income being £108.30): *Professors' fees books, UCL Sessions [sic] 1881–82*, UCL Records Office, CA/UCL/Prof Fee Bks/1 f.121. Pollock's successor, Alexander Henry, attracted nineteen students and was paid £110.50 (the overall income being £131.15): *Professors' fees books, UCL Session 1883–84*, UCL Records Office, CA/UCL/Prof Fee Bks/3 f.118. Apparently, UCL 'produced only 135 LL.B.s in the nineteenth century', and a 'majority of those . . . studied privately'. W. L. Twining, 'Laws', in *The University of London and the World of Learning, 1836–1986*, ed. F. M. L. Thompson (London: Hambledon Press, 1990), 81–114 at 96.

[184] For Pollock's notes, see 'Lectures, M[ichaelmas] T[erm] 1882, Liverpool and Univ. Coll; London', in Pollock notebooks, Misc. 793, 20–59. The lectures are titled: I. Introductory; II. Form of Positive Law; III & IV. System of Judicial Precedents; V & VI. Systematic Legislation in England, and Movements towards Codification; VII. Matter of Positive Law; VIII & IX. Public and Private Law; X. Duty and Sovereignty.

[185] Frederick Pollock, 'The Methods of Jurisprudence' (1882) 8 *Law Magazine & Rev. (4th Ser.)* 25–53 at 48. The article is Pollock's introductory lecture delivered at University College London on 31 October 1882 (repr. *OLOD* 1–36). Citations here are to the original article.

[186] Pollock, 'The Methods of Jurisprudence', ibid. 37. 'Bluntschli' = Johann Caspar Bluntschli (1808–81), Swiss jurist and political scientist, and student of Savigny. The first part of his *Lehre vom modernen Staat*, 2 vols. (Stuttgart: Cotta, 1851–2) was fairly soon to be published in English: J. C. Bluntschli, *The Theory of the State*, trans. D. G. Ritchie, P. E. Matheson, and R. Lodge (Oxford: Clarendon Press, 1885). On Bluntschli, see Martti Koskenniemi, *The Gentle Civilizer of Nations: The Rise and Fall of International Law 1870–1960* (Cambridge: Cambridge UP, 2001), 42–7 and the centennial celebration by Friedrich Meili, *J. C. Bluntschli und seine Bedeutung für die moderne Rechtswissenschaft* (Zurich: Fussli, 1908).

[187] Pollock, 'The Methods of Jurisprudence', above n.185, 40.

second term of 1882–3, he lectured to the UCL students on the topic of civil liability.[188] While his notes for these lectures suggest that they would by no means have been easy going, they are certainly less recondite than those delivered in the first term. By the second term, however, the damage had most likely been done and the students put off.

It seems almost ironic that, today, the Faculty of Laws at University College London should award a scholarship bearing Pollock's name,[189] for Pollock lasted but one year in Austin's chair. Perhaps part of the problem for him was that, by 1882, it really was Austin's chair: Austin was by this time a legal philosopher held in high—Pollock would have said inordinately high—regard. Austin's jurisprudence, he told his students, was 'too much in the air'. Those who follow Austin's route 'run an appreciable risk . . . of regarding legal science as a thing apart from legal practice.'[190] That Pollock felt the need to say as much indicates, nevertheless, that, by this point in time, Austin's route was being travelled.[191] Perhaps Pollock was unhappy to find himself in the long shadow cast by a man for whom he had very little intellectual respect. For whatever reason, his association with UCL did not work out. As early as March 1883 it was determined that Alexander Henry, a jurist in the Austinian tradition, would succeed Pollock to the re-named Professorship of Jurisprudence and Indian Law.[192]

Given that Pollock switched from London to Oxford, it is tempting to conclude that aspiration rather than exasperation must have caused him to leave. Pollock's son, writing in his seventies and professing to have an impressive long-term memory, believed that his father did not jump but was pushed: 'his post as Professor of Jurisprudence at University College, London . . . was an annual appointment, but considered a permanency. Though then only four, I have a vivid recollection of my father's anger and my mother's consternation when he came back one afternoon from Lincoln's Inn and told her that the post had been filched from him by a personal intrigue.'[193] The father's disparagement—

[188] See Pollock notebooks, Misc. 793, 61–121. The lectures are untitled and the last one is dated 9 April 1883. It appears that Pollock presented the lectures in updated form at Oxford in the Hilary Term of 1885: see Pollock notebooks, Misc. 793, 123–43.

[189] 'The Sir Frederick Pollock Scholarship for Students from North America' can be found advertised on the UCL website at http://www.ucl.ac.uk/laws/prospective/graduate/index.shtml?scholarships (last visited 4 April 2004).

[190] Pollock, 'The Methods of Jurisprudence', above n.185, 52.

[191] On the late nineteenth-century reception of Austin, see Collini, above n.26, 268; and Morison, above n.169, 151–3.

[192] University College London, Minutes of Senate, 8 March 1883, in *University College London: Minutes of Senate, No. 5*, UCL Records Office, CA/UOL/Mins/Sen/5, 96. The Committee which recommended the appointment of Henry included Pollock: Minutes of Senate, 22 February 1883, ibid. 94. For Henry, see Alexander Henry, *Jurisprudence: or, the Science of Law, its Objects and Methods. An Introductory Lecture, delivered at University College, on 2nd November, 1883* (London: Stevens, 1884); and also Schofield, above n.170, 82–3. Henry is perhaps primarily of historical note for having been John Salmond's jurisprudence teacher at UCL: see Alex Frame, *Salmond: Southern Jurist* (Wellington, NZ: Victoria UP, 1995), 24–7.

[193] John Pollock, *Time's Chariot*, above n.4, 78.

in a letter to Holmes written eleven years after departing UCL—of 'the sham University of London' possibly indicates some sort of residual bitterness.[194] But the fact is that Pollock left UCL of his own accord: in February 1883, Senate accepted his resignation.[195] There was, nevertheless, reason for him to feel resentful: Pollock had wanted to vacate the Chair of Jurisprudence during the 1882–3 session but was refused permission to do so.[196] The most intriguing question—and the one to which there is no obvious answer—is why he should have wanted to quit the post so quickly.

What is certain is that by the end of his year at UCL, Pollock did not want to be there. We also know that, as early as 1882, he was pursuing a chair at Oxford.[197] In that year, A. V. Dicey was elected to the Vinerian Chair of English Law. Although a later incumbent of that post discussed the election of Dicey as if it had been a formality,[198] it in fact took the search committee two years to decide in Dicey's favour.[199] Pollock was an unsuccessful contender. 'I was sorely disturbed when in London,' Holmes wrote to Pollock of his visit there in 1882, 'to think that two friends whom I value as I do you and Dicey should find themselves in competition.'[200] Fortunately, for Pollock, there was another route to Oxford. After holding the Corpus Professorship of Jurisprudence for the best part of a decade, Sir Henry Maine resigned the post in 1878, having accepted an invitation to become Master of Trinity Hall, Cambridge. Maine appeared to have no doubt about whom his successor should be. 'I trust F. Pollock Jr., whom I think you know, will be elected', he wrote to Holmes in 1878. 'He is of all men in this country most likely to rewrite the history of English law, which urgently needs re-writing.'[201] Pollock and Maine

[194] Pollock to Holmes, 9 August 1893, in *PHL* i. 45. Not that Pollock shunned UCL for the rest of his life: see Pollock to Holmes, 11 February 1924, in *PHL* ii. 127. Although when he did revisit there to lecture, the experience seemed hardly to invigorate him: see Pollock to Holmes, 24 March 1924, ibid. 131.

[195] Minutes of Senate, 22 February 1883, in *University College London: Minutes of Senate, No. 5*, above n.192, 91–2.

[196] Council Minutes, 14 April 1883, in *University of London: Council Minutes 1876–83, vii*, UCL Records Office, CA/UOL/Cmins/7: 'Read letters from Professor Pollock asking to be allowed to give up the duties of his Professorship at once and proposing that Mr Robert Campbell should be appointed as his substitute for the remainder of the Session. Resolved that Professor Pollock be informed that the Council regret that they are unable to accede to his request.'

[197] Indeed, he only accepted the UCL post once he was sure that to do so would not frustrate this pursuit: see Frederick Pollock to Mr [W. A.?] Hunter, 8 May [1882], in Pollock correspondence (Appointments. 1882: Jurisprudence): '. . . about the Univ. Coll. chair of Jurisprudence. I wrote to a trustworthy authority at Oxford to telegraph dissent if the thing would be against me there—having heard nothing I hold myself free to accept and do accept.'

[198] 'When all was ready for the reception of the new professor, . . . the Board realized that a search would be superfluous, if only Dicey could be persuaded to stand.' Harold G. Hanbury, *The Vinerian Chair and Legal Education* (Oxford: Blackwell, 1958), 100.

[199] See Richard A. Cosgrove, *The Rule of Law: Albert Venn Dicey, Victorian Jurist* (Chapel Hill: University of North Carolina Press, 1980), 46.

[200] Holmes to Pollock, 25 March 1883, in *PHL* i. 20.

[201] H. S. Maine to O. W. Holmes, Jr., 24 August 1878, in Holmes papers, Harvard Law Library, cited after Feaver, above n.27, 306 n.2.

became acquainted through the Apostles, and in 1870 Pollock had attended Maine's Oxford lectures on 'Village Communities in the East and West.'[202] Like Ilbert and James Fitzjames Stephen, Maine served as legal member of the Governor-General's council in India (1862–9), and he shared with them and with Pollock a strong faith in the Anglo-Indian codification initiative.[203] He also shared with Pollock—or rather, Pollock shared with him—a belief in the aims and methods of comparative jurisprudence.

In 1883, Pollock succeeded Maine as the Corpus Christi Professor of Jurisprudence in the University of Oxford. '[Y]ou have become more vested than ever and having had the animus to profess the law in Oxford have now the Corpus also', Maitland quipped in his congratulatory letter.[204] Why it should have taken five years to appoint a successor to Maine is unclear. One possible reason was Oxonian doziness: on 'my election to the Chair of Jurisprudence', Pollock recalled, '[m]y predecessor, Maine, being an elector, sent me a private telegram, but I never had a word from the Vice-Chancellor or any other University officer. The only regular evidence of my appointment that ever came to my immediate knowledge was the fact of being admitted to a fellowship in my new College by the President of Corpus.'[205] In April 1883, in his eye-catchingly titled inaugural lecture, *Can English Law be Taught at the Universities?*, Oxford's new Vinerian Professor of English Law, A. V. Dicey, was already referring to Pollock as a colleague.[206] 'If youthful learners are capable of gratitude,' Dicey proclaimed, 'there must surely be a large class of students who render daily thanks to Sir William Anson and Professor Pollock' for enabling 'them to see that law is a rational study, and can be treated like other sciences in a clear, rational, and interesting manner.'[207] Six months later, Pollock began his own (rather less snappily-titled) inaugural lecture by repaying the compliment.[208]

Neither of these lectures, however, was merely an exercise in back-slapping. Indeed, both men delivered a similarly stark message. Dicey's tone was essentially hortatory, emphasizing what he believed university lawyers to be capable of achieving: '[i]t is for professors to set forth the law as a coherent whole—

[202] See Feaver, ibid. 119. The lectures were published the following year: *Village Communities in the East and West* (London: Murray, 1871).

[203] See R. C. J. Cocks, *Sir Henry Maine: A Study in Victorian Jurisprudence* (Cambridge: Cambridge UP, 1988), 83–8.

[204] F. W. Maitland to Frederick Pollock, [probably March 1883], in *The Letters of Frederic William Maitland*, above n.22, 11. The post ceased to be called the Corpus Professorship when it was transferred from Corpus Christi to University College in the mid-1920s: see Lawson, above n.115, 126 n.5.

[205] *FMG* 20.

[206] A. V. Dicey, *Can English Law be Taught at the Universities?* (London: Macmillan & Co., 1883), 23. On the title, see A. V. Dicey to E. A. Freeman, 2 August 1883, in Freeman papers: 'I hope my inaugural lecture has safely reached you. . . . Many of my friends blame the title, thinking it I suppose wanting in dignity. But as the whole object of a title appears to be to state as plainly as may be the contents of a book or pamphlet I cannot see why I should be blamed for stating the subject of the lecture in the plainest terms.'

[207] Dicey, *Can English Law be Taught at the Universities?*, above n.206, 23.

[208] See *EOD* 3–5.

to analyse and define legal conceptions—to reduce the mass of legal rules to an orderly series of principles, and to aid, stimulate, and guide the reform or renovation of legal literature.'[209] But these could not yet be called achievements. 'We have no history of English law as a whole deserving the name,' he remarked. 'If our wealth in reports is the standing memorial to the greatness of our judges, the poverty of our legal literature is surely one result of the non-existence till recent years of any legal professoriate.'[210] For Pollock, university law was under-appreciated as well as underdeveloped: 'the scientific and systematic study of law', he claimed, is 'a pursuit still followed in this land by few, scorned or depreciated by many'.[211]

But how, according to Pollock, ought law in the universities to be advanced? In his inaugural lecture, Pollock's basic message was that it is important to keep faith with the project of his predecessor. 'I understand that a certain sort of clever young men, anxious to say something new and surprising, are already going about to disparage Sir Henry Maine's way of research as a thing out of date.'[212] Such disparagement Pollock did not deign to accord serious treatment. Instead, he offered defiant support for Maine's project. 'The historical and comparative treatment of jurisprudence . . . is the newest and most powerful instrument, not only of the moral and political sciences, but of a great part of the natural sciences, and its range is daily increasing.'[213] Darwin's theory of evolution, he added, 'is nothing else than the historical method applied to the fact of nature.'[214] In later years, he would write more in tribute to Maine, and would be responsible for ensuring numerous reprints of Maine's classic, *Ancient Law* (first published in 1861).[215] Such words and deeds make the

[209] Dicey, *Can English Law be Taught at the Universities?*, above n.206, 18. [210] Ibid. 22.

[211] *EOD* 5. [212] *EOD* 7.

[213] *EOD* 6–7. Pollock's argument in this passage is examined in chapter 3. [214] *EOD* 7.

[215] See Frederick Pollock, 'Sir Henry Maine and His Work' (February 1889) 55 *Contemporary Rev.* 265–76; 'Sir Henry Maine as Jurist' (July 1893) 178 *Edinburgh Rev.* 100–21; 'Introduction', in Sir Henry Sumner Maine, *Ancient Law: Its Connection with the Early History of Society and its Relation to Modern Ideas*, new impression (London: Murray, 1909), xiii–xxiv at xxiii; also Cocks, above n.203, 185; and Holmes to Pollock, 26 July 1930, in *PHL* ii. 272.

It is clear from Pollock's correspondence with the publisher, John Murray, that by the early 1890s Murray was looking for someone to edit a new edition of *Ancient Law*. Pollock approved of the idea but was unenthusiastic about all of Murray's proposed editors (Frederick Pollock to John Murray, 14 August 1890; 12 July 1892; 22 July 1892, in Pollock correspondence (Murray)). By 1894, an agreement had been reached whereby Murray was to publish a new edition of *Ancient Law* incorporating Pollock's article on Maine from the July 1893 *Edinburgh Review* (C. J. Longman to John Murray, 15 August 1894, in Pollock correspondence (Murray)). Around October 1894, however, it appears that Maine's widow objected to the inclusion of Pollock's essay in this new edition. The episode is interesting if only because it might cause anyone who has speculated about how history might have viewed John Austin's work but for the endeavours of his wife to wonder about the extent to which the history of English jurisprudence generally is a story of men supported by strong-minded women.

Not that Pollock speculated thus. 'I consider the objection quite perverse and unreasonable,' he wrote. 'If Lady Maine were a man I should have some observations to make on her conduct', though he added that it would be wrong to 'act against Lady Maine's wish in such a matter'. (Frederick Pollock to John Murray, 12 November 1894; and 16 November 1894, in Pollock correspondence (Murray)). Just how Lady Maine objected is not clear from the available correspondence, but Pollock was clearly stung. In 1903 he wrote to Murray that he had written some notes on Maine which he had used in lectures

conclusion of one modern legal historian—that 'Pollock never relented in his attempt to restrict the relevance of Maine's work' and seemed to want 'to write Maine's ideas out of English legal thought'[216]—appear highly questionable.

Yet even if the conclusion is questionable, the fact that it should have been reached is not entirely surprising. Although it would be difficult to argue convincingly that Pollock opposed the comparative jurisprudential project, it is not clear that he was ever thoroughly devoted to it. He could certainly be scathing when he considered the project to have been undertaken badly.[217] Significantly, in his inaugural lecture delivered in March 1904, Paul Vinogradoff, Pollock's successor as Corpus Professor, nodded politely towards the achievements of his predecessor but chose as his theme 'The Teaching of Sir Henry Maine'.[218] Unlike Pollock, Vinogradoff was Maine's natural heir; unlike either Maine or Vinogradoff, Pollock was not really a card-carrying comparative jurisprudent. In the next chapter, we will see that Pollock equivocally opposed analytical jurisprudence and wrote equivocally in support of comparative jurisprudence. The equivocations, it will be argued, are actually very important for the purpose of understanding the development of English jurisprudential thought. But if Pollock was not a dyed in the wool disciple of Maine, if he lacked commitment to comparative jurisprudence as a project, why did he defend it?

Pollock probably felt duty-bound to do so. Advancing comparative jurisprudence was part of the job description: '[t]he [Corpus] Professor will be required to lecture and give instruction in the History of Laws and the Comparative Jurisprudence of different Nations'.[219] Certainly Pollock took the requirement seriously. 'The historical and comparative treatment of jurisprudence is the function properly assigned to the Corpus Professor', he noted.[220] 'This imposes on me,' he added on Maine's death, 'and those who may come after me in this Chair, the duty, no facile one, but therefore the more honourable, of working, so far as our powers extend, in the spirit of the illustrious leader whom we have this year lost.'[221]

at Oxford and 'which might do to publish one day, but not in Lady Maine's lifetime, as she would be offended by even the most reverent criticism.' (Frederick Pollock to John Murray, 8 June 1903, ibid.). The storm eventually blew over: 'I have seen Lady Maine,' he wrote to Murray a year later, 'and she now has no objection to "Ancient Law" being republished with a commentary, and in fact has given me a free hand in the matter.' (Frederick Pollock to John Murray, 17 December 1904, ibid.).

216 Cocks, above n.203, 185.

217 For example, when one comparatist scholar produced an article on the origin of the word *busones*, purporting to trace it to the Icelandic *búi*, Pollock, writing to William Paley Baildon, was forthright: 'If you want to see some real wild-cat nonsense I commend to you A. Betts's Icelandic derivation of *busones* (Juridical Review)'. Frederick Pollock to W. P. Baildon, 9 March 1915, in Baildon papers (WPB 4/348), referring to Arthur Betts, 'Busones' (1915) 27 *Juridical Rev.* 98–108 at 104–5. For Pollock's reservations over comparativism, see also Holdsworth, *Some Makers of English Law*, above n.4, 284.

218 'The Teaching of Sir Henry Maine', in *The Collected Papers of Paul Vinogradoff. Volume i: Historical. Volume ii: Jurisprudence* (Oxford: Clarendon Press, 1928), ii. 173–89. Vinogradoff says all that he has to say about Pollock in the opening paragraph.

219 Cited after H. A. L. Fisher, 'Paul Vinogradoff: A Memoir', in *Collected Papers*, ibid. i. 1–74 at 31.

220 *EOD* 6.

221 Pollock, 'Sir Henry Maine and His Work', above n.215, 265.

That he should have laid on with a trowel this idea of duty to the past is somewhat ironic, given that executing the obligations of the Corpus Professor rarely if ever put Pollock under much strain. There were few students with whom to deal, lectures to be delivered, or examinations to set.[222] College teaching was done by assorted drifting clouds—tutors who more often than not lacked either legal training or academic ambition, and who would probably never have met Pollock or any other Oxford law professor.[223] Holmes asserted on more than one occasion that academic life is but a 'half-life', meaning that academics tend to be a cloistered bunch who miss out on a great deal of commonplace experience.[224] Pollock's life as an Oxford professor was something like a half-life, but not in the way that Holmes had intended the phrase. Little of Pollock's life seems to have been taken up with Oxford, and throughout his time as Corpus Professor he was significantly preoccupied with various other undertakings.

Only one year after being appointed to the Corpus Chair, for example, he felt able to take on an additional academic post. In 1873, the Council of Legal Education had established at the Inns of Court four professorships—in Jurisprudence, Common Law, Property Law, and Equity—appointees to which would normally serve for three years. Pollock served as Professor of Common Law at the Inns of Court between 1884 and 1890.[225] Whether he did all that much to advance legal education at the Inns of Court is not clear—accounts of his teaching at Oxford, we will see presently, make it seem unlikely

[222] For a sense of how little there would have been for Pollock to do, see Barry Nicholas, 'Jurisprudence', in *The History of the University of Oxford. Volume ii: Nineteenth-Century Oxford, Part 2*, eds. M. G. Brock and M. C. Curthoys (Oxford: Clarendon Press, 2000), 385–96 at 385–6.

[223] See Nicholas, above n.222, 392–3; Lawson, above n.115, 46, 50–1.

[224] See Oliver Wendell Holmes, 'Law in Science and Science in Law' (1899) 12 *Harvard L. Rev.* 443–63 at 452; also Oliver Wendell Holmes, Jr., to Felix Frankfurter, 15 July 1913, in *Holmes and Frankfurter: Their Correspondence, 1912–1934*, eds. R. M. Mennel and C. L. Compston (Hanover: University Press of New England, 1996), 12. Life, for Holmes, could be but a half-life for reasons other than being wedded to academia: see Oliver Wendell Holmes, Jr. to John C. H. Wu, 16 June 1930, in 'Some Unpublished Letters of Justice Holmes' (1935) 1 *T'ien Hsia Monthly* 251–302 at 298.

[225] One of Pollock's notebooks (Misc. 797) is entitled 'Inns of Court 1884–7' and contains his 1884 October Term and Michaelmas Term lecture notes on the 'Principles of the Law of Torts' (1–75), his 1885 Michaelmas Term notes on 'The Methods and Authorities of the Common Law' (76–103), his 1885 Hilary Term notes on 'Possession and Trespass' (104–22), his notes for the 1886 Easter and Trinity terms on 'The Relations of Contract and Tort' (124–32), his 1886 Michaelmas Term notes on 'The Law of Contract—with special reference to Finch's Select Cases' (133–8), and his 1887 Hilary Term (untitled) notes on contracts (139–48). One half of another notebook (Misc. 798) is entitled 'Inns of Court 1887–9: Contracts, Possession, Sale of Goods' and contains Pollock's 1887 Easter Term lecture notes on 'Law of Contract (continued)' (1–21), his 1887 Michaelmas Term notes on 'The Performance and Discharge of Contracts' (not paginated [22–47]), his notes for the 1888 Easter and Trinity terms on 'Possession and Delivery' (not paginated [48–53]), his 1888 Michaelmas Term notes on 'The Law of Wrongs and Offences against Possession' (not paginated [54–63]), his 1889 Hilary Term notes on 'The Sale of Goods' (not paginated [55–66]), his notes for the 1889 Easter and Trinity terms on 'Sale of Goods, cont'd.' (not paginated [67–79]), and his 1889 Michaelmas Term notes on 'Sale of Goods' (not paginated [80–8]). All of the notes appear in Pollock's hand and at various points contain insertions of extra notes, letters, and advertisements for moots at the Inns of Court. It is evident from the notes for the later courses—which are often scrappy by Pollock's standards—that he gradually spent less time preparing lectures.

that he would have done. What is clear is that he was by no means enamoured of the institution which he served: in his final year as a Professor at the Inns of Court, he produced a note in the *LQR* summarizing the system of legal education there and observing that it was 'felt by a considerable proportion of . . . Benchers . . . to be far from satisfactory.'[226] It seems improbable that Pollock would have made the system any more satisfactory had his professorship at the Inns of Court been extended—all that is certain is that it was not through his choice that his tenure came to an end.[227]

In 1896, he published in the *LQR* a memorandum on law teaching in the universities, prepared by his Oxford colleague, Henry Goudy, which criticized the Inns of Court for failing to acknowledge honours degrees in law as sufficient evidence of theoretical training in the subject.[228] Pollock appended to the memorandum notes of his own, which he had already circulated to colleagues and acquaintances at both Oxford and Cambridge and at the Inns of Court, and in relation to which he claimed he had 'received indications of a considerable amount of assent.'[229] Convinced that the Council of Legal Education was slighting the universities, he railed against its 'insane policy'[230] on law teaching and 'the present absurd system of the Inns of Court'.[231] That Pollock should have written in this way about legal education at the Inns of Court hardly suggests that he would have contemplated his tenure there with fondness. Nor could he console himself with the assurance that his criticisms worked to the good. By 1902 he confessed to '[b]eing weary of protesting in the wilderness' about the Inns of Court.[232] 'To the majority of the Benchers and the Council of Legal Education it is useless to appeal',[233] for 'the bulk of the legal profession in England remains in its usual and deplorable state of profound indifference and ignorance on the whole matter.'[234]

Of course, while Pollock wrote resignedly about the failures of the Inns of Court, there was no need for him to despair too much. His principal post, after all, was at Oxford; and about the state of teaching there he could be decidedly more positive. In May 1886 he delivered an address at Oxford—essentially a Victorian mission statement—in which he considered the point

[226] (1890) 6 *LQR* 228. He continued in much the same vein in later years: see the account of Charles Noble Gregory, 'The State of Legal Education in the World' (1900) 34 *American L. Rev.* 841–55 at 846, 849.

[227] Frederick Pollock to James Barr Ames, 7 December 1889, in Ames correspondence, box 1, folder 32 ('A day or two after you get this it will be decided whether I am to retain my professorship in the Inns of Court, or vacate it according to a strict interpretation of a strange rule made by people who must have known very little about teaching. The notion of making a Law School by changing the teachers every three years is somewhat grotesque. However, things cannot remain on the present precarious footing very long'). We might ask, of course, why Pollock should have wanted to retain his post at an institution for which he had so little regard. An answer is suggested in chapter 6.

[228] See (1896) 12 *LQR* 1–3.

[229] (1896) 12 *LQR* 3. An anonymous, neutral report on Pollock's notes appears as 'The Movement in Legal Education' (1896) 100 *Law Times* 262–3.

[230] (1898) 14 *LQR* 232.

[231] (1898) 14 *LQR* 127.

[232] (1902) 18 *LQR* 236.

[233] (1898) 14 *LQR* 127.

[234] (1892) 8 *LQR* 20.

of law within a university curriculum and, in the course of so doing, noted the achievements of certain of his colleagues.[235] Universities, he began, can never guarantee to produce, and should not make it their objective to produce, successful lawyers. The profession of law requires 'the undertaking of a high duty to mankind', and so a 'function of the University' should be to demonstrate to the would-be lawyer 'that there is a science as well as a practice of law'.[236] If this science is well taught, the intending lawyer will learn 'that there are such things as general principles of law' and 'that the multitude of particulars in which he must inevitably be versed . . . are not really a chaos'.[237] While universities cannot guarantee that the prospective lawyer will be successful at 'bargain and bread-winning',[238] they 'can aid him to form the scholarly habit which makes the difference in practice between sure-handed and slovenly execution.'[239] Furthermore, they 'can aid him to form tastes which . . . will lead him to enjoy the fruits of higher learning'[240] and to discover 'joy . . . in the lucid expression of broad legal principles, or in the conduct of a finely reasoned argument on their application to a disputed point.'[241]

Although Pollock might have believed that the universities could improve legal minds, he seemed, in private at least, to doubt that they were fulfilling their potential. 'We brought out the B.C.L. list by 1.30 today', he wrote to Bryce in 1890. 'The men were a poor lot. We could not make a first class and had to pluck six out of twenty one.'[242] But all was not lost. Oxford's graduates may have caused Pollock to despair, but its jurists made him proud. Colleagues past and present—the likes of Maine, Bryce, Markby, Holland, Dicey, and Anson—had advanced their subject areas significantly: 'considering the moderate number of years for which our Law School has been in existence in its present form, we think we can show fairly acceptable results.'[243] Such scholarship, Pollock maintained, is integral to good learning. Nutshells and the like, by contrast, are not: 'attempts to dispense with first-hand reading and digesting by printed summaries and other like devices . . . are absolutely to be rejected. No man ever became a lawyer by putting his trust in such things. . . . It is of course needless to say this to scholars.'[244] Through 'contact with scholarship' the undergraduate will come to learn and most likely to love the law. The apprenticeship may be 'long, . . . technical, . . . laborious, and . . . ungenial', but with proper commitment it will prove fulfilling.[245]

[235] Frederick Pollock, 'Oxford Law Studies' (1886) 2 *LQR* 453–64; repr. *OLOD* 91–111.
[236] *OLOD* 92–3. [237] *OLOD* 94. [238] *OLOD* 93.
[239] *OLOD* 104. [240] *OLOD* 102. [241] *OLOD* 110.
[242] Frederick Pollock to James Bryce, 12 June 1890, in Bryce papers, MSS. Bryce 120 f.33. See also James Barr Ames, 'The Vocation of the Law Professor' (1900) n.s. 39 *American Law Register* 129–46 at 133 ('. . . the ancient universities made a grave mistake when they placed law among the subjects that qualify for the degree of B.A. . . . Sir Frederick Pollock considers this mistake irrevocable').
[243] *OLOD* 96.
[244] *OLOD* 105. Scholars, that is, as opposed to 'short-sighted learners and unscrupulous teachers, who substitute for the pursuit of knowledge the pursuit of examinations' (103).
[245] *OLOD* 109.

One can only wonder how any undergraduate attending Pollock's address in search of advice and instruction would have received his message. We cannot guarantee to turn you into a successful lawyer, he seemed to be saying, but if you revere scholarship and immerse yourself in the literature of the law, your experience of professional training will at least be ennobled and enriched. At points, the performance was worthy of a Zen master: the riches available through abandonment to legal science 'may come to you, or they may not. If they come, it may be sooner or later; it may be through your own desert, or by the aid of quite extraneous causes.'[246] There are no guarantees to legal success, but those who come to enjoy the law will probably enjoy practising it, and those who enjoy what they do are perhaps more likely to be successful at what they do. 'Trust me!'—hardly a phrase that Pollock was ever likely to utter—would not have been an inapt injunction.

The problem for most students would have been that they would have struggled so much as to approach Pollock, let alone trust him. In his 1886 address, he made particular reference to postgraduates: 'a University has regard to the mature worker as well as to the novice.'[247] Postgraduates, certain of those close to him implied, were the only students with whom he could make any meaningful connection. 'Pollock was essentially a teacher for advanced students, and for those who were interested in legal research. His lectures were never frequented by the ordinary undergraduate.'[248] Inspiring postgraduates is most welcome when an institution has postgraduates to be inspired; but 'until very near the end of his tenure of the Corpus Chair', Lawson claims, 'there were no advanced students of law in Oxford with whom he could have come into contact.'[249] Even if there had been, Lawson clearly doubts that Pollock would have been of much help to them. '[I]t would have made little difference to the teaching of law in Oxford if Pollock had never been there. He was a bad lecturer who drew very poor audiences; so far as can be ascertained, he never taught any undergraduate in a private tutorial hour'; and his 'well-known difficulty of making oral communication with anyone with whom he was not naturally *en rapport* made him to all intents and purposes useless as a teacher.'[250]

If students had found Pollock difficult to approach, it would not only have been because of his manner. As Corpus Professor, Maine had an arrangement whereby his teaching and other duties were made to fit the circumstances of his professional life in London.[251] Although he was apparently conscientious

[246] *OLOD* 108. [247] *OLOD* 95.

[248] Holdsworth (1937) 53 *LQR* 180. See also Hazeltine, above n.4, 240.

[249] Lawson, above n.115, 72.

[250] Ibid. 72–3. See also F. W. Maitland to Henry Jackson, 10 January 1904, in *The Letters of Frederic William Maitland*, above n.22, 372 ('I think that he had difficulty in obtaining hearers—or rather that he would not make any effort to obtain them. He has no notion of adapting supply to demand: you must take what he thinks good for you or leave it alone, and the young gents with examinations before them left it alone').

[251] See Feaver, above n.27, 171.

and came up regularly to give lectures and hold classes, he was not often present in Oxford.[252] It seems that, on Maine's retirement, there emerged an expectation at Oxford that the Corpus Chair 'was thereafter to be held by a resident professor engaged fulltime in the life of the University.'[253] Whether or not this was a genuine expectation, it was certainly not fulfilled. Like Maine, Pollock was non-residential: 'he continued to live in London, where his main professional activity was that of editing the *Law Reports*, and came up to Oxford only once or twice a week to deliver his lectures.'[254] 'I am living in the hope that Pollock's successor at Oxford may be Vinogradoff', Maitland wrote in the year of Pollock's resignation from the Corpus Chair. 'My own belief is that he will make a better professor than either F. P. or Sir H. M.'[255] At least part of the reason for Maitland's holding this belief seems to have been that he doubted Pollock's commitment to the post. Knowing, in 1902, that Pollock was about to vacate the Corpus Chair, Maitland wrote to his colleague C. S. Kenny emphasizing the attractiveness of succeeding Pollock: 'it is by no means an uneasy chair, [given] that its present occupant has given per ann. about 1/5th. as many lectures as you habitually give, [and] that Jurisprudence covers all sorts of legal knowledge. . . . The tenure is not freehold but renewable leasehold—however, it has been renewed several times in the person of F. P. despite non-residence and lectures few and far between.'[256]

Normally absent from Oxford, and intimidating to approach when not, it is hardly surprising that Pollock should not have connected with the students. One senses that at times he fared no better with the dons. There is a story—though perhaps it is no more than that—which has various Oxford academics attempting in the Senior Common Room to dent Pollock's ego by extolling the scholarship of Maitland.[257] Bearing in mind Pollock's manner, the story is certainly believable (plausibility is stretched most by the suggestion that he bothered with the Senior Common Room). It is important to emphasize also, none the less, that there is no shortage of information pushing in the opposite direction. First of all, as Maitland noted, the Corpus Chair was held for a fixed term rather than in perpetuity. Pollock had been elected to the Chair for a five-year period subject to re-election. He was to be elected for three further terms.[258] Of course, this observation counts for little if such re-elections were merely a formality; yet there is evidence that Pollock did not

[252] See Feaver, above n. 27, 113–14; also Collini, above n.26, 47 ('Maine was appointed to . . . a non-resident post which only required one overnight stay in Oxford during term').

[253] Feaver, above n.252, 171. [254] Lawson, above n.115, 73.

[255] F. W. Maitland to Henry Jackson, 13 December 1903, in *The Letters of Frederic William Maitland*, above n.22, 288; and cf. Nicholas, above n.222, 395.

[256] F. W. Maitland to C. S. Kenny, 19 November 1902, in *The Letters of Frederic William Maitland: Volume ii*, ed. P. N. R. Zutshi (London: Selden Society, 1995), 189.

[257] See G. H. Jones, above n.4, 422.

[258] When Pollock's fourth term as Corpus Professor expired on 1 February 1903, he did not seek re-election: see (1903) 19 *LQR* 1.

regard them thus[259]—which is perhaps not surprising, given his experience of University College London.

Secondly, there are indications that Pollock was not wholly disconnected from his Oxford colleagues. The eleventh Vinerian Professor was under the impression that Pollock, although 'greatly respected and loved' at Oxford, had about him 'a certain Olympian quality'.[260] It seems doubtful that he was either very much loved or thoroughly aloof. The pragmatist philosopher, F. C. S. Schiller, had studied at Oxford and returned there in 1897 to teach at Corpus Christi College. When, over a decade later, Schiller sought appointment to Oxford's Waynflete Professorship of Moral and Metaphysical Philosophy, Pollock was called upon to act as one of his referees. 'I know enough of Dr Schiller and his performance to affirm without rashness that he has strong claims upon your consideration', Pollock wrote. 'You can see for yourselves that his dialectic is brilliant, and to my mind at least the primary consideration is not whether one agrees with his results, but whether his work and method are genuine and of the kind that make other people think, whether with him or otherwise as it may turn out, but in any case for themselves and in disinterested pursuit of truth.'[261] Over two decades later again, Pollock reiterated this assessment of Schiller in his memoirs and drew attention to the fact that at Corpus Christi the two of them had become friends.[262]

Oxford brought numerous other friendships—with four successive Regius professors of modern history (William Stubbs, E. A. Freeman, J. A. Froude, and F. Y. Powell), for example, as well as with the President of Corpus Christi, Thomas Fowler, and the jurist, Sir William Anson (with whom Pollock was already familiar from Eton days).[263] Perhaps the most intriguing friendship was that which Pollock enjoyed with Dicey. On various issues the two men found themselves at loggerheads. On more than one occasion they crossed swords in the *LQR* over matters of private international law.[264] They also disagreed over the degree to which the military could be responsible for harm done to civilians in times of emergency, Pollock being of the view that in such times many legal rights are necessarily suspended.[265] ('My private opinion is that there is no liberty of the subject in time of war within the realm', he wrote to Holmes.[266]) Taking issue with Pollock, Dicey argued that criminality cloaked

[259] See Pollock to Holmes, 28 December 1897, in *PHL* i. 81 ('if I am re-elected . . .'); also F. W. Maitland to J. H. Round, 22 March 1898, in *The Letters of Frederic William Maitland*, above n.22, 173.

[260] Hanbury, above n.198, 245.

[261] Frederick Pollock to My Lords and Gentlemen, 18 February 1910, in Schiller papers, collection 191, box 3.

[262] *FMG* 44–5. [263] See generally *FMG* 42–50.

[264] See the exchanges at (1903) 19 *LQR* 244–7 and (1912) 28 *LQR* 227–8.

[265] See Frederick Pollock, 'Martial Law' (1902) 19 *S. African L. J.* 142–9; slightly different version repr. as 'What is Martial Law?' (1902) 18 *LQR* 152–8. See also *The Times* (letters), 5 April 1906, 8, col. B.

[266] Pollock to Holmes, 14 May 1917, in *PHL* i. 245. See also Sir Frederick Pollock, 'Introduction', in *The Progress of Continental Law in the Nineteenth Century*, John Henry Wigmore et al. (London: Murray, 1918), xli–xlix at xlviii ('The liberty of the subject is good in time of peace, but must give place when

by martial law ultimately must come before a court of justice.[267] In letters to Holmes, Laski refers repeatedly to this particular disagreement as if it represented some kind of donnybrook.[268] But while the disagreement was not insignificant—particularly since it evolved against the backdrop of the Boer War[269]—it was rooted in technicalities rather than personalities. Pollock generally lamented Dicey's willingness to accommodate certain Austinian ideas but recognized him to be a highly original scholar.[270] When Dicey's *A Digest of the Law of England With Reference to the Conflict of Laws* was published in 1896, Pollock wrote to Dicey complimenting him on what he had achieved and subjected the book to a serious but very positive review in *The Spectator*.[271] Besides being Oxford law professors, Pollock and Dicey inhabited overlapping London social circles (Dicey was a cousin of Leslie Stephen and a long standing friend of James Bryce). They also shared a love of the United States, and particularly of the Harvard Law School, an institution with which both men developed close links.[272]

The two men also appeared to be in broad agreement on what was perhaps the most intellectually divisive issue of the late Victorian period. 'I am more and more convinced of the truth of the doctrine which I have preached in season and out of season for thirty years,' Dicey wrote to one of his publishers in 1914, 'that any plan of Home Rule would be more injurious to England than Irish independence.'[273] Whereas Dicey vehemently and very publicly rejected Home Rule and Gladstonian Liberalism, Pollock was rather more cagey. Certainly he showed no enthusiasm for either Irish nationalism

the free peoples of the earth are fighting for their very life and liberty against the most wicked and relentless despotism that ever set out on the adventure of subduing all things to its evil will').

267 See A. V. Dicey, *Introduction to the Study of the Law of the Constitution*, 7th edn. (London: Macmillan, 1908), Appendix, 551.

268 See Harold J. Laski to O. W. Holmes, 23 October 1923, in *Holmes-Laski Letters*, above n.116, i. 553; Laski to Holmes, 25 May 1924, ibid. 621; 13 July 1925, ibid. 764; 28 July 1925, ibid. 771–2; 20 August 1929, ibid. ii. 1176. Laski vacillates on the matter of which of the two men holds the more persuasive view.

269 See Richard A. Cosgrove, 'The Boer War and the Modernization of British Martial Law' (1980) 44 *Military Affairs* 124–7 at 126.

270 See *FBJ* 260 n.1; Pollock to Holmes, 2 October 1896, in *PHL* i. 71.

271 Frederick Pollock to A. V. Dicey, 16 September 1896, in Dicey correspondence and papers (MS Gen. 508/3): 'Since I came back from South Germany at the end of last month I have been reading your Conflict of Laws. I think it will be the work of authority (so far as any new book can be authoritative) for our time at any rate, and fully justifies the amount of work you have put into it.' See also [Frederick Pollock], 'Dicey on the Conflict of Laws' (3 October 1896) 77 *Spectator* 433–5. At more or less the same time, Dicey wrote a similarly serious but flattering review of Pollock's *FBJ*: see [A. V. Dicey], 'An Introduction to Jurisprudence' (24 September 1896) 63 *The Nation*, 234–5.

272 On Pollock and Harvard see 64–7. With regard to Dicey, see Richard A. Cosgrove, 'A. V. Dicey at the Harvard Law School, 1898: A Study in the Anglo-American Legal Community' (1978) 26 *Harvard Library Bulletin* 325–35. And on the affection which evolved among the Victorian intelligentsia towards the United States, see H. A. Tulloch, 'Changing British Attitudes Towards the United States in the 1880s' (1977) 20 *Historical Jnl.* 825–40. (Tulloch's study focuses on Bryce, Dicey, and Maine, but does not deal with Pollock.)

273 A. V. Dicey to Sir Frederick Macmillan, 24 February 1914, in *Letters to Macmillan*, ed. S. Nowell-Smith (London: Macmillan, 1967), 181. On Dicey's opposition to Home Rule, see generally Cosgrove, above n.199, 114–69; and Christopher Harvie, 'Ideology and Home Rule: James Bryce, A. V. Dicey and Ireland, 1880–1887' (1976) 91 *English Historical Rev.* 298–314.

or Liberal attempts at legislative appeasement over the Irish question; but he was also disinclined, in the long term, to turn his back on general Liberal policies.[274] Constitutional and political complications would result from Home Rule, he argued in the late 1880s: 'Ireland is divided by bitterly hostile parties. . . . Any Home Rule constitution settled by the Imperial Parliament would, by the nature of the case, aim at compromise between parties of whom neither has shown much of the spirit of compromise, and each of them would find matter of offence in some part of it.'[275] Leaving aside such complications, he continued, the British government ought to consider the maintenance of union with Ireland to be one of 'our imperial duties'.[276] 'If we do not know how to govern Ireland, we must learn. It is a duty we cannot shuffle off. Remissness in this duty gives the demand for Home Rule its only real strength.'[277] By the early 1900s, Pollock appeared to be estranged from the Liberal Party and was serving as president of one of the London Liberal Unionist Committees.[278] By 1910, however, he was back within the fold: indeed, in that year he stood unsuccessfully as a Liberal candidate, running on the free trade ticket, in the Universities of Glasgow and Aberdeen constituency (an episode which he seemed to view with amused detachment).[279] In Dicey's eyes, Pollock remained an ally. Congratulating Pollock on his admission to the Privy Council in 1911, Dicey added a confession: 'I should have liked that all Unionists had come to an agreement not to accept any honours which were offered them thro' the hands of the present government'—although, he continued, 'this delusion or heresy does not diminish

[274] For Pollock's views in this context, see Christopher Harvie, *The Lights of Liberalism: University Liberals and the Challenge of Democracy 1860–86* (London: Allen Lane, 1976), 237; Lubenow, above n.6, 192–3; and cf. also Pollock to Holmes, 18 April 1918, in *PHL* i. 264 ('The British Government that does not make a mess of Ireland has yet, I fear, to be born,—not much distinction of parties to my mind'); 13 February 1922, in *PHL* ii. 89. More generally, on Home Rule and the divisions and contradictions that it generated among Pollock's contemporaries, see Alvin Jackson, *Home Rule: An Irish History, 1800–2000* (London: Weidenfeld & Nicolson, 2003), 38–105; Christopher Kent, *Brains and Numbers: Elitism, Comtism, and Democracy in Mid-Victorian England* (Toronto: University of Toronto Press, 1978), 163–5; and John Roach, 'Liberalism and the Victorian Intelligentsia' (1957) 13 *Cambridge Historical Jnl.* 58–81 at 80–1.

[275] Frederick Pollock, 'Home Rule and Imperial Sovereignty', in *The Truth about Home Rule: Papers on the Irish Question*, 2nd edn., G. Baden-Powell (Edinburgh: Blackwood & Sons, 1888), 79–104 at 90.

[276] Ibid. 100. See also Frederick Pollock, 'A Fresh Puzzle of Home Rule' (August 1893) 21 *National Rev.* 841–4 at 843.

[277] Pollock, above n.275, 103–4. This line of reasoning, a reviewer in the *New York Times* remarked, 'shows how far [Pollock] is from understanding what people who have modern ideas and the suffrage want and mean to have.' Anon., 'A Legal Baronet' in *New York Times*, 14 June 1891, 19, col. 3.

[278] According to F. R. Jones, writing in 1904 (above n.4, 3), 'he has taken an active interest in politics, and is the president of one of the London Liberal Unionist Committees, being driven from the Liberal party by Mr Gladstone's Home Rule policy.' Pollock's Unionist sympathies seem, in fact, to have been long-standing: see Frederick Pollock to John Tyndall, 6 August 1892, in Tyndall papers, Add. 53715 f.70 ('I had a merry time in Dublin and found my Unionist friends (including some new ones, my excellent hosts) in good heart'); and Frederick Pollock, review of A. J. Balfour, *The Foundations of Belief* (1895) 4 *Mind* 376–84 at 378 ('being myself a convinced Unionist . . .').

[279] See Pollock to Holmes, 20 January 1910, in *PHL* i. 158. On the ambivalent attitude of many late-Victorian intellectuals towards Liberalism, see Collini, above n.26, 189.

my personal satisfaction & pleasure in the deserved honour done to you.'[280]

It would be silly and inaccurate to present Pollock as if he were somehow at the heart of Oxford affairs. He was not. But the point again is that to portray him as detached or atomistic is to miss something of his character. Holdsworth's claims that '[t]o any serious student [Pollock] was kindness itself' and that in his dealings with such students 'he proved himself a great teacher'[281] require, if they are to be believed, a substantial amount of benevolence. But there seems little doubt that Pollock took his duties as a lecturer seriously. This much becomes apparent from examination of his lecture notes. In October 1883 he began a course of lectures on 'Forms and Authorities of Law'[282] and followed these in January 1884 with a course on 'The Arrangement of Private Law'.[283] The following January, he delivered lectures on the 'Theory of Civil Liability',[284] and in the Michaelmas and Hilary terms of 1886 he lectured on the topics of possession and trespass (the lectures on possession were repeated in 1888 and 1890).[285] Some of these lecture courses largely replicate those he presented at the Inns of Court throughout the same period.[286] But certain of the courses were unique to Oxford: in the Hilary Term of 1889 he delivered a detailed series of lectures on 'Analytical Jurisprudence';[287] in 1898 he presented for the first time a course of lectures entitled 'Theory of the State in English Publicists', in which he rehearsed the critical assessments of Hobbes, Locke, Bentham, and Austin which would eventually appear, in 1890, in the first edition of *An Introduction to the History of the Science of Politics*;[288] and in the Hilary Term of 1899 he first delivered lectures on the 'History of Courts and Procedure in England'.[289] The marginal notes and insertions to be found in these various sets of notes indicate clearly that Pollock would often update his lectures for repeated presentation. It is also clear that he connected teaching and scholarship: on the front page of one of his notebooks containing Oxford lectures he included the words 'Almost the whole of this has been worked into published books'.[290] Invariably his lectures are carefully written and devised, and although they contain plenty of evidence of Pollock's

[280] A. V. Dicey to Frederick Pollock, 25 June 1911, in Pollock correspondence, box 1, folder 19. For Pollock's continued opposition to Home Rule, see *The Times* (letters), 13 July 1912, 10, col. C.

[281] Holdsworth (1937) 53 *LQR* 180.

[282] Pollock notebooks, Misc. 795, 1–42. [283] Ibid. 43–63. [284] Ibid. 64–77.

[285] Ibid. 102–19. Pollock mentions that these lectures were repeated in the October terms of 1888 and 1890, ibid. 137.

[286] For details of Pollock's Inns of Court lectures, see n.225 above.

[287] Pollock notebooks, Misc. 795, 137–75.

[288] Pollock notebooks, Misc. 798, 1–20. He had already offered an assessment of Hobbes in a lecture delivered at Oxford in August 1894, published as Frederick Pollock, 'Hobbes' (September 1894) 24 *National Rev.* 29–41.

[289] Ibid. 21–35.

[290] Misc. 795, opening page. Note also that, on completion of the manuscript for *FBJ*, Pollock wrote to his publishers that '[t]he second part of it is in a notebook because it was worked up from rougher notes which I had used for lectures, and used, during that process, for a repetition of the course.' Frederick Pollock to Messrs. Macmillan & Co., 30 March 1896, in Macmillan Archive, Add. 55083 f.81.

cold-fish formality they are rarely as abstruse as was his introductory lecture at UCL. When discoursing on doctrinal topics, indeed, he appears from his notes to have been a fairly straightforward, if by no means the most engrossing, lecturer. It seems, hardly surprisingly, that the more he lectured, the better he became at assessing what his audience would and would not already understand.

The common assessment of Pollock as an Oxford professor is that he was a distinguished jurist who left little or no mark as a teacher. Lecturing seems to have been for him a matter of duty, something which had to be undertaken and accomplished professionally but which did not require much in the way of engagement with or commitment to one's institution. Even a stalwart friend like Maitland, we have seen, doubted that Pollock could be bothered to break sweat in fulfilling his obligations as Corpus Professor. But we should not deduce from Pollock's apparent indifference to lecturing that his university career was insignificant. His career was significant, first of all, because it was just that: Pollock belonged to that era during which reference to occupation within a university as a career became meaningful. Maine apparently claimed that he had himself continued to practise law while holding the Corpus Chair because he could not survive on what Oxford paid.[291] Various reforms of the 1860s and 1870s—in particular, the removal of the celibacy restriction on Oxbridge Fellowships and the general improvement of salaries—made the life of the don a more attractive proposition for the Victorian gentleman with a secular intellectual disposition and an inadequate private income.[292] Throughout these two decades, Pollock was earning money from a variety of pursuits—journalism, the writing of books, teaching at the Inns of Court, and examining, among others[293]—and it is far from obvious that he would have taken the Corpus Chair primarily for the salary. But the point to be stressed is that this was a Chair to which there attached a salary. A law professorship—the history of the Chair of Jurisprudence at UCL is evidence of this much—had not always been a salaried post. The Corpus Chair provided Pollock—a scholar at heart, who would happily have remained at Cambridge as a classicist—the opportunity to pursue in a professional capacity the activity he loved most dearly. As Corpus Professor, he had a career as an academic lawyer.

But what did this career involve? Being in Oxford and available to undergraduates was clearly not integral to the job specification as Pollock understood it. Is it not the case that he only nominally had a university career? Did

[291] See Sheldon Rothblatt, 'The Diversification of Higher Education in England', in *The Transformation of Higher Learning 1860–1930: Expansion, Diversification, Social Opening and Professionalization in England, Germany, Russia and the United States*, ed. K. H. Jarausch (Stuttgart: Klett-Kotta, 1982), 131–48 at 134.

[292] See generally A. J. Engel, *From Clergyman to Don: The Rise of the Academic Profession in Nineteenth-Century Oxford* (Oxford: Clarendon Press, 1983), 106–285; and Rothblatt, above n.154, 181–247.

[293] All of these pursuits have been at least mentioned here already, with the exception of examining. Pollock was an examiner for the Cambridge Law Tripos (1879–81) and a public examiner (1881–4). See Foster, above n.4, 370. On the money to be earned from examining during this period, see Collini, above n.26, 44.

he not resist the tide of academic professionalization, in other words, by treating his professorship as a more or less part-time pursuit? To answer this last question in the affirmative is to fail to understand what professionalization means in this context. For one contributor to the *Oxford Magazine*, Pollock's resignation as Corpus Professor in 1903 raised a 'perplexing question', namely:

> [w]hat ought an ideal Oxford Professor to do? Is his main duty to teach undergraduates or, as Professor Freeman is said to have held, to teach the teachers? Is it to spend his time in research, thereby increasing knowledge? Or is a Professorship rightly considered, a reward of previous meritorious activities, endowing the holder and affording him the leisure and the prestige to employ his time elsewhere with profit to himself?[294]

Pollock would not have considered these possibilities mutually exclusive. The Corpus Chair certainly afforded him plenty of time to engage in profitable pursuits away from Oxford—teaching at the Inns of Court is perhaps the most obvious of these. But the Chair also afforded him time to develop his scholarly objectives. That he would have accomplished many of these objectives irrespective of his holding the Corpus Professorship is beside the point. What matters is that, in pursuing them, he played a role typically ascribed to the late nineteenth-century professional academic. But what was that role? Before considering how Pollock managed to fulfil the role, it is important to try to develop some understanding of what the role was.

By the late nineteenth century, the idea of the academic as both researcher and expert—responsible for mastering the technicalities and ensuring the advancement of his discipline, as well as for providing specialist knowledge—was generally accepted.[295] At Oxford and Cambridge by the mid-1880s, Heyck claims, 'research had been accepted as a primary function of a university and had become a central occupation of fellows as well as professors', notwithstanding that many felt overburdened with teaching.[296] Heyck perhaps puts the point a little too starkly. Writing specifically about history as a discipline, Jann argues that '[t]he triumph of the research ideal was in many ways more apparent than real; especially at the ancient universities, the enduring vitality of liberal education provided a medium in which traditional assumptions about history's practical and moral importance continued to thrive.'[297] History, Collini notes, was not the only discipline suffering from tensions. While 'the establishment of the university study of law . . . encourage[d] the writing of legal texts and create[d] the role of the legal professor as a figure of some

[294] *Oxford Magazine*, 28 January 1903, cited after Lawson, above n.115, 157.

[295] See Reba N. Soffer, *Discipline and Power: The University, History, and the Making of an English Elite, 1870–1930* (Stanford: Stanford UP, 1994), 25–6.

[296] T. W. Heyck, *The Transformation of Intellectual Life in Victorian England* (London: Croom Helm, 1982), 186.

[297] Rosemary Jann, *The Art and Science of Victorian History* (Columbus: Ohio State UP, 1985), 224.

public standing', it also 'set in train a process which was increasingly responsive to the practical requirements' of the legal profession.[298] Responding to the requirements of the profession jarred with teaching as well as with research ideals. 'The academic teacher of law inevitably found himself in a somewhat different position from other teachers: he needed simultaneously to justify law's place in a liberal education to a sceptical university and to justify the usefulness of academic study to a sceptical profession.'[299] Pollock, we have seen, remained defiant in the face of these tensions: for him, universities are not production lines for the legal profession. That he defied the tensions, however, does not mean that he put an end to them.

Adding flesh to the bones of this last assertion requires a fairly labyrinthine inquiry. Let us start with Pollock's defiance of the tensions. Pollock wanted to contribute to the practical development and application of the law while maintaining a scholarly or scientific detachment from it. The two exercises he regarded as complementary rather than incompatible: 'there is a science as well as a practice of law; a science inseparable from the practical art, or separable only at the cost of ceasing to be versed in real matter.'[300] Prioritize the pursuit of scholarship and the development of legal science, he believed, and natural by-products of the exercise will very likely be the provision of both a liberal education for students of law and the sorts of doctrinal insight and expertise valued by the profession. Pollock's conception of legal science will be considered in more detail in due course,[301] but it is worth noting at this point that his understanding of science connects with the idea of progress. When Pollock asserted that law is a science, Sugarman has observed, he 'seems to have meant little more than that law was clear, rational, internally coherent and systematized'.[302] In fact, Pollock insisted that there is no single legal science. 'Taking legal science in its widest extent, we find that it has different branches aiming at distinct objects.'[303] Certainly his notion of jurisprudence as legal science encapsulated some of the qualities to which Sugarman refers.[304] When developing a broader conception of legal science, however, Pollock emphasized that law could be scientific notwithstanding that it might also be unclear and unsystematic.

In fact, if, as Pollock believed, 'the law is a living science'[305]—an evolutionary process—then we may *expect* that it will exhibit irrationality, incoherence, lack of clarity, and the like. For the scientific character of the law, on this account, rests not so much in its accomplishments as in its ideals and aspirations. To recognize that 'in a civilised commonwealth law must inevitably become a science', Pollock wrote in 1896, is to appreciate that 'the law is in a constant process of approximation to an ideal certainty which . . . can never

[298] Collini, above n.26, 301. [299] Ibid. 269. [300] *OLOD* 92.

[301] See chapter 3, 116–23.

[302] David Sugarman, 'Legal Theory, the Common Law Mind and the Making of the Textbook Tradition', in *Legal Theory and the Common Law*, ed. W. Twining (Oxford: Blackwell, 1986), 26–61 at 30.

[303] *EJE* 262. [304] See, e.g., *EJE* 27. [305] *OLOD* 105.

be perfectly attained at any given moment.' '[I]t must be remembered', he added, 'that the political sciences do not claim to be exact in either a speculative or a practical point of view.'[306] Note the link between science and civilization. '[F]aith in the science of law,' he would insist in due course, 'has to do not with a mere intellectual craft but with a vital aspect of human and national history.'[307] This is classic late Victorian scientific naturalism. In his first edition of *The Grammar of Science*, published in 1892, Karl Pearson claimed that 'the scientific habit of mind'—those last three words, it should become clear in due course, might well be underlined, italicised, and put in bold—was 'an essential for good citizenship'.[308] The equation of scientific progress with the progress of civilization ran throughout many of the writings of two of Pollock's close friends, William Kingdon Clifford (to whom Pollock dedicated his principal book on Spinoza) and the French philosopher and historian, Ernest Renan (to whom Pollock dedicated *Essays in Jurisprudence and Ethics*).[309] In tributes to both men, Pollock emphasizes the complementary nature of scientific and philosophical modes of inquiry. Pollock praises Clifford for showing 'that, as the frank application of the right method of search to the physical sciences has put them on a footing of steady progress, . . . so the like effects might be expected when philosophical speculation was taken in hand by the light of science and with scientific impartiality and earnestness.'[310] Renan, treated to a less prolix assessment, is lauded for having been 'an idealist in philosophy and a scientific optimist in practice'.[311] Each, in Pollock's eyes, deserves our admiration for lending substance to the intuition that, more often than not, to make progress with science is to ensure progress for mankind.

Pollock's defiant response to the tensions inherent in teaching and researching law within the university took the form of a paean to legal science: if university lawyers treat, respect, and endeavour to advance their discipline as a science, it is unlikely that either law students or the profession will be ill-served. The message was clear, but was it persuasive? We have noted already Jann's observation with regard to the study of history in the Victorian universities. Regarding law in the universities throughout this period, it seems similarly inappropriate to refer to the triumph of the research ideal. As was noted earlier, Pollock lamented in his Oxford inaugural that, in England, the scientific study of law was a pursuit followed by few and scorned by many.[312] Almost a decade later, in his valedictory lecture, Bryce lamented the failure of Oxford

[306] *FBJ* 41–2. [307] *GCL* 1.

[308] Karl Pearson, *The Grammar of Science* (London: Dent, 1951 [1892]), 12. On Pearson's scientific naturalism, see George Levine, *Dying to Know: Scientific Epistemology and Narrative in Victorian England* (Chicago: University of Chicago Press, 2002), 220–43.

[309] For relevant discussions of both Clifford and Renan, see Frank Miller Turner, *Between Science and Religion: The Reaction to Scientific Naturalism in Late Victorian England* (New Haven: Yale UP, 1974), 12–14; *Contesting Cultural Authority: Essays in Victorian Intellectual Life* (Cambridge: Cambridge UP, 1993), 203–5.

[310] Pollock, 'Introduction', above n.22, 28.

[311] Frederick Pollock, 'Some Recollections of Ernest Renan' (November 1892) 32 *Nineteenth Century* 711–19 at 714.

[312] See *EOD* 5.

to attract 'a band of young lawyers' with 'an interest in legal history and juristic speculation'. 'The number of persons in England who care for either subject', he continued, 'increases so slowly as to seem to discredit the efforts of the Universities.'[313]

Yet we have seen that, in between Pollock's inaugural and Bryce's valedictory, Pollock delivered an address which offered a fairly positive assessment of research at Oxford in the mid-1880s. After his resignation from Oxford, however, he came to be of the view that research had lost out to teaching. In 1909, responding to Harold Hazeltine's address to the American Bar Association on the state of legal education in England, Pollock chided Hazeltine for painting too rosy a picture.[314] Of Oxford undergraduates—never a group that had set his pulse racing—he was clearly unenamoured. 'I have seen an Oxford man presenting himself for a law degree who could not construe a sentence from Justinian when the book was put in his hand.'[315] Undergraduate education, furthermore, was largely unsystematic: 'there is not in any law school in England what you [i.e., an American lawyer] would call a prescribed course of study.' Neither Oxford nor Cambridge requires 'a candidate for a law degree, or for any degree, to have actually taken any course of lectures', and preparation for examinations is purely a matter of personal initiative. '[M]any of us' wonder, Pollock continued,

> whether it was a good thing when, some thirty-five years ago, our universities undertook to teach law at all to our undergraduates. Personally, I very much question whether many men at the undergraduate age are capable of acquiring a legal habit of mind, and of understanding that law cannot be learned out of text-books and in examinations, but is concerned with men's living business, and with the decisions of live judges in very active courts . . . Now they are beginning to teach law in an academic manner to undergraduates, but the results are very doubtful, and I gravely question whether it does not divert a man from the serious study and practice of the law.[316]

The only saving grace for Oxford specifically, he continued, was the B.C.L. degree, which had been reformed in the 1870s. 'That is, I think, the most valuable academic institution that we have at present in England for the

[313] James Bryce, 'Legal Studies in the University of Oxford' (1893), in his *Studies in History and Jurisprudence*, 2 vols. (Oxford: Clarendon Press, 1901), ii. 504–25 at 518.

[314] See the remarks of Sir Frederick Pollock, in the *Report of the Thirty-Second Annual Meeting of the American Bar Association held at Detroit, Michigan. August 24, 25, 26 and 27, 1909* (Baltimore: The Lord Baltimore Press, 1909), 832–6.

[315] Pollock, ibid. 835; cf. also *PCLE(3)* x. For details of the examination method to which Pollock refers, see Nicholas, above n.222, 386–7; and, regarding the general sentiment on display in Pollock's comment, see Françoise Waquet, *Latin or the Empire of a Sign: From the Sixteenth to the Twentieth Centuries*, trans. J. Howe (London: Verso, 2001), 178–206.

[316] Pollock, above n.314, 833. These views Pollock had held for at least a decade—see Ames, above n.242, 132–3—although by 1924, speaking in front of an English university audience, his outlook was far less gloomy: see 'Learning the Law', above n.47, 290.

university study of law and the encouragement of legal research.'[317] The more general message, however, was that research goals had been sacrificed. Promoting the value and teaching the methods of legal science are likely to have progressive and beneficial consequences where the university is dominated by research objectives; but in an environment overpopulated by undergraduates, the legal scientist will probably encounter too much of an uphill struggle. If this last proposition is an accurate distillation of Pollock's view of law in the universities by the early 1900s, it is small wonder that he vacated the Corpus Chair when he did.

v. After Oxford

Pollock was in his late fifties when he did resign. Apparently he felt that twenty years was a sufficiently long time for anyone to occupy a jurisprudence chair.[318] *Who Was Who*, *Burke's Peerage*, and other reference works about the great and the good record that a plethora of honorary degrees and academic gongs awaited him in later years. But by 1903 his university career was at an end. What would he do with the rest of his life?

One of the first things he would do is go west. Teaching in the American law schools seemed to generate in him an enthusiasm that teaching in England could not. '[T]he science of law is still as much alive in England as ever', Pollock remarked in 1895, '[o]nly we need, it seems to me, a little more self-confidence.'[319] In America he detected that self-confidence. '[T]he present generation of scientific American lawyers', he observed in his introductory lecture at UCL, 'have shown a disposition for historical research and exposition which has already borne excellent fruit.'[320] One of his 'pet wishes', apparently, was that his son study at the Harvard Law School.[321] On the twenty-fifth anniversary of Christopher Columbus Langdell's deanship at Harvard—the Langdellian approach to legal education having by this point secured its grip on many of the major American law schools[322]—Pollock had visited the

[317] Pollock, above n.314, 834. On the reform of the B.C.L. (which was introduced at Oxford in 1851), see Nicholas, above n.222, 395.

[318] See Anon., 'Sir F. Pollock, 91, Legal Expert', above n.4; F. R. Jones, above n.4, 3.

[319] *ECL* 8. Regarding this lack of self-confidence, see further *ECL* 11: 'It appears to us quite natural that Roman law should have its proper conceptions and terminology. . . . What I desire to suggest is that, as we allow this liberty to others as a matter of right, we should not be afraid of claiming it for ourselves; that, if English-speaking lawyers are really to believe in their own science, they must seek a genuine philosophy of the Common Law.'

[320] Pollock, 'The Methods of Jurisprudence', above n.185, 51. See also Pollock, 'Bigelow's Placita Anglo-Normannica', above n.26, 327 ('. . . while work like Mr Bigelow's does honour to American learning, it is not exactly an honour to English learning and jurisprudence that we leave our brethren on the other side of the Atlantic to compete almost unaided with the insatiable industry of German scholars for the elucidation of our own legal antiquities').

[321] John Pollock, *Time's Chariot*, above n.4, 184.

[322] See William P. LaPiana, *Logic and Experience: The Origin of Modern American Legal Education* (New York: Oxford UP, 1994), 79–109.

School to pay tribute to Langdell's achievement.[323] The case method of instruction, Pollock contended, 'is the best way, if not the only one, to learn law.'[324] For 'at the root of Mr Langdell's work' is the conviction that 'principle is the touchstone by which particular decisions have to be tried.' While 'several of us have dissented, now and again, from this or that opinion of Mr Langdell's', in general 'appreciation of his point of view was sure to bring one nearer to the heart of the Common Law', since 'he gives us the method and the power that can test the reason of rules.'[325] Two years after this public tribute, Pollock privately disparaged 'the Langdellian ether of a super-terrestrial Common Law where authority does not count'[326]—words which make the tribute ring a little hollow.[327] Whether, furthermore, he endorsed the Socratic approach to teaching—an approach which it is almost impossible to imagine him undertaking—is not clear.[328] It is clear, however, that his general assessment of Langdell complements some of the modern revisionist appraisals of Langdellian legal science,[329] and that he considered Langdell and

[323] For a report on his visit and a synopsis of his lecture, see Anon., 'Sir Frederick Pollock in America' (1895) 99 *Law Times* 314–16.

[324] *ECL* 6; and see also *FMG* 194. For a modern description of the case method of legal instruction, see Patrick Atiyah, 'An Autobiographical Fragment', in *Frontiers of Legal Scholarship*, ed. G. P. Wilson (Chichester: Wiley, 1995), 34–46 at 40 ('[M]ost law teaching in America is done through the Casebook, and at its best and most effective, the class hour is spent in Socratic question and answer style. The students are expected to, and (at any rate in their first year) they do prepare for every class very thoroughly, so that the teacher can ask a series of searching questions, going from one student to another. In this way, answers emerge slowly and—if the exercise is done with real skill—the reasons for them emerge as the answers themselves emerge. What is more, the student is made to see that there are always alternative possible answers, and he is made to examine the advantages and disadvantages of each possible answer'). Other than that Langdell and his immediate followers were probably not too interested in having students consider 'alternative possible answers', this description of the case method is probably as apt for the late nineteenth century as for the late twentieth.

[325] *ECL* 7. See also F. R. Jones, above n.4, 1: 'Sir Frederick Pollock . . . was the first English legal publicist to recognize the worth of the system of legal teaching evolved by Professor Langdell of Harvard, and of the consequent advantages enjoyed by the profession in the United States.'

[326] Pollock to Holmes, 17 September 1897, in *PHL* i. 80.

[327] Though it is perhaps stretching matters to conclude that 'Pollock . . . regarded . . . Langdellian jurisprudence . . . as hopelessly detached from life's legal realities'. K. J. M. Smith and J. P. S. McLaren, 'History's Living Legacy: An Outline of "Modern" Historiography of the Common Law' (2001) 21 *Legal Studies* 251–324 at 262.

[328] See *TLT* vi: 'Of Harvard and its Law School I will say only this, that I have endeavoured to turn to practical account the lessons of what I saw and heard there, and that this present book is in some measure the outcome of that endeavour. It contains the substance of between two and three years lectures in the Inns of Court, and nearly everything advanced in it has been put into shape after, or concurrently with, free oral exposition and discussion of the leading cases.' Although Pollock's Inns of Court lecture notes on tort (Pollock notebooks, Misc. 797, 1–75) do not provide any indication of his having put questions to his audiences, they are notes rather than lectures and would have allowed for improvisation in delivery. The difficulty lies in imagining Pollock improvising in the lecture hall—though he did insist near the end of his life that 'it is really more important for a teacher to be able to talk to his pupils informally than to be a good formal lecturer' (above n.111, 9). For a confident assertion that Pollock did use Langdell's teaching methods, see Cosgrove, above n.4, 139–40.

[329] See, e.g., Bruce A. Kimball, '"Warn Students That I Entertain Heretical Opinions, Which They Are Not to Take as Law": The Inception of Case Method Teaching in the Classrooms of the Early C. C. Langdell, 1870–1883' (1999) 17 *Law & History Rev.* 57–140; and W. Burlette Carter, 'Reconstructing Langdell' (1997) 32 *Georgia L. Rev.* 1–139.

Holmes to be allied to the same basic cause—that of advancing the science of the Common Law.[330]

A few months after his resignation from Oxford, Pollock embarked on a lecture tour of North American and Canadian law schools, returning to Harvard and also speaking at Yale, Michigan, Toronto, Chicago, Columbia, and Iowa (he also fitted in a trip to Hot Springs, Virginia, to attend the meeting of the American Bar Association).[331] Numerous other trips to the United States would follow, Pollock's last visit taking place in 1930. In preparing for these visits, he produced some of his most confident, reflective, provocative, and valuable work. When writing for an audience uninitiated in the technicalities of English legal doctrine he would tend to discuss the common law tradition in terms of history, science, and principles, making comparisons not only between the English and American systems but also offering insightful cross-references to Hindu and Roman law. Two works from this period are particularly important. Largely the product of a 1903 lecture tour, *The Expansion of the Common Law*—the title is redolent of that which J. R. Seeley had given to his highly popular lectures on colonialism two decades earlier[332]—is the first book by Pollock in which he adopts the role of the grandee jurist, looking back at what he has achieved and situating those achievements within a broader jurisprudential history. Avoiding doctrinal discussion, Pollock focuses on that which he considers fundamental to a proper grasp of the common law tradition: 'our business here is to understand the strength of the root, not to justify the growth of all its branches.'[333] Like most of Pollock's major works, the book builds to a stirring crescendo, calling upon young American lawyers to recognize their duty to their vocation: '[t]he Common Law, here and in England and round the world, looks to your youth and strength to improve it as good husbandmen.'[334] This notion of duty to the common law is taken up again by Pollock in his 1911 Carpentier Lectures at Columbia University: '[w]e are here to do homage to our lady the Common Law', he wrote; 'we are her men of life and limb and earthly worship. But we do not worship her as a goddess exempt from human judgment or above human sympathy.'[335] Originally published as articles in the *Columbia Law Review* (in 1912 they would be collected together as *The Genius of the Common Law*), these lectures were apparently dubbed by the Secretary of the journal's Editorial Board 'the love story of the common law.'[336] In fact, they pale somewhat when stood in the light of Pollock's 1903 lectures. The tone of *The Genius of the Common Law* may be more

[330] See *EOL* 8. [331] See *FMG* 196–7; Pollock to Holmes, 17 January 1903, in *PHL* i. 111–12.

[332] J. R. Seeley, *The Expansion of England: Two Courses of Lectures* (London: Macmillan, 1883). Seeley was Regius Professor of Modern History at the University of Cambridge, where these lectures were delivered.

[333] *ECL* 60. [334] *ECL* 137. [335] *GCL* 2.

[336] See Barbara Aronstein Black, 'From the Archives (Such as They Are)' (2000) 100 *Columbia L. Rev.* 1–15 at 15. In 1911, the lectures were rather dreadfully abridged by an anonymous reporter relying for information on the coverage of them in the *New York Times*: 'Sir Frederick Pollock on "The Genius of the Common Law"' (1911) 23 *Green Bag* 626–34.

authoritative, and possibly more passionate, but the volume is not as insightful as the earlier one, and Pollock exploits the imagery of 'our lady' the common law to the point where it begins to grate like a dentist's drill. To emphasize this comparison, however, would be to overlook the essential point: both of these books brim with juristic insight, and will demand fuller attention when we come to study Pollock's philosophy of the common law.

Pollock was especially fond of Harvard. In various ways, and on numerous occasions, he signalled his loyalty to the Harvard Law School.[337] Had it been possible, he would have spent more time there. In 1898, Dicey accepted an invitation from the President of Harvard, Charles Eliot, to deliver a series of student lectures on law and public opinion in England.[338] Eliot wanted Pollock to deliver a similar lecture series, but the responsibility of editing the Law Reports meant that Pollock could not find enough time to put aside for such a venture.[339] At Harvard, perhaps more than at any other academic institution, he found soul mates of sorts. In the Harvard Law School Library we find in the papers of two successive deans, Langdell and James Barr Ames, letters to Pollock paying tribute to his research achievements.[340] Ames's correspondence is especially significant because it comes six years after the two men had disagreed over the meaning and scope of consideration in the law of contract.[341] Pollock himself was particularly impressed by Ames's work on the history of assumpsit,[342] and his concern over Ames's health just before Ames died seems to indicate that over time the two men became good friends. That Pollock's principal intellectual home was Cambridge, England, has been noted; that his second such home may have been Cambridge, Massachusetts, is not impossible. After the *Law Quarterly Review*, the *Harvard Law Review* published more of Pollock's essays than did any other law journal. When Harvard awarded him an honorary LL.D., he was especially delighted.[343]

The basic point to be emphasized here is that, when Pollock ended his university career, he did not abandon intellectual life. He was a jurist before, throughout, and after his years at Oxford. Not only was he always working on new projects, but he regularly revised his principal texts: *The Law of Torts* went

[337] For examples, see Cosgrove, above n.4, 140.

[338] A. V. Dicey, *Lectures on the Relation between Law and Public Opinion in England during the Nineteenth Century* (London: Macmillan, 1905); and see further Cosgrove, above n.199, 170–94.

[339] See Frederick Pollock to President Charles W. Eliot, 30 October 1900, in President's papers: Charles W. Eliot, box 130, folder 7/7: 'It would be most agreeable to me, if it were possible, to give a course of lectures at the Harvard Law School: but unfortunately it is not possible for me to leave England for so long together while I am editor of the Law Reports, which, except in part of the Long Vacation, require my personal attention for several days in each month.'

[340] C. C. Langdell to Frederick Pollock, 30 March 1902, in Pollock correspondence, box 1, folder 43; James Barr Ames to Frederick Pollock, 31 August 1905, ibid., folder 2.

[341] See chapter 5, 208–15.

[342] Frederick Pollock to James Barr Ames, 23 June 1888, in Ames correspondence, box 1, folder 32; John Chipman Gray to Frederick Pollock, 27 February 1910, in Pollock correspondence, box 1, folder 26 (Gray responding to an enquiry from Pollock regarding Ames's health).

[343] See Pollock to Holmes, 11 December 1919, in *PHL* ii. 33.

into thirteen editions during his lifetime, the *Digest of the Law of Partnership* into twelve, *Principles of Contract* into nine, and *A First Book of Jurisprudence* into six.[344] There was also his work as an editor. Pollock's editorship of the *Law Quarterly Review*, which he had undertaken during his early years at Oxford, was to continue until 1919 (with a brief stint as 'emergency' editor in 1925[345]). He also served as the General Editor of the *Revised Reports*, all 149 volumes of which were published between 1891 and 1917. These reports 'republish the old Reports of our Superior Courts of Common law and Equity which are modern enough to be still of frequent practical utility, reducing them to a manageable bulk and cost by the omission of obsolete and unimportant matter.'[346] Each volume contains a short preface by Pollock, and the entire collection covers cases decided between 1785 and 1865. The workload turned out to be greater than he had expected. Having initially intended only to reproduce cases, Pollock, ever the editor, found himself correcting large numbers of original reporting errors.[347] The task probably provided good training for his much more significant law-reporting role: as Editor-in-Chief of the Law Reports from 1895 through to 1935. Pollock's work as an editor is analysed in some detail in chapter 6. For now it is enough to note that his careers as both writer and editor were something apart from his career as an academic.

From the time of his resigning the Corpus Chair through to the end of his life, Pollock became increasingly involved in the administration of the law and the affairs of the state. It should not be assumed, however, that he was turning his back on one goal so as to begin pursuing another. Just as the end of Pollock's academic career did not signal the end of his juristic ambitions, so too it did not mark the beginning of his endeavours as a lawyer-statesman. From 1891 to 1894, he had served as a member of the Royal Commission on Labour, his primary task being to render coherent the law of trade combinations. During this time he also travelled to the West Indies as a member of a special commission appointed to report on the administration of justice by the Supreme Court of Trinidad.

In his memoirs, Pollock recounts the trip to Trinidad as if the only notable feature about it was the weather.[348] 'Our commission . . . is probably forgotten even on the spot by this time.'[349] In fact, on Trinidad a specific judicial difficulty had arisen. During the 1880s, the Chief Justice of the Supreme Court, Sir John Gorrie, had begun, without any effective opposition from his brethren, to adopt the role of a judicial Robin Hood, using his decision-making capacities to champion the causes of the island's non-white popula-

[344] Not that the new editions always involved significant revision. See, e.g., Frederick Pollock to Messrs. Macmillan & Co., 8 April 1911, in Macmillan Archive Add. 55083 f.108: 'The alterations for a third edition [of *FBJ*] will not be considerable.' The fourth, fifth, and sixth editions of *FBJ* do not differ much from the third.

[345] See chapter 6, 310.

[346] F[rederick] P[ollock], 'General Introduction' (1891) 1 *Revised Reports* v–x at v.

[347] F[rederick] P[ollock], 'Preface to Vol. CXLIX' (1917) 149 *Revised Reports* v–vi at v.

[348] See *FMG* 207–8. [349] *FMG* 208.

tion. Gorrie met his nemesis in the form of Richard Anderson, a prominent citizen of the white community. In 1890, an action was brought against Anderson by one of his crop-workers or *metayers*. Since the 1840s, *metayers* on Trinidad and Tobago had regularly complained about the erosion of their customary rights—it had become common for crop-holders to withhold payment for work and to issue summary dismissals—and when Anderson evicted Joseph Frank, a 73-year-old *metayer* with forty-five years of service, the dispute between the two men was heard in the Supreme Court. Presided over by Gorrie, the Court in effect held that Frank had security of tenure. When Anderson unsuccessfully petitioned for leave to appeal the case to the Privy Council, he turned his attention to the Court itself, issuing a writ against Gorrie and his colleagues and claiming damages of £10,000.[350]

Unfortunately for Anderson, Gorrie and his colleagues turned out to be fireproof. The English Court of Appeal held unanimously in *Anderson v Gorrie* that no action lies against a judge of the Supreme Court of a colony in respect of any act done by him in his judicial capacity.[351] While Gorrie could not be touched, however, he could still be damned. 'It cannot be denied', Kay L. J. remarked, 'that all the acts complained of were done by the defendant in his capacity as judge,' that 'he acted maliciously and for the purposes of gratifying private spleen.'[352] Reaching this conclusion had probably been made all the easier because of the report produced principally by Pollock. On arriving in Trinidad in April 1891, Pollock's co-commissioner, Sir William Markby, had fallen sick, leaving Pollock with the lion's share of the work to do. With Pollock, Gorrie's portrayal of himself as a champion of the oppressed cut no ice at all. While '[t]he Chief Justice has over and over again asserted' that under his administration 'the poor and illiterate have a chance now which they had not before of asserting their just rights', Pollock observed, he seems not to appreciate that 'civilized nations' agree 'that there shall be limits to judicial discretion. . . . If he seeks to justify himself by saying that in his opinion the result has been beneficial to the community, the answer is that in a civilised community the first duty of judges, as of other citizens, is to obey the law.'[353]

That discretion and valour must be tempered by constraint was, we will see in chapter 4, very much Pollock's general philosophy of adjudication. More immediately significant is the fact that his report into the administration of justice in Trinidad would have played directly into the hands of the Colonial Office, which by the 1890s had become seriously concerned about Gorrie's

[350] For the episode in more detail, see Patrick Polden, 'Doctor in Trouble: *Anderson v Gorrie* and the Extension of Judicial Immunity from Suit in the 1890s' (2001) 22 *Jnl. Leg. Hist.* 37–68 at 40–4.

[351] *Anderson v Gorrie* [1895] 1 QB 668. [352] Ibid. 672.

[353] *Report of the Judicial Enquiry Commission on the Administration of Justice in the Colony, 15 June 1892*, HL 328 (1893–4), part 8; extract published as 'Our Colonial Judiciary' (1892–93) 94 *Law Times* 202–5 (quoted passage at 204). For Gorrie's efforts at self-justification, and his exasperation with the Commission, throughout this episode see Bridget Brereton, *Law, Justice and Empire* (Barbados: University Press of the West Indies, 1997), 300–6.

decision-making.[354] This was not the only instance in which Pollock's efforts worked to the good of the Colonial Office. In 1896, he advised the British Government in its effort to resolve a boundary dispute between Venezuela and British Guiana. The advice that he offered would have been music to the ears of any British colonialist: not only, he claimed, had the British Government 'been willing to agree to a boundary within those limits which would give to Venezuela far more territory than that to which she can show any title', but 'the claim of Venezuela . . . has been based upon contentions which are in no way supported by the facts and cannot be justified upon any reasonable ground.'[355]

The then Attorney-General declared Pollock's report on the dispute to be informative, 'though not in a form suitable for a case before arbitrators'.[356] Notwithstanding that Pollock's son believed that the report forced the dispute into arbitration and removed the danger of war,[357] its purpose had not, in fact, been to assist arbitrators but to supply information to the Colonial Office: to assess it in terms of its suitability as a mediation document was to judge it according to a standard it was never intended to meet. But the report proved objectionable even when considered purely as a source of information. The case that Pollock had made for British territorial ownership over the competing Venezuelan claim was, the *New York Times* declared in March 1896, 'irrefragable'.[358] Although the report 'makes very sweeping claims,' it was noted, 'the evidence . . . is presented entirely on its merits.'[359] Within weeks, however, the Venezuelan government was asserting not only that there were 'inaccuracies . . . in Prof. Pollock's . . . presentation of all the evidence in the case',[360] but that these 'errors . . . were intentionally made to bolster up a weak cause.'[361] The allegation that the report contained inaccuracies was, according to the British Foreign Office, not without foundation,[362] and the Colonial Office, with Pollock's involvement, subsequently produced a list of corrections.[363] Excuses were issued on Pollock's behalf—that he had been required

[354] See Polden, above n.350, 41.

[355] *Documents and Correspondence relating to the Question of the Boundary between British Guiana and Venezuela* C 7972 (London: HMSO, 1896), 38–9.

[356] Lord Alverstone, *Recollections of Bar and Bench* (London: Arnold, 1914), 237.

[357] John Pollock, *Time's Chariot*, above n.4, 90; and cf. Hazeltine, above n.4, 243–4.

[358] Anon., 'England's Case Made Up. Sir Frederick Pollock's Report on the Venezuelan Controversy', in *New York Times*, 5 March 1896, 5, col. 3.

[359] Anon., 'British Venezuela Blue Book. The Evidence of Great Britain in its Context for Territory Arranged in a Very Clear Way', in *New York Times*, 19 March 1896, 4, col. 3.

[360] Anon., 'Blue Book Unreliable. Important Evidence as to the Venezuelan Case Suppressed', in *New York Times*, 18 April 1896, 3, col. 4.

[361] Anon., 'Guiana and Venezuela. Blunders in Blue Book to be Corrected by Memorandum', in *New York Times*, 22 March 1896, 5, col. 1.

[362] Anon., 'That Erring Blue Book. Lord Salisbury Wants a Report as to Who Made the Blunders', in *New York Times*, 22 March 1896, 17, col. 2.

[363] See Anon., 'The Blue Book Amended. Alterations in the Report on the Venezuelan Boundary', in *New York Times*, 26 March 1896, 5, col. 2; 'Guiana Negotiations Process. Document Amending the Blue Book Will Soon Be Ready', in *New York Times*, 29 March 1896, 5, col. 2.

to produce the report hastily, that it was mistakenly assumed that he had the linguistic competence to assess the Venezuelan documentation[364]—but he could hardly have been anything other than embarrassed.

It is noteworthy that the *New York Times* was so interested in this affair. Perhaps the most significant point to observe about the controversy is that arbitration was conducted not between Great Britain and Venezuela, but between Great Britain and the United States, who supported Venezuela's claims. In 1896, there apparently was some talk of Britain and the United States going to war over the controversy, though the storm blew over quickly once it transpired that the territory in dispute did not, contrary to earlier reports, contain gold.[365] The eventual decision of the arbitration tribunal, which generally supported British claims, was met with widespread indifference. None the less, for Pollock—who, in preparing his report, had studied the correspondence between the U.S. Government and the British Foreign Office[366]—the controversy provided an opportunity for assessing Anglo-American relations. One claim put forward by the U.S. Secretary of State in the course of this correspondence was that the dispute ought to have been resolved through the application of the so-called 'Monroe Doctrine'—the principle, that is, that any intervention by external powers in the politics of the Americas is a potentially hostile act against the United States.[367] For Pollock, this was a dispute to which the Monroe Doctrine did not apply.[368] However, to claim as much was not, he insisted, to reject the Doctrine altogether. 'Monroe's declaration was received with no uncertain welcome in England',[369] and even at the beginning of the twentieth century '[p]ublic opinion in England was no less decisively in favour of' the spirit of the Doctrine—even if 'the name is no longer useful'—'than it had been in favour of Monroe's original declaration in 1824.'[370] Quoting approvingly from a letter to *The Times*, Pollock emphasized that the British position regarding the Doctrine 'is quite simple . . . "We have no reason to object to the protest of the United States

[364] See Anon., 'Venezuelan Blue Book Errors. Government Explains Misquotations by Haste in Preparation', in *New York Times*, 14 March 1896, 5, col. 2; 'That Erring Blue Book', above n.362.

[365] See Edward D. Mathews, *British Guiana and Venezuela* (London: Straker, 1888), 1–3.

[366] For details of Pollock's preparation of the report, see John Pollock, *Time's Chariot*, above n.4, 90–1; and Hazeltine, above n.4, 243–4. Both assert that Pollock produced the report within forty-eight hours, though Pollock himself claimed to work on it for three weeks: see Pollock to Holmes, 1 February 1896, in *PHL* i. 68–9.

[367] See *Parl. Papers., U.S.* No. 1. C 7926 (London: HMSO, 1896), 15 (Mr Olney, Secretary of State).

[368] Frederick Pollock, 'The Monroe Doctrine' (October 1902) 52 *The Nineteenth Century and After* 533–53 at 546–7.

[369] Ibid. 542.

[370] Ibid. 552–3. In the United States, Pollock's assertions were generally received warmly—though it was also appreciated that he tended mistakenly to assume that all British people shared his affection for Americans. See Anon., '"Keystone of an Alliance". Sir F. Pollock on the Conditions Which Should Govern an Anglo-American Entente', in *New York Times*, 19 April 1898, 3, col. 5; 'An Anglo-American Monroe Doctrine', in *New York Times*, 20 April 1898, 6, col. 3; 'Monroe Doctrine Indorsed. London Spectator Commends Sir Frederick Pollock's Speech—The Saturday Review Denounces it', in *New York Times*, 15 June 1902, 18, col. 4.

against the acquisition of new territorial rights in North or South America by any European Powers." '[371]

Certainly by the beginning of the twentieth century, this idea that Britain must be seen to be generally supportive of the United States had become particularly important to Pollock. That the idea had become so important to him is probably due in part to the fact that, by this point, he had forged close bonds with a number of American lawyers. But this is by no means the entire explanation for his outlook. By the early 1900s, trouble was clearly afoot—trouble in the form of Austro-German efforts to undermine the Anglo-American alliance. If continued British support for the Monroe Doctrine was likely to be an effective way of demonstrating commitment to the alliance, Pollock believed, then the support should be forthcoming. Any hint of schism, after all, may play straight into enemy hands:

> The enemies of light and freedom are neither dead nor sleeping; they are vigilant, active, militant, and astute. It is certain that any serious discord between the United States and Great Britain would be an opportunity for those enemies all over the world; and, that being so, harmony should be among the first objects of citizens of both countries. There is no need to talk of any formal convention or declarations. If the spirit is there, the letter can be provided when the time calls for it. A generally understood accord on the greater matters of policy will suffice. It is the business of the present generation, wherever the English tongue runs, to make that accord so firm that for generations to come it may be the best security for peace and progress.[372]

Pollock was still an Oxford professor when he wrote these words. In the years following Oxford, he found reason to write much more in the same vein. It was noted at the outset of chapter 1 that the First World War and its aftermath inspired Pollock's best impression of a public moralist. Much of his writing in this context was technical, explaining both the history and structure of international law and—one of his favourite topics—the legal principles underscoring the Covenant of the League of Nations.[373] The technicality of the Covenant, he insisted, does not mean that it demands some sort of rigid formalism in the solution of international disputes: 'a wide and elastic discretion is left in justiciable matters to the parties and in others to the Council [of the League]. Critics of the school that loves cut and dry formulas will no doubt

[371] Pollock, above n.368, 536. [372] Ibid. 553.

[373] See, e.g., Frederick Pollock, *League of Nations Covenant: A Summary with Comments* (London: The League of Nations Union, n.d.); *LNCR*; *LN*; *LN(2)*; also [Frederick Pollock], 'The Modern Law of Nations and the Prevention of War', in *The Cambridge Modern History. Volume xii: The Latest Age*, eds. A. W. Ward, G. W. Prothero, and S. Leathes (Cambridge: Cambridge UP, 1910), 703–29. The seeds of this last essay can be found in Frederick Pollock, 'The Sources of International Law' (1902) 18 *LQR* 418–28 (repr. (1902) 2 *Columbia L. Rev.* 511–24).

complain of vagueness, but to the present writer's mind this is among the chief merits of the scheme.'[374] Pollock supported the establishment of a League of Nations almost as fervently as Dicey had opposed Home Rule, as is especially clear not from Pollock's principal writings about the League—all of which tend to be fairly arid—but from his numerous pamphlets and minor essays on the subject.

His reflections on the Monroe Doctrine had set the tone. International difficulties, he believed, must be resolved by collective resolutions and plans of action. This attitude underscored his initiatives in the early 1900s, when he was one of the loudest voices urging the establishment of an imperial council of the British Empire—a recommendation which became the basis of Conservative Party policy.[375] During the First World War, he reiterated the importance of trying to ensure the involvement of the United States in securing peace. William Howard Taft's scheme for an international jurisdiction, as advocated by the American League to Enforce Peace, was, Pollock argued in 1916, the most 'eminently practical' proposal for securing an end to the War.[376] However, 'the League must spring out of the Alliance.'[377] While it is not necessary to the effectiveness of a League of Peace that the United States be a member, he wrote, such membership 'seems very desirable. The prospects of success would be much greater, and there would be much less plausible excuse for refusal to join, if the United States took the first steps towards the formation of such a league.'[378] Encouraging unity in the face of despotism, after all, was crucial: 'when great Powers commit themselves to principles of anarchic tyranny, that is the very reason why those who still believe in the rule of law should reassert and republish their faith as the most dignified form of protest,

[374] *LN* 133; *LN(2)* 139; and see also *League of Nations Covenant*, above n.373, 1–2 ('Doctrinaires may object to the lack of hard and fast rules, but this is the last country from which objections of that kind should come, for it is an eminently English habit, and, in my judgment, a sound one, not to fetter experiment overmuch by rules made in advance, but to work out your rules according to the results of experience').

[375] On this matter, see Pollock's various letters to *The Times*: 19 October 1906, 6, col. A; 14 February 1907, 4, col. E; 20 May 1907, 6, col. A; 14 March 1907, 8, col. C; also Richard Symonds, 'Oxford and the Empire', in *The History of the University of Oxford*, above n.222, 689–716 at 695, 705; and Frederick Pollock to Herbert Samuel, 15 February 1905, in Samuel papers (SAM/A/155/3), f.38 ('I am glad to learn that you are in general sympathy with the movement for imperial organization. . . . One of our objects is to show how much can be done without legislation, without applying to Parliament except for the necessary grant to provide for a secretary and clerks, and without directly asking the Colonial Governments to do anything. My impression is that the present [Conservative] government is favourably disposed').

[376] See Frederick Pollock, 'Cosmopolitan Custom and International Law' (1916) 29 *Harvard L. Rev.* 565–81 at 579–81. Certain of the proposals concerning how the scheme would be enforced were formulated by A. Lawrence Lowell, President of Harvard University. Pollock found Lowell's proposals to be 'eminently reasonable and proper': see Sir Frederick Pollock, 'The American Plan for Enforcing Peace' (May 1917) 119 *Atlantic Monthly* 650–5 at 651. A decade later, Pollock was similarly positive about Lowell's report recommending that the Supreme Court of Massachusetts refuse clemency in the Sacco-Vanzetti case: see Cosgrove, above n.4, 140; and cf. Pollock to Holmes, 29 August 1927, in *PHL* ii. 204.

[377] Pollock, 'The American Plan for Enforcing Peace', above n.376, 655.

[378] Pollock, 'A League of Peace', above n.49, 134.

and in the long run not the least effectual.'[379] The distribution in the United States of a German propaganda pamphlet attempting to undermine Anglo-American relations prompted Pollock to respond in splenetic mode: '[a]ll the world knows what has been reported from the smaller places captured and occupied by German soldiery. . . . The German horde has not gone from Belgium. But it will go perforce; and if there be any people on the earth so deceived as to send any blessing after the defeated host of William the Hun, it will not be the American.'[380] Once the War was over and the League of Nations established, his tone was hardly less robust. 'There are militarists who refuse to believe that war can be restrained at all' and '[t]here are pacifists who refuse to believe that an effective community of nations must have means of self-preservation'—the objectives of the League, he insisted, must not be frustrated by either group.[381] Nor must those objectives be jeopardized by nit-picking legalists: 'the law of nations is cosmopolitan custom, very good custom so far as it has gone,' and 'the Covenant of the League of Nations is probably the most cosmopolitan of all treaties. . . . Enlightened common sense as well as good faith is no more than the authors of [the Covenant] may reasonably require us to bring to the study of their work. . . . Hasty zeal for defining all points [of the Constitution] at once might easily have ruined the union of the American states, and might well ruin the League of Nations if some of our latter-day zealots had their way.'[382]

It is a task of the legal profession, Pollock believed, to try to save the League of Nations from the contrivances of such zealots. '[T]he evils due to formalism', he insisted, are 'not always due to the lawyers'[383]—while lawyers may, unlike laymen, be too willing to acquiesce in the imperfections of the law,[384] laymen, as compared with lawyers, 'are far more hide-bound as interpreters, far more in peril of being enslaved to the mere letter.'[385] 'There is much to be done in setting forth the facts of the League's activity so that they may be generally understood.'[386] '[L]awyers may fairly be called upon to take a leading part in the education of public opinion' and in saving the interpretation of the Covenant of the League from 'clever novices full of a little learning'.[387] The deeper objective, of course, was to ensure lasting peace through collective reaffirmation of the rule of law. Whereas some politicians and intellectuals expressed anxiety over the emergence of the United States as the

[379] Sir Frederick Pollock, 'Introduction', in Coleman Phillipson, *Wheaton's Elements of International Law*, 5th English edn. (London: Stevens & Sons, 1916), xxxix–xliv at xl. *Wheaton's Elements* was the classic nineteenth-century American treatise on international law.

[380] Sir Frederick Pollock, *German 'Truth' and European Facts about the War* (London: The Central Committee for National Patriotic Organizations, 1915), 12. See also *The Times* (letters), 7 March 1917, 7, col. C.

[381] Sir Frederick Pollock, *The Covenant and the Protocol* (London: League of Nations Union, 1924), 5–6.

[382] Sir Frederick Pollock, *Lawyers' Place in the League of Nations* (London: privately printed by C. F. Roworth, n.d.), 3–4.

[383] *GCL* 63.

[384] See (1901) 17 *LQR* 356.

[385] Pollock, above n.382, 2.

[386] Ibid. 6.

[387] Ibid. 5, 3.

world's great power in the aftermath of the First World War,[388] Pollock was never in doubt that Americans could be trusted to lead from the front in this process of reaffirmation. That he felt this way is hardly surprising, since he regarded the legal values of the Americans and the English as basically indistinguishable. Near the end of his life he received a rather bizarre letter from a law clerk of a Justice of the Supreme Court asking whether it was true that the United States and Great Britain were soon to reunify. 'There has been no serious suggestion here of any such wild cat project as reunion', Pollock replied. But then, even if reunification were technically feasible, it would be unnecessary, since the two nations share 'above all the common tradition of law and liberty. On that tradition is founded the informal understanding with the U.S. which is really more stable than any formal alliance.'[389] The special legal mindset that Pollock attributed to the English, we will see later, he accorded equally to the Americans.

Previous accounts of Pollock's career have tended to pay little or no attention to the work that he undertook in response to and in the aftermath of the First World War. Possibly this is because this work, *engagé* as it was, does not fit easily with the familiar image of Pollock as a sagacious man of affairs, reflecting upon and writing about, but ultimately standing aloft from, matters of law and state. In fact, Pollock's War-related work speaks volumes about his character, indicative as it is of his faith in the remedial powers of law and lawyers, of his strong Hobbesian sentiment that the covenant counts for little without the sword, of his public moralist instincts, and of the fact that, as regards emotions, he did have a pulse. While it would be going too far to claim that Pollock actually enjoyed wartime conditions, there is no doubt that he considered war to bring out the best in people—or certainly in English people. Wartime worries over air raids, and post-War complaints about rationing, tended to leave him unmoved.[390] All that really saddened him, it seems, was 'the contra-natural selection of war': '[m]y complaint against war is not that it kills men but that it kills the wrong ones, taking an undue proportion of the strong and adventurous and leaving too many weaklings and shirkers, thus working a perverse artificial selection of those who are least fitted to adorn or improve the commonwealth.'[391]

[388] See Richard L. Rapson, *Britons View America: Travel Commentary, 1860–1935* (Seattle: University of Washington Press, 1971), 141–3.

[389] F. Pollock to John Knox, 5 September 1936, in Knox papers, MS 10240-K. Knox served as a law clerk for Justice James C. McReynolds. For Knox's own account of his clerkship—an account which reveals as much about his chutzpah and eccentricity as it does about the unpopular and rather lazy McReynolds—see John Knox, *The Forgotten Memoir of John Knox: A Year in the Life of a Supreme Court Clerk in FDR's Washington*, eds. D. J. Garrow and D. J. Hutchinson (Chicago: University of Chicago Press, 2002); and for an arresting conspectus of the relationship, see Barry Cushman, 'Clerking for Scrooge' (2003) 70 *Univ. Chicago L. Rev.* 721–49.

[390] See Pollock to Holmes, 15 October 1917, in *PHL* i. 249; 18 April 1918, ibid. 263; 14 October 1918, ibid. 269–70; and cf. Pollock to Holmes, 30 January 1916, ibid. 230 ('people cry aloud not when they are worst off but when a beginning of better things has given them a little spare strength to cry with').

[391] Pollock to Holmes, 14 April 1920, in *PHL* ii. 43; 11 April 1920, ibid. 39.

Other tasks undertaken by Pollock in the last three decades of his life are perhaps easier to square with the familiar image of the man. Certain of these tasks—his appointment as a curator of the *Societas Spinoza* in the 1920s, his work as Literary Director of the Selden Society[392]—were largely the exercises of a philosopher-jurist without portfolio. Generally, the roles to which he agreed were of a type unsuited to anyone likely to be fazed by large amounts of administration and paperwork. In November 1910, we find Pollock writing to his publishers about how he wanted to complete his new edition of *An Introduction to the History of the Science of Politics* 'before I go into the mill of the Commission on Public Records'.[393] He had been officially named Chairman of the Royal Commission on Public Records in the previous month and, even though the Commission's first report would be published in September 1912,[394] he was still caught up in public records matters as late as 1918.[395] Only from Pollock's legal writing, interestingly enough, do we acquire any sense of his becoming less productive as the years progress. After 1922 he wrote no new major legal text—though he returned to and revised his established works on contract, torts, and partnership—and the new books which he did produce from then onwards are for the most part, to borrow the title of one of them, concerned with matters outside the law. This is not particularly surprising. By 1922 his major projects and ideas were in print, and it is unlikely that he would have felt that he had very much new to say.[396]

[392] Pollock was joint Literary Director of the Selden Society (with Paul Vinogradoff) 1908–18 and sole Literary Director 1919–37. In 1938, he was succeeded by W. S. Holdsworth, T. F. T. Plucknett, and G. S. Turner. Pollock himself contributed to the Society's publications Selden's *Table Talk*, based upon a previously unpublished Lincoln's Inn Library manuscript: see *Table Talk of John Selden*, ed. F. Pollock (London: Quaritch, 1927). '[T]he *Table Talk*', Pollock comments in his Introduction (vii–xxiv at viii), 'has been a favourite book of mine for more than half a century.'

[393] Frederick Pollock to Messrs. Macmillan & Co., 3 November 1910, in Macmillan Archive, Add. 55083 f.104.

[394] *First Report of the Royal Commission on Public Records appointed to Inquire into and Report on the State of the Public Records and Local Records of a Public Nature of England and Wales*, Cd. 6361 (London: HMSO, 1912).

[395] See Pollock to Holmes, 16 September 1910, in *PHL* i. 169; 30 January 1912, ibid. 188–9; 1 March 1913, ibid. 207; 19 May 1915, ibid. 228. Although Pollock had hoped the Commission's work would be concluded before the outbreak of war (Frederick Pollock to Malcolm Ramsay, 12 January 1918, PRO: T1/12391), the project was not concluded until the spring of 1918. In September 1915, the Treasury had awarded the Commission £400 to complete its work within twelve months, though by June the following year less than a quarter of this sum had been spent and little of the work had been done. At this stage, the Treasury threatened, among other things, to withhold the remainder of the funding if the Commission did not complete the work quickly. Up until January 1918, various time extensions were granted to the Commission, at which point the Treasury issued its final ultimatum: 'the final report and appendices to be completed and signed by the 31st March next' (John Bradbury to Frederick Pollock, 12 January 1918, PRO: T1/12391). 'It is possible that the actual signing of the [Third and Final] Report by all of the Commissioners may not be practicable till some days later than March 31,' Pollock responded, 'but I will undertake that no expense shall be incurred after that date. . . . You can be assured that no one can be more anxious than I am—and I think I may add my colleagues—to avoid needless expense or delay' (Frederick Pollock to Malcolm Ramsay, 8 January 1918, PRO: T1/12391). The Commission's final report was completed and signed in April 1918.

[396] In his presidential address to The Holdsworth Club in May 1932 (above n.111, 1), Pollock basically conceded as much: 'It is a common observation that after the age of about fifty a man ceases to

Had he much new to say, he would probably have said it—for the diminution in juristic output does not reflect a more general letting up on Pollock's part. Plenty of vacations were taken, but their purpose and effect seems to have been to ensure, as Louis Brandeis might have put it, that Pollock would achieve at least as much in eleven months as he ever could in twelve.[397] At the beginning of the 1930s he was still working hard—and, as he sometimes saw it, in defiance of ignorant and dictatorial printers[398]—editing the Law Reports so that the decisions of the appeal courts would be fit for public consumption. His encounters with Indian law reporting proved even more exasperating. From 1905 through to the beginning of the 1930s Pollock had, with Sir Dinshah Mulla, produced six editions of what would nowadays be called a cases and materials book on the Indian Contract Act 1872. When, in the early 1930s, Mulla was co-opted to the Indian Legislative Department, Pollock had to work on the next edition more or less on his own. His principal difficulty, as he noted it, was that the Indian law reports 'are produced by reporters who don't know the elements of reporting, not even that a decision on a question of pure fact is not authority.'[399] Revising the volume on the Indian Contract Act from another continent and without Mulla's involvement clearly tried Pollock. To Holmes he was candid: 'Indian imbecility (of reporters I mean) is now vexing my professional soul only within tolerable limits.'[400]

In the 1930s, writing seemed to become for Pollock more of a leisurely pastime and less of a professional pursuit. His written style—'coloured', as Lord Wright would observe, 'by the philosophical and literary culture in which he was steeped'[401]—never pandered to a popular readership, and even in his least stiff-collared works one finds the characteristic plummy prose and attention to detail. But as the years progressed the style became less embellished—less Victorian—and somewhat more relaxed. His works of note from the 1930s—his remembrances, his vignette on Spinoza, and various elegant arabesques covering a range of topics—did not require strenuous research and would have been a pleasure to write. One such work—derived from an extempore address at a Lincoln's Inn dinner—is sometimes held up as an illustration of how impressive Pollock could be when forced to think and talk on his feet, though by the time the address made it into print it carried

acquire any new ideas; he is by then pretty well settled in his outlook on life and learning. He may still find occasions for new applications of the ideas he has already formed, but he is extremely unlikely to discover anything new in substance. So that what I shall endeavour to do to-day is not to attempt to tell you anything new but to take an old text and just gossip about it.'

[397] Various sources report Brandeis as having said that he could do twelve months' work in eleven months but not in twelve: see, e.g., Alpheus T. Mason, *Brandeis: A Free Man's Life* (New York: Viking Press, 1946), 78; and Richard A. Posner, *Overcoming Law* (Cambridge, Mass.: Harvard UP, 1995), 137.

[398] See, e.g., Pollock to Holmes, 16 July 1931, in *PHL* ii. 290–1; and chapter 6, 299–300.

[399] Pollock to Holmes, 20 July 1930, in *PHL* ii. 274.

[400] Pollock to Holmes, 19 June 1930, in *PHL* ii. 269.

[401] Lord Wright, obituary for W. S. Holdsworth (1944) 60 *LQR* 139–46 at 142.

an appendix and read like more or less any other essay to have come from his pen.[402]

Pollock presented this address in his capacity as Treasurer of Lincoln's Inn, a one-year office to which he was elected for 1931. The post, as Pollock himself noted, was no sinecure, and by the end of October he was looking forward to the end of his tenure.[403] As his period of office came to an end, he professed himself to be in a good state. 'Here I am *aet.* 86 today,' he quipped to Holmes, 'not feeling decrepit and encouraged by your example.'[404] Indeed, at this point he still had two books left in him. By 1934, however, there were indications of failing powers. Pollock entered around this time into a fairly protracted correspondence with an American Spinoza specialist, Adolph Oko. The correspondence between the two men reveals Oko to be anything but shy about asking questions. Although Pollock drops his guard little, Oko's sheer forthrightness forces him to be more revealing than he is with most other correspondents. When Oko wrote to Pollock purporting to be worried that Pollock's silence—he had not written to Oko for almost a month!—indicated that Oko had offended him, Pollock dismissed the apprehension as 'groundless'. His explanation as to why it was groundless is a piece of perfect Pollockian pomposity:

> Probably you are not aware that the editor of the Law Reports—a publication you may well never have heard of, but of some importance to English-speaking lawyers—has to attend to Spinoza, not to mention keeping up with humane letters in general, in such time as he can spare or it may be steal from his professional duties.[405]

The reply is significant not only for the fact that it was required—it is unlikely that anyone had ever before suggested that Pollock was a tardy correspondent—but also because Pollock makes it clear that he is busy. This, generally, was not Pollock's style. Pollock worked very hard nearly all his life, but was not in the habit of giving the impression that he was overworked. Indeed, one senses that he generally considered it unbecoming to protest to being busy. 'That doughty Nestor, Sir Frederick Pollock,' Lord Sankey wrote with affection in November 1934.[406] By then, however, Pollock appeared to be struggling.

March 1935 saw the death of his wife. The day after her death he was at his desk—replying to the latest missive from Oko, among other things: 'Last

[402] *The Origins of the Inns of Court: An Address Given to Guests at Lincoln's Inn by the Rt. Hon. Sir F. Pollock, P.C. LL.D., D.C.L., Treasurer of the Society, July 21, 1931* (Oxford: Oxford UP, 1931); repr. at (1932) 48 *LQR* 163–70. On the reception of the address, see Lord Maugham (1937) 53 *LQR* 170–1; Goodhart, 'Introduction', in *JLE* ix–xlviii at xxii; and cf. Pollock to Holmes, 5 August 1931, in *PHL* ii. 293.

[403] See Pollock to Holmes, 29 January 1931, in *PHL* ii. 275; 9 March 1931, ibid. 282; 23 April 1931, ibid. 284; 29 October 1931, ibid. 296; 17 December 1931, ibid. 300.

[404] Pollock to Holmes, 10 December 1931, in *PHL* ii. 299.

[405] Frederick Pollock to Adolph S. Oko, 22 November 1934 (no. 2–261), in Oko papers, MS 14, box 5, file 13.

[406] Lord Sankey, 'Foreword' (1935) 51 *LQR* 1–3 at 2.

night I lost my wife after more than sixty years of a most happy marriage. There was no long illness, only failure at her age to resist the shock of what for a person younger and stronger would have been merely a passing indisposition.'[407] Pollock's letters to Oko after her death reveal Pollock succumbing to numerous ailments, struggling to recuperate, and needing the constant supervision of a nurse.[408] It is not at all surprising that, by the end of 1935, he had forfeited the chief editorship of the Law Reports.

Pollock fell seriously ill soon after his ninety-first birthday in December 1936. It appears that he performed one last, apparently impromptu act of statesmanship just weeks before his death. The abdication of Edward VIII on 11 December 1936 was given effect by an act of parliament which passed through all its stages in a single day.[409] 'Immediately upon the Royal Assent being signified to this Act', s 1(1) of the statute reads, 'His Majesty shall cease to be King and there shall be a demise of the Crown, and accordingly the member of the Royal Family then next in succession to the Throne shall succeed thereto and to all the rights, privileges, and dignities thereunto belonging.' Pollock, well-versed in matters monarchical and experienced in legislative drafting, apparently wrote to the Home Secretary, Sir John Simon, offering advice on the form that the Abdication Act should take. According to one account, he produced his notes from his sick bed, relying on memory alone; according to another, the wording of the Act largely replicated those notes.[410] Even if both stories are the stuff of legend, they round off Pollock's life in a manner that seems somehow appropriate to the man.

vi. Concluding reflections

When, soon after Pollock's death in 1937, Adolph Oko wrote to Pollock's son proposing to write a book about his father, the son's reply was candid: 'I feel bound to suggest that you should not allow whatever form you ultimately give your monograph to have the appearance or title of a Life. My father had a horror of biographies of people who had "done nothing", as he said. He thought biography should be restricted to men of action.'[411] While the thrust

[407] Frederick Pollock to Adolph S. Oko, 31 March 1935 (no. 2–149), in Oko papers, MS 14, box 5, file 13.

[408] Frederick Pollock to Adolph S. Oko, 16 May 1935 (no. 2–231); 9 June 1935 (no. 2–230); 4 July 1935 (no. 2–228); 24 August 1935 (no. 2–224); 22 September 1935 (no. 2–211); 18 December 1935 (no. 2–197); 27 January 1936 (no. 2–193), in Oko papers, MS 14, box 5, file 15.

[409] His Majesty's Declaration of Abdication Act 1936. On the complexities of determining the appropriate legislation in this instance, see S. M. Cretney, 'The King and the King's Proctor: The Abdication Crisis and the Divorce Laws 1936–1937' (2000) 116 *LQR* 583–620 at 589–90.

[410] 'Sir Frederick Pollock, K.C.: The "Old Broad Culture"', above n.4; John Pollock, *Time's Chariot*, above n.4, 51–2. Fifoot, above n.19, 12 states not that Pollock volunteered advice but that 'his opinion was sought on the legislation'.

[411] John Pollock to Adolph S. Oko, 12 February 1937 (no. 2–304), in Oko papers, MS 14, box 3, file 15.

of this chapter has been biographical, the study as a whole perhaps would not have offended against Pollock's wishes. Its principal focus, after all, is not Pollock but his work and ideas; by no means will one find here a comprehensive account of his life. And in so far as this chapter has been used to consider his life, the task has deliberately been left uncompleted: certain of Pollock's objectives and achievements are deferred until later, since to include them now would, as a matter of style, be less satisfactory than allowing them to emerge as the analysis unfolds.

Anyone who should decide to ignore Pollock's wishes will have their work cut out. His life was long and full—meaning that, from a biographer's point of view, it was complex. Of course, the fact that his life was complex does not mean that his character must have been complex; but then even the most straightforward personalities are likely to exhibit complexity the more one delves into them. To conclude that Pollock was a complex character would be trite. It would be better to conclude by reflecting on the nature of his complexity. The development of such a conclusion seems to lead towards two general propositions. The first is that Pollock's complexity was largely behavioural. Like most of us, he could blow hot and cold on a multitude of matters. The second is that Pollock's complexity is largely attributable to what others have projected on to him. Like many other jurists, he has been subjected to diverse interpretations and assessments. Yet out of those interpretations and assessments there emerges a rather crude claim: that Pollock, whatever his qualities, lacked the spark of genius. The purpose of this study is not to dispute that claim. Rather, it is argued that an understanding of Pollock's significance within the English juristic tradition requires, peculiarly enough, an appreciation of the essentially non-mercurial nature of his character and accomplishments.

The first proposition is easy to elaborate. People are not always consistent. (The so-called American legal realists invested this observation with jurisprudential significance when they suggested that a legal outcome might sometimes depend on what the judge ate for breakfast that morning.[412])

[412] The provenance of this image is difficult to determine. Dworkin asserts that '[s]ome realists . . . said . . . that law is only a matter of what the judge had for breakfast', but unfortunately mentions no names and provides no sources. See Ronald Dworkin, *Law's Empire* (London: Fontana, 1986), 36; and cf. Charles M. Yablon, 'Justifying the Judge's Hunch: An Essay on Discretion' (1990) 41 *Hastings L. J.* 231–79 at 236. The image may have been developed from Pound's description of 'the oriental cadi administering justice at the city gate by the light of nature tempered by the state of his digestion'. Roscoe Pound, 'The Decadence of Equity' (1905) 5 *Columbia L. Rev.* 20–35 at 21. Frank borrows the imagery from Pound around a quarter of a century later—see Jerome Frank, 'Are Judges Human?' (1931) 80 *Univ. Pennsylvania L. Rev.* 17–53, 233–67 at 24—and the theory for which the image is taken to stand is dismissed (though again, no names or sources are mentioned) by William L. King, 'The Breakfast Theory of Jurisprudence' (1936) 18 *Chicago Bar Record* 15–17. One Harvard Law School graduate from the 1930s recalls Thomas Reed Powell in his 1935 constitutional law class observing 'that cases usually turn on "the nature of the breakfast the judges have in the morning".' Joseph L. Rauh, 'Lawyers and the Legislation of the Early New Deal' (1983) 96 *Harvard L. Rev.* 947–59 at 950. Possibly Powell too had taken the image from Pound, who was still Dean at Harvard in 1935 and under whom Powell had worked for a decade.

Inconsistency, of course, is usually a matter of degree. 'In so many people', Proust observed in one of his pithier moments, 'there are different strata which are not alike'. Sometimes the strata seem to diverge radically, so that dealings with some people can put one in mind 'of those countries with which one dare not form an alliance because of their too frequent changes of government.'[413] In others, like Pollock, the divergences are mild. The man with standoffish proclivities, we have seen, was also the man capable of forming especially strong and close bonds. His marriage, which surpassed its diamond wedding year and was by all accounts happy throughout, indicates as much. Equally significant is the friendship he enjoyed with Holmes. 'There was no stage of acquaintance ripening into friendship; we understood one another and were friends without more ado', he wrote on the death of Holmes.[414] In Pollock's eyes, Holmes deserved the highest accolade: he had that 'undefinable yet controlling power which we call character'.[415] 'The dignity of his bearing was wholly free from arrogance, the brilliance of his intellect from vanity. Both were inspired by fervid and constant faith in the pursuit of truth.'[416] When Pollock submitted the obituary in which this last passage appears for publication in the *LQR*, the editor wrote back proclaiming it one of the most beautiful things Pollock had ever written.[417]

Various accounts of Pollock create the impression that he was miserly. The truth, however, is not quite so simple. Sometimes he behaved like a penny-pincher, on other occasions he could be very generous. There is a popular story surrounding *The History of English Law* which has been used by a number of commentators both to illustrate Maitland's placidness and to portray Pollock as niggardly and vain.[418] Pollock wrote roughly 10 per cent of *The*

[413] Marcel Proust, *Remembrance of Things Past*, 3 vols., trans. C. K. Scott Moncrieff, T. Kilmartin, and A. Mayor (Harmondsworth: Penguin, 1983 [1954]), iii. 710.

[414] Frederick Pollock, 'Mr Justice Holmes' (1935) 48 *Harvard L. Rev.* 1277–8 at 1277. In his introduction to the American edition of the *Holmes–Pollock Letters*—note the ordering of the names—Palfrey suggests that when Holmes and Pollock met they may have found friendship easy because they had much in common. 'At this time the positions in the world of the two men were similar. Both had been recently married, Holmes in 1872 and Pollock in 1873. They were in the early stages of law practice, Holmes more actively than Pollock, and both were becoming legal scholars of the first magnitude.' John Gorham Palfrey, 'Introduction', in *Holmes–Pollock Letters: The Correspondence of Mr Justice Holmes and Sir Frederick Pollock, 1874–1932*, ed. M. DeWolfe Howe (Cambridge, Mass.: Harvard University Press, 1942), xiii–xxii at xv. Possibly the friendship was also sustained owing to the fact that the two met and began their correspondence before either had achieved significant professional status: see Sanford Levinson, 'Fan Letters' (1997) 75 *Texas L. Rev.* 1471–86 at 1472, n.10.

[415] Pollock, above n.414, 1278.

[416] Frederick Pollock, 'In Memoriam: Mr Justice Oliver Wendell Holmes' (1935) 51 *LQR* 263–4 at 264. Pollock nearly always regarded Holmes primarily as a truth-seeker rather than as a sceptic.

[417] A. L. Goodhart to Sir Frederick Pollock, 12 March 1935, uncollected letter inserted in Pollock's copy of Holmes, *Collected Legal Papers* (see above n.147): 'I hope that you will not consider it impertinent of me to say that I think your memorial of Mr Justice Holmes is one of the most beautiful things you have ever written.'

[418] See, e.g., the entries for both men in the *Biographical Dictionary of the Common Law*, above n.4; Fifoot, above n.19, 16; and H. E. Bell, *Maitland: A Critical Examination and Assessment* (London: Black, 1965), 62–3.

History of English Law and Maitland allowed him approximately 20 per cent of the royalties.[419] Pollock was candid about his limited contribution to the book.[420] Yet its title page announces it as a book 'by Sir Frederick Pollock and Frederic William Maitland'. Why was it not by Maitland and Pollock? Pollock's answer was that the order of names accorded with convention, reflecting the seniority of each man at the Bar.[421] Curiously, he had not applied this rationale a decade earlier when R. S. Wright—called to the Bar six years before Pollock—wrote roughly half of *An Essay on Possession in the Common Law* but, like Maitland, was listed as second author. Pollock's attitude towards the royalties for *The History of English Law* seems just as graceless as his attitude towards co-author accreditation, though on the matter of royalties it should be noted that Pollock—as various of his letters to Macmillan & Co. reveal—always drove a hard bargain.[422] Although he could fight hard for money, furthermore, it would be wrong to assume that he could not be parted from it. To various causes—particularly his cherished Apostles—he donated considerably.[423] For Pollock, looking after one's own was an

[419] Maitland's papers—see Add. 2766(16)—contain an undated note, unsigned but clearly in Maitland's hand, indicating that Pollock wrote 133 pages and Maitland 1,267 pages of *HEL* (presumably the first edition) and containing the words: 'Say F.P. 1/10th F.W.M. 9/10ths'.

[420] See *HEL* i. vi; Pollock to Holmes, 23 August 1895, in *PHL* i. 60–1 (Pollock stating that he wrote 'the Introduction (not quite all), the chapter on Anglo-Saxon law [i. 25–63], and the bulk, not the whole, of the chapter on Early History of Contract [ii. 184–239], which is expounded and rearranged from [his unsigned article, 'Contracts in Early English Law' (1893) 6 *Harvard L. Rev.* 389–404]'). Cf. James R. Cameron, *Frederick [sic] William Maitland and the History of English Law* (Norman: University of Oklahoma Press, 1961), 4–5; and Fifoot, above n.19, 16.

[421] Pollock, 'Frederic William Maitland', above n.10, 412.

[422] See, e.g., Frederick Pollock to Messrs. Macmillan & Co., 5 September 1881, in Macmillan Archive, Add. 55083 f.16: 'As to terms [for the publication of *EJE*], I think the form of agreement you suggest is much the best. But if I remember right your practice is to give the author a royalty of one *fifth* if you really think a book is likely to come to much good. And if you do not think so of mine, I would rather leave it alone for the present (having indeed no lack of other things to do in the near future) than be at the pains of putting it into shape.' As a representative of the Incorporated Society of Authors, Pollock often adopted a hawkish attitude towards publishers over royalties and other matters: see Pollock to Macmillan & Co., 13 April 1893; 22 May 1894; 3 June 1894, all in Macmillan Archive, Add. 55083 ff.56, 62, 64; also Sir Frederick Pollock, 'The Profession of Authorship', in *The Grievances Between Authors & Publishers, being the Report of the Conferences of the Incorporated Society of Authors held at Willis's Rooms, in March 1887* (London: Field & Tuer, 1887), 52–62; 'Anglo-American Copyright' (April 1891) 59 *Contemporary Rev.* 602–8; and 'Some Considerations on Publishing' (June 1893) 4 *Author* 5–15. It appears that the initiatives of the Incorporated Society of Authors, along with those of the Authors' Syndicate (with which the Society was closely connected from 1890 to 1898), were rarely fruitful: see David Finkelstein, *The House of Blackwood: Author-Publisher Relations in the Victorian Era* (University Park, PA: Pennsylvania State University Press, 2002), 132, 138; and Robert A. Colby, '"What Fools Authors Be!": The Authors' Syndicate, 1890–1920' (1986) 35 *Library Chronicle of the University of Texas* 60–87.

[423] On Pollock's fund-raising for the Apostles, see Lubenow, above n.6, 133. See also Frederick Pollock to Henry Sidgwick, 3 April 1876, in Pollock correspondence (Wren), Add. MS c. 95, 38 ('[William Kingdon] Clifford is seriously ill—threatened with lung disease—the best thing for him, by medical advice and the common opinion of all who know him, will be to get away for a good long time and have complete rest and change of life. We are about to raise a fund to make this possible. . . . Any help from you and other friends in Cambridge will be most welcome').

indication of good character, of willingness to face up to one's duties.[424]

The general point for emphasis here is simple: Pollock was indeed on occasions aloof, pompous, miserly, vain, and so on, but it would be foolish to assume that such qualities somehow capture him. To reduce any person to a series of adjectives is to withhold dimension from character: the exercise may make for good reading, but the resulting analysis is likely to be incomplete or distorted. In providing an account of Pollock's character, the objective in this chapter has been to guard against adjectival history. From this point onwards, we shall concern ourselves little with Pollock's character and pay far more attention to his work. As a conclusion to this chapter, and as a preamble to the ones that follow, it is worth considering briefly some general assessments of that work.

Inevitably, those who have offered such assessments do not speak with a single voice. Plaudits abound: 'many thought him the most completely learned man of his time';[425] 'he [was] one of the greatest of that select band of professors whose work places them amongst the Makers of English Law';[426] 'all lawyers in the world now bow before this gigantic figure'.[427] But there are cooler assessments, too: 'distinguished as is much of his work, probably none of it adequately represents his great natural powers';[428] 'it is more than strange that his influence and reputation should be greater in the United States than in England';[429] 'however interesting and rich a personality, [he was] merely a very good second-rater.'[430] The two sets of statements do not actually contradict one another. His erudition, his prodigious scholarly output, his precise command of facts, and his virtuosity in a variety of fields are, as Holmes recognized, immensely impressive. Reading Pollock, however, rarely generates the sense that one has encountered something very special. While he was, as we will see later, a remarkably influential jurist, his influence was usually the result of solid analyses carefully pursued—of indefatigable labour in some instances—rather than of astounding insights. Even the most devoted student of Pollock is unlikely to uncover a genius.

Oddly enough, it is this failure of his ideas to ignite that makes his jurisprudential work not only intriguing but also significant. For in the field of jurisprudence it really should not have been this way. Everything was stacked in Pollock's favour. He held the Corpus Professorship of Jurisprudence, directly inherited Maine's intellectual legacy, occupied a position of considerable academic importance; yet his influence upon the future development of jurisprudence would be negligible. Far more crucial to the evolution of jurisprudence

[424] 'Lord Hanworth said that Sir Frederick did what he felt to be his duty as head of the Pollock family, and that any member who brought his troubles to him experienced unbounded unselfishness and generosity.' Hollond, above n.4, 50.

[425] Levy, above n.6, 81.

[426] Holdsworth, *Some Makers of English Law*, above n.4, 290.

[427] Sarfatti, above n.4, 6.

[428] 'Sir Frederick Pollock: A Distinguished Jurist', above n.4.

[429] F. R. Jones, above n.4, 1.

[430] Max Lerner, review of *PHL* (1942) 55 *Harvard L. Rev.* 1069–73 at 1071.

in England was that rather pitiable, Eeyore figure that we encountered approximately midway through this chapter, the author of *The Province of Jurisprudence Determined*, a book which Lord Melbourne apparently pronounced 'the dullest . . . he ever read'.[431] How did Pollock come to represent the road not taken? It was certainly not for want of effort. While never central to the affairs of any university, Pollock took the idea of legal science seriously and was very clearly committed to the values which have traditionally been at the heart of university culture. But dedication to the pursuit of truth, the advancement of knowledge, and the production of rigorous and open-minded scholarship were not qualities sufficient to ensure that Pollock would influence jurisprudential thought in any significant way. In this context, he failed. The core purpose of the next chapter is to show that it is instructive to develop some insight into why he failed.

[431] *The Greville Memoirs 1840–1860. Volume iii: January 1834 to December 1837*, eds. L. Strachey and R. Fulford (London: Macmillan & Co., 1938), 88.

3

WHY ENGLISH JURISPRUDENCE IS ANALYTICAL

A particularly careful chronicler of Anglo-American jurisprudential history has remarked in recent years that Pollock was one of a band of Victorian jurists 'who were suspicious of philosophy'.[1] As applied to Pollock, this seems at first glance to be a startling, indeed glaringly inaccurate, observation. Pollock was a skilled exponent of philosophical ideas, a major authority on Spinoza, and, when the mood took him, a competent philosopher in his own right. He could be defensive in the face of those who denigrated philosophy as a pursuit,[2] and it is not uncommon to find political philosophers and Spinozists referring to him first and foremost as a philosopher rather than as a jurist.[3] In Pollock's eyes, law and philosophy often go hand in hand. Not only did he believe that political philosophy contributes significantly to our understanding of law, but he also insisted that some of the driest legal doctrine raises important questions of metaphysics.[4] Questions such as 'what is a thing?', 'what is a place?', and 'what is a cause of action?'—questions to which the very best lawyers want answers—are most profitably approached, Pollock believed, through the lens of philosophy.[5] The claim that he was suspicious of philosophy seems to invite an obvious retort: if only more jurists were so suspicious.

Yet the remark by no means defies belief. 'It's a cranky world,' Pollock wrote to Holmes in 1931. 'The last crank in music is one [Alexandre] Mossolov, a young Russian who has made a piece of so-called Music of Machines, inspired

[1] William Twining, *Globalisation and Legal Theory* (London: Butterworths, 2000), 33.

[2] See, e.g., Frederick Pollock, review of A. J. Balfour, *The Foundations of Belief* (1895) 4 *Mind* 376–84 at 378–9.

[3] See, e.g., [René de Kérallain], 'Note du traducteur', in Frederick Pollock, *Introduction à l'étude de la science politique. Essais et conférences* (Paris: Thorin et fils, 1893), i–vi at ii–iii; and [Adolph S. Oko], 'Sir Frederick Pollock, Bt. (1845–1937)', paper presented to the Quarto Club, 24 October [1943?], in Oko papers, MS 14, box 9, file 23.

[4] See *EOL* 19–20; (1887) 3 *LQR* 359; (1901) 17 *LQR* 114.

[5] See (1885) 1 *LQR* 279; (1886) 2 *LQR* 116; (1898) 14 *LQR* 228; and cf. *S* 204–6.

by the noises of a big factory. We heard it last night. Either M. has not done justice to the factory he studied or the manager should be sacked for not seeing that the machinery is better oiled.'[6] Pollock's attitude to Mossolov's machine music epitomizes his attitude towards a good deal of philosophy: invariably he was prepared to listen—he would strive to be receptive and open-minded[7]—but more often than not he would profess disappointment with what he heard. In his correspondence with Holmes, he not only refers to many philosophical works but in most instances shows that he has read them—something about which, as we noted in the previous chapter, Holmes professed awe. But Pollock's assessments are rarely enthusiastic: one philosophy is 'the clever sort of nonsense that might make sense in some other world'; another, similarly, 'is bosh because it won't fit into the conduct of life'; about yet another we might 'have a suspicion of *squish*'; while others are faulted for lacking 'a beginning middle and end', or 'preaching to the converted.'[8] Not that all philosophers are disparaged thus. 'Rousseau's *Contrat Social* is awfully clever', William James could produce fruitful work when not sidetracked by 'the Pragmatism business', George Santayana could be 'brilliant' (although 'somehow there is something elusive about him'), as could Bertrand Russell (though he seems to be 'angry with the gods for not existing, because if they did he would like to break their windows'), and there are plenty of unsung philosophical worker-bees producing 'solid stuff without any nonsense'.[9] More often than not, however, the efforts of other philosophers brought out a cynical streak in Pollock. He gave short shrift to the concept of 'the Absolute', to 'materialists who talk of epiphenomenon', and to 'jeremiads about the world being in chaos'.[10] It is noticeable in *The Pollock–Holmes Letters* that when Holmes wrote about the cosmos it was usually in his letters to Pollock's wife.[11] Pollock himself found talk of cosmic significance uninteresting.[12] While content to read philosophy, he never regarded himself as, nor wanted to be, a philosopher.[13] 'He liked', Fifoot has observed, 'to exercise the muscles of his mind in meta-

[6] Pollock to Holmes, 26 February 1931, in *PHL* ii. 280.

[7] See, e.g., Pollock to Holmes, 3 February 1930, in *PHL* ii. 258 ('My own way has been . . . to converse with people of the best in their nations and callings'); and 23 November 1931, ibid. 299 ('Thought transference . . . as to which I have an open mind . . .').

[8] Pollock to Holmes, 17 December 1910, in *PHL* i. 171; 19 July 1911, ibid. 182; 20 May 1914, ibid. 215; 2 May 1929, in *PHL* ii. 242; and 17 December 1931, ibid. 300.

[9] Pollock to Holmes, 3 September 1919, in *PHL* ii. 23; 20 July 1912, in *PHL* i. 195; 9 January 1914, ibid. 210; 3 February 1918, ibid. 259; 30 May 1918, ibid. 266; 18 May 1925, in *PHL* ii. 159–60; 2 July 1928, ibid. 224; 15 August 1920, ibid. 51; also 12 September 1920, ibid. 54.

[10] Pollock to Holmes, 24 February 1925, in *PHL* ii. 153; 15 August 1920, ibid. 50; and 7 March 1932, ibid. 305.

[11] See, e.g., Holmes to Georgina Pollock, 27 October 1901, in *PHL* i. 99–100; 31 July 1902, ibid. 100–2.

[12] See Pollock to Holmes, 7 July 1919, in *PHL* ii. 16; also 24 February 1904, in *PHL* i. 117; and cf. Frederick Pollock, 'The Uniformity of Nature' (1876) 1 *Mind* 425–6 at 426; 'A Recent Work on Cosmic Philosophy' (May 1875) n.s. 17 *Fortnightly Rev.* 725–38 at 726–31; *EL* 147.

[13] See *FMG* 109–10.

physical gymnastics; but he distrusted grandiose attempts to construct a synthesis or to frame a creed.'[14] While, in reality, '[n]o philosopher can give you more than a world-poem', Pollock claimed, many 'have their own fourteenth hour at which they expect to find noon, and when they don't they sit down and cry or else fudge the clock.'[15] Thus it is that philosophers often end up either 'crying over spilt milk' or developing theories 'to justify the motives they have already'.[16]

It was not only philosophy that Pollock rinsed with cynical acid. Research for his introduction to the 1906 edition of Maine's *Ancient Law* did not increase his 'respect for the average common sense of professed anthropologists'.[17] While Sir James Frazer 'tells a story mighty well', the universalizing thrust of his evolutionist cultural anthropology—Frazer argued that a belief in magic always precedes religion—left Pollock unconvinced. 'He constantly omits to consider whether his key is the only one that fits,' Pollock declared to Holmes, 'or whether it is a matter of one key at all.'[18] His most withering assessment he saved for W. G. Sumner's *Folkways*: '[i]t looks like the workshop of a man so much overweighted by book-learning that his selective judgment was dulled and his critical faculty blunted and he forgot how to keep his own eyes open. Not a very human man unless (as many do) he lived in water-tight compartments and hung up the live man outside the study door.'[19] Armchair anthropology clearly irked Pollock: 'too many anthropologists are like the kind of real property lawyer who has never seen an original medieval charter and could not read a word of it if he did.'[20] The real source of his ire, however, seemed to be not the failure of many anthropologists satisfactorily to acquire and interpret what they would nowadays call local knowledge, but their hubris—much the same hubris as Pollock detected among philosophers—in believing that they were capable of producing, and in some instances believing that they had produced, universally applicable theories. To claim that Pollock was suspicious of philosophy does not quite reach the heart of the matter: he was inclined to distrust all grand schemes and systems, be they created by philosophers,

[14] Cecil Fifoot, *Pollock and Maitland* (Glasgow: University of Glasgow (Murray Foundation Lecture no. 31), 1971), 12.

[15] Pollock to Holmes, 24 August 1921, in *PHL* ii. 76; 24 February 1925, ibid. 153.

[16] Pollock to Holmes, 24 February 1921, in *PHL* ii. 65; 13 April 1910, in *PHL* i. 161.

[17] Pollock to Holmes, 15 July 1905, in *PHL* i. 120.

[18] Pollock to Holmes, 5 February 1923, in *PHL* ii. 112. Pollock was candid about Frazer in his correspondence with him. 'Many thanks for your little book of addresses on Renan, delightful both in substance and in form', he wrote on one occasion. (Frederick Pollock to J. G. Frazer, 26 October 1924, in Pollock correspondence (Wren), Add. MS c. 59, 91(1).) But while he was happy to compliment Frazer on his style, he was equally forthright in drawing attention to likely inaccuracies: see, e.g., Frederick Pollock to J. G. Frazer, 4 May 1921, in Pollock correspondence (Wren), Add. MS c. 59, 90(1) ('[Y]ou seem to assume that the fox was already established as a sacred animal temp. Queen Anne. This seems hardly credible . . .'); also Frederick Pollock to J. G. Frazer, 5 November 1900, in Pollock correspondence (Wren), Add. MS c. 59, 88(1).

[19] Pollock to Holmes, 22 July 1929, in *PHL* ii. 247. [20] Ibid.

anthropologists, or anyone else. His style was very much that of the fox rather than the hedgehog.[21]

It is significant, even if it is not particularly surprising, that this distrust of the grandiose and the systematic characterizes Pollock's attitude towards jurisprudence. The French understanding of jurisprudence—jurisprudence meaning the case law of the courts—seemed to appeal to Pollock rather more than did the idea of jurisprudence as legal philosophy.[22] While a comprehensive liberal education was, he believed, an advantage to any lawyer,[23] efforts to conceptualize legal phenomena in accordance with some philosophical scheme or model generally left him unimpressed. Jurists 'who think you can reduce law to rigorous chess problems' exasperated him,[24] so it is hardly surprising that Wesley Newcomb Hohfeld's analysis of jural relations should not have been to his taste: 'it is strange', he declared apropos of Hohfeld, 'how many rational beings believe the ultimate truths of the universe to be reducible to patterns on a blackboard.'[25] The concept of 'right' and efforts to explicate it he would happily have seen banished from jurisprudence.[26] Much better, he believed, that jurisprudence be kept straightforward, easily intelligible, free from the technical vocabulary of professional philosophers. '[T]he older I grow', he declared to the law students of the University of Birmingham in May 1932,

> the less inclined I am to trust any general theories of jurisprudence. For my part I have only one dogma about jurisprudence, which I will entrust to you in confidence. When you see a proposition of law which cannot be made intelligible to a jury of educated laymen, I think you may fairly presume that there must be something unsound about it. That dogma I am prepared to defend against all mankind.[27]

It is worth recalling just who was saying all of this. Pollock was for twenty years a professor—*the* professor—of jurisprudence at Oxford. Yet jurispru-

[21] '[T]here exists a great chasm between those, on the one side, who relate everything to a single central vision, one system less or more coherent or articulate, in terms of which they understand, think and feel—a single, universal, organizing principle in terms of which alone all that they are and say has significance—and, on the other side, those who pursue many ends, often unrelated and even contradictory, connected, if at all, only in some *de facto* way, for some psychological or physiological cause, related by no moral or aesthetic principle . . . The first kind of intellectual and artistic personality belongs to the hedgehogs, the second to the foxes.' Isaiah Berlin, *The Hedgehog and the Fox: An Essay on Tolstoy's View of History* (London: Weidenfeld & Nicolson, 1953), 1–2.

[22] Thus it is that he wrote privately of his preference for jurisprudence 'in its proper sense of development of the law by the living voice of the courts'. Frederick Pollock to Adolph S. Oko, 20 April 1936 (no. 2–187), in Oko papers, MS 14, box 5, file 13.

[23] See *OLOD* 108.

[24] Pollock to Holmes, March 1916, in *PHL* i. 234. See also Pollock to Holmes, 30 June 1924, in *PHL* ii. 138 (lamenting how 'seemingly no Continental jurist will believe that any writer . . . does not intend to lay down a complete deductive system').

[25] Pollock to Holmes, 9 February 1921, in *PHL* ii. 63.

[26] See Pollock to Holmes, 21 January 1929, ibid. 236.

[27] Sir Frederick Pollock, *The Talkative Profession* (Birmingham: The Holdsworth Club of the University of Birmingham, 1932), 11.

dence—certainly if taken to mean legal philosophy—was, like philosophy generally, a subject which he approached with considerable suspicion. His detachment from philosophy and his tendency to look askance at the work of many philosophers can be explained: he was, he always insisted, nothing more than 'an amateur in philosophy',[28] an outsider looking in—and regularly bemused by what he found. But he was no amateur jurisprudent. John Chipman Gray wrote to Pollock in 1911, for example, about how *A First Book of Jurisprudence* was inappropriately titled, given how much professional jurists could learn from it.[29] Yet Pollock seemed largely exasperated by the intellectual pursuit over which he was supposed to be a master. How are we to explain this?

The essence of the explanation is that he had serious reservations about a particular type of jurisprudence, analytical jurisprudence. The difficulty with this claim, notwithstanding that it is indisputable, is that it simplifies his position. Pollock's dislike of the analytical project was, we will see, not unequivocal. And although historical and comparative jurisprudence was more to his taste he was, as we saw in chapter 2, not wholly wedded to that project either. About jurisprudence in general he could be markedly ambivalent. The general objective of this chapter is to try to show that, for the purpose of understanding the intellectual history of modern English jurisprudence, this ambivalence turns out to be significant.

We begin by considering Pollock's principal contributions to philosophical debate. Although there is not a great deal to be said about these contributions, they are worth examining because they provide some insight into his philosophical preferences. Not that this exercise reveals much about Pollock's jurisprudential preferences, for he tended to treat his philosophical studies and his work as a jurist as separate exercises. It is unlikely that anyone would ever guess from reading Pollock's legal texts, for example, that he was intimately versed in the philosophy of Spinoza—throughout those texts there are more clues that he loved fencing and mountaineering. For Pollock, the juristic work was just that—work—while philosophy was a hobby, a pleasant distraction from work. Given his belief that doctrinal problems can be illuminated by philosophy, it seems odd that he should have maintained this separation.

If it is hardly possible to ascertain Pollock's jurisprudential preferences from his philosophical studies, determining those preferences from what he had to

[28] *FMG* 109–10.

[29] John Chipman Gray to Frederick Pollock, 10 December 1911, in Pollock correspondence, box 1, folder 26. See also Arthur L. Goodhart, *English Contributions to the Philosophy of Law: The Seventh Annual Benjamin N. Cardozo Lecture Delivered before the Association of the Bar of the City of New York, 25 May 1948* (New York: Oxford UP, 1948), 42–3 ('. . . his *First Book of Jurisprudence*, based primarily on the common law, contains more original ideas than do the far lengthier tomes of many other writers'). Pollock seemed more or less to concur with the assessment offered by Gray: see Pollock to Holmes, 1 November 1917, in *PHL* i. 252 ('. . . a book which does not cater for the examination appetite or pretend to make hard things easy'). Some reviewers similarly concurred—see, e.g., (1896) 43 *The Nation* 234–5—though there were also those, particularly writing for the practitioner-oriented journals, who found the book 'too far removed from the working of the law': Anon., 'Legal Education' (15 August 1896) 101 *Law Times* 367.

say about jurisprudence is not much easier. His reservations about specific perspectives and schools are, we have already noted, often quite easily discernible; determining where his beliefs and enthusiasms lay, however, proves more difficult. Science provides the exception to this assessment: Pollock, like other Victorian jurists, was keen to see the study of law accorded scientific status—an enthusiasm of sorts—and while his analysis of law as a science never generated anything so grandiose as a theory, it is certainly possible to find within his work an argument to the effect that case law develops in accordance with scientific criteria. We will see, however, that the argument which Pollock developed is rather uninspired and anaemic, especially when considered alongside a similar line of argument elaborated around the same time by Holmes. Believing in the idea of law as a science is easy as compared with the task of developing a vision which makes the idea compelling: Pollock believed in the idea, but performed the task half-heartedly.

This is hardly surprising. Pollock, as we know, disliked ambitious efforts at systematization. He resisted the idea of reducing law to some sort of model. But—and this brings us to an argument which is central to this chapter—late nineteenth- and twentieth-century juristic thought evolved mainly within a university culture which emphasized rigorous inquiry and the systematization of knowledge. The analytical tradition, for all its shortcomings, fitted well within this culture: it provided a framework within which to try to provide insight into the nature of legal validity. Jurists were able to modify the framework on offer—indeed, eventually analytical jurists would no longer be modifying the Austinian model but rejecting it. But the basic questions inspired by the analytical project—Why does law bind citizens? To what extent, if at all, does the binding force of law depend upon the moral quality of law?—remained constant and intriguing. Analytical jurisprudence set an identifiable agenda.

By contrast, the goals of historical and comparative jurisprudence—which we will often refer to (as did Pollock) simply as comparative jurisprudence—were for the most part diffuse. This is not to claim that Maine, Vinogradoff, and other proponents of comparative jurisprudence had nothing of interest to say; but, without a distinct jurisprudential agenda, none of them was likely to capture to a significant degree the imaginations of later legal theorists. In this respect, jurisprudence was not alone: the 'comparative method' generally, it has been argued,

> left remarkably little direct legacy; the bandwagon ran into the sand and even the ruts have been almost covered by oblivion. Anthropology, perhaps, has testified best to its sense of continuity; Maine and Tylor are still occasionally invoked, and ritual slayings of Sir James Frazer were still in order up to a few years ago. In other disciplines, figures such as Max Müller, Pollock, Vinogradoff, Cliffe Leslie, or Freeman have not within

living memory been keepers of an academic golden bough worth even the least ambitious aspirant's acquisition.[30]

Pollock may not have been an unequivocal purveyor of the comparative method, but his jurisprudence was rooted in that tradition and was to meet with much the same fate as awaited the works of many other comparatists of his era. His jurisprudential perspective—if, indeed, it is accurate to describe it as a perspective—set no obviously discernible or pressing tasks. Rather than identifying fundamental jurisprudential problems and proposing some sort of framework within which to tackle those problems, he left a tangled web of often interesting if invariably modest reflections on a variety of secondary jurisprudential quandaries. Besides tending to sidestep larger jurisprudential difficulties, Pollock was also convinced that no theory or method or system could prove as enlightening for the purposes of legal inquiry as could straightforward scholarly sincerity, assiduousness, and good sense. If any approach to jurisprudence was to complement the evolving university culture of the late nineteenth and early twentieth centuries, it would have to set itself a clearer agenda than anything suggested by the works of Maine, Vinogradoff, or Pollock. These men may well have been Oxford professors of jurisprudence, but their reflections on the subject were insufficiently well structured and focused to ensure that their own jurisprudential achievements would have lasting appeal. Ultimately, this judgement would be traceable to Oxford itself: in due course, jurisprudence there would shake off its comparatist associations and not only embrace the analytical tradition, but, more significantly, take charge of it.

i. Cul-de-sac

A significant number of Pollock's books begin with the same pre-emptive confession: this work, he is fond of telling the reader, is aimed at a non-specialist audience and therefore deliberately avoids many details and technicalities, particularly references to relevant sources.[31] The confession is usually appropriate. Many of Pollock's intellectual contemporaries produced books which were candidly presented as lectures on one or another topic—this manner of presentation affording a means by which authors could exculpate themselves

[30] Stefan Collini, Donald Winch, and John Burrow, *That Noble Science of Politics: A Study in Nineteenth-century Intellectual History* (Cambridge: Cambridge UP, 1983), 209.

[31] See, e.g., *OLOD* vii; *LL(3)* vii; *ECL* v; *FBJ* vi–vii; *GCL* preface; *OL* advertisement; *S* 7. The exceptions are Pollock's treatises, *PCLE* and *TLT*, although even those are economical with references as compared with most modern legal textbooks. Writing soon after the appearance of the first edition of *TLT*, one American treatise writer warned that 'insect annotation' and '[o]verloaded notes' would be the death of Anglo-American legal scholarship. James Schouler, 'Text and Citations' (1888) 22 *American L. Rev.* 66–73 at 72–3. Of course, the warning was never much heeded and the death never occurred.

from a duty to explore themes in a more rigorous or searching fashion.[32] Pollock did not shun this trend; indeed, the works in which he confesses to be writing for non-specialists are usually those which began life as lectures. One of his books, however, presents a rather different case.

Pollock begins his study of the seventeenth-century Dutch philosopher, Benedict (Baruch) de Spinoza, with his trademark claim that it is intended to be 'understood by those who have not made a special study of the subject'.[33] In this instance, however, the reader is not to be spared of detailed references to authorities and sources. The book, unlike most of Pollock's other books, is neither an introductory textbook nor a reworking of lectures but an extensively footnoted, patiently prepared, rigorously researched monograph. Indeed, although Pollock may have considered himself an amateur in philosophy, it is arguably his most impressive scholarly accomplishment. Most of Spinoza's work languished in obscurity for almost two centuries after his death.[34] In the nineteenth century, the pantheist strain in his philosophy was discovered by, and was to influence, Coleridge, Wordsworth, and other Romantic writers. Pollock was one of the first nineteenth-century intellectuals to recognize that Spinoza's philosophy was composed of more than just pantheism. '[I]f we turn Spinoza's thought into a guide for action,' he asks, 'what is the outcome?' The answer he finds easy to summarize:

> Seek the truth, fear not and spare not: this first, this for its own sake, this only; and the truth itself is your reward, a reward not measured by length of days nor by any reckoning of men. This lesson assuredly is not an idle one, or unworthy to be set forth with fervent and solemn words. And if any man ever had a special title so to repeat the lesson, that man was Spinoza, whose whole life was an example of it.[35]

Simply to treat Spinoza's philosophy as an exercise in mysticism would, in Pollock's eyes, be unwise. Given that 'the groundwork of [Spinoza's] doctrine is the Aristotelian theory that contemplative knowledge is the highest and most proper function of the mind,' he 'is no more a mystic than Aristotle.'[36] Not that Pollock was dismissive of mystical philosophy. According to his son, Pollock had an 'abiding sense of the one-ness of all things' and 'a firm faith that by conscious improvement man can realize his place in the divine infinitude.'[37] During the later decades of his life he apparently discussed mysticism regularly with one of its chief popularizers, Evelyn Underhill.[38] For a man gen-

[32] See Stefan Collini, *Public Moralists: Political Thought and Public Life in Britain 1850–1930* (Oxford: Clarendon Press, 1991), 225–6.

[33] *SHLP* vii.

[34] See Stuart Hampshire, *Spinoza* (Harmondsworth: Penguin, 1951), 234.

[35] *SHLP* 282–3.

[36] *SHLP* 283.

[37] Sir John Pollock, *Time's Chariot* (London: Murray, 1950), 73–4.

[38] See ibid. 74. Underhill wrote numerous books about mysticism, including *Mysticism: A Study in the Nature and Development of Man's Spiritual Consciousness* (London: Methuen & Co., 1911); *Practical Mysticism: A Little Book for Normal People* (London: Dent, 1914); and *The Essentials of Mysticism and Other Essays*

erally uninterested in talk of cosmic significance, both the sentiments and the choice of company seem strange. This interest in mysticism seems even odder, furthermore, when one considers that the popularity of mysticism in Europe of the late nineteenth and early twentieth centuries is often taken to be indicative of disenchantment with reason.[39] Pollock, as we will see presently, did not share this disenchantment. What, then, explains his attraction to mysticism?

The answer, in essence, seems to be that he considered mysticism not only interesting, but also maligned. '[T]he philosophical bearing of mysticism has been misunderstood by superficial modern criticism in much the same sort as the mediaeval doctrine of the law of nature.'[40] Although 'we have no warrant for saying that there is any such thing as an exclusive or definite mystical philosophy',[41] proponents of mysticism have cautioned regularly about both the need for scepticism in inquiry and the redundancy of worrying over one's place in the cosmos.[42] The pursuit of reason in fact often entails mystical experience. No longer is it 'assumed as a matter of course that the key to all the secrets of the universe' is 'in man's hands'—'[s]cience has for good and all abandoned the dream of finality.'[43] Modern scholars, encountering the thresholds of their knowledge, will often pass 'through stages of something resembling in quality, if not in intensity, the "dryness" or "dark night of the soul"

(London: Dent, 1920). Like Pollock, she was a member of Younghusband's Fight for Right movement: see Evelyn Underhill, 'The Consecration of England', in *For the Right: Essays and Addresses by Members of the 'Fight for Right Movement'* (London: T. Fisher Unwin, 1916), 219–28. For Underhill, the First World War was a 'struggle between that power within the universe which makes for moral beauty and the unsubdued physical force which resists it. . . . To England and her Allies have been given the great honour and great responsibility of fighting on the side of moral beauty' (ibid. 220). Resisting Germany she considered at this time to be a necessity—'[w]e must fight; . . . [w]e . . . must take our risks and accept our honourable wounds' (ibid. 225)—though by the time of the Second World War she had become a pacifist: see Evelyn Underhill to Geoffrey Curtis, 18 January 1940, in *The Letters of Evelyn Underhill*, ed. C. Williams (London: Longmans, Green & Co., 1943), 286 ('I am still entirely pacifist and more and more convinced that the idea that this or any other war is "righteous" or will achieve any creative result of a durable kind, is an illusion').

[39] See J. W. Burrow, *The Crisis of Reason: European Thought, 1848–1914* (New Haven: Yale UP, 2000), 225–33. After 1914 interest in mysticism, and particularly in spiritualism, was largely sustained by widespread bereavement: many of those who lost loved ones during the War looked to mystic and spiritual philosophies for the consoling possibility of a hereafter. Even before the War, we find Pollock's relative, E. S. P. Haynes, writing at length about the possibility of life after death. '[T]here is a kind of heroic virtue in believing in what we should never accept on rational grounds in ordinary life', he wrote in 1913. 'We have all experienced the shiver of being face to face with the death of those dearest to us, and some of us know what it is to have faced almost certain death in person. At such moments surely our only fortifying thought is that the whole is greater than the part, and that all that in which and for which we have lived will survive our individual selves, perishable organisms as we are. . . . Our religious friends will no doubt tell us that all this is hollow. . . . But the time is fast coming when modern men and women . . . will demand, and obtain, a larger view of the universe than the Christian cosmogony.' E. S. P. Haynes, *The Belief in Personal Immortality* (London: Watts & Co., 1913), 147–51.

[40] *OL* 24–5. [41] *OL* 23.

[42] See *OL* 10 ('It is common knowledge that the great mystics . . . have warned novices, over and over again, of the need for scrutinising visions, auditions, and the like') and 11 ('competent students rank Joan of Arc high among the mystics, and yet her mission was neither religious nor philosophical, and I never read that she was exercised about her own soul at all').

[43] *SHLP* 76–7.

so familiar in mystical writings. . . . There are days . . . when reason maintains that something is bound to come out, but one cannot feel as if it would be anything but some dressing and patching up of old unsatisfying forms.'[44] Understood in this light, mystical thought can be seen to have 'had a rational and anti-dogmatic operation'.[45]

Properly to understand the mystical element in Spinoza's philosophy requires an appreciation that mysticism is not antithetical to scientific inquiry. '[E]ven when Spinoza goes farthest in overleaping the bounds of experience, it is still the scientific element that gives consistence and definition to his work.'[46] Indeed, 'we find almost everywhere in his work scientific and essentially modern thought clothed in the semblance of scholastic forms.'[47] The scientific thrust of his philosophy, furthermore, whatever its relationship to mystical thought, is always generated by a faith in reason. 'Belief in the nature of things is the mainspring of all science and the condition of all sound thinking, unless there be some kind of sound thinking which diverges from sound reason. . . . Spinoza's philosophy is the enthronement of reason, and it is this belief that he requires.'[48] Although this depiction of Spinoza's philosophy as simultaneously embracing science, secular reason, and mysticism may seem rather odd, it is not, Pollock insists, implausible. Certainly it is a difficult philosophy to piece together—'[t]he metaphysical parts of Spinoza's philosophy are expressed, it must be allowed, in a manner not congenial to English habits of thought'—and the 'peculiar vocabulary' sometimes leaves us guessing at what might have been meant.[49] So long, however, as it is appreciated that mystical sentiments can exist and indeed flourish within a system of thought which emphasizes scientific inquiry and secular reason, Spinoza's philosophy, for all its complexity, need not be adjudged incoherent. The trick is to determine how the philosophy is able to accommodate, indeed be founded upon, apparently disparate ideas.

> In any scheme of philosophy . . . which is worth serious consideration, there is a vital core of ideas embodied in a frame of more or less artificial construction. It is the task of the history of philosophy to trace . . . the life and growth of these ideas; to disengage them from their local and temporary incidents; and thereby to keep a clear pathway for the work of philosophy itself. This is the spirit in which we . . . approach . . . Spinoza.[50]

Pollock did not read Spinoza uncritically.[51] His principal concern, none the less, was to demonstrate that Spinoza developed a coherent, if remarkably

[44] *OL* 11–12.
[45] *OL* 25. See also *EL* 171–2; and cf. Frederick Pollock, 'Notes on the Philosophy of Spinoza' (1878) 3 *Mind* 195–212 at 210–11.
[46] *SHLP* 158. [47] *SHLP* 147.
[48] *SHLP* 134; see also ibid. 237–40, 268, 288; and cf. Frederick Pollock, 'Marcus Aurelius and the Stoic Philosophy' (1879) 4 *Mind* 47–68 at 56.
[49] *SHLP* 289, 172, 269. [50] *SHLP* 79. [51] See, e.g., *SHLP* 123, 197.

complex and recondite, philosophy. This task he considered to be reconstructive: he regarded himself not as a philosopher but as a handmaiden at the service of other philosophers; he would save these philosophers the labour of having to piece together Spinoza's philosophy, so that they could get straight to the work of reflecting upon it. It was a useful task to perform, and certainly appreciated—many subsequent studies of Spinoza acknowledge the value of Pollock's endeavour.[52] His work revealed that there was much more to Spinoza's philosophy than pantheism, that it was a scientifically grounded philosophy of considerable complexity and nuance. Pollock claimed that his reading of Spinoza was largely attributable to William Kingdon Clifford: '[t]he interpretation of Spinoza's philosophy which I have put forward', he wrote just before the publication of the first edition of his main book on Spinoza, 'I owe very much to him.'[53] The more interesting question is that of what Pollock owes to Spinoza. One might reasonably anticipate that Pollock would dismiss Spinoza's work as yet another illustration of the capacity of philosophers to produce clever nonsense. For some reason, however, Spinoza appealed to him. Why?

Part of the appeal was the opportunity to practise what Fifoot called metaphysical gymnastics. It is clear from Pollock's writings on Spinoza that he relished the challenge of rendering Spinoza's philosophy less abstruse. There is also the fact that Pollock genuinely revered Spinoza as a genius: 'the secret workings of nature which bring it to pass that an Aeschylus, a Leonardo, a Faraday, a Kant, or a Spinoza is born upon the earth, are as obscure now as they were a thousand years ago. The power of these men still bears with it the reverence and awe that belong to great things unaccountable.'[54] Most significantly of all, some of the qualities that Pollock identified in the work of Spinoza are among those he commended in his juristic writings. The most obvious of these qualities is reason. Pollock was no less dedicated to the enthronement of reason than was Spinoza. The common law, Pollock insisted, embodies 'the common reason of mankind'[55]—is dedicated, indeed, to 'the perfection of reason'.[56] His preoccupation with reason will be examined in due course, but for now it need only be noted that his attraction to the philosophy of Spinoza was partly attributable to the fact that he considered it to extol one of the human capacities which, as a jurist, he emphasized and indeed cherished. Reason was not the only attractive juristic quality, furthermore, that Pollock found in Spinoza's philosophy. Pollock

[52] See, e.g., Hampshire, above n. 34, 10; and Roger Scruton, *Spinoza* (Oxford: Oxford UP, 1986), 118; although cf. Alan Donagan, *Spinoza* (London: Harvester, 1988), 126–7.

[53] Frederick Pollock, 'Introduction', in *Lectures and Essays by the Late William Kingdon Clifford*, 2 vols., eds. L. Stephen and F. Pollock (London: Macmillan, 1879), i. 1–72 at 39.

[54] *SHLP* 2. Cf. also Frederick Pollock, 'Benedict de Spinoza' (February 1878) 3 *Nineteenth Century* 330–54 at 354 ('. . . the worth of a philosopher to the world is measured not by the number of people who accept his system, or by the failure of criticism to detect logical flaws in it, but by the life and strength of the ideas he sets stirring in men's minds. . . . Judged by this test, Spinoza stands on a height of eminence such as very few other thinkers have attained').

[55] *OLOD* 21. [56] *GCL* 2.

interpreted and indeed admired Spinoza as a political philosopher in the Hobbesian cast. Although Spinoza was 'not actually a disciple of Hobbes'—according to Pollock, he only ever mentions Hobbes once throughout his writings—he 'so closely follows' Hobbes that his views on law and government might be said to belong 'to the general doctrine characteristic of the English school of jurisprudence'.[57] Indeed, for Pollock, Spinoza developed an essentially Hobbesian political theory which, as compared with that developed by Hobbes himself, 'rests on a wider and most generous view of human life', 'is less encumbered with fictions', and 'aims at a higher mark'.[58]

Given Pollock's admiration for and knowledge of Spinoza's philosophy, one might expect some of Spinoza's preoccupations and ideas to surface clearly in his juristic work. The Austro-Hungarian international lawyer, Hersch Lauterpacht, was likewise an admirer of Spinoza, and when he wrote about him it was in an effort to demonstrate that 'his teaching may not be altogether without advantage for the student of the history and the theory of international law.'[59] Pollock himself was generally dismissive of Spinoza's views on international law.[60] Lauterpacht and Pollock make an interesting contrast, however, not because of their differing estimations of Spinoza's contribution to the theory of international law, but because of what they derive from Spinoza for juristic purposes. Lauterpacht's interest in Spinoza's philosophy is instrumental: he considers Spinoza to make a distinctive juristic contribution. Pollock, by contrast, values Spinoza's philosophy for its own sake: while he finds in Spinoza's writings a number of insights with juristic significance, he never claims that Spinoza provides unique enrichment for those who study the law. Certainly, as a jurist, he sometimes asked questions which Spinoza might well have asked.[61] But his juristic writings rarely refer to or draw upon Spinoza. One would expect to find Pollock's jurisprudence inspired to a notable degree by the philosopher who engaged him most, especially since certain of the inquiries undertaken by that philosopher were, as Pollock recognized, not without jurisprudential relevance. Yet Pollock's jurisprudential analyses

[57] *SHLP* 289, 291, and see also 183.

[58] *SHLP* 316. Pollock also detected a strand of Machiavellian political theory in Spinoza's work, although he clearly found this to be neither as pronounced nor as admirable as Spinoza's Hobbesian outlook: see Sir Frederick Pollock, 'Spinoza et le Machiavelisme' (January–February 1919) 11 *Revue politique internationale* 3–11; also *SHLP* 309; Pollock to Holmes, 14 October 1918, in *PHL* i. 269.

[59] Hersch Lauterpacht, 'Spinoza and International Law' (1927) 8 *British Year Book of International Law* 89–107 at 90. See also Martti Koskenniemi, 'Lauterpacht: The Victorian Tradition in International law' (1997) 8 *European Jnl. of International Law* 215–65 at 220.

[60] Sir Frederick Pollock, 'Spinoza's Political Doctrine with Special Regard to his Relation to English Publicists' (1921) 1 *Chronicon Spinozanum* 45–57 at 52 ('Spinoza's ideas of international relations are in general as crude and archaic as those of Hobbes; he had no conception of any rules being possible otherwise than by agreements in the nature of alliance').

[61] See, e.g., Frederick Pollock, 'What is a Thing?' (1894) 10 *LQR* 318–22; and cf. *SHLP* 204–5. Though it should be noted that some of these questions were also being asked by other jurists. Regarding 'what is a thing?', for example, see John Austin, *Lectures on Jurisprudence or the Philosophy of Positive Law*, 2 vols., 5th edn. R. Campbell (London: Murray, 1885), i. 357–64.

proceed as if Spinoza had never existed. To understand Pollock's jurisprudence, it is necessary that we jettison Spinoza and begin to look elsewhere.

So, where else do we look? Pollock hardly distinguished himself from his Victorian juristic contemporaries by connecting law with science. Indeed, the remarkable Victorian jurist would be the one who did not posit any such connection.[62] The presence of a shared goal, however, is not necessarily indicative of a shared outlook. During the nineteenth and early twentieth centuries, English jurists supported and promoted the idea of law as a science in a variety of ways. The various perspectives articulated throughout this period generally broke down into those two distinct though not wholly incompatible categories of thought which, for convenience, we have labelled analytical jurisprudence and comparative jurisprudence. Pollock's understanding of legal science belonged more to the latter than to the former category. But not entirely so: indeed, as noted already, Pollock was neither an unequivocal advocate of comparative jurisprudence nor, despite his many vituperative condemnations of the work of John Austin, an out-and-out opponent of the analytical project. '[T]he closer one looks,' it has been remarked, 'the harder it is to find the "English School of Jurisprudence".'[63] Pollock certainly did not make the task any easier, so committed was he to equivocating on the subject of legal science. Understanding his jurisprudence requires that we try to uncover and explain his arguments on that subject. But this is not the only or even the most valuable task at stake here. By putting these arguments in context, and by trying to show why, ultimately, they fell on deaf ears, we might also gain some insight into why English jurisprudence generally took the analytical rather than the comparative route.

ii. Rechtswissenschaft, *English-style*

The jurisprudence of John Austin has been the subject of so many nuanced and revisionist analyses that one hesitates to say anything straightforward about it. Yet one hardly goes out on a limb in claiming that Austin wanted to accord scientific status to the study of positive law. 'Though every system of law has its specific and characteristic differences,' he claimed, 'there are prin-

[62] A point adverted to by Buckland, looking back in his eighty-fifth year on the history of modern jurisprudence: see W. W. Buckland, *Some Reflections on Jurisprudence* (Cambridge: Cambridge UP, 1945), 40–1. Curiously, over half a century earlier Buckland had been more sceptical than most about what he considered to be the universalizing pretensions of a good deal of Victorian legal science: see W. W. Buckland, 'Difficulties of Abstract Jurisprudence' (1890) 6 *LQR* 436–45. While not wholly disparaging of legal science—Buckland acknowledged, for example, 'the enormous service rendered by historical study to the science of law' (ibid. 443)—he professed to be 'doubtful whether any claim of universality is maintainable or useful' (ibid. 445), given that principles of law often differ between and change within legal systems. He was no less doubtful by 1945: cf. *Some Reflections on Jurisprudence*, 68.

[63] Michael Lobban, 'Was there a Nineteenth Century "English School of Jurisprudence"?' (1995) 16 *Jnl. Leg. Hist.* 34–62 at 53.

ciples, notions, and distinctions common to various systems, and forming analogies or likenesses by which systems are allied.'[64] The purpose of jurisprudence as Austin preferred it to be conceived was to identify, clarify, and arrange these general principles—'General Jurisprudence', indeed, was his description of the task. '[T]he various principles common to maturer systems', he wrote, 'are the subject of an extensive science . . . named General . . . Jurisprudence, or the philosophy . . . of positive law.'[65] A satisfactory definition of 'General Jurisprudence', he added, might be 'the science concerned with the exposition of the principles, notions, and distinctions which are common to systems of law'.[66] This conception of jurisprudence is, to use Bentham's terminology, expository rather than censorial, concerned with what law is rather than what it ought to be. 'The *science of jurisprudence*', Austin confirmed, 'is concerned with positive laws, or with laws strictly so called, as considered without regard to their goodness or badness.'[67] Disregarding the quality of positive laws made good sense to Austin: 'the goodness or badness of a human law is a phrase of relative and varying import',[68] and so those concerned with developing the science of jurisprudence ought to address 'the existence of law' rather than 'its merit or demerit'.[69] Such development requires an appreciation of the fact that 'laws or rules, properly so called, are a *species* of commands'[70]—commands which are issued by a sovereign and which 'the *bulk* of the given society' habitually obeys.[71] Appreciation of as much holds 'the *key* to the sciences of jurisprudence and morals'.[72]

Paradoxically, we might say, Austinian jurisprudence, being focused on general principles common to legal systems but detached from normative or censorial considerations, is at once broad and narrow. Both the breadth and the narrowness came to be considered faults. Indeed, after the publication of the second edition of Austin's *The Province of Jurisprudence Determined* and his *Lectures on Jurisprudence or the Philosophy of Law* in the early 1860s, critics gradually developed a range of objections to his legal philosophy.[73] '[F]or the student in the days of my youth', Buckland recalled in 1945, 'Austin . . . was a religion; to-day he seems to be regarded rather as a disease.'[74] By the early 1960s, the disease appeared to have been eradicated. 'Austin wrongly claimed to have found in the notion of coercive orders . . . "the key to the science of jurisprudence" [*sic*]', H. L. A. Hart wrote in 1961.[75] Unfortunately, 'the simple, Aus-

[64] Austin, above n. 61, ii. 1072. [65] Ibid. [66] Ibid. 1073.

[67] Ibid. i. 172. [68] Ibid. 174; and, in a similar vein, see ibid. 218, 268.

[69] Ibid. 214. [70] Ibid. 88. [71] Ibid. 220–1. [72] Ibid. 88.

[73] See Richard A. Cosgrove, 'The Reception of Analytic Jurisprudence: The Victorian Debate on the Separation of Law and Morality, 1860–1900' (1981) 74 *Durham Univ. Jnl.* 47–56; and Albert Kocourek, 'The Century of Analytic Jurisprudence Since John Austin', in *Law. A Century of Progress, 1835–1935: Contributions in Celebration of the 100th Anniversary of the Founding of the School of Law of New York University*, 3 vols. (New York: New York UP, 1937), ii. 195–230 at 199–201.

[74] Buckland, *Some Reflections on Jurisprudence*, above n.62, 2.

[75] H. L. A. Hart, *The Concept of Law*, 2nd edn. (Oxford: Clarendon Press, 1994; 1st edn. publ. 1961), 81.

tinian formula of a general habit of obedience . . . only caters for what we may term the "end product" of the legal system.'[76] We need, Hart claimed, 'greater clarity', 'a fresh start', an acknowledgement of 'the deficiencies of the theory which has dominated so much English jurisprudence since Austin expounded it', and the courage 'to learn from our failure'.[77] Among other things, we ought to concede that the notion of 'a general habit of obedience' is neither sufficiently powerful nor precise to explain the validity of legal systems,[78] that legal obligation is not merely a matter of orders backed by threats,[79] that legal rules may confer powers as well as impose duties,[80] that 'the judge's own statement that a particular rule is valid . . . is an internal statement recognizing that the rule satisfies the tests for identifying what is to count as law',[81] and that internalization of a legal rule means looking upon it 'as a legal standard of conduct,' to be referred to 'in criticizing others, or in justifying demands'.[82] It is now necessary, Hart insisted, 'to advance legal theory by providing an improved analysis of the distinctive structure of a municipal legal system and a better understanding of the resemblances and differences between law, coercion, and morality, as types of social phenomena.'[83] By the later decades of the twentieth century, notwithstanding the occasional (and often unconvincing) claim that Austin suffered harshly at the hands of modern legal philosophers,[84] the Austinian vision of a science of jurisprudence was but a reminder of a bygone age.

The general decline in the significance of Austinian jurisprudence ought to be considered in the light of two fairly obvious yet, for our purposes, crucial points. The first of these is that although Hart discredited the Austinian project, by no means did he undermine analytical jurisprudence generally. Hart recognized two phases of analytical jurisprudence, the first phase being that associated with Bentham and Austin and the second, modern phase having been inspired by the linguistic philosophies of Ludwig Wittgenstein and the Oxford moral philosopher, John L. Austin.[85] Hart himself, being the preeminent representative of this modern phase, was very much responsible for the survival and the popularity of analytical jurisprudence in the second half of the twentieth century. The second point to note is that when Hart set about dismantling Austin's theory of law as coercive orders, the exercise was considered to be jurisprudentially worthwhile: Austin's theory may not have been the potent force that it once was, but its domination of English jurisprudence throughout an earlier era meant that subjecting it to sustained critique was not tantamount to attacking a figure of straw. Hart was able successfully

[76] Ibid. 112. [77] Ibid. 6, 80, 16, 20. [78] Ibid. 23–4, 51–5, 68–71.
[79] Ibid. 28, 48. [80] Ibid. 27–9, 40–2, 77, 153. [81] Ibid. 105.
[82] Ibid. 138; and also, on internalization generally, ibid. 55–8, 82–91. [83] Ibid. 17.
[84] See, e.g., Thomas Broden, Jr., 'The Straw Man of Legal Positivism' (1958–9) 34 *Notre Dame Lawyer* 530–55 at 531–5; Robert N. Moles, *Definition and Rule in Legal Theory: A Reassessment of H. L. A. Hart and the Positivist Tradition* (Oxford: Blackwell, 1987).
[85] See H. L. A. Hart, 'Jhering's Heaven of Concepts and Modern Analytical Jurisprudence' (1970), in his, *Essays in Jurisprudence and Philosophy* (Oxford: Clarendon Press, 1983), 265–77 at 271–7.

to advance the second phase of analytical jurisprudence precisely because the first phase, for all its limitations, provided solid enough foundations upon which to build: it was, as Hart put it, the 'type of theory which has perennial attractions whatever its defects may be'.[86]

It is important to keep in mind, in other words, that Austinian jurisprudence was sufficiently potent to be a religion as a well as a disease. Even more importantly, the period during which it was more worshipped than dreaded coincided with that during which jurisprudence preoccupied Pollock. Austin was certainly not without his critics throughout this period—John Dewey, for example, argued at length that Austin's jurisprudence was both derivative (particularly from Hobbes) and premised on 'a radical error concerning the mode in which sovereignty is exercised'[87]—and even those who lauded his theory rarely did so unequivocally. The point, however, is that during the second half of the nineteenth century, Austin's jurisprudence *was* being widely lauded. The publication of the second edition of *The Province of Jurisprudence Determined* in 1861 coincided with the publication of Maine's *Ancient Law*. In reviewing the two books together, James Fitzjames Stephen clearly found Austin's work to be the more stimulating. 'Maine . . . confines himself most cautiously and studiously to the investigation of facts; he puts forward no philosophical theories at all. . . . The light by which his book should be read is supplied by Bentham and Mr Austin, who have analysed with a precision, which leaves hardly anything to be desired, the fundamental notions which lie at the bottom of jurisprudence.'[88] Indeed, 'Austin's propositions on jurisprudence have as much precision, and will in all probability be seen hereafter to have as much importance, as the propositions of Adam Smith and Ricardo on rent, profits, and value.'[89] 'No writer whom we know had more of the qualities needed for initiating and disciplining other minds in the difficult art of precise thought', John Stuart Mill wrote upon the publication of Austin's *Lectures on Jurisprudence* two years later (echoing sentiments he had originally expressed when reviewing the first edition of *The Province of Jurisprudence Determined* thirty years earlier).[90] '[T]he remains which [Austin] has left, fragmentary though much

[86] Hart, above n.75, 18. See also H. L. A. Hart, 'Positivism and the Separation of Law and Morals' (1958) 71 *Harvard L. Rev.* 593–629 at 593 ('Like our own Austin, . . . Holmes was sometimes clearly wrong; but, again like Austin, when this was so he was always wrong clearly. This surely is a sovereign virtue in jurisprudence'). Colin Tapper, 'Austin on Sanctions' [1965] *Cambridge L. J.* 271–87, begins by contending, *pace* Hart, that 'the conventional view of Austin as a careful and painstaking manipulator of hard concepts is quite unjustified' and 'that time spent shooting at Austin is invariably successful, and invariably unrewarding' (ibid. 271). As Tapper's essay proceeds, nevertheless, he becomes gradually more charitable towards Austin, concluding ultimately that Austin was 'an honest and often perceptive explorer into the foundations of law' and that 'he left work . . . for which his successors should be profoundly grateful' (ibid. 287).

[87] John Dewey, 'Austin's Theory of Sovereignty' (1894) 9 *Pol. Sci. Q.* 31–52 at 34.

[88] [James Fitzjames Stephen], 'English Jurisprudence' (October 1861) 114 *Edinburgh Rev.* 456–86 at 484.

[89] Ibid. 466–7.

[90] [John Stuart Mill], 'Austin on Jurisprudence' (October 1863) 118 *Edinburgh Rev.* 439–82 at 439; and cf. [John Stuart Mill], 'Austin's Lectures on Jurisprudence' (1832) 2 *Tait's Edinburgh Magazine* 343–8

of them be, are a mine of material for the future.'[91] Echoing Mill, Cliffe Leslie judged the *Lectures* to be a 'mighty work', the 'momentousness' of which will be 'difficult to overestimate'.[92] Such assessments did not dry up during the later decades of the nineteenth century. Austin's *Province*, T. E. Holland claimed in the first edition of *The Elements of Jurisprudence*, 'is a book which no one can read without improvement. It presents the spectacle of a powerful and conscientious mind struggling with an intractable and rarely handled material. . . . [T]hose distinctions upon which Austin . . . bestows most labour are put in so clear a light that they can hardly again be lost sight of.'[93] For E. C. Clark, Austin's jurisprudence had, by the early 1880s, become 'the staple of jurisprudence in all our systems of legal education.'[94] 'If the student be engaged upon a body of law which is capable of scientific exposition, . . . it would . . . seem desirable . . . to establish in the mind of the learner . . . some general system or outline. . . . For this purpose, it may be questioned whether a better scheme can be suggested than that of Austin's Lectures.'[95] Critical reverence—a distinctly oxymoronic term—was, during the late nineteenth and early twentieth centuries, the predominant attitude towards Austin's project. It was an

at 344 ('Mr Austin's work is part of the grammar of a science. As such, it is not a book for any but persons who are really anxious to learn; but to them, it is such a book as they delight in. The author's style is a model of perspicuity: the concatenation of his propositions is free from all obscurity; and the reader will find no difficulty but that which is inseparable from the attempt to communicate precise ideas'). The latter review is essentially an advertisement for Austin's *Province*, as Mill himself conceded: see Collini, above n.32, 259–60.

[91] Mill, 'Austin on Jurisprudence', above n.90, 480.

[92] [T. E. Cliffe Leslie], 'Modern Phases of Jurisprudence in England' (1864) n.s. 26 *Westminster Rev.* 261–76 at 276.

[93] Sir Thomas Erskine Holland, *The Elements of Jurisprudence*, 13th edn. (Oxford: Clarendon Press, 1924; 1st edn. publ. 1880), vii (preface to first edition).

[94] E. C. Clark, *Practical Jurisprudence: A Comment on Austin* (Cambridge: Cambridge UP, 1883), 5. For a critique of Clark on Austin, see F. M. Maxwell, 'Austin's Jurisprudence and its Latest Critic' (1884–5) 10 *Law Magazine & Rev. (4th Ser.)* 167–93.

[95] E. C. Clark, 'Jurisprudence; Its Use and Its Place in Legal Education' (1885) 1 *LQR* 201–6 at 204. Clark was one of a number of late nineteenth- and early twentieth-century authors who produced books which, while rarely uncritical, were devoted to spreading the Austinian faith: for other examples, see W. Jethro Brown, *The Austinian Theory of Law, being an Edition of Lectures I, V, and VI of Austin's 'Jurisprudence,' and of Austin's 'Essay on the Uses of the Study of Jurisprudence' with Critical Notes and Excursus* (London: Murray, 1906); R. A. Eastwood, *A Brief Introduction to Austin's Theory of Law and Sovereignty* (London: Sweet & Maxwell, 1916); and R. A. Eastwood and G. W. Keeton, *The Austinian Theories of Law and Sovereignty* (London: Methuen & Co., 1929). The Preface to Eastwood's *A Brief Introduction to Austin's Theory of Law and Sovereignty* exemplifies the basic style of these books: '[n]ine out of every ten students who take up the study of Jurisprudence are set to read Austin. Yet it can hardly be said that the result is always satisfactory. The student . . . at the outset of his legal studies . . . accepts easily enough the masterful arguments of Austin. And then, after a time, comes a complete revulsion. . . . He treats the Austinian doctrines as matters to be dismissed with a contemptuous shrug, and he mistakes abuse for criticism. Much of this might be avoided if he . . . could realise at the beginning that Austin's work does not now stand alone, but is more properly to be surveyed in connection with the volume of criticism and counter criticism to which it has given rise' (iii–iv). Cf. the intriguing American essay by Charles Malcom Platt, 'The Character and Scope of Analytical Jurisprudence' (1890) 24 *American L. Rev.* 603–15, which basically reprimands Holland and Clark for being excessively critical of, and insufficiently reverential towards, Austin.

attitude that formed the backdrop, so to speak, against which Pollock developed his own thoughts on the scientific nature of law.

Some jurists of this era were perhaps inevitably more critical than reverent when writing about Austin, and the classic line of late-Victorian critique was that Austin tended to be insensitive to history.[96] Sir Henry Maine had anticipated this line of critique as early as 1861 in his *Ancient Law*. '[T]he farther we penetrate into the primitive history of thought,' he wrote, 'the farther we find ourselves from a conception of law which at all resembles' those developed by either Bentham or Austin.[97] This critique he elaborated in his final two *Lectures on the Early History of Institutions*, delivered at Oxford in the early 1870s. Within the lectures there is no shortage of the customary reverence: '[Austin's *Province*] has long been one of the higher class-books in this University; and . . . it must always, or for a long time to come, be the mainstay of the studies prosecuted in this Department.'[98] But the analysis quickly becomes critical:

> the Austinian view of sovereignty . . . is arrived at by throwing aside all the characteristics and attributes of Government and Society except one, and by connecting all forms of political superiority together through their common possession of force. . . . [I]t is its history, the entire mass of its historical antecedents, which in each community determines how the Sovereign shall exercise or forbear from exercising his irresistible coercive power. All that constitutes this . . . is rejected by the Analytical Jurists.[99]

The argument that Austinian sovereignty theory generally ignored the actual history of legal systems was reiterated by other Victorian jurists, and remained popular well into the twentieth century.[100] Pollock was among those

[96] 'The ideas of Bentham and Austin attracted an enthusiastic following among liberal thinkers who favoured law reform. Those who opposed them had to find respectable counter-arguments. They concentrated on the failure of the Benthamites to give adequate consideration to historical factors.' Peter Stein, *Legal Evolution: The Story of An Idea* (Cambridge: Cambridge UP, 1980), 72.

[97] Henry Sumner Maine, *Ancient Law: Its Connection with the Early History of Society, and its Relation to Modern Ideas* (London: Murray, 1861), 7–8. See also George Feaver, 'The Victorian Values of Sir Henry Maine', in *The Victorian Achievement of Sir Henry Maine: A Centennial Reappraisal*, ed. A. Diamond (Cambridge: Cambridge UP, 1991), 28–52 at 41–2.

[98] Sir Henry Sumner Maine, *Lectures on the Early History of Institutions* (London: Murray, 1875), 345.

[99] Ibid. 359–60. For a vigorous defence of Austin against Maine's critique, see W. Markby, 'Analytical Jurisprudence' (1876) n.s. 1 *Law Magazine & Rev.* 617–30; and cf. also William Graham, *English Political Philosophy from Hobbes to Maine* (London: Arnold, 1926), a work which acknowledges as significant Maine's critique of Austin (ibid. 349–50) but which also criticizes Maine for being insufficiently attentive to the lessons of natural law jurisprudence (ibid. 375–7).

[100] See, e.g., Frederic Harrison, 'The English School of Jurisprudence' (1878) n.s. 24 *Fortnightly Rev.* 475–92, 682–703; (1879) n.s. 25 *Fortnightly Rev.* 114–30, part i, at 487 ('The analysis of sovereignty, . . . contained in Austin's *Province of Jurisprudence*, is of the highest value provided that we recognize its relative character. . . . [F]rom the point of view of scientific history and scientific politics, the [analysis] requires so much qualification and correction, that it ceases to be a complete account of the matter at all'); James Bryce, 'The Nature of Sovereignty', in his *Studies in History and Jurisprudence*, 2 vols. (Oxford: Clarendon Press, 1901), ii. 49–111 at 89–97, and 'The Methods of Legal Science', ibid. 172–208 at 180–4; Carleton Kemp Allen, *Legal Duties and Other Essays in Jurisprudence* (Oxford: Clarendon Press, 1931), 141–2 ('Neglect of history . . . produced in England a theory of law which is chiefly associated

who elaborated this argument. The critique of Austin to be found in the *Early History of Institutions* was, he proclaimed, 'the very foundation of sound judgement.'[101] Thanks to Maine, it had become clear that 'the analytical school . . . could not lead to any rational explanation of an actual historical system.'[102] The problem, for Pollock, was not just that Austin 'absolutely ignored history'[103]; it was also that he failed to appreciate that a system of public international law is genuinely law, 'regard[ed] legal science as a thing apart from legal practice', and was a 'thoroughly amateurish' lawyer, being 'seldom well informed or accurate in the details of either English or Roman law'.[104] Austin's conception of law as command demanded the conclusion that statutes which are obsolete but have never been repealed must be treated as binding on citizens.[105] It also necessitated the conclusion that custom can never be law—had Austin explored Maine's Indian village, indeed, he would have determined that no laws existed there.[106] '[I]f one is to hold fast to the conception of law as command, and follow it into its consequences, the last result is this: that in British India, or in any other part of the world where a dominant race is strong enough to govern, but not strong enough to abolish institutions it found existing, there is so far as concerns those institutions no real positive law at all.'[107]

To some degree, this distaste for Austin's jurisprudence was part and parcel of a broader critique of the analytical tradition.[108] 'Just now', Pollock wrote to Holmes in 1894, 'I am involved in a course of lectures on "Jurisprudence"' —lectures which would eventually comprise part of Pollock's *A First Book of*

with the names of Hobbes and Austin. . . . It may conveniently be called the imperative theory of law and sovereignty. . . . It is still much canvassed in England, though scarcely anywhere else; but there is at least general agreement that its exclusion of historical considerations from the province of jurisprudence led it into the radical fallacy of regarding all systems of law as being typified by Western European monarchical states'); and Andreas B. Schwarz, 'John Austin and the German Jurisprudence of His Time' (1934–35) 1 *Politica* 178–99 at 187–9; although cf. Stephen, above n.88, 482 ('Mr Maine does not recognise the necessity of analysis as expressly as Mr Austin recognises the necessity of history'); and Wilfrid Rumble, 'John Austin and His Nineteenth Century Critics: The Case of Henry Sumner Maine' (1988) 39 *N. Ire. Leg. Q.* 119–49, who, while noting the Maineian critique of Austinian ahistoricism, argues that Maine and Austin turn out to be agreed on many legal and political issues.

[101] [Sir Frederick Pollock], 'Sir Henry Maine as a Jurist' (July 1893) 178 *Edinburgh Rev.* 100–21 at 120.

[102] Frederick Pollock, 'Sir Henry Maine and His Work' (Feb. 1889) 55 *Contemporary Rev.* 265–76 at 271.

[103] *IHSP* 111; and see also *ECL* 4.

[104] *ECL* 119–20; *OLOD* 35; *PHL* i. 94; *EIL* 158 n.2.

[105] Frederick Pollock, 'Law and Command' (1872) n.s. 1 *Law Magazine & Rev.* 189–205. Pollock would later declare the tone of this article 'immature', though he never departed from its arguments: see (1895) 11 *LQR* 105.

[106] See Pollock, 'Law and Command', above n.105, 192–5; and cf. Henry Sumner Maine, *Village-Communities in the East and West. Six Lectures Delivered at Oxford* (London: Murray, 1871), 29–62, 101–28.

[107] Pollock, 'Law and Command', above n.105, 196.

[108] See, e.g., Pollock, ibid. 204 (concluding from his critique of Austin that 'the analytical jurists have not succeeded in giving us a sufficient or final conception of the nature of law'); *OLOD* 11, 98; *EJE* ix–x. The distaste was shared by, among others, Bryce: see his *Studies in History and Jurisprudence*, above n.100, ii. 96 ('This besetting sin of those who frame logical classifications upon the basis of abstract notions has led the so-called Analytic School of jurists sometimes to ignore the most material facts').

Jurisprudence—'in which I am deliberately burning the gods of the so-called English school.'[109] Although Pollock distanced himself from this school, however, he was very much inspired by Hobbes and an ambivalent admirer of Bentham, whom he considered to have pioneered the analytical approach.[110] The fact is that he reserved for Austin an especial vehemence; indeed, leaving aside the occasional begrudging compliment,[111] Pollock could rarely resist denigrating him. 'I love him not', he wrote to Holmes; in print, he was willing to declare 'Austin's manner . . . so repulsive . . . that it is hard to be quite just to his matter.'[112] When, in April 1893, a commentator in the *Juridical Review* concluded that there is a need for more careful study of Austinian jurisprudence, Pollock's response was perfect in its curtness: '[i]t appears to us that what we have to do at present, if we are to have any adequate theory of law, is to forget it as soon as possible.'[113] 'Last night I greatly missed you at the Law Club,' he wrote to Bryce two years later, 'for Anson read a paper which amounted to a direct challenge to me to say what I really thought of Austin; and so I did—to

[109] Pollock to Holmes, 11 May 1894, in *PHL* i. 51–2.

[110] See Pollock, 'Law and Command', above n.105, 198 n* ('Hobbes' view as to the nature of law, though very near to that of Bentham and Austin, is in truth to be distinguished from it. For the sovereign power, as conceived by Hobbes, is far more than a political superior'); *FBJ* vii ('[T]he philosophy of the English or "analytical" school is not mine; nevertheless I have learned much from Hobbes. . . . It may be that I love Hobbes a little too well to be perfectly just to his successors, who, to my thinking, have often got more praise than they deserved for repeating Hobbes's ideas in clumsier and really less exact words'). Pollock held the political philosophy of Jean Bodin in similarly high regard: see, e.g., *FBJ* 248–9; *IHSP* 53–6; 'Sovereignty in English Law' (1894) 8 *Harvard L. Rev* 243–51 at 244–5. Peculiarly, he was able to write of Bentham that his work displays 'trenchant clearness' (*OLOD* 23), yet also that '[n]o man ever laboured more assiduously . . . to make the outward form of his thoughts repulsive or ridiculous to the public' (*IHSP* 102). More often than not, his assessments of Bentham tend towards the positive. Although Bentham, like other English utilitarians, showed himself to be ignorant of history (*ECL* 128), he modernized English jurisprudence and pioneered the analytical form (*OLOD* 29, 26). 'Bentham has,' Pollock believed, 'a decided and confident theory as to the purpose for which governments exist' and is almost entirely to be credited for '[t]he change which has come over the spirit and methods of law-making in the last few generations' (*IHSP* 106, 108). In a similar vein, see F. Pollock, review of M. Guyau, *La Morale anglaise contemporaine* (1880) 5 *Mind* 280–8 at 281 ('Guyau . . . seems to me to underrate considerably the importance of the legal and political aspects of Bentham's system. [He] probably does not know the extent of Bentham's influence in England, not only on the scientific study of law but on the actual course of law reform and the general habit of modern legislation'); also Frederick Pollock to Henry Sidgwick, 14 November 1898, in Pollock correspondence (Wren), Add. MS c. 95, 39(1–2) ('What is [Austin] supposed to have added to Bentham's Fragment on Government, or how to have improved on it? My opinion is that Austin's departures from Bentham are for the worse in both matter and form. . . . What I do think Austin did, for what it may be worth, was to formulate the conception of a pure or a historical science of positive law').

[111] Which, compiled, appear to amount to the observation that Austin was 'an acute dialectician' who 'did useful work in his own country and generation'. *EIL* 158 n.2; *IHSP* 110. Elsewhere, he observes that the dialectic, while acute, was 'extremely narrow and ill-informed'. F[rederick] P[ollock], review of H. J. Laski, *The Foundations of Sovereignty* (1922) 38 *LQR* 242–3 at 242. In a similar vein, see also *PCLE(3)* ix-x.

[112] Pollock to Holmes, 20 September 1919, in *PHL* ii. 26; *IHSP* 109 n.2.

[113] (1893) 9 *LQR* 200; and cf. M. J. Farrelly, 'The New Italian School of Private International Law' (1893) 5 *Juridical Rev.* 105–24, 197–211 at 122–4.

wit, that when a man goes about to make a philosophy of law not knowing any law and being neither unable nor unwilling to understand any philosophy, the result is naturally pretty bad.'[114]

This was not simply a case of character assassination. With Austin, legal science took what Pollock considered to be a wrong turn. To understand how this occurred, he claimed, we must first of all revisit Hobbes. In essence, Hobbes laid down two principles: 'the principle of sovereignty' and 'the theory of the origin of civil society in contract'.[115] Hobbes's mistake was to try too hard 'to fortify the doctrine of sovereignty and to leave no excuse for disputing the authority of the State', one consequence of which is that he provided an elaborate account of the construction of the State by reference to an imaginary original covenant between its members.[116] In fact, Pollock argues, Hobbes had no need to employ his imagination thus: firm support for contractarian political thought could be traced back to Ancient Greece via the Reformation.[117] 'Hobbes . . . supported a plain and sound doctrine by needless and untenable fiction, and for the purpose of deducing consequences from it which it would not bear.'[118] The correct way for political philosophy to proceed after Hobbes was to refine the doctrine of sovereignty, to learn from Hobbes's mistakes. Austin, however, reinforced Hobbes's mistakes: whereas he ought to have made 'the doctrine of sovereignty the starting-point of fresh criticism and construction,' he continued with Hobbes's wrongheaded endeavour 'to swallow up policy, and to a considerable extent even morality, in positive law.'[119] In short, he accentuated 'the wrong part of Hobbes's work'.[120]

After Austin, Pollock believed, English legal science continued to proceed down the wrong path. Principally to blame for this state of affairs was Thomas Erskine Holland. Pollock admired Holland's jurisprudence much more than he did Austin's, not least because Holland rendered so many of Austin's arguments comprehensible.[121] Ultimately, however, Holland could be seen to belong to a jurisprudential tradition to which Pollock professed considerable aversion. Occasionally, Holland seemed to recognize the right direction—to appreciate, that is, that a satisfactory theory of sovereignty must embrace the history and comparison of legal phenomena—but he never reoriented accordingly.[122] Pollock would have to do the work for himself. Both 'the historical and the analytical manner of considering legal phenomena . . . are in truth useful

[114] Frederick Pollock to James Bryce, 3 March 1895, in Bryce papers, MSS. Bryce 120, ff.44–5. The letter continues: '[a] lively discussion ensued, in which I thought the only words that showed any adequate grasp of the subject as a whole were Raleigh's. Those who are in the gall of so-called "analysis" were in a majority. Dicey, rather to my surprise, is still shocked when you say that Austin was no lawyer. Holland did not seem to mind.' Ibid. (Raleigh = Sir Thomas Raleigh, Reader in English Law at Oxford, 1884–96.)

[115] *IHSP* 59. [116] *IHSP* 59–60. [117] See *IHSP* 60, 30–1.

[118] *IHSP* 60. [119] *IHSP* 67–8. [120] *IHSP* 67. See also (1915) 31 *LQR* 375.

[121] See, e.g., *OLOD* 98; *FBJ* 75, 107; *ECL* 13; *EJE* 1–2.

[122] See *EJE* 3–6.

and necessary,' he observed in 1882, 'and either of them alone is imperfect.'[123] 'There is a want of effectual contact and influence' between the two approaches, he remarked in the same year, and so '[o]ur most useful ambition . . . will be to supply this want'. '[I]t will be my endeavour,' he declared, 'to work in this direction.'[124]

By shifting our attention away from Spinoza and towards Austinian legal science, we have acquired our first proper glimpse of Pollock's own jurisprudential project. Pollock wanted to discredit what he considered the least appealing elements of the analytical tradition—Austin's contributions to it, in essence—and integrate what remained with comparative jurisprudence. This observation, however, raises at least three other questions. How was Pollock inspired by the analytical tradition? Did he successfully connect—and, if so, how did he connect—the analytical and comparative perspectives? And, most importantly of all for our purposes, in what way could Pollock's effort to forge this connection be said to amount to a legal science? Addressing these last two questions will, in due course, move us towards a broader line of inquiry concerning what might tersely be described as the limitations of comparative legal science as a jurisprudential project. But that line of inquiry is still some way in the distance. First of all, we need to consider the questions that we have just posed.

a. The utility of analysis

According to Pollock, 'jurisprudence or legal science'—he treated the terms as synonymous—is best understood as 'a branch of politics'.[125] Jurisprudence itself, furthermore, splits into a variety of branches—historical and comparative jurisprudence, analytical jurisprudence, ethical jurisprudence (or natural law), and international jurisprudence, among others.[126] Pollock had something to say about all the branches that he identified, although what he had to say was not always enlightening. On the matter of what he called international jurisprudence, for example, he seemed thoroughly muddled. 'International Law . . . is a true branch of jurisprudence,' he proclaimed in 1882, 'notwithstanding all that may be said about its want of sovereign power and a tribunal. You may define it as "positive international morality" not having the nature of law, but if you do the facts are against you.'[127] Some sixteen years later, by contrast, he was of the opinion that the rules of international law 'have not fully acquired the character of law, but are on the way to become law'.[128]

123 *EJE* viii. 124 *OLOD* 35–6.

125 *OLOD* 4; *EJE* 27; *IHSP* 32. 126 See *OLOD* 19–20.

127 Frederick Pollock, 'The Methods of Jurisprudence' (1882) 8 *Law Magazine & Rev. (4th Ser.)* 25–53 at 38.

128 *FBJ* 13; also Frederick Pollock, 'The Annual Digest of International Law Cases' (1930) 46 *LQR* 46–8 at 47–8; and cf. D. H. N. Johnson, 'The English Tradition in International Law' (1962) 11 *Inter-*

Whereas Pollock's position on the question of whether international law is really law was unsettled, his estimation of natural law, although on first impression equally ambiguous, was subtler and might profitably be explored before we move on to the jurisprudential themes which occupied him at greater length. Pollock was of the view that natural law—that body of 'rules of conduct which the light of reason . . . can discover as generally applicable to man as a rational being'[129]—has suffered at the hands of English lawyers. '[S]ome English writers, half a century behind their time, still maintain the obsolete Benthamite aversion to its name.'[130] Yet although 'Bentham and his followers suppose[d] . . . that the Law of Nature meant nothing but individual fancy', it could be argued, Pollock believed, that 'the doctrine of the English utilitarians' was 'the most dogmatic of all systems of natural law'.[131] However systematized, natural law philosophy met with Pollock's reserve: '[s]o far as my acquaintance with it goes, it appears to me to lump together in a cumbrous and over-ambitious manner a good many topics in the theory of government, politics, and legislation, which are better treated separately.'[132] Although he was wary of natural law devised as a distinctive philosophy, however, he did not renounce natural law as a phenomenon: about ethical jurisprudence he was cool, about the law of nature he was enthusiastic. 'The Common Law . . . has largely enriched and is still enriching itself by associating the Law of Nature with its authority'; indeed, 'in the course of the seventeenth century . . . the ideas of reasonableness and natural justice, which . . . belong to the Law of Nature[,] . . . became the vehicle for spreading the distinctive principles and methods of the Common Law in lands where it did not and could not formally claim any jurisdiction.'[133] Note the link that Pollock makes between the law of nature and reasonableness. In so far as he is attracted to natural law, it is because he regards the law of nature and reason—that most precious of entities, in Pollock's eyes—as essentially synonymous.[134] Common law notions of 'reason' and 'reasonable'—as St German had discerned in the sixteenth century—are simply 'ideas which the civilian or canonist puts under the head of "Law of Nature." Thus natural law may fairly

national and Comparative Law Quarterly 416–45 at 421–2, where Pollock's contribution to the jurisprudence of international law is commended—though it is also noted that his critique of 'Austin's contention that, because they did not stem from a sovereign authority, the rules of international law were not legal rules at all' was 'exaggerated' (ibid. 422).

[129] *EIL* 86. [130] *ECL* 130.

[131] *EIL*, 62, 23; cf. also 47 ('If Bentham had known what the Law of Nature was really like in the Middle Ages, he would have had to speak of it with more respect') and 65 ('If any one ever did lay down a dogmatic and immutable code of *Naturrecht*, it was not the schoolmen, but the utilitarians'); and F. Pollock, 'Happiness or Welfare' (1877) 2 *Mind* 269–72 (on Sidgwick). Unsurprisingly, Pollock considered Austin to be among those to blame for this dogmatism: see (1894) 10 *LQR* 100. In describing the Benthamite jurisprudential tradition as a natural law tradition, John Dewey pointed out, Pollock 'fails to note that the ethical criterion of utilitarianism is prospective, future, based on foreseeable consequences, while that of other systems of natural law had been found in some antecedent state of affairs'. John Dewey, review of *EIL* (1923) 23 *Columbia L. Rev.* 316–18 at 317–18.

[132] *OLOD* 15. [133] *ECL* 132; *EIL* 62–3. [134] See *EIL* 31, 78.

claim, in principle though not by name, the reasonable man of English and American law.'[135]

While Pollock paid tribute to natural law, to have described himself as a natural lawyer would have meant nailing his colours to a particular jurisprudential mast; and for someone inherently suspicious of grand visions and organizing theories, this was probably too bold a proclamation to make.[136] To commit to a definite perspective—to declare oneself a particular type of '*ist*' or subscriber to some form of '*ism*'—simply was not Pollock's style. His writings are often distinctly pragmatic, praising, for example, 'practical instinct' as 'the spirit of the law and the true lawyer' and emphasizing experience as preferable to idealism and logic;[137] as we have seen already, furthermore, he admired the writings of pragmatist philosophers such as O. W. Holmes, Jr., William James, and F. C. S. Schiller. Yet, as we have also seen already, he would have baulked at being labelled a pragmatist. Identification with credos was, for Pollock, unsubtle and intellectually suspicious.

This observation might be used to explain his refusal to commit to a specific jurisprudential perspective. But in fact this refusal warrants a deeper explanation. Pollock, whether because of a lack of confidence or because he genuinely believed that there is something to be salvaged from even the most wayward theories, seemed unwilling to reject any jurisprudential perspective for good. Every view, it seems, has, in his eyes, the potential to bear fruit. Thus it is that he set himself up in what, at first glance, seems to be the unlikely role of conciliator in the jurisprudence family. Of course there are feuds and factions, he appreciated, but no member of the family is worthless. Indeed, 'the several methods of jurisprudence . . . need not and should not be positively hostile to one another'—quite a claim from a man who made a hobby out of vilifying Austin—since 'none of them can really subsist alone'.[138] Pollock was keen to build bridges and urge breadth of perspective: so far as the advancement of jurisprudence was concerned, he maintained, only good could come of such an initiative. Yet the quest for a catholic approach seemed, with Pollock, to lead not to greater jurisprudential ambition or insight but to a dilution of ideas. Austin may have been too unsubtle for Pollock, but Pollock's own effort to supply what Austin had missed resulted—and here we are simply anticipating a line of critique which will unfold in due course—in a jurisprudential project marred by excessive guardedness, inordinate embellishment, a lack of critical focus, and a tendency to fall between two stools.

[135] *EIL* 69, and see also 17, 57–8.

[136] A year before Pollock died, his wavering attitude towards natural law doctrine in particular was criticized by Radbruch in the *LQR*: see Gustav Radbruch, 'Anglo-American Jurisprudence through Continental Eyes' (1936) 52 *LQR* 530–45 at 540. Radbruch's article pulls few punches—its opening line ('The development of English legal philosophy shows the insular character of England') rather sets the tone—and one wonders whether the *LQR* (ten years into A. L. Goodhart's editorship) would have published the piece were it not that by 1936 Radbruch himself (d. 1949) was one of the elder statesmen of jurisprudence.

[137] *FBJ* 71; *GCL* 113; also *EIL* 258–9; *IHSP* viii.

[138] Pollock, above n.127, 44, 40.

Analytical and comparative jurisprudence—the two stools in question—Pollock categorized together as perspectives on positive law.[139] While he preferred comparative jurisprudence, he recognized the utility of and was often willing to adopt an analytical perspective—'[w]e analyse', after all, 'to supply our want of clear terms and correct instinct.'[140] Certainly one chapter of *A First Book of Jurisprudence* is devoted to showing how the closely related notions of control, enjoyment, ownership, possession, and title are analytically distinct;[141] indeed, even though Pollock cautions against turning jurisprudence into taxonomy,[142] he concedes that his approach to these notions is 'analytical'.[143] Yet his taste for analytical distinction is revealed not, in the main, in his general writings on jurisprudence but in his work on possession. In Parts I and II of *An Essay on Possession in the Common Law*, Pollock set out to clarify the legal concept of possession through analysis.[144] Possession is not only distinguishable from cognate concepts (such as enjoyment, control, and title), but in itself permits of distinctions: for example, it is possible to differentiate a right *to* possession and a right *of* possession.[145] Behind the concept of possession, furthermore, there lie various distinct 'remedies for wrongs to possessory rights' (trespass, conversion, trover, larceny).[146] Most importantly of all, there is an analytical exercise to be undertaken for the purpose of distinguishing possession as a matter of fact and possession as a matter of right.[147] And just as the concept of possession demands analysis if it is to be grasped, so too does the notion of relinquishing possession, which can be effected in a variety of distinct ways (such as delivery and abandonment).[148]

To Pollock's eyes, then, there is something to be gained from analysing possession in a manner akin to that which a philosopher might adopt. 'Jurisprudence,' generally speaking, 'must partake of the nature of Philosophy.'[149] But we must be careful not to overvalue philosophy. It is all fine and good, for example, to produce fine-grained philosophical analyses of the concept of possession, but 'the practising lawyer's instinct' will often serve us as well as, if not better than, any philosophy.[150] The insightful practitioner is, as compared with

[139] Ibid. 40; and cf. Wesley Newcomb Hohfeld, 'A Vital School of Jurisprudence and Law: Have American Universities Awakened to the Enlarged Opportunities and Responsibilities of the Present Day?' [1914] *Association of American Law Schools Proceedings* 76–139 at 82–3. While Hohfeld categorizes analytical and comparative jurisprudence in a fashion similar to how Pollock categorizes them, in Hohfeld's essay there is a difference in emphasis: certainly he has polite observations to make about what he terms 'comparative, or eclectic, jurisprudence' (see ibid. 86–96), but about analytical jurisprudence he is distinctly more enthusiastic. '[T]o equip our future professional teachers of law there must be comprehensive courses in analytical jurisprudence', he contends, since 'nothing conduces more to the perception of fundamental identities in legal problems' (ibid. 98, 97).

[140] Pollock, above n.127, 30. [141] See *FBJ* 160–78.

[142] See *FBJ* 80, 89. [143] *FBJ* 176.

[144] The book is the composite, but not the joint, work of Pollock and R. S. Wright: see *PCL* v. Wright wrote Part III of the book. On Pollock's and Wright's collaboration over this project, see C. H. S. Fifoot, *Judge and Jurist in the Reign of Victoria* (London: Stevens and Sons, 1959), 91–2.

[145] *PCL* 2. [146] *PCL* 5. [147] See *PCL* 10–20.

[148] See *PCL* 43–4. [149] *OLOD* 63. [150] *PCL* 6.

the philosopher, less likely to lose sight of legal objectives when pursuing and formulating analytical distinctions; and it is important, Pollock insisted, to keep in mind that the primary purpose of the exercise is to make sense of the law rather than to advance the philosophy of possession. Law, in short, must come first: 'the comparative worth of the philosophical or semi-philosophical theories of Possession cannot be weighed to much purpose until one has mastered in some detail the actual contents of the law.'[151] 'General Jurisprudence' may well be analytical jurisprudence: the analytical impulse might lead us to 'attempt a general definition of such ideas as Duty, Intent, Negligence, Ownership, Possession, or (boldest ambition of all) of Law itself.'[152] But General Jurisprudence need not be—indeed, preferably, will not be—exclusively analytical. If our jurisprudential inquiries are to be firmly grounded in, and to provide valuable insights into the composition and functioning of, real legal systems, we would do well to treat the techniques of the analytical philosopher only as supplemental to some broader perspective.

b. The centrality of comparison

While analytical perspectives must not be ignored, Pollock believed, equally they must never be regarded as anything other than ancillary to the methods of historical and comparative jurisprudence. History and comparison, although distinguishable as forms of jurisprudential inquiry, in fact go hand-in-hand: the primary lesson to be learned from Maine's *Ancient Law* was that 'intimate alliance between comparative and historical research is not only natural and desirable, but necessary for either branch of work being efficiently done.'[153] Until 1869, when Maine was appointed as the first Professor of Historical and Comparative Jurisprudence at Oxford, the comparative jurisprudential project had 'suffered . . . a somewhat cold and unintelligent reception from . . . the surviving high priests of a moribund utilitarian orthodoxy'.[154] In his Oxford farewell lecture, delivered in January 1903, Pollock expressed confidence that the project had weathered the storm and was flourishing. The twentieth century, it seemed, would belong to the comparatists. '[O]ur master Maine', Pollock concluded, 'taught us to understand what it is that we inherit.'

The work of the present generation in the field of comparative jurisprudence is mostly work of detail. . . . But there is no rest for knowledge, and for our children, if not for

[151] *PCL* 4. One commentator, having apparently consulted only a handful of Pollock's writings (and apparently having not consulted *PCL*), reaches the simplistic conclusion that Pollock's analysis of possession 'confirm[s] his belief in natural law'. Robert G. Bone, 'Normative Theory and Legal Doctrine in American Nuisance Law: 1850–1920' (1986) 59 *Southern California L. Rev.* 1101–226 at 1120.

[152] Pollock, above n.127, 33.

[153] *EIL* 4. For Pollock's acknowledgement that the historical and the comparative exercises can be treated as jurisprudentially distinct, see above n.127, 33.

[154] *EIL* 25.

us, there will again be a time of large adventure. They will go forth to conquests, perhaps armed with the weapons we have forged for them, perhaps with others of such fashion and power as we cannot even guess. . . . [T]he victory will be to truth; neither will our sons forget in their triumphs that we wrought, as best we might, to prepare the way for them.[155]

In his addresses, Pollock never tired of concluding with a crescendo. So wedded was he to this style, indeed, that there is always good reason to assume that the last few pages of a Pollock lecture will be strong on hyperbole, and will therefore play well into the hands of the interpreter who wishes to present Pollock as a jurist prone to exaggeration and averse to subtlety. The passage quoted above—for all that it conforms to the style just described, and therefore ought to be treated with caution—contains two noteworthy observations. First, it points to the future: we can be confident, according to Pollock, that comparative jurisprudents of the twentieth century will do great work. Secondly, the passage intimates about past achievements. Maine's heirs—Pollock being the most conspicuous of this group—had nurtured something powerful upon which later generations could build. Of course, Maine's own comparative-jurisprudential legacy is well known.[156] But what did Pollock bequeath? After twenty years as the second Professor of Historical and Comparative Jurisprudence at Oxford, had he produced anything to compare with *Ancient Law*, or with Maine's lectures on village communities and on the early history of institutions, or even—to switch from Maine to Maine's real jurisprudential successor—with Vinogradoff's work on villeinage in early medieval England?

The momentum of the previous paragraph clearly invites a negative answer. In fact, this is the only conceivable answer. Santayana—one of the few philosopher-contemporaries, we noted earlier, for whom Pollock expressed any admiration—observed that comparison is often the tactic of those who cannot reach the heart of a matter.[157] To read Pollock on comparative jurisprudence is to see this observation come alive. While 'comparative study discloses a certain amount of groundwork and typical conceptions which are common to all legal systems,' it must be remembered that '[s]imilarity of laws . . . is only a guide to inquiry; it is not conclusive evidence of dependence or of a common origin.'[158] If comparative investigation is to prove valuable, then, it

[155] *EIL* 29. The lecture ('The History of Comparative Jurisprudence') was first published at (1903) 5 *Jnl. of the Society of Comparative Legislation* 74–89 (the quoted passage appears at 88–9).

[156] For a good summary of just what Maine bequeathed, see Collini, Winch, and Burrow, above n.30, 210–11, 252–3.

[157] 'Comparison is the expedient of those who cannot reach the heart of the things compared'. George Santayana, *Character and Opinion in the United States: With Reminiscences of William James and Josiah Royce and Academic Life in America* (New York: Scribner, 1924 [1920]), 166. Cf. F. W. Maitland, 'Why the History of English Law is not Written' (1888), in *The Collected Papers of Frederic William Maitland*, 3 vols., ed. H. A. L. Fisher (Cambridge: Cambridge UP, 1911), i. 480–97 at 489.

[158] *OLOD* 10, 164; cf. also *GCL* 116–17; and Sir William Holdsworth, *Some Makers of English Law: The Tagore Lectures, 1937–38* (Cambridge: Cambridge UP, 1938), 284.

must be undertaken with sensitivity and circumspection. Pollock approaches the matter of comparison with such delicacy, however, that the investigative part of the project never gets off the ground. Most of what he has to say about the project can be found in the two lectures which mark the beginning and the end of his professorship at Oxford. His inaugural lecture of 1883 contains numerous assertions concerning how the English can learn much from comparing their legal arrangements with those to be found in the United States, India, Scotland, in Roman law, and even with those of the minor jurisdictions of the British Isles ('[h]ere are opportunities of fruitful comparison . . . going to waste at our own door').[159] Yet only once in this lecture—when demonstrating the relevance of the Roman use of oaths to the treatment of promises in English contract law[160]—does Pollock try to show how comparative inquiry can prove jurisprudentially valuable. For the most part, his discussion takes the hortatory form: not 'this is what comparative inquiry achieves', but 'just imagine what comparative inquiry might achieve were we to engage in it'. As to the question of whether the comparative approach really will deliver the goods, Pollock's answer is basically that we should take his, or better still take Maine's, word for it.[161]

Leaving aside Pollock's dreams about the revenue that might be raised from comparative inquiries, his general paean to historical and comparative jurisprudence becomes yet more disappointing when he purports to promote some distinct methodology. For Pollock, there are such distinct entities as '[t]he historical method' and 'the modern comparative method'.[162] John Dewey professed to uncertainty over what Pollock meant when he referred to these methods, adding that Pollock's understanding of them, in so far as it could be ascertained, seemed incorrect.[163] In fact, Pollock is unequivocal about what 'the historical method' in particular should be taken to mean: 'the historical method is nothing else than the doctrine of evolution applied to human soci-

[159] *OLOD* 50. Cf. also Sir Frederick Pollock, 'The Judicial Committee of the Privy Council' (1905) 4 *Canadian L. Rev.* 508–13 at 510. For the various suggestions for comparison, see *OLOD* 47–58.

[160] *OLOD* 58–9. For his treatment of oaths, sureties, and pledges, see generally Frederick Pollock, 'Archaism in Modern Law' (1893) 9 *LQR* 271–84.

[161] *OLOD* 62 ('To pursue this subject . . . would take us I know not where, certainly as far as India. Therefore I shall be your suitor that these bare indications may suffice, and I will make an end by claiming as good company and alliance for the studies assigned to this Chair as at the beginning I did for my own person').

[162] *OLOD* 41; *EIL* 23 n.1. See also M. H. Hoeflich, *Roman Law and Civil Law and the Development of Anglo-American Jurisprudence in the Nineteenth Century* (Athens, Ga.: University of Georgia Press, 1997), 82–3.

[163] Dewey, above n.131, 317 ('Pollock appears to share the notion that the historical method, and the possibility of employing the comparative method in law, implies the notion of stages of evolution through which societies pass, some of course being more advanced than others. I think the tendency of present competent specialists is to hold that the doctrine of parallel stages is but a refined survival of the older tendency, rejected of course by Pollock, to draw comparisons without reference to the past histories of the things compared'). See also G. Valbert, 'Sir Frederick Pollock et sa théorie de la persécution' (1893) 118 *Revue des deux mondes* 694–705, who discerns a tension between Pollock as a proponent of historical-evolutionary method and Pollock '[comme] un conservateur libéral' (ibid. 694–5). Cf. *EJE* 144–75.

eties and institutions.'[164] Certainly as applied to Maine, this depiction of the method has some resonance to it: it was Maine, after all, who purported to discern in 'progressive societies' a 'gradual dissolution of family dependency', and, in the place of such dependency, 'the growth of obligation'—the evolution 'from status to contract', to use the classic Maineian epigram.[165] Pollock had a problem not with summarizing method, however, but with developing it. 'I have used by preference the historical method,' he declared in the Preface to his *Essays in Jurisprudence and Ethics*.[166] Neither throughout that work nor any of his other works does it become clear just how he used this method. The only thing that is ever clear is that he was besotted by it. 'The historical method', he observed in 1883,

> is the newest and most powerful instrument, not only of the moral and political sciences, but of a great part of the natural sciences, and its range is daily increasing. . . . That such a method should not be fruitful when applied to jurisprudence . . . would be a thing contrary to all rational expectation. . . . [A]lready we have ample fruit, and ample promise of more. Enough, however, of these things in general. If any man is wilfully blind, let us leave him to his blindness. It will not be convenient for us, I think, to consider, not what may be done by historical and comparative jurisprudence in the abstract, but what we as Englishmen, here and now, have special opportunities for making of it. . . .[167]

Note the absence of specifics from this passage. Only the 'wilfully blind', it seems, would doubt its correctness, so why bother to elaborate? Pollock's sole concession to elaboration is to sandwich the passage between references to some of those he credited with advancing the historical method—Savigny, Burke, Holmes, Stubbs, Fitzjames Stephen, and the pioneer of the method, Montesquieu.[168] The nature and details of what unites these men are never made clear. Perhaps this is only to be expected, for Pollock insisted that his goal was not to assess what had been achieved in the name of the historical method but to consider the opportunities for putting it to still greater use. But the point to be stressed is that Pollock himself never put the method to greater use.

The fundamental problem with 'that great vogue for the Comparative and Historical Method', Collini, Winch, and Burrow have observed, was that 'there was no single method, nor were the various fashions loosely grouped

[164] *OLOD* 41. For what is essentially an elaboration of this statement—an elaboration of the type that Pollock signally did not provide—see Ernest Barker, *Political Thought in England from Herbert Spencer to the Present Day* (London: Williams and Norgate, 1915), 161–83.

[165] Maine, above n.97, 168–70. It would be wrong, however, to assume that Maine's *Ancient Law* (1861) was specifically indebted to Darwin's *Origin of Species* (1859). The manuscript for the former text appears to have been completed before the publication of the latter: see Stein, above n.96, 88 n.24, 100.

[166] *EJE* viii. [167] *OLOD* 41–3. [168] See *OLOD* 41–6.

under this label always as novel as their proponents liked to claim; but what helped to generate an exaggerated sense of a coherent approach was a common contrast with the method of deductive Utilitarianism, supposedly, though never actually, dominant in the previous generation.'[169] Pollock corroborates this assessment, keen as he was both to exalt 'the method' and to emphasize its superiority to the jurisprudential tradition of Bentham and Austin. Forty years after the occasion of his inaugural lecture, he was, after a fashion, still toeing the same line: 'the application of methodical historical criticism (from whatever school derived) to commonly accepted statements has exploded one baseless legend after another to the confusion of partisan writers and the relief of honest students.'[170] By this point in time, however, the jurisprudential landscape had changed. '[N]ot without cause', Pollock had claimed in 1918, the principal lessons of Maine's historical-jurisprudential project were being approached with suspicion.[171] Although Maine's achievements as a jurist were beyond doubt, this did not necessarily make him a good historian; indeed, as early as 1901, Maitland had cautioned Pollock about treating him as such.[172] Moreover, the inheritors of Maine's legacy could no longer be optimistic about the twentieth century belonging to them. 'The stubborn remnant' of the historical and comparative school, Pollock remarked gloomily at the end of the First World War, 'may console itself, if it can, with the reflection that the newer teaching now in vogue may prove not much more adequate to cope with the problems of a world which, for better or worse, will be transformed when it stands clear of the present confusion.'[173] Five years after the War, however, Pollock, although still romanticizing the glorious yesteryears of comparative jurisprudence, seemed more eager to discredit than to commend the revival of the historical method. When Roscoe Pound, in his *Interpretations of Legal History*, emphasized with notable passion the achievements of 'the historical school'—its having 'laid the foundations of a sound comparative legal history in place of the brilliant superficiality of the eighteenth-century universal legal history', 'its unification of jurisprudence and politics', its having 'led to the idea of the legal order as part of a wider social control from which it cannot be dissociated', its having 'prepared the way for the functional attitude of the legal science of today'[174]—Pollock produced a snooty, quibbling response.

[169] Collini, Winch, and Burrow, above n.30, 145.

[170] Frederick Pollock, 'A Plea for Historical Interpretation' (1923) 39 *LQR* 163–9 at 168.

[171] Sir Frederick Pollock, 'Introduction', in *The Progress of Continental Law in the Nineteenth Century*, J. H. Wigmore et al. (London: Murray, 1918), xli–xlix at xlix.

[172] 'You spoke of Maine. Well, I always talk of him with reluctance, for on the few occasions on which I sought to verify his statements of fact I came to the conclusion that he trusted too much to a memory that played him tricks and rarely looked back at a book that he had once read.' F. W. Maitland to Frederick Pollock, 21 January 1901, in *The Letters of Frederic William Maitland*, ed. C. H. S. Fifoot (London: Selden Society, 1965), 222. For Maitland's general reservations about historical jurisprudence, see C. H. S. Fifoot, *Frederic William Maitland: A Life* (Cambridge, Mass.: Harvard UP, 1971), 143.

[173] Pollock, above n.171, xlix.

[174] Roscoe Pound, *Interpretations of Legal History* (Cambridge: Cambridge UP, 1923), 68.

My own memory, fallible certainly, but founded on half a century's observation, is that any domination of the historical school in English law covered not the whole of the nineteenth century but only the last quarter of it or at most the last thirty years. . . . So, when I am confronted with Professor Pound's unqualified assertion that a historical-metaphysical doctrine 'was dominant in the science of law throughout the century,' I feel tempted to ask which one of us is standing on his head.[175]

Never mind that Pound was, as it were, on Pollock's side, eager to accord the historical school its place in the jurisprudential pantheon. Rather than credit Pound for his effort, it was better to berate him for 'not looking in quite the right places'[176] and giving the school more prominence than it deserved. Shooting at allies would, in due course, become a part of Pound's *modus operandi* also, although that story is not relevant here.[177] But what is relevant is the question of why Pollock should have reacted thus. Although most of his criticisms of Pound concern footling points, the overall tenor of his attack seems to be that he disliked Pound's insistence—and it is certainly correct to claim that Pound did insist[178]—on ascribing method to the historical method. 'Professor Pound . . . saddles the historical school with excessive insistence . . . on the fulfilment of individual will or intention as a motive of legal decision.'[179] Methods, in Pollock's eyes, ought ultimately to be treated like all grand schemes and systems—with suspicion. The historical method should be valued not as a method, he appeared to believe, but as *bricolage*—as an exercise in rummaging through the past or through other legal systems to find new ways of exhibiting the genius of the common law.[180]

Pollock's claim that the analytical and comparative perspectives could survive symbiotically turns out to be hollow. The point is not that the two perspectives could never feed off one another. No doubt they could: even Austin devised a conceptual apparatus which allows for the historical evolution of law from custom through judicial legislation—a view more readily associated with the historical and comparative school than with analytical jurisprudence.[181] But Pollock himself, for all his talk about how the connection between the analytical and the comparative could bear fruit, never showed how that connection might be forged. In fact it is never clear with what, in Pollock's eyes, analytical jurisprudence would find itself connected.

This last observation points to an irony of sorts: while Pollock showed limited enthusiasm for the methods of analytical jurisprudence, it is at least clear where he uses them; for all his numerous erudite essays on legal history,

175 Pollock, above n.170, 164. 176 Ibid. 169.

177 See Roscoe Pound, 'The Call for a Realist Jurisprudence' (1931) 44 *Harvard L. Rev.* 697–711; and, for the story in detail, see N. E. H. Hull, *Roscoe Pound and Karl Llewellyn: Searching for an American Jurisprudence* (Chicago: University of Chicago Press, 1997).

178 See Pound, above n.174, 12–18. 179 Pollock, above n.170, 165. 180 See *GCL* 110–11.

181 See Michael Lobban, *The Common Law and English Jurisprudence 1760–1850* (Oxford: Clarendon Press, 1991), 227–34.

and for all his eagerness to refer to the rewards that might be had from comparing legal systems, he never explained the historical and comparative project by reference to methods. Methodologically speaking, we might say, he was more clearly identifiable as an analytical rather than as a comparative jurisprudent. Pollock, of course, would never have accepted this characterization. The historical and comparative project, as we have seen, was more to his liking. Yet he approached that project in a literalistic and decidedly limited fashion, establishing hardly anything more than that it is often worthwhile to look backwards and outwards and compare one's own legal arrangements with what one finds elsewhere.

c. The reliance on science

There is more to be said about comparative jurisprudence. Specifically, we need to provide the explanation promised by the title of this chapter, and to do this requires an inquiry into why English jurisprudence eschewed the comparative route. It is necessary, however, to postpone that task until section iii, since we have yet to address properly the issue of legal science. So far, in this section, we have tried to establish four basic points: that Austin had a vision of the science of jurisprudence; that Maine disliked that vision and set about devising an alternative; that this alternative made a positive impression on Pollock; and that, although duly impressed by the historical method, Pollock did not significantly contribute to its advancement. If Pollock was more or less inarticulate over matters of method, it surely follows that he would have nothing significant to say on the subject of legal science. Indeed, had not Maine said it all? As Pollock appreciated, Maine epitomized the late nineteenth-century trend of equating science with the theory of evolution. Since Pollock failed to make any methodological advance on Maine, can we not confidently anticipate that Pollock's notion of legal science will be identical to Maine's? While we might anticipate as much, it turns out that Pollock does not play by the script.

'The connection between jurisprudence and political theory', Ernest Barker wrote in 1915, 'is close and obvious. . . . [I]t was law which produced the radical doctrine of the Social Contract, and it is law, as interpreted by Maitland, which has of late years added new and radical ideas to the content of political theory.'[182] Although Barker would later question just how close this connection really was,[183] he was surely correct to posit it. For many Victorian intellectuals, Collini, Winch, and Burrow have observed,

> the language of the law constituted something of a *lingua franca*. . . . The study of the law, it hardly needs to be said, commanded a guaranteed audience both within and

[182] Barker, above n.164, 15. [183] See Collini, above n.32, 251–2.

without the universities, but the teaching of jurisprudence at Oxford and Cambridge was not yet the narrowly professional training it was soon to become; in this period it managed to accommodate the authors of several of the most widely cited works of political science, such as Maine, Bryce, Dicey and Pollock, as Professors of Law. There is an appropriateness in the fact that the standard introduction to the history of the science of politics should have been written by the man who succeeded Maine as Professor of Jurisprudence at Oxford . . . , who collaborated with Maitland on the classic *History of English Law*, and who became the first editor of *The Law Quarterly Review*.[184]

Of course, that collaboration with Maitland on *The History of English Law* was, as we saw in chapter 2, for the most part nominal. But the Introduction to the work, most of which Pollock claimed to have written, offers within its first page the following, intriguing assertion:

It has been usual for writers commencing the exposition of any particular system of law to undertake, to a greater or less extent, philosophical discussion of the nature of laws in general, and definition of the most general notions of jurisprudence. We purposely refrain from any such undertaking. The philosophical analysis and definition of law belongs, in our judgment, neither to the historical nor to the dogmatic science of law, but to the theoretical part of politics. . . . The matter of legal science is not an ideal result of ethical or political analysis; it is the actual result of facts of human nature and history.[185]

As Collini, Winch, and Burrow note, not only did Pollock belong to a generation of jurists that was uninhibited by disciplinary boundaries, but he personally seemed thoroughly confident about venturing into and expounding upon the history of political science. It was not that the barriers were there to be straddled; the barriers simply did not exist. While jurists might profitably comment on political science, however, it must not be assumed, Pollock insisted, that there is anything to be gained from a branch of political science taking control of legal science. Pollock, we have seen, was keen to refer to the various branches of jurisprudence as if they made up one big happy family. But analytical jurisprudence—this much being clear from the quotation just taken from *The History of English Law*—was a science not of law but of politics.[186] At this point, we find the barriers erected. In his more bullish moments, Pollock was even churlish about according analytical jurisprudence the title of jurisprudence: 'Austin's second, third, and fourth Lectures'—a significant chunk of *The Province of Jurisprudence Determined*—'are not jurisprudence at all,'

[184] Collini, Winch, and Burrow, above n.30, 359.
[185] *HEL* i. xciii. [186] In a similar vein, see *IHSP* 32.

he complained, 'but ethics out of place.'[187] The language of the law might well have constituted something of a *lingua franca*, but the language of legal science was a different matter. Whatever analytical jurists might have claimed, their project belonged to political rather than legal science. Dominion over legal science resided elsewhere.

Where, then, did it reside? Of course, comparative jurisprudence could stake a legitimate claim to scientific status—Pollock had no doubt that Maine and Vinogradoff were genuine legal scientists.[188] But he resisted identifying legal science exclusively with comparative jurisprudence.[189] When legal science is equated with one or another method, Pollock believed, the enterprise is easily corrupted by charlatans: 'I really do think there is less danger to legal science from the frank and shameless ignorance of the illiterate practitioner than from the sciolism and wild guesswork of the half-trained amateur. . . . What is more, the lay people may take those deluded adventurers for real explorers and discoverers.'[190] Even if a particular method is mastered, there is no guarantee that convincing legal science will follow—'faith in the science of law' is about more than 'mere intellectual craft'.[191] We saw in chapter 2 that Pollock linked science in general not with a belief in method or system but with the progress of civilization; if science is conceived thus, he claimed, no one form of juristic inquiry will be entitled to hold the title of legal science.[192] But in chapter 2 we deliberately avoided trying to identify Pollock's own conception of legal science. Did he, in fact, have a conception of legal science?

It seems odd that, in order to find anything akin to method in Pollock's jurisprudence, we should have to look not to what he had to say about the virtues of history and comparison, but to what he says specifically about the scientific study of law—and it ought to be noted immediately that while comparative jurisprudence may, in Pollock's eyes, be tantamount to the scientific study of law, it is not really what he has in mind when he refers to such study. Pollock did indeed have a conception of legal science—though to call it his own would be to distort its provenance. It was noted above that Holmes was among those whom Pollock associated with the historical method. The association, while easily overemphasized, was by no means inapt.[193] But when

[187] *OLOD* 17. Pollock did not always take this view of analytical jurisprudence: see, e.g., his discussion of Holland in *IHSP* 67; also *EJE* 27, 262.

[188] See Pollock, above n.102, 270 ('Maine was determined . . . that his science should speak the language of a scholar and a gentleman'). For Pollock on Vinogradoff see, e.g., *LL(3)* 21.

[189] See *EJE* 262–8. Others resisted similarly: see Collini, Winch, and Burrow, above n.30, 40–1.

[190] *EIL* 238; and cf. also *EJE* 6.

[191] *GCL* 1.

[192] See chapter 2, 61–2.

[193] For Holmes and the historical method, see J. W. Burrow, 'Holmes in His Intellectual Milieu', in *The Legacy of Oliver Wendell Holmes, Jr.*, ed. R. W. Gordon (Edinburgh: Edinburgh UP, 1992), 17–30 at 25–8. For an illustration of overemphasis in this context, see Stephen G. Utz, 'Maine's *Ancient Law* and Legal Theory' (1984) 16 *Connecticut L. Rev.* 821–52 at 844 ('Holmes's . . . essay, *The Path of the Law*, might almost have been ghostwritten by Maine'). Soon after Maine's death, Holmes offered an assessment of Maine's abilities as an historian which was not very different from that which Maitland was to offer in 1901: see above n.172; and cf. Holmes to Pollock, 4 March 1888, in *PHL* i. 31.

Pollock reviewed *The Common Law* in 1881, he wanted to emphasize how Holmes 'belong[ed] to an American school of legal criticism distinguishable from anything that has yet taken root [in England]'.[194] As is well known, in *The Common Law* Holmes contends that issues of civil and criminal liability must be determined by reference not to private or internal moral standards but to the shared or external standards of the community. 'The standards of the law are standards of general application. . . . The law considers, in other words, what would be blameworthy in the average man, the man of ordinary intelligence and prudence, and determines liability by that.'[195] Although Pollock, in his review of the book, purported to be not entirely convinced by Holmes's treatment of external standards as objective standards,[196] in his first ever letter to Holmes—some seven years earlier—he was already edging towards Holmes's position: 'I am glad you so clearly expose the fallacy of treating legal negligence as a state of the negligent's consciousness', Pollock wrote in 1874; 'the true theory is that all attempts to get a scientific measure are out of place and we can only seek a rough measure in "the average opinion of the community"—or such of the community as are accustomed to dealings of the kind in question.'[197]

By the time that *The Common Law* was published, Pollock's position was still closer to Holmes's. When employing 'an external standard', he observes in *Essays in Jurisprudence and Ethics*, 'I judge not merely as an individual expressing my personal feeling . . . but as a citizen expressing a fellow-feeling as to things which concern the good or harm of my fellow-citizens.'[198] Pollock also at this point complicates the notion of an external standard slightly by connecting it to another classic Holmesian theme: that of prediction. An appeal to an external standard, he argues, may require a 'prediction of like judgments in like future cases, founded on an assumption of uniformity'[199]—a prediction, that is, about how our fellow citizens are likely to feel in particular circumstances, this prediction being derived from our experience of how citizens have felt in similar circumstances in the past. 'The predictions of that part of legal science which is called case law rest on the assumption that within the range of the particular system of law the same legal judgment will be passed by every competent court upon the same facts.'[200] Within the English common law tradition, Pollock believed, it is safe to make this assumption of uniformity, for the English do indeed conform to collective standards. There is nothing at all controversial about appealing 'to the moral sense of Englishmen', because it is 'a matter of fact . . . that the moral judgment of an average-

194 [Frederick Pollock], 'Holmes on the Common Law' (11 June 1881) 51 *Saturday Rev.* 758–9 at 758.

195 Oliver Wendell Holmes, Jr., *The Common Law* (Boston: Little, Brown & Co., 1881), 108.

196 '[T]he prudence required [to satisfy this standard] is not exactly the prudence of a common man, but the prudence of a man such as would commonly and properly be concerned in the matter in hand.' Pollock, above n.194, 759.

197 Pollock to Holmes, 3 July 1874, in *PHL* i. 3–4 (apropos of [O. W. Holmes, Jr.], 'The Theory of Torts' (1873) 7 *American L. Rev.* 652–63).

198 *EJE* 268–9. 199 *EJE* 269. 200 *EJE* 268.

right-minded man does, on the whole, follow precedents, and is guided by settled principles.'[201] For Pollock, it is the English commitment to a collection of shared moral standards that makes the prospect of predicting future legal judgments seem so reasonable.

The significance of English character and temperament to the nature of the common law system is a theme to which Pollock devotes considerable attention, and we will examine it in chapter 4. At this point it features only because it is integral to Pollock's understanding of law and prediction. During the 1870s, Pollock made prediction central to his own conception of legal science. The timing is interesting. Commonly, the so-called prediction theory of law is associated with Holmes's famous 1897 address, 'The Path of the Law'.[202] While it is quite correct to attribute the theory to Holmes, it is wrong to believe that he developed it in the late 1890s. The germ of the theory in fact emerges during the early 1870s, and does so out of his engagement with Pollock's early work on Austin. In April 1871, Holmes was appointed University Lecturer on Jurisprudence at Harvard College for the following year. The lectures that he delivered in April and May of 1872 were structured around Austin's *Lectures on Jurisprudence*.[203] In that same year, Holmes published in the *American Law Review* a short notice dealing with Pollock's article on the command theory of law.[204] Pollock's conclusions about the command theory largely coincide with those which Holmes had already reached in his jurisprudence lectures.[205] But when one looks carefully at what Holmes and Pollock wrote, some significant differences begin to emerge. Pollock had concluded his article with a decidedly Savigny-esque definition of law: '. . . a condition, or assemblage of conditions, under which the evolution of a society proceeds, and the determination of which is part of the collective consciousness of that society.'[206] Holmes, by contrast, was making no appeals to the *Volksgeist*. Even in his note of 1872, Menand observes, 'Holmes's view of law was premised on the assumption that law is simply and empirically judicial behavior. A rule may be written down, it may express the

[201] *EJE* 270; and cf. also *EJE* 277 ('[W]hen admitted principles have to be applied to a complex particular case the conclusions of right-minded men may differ. Hence there is a discrepance of moral judgments within certain limits; . . . here, . . . the comparison of case law will still be helpful').

[202] Oliver Wendell Holmes, Jr., 'The Path of the Law' (1897) 10 *Harvard L. Rev.* 457–78; and see also David H. Moskowitz, 'The Prediction Theory of Law' (1966) 39 *Temple L. Q.* 413–31 at 413–17. For Moskowitz, the theory is born with Holmes's address.

[203] See M. H. Fisch, 'Justice Holmes, The Prediction Theory of Law, and Pragmatism' (1942) 39 *Jnl. of Philosophy* 85–97 at 92; G. Edward White, *Justice Oliver Wendell Holmes: Law and the Inner Self* (New York: Oxford UP, 1993), 119.

[204] [O. W. Holmes, Jr.], review of *The Law Magazine & Rev.* (1871–2) 6 *American L. Rev.* 723–5.

[205] Holmes was keen to stress that Pollock's article, which appeared in the April 1872 issue of the *Law Magazine and Review*, 'was going through the press' at the time that his jurisprudence lectures were being delivered: Holmes, above n.204, 723. Apparently, Holmes wrote his lectures 'in the fall of 1871 and the early spring of 1872': White, above n.203, 119. On the evolution of Holmes's critique of Austinian jurisprudence, see Frederic Rogers Kellogg, *The Formative Essays of Justice Holmes: The Making of an American Legal Philosophy* (Westport, Conn.: Greenwood Press, 1984), 23–9.

[206] Pollock, above n.105, 205.

will of the sovereign, it may be justified by logic or approved by custom; but if courts will not enforce it, it is not the law, and lawyers who bet their cases on it will lose.'[207] As Holmes himself explained:

It must be remembered . . . that in a civilized state it is not the will of the sovereign that makes lawyers' law, even when that is its source, but what a body of subjects, namely, the judges, by whom it is enforced, *say* is his will. The judges have other motives for decision, outside their own arbitrary will, beside the commands of their sovereign. And whether those motives are, or are not, equally compulsory, is immaterial, if they are sufficiently likely to prevail to afford a ground for prediction. The only question for the lawyer is, how will the judges act? Any motive for their action, be it constitution, statute, custom, or precedent, which can be relied upon as likely in the generality of cases to prevail, is worthy of consideration as one of the sources of law. . . .[208]

This passage is particularly interesting because it is possibly the first occasion on which Holmes explained law by reference to the prediction of judicial action.[209] The likelihood is that he further explored the implications of the prediction theory in his contributions to the meetings of the 'Metaphysical Club' during the early 1870s.[210] Pollock, in his 1872 article on the command theory, never so much as mentions prediction. By 1874, however, he too was considering the jurisprudential implications of the idea. In his series of articles on 'Case Law and Inductive Science', first published during that year in the *Pall Mall Gazette*,[211] Pollock stamps his own mark on a Holmesian theme by arguing that the notion of prediction is crucial to the development of a science of judicial decision-making. Whether it would be right to assume that Pollock simply followed Holmes in linking science and prediction is open to question. In August 1872 Pollock's friend and fellow Apostle, William Kingdon Clifford, made precisely the same link in his lecture to the British Association:

[t]he aim of scientific thought . . . is to apply past experience to new circumstances; the instrument is an observed uniformity in the course of events. By the use of this instrument it gives us information transcending our experience, it enables us to infer things that we have not seen from things that we have seen; and the evidence for the

[207] Louis Menand, *The Metaphysical Club* (New York: Farrar, Straus and Giroux, 2001), 343.

[208] Holmes, above n.204, 724. [209] See Fisch, above n.203, 94.

[210] See Max H. Fisch, 'Was There a Metaphysical Club in Cambridge?', in *Studies in the Philosophy of Charles Sanders Peirce. Second Series*, eds. E. C. Moore and R. S. Robin (Amherst: University of Massachusetts Press, 1964), 3–32 at 20; and Marcia J. Speziale, 'By Their Fruits You Shall Know Them: Pragmaticism and the Prediction Theory of Law' (1978) 9 *Manitoba L. J.* 29–51 at 31.

[211] See Pollock to Holmes 26 July 1877, in *PHL* i. 7. The articles were reprinted as chapter 9 of *EJE*.

truth of that information depends on our supposing that the uniformity holds good beyond our experience.[212]

It is very likely that Pollock would have been aware of this lecture when he wrote 'Case Law and Inductive Science'.[213] Possibly he was more influenced by Clifford than by Holmes in connecting science and prediction; though in fact such speculation is hardly crucial, for what is clear is that the argument which Pollock develops, even if it was inspired by Holmes, is far from Holmesian in spirit.

Although '[m]uch has been said and written lately about making English law more scientific', Pollock begins, many of 'those who expound a so-called science of law' produce schemes which appear 'to have little to do with science, and less with the law of England.'[214] These schemes devote surprisingly little attention 'to the scientific character' of 'the records of decided cases', upon 'which a great part of English law has actually been built up, and by which it is still administered and developed.'[215] Demonstrating that judicial decision-making, and the reporting of judicial decisions, 'have a truly scientific character'[216] requires that we make use of the notion of prediction.

The object of both natural science and legal science 'is to predict events'—in the case of legal science, it is 'to predict . . . the decisions of courts of justice'.[217] Predicting legal results requires that we 'suppose that the same decision is always given on the same facts'.[218] Pollock considered it reasonable to make such an assumption.[219] Although it may be objected that 'the legal order of things has only a relative and limited uniformity, whereas the order of nature has an absolute uniformity', the fact is that 'we do not know the order of nature to be absolutely uniform'[220] and we have no reason to believe the legal order to be any less uniform. Granted, 'judges and lawyers are human, and their legal judgment is sometimes influenced by unscientific motives'; 'the want of a complete and homogeneous system of appeals', furthermore,

[212] W. K. Clifford, 'On the Aims and Instruments of Scientific Thought' (1872), in his *The Ethics of Belief and Other Essays*, eds. F. Pollock and L. Stephen (London: Watts & Co., [1947]), 1–27 at 7. The editorial history of this collection is a mystery, as both Pollock and Leslie Stephen had been long dead by the time of its appearance. The collection contains an Introduction by Archibald Robertson (ibid. vii–x) which offers no clues.

[213] Five years after this lecture was first printed (in *Macmillan's Magazine*, October 1872), it was included in the *Lectures and Essays by the Late William Kingdon Clifford*, above n.53, i. 124–57. Clifford died 3 March 1879. Although it is not known when Pollock and Stephen compiled *The Ethics of Belief* (above n.212), it is most likely that the *Lectures and Essays* mark the first time that Pollock dealt with 'On the Aims and Instruments of Scientific Thought' in an editorial capacity.

[214] *EJE* 237. [215] *EJE* 237. [216] *EJE* 238. [217] *EJE* 238. [218] *EJE* 239.

[219] See David Ibbetson, 'Historical Research in Law', in *The Oxford Handbook of Legal Studies*, eds. P. Cane and M. Tushnet (Oxford: Oxford UP, 2003), 863–79 at 866 ('. . . a lawyer like Pollock could openly hold to the position that the lawyers' authorities were like the data of natural scientists, with the result that just as the natural scientists' laws were based upon an observed congruity of single instances, so the lawyers' rules were to be discovered from the observation of similar results in similar lawsuits').

[220] *EJE* 253.

'leaves room . . . for conflicts and inconsistencies'.[221] 'But . . . our comparison [between natural and legal science] is not the worse but the better for the approximate character of legal predictions. For no general proposition of science is known to be more than approximately true, nor is any prediction known to be more than approximately accurate.'[222] The claim that predictions regarding the decisions of courts are no more approximate than predictions regarding the laws of nature—as if the outcome of a case will be no less easily foreseeable than the consequence of an apple disconnecting from its branch—is unconvincing. Moreover, even if it is reasonable to assume approximate uniformity—to assume that similar cases are treated similarly—in judicial decision-making, what guarantees as much? Pollock's answer, laconic but intriguing, is that 'legal uniformity . . . springs from unconsciously formed habits of mind.'[223] Behind this statement lie two assumptions. First, there is the assumption that the promotion of uniformity will be a by-product of the activities of both lawyers and judges: those who hold these offices, after all, 'must select the right kind of cases for comparison with the case before [them]' and 'must observe the right points of likeness and unlikeness in the cases [they] compare[]'.[224] Over time, '[e]xperts acquire an unconscious habit of looking at the matters of their own art in the right way.'[225] Secondly, there is that matter of the English character to which we adverted earlier. Although Pollock did not pursue this matter in 'Case Law and Inductive Science', he would later argue that bound up in this character there is a belief in 'the sanctity of precedent'.[226] 'We and our kinsfolk in America love to think of ourselves as a law-abiding people. We like to have the sanction, or at least the analogy, of precedent and law for whatever we do. . . . [T]his habit of mind . . . is the foundation of our modern jurisprudence.'[227] Where citizens are inclined to respect the decisions of the past, it is almost inevitable that there will be a marked degree of uniformity in judicial decision-making.

'[C]ase-law', then, 'has a scientific aim, namely, the prediction of events by means of past experience.'[228] This is as close as Pollock ever came to stipulating his own conception of legal science. Note how the conception depends on two classic Holmesian motifs: prediction and external standards. The resort to prediction proves unconvincing. Holmes used the notion to articulate a crucial insight: if we can predict that a law will not be enforced, its legal validity counts for nothing. Pollock, by contrast, seemed to settle upon the idea of prediction so that he could suck the life out of it. His thesis, in essence, is that law deserves recognition as a science because we can confidently predict that like cases will be treated more or less alike. Whereas Holmes was candid about judicial power—whereas he recognized that a judicial decision might be

[221] *EJE* 255. [222] *EJE* 255.
[223] *EJE* 255. [224] *EJE* 249. [225] *EJE* 249.
[226] Frederick Pollock, 'The History of English Law as a Branch of Politics' (October 1881) n.s. 30 *Fortnightly Rev.* 478–98 at 487.
[227] Ibid. 486–7. [228] *EJE* 246.

motivated by a variety of factors—Pollock depicted a decidedly more benign process whereby stalwart judges can be trusted to apply appropriate precedents. The resort to the notion of external standards, certainly in *Essays in Jurisprudence and Ethics*, fares little better. Holmes employed the notion in order to make a distinction between law and morality—to show that personal moral blameworthiness is not generally an ingredient of liability. When Pollock relies on the idea of an external standard, however, the distinction between law and morality is sometimes blurred. To some extent, this was a matter of disagreement. Indeed we will see in chapter 5 that, when writing about contractual obligations, Pollock simply did not accept Holmes's theory of liability.[229] In *Essays in Jurisprudence and Ethics*, however, it is noticeable that although Pollock adopts the notion of external standards, he departs from Holmes by treating them not primarily as objective but as moral standards—as embodying 'the moral sense of Englishmen', no less. Reviewing Pollock's book, W. L. Courtenay professed to being confused: was Pollock trying to emphasize, or was he against making too much of, the role of morality in law? 'He is troubled with many doubts, especially on two points—the bearing of scientific ethics on practical morality, and the relation of moral ideals to contemporary practice. And so it is not unnatural to find in his essays sentences which are not obviously consistent.'[230]

Whereas, from the early 1880s onwards, Pollock basically jettisoned the idea of prediction, the notion of external standards continued to preoccupy him. Sometimes he was careful to emphasize that his use of the notion did not conform to the way in which Holmes had employed it.[231] But on other occasions the Holmesian signature was pronounced. During the Hilary Term of 1889, Pollock delivered a series of lectures at Oxford on 'Analytical Jurisprudence'.[232] Notwithstanding his criticisms of the Austinian tradition, he was keen in these lectures to capture the many ways in which law and morality diverge.[233] But in trying to capture these divergences he drew inspiration not from Austin, but from Holmes. Law, Pollock proclaimed,

> is a distinct science. For, even if we assume that morality is capable of scientific definition, the subject-matter of law is not the same. Its field neither coincides with nor is included in the field of moral rules. Law does not aim directly at the perfection of individual character, but only at regulating social relations. It judges, as a rule, the conformity or otherwise of human conduct to an 'external standard', not the motive from which conduct proceeds.[234]

The conception of external standard that Pollock employs in this instance is very clearly Holmes's, rather than some modified version which makes ref-

[229] See chapter 5, 208–9.
[230] W. L. Courtenay, 'Modern Ethics' (April 1883) 157 *Edinburgh Rev.* 423–58 at 446–7.
[231] See, e.g., *GCL* 17. [232] Pollock notebooks, Misc. 795, 137–75.
[233] Ibid. 146–7. [234] Ibid. 145–6.

erence to the morality of the common law mind. It is noticeable too that although Pollock's argument is Holmesian, the purpose of its application is to establish an analytical-jurisprudential proposition: that law is a science because it does not necessarily correlate with morality. In *The History of English Law*, in a passage written by Pollock, we find this manoeuvre more or less repeated. When Holmes wrote of the life of the law being not logic but experience, he seemed to echo Rudolph von Jhering.[235] Pollock and Maitland—though concerned with the hazards of reducing law to metaphysics rather than logic—seemed, in turn, to echo Holmes when they observed that '[l]aw, such as we know it in the conduct of life, is matter of fact; not a thing which can be seen or handled, but a thing perceived in many ways of practical experience.'[236] This passage is intriguing for our purposes because it shows Pollock again adopting a broadly Holmesian perspective in order to differentiate law and morality. '[T]here are and must be rules of law beyond or outside the direct precepts of morality', he continues, just as 'there are, and must be, rules of morality beyond the commandments of law.'[237] Practical experience teaches us that legal rules are often necessary to coordinate pursuits. Such rules, Pollock contends in both the *History of English Law* and elsewhere, may have no moral dimension. 'In England men drive on the left-hand side of the road . . . Morality has nothing to say to this, except that those who use the roads ought to know and observe the rule.'[238] Law and morality may often overlap, but they are not reducible to one another.

Yet again we see that Pollock was not wholly unsympathetic to the aims of analytical jurisprudence. He makes the rather bewildering move, however, of distinguishing law from morality while also insisting that what makes the common law unique is the fact that it is grounded in distinctive moral sentiments—more specifically, in the moral consciousness of the judiciary. In short, as Lobban puts it, Pollock 'smudged over the line between positivism and intuitionism'.[239] While this seems fair comment, it ought to be emphasized that the move which Pollock makes, although somewhat puzzling, is not incoherent. Pollock believed that many laws are created for non-moral reasons. There is no inconsistency in the fact that he also believed (as we have already seen)

[235] See Holmes, above n.195, 1; and cf. Peter Stein, 'Logic and Experience in Roman and Common Law' (1979) 59 *Boston Univ. L. Rev.* 433–51 at 437.

[236] *HEL* i. xcv. The words quoted in this sentence were used by Pollock five years before the first edition of *HEL* was published. See Frederick Pollock, 'The Origins of the Common Law' (December 1890) 58 *Contemporary Rev.* 849–62 at 850. Holmes is perhaps not the only one whom Pollock is echoing: cf. *Case of the Duchy of Lancaster* (1561) 1 Plowden 212, 213 ('For the King has in him two bodies, viz., a body natural, and a body politic . . . But his body politic is a body that cannot be seen or handled . . .').

[237] *HEL* i. xcv–xcvi; and cf. K. J. M. Smith, *James Fitzjames Stephen: Portrait of a Victorian Rationalist* (Cambridge: Cambridge UP, 1988), 56. On at least one occasion, Pollock suggests that moral rectitude is largely a matter of good manners: see *EJE* 373.

[238] *HEL* i. xcvi. In the same vein, see *FBJ* 49; *EIL* 33; and cf. Frederick Pollock, 'Locke's Theory of the State' (1904) 2 *Proc. Brit. Acad.* 237–49 at 242–4.

[239] Lobban, above n.63, 52.

that judges apply the law with some unconsciously acquired *Rechtsgefühl*—with the innate good legal sense of a 'right-minded man'.[240]

Just as law is not reducible to morality, equally, for Pollock, it is not reducible to politics. '[L]aw is not law merely because the State enforces it,' he was to claim on more than one occasion, 'but on the contrary the State enforces it because it is law.'[241] A. L. Goodhart considered this proposition to be 'the most important one that Pollock ever wrote', marking, as it does, 'a complete separation from the theory of law accepted by his three colleagues at Oxford—Sir Thomas Erskine Holland, Sir William Anson, and Professor A. V. Dicey'.[242] Yet Goodhart also considered the proposition exasperating. On the occasions that Pollock made the claim he immediately ducked out of discussing it, professing in one instance that 'the further pursuit of this subject seems to belong to the philosophy of Politics rather than of Law.'[243]

The basic purpose of the proposition seems to be to distinguish Pollock's understanding of law from Austin's command theory or any of its derivatives. But that is not its only purpose. For Pollock, law—certainly the English common law—could never be tantamount to State authority. 'The Common Law', he wrote to Lytton Strachey in 1918, 'is older than our political institutions and—not being tied to dogmas—will live to see them transformed.'[244] To treat the common law as but part of the political apparatus would be to ignore the fact that the common law is very much the product of a special mindset. 'Law . . . means . . . the sum of those rules of conduct which courts of justice enforce, the conditions on which they become applicable, and the manner and consequences of their application. This is a matter of fact not in any way dependent on the view that we may take of the political and ethical foundations of government and positive law.'[245] Note the equation of law not just with rules, but also with the conditions and the manner of their application. Pollock's principal concern was with 'the permanent mind and temper of the common law', with the way in which lawyers and judges think and work, rather than with 'the particular rules which judges administer to-day'.[246] The autonomy of law—the reason that it can be the subject of a distinct science—is traceable 'to a certain continuous drift of thought which is called the legal habit of mind'.[247] We get to the heart of a legal system, in short, by understanding the minds of its legal officials. About this we will have more to

[240] *EJE* 295. [241] *SHLP* 304; and see also *FBJ* 27.

[242] A. L. Goodhart, 'Introduction', in *JLE* ix–xlviii at xxv.

[243] *FBJ* 27; and see also *SHLP* 304 ('I am not here concerned to set forth my own opinions'). On at least one occasion, furthermore, he appeared to contradict the claim: see Frederick Pollock, 'The Continuity of the Common Law' (1898) 11 *Harvard L. Rev.* 423–33 at 424 ('When we speak of law we mean, for all practical purposes, those rules of conduct which the State deems binding on citizens, not merely as rational and moral beings but as members of that State, and accordingly thinks fit to enforce by public authority: in other words, the rules which are administered and applied by courts of justice').

[244] Frederick Pollock to G. L. Strachey, 15 June 1918, in Strachey papers, Add. 60691 f.71.

[245] *FBJ* 217. [246] *GCL* 8.

[247] *EJE* 278; and, for Pollock on the automony of law ('a perfectly distinct art'), see above n.127, 25.

say in chapter 4. For now we need only note that the significance that Pollock attaches to the existence of a peculiarly legal habit of mind is part and parcel of his effort to visualize a science of the common law.

iii. The path of modern jurisprudence

Fundamental to Pollock's own vision of legal science is the idea of rectitude. A single reason explains why we can plausibly conceive of external standards of liability, why it is possible to predict legal outcomes, and why we must see law as something distinct from morality and politics: the common law tradition has its own correct ways of doing things. Lawyers working within that tradition, if they are to do things correctly, must develop appropriate habits of thought. At first glance, this seems to be a reiteration of Sir Edward Coke's point about artificial reason.[248] But it is not exactly the same.[249] For Pollock, 'getting things right' as a lawyer is not guaranteed by years of study and experience;[250] the quality of rightness requires good sense as well as expertise.

This link between rectitude and good sense Pollock made when reflecting on scholarship as well as on the practice of law.[251] Scholarship, like law, demands a special temperament and mentality, as well as the acquisition of special skills. Scholarly talent ought to be more highly appreciated—Pollock feared for 'the poor scholar of Cambridge or Oxford who has a mind to be a *vir doctus* just for learning's sake'[252]—although 'on the whole really good work does count even in this world.'[253] Meeting the demands of scholarship is more than a matter of becoming versed in method or theory. As we have noted, Pollock seemed only minimally interested in the methods of comparative jurisprudence precisely because he was no lover of methods in general.

[248] *Twelfth Reports, Prohibitions del Roy* (1607) 12 Co. Rep. 63, 64.

[249] Cf. John Underwood Lewis, 'Sir Edward Coke (1552–1633): His Theory of "Artificial Reason" as a Context for Modern Basic Legal Theory' (1968) 84 *LQR* 330–42 at 340–1.

[250] Introducing *FBJ*, Pollock declared his belief that '[n]o practical art can really be taught' (viii–ix). From this we might deduce that his position was closer to that of Michael Oakeshott than that of Coke. See Michael Oakeshott, *Rationalism in Politics and Other Essays* (Indianapolis: Liberty Press, 1991 [1962]), 15 ('practical knowledge can neither be taught nor learned, but only imparted and acquired. It exists only in practice, and the only way to acquire it is by apprenticeship to a master—not because the master can teach it (he cannot), but because it can be acquired only by continuous contact with one who is perpetually practising it').

[251] Pollock's principal reservation about Coke, ironically, was that Coke lacked the scholarly good sense that is required of the very best legal minds: see *FBJ* 250; *GCL* 76. He did recognize, none the less, that Coke appreciated the jurisprudential value of historical research. See Pollock notebooks, Misc. 799, 'H': 'Historical research commended by Coke (Co. Lit. 43a). It is to be observed, that oftentimes for the better understanding of our books the advised reader must take light from history and chronicles, especially for distinction of times.'

[252] *OLOD* 230; Frederick Pollock, 'The Sacrifice of Education' (February 1889) 25 *Nineteenth Century* 291–300 at 298 (same). See also Pollock to Holmes, 2 January 1921, in *PHL* ii. 60 ('there is much more respect for learning in the US and Canada than in England (I don't say Scotland)').

[253] *GCL* 112.

Historical scholarship he regarded very much as a craft—one which is attributable not to method but to scholarly ability—and he wrote about genuine historians (William Stubbs he seemed to revere most[254]) rather as one might in modern times refer, albeit usually tongue-in-cheek, to 'real men'. Hence, genuine historians have an eye for nuance,[255] eschew speculation,[256] know the value of a 'considered opinion',[257] are 'careful . . . not to be misled into making familiar historical words bear a purely modern significance',[258] and recognize the 'danger . . . of overrating . . . the trustworthiness of written documents'.[259] Beware, Pollock warns, of those who are not the genuine article, who in fact contribute to 'the general lowering of tone in matters of intellect'.[260] Often, those most responsible for the degradation of scholarly standards are eminent lawyers: '[s]ome of the worst nonsense I have met with about historical evidence was written by respectable lawyers from Coke downwards.'[261] The best legal historians, the true craftsmen, 'are not frightened by the difficulties of legal history'.[262] They appreciate that 'tracing the pedigree of legal ideas is ticklish work', that '[t]he most tempting resemblances of modern to ancient forms are often fallacious, and [that] ideas which are really of great antiquity may . . . lie comfortably concealed in modern terminology.'[263]

Pollock, of course, placed himself among the craftsmen. Part of his self-conceived task was to dispel legal myths accepted by those who cannot be expected to know better. While law 'must have its proper terms, which can be understood only by training[,] . . . there is no reason why its broad principles . . . should not be set forth in language intelligible to all educated men'.[264] A proper task of jurisprudence, therefore, is to correct 'certain false opinions' which 'easily occur to the first thoughts of a reasonable but uninstructed layman'.[265] But the bigger task was to combat egregious scholarship, to maintain standards. Why, Pollock wondered, were certain legal historians noticeably inclined to denigrate a juristic opinion when its originator was no longer around to defend it? 'I have an odd prejudice', he declared, 'in favour of making sense of what has been said by men who . . . were not likely to talk nonsense.'[266] Bewilderment was often his response when faced with what he considered to be departures from scholarly norms. When a Belgian interna-

[254] See, e.g., Pollock, above n.226, 479–80, also 483 n.1 ('I am content to be inaccurate, if inaccuracy there is, in Professor Stubbs's company').

[255] See *ECL* 38 n.*a*. [256] See *ECL* 86, 90. [257] *OLOD* 216. [258] *GCL* 95.

[259] *HEL* i. 25. These words appear on the first page of a chapter to which Pollock only contributed, and so may well have been written by Maitland.

[260] *OLOD* 228; 'The Sacrifice of Education', above n.252, 297 (same). Legal-historical scholarship which, in Pollock's view, did lower the tone was granted no mercy: see, e.g., his annihilation of the work of Sir Travers Twiss: *PCLE(3)* vii–viii; and 'Sir Travers Twiss's Bracton', *Saturday Rev.*, 1 February 1879, 153–4.

[261] *EIL* 265.

[262] *EJE* 201. See also Frederick Pollock, review of Vinogradoff et al. (1914) 30 *LQR* 502–3.

[263] *EIL* 221. [264] *EIL* 278. [265] *EIL* 258.

[266] *OLOD* 22. See also *EJE* 59 ('We . . . shall do much amiss if . . . we despise our fathers for not having known better').

tional lawyer wrote to Pollock asking if he would arrange for the translation of an article and for its publication in the *Law Quarterly Review*, Pollock refused to do so, relaying the explanation for his decision to T. E. Holland in the form of a simple question: '[s]urely everybody who cares about the history of international law can read French?'[267] The world of 'Maine, Pollock, Bryce, and Vinogradoff', it has been suggested, 'was one of scholarship, of learned languages, of documents, of critical historical methods and legal technicalities'; 'they represented a genuine, if snobbish commitment to a conception of respectable scholarship. The adherence to "history" was deep, the language of "science" usually perfunctory.'[268] As an assessment of Pollock, this is to some extent inaccurate and misleading: scholarship was only a segment of his world, and within that segment there was little room for 'critical historical methods'. For the most part, however, the quotation is right. Pollock insisted on, and could barely tolerate departures from, scholarly correctness: far more concerned was he with the notion of proper historical inquiry than with the notion of legal science.

Rectitude, then, was very much a matter of proper form rather than analytical precision. Austin had always sought to be precise—it was his desire to be precise that often made him near unreadable—but he was, in Pollock's eyes, a poor lawyer and historian who produced lectures littered with 'damnable heresies'.[269] To some extent, this was an issue of aesthetics. Pollock's idea of polishing his prose was to bring flamboyance to it—to find the most felicitous phrases and the most learned allusions, to find an epithet in (say) Persian to summarize a point.[270] For Austin, as for many analytical jurists since, polishing was first and foremost about attending to technicalities—about ensuring that phrases and arguments are carefully employed, developed, and (where necessary) qualified. But there was more than just aesthetics at stake. Juristic elegance meant, for Pollock, immersion in legal history and doctrine, and an ability to interpret this history and doctrine with discrimination: it is 'inelegant . . . for the law as a science' when a court 'talk[s] too much and about too many things'.[271] Analytical jurisprudence, being a species of 'General Jurisprudence', breeds inelegance. Of course, law 'has all the marks of a distinct science';[272] but capturing the elegance of this science requires that we

[267] Frederick Pollock to T. E. Holland, 10 October 1898, in Pollock correspondence, box 1, folder 34. The explanation was sincere: Pollock had already published international law scholarship in the *LQR* in the original French. See Ernest Nys, 'Notes inédites de Bentham sur le Droit International' (1885) 1 *LQR* 225–31.

[268] Collini, Winch, and Burrow, above n.30, 213.

[269] Pollock to Holmes, 2 October 1896, in *PHL* i. 71.

[270] Of course, Pollock hardly differed from other Victorian jurists in using a variety of languages. His attraction to Persian, none the less, did rather single him out. For Pollock's love of Persian, see Sir Frederick Pollock, *A Little Persian Not a Dangerous Thing* (London: Hogg, 1913).

[271] Pollock to Holmes, 30 March 1898, in *PHL* i. 84. 'Etymologically, elegance is connected with *eligere*, to choose, and essentially it suggests choice, a discriminating choice, choice governed by a nicety of feeling.' Peter Stein, 'Elegance in Law' (1961) 77 *LQR* 242–56 at 242.

[272] *OLOD* 3.

conceive of it not, primarily, as a philosophical abstraction but as a mass of historical and doctrinal detail in need of judicious interpretation.[273]

It is tempting, of course, to ask: who was right? Or, to put the question only slightly less crudely, who, as between Austin and the analytical tradition and Pollock and the comparative tradition, had the better jurisprudential project? Pollock, as compared with Austin, was the more accomplished legal technician and the better writer. He was also writing as a critic, pointing out the shortcomings of the Austinian project and suggesting how jurisprudence could, if diverted from that project, prove so much more fruitful. Certainly the comparative perspective represents the path not chosen. Should we not lament this? Would not modern jurisprudence be considerably more enlightening had we eschewed the analytical tradition and dedicated ourselves instead to the complexities of the historical and comparative quest?

The first two questions in the last paragraph not only permit of no satisfactory answer but also point us in the wrong direction. What we need to know is not which of the two traditions offered the 'better' project, but why one tradition should have proved more resilient than the other. Most of the remainder of this chapter will be devoted to explaining why this should have happened. As for the last two questions in the previous paragraph, it should become clear below that there is no compelling reason to assume either is best answered in the affirmative. Not that everyone would agree with this claim. Whereas we are concerned with the question of why English jurisprudence should be analytical, Morton Horwitz, in his Hart Lecture of 1995, poses more or less the obverse question: 'why is Anglo-American jurisprudence unhistorical?'[274] When Horwitz elaborates this question, it becomes clear that he regards the capacity of 'analytical jurisprudence . . . successfully to resist the challenge of historicism'[275] to be a cause for lament. 'Why,' he asks, has Anglo-American jurisprudence remained 'staunchly indifferent to history? How has it been able to maintain its confident assumption that the analytical and the historical can be neatly separated; and that one can engage in the analysis of concepts whose meaning is thought to be understood independently of the historical context in which those concepts are conceived, developed and deployed in argument?'[276] The rather convoluted syntax does not disguise Horwitz's disappointment that the analytical project should have been so successful. '[A]nalytical jurisprudence has been able to resist the historicist challenge to its static and monolithic conception of meaning.'[277] By separating law from history, furthermore, it became 'a tool for promoting conservative politics'.[278]

[273] On juristic elegance as 'exact historical scholarship', see H. F. Jolowicz, 'Utility and Elegance in Civil Law Studies' (1949) 65 *LQR* 322–36 (quotation at 336).

[274] Morton J. Horwitz, 'Why is Anglo-American Jurisprudence Unhistorical?' (1997) 17 *Oxf. Jnl. Leg. Studs.* 551–86.

[275] Ibid. 552. [276] Ibid. 553–4. [277] Ibid. 558. [278] Ibid. 568.

So much for Horwitz's dismay that analytical jurisprudence should have proved so potent at resisting history. Why should it have proved so potent? Credit—perhaps that should be blame—is due first of all to Austin, who succeeded in depoliticizing Benthamite jurisprudence: 'as Austin's jurisprudence separated itself over time from Benthamite radicalism it became more politically acceptable because it was increasingly being read—and taught—apolitically.'[279] Later, Hart 'followed in Austin's path' and sought 'to distinguish law from history and politics'.[280] The notion that Austin depoliticized Benthamite jurisprudence is a familiar one, as, indeed, is the idea that Hart continued in the same vein.[281] The most important point to note for our purposes is that, for Horwitz, Anglo-American jurisprudence is analytical because of the success of Austin and Hart in advancing their anti-historical, depoliticizing initiatives. Our objective here is not to question that account but to offer a different one. Certainly analytical jurisprudence is a success story (though the success which we discuss here is rather different from that which Horwitz purports to identify); but, by the same token, comparative jurisprudence was not a success story. Properly to explain the success of the analytical project requires that we understand the failure of the comparative project. To understand this failure, we do well to look to Pollock. Before returning to him, however, it is worth reflecting briefly on the intellectual culture of the late-Victorian universities.

'The modern university,' it has been observed, 'began with the Victorians.'[282] It would also be true to say that the modern university evolved with the Victorians, for university culture throughout the Victorian period did not remain static. Not until the 1860s, for example, did academic activity begin

[279] Ibid. 564. [280] Ibid. 573, 577.

[281] On Austin see, e.g., Philip Schofield, 'Jeremy Bentham and Nineteenth-Century English Jurisprudence' (1991) 12 *Jnl. Leg. Hist.* 58–88 at 61–5. On Hart see, e.g., Peter Goodrich, *Legal Discourse: Studies in Linguistics, Rhetoric and Legal Analysis* (London: Macmillan, 1987), 44–9. Horwitz's discussion of what he considers to be Hart's depoliticizing tendencies is heavily reliant on speculation and proves difficult to follow. For Horwitz, 'Hart *surely* was . . . struck by the way in which the vague constitutional argument [of 1931, when the Prime Minister, Ramsay MacDonald, sought a 'doctor's mandate', i.e. a blank authority for the National government to do whatever it could agree on] was deployed in order to justify depriving Labour of its electoral advantage. . . . The Crisis of 1931 reminded young Labour Party supporters like Hart that the English Constitution had . . . been invoked by conservatism as a defence against democracy' (Horwitz, above n.274, 578–9, emphasis added). Having read Hart's mind thus, Horwitz concludes that 'one might now understand why . . . Hart would wish to avoid deriving the rule of recognition from history' (ibid. 580). In fact, even if Horwitz's speculations are correct, it is not at all clear why we might deduce from them that Hart would be keen to emphasize law's autonomy; if anything, we might expect Hart to want to do just the opposite. For a study which attempts a manoeuvre comparable with Horwitz's, setting Hart's jurisprudence against the backdrop of post-Second World War British Labourism (which apparently 'entailed a belief in the withering away of class'), see Brendan Edgeworth, 'H. L. A. Hart, Legal Positivism and Post-War British Labourism' (1989) 19 *Univ. Western Australia L. Rev.* 275–300 (quotation at 294).

[282] A. H. Halsey, *The Decline of Donnish Dominion: The British Academic Professions in the Twentieth Century*, rev. edn. (Oxford: Clarendon Press, 1995), 23. See also Harold Perkin, *The Origins of Modern English Society 1780–1880* (London: Routledge & Kegan Paul, 1969), 121.

properly to acquire its identity as professional activity.[283] Furthermore, the research ideals of the late-Victorian period were hardly present in the early nineteenth century. In 1845, John Stuart Mill lamented the English lack of intellectual rigour. 'If we open an English book of history, jurisprudence, or any similar subject, we seldom find in it the real foundation, the ultimate reason of things. In all matters, and especially in politics, pure doctrine and philosophy—science properly so called—have prospered far more on the Continent than in England.'[284] Note that we 'seldom' find among the English the intellectual qualities that Mill so admired: John Austin—who undertook much of his juristic training in Germany in the late 1820s, and for whom Mill had considerable admiration—would probably have been considered by Mill to be an exception to this generalization.[285] But then Austin was an exception in more ways than one. His career was, famously, one long false start. Although Mill might have welcomed the exceptional quality of Austin's work, not until the 1860s did that work begin to resonate. 'Part of the poignancy of Austin's career comes from the fact that he was by nature a professor, but that he lived in a society which had not yet conceived the need for the academic treatment of his subject.'[286] By the time of his death in 1859, however, the need for work of the type that Austin had produced was beginning to be felt.

Why so? Why, that is, should Austin's jurisprudence have been neglected in the early 1830s yet very much a topic for discussion by the late 1860s? To begin to answer this question, it is important to have some appreciation of the epistemic requirements of the late-Victorian universities. The second half of the nineteenth century witnessed what we might term a hardening of knowledge. The inquiries of economists, historians, and philosophers were becoming gradually more technical, their analyses more hard-wired and robust. 'It became very important,' Soffer remarks, 'to agree upon the criteria for recognizing truth.'[287] In economics, there was an ever more intense emphasis on measurement.[288] '[U]niversity historians . . . [b]y the end of the nineteenth century . . . were expected to recognize the objective evidence that was there for every student who sought it out.'[289] According to Harvie, similarly with philosophy: in the 1870s, he claims,

[283] See T. W. Heyck, *The Transformation of Intellectual Life in Victorian England* (London: Croom Helm, 1982), 155–89; and W. J. Reader, *Professional Men: The Rise of the Professional Classes in Nineteenth-Century England* (London: Weidenfeld and Nicolson, 1966), 127–45.

[284] John Stuart Mill, 'Guizot's Essays and Lectures on History' (1845), in his *Dissertations and Discussions: Political, Philosophical, and Historical*, 4 vols. (3rd edn., London: Longman's Green, Reader, and Dyer, 1875), ii. 218–82 at 282.

[285] On Austin's German training, see Schwarz, above n.100, 180–92. On Mill's admiration for Austin, see Collini, above n.32, 260–1.

[286] Collini, above n.32, 262.

[287] Reba N. Soffer, *Discipline and Power: The University, History, and the Making of an English Elite, 1870–1930* (Stanford: Stanford UP, 1994), 31.

[288] See Collini, Winch, and Burrow, above n.30, 316–20.

[289] Soffer, above n.287, 38.

the desire to produce a simple serviceable ethics slackened, to be replaced by more rigorous intellectual debates about fundamental questions of philosophy. . . . Philosophy was maturing as a profession at the universities—henceforth, even when philosophers remained concerned with politics, fundamental postulates about the nature of mind and the analysis of concepts and relationships played a much greater part in forming their ideas. . . . The nature of authority at the universities was changing. . . . Politics as a lived experience declined in importance, intellectual values were enhanced. The university was increasingly a separate, internally satisfying world.[290]

The second half of the nineteenth century marked the end of 'an age', as Milsom has put it, 'when have-a-go scholars of independent means and independent mind did it their way.'[291] In the late-Victorian universities, the casual erudition of many such scholars was rather out of place. Professionalized scholarship—research—entailed rigour and precision; erudition would always be an advantage for an academic, but from the late nineteenth century onwards it would never again be enough.[292] Sidgwick, in *The Elements of Politics*, first published in 1891, captured the tone of this new era as he set about explaining the 'fundamental conceptions' of politics: '[t]o obtain clear and precise definitions of leading terms is an important, and not altogether easy, achievement in all departments of scientific inquiry: but it is especially important in our present subject.'[293] As noteworthy as Sidgwick's emphasis on clarity and precision is the fact that the 'present subject' to which he referred was notionally politics, but in reality jurisprudence—indeed, *The Elements of Politics* is one of the great jurisprudential studies never to have been identified as such. Sidgwick wanted 'to examine what is essentially involved in the terms "property," "contract," "executive" and "legislative" organs and functions' and to explain what is meant by 'the fundamental conceptions Government, Law, Right, [and] Obligation'.[294] How was one to set about providing precise definitions and rooting out essences? For Sidgwick, the answer was obvious: one starts with Austinian jurisprudence.[295]

Recall our earlier notion of critical reverence. The point is not that Sidgwick and others followed Austin slavishly. Rather, the point is that analytical jurispru-

[290] Christopher Harvie, *The Lights of Liberalism: University Liberals and the Challenge of Democracy 1860–86* (London: Allen Lane, 1976), 202–3.

[291] S. F. C. Milsom, 'Maitland' (2001) 60 *Cambridge L. J.* 265–70 at 268. See generally Reba N. Soffer, 'The Modern University and National Values, 1850–1930' (1987) 60 *Historical Research* 166–87; also George C. Brodrick, 'A Nation of Amateurs' (1900) 48 *Nineteenth Century* 521–35.

[292] See Collini, above n.32, 21, 23, 212–13. Cf. also Harold Perkin, *The Rise of Professional Society: England since 1880* (London: Routledge, 1889), 87 ('[T]he average Oxford and Cambridge don was transformed during the late Victorian age from a celibate clergyman awaiting a college . . . to a career-oriented, and usually married, teacher and scholar or scientist').

[293] Henry Sidgwick, *The Elements of Politics* (London: Macmillan, 1891), 15.

[294] Ibid. [295] Ibid. 15–28.

dence complemented the late nineteenth-century quest for greater rigour, robustness, precision, technicality, and the like. Even when those who epitomized the culture of the late-Victorian universities rejected Austinian analysis, they still tended to recognize its congeniality to the intellectual attitudes of that period. Austinian jurisprudence was a success story because, broadly speaking, it turned out to satisfy the epistemic requirements of late-Victorian university culture. Even Pollock appeared to appreciate as much, notwithstanding that he was never a member of the critical reverence club.

Pollock seemed to be irritated by Austin not only because he felt he could see through Austin's work, but also because he felt that others who ought to have been able to do the same did not.[296] Of course, to some extent, Pollock did see through Austin—he was as astute as was Maine, and more hawkish, in highlighting the disparity between the Austinian analysis of the basis of legal validity and the facts about validity as revealed by the histories of a variety of legal systems.[297] But Pollock's jurisprudential critique was never likely to meet the requirements of late-Victorian university culture in the way that Austin's did. For critique was the sum of it: Pollock offered no distinctive method, system, framework, agenda, or criteria. Austin's jurisprudential writing—despite its many vacillations, circumlocutions, and eye-glazing embellishments ('law properly or strictly so called', 'law improperly so called', and so on)—contains a set of unequivocal arguments: '[l]aws properly so called are a species of *commands*'; 'customary laws, considered as positive law, are not commands'; 'every law properly so called is a *positive* law'; '[t]he matter of jurisprudence is positive law'; '[e]very positive law . . . is set . . . by a sovereign person or body, to a member or members of the . . . society wherein that person or body is sovereign'.[298] The arguments are as easily multiplied as they are disputed. But then this is the key to understanding the longevity of Austinian jurisprudence: Austin provided a great deal with which natural lawyers, proponents of comparative jurisprudence, and even other legal positivists could take issue. The comparative project—even in Maine's hands, let alone Pollock's—never engaged an audience to the degree that Austin's eventually did.

Modern sympathizers with the comparative jurisprudential tradition—the breed is not quite extinct—sometimes paint a somewhat different picture. 'Maine's comparative historical analysis inspired over half a century of scholarship in history and political science,' two such sympathizers have recently claimed, 'establishing itself as an analytical method to rival Austinian

[296] See, e.g., Pollock to Holmes, 2 October 1896, in *PHL* i. 71; 5 July 1899, ibid. 94 ('I am a little bit disappointed that you only say Austin did not know *enough* law').

[297] Though Pollock did have a tendency to argue this point without any regard to how an Austinian might respond to it: see Glanville L. Williams, 'International Law and the Controversy Concerning the Word "Law"' (1945) 22 *British Yearbook of International Law* 146–63 at 149–51. For Williams, Pollock was as mistaken as was Austin in assuming that there is a proper way of using the word 'law'.

[298] Austin, above n.61, i. 178, 101, 171, 86, 263.

"autonomous analytical" jurisprudence.'[299] While the first part of the quotation is more or less correct, the second part seems rather exaggerated.[300] As an illustration of the point, consider the claim that we have just made concerning how Maine's ideas ultimately failed to engage an audience as did Austin's. This claim can be interpreted literally. When Maine lectured Oxford undergraduates on historical and comparative jurisprudence, attendances dwindled.[301] '[T]he only lectures which draw a large number of undergraduates to my class are lectures on elementary Austinism,' he complained to Bryce in 1875.[302] As Dicey proclaimed four years later, the reality was that 'the study of jurisprudence . . . generally and inevitably meant the study of Austin.'[303] 'The Oxford school of historical jurisprudence' may well have 'broke[n] new ground in the transformation of Law into a university discipline.'[304] But it failed, in the long term, to hold the attention of those studying law within the university. Pollock, implicitly, was willing to concede as much. About Maine he was prepared to declare in 1888 that 'I do not think [he] will leave much mark on the actual structure of jurisprudence.'[305] About Austin, over forty years later, he could not but admit, albeit sourly, that a mark had been left: '[o]ne reason of his success in English law schools may be that a cocksure dogmatic theory, however bad, is good stuff to examine, and cram for examinations, upon.'[306]

If Austinian jurisprudence turned out to be a story of triumph, can we conclude also that the comparative project was an unequivocal failure? To do so would be rash: contemporary academics who look sympathetically upon the comparative tradition fairly point out that it has not left the grammar of

[299] K. J. M. Smith and J. P. S. McLaren, 'History's Living Legacy: An Outline of "Modern" Historiography of the Common Law' (2001) 21 *Legal Studies* 251–343 at 257–8.

[300] To support the claim made in the first part of the citation, Smith and McLaren cite chapter 7 of Collini, above n.32: see Smith and McLaren, above n.299, 257 n.28. In fact, in that chapter Collini is primarily concerned with Maine's advancement of the notion of 'character' and the way in which Maine's 'prose invokes . . . a kind of moral authority' (above n.32, 276). On the matter of Maine's influence, Collini acknowledges that 'Maine's intellectual authority'—which 'only partly rested on his standing as a lawyer'—'was . . . widely felt in the 1870s' (ibid. 287); but he also argues that 'the Common Law tradition, always suspicious of "theorizing" as alien or at least irrelevant, had never been particularly responsive to the likes . . . of Maine', and subsequently 'entrenched rather than undermined these attitudes' (ibid. 307). Certainly Collini does not deny (though he is not particularly concerned with) Maine's influence upon history and political science; but he seems far from convinced that Maine significantly influenced thinking about law: 'notwithstanding his celebrated dicta about the modernity of societies based upon contract, it could not be said that he furnished his lay readers with any distinctively *legal* understanding of the nature of the English polity' (ibid. 287).

[301] See Collini, Winch, and Burrow, above n.30, 357.

[302] Henry Sumner Maine to James Bryce, 25 November 1875, quoted in F. H. Lawson, *The Oxford Law School, 1850–1965* (Oxford: Clarendon Press, 1968), 49.

[303] A. V. Dicey, 'The Study of Jurisprudence' (1879–80) n.s. 5 *Law Magazine & Rev.* 382–401 at 386.

[304] Janet Howarth, 'The Self-Governing University, 1882–1914', in *The History of the University of Oxford. Volume ii: Nineteenth-Century Oxford, Part 2*, eds. M. G. Brock and M. C. Curthoys (Oxford: Clarendon Press, 2000), 599–643 at 617.

[305] Pollock to Holmes, 4 March 1888, in *PHL* i. 31.

[306] Pollock to Holmes, 17 April 1930, in *PHL* ii. 263.

general jurisprudence entirely unaffected, that the eclecticism of Maine and his successors at least partially paved the way for modern interdisciplinary legal scholarship, and that the methodology of modern comparative law remains rooted in standard historical-jurisprudential inquiries and debates concerning the evolution of law and the identification of legal families.[307] In England from the late nineteenth century onwards, nevertheless, the tendency increasingly to identify the discipline of jurisprudence with the philosophy of law meant that the belief that jurisprudence should be grounded in history and comparison would become ever more marginalized. Frederic Harrison went so far as to declare in 1878 that 'the historical spirit is in strong contrast to the true spirit of jurisprudence.'[308] While the historical method may be 'a potent and fruitful instrument of jurisprudence,' he continued, we must recognize that it is 'merely an instrument of jurisprudence, and never take it for jurisprudence itself.'[309] For 'the historical method, if left unqualified, is perpetually tending to carry us off the field of law into the field of social history or political antiquities'—onto a terrain, in other words, 'most alien to the scientific aspect of law'.[310] Looking to the historical school to discover where the action is could not, so far as Harrison was concerned, be considered a sound strategy for the student of jurisprudence.

The notion that the historical and comparative method was somehow suspect—that it offered plenty by way of exhortation, suggestion, and story-line, but comparatively little insight—spread beyond law. In November 1876 we find W. S. Jevons, the newly appointed Professor of Political Economy at UCL, proclaiming that 'the historical treatment of our science . . . may very properly do for political economy what Sir Henry Maine has done for jurisprudence'.[311] Not ten years had passed, however, before Henry Sidgwick sensed a false alarm: '[t]he proof of the pudding, as the proverb says, is in the eating; but our historical friends make no attempt to set before us the new economic pudding which their large phrases seemed to promise. It is only the old pudding with a little more ethical sauce and a little more garnish of historical illustrations.'[312] Among those who felt wary about the historical and com-

[307] For a representative sample of sympathetic literature, see Peter Stein, 'The Tasks of Historical Jurisprudence', in *The Legal Mind: Essays for Tony Honoré*, eds. N. MacCormick and P. Birks (Oxford: Clarendon Press, 1986), 293–305; *Legal Evolution*, above n.96, 124–7; and Geoffrey Samuel, 'Science, Law and History: Historical Jurisprudence and Modern Legal Theory' (1990) 41 *N. Ire. Leg. Q.* 1–21.

[308] Harrison, above n.100, iii. 120.

[309] Ibid. 125, 124. [310] Ibid. 122.

[311] W. Stanley Jevons, 'The Future of Political Economy' (1876), in his *The Principles of Economics: A Fragment of a Treatise on the Industrial Mechanism of Society and Other Papers*, ed. H. Higgs (London: Macmillan & Co., 1905), 185–206 at 195.

[312] Henry Sidgwick, 'The Scope and Method of Economic Science' (1885), in *Essays in Economic Method: Selected Papers read to Section F of the British Association for the Advancement of Science, 1860–1913*, ed. R. L. Smyth (London: Duckworth, 1962), 73–97 at 88. Whereas Sidgwick was unenamoured of what he considered to be the superficiality of historical method, historians of this period were sometimes similarly disparaging about the methods of jurists. 'The lawyer's vision', J. H. Round wrote in 1910, 'is bounded by his "books;" the historian goes behind his books and studies the facts for himself.' J. Horace Round, *Peerage and Pedigree: Studies in Peerage Law and Family History*, 2 vols. (London: Nisbet,

parative method we can, of course, count Pollock. But note that Pollock was neither a Harrison nor a Sidgwick. '[T]he keynote of [Harrison's] career', according to Kent, was 'amateurism': while 'not quite a full eccentric,' he was 'a licensed irregular whose views were treated with the respect due to his sincerity, intelligence, and education, as well as his means and his numerous and important personal connections.'[313] Sidgwick, by contrast, was very much the professional academic; like Harrison, however, he was no votary of the historical and comparative school. Pollock, let us remind ourselves, was for twenty years Oxford's professor of historical and comparative jurisprudence[314]—a professor of jurisprudence who seemed to distrust, and who certainly showed little faith in, historical and comparative methods. That the analytical tradition should have dominated over the comparative tradition in English jurisprudence is perhaps inevitable, given the requirements of late nineteenth-century university culture. All the same, the historical and comparative project cannot have been aided by the fact that the man who for two decades was responsible for its advancement at Oxford seemed paralysed by his subject matter—capable of writing, certainly, but frozen by a fear of jurisprudential perspectives. It is difficult to avoid the conclusion that Pollock simply could not do jurisprudence. His opinions on the subject were neither here nor there. To no perspective did he commit, just as there was apparently none that he would reject. Even if Maine's successor had pursued historical and comparative inquiries as vigorously and successfully as had Maine himself, it is doubtful that English jurisprudence would not have turned out to be predominantly analytical. Given the non-event that was Pollock's jurisprudential career, the dominance of analysis seems almost inevitable.

iv. Conclusion

By no means did the whole of Pollock's career prove so undistinguished, and from the next chapter onwards we will begin to strike some more positive notes. At this point, none the less, the reader might be forgiven for feeling slightly baffled, if not duped. Why such a long chapter to report what has ultimately been adjudged a non-event? The answer is that Pollock's failure as a jurisprudential writer is historically significant. His work embodied many of the least satisfactory elements—the ambiguousness, the lack of vision, indeed,

1910), i. ix. Cf. Maitland, above n.157, 491; and see generally Reba Soffer, 'Nation, Duty, Character and Confidence: History at Oxford, 1850–1914' (1987) 30 *Historical Jnl.* 77–104 at 81–2; P. B. M. Blaas, *Continuity and Anachronism: Parliamentary and Constitutional Development in Whig Historiography and in the Anti-Whig Reaction between 1890 and 1930* (The Hague: Nijhoff, 1978), 258–62.

313 Christopher Kent, *Brains and Numbers: Elitism, Comtism, and Democracy in Mid-Victorian England* (Toronto: University of Toronto Press, 1978), 159, 157.

314 See *EOD* 6 for Pollock's own description of the post (and his duties) in these terms.

after Maine, the largely unambitious nature—of the historical and comparative project. If comparative jurisprudence was to compete convincingly with analytical jurisprudence in the late nineteenth century, the inheritor of Maine's mantle needed to ensure that the project directly addressed the epistemic requirements of the evolving university culture. Rather than investing the project with such directness, however, Pollock, ever suspicious of methods and systems, more or less guaranteed its consignment to the margins of English jurisprudence. Why is English jurisprudence analytical? Primarily because it taught some challenging and (from a late nineteenth-century perspective) pertinent lessons, but also—and this has been the point of this chapter—because a similar quality of lesson was not being taught by Maine's principal successor.

Pollock did have messages that he wanted to communicate, of course. He wanted the world to understand that Austin's jurisprudence was seriously flawed and ought to be more soberly assessed. He wanted to emphasize the value and the virtue of scholarly good sense. He had, and indeed articulated, a vision—modest and somewhat derivative, but a vision all the same—of the science of the common law. But this mixture of critique and exhortation did not amount to a distinctive jurisprudential position. So it is that we draw to a rather dour conclusion. In the next chapter, however, the mood will shift. The qualities that made Pollock a rather poor jurisprudent—his penchant for low-level critique, his distrust of system-builders, his hortatory style—are precisely those exhibited by the very best champions of the common law tradition. Pollock the jurisprudent may have been a rather passionless creature, but Pollock the common law jurist is a different proposition.

4

THE SANCTIFICATION OF THE COMMON LAW

Arthur Lehman Goodhart was never an especially convincing jurisprudence professor. He was certainly an astute and highly regarded common law jurist—'the greatest living jurist of our time', in Lord Denning's eyes[1]—but when, in 1931, he renounced his fellowship at Corpus Christi College, Cambridge, in order to become a professor at Oxford, he would have been better suited to, and by his own admission would have preferred, the Vinerian Professorship of English Law to the Corpus Professorship of Jurisprudence.[2] 'It was his achievement to introduce the common law into jurisprudence,' wrote his *Times* obituarist.[3] Although he 'filled a gap in the faculty teaching arrangements [at Oxford] by lecturing in jurisprudence,' according to the *Dictionary of National Biography*, he was 'never much interested in theory' and 'took jurisprudence to be mainly concerned with the general principles that underlie the common law'.[4] Goodhart's *Essays in Jurisprudence and the Common Law* epitomize his preferences: one of the essays is a study of 'recent tendencies in English jurisprudence', and the remaining twelve concern the Anglo-American common law tradition.[5]

In this respect, as in others, Goodhart mirrored Pollock. Rather uneasy in the role of jurisprudence professor, Pollock too had coveted the Vinerian Professorship. Although we can say for sure only that the Corpus Professorship was Pollock's second choice rather than his idea of second-best—Dicey, we saw in chapter 2, was elected Vinerian Professor in preference to Pollock in 1882—it seems reasonable to speculate that Pollock would have felt more at

[1] Lord Denning, '1885–1984' (1984) 100 *LQR* 513–14 at 514.

[2] On Goodhart's preference for the Vinerian Chair, see R. F. V. H[euston], 'Goodhart, Arthur Lehman', in *Biographical Dictionary of the Common Law*, ed. A. W. B. Simpson (London: Butterworths, 1984), 211–12 at 212.

[3] Anon., 'Professor A. L. Goodhart: Influence on Law in Britain', in *The Times*, 11 November 1978, 16, col. F.

[4] Tony Honoré, 'Goodhart, Arthur Lehman', in *DNB (1971–1980)*, 350–1 at 350.

[5] See Arthur L. Goodhart, *Essays in Jurisprudence and the Common Law* (Cambridge: Cambridge UP, 1931). The essay on jurisprudence (ibid. 27–49) first appeared two years earlier: 'Recent Tendencies in English Jurisprudence' (1929) 7 *Canadian Bar Rev.* 275–93.

home in the latter post. For Pollock, like Goodhart, was essentially a common law jurist who would sometimes clothe in the language of jurisprudence his discourses on common law doctrine. Both men wrote books about the common law but with jurisprudence in the title. Indeed, as Fifoot has observed, '[e]ven when [Pollock] had committed himself to write *A First Book of Jurisprudence*, he took care to save it from reproach by devoting half its pages to the sources and methods of the Common Law.'[6] The organization of the book, Pollock himself remarked, was 'intended as a protest against the habit of regarding "jurisprudence" as something associated with a little knowledge of the laws of every country but one's own.'[7] Steeped as he was in the detail of the English common law, and immensely knowledgeable about a vast range of legal topics (not to mention systems), Pollock generally sought to anchor his jurisprudential discussions in the law that he knew: rather than start with abstractions and work inwards towards the substance of the law—this being the approach which he considered to be at work (and which he so disliked) in the writings of Bentham and Austin—he would start with the substance of the law and generalize outwards.[8] The reason this procedure tended not to produce particularly interesting jurisprudence is that the legal substance would tend to swallow up the generalizations: no sooner would Pollock offer a proposition than he would be citing some piece of legal evidence qualifying it. His lawyerly eye for provisos and exceptions meant that, even had he tried, he could never have been comfortable producing General Jurisprudence in the manner of Bentham and Austin. Respecting particulars was his sworn way of life.

The jurisprudence professor who does not really feel comfortable doing jurisprudence is an intriguing and by no means uncommon character. Pollock played the part near to perfection, and one way to continue at this point would be to focus on some of his acolytes. 'From 1900 to 1950', according to Twining, 'nearly all chairs of jurisprudence were occupied by men who were lawyers first and foremost, often without very serious claims to being theorists of any kind.'[9] MacCormick concurs: '[b]y the middle part of [the twentieth] century, lawyers had stopped being interested in philosophy, philosophers in law. Jurisprudence in the universities had become a routine reading and re-reading of a canon of texts and text-books. Excepting a handful of brilliant excep-

[6] Cecil Fifoot, *Pollock and Maitland* (Glasgow: University of Glasgow (Murray Foundation Lecture no. 31), 1971), 13.

[7] *FBJ* x. Goodhart approved: see (1937) 53 *LQR* 205; and 'Recent Tendencies in English Jurisprudence', above n.5, 278.

[8] Although this chapter generally cautions against seeing connections between Pollock's approach to law and Dworkin's, on this matter there is clearly an affinity between the two men. For Dworkin's advocacy of 'inside out' over 'outside in' theorizing, see Ronald Dworkin, *Life's Dominion: An Argument about Abortion and Euthanasia* (London: HarperCollins, 1993), 29.

[9] William Twining, 'Academic Law and Legal Philosophy: The Significance of Herbert Hart' (1979) 95 *LQR* 557–80 at 559.

tions, the subject was moribund.'[10] The temptation here is to lapse into threnody, to tell a sorry tale of how, for the first half of the twentieth century, English jurisprudence resisted innovation and clung tenaciously to its past. But this is not the path we will take. Having considered Pollock's anticlimactic contribution to English jurisprudence, we move now to a happier story. In short, what jurisprudence lost the common law gained; for Pollock's writings on the common law are invariably bold, forceful, and unequivocal—altogether different from his meanderings around jurisprudence.

There is no shortage of tributes reinforcing this last claim. Pollock's work—'steeped in the principles of the common law of England'[11]—exhibits, according to Holdsworth, 'reverence for and mastery of the law, the . . . power to illuminate the dark places of the law, and the . . . sense of the need to keep the law in touch with the realities of life. . . . [H]e is one of the greatest of that select band of professors whose work places them amongst the Makers of English Law.'[12] For Winfield, 'Pollock was, above all, a great Common Lawyer. He had the ability to pick out from the confused kaleidoscope of decisions that surrounds many a legal principle the pattern of the principle itself.'[13] 'He accepted little on faith,' Cosgrove remarks, 'except for the excellence of the common law itself.'[14] This small sample of praise should suffice to convey the basic message: Pollock is widely considered to be one of the great common law jurists. The point of this chapter is certainly not to contest this assessment—the tributes are indeed justified. But what lies behind them? What was Pollock's contribution to common law thought? From where did he draw his inspiration? What did he argue?

Taking a fairly circuitous route, this chapter provides answers to these questions. The route is necessarily circuitous because the questions conceal a considerable amount of detail and complexity. But the route is there, and it makes sense to sketch it at the outset. We begin by considering those features of the English common law tradition which turn out to be of especial concern to Pollock. Many modern English jurists have been preoccupied with the question of what makes for legal authority within the common law tradition, and we will see that Pollock is no exception to this trend. In line with the received wisdom of his era, he maintained that the works of living jurists could never be legal authorities—something of an ironic stance for him to take, given that the courts considered some of his writings to be as close to legal authority as juristic work might ever get. Of more interest to Pollock than the notion of

[10] Neil MacCormick, *H. L. A. Hart* (London: Arnold, 1981), 19.

[11] Anon., 'Sir Frederick Pollock, K.C.: The "Old Broad Culture"', in *The Times*, 19 January 1937, 14, col. B.

[12] Sir William Holdsworth, *Some Makers of English Law: The Tagore Lectures, 1937–38* (Cambridge: Cambridge UP, 1938), 290.

[13] Comment attributed to Sir Percy Winfield by H. D. Hazeltine, 'Sir Frederick Pollock, Bart., 1845–1937' (1949) 35 *Proc. Brit. Acad.* 233–56 at 246.

[14] Richard A. Cosgrove, *Our Lady the Common Law: An Anglo-American Legal Community, 1870–1930* (New York: New York UP, 1987), 141.

authority was the notion of reason: like so many English jurists before him, he wished to show that the common law is intrinsically reasonable. But how might it be reasonable? The common law is reasonable, first of all, because it is the English common law, and the English are reasonable people. Indeed, so far as Pollock was concerned, the English have many virtues—virtues which are reflected in, and sometimes exemplified by, their common law tradition. But he appreciated that one does not demonstrate the essentially reasonable quality of the common law simply by proclaiming, or even showing, that it is rooted in the English character. And so he offers two further lines of argument. The first is that the common law is reasonable because it invariably encapsulates common sense perspectives. This argument, we will see, is easy to criticize; it will also be suggested, however, that the argument has some sense about it when considered in historical context. The second argument is that the common law is reasonable because it makes great use of what is probably the finest instrument of reason: principle. It is important to emphasize that this argument, too, has an historical context, and that it would be wrong to jump to the conclusion that Pollock might profitably be read as a precursor to Dworkinian interpretativism, or, for that matter, to any other modern jurisprudence centred upon the notion of principle.

Generally, Pollock sanctified the common law because he regarded it as an accumulation of reason, as the sedimentation of sound principles of justice. He did not believe that legislation could be regarded thus. Indeed, the best way to understand what Pollock loved about the common law is to consider what he disliked about legislation. For Pollock, legislation is too often lacking in qualities such as common sense and principle, and too often fuelled by *dirigisme*, hubris, and misplaced good intentions. Of course, legislation tends also to be politically motivated, and it is tempting to assume that Pollock would have cited as further evidence of the superiority of the common law its apolitical character. But he did not take it for granted that the common law possesses this character. Rather, he argued that the common law is apolitical only in the sense that it has no unique political affiliations and excludes no particular political perspective. Never did he deny that the common law will accommodate arguments which align with particular political positions—indeed, he went so far as to claim that within the English common law tradition it is possible to discern both the politics of the free market and the politics of socialism. His only insistence was that the common law was impartial as between such positions: the common law is not political because it has the potential to embrace a variety of perspectives.

i. Authority and reason

There is no shortage of generalizations about the character of the common law. Many such generalizations are accurate and convincing, and there is often something engaging about those studies—Pollock penned his fair share—which have at their heart the goal of identifying a fundamental common law mindset, voice, attitude, worldview, or whatever. Note, however, that this observation is cast in the plural: there really are numerous plausible, indeed often complementary, generalizations about the nature of the common law because the philosophy of the common law admits of a variety of convincing constructions.

As an illustration of this point, consider two generalizations that are often made about the common law tradition. The first is what we might term the conception of common law rules as immemorial custom. During the seventeenth century, according to Pocock, 'common lawyers . . . came to believe that the common law, and with it the constitution, had always been exactly what they were now, that they were immemorial . . . in the precise legal sense of dating from time beyond memory.'[15] Various jurists of the seventeenth and eighteenth centuries wrote eloquently in support of this idea.[16] Sir Henry Finch observed in 1627 that 'the common law of England is a law used time out of mind'[17]—a notion replicated almost 150 years later by Blackstone when he wrote of how 'the common law, or *lex non scripta*, of this kingdom' derives 'weight and authority' from 'its having been used time out of mind; or, in the solemnity of our legal phrase, time whereof the memory of man runneth not to the contrary.'[18] Note that Blackstone refers to the immemorial quality of common law rules to explain their authority. '[T]he only method of proving that this or that maxim is a rule of the common law,' he believed, 'is by shewing that it hath been always the custom to observe it.'[19] Sir Matthew Hale had made much the same connection between the authoritative and the immemorial in the seventeenth century when he wrote of how 'the law *leges non scriptae* . . . have acquired their binding power and force of laws, by a long and immemorial usage.'[20] The common law, on this account, derives its authority

[15] J. G. A. Pocock, *The Ancient Constitution and the Feudal Law: A Study of English Historical Thought in the Seventeenth Century. A Reissue with a Retrospect* (Cambridge: Cambridge UP, 1987 [1957]), 36, and cf. also 274–5 (where Pocock emphasizes that he means not 'that the whole body of the law was held to be immemorial' but 'that any element in it could be held immemorial at will').

[16] See generally ibid. 30–55.

[17] Sir Henry Finch, *Law, or a Discourse thereof* . . . (London: Society of Stationers, 1627), 77. More generally on Finch, see Wilfrid Prest, 'The Dialectical Origins of Finch's *Law*' (1977) 36 *Cambridge L. J.* 326–52.

[18] Sir William Blackstone, *Commentaries on the Laws of England*, i. 67. The notion of common law rules being used 'time out of mind', or for longer than anyone can remember, was a commonplace in juristic writings of this era: see Pocock, above n.15, 37–8; and J. W. Tubbs, *The Common Law Mind: Medieval and Early Modern Conceptions* (Baltimore: Johns Hopkins UP, 2000), 153–4. It can be traced certainly as far back as Littleton in the second half of the fifteenth century: see Sir Thomas Littleton, *Tenures* [*c.*1465–75], ed. E. Wambaugh (Washington, DC: John Byrne, 1903), s.170 ('no custome is to bee allowed, but such custome, as hath bin used by title of prescription, that is to say, from time out of minde').

[19] Blackstone, *Commentaries*, i. 68.

[20] Sir Matthew Hale, *The History of the Common Law of England*, 6th edn. (London: Butterworth, 1820; orig. publ. 1713), 21. The book appeared posthumously (Hale died in 1676).

from the fact that things always appear to have been thus, that nobody remembers a time when matters were otherwise.[21] As Burke would have it, English lawyers, indeed the English generally, exhibit a 'powerful prepossession towards antiquity'.[22]

However persuasive this characterization of the common law may have been in the seventeenth and eighteenth centuries, it is unlikely, as Simpson observes, that anyone would subscribe to it today.[23] 'Formulations of the common law . . . are inherently corrigible, for it is always possible that they may be improved upon, or require modification as what they describe changes.'[24] The fluidity of the common law means that its principles cannot simply be considered to be of immemorial antiquity; the principles need to be documented, and their modification recorded. But this is a far from straightforward task.[25] Can only courts—and, if so, should only some courts—be permitted to deal with matters of legal principle? How are we to distinguish between the *ratio decidendi* of and *obiter dicta* in a judicial decision? Can textbooks and treatises be considered sources of legal authority? The movement away from the belief that common law principles derive their authority from being grounded in immemorial antiquity coincided with a growing preoccupation with the development of conventions to determine just what does constitute legal authority. Thus—to take one such convention—we find that, by the early nineteenth century, English courts are moving towards a requirement that counsel avoid citing living writers as authority for a legal proposition.[26] The complexity of this convention rather eluded the courts. Was it to apply to all living writers, or just some? What about subsequent editions of books by long-dead authors? 'Can I look at this book?', asked Clauson J. in *Re Thompson* after counsel for the trustees had cited the sixth edition of Dymond on *Estate Duties*. 'I thought the practice of the Court was to look only at text-books prepared by members of the Bar, which this book is not.'[27] Clauson passed no comment when, during the same proceedings, counsel for

[21] If anyone could remember otherwise, the authority of the relevant rule would of course be open to question: see Blackstone, *Commentaries*, i. 77 ('being immemorially disputed . . . is a proof that such consent was wanting').

[22] See Edmund Burke, *Reflections on the Revolution in France, And on the Proceedings in Certain Societies in London Relative to that Event*, ed. C. C. O'Brien (Harmondsworth: Penguin, 1968 [1790]), 117–18; also J. G. A. Pocock, 'Burke and the Ancient Constitution: A Problem in the History of Ideas' (1960) 1 *Historical Jnl.* 125–43; and cf. F. W. Maitland, *The Forms of Action at Common Law: A Course of Lectures*, eds. A. H. Chaytor and W. J. Whittaker (Cambridge: Cambridge UP, 1936; orig. publ. 1909), 8–9.

[23] See A. W. B. Simpson, 'The Common Law and Legal Theory', in *Oxford Essays in Jurisprudence (Second Series)*, ed. A. W. B. Simpson (Oxford: Clarendon Press, 1973), 77–99 at 93–4.

[24] Ibid. 94.

[25] See J. H. Baker, *The Law's Two Bodies: Some Evidential Problems in English Legal History* (Oxford: Oxford UP, 2001), 9–17; also Carleton Kemp Allen, *Law in the Making*, 3rd edn. (Oxford: Clarendon Press, 1939), 212–24; and Sir Frederick Pollock, 'Introduction', in *The Progress of Continental Law in the Nineteenth Century*, J. H. Wigmore et al. (London: Murray, 1918), xli–xlix at xlii–xliii.

[26] See, e.g., *Johnes v Johnes* (1814) 3 Dow 1, 15; *Taylor v Curtis* (1816) 6 Taunt. 608, 610; also Percy H. Winfield, *The Chief Sources of English Legal History* (Cambridge, Mass.: Harvard UP, 1925), 255–6.

[27] *Re Thompson* [1936] Ch. 676, 680.

the legatee cited the 21st edition of Snell's *Equity*—this edition having been prepared by a solicitor.[28] The point for emphasis is not that the judiciary struggled with this particular convention, but that the development of rules and criteria to determine what constitutes, and how to use, authority in legal argument generated a new set of problems—problems which the courts tended to underestimate or neglect rather than resolve.

For Simpson, rules about legal authority—determining, among other things, 'what courts are bound by what decisions, how one is to distinguish authoritative statements of law from statements of no authority, what law reports should be used and what difference, if any, it makes if a writer is dead or alive'—are not only 'notoriously controversial' and inconsistently applied but also 'commonly vague or qualified by escape clauses'; in fact, 'on very many matters no rules can be said to exist at all.'[29] Although Pollock's language was never quite as forthright as is Simpson's—although, indeed, Pollock more regularly lauds than he criticizes the operation of the common law—he was largely in agreement with these sentiments. 'No general description can be given of what constitutes a "book of authority",' he observed apropos of non-judicial expositions of law; 'being written by a judge does not make a book authoritative'.[30] Even if one shifts attention from the books that judges occasionally write to the decisions that they reach, the problem of determining authority does not disappear, 'for the great proportion of our case law . . . professes . . . to develop and apply principles that have never been committed to any authentic form of words.'[31] Simpson uses this last passage to support the proposition that the common law cannot be understood as a precise and finite set of rules,[32] though it also shows that Pollock appreciated the hazards of determining authoritative legal sources. The nature of Pollock's own preoccupation with authoritative sources will be considered briefly later in this chapter.

A second, and for our purposes equally significant, generalization about the common law highlights the place of reason in its history. Within the English juristic tradition, certainly onwards from the thirteenth century and the earliest Year Book cases, the common law has been regularly and closely associated with reason. Although not everyone has recognized this partnership—Bentham certainly did not[33]—the history of English law has been more inclined to defend rather than to mock the idea that the common law is fundamentally reasonable.[34] Coke, as is well known, was of the view that 'Reason is the life of the law,' that 'the Common Law itself is nothing

[28] See ibid. 679. [29] Simpson, above n.23, 87. [30] *FBJ* 236.

[31] *FBJ* 239. [32] See Simpson, above n.23, 88–9.

[33] See Gerald J. Postema, *Bentham and the Common Law Tradition* (Oxford: Clarendon Press, 1986), 269; and Simpson, above n.23, 88–91.

[34] 'The mantra of classical common lawyers', as Postema (providing a range of sources) puts it, 'was: "the common law is no other than common reason"'. Gerald J. Postema, 'The Philosophy of the Common Law', in *The Oxford Handbook of Jurisprudence and Philosophy of Law*, eds. J. Coleman and S. Shapiro (Oxford: Oxford UP, 2002), 588–622 at 592–3.

else but Reason . . . fined and refined by an infinite number of grave and learned men'.[35] But it is also well known that Coke considered reason to take more than one form. Of course the law is founded on reason, and of course the King possessed reason, Coke observed in his famous account of his 1608 discussion with James I, but 'His Majesty was not learned in the laws of the realm of England, and causes . . . are not to be decided by natural reason but by the artificial reason and judgment of the law, . . . which requires long study and experience, before that a man can attain to the cognizance of it.'[36] If reason is the life of the law, it is a complicated life, for reason assumes numerous identities. In one such guise, reason clearly connects with the notion of immemorial antiquity: the common law is not merely reason, Thomas Hedley claimed in a speech to the House of Commons in 1610, but 'must be tried reason, . . . allowed by the wisdom of time from many ages to be good and profitable for the commonwealth'.[37] '[T]his time'—which 'is wiser than the judges, wiser than the parliament, nay wiser than the wit of man'—'must not be such as statute laws are tried by, . . . but such time whereof the memory of man is not to the contrary, time out of mind.'[38]

Hedley appreciated that there are many other competing conceptions of the reasonableness of the common law—certain of which he himself rejected[39]—and while it would involve too much of a detour to review these conceptions here, we should at least mention that jurists who have analysed common law reason have variously portrayed the common law as an accretion of collective wisdom, a reservoir of common experience, and a repository of general principles.[40] This last characterization was very much favoured by Lord Mansfield, perhaps the greatest eighteenth-century defender of the view that the common law is founded upon reason and principle and a judge for whom Pollock expressed a great deal of admiration.[41] The common law, according to Mansfield, 'does not consist in particular cases, but in general principles which run through cases and govern the decision of them'.[42] While precedents may 'serve to fix Principles,' a 'precedent, though it be Evidence of law, is not law itself'; indeed, 'the Law would be a strange science if it rested

[35] Sir Edward Coke, *Institutes of the Laws of England* (1787), i. 97b.

[36] *Twelfth Reports, Prohibitions del Roy* (1607) 12 Co. Rep. 63, 64.

[37] Thomas Hedley, speech to the House of Commons, 28 June 1610, in *Proceedings in Parliament 1610: Vol. ii: House of Commons*, ed. E. R. Foster (New Haven: Yale UP, 1966), 170–97 at 176.

[38] Ibid. 175.

[39] See ibid. 173–4. On Hedley's conception of the common law and variations on it, see Gerald J. Postema, 'Classical Common Law Jurisprudence (Part I)' (2003) 2 *Oxford Univ. Commonwealth L. J.* 155–80 at 167–76.

[40] See, generally, Postema, above n.33, 3–80.

[41] For Pollock on Mansfield, see *EIL* 60, 67–8; *ECL* 118–19; *LCDE* 20.

[42] *Rust v Cooper* (1774) Cowp. 629, 632, cited after David Liebermann, *The Province of Legislation Determined: Legal Theory in Eighteenth-Century Britain* (Cambridge: Cambridge UP, 1989), 126; and Postema, above n.33, 35. Cf. Pollock, above n.25, xliv ('Judicial authority belongs not to the exact words used in this or that judgment, nor even to all the reasons given, but only to the principles recognized and applied as necessary grounds for the decision').

solely upon cases'.[43] Proper appreciation of this and other depictions of the common law would require detailed study not only of Mansfield but also of jurists such as Fortescue, St German, Blackstone, and Coke. Such a task is well beyond this particular project.[44] What of course lies very much within this project is Pollock's contribution to the juristic tradition that equates the common law with reason. Differences of perspective among those jurists who make this equation are often difficult to discern—divergences over just what is common law reason are often subtle—and Pollock's own contribution is reminiscent of and certainly indebted to arguments advanced by others (particularly Mansfield). It would be wrong, however, to suggest that Pollock lacked a voice of his own when writing about the reasonableness of the common law, and a basic objective of this chapter is to determine just what he had to say.

ii. The qualities of the common law

Throughout Pollock's writings we find a phrase which seems to recur more than any other, a phrase which we have encountered already in this book but which we have not yet properly analysed. It is not often that we find modern writers referring to 'habits of mind'; but in Pollock's day the phrase was in common usage, as was its close relative, 'habits of thought'. Pollock, like others, used 'habits of mind' for a variety of purposes.[45] More often than not, however, he used it for a very specific purpose: to capture the virtues of the common law and the common lawyer.

Some Victorian social commentators and theorists were inclined to treat the general notion of habit as indicative of moral weakness, whereas others associated it with strength of character. Various Victorian psychologists and physiologists appealed to what Collini has called 'a diluted Lamarckianism', according to which the individual, by 'properly exercising the muscles of the will', might acquire 'a new capacity that could operate instinctively on future occasions and . . . could determine the behaviour of future generations.'[46]

[43] *Jones v Randall* (1774) Lofft 383, 385, cited after Liebermann, above n.42, 126; and Postema, above n.33, 35. More generally, on Mansfield's promotion of principle over precedent, see C. H. S. Fifoot, *Lord Mansfield* (Oxford: Clarendon Press, 1936), 224–9; and Gerald J. Postema, 'Classical Common Law Jurisprudence (Part II)' (2003) 3 *Oxford Univ. Commonwealth L. J.* 1–28 at 14–15.

[44] Though it has been undertaken with considerable success by others: see, e.g., Tubbs, above n.18, 53–109, 141–95; and Liebermann, above n.42, 71–143.

[45] See, e.g., *FBJ* v; *EIL* 57; *EJE* 116, 215, 216, 255, 278; *SHLP* 349. He was less wedded to 'habits of thought', but would occasionally use that, too: see, e.g., *LL(3)* 2; *SHLP* 145, 289; *ECL* 4.

[46] Stefan Collini, 'The Idea of 'Character' in Victorian Political Thought' (1985) 35 *Transactions of the Royal Historical Society* 29–50 at 35. To call this 'diluted' Lamarckianism is perhaps charitable. Collini's point appears to be that many Victorian psychologists and physiologists accepted a standard version of Lamarckianism as the idea that organisms survive by passing on their acquired characteristics to their offspring. Lamarck in fact believed something more complex: that organisms are not passively altered by their environment, but that changes in the environment cause changes in the needs of organisms living in that environment, which in turn causes changes in their behaviour. Altered behaviour

Habits—physical habits or habits of the mind—'could modify or leave a deposit in the nervous system itself';[47] and these modifications or deposits might be to good effect or ill. If habits are to be regarded as acquired characteristics, capable of being inherited by successive generations, then we might expect some bad habits—for example habits which, although conducive to survival, are considered unsociable—to regenerate along with acceptable ones.[48] Hence the Victorian 'anxiety about the insidiously corrosive power of habit'.[49] During the nineteenth century, however, the notion of habit was not always invested with negative connotations. Within Victorian political thought, Collini points out, the formation of habit was often equated with the idea of restraint, with the reining in of individual will: 'the assumption', in essence, was 'that the possession of settled dispositions indicated a certain habit of restraining one's impulses. The contrast was with behaviour which was random, impulsive, feckless.'[50]

Pollock took something akin to this latter route, and used the notion of habit to depict how he considered the English to blend an appreciation of rules and restraint with an instinctive distrust of authoritarianism. Not only have 'legal habits of thought . . . entered into the very marrow of our political history', he argued, but 'the current opinions and habits of mind of lawyers from generation to generation have a history of their own'.[51] Understanding this latter branch of history draws us closer to the common law psyche. Among other

leads to greater or lesser use of a given structure or organ; use would cause the structure to increase in size over several generations, whereas disuse would cause it to shrink or disappear. Thus, giraffes' necks became long, according to this theory, because they kept stretching them in order to reach high leaves on trees. Change occurs because an animal passes on to its offspring physiological changes it had undergone in its own lifetime, changes which came about by its responding to its survival needs. The Victorian equation of habits with Lamarckian acquired characteristics might be called a dilution of the basic idea, though distortion would seem the better word. For Lamarck's evolutionary theory, see Jean-Baptiste Lamarck, *Zoological Philosophy: An Exposition with Regard to the Natural History of Animals*, trans. H. Elliot (Chicago: University of Chicago Press, 1984 [1809]); and, for general studies, see Madeleine Barthélemy-Madaule, *Lamarck, the Mythical Precursor: A Study of the Relations Between Science and Ideology*, trans. M. H. Shank (Cambridge, Mass.: MIT Press, 1982); and Richard W. Burkhardt, Jr., *The Spirit of System: Lamarck and Evolutionary Biology*, rev. edn. (Cambridge, Mass: Harvard UP, 1995 [1977]).

[47] Collini, above n.46, 35.

[48] Of course, this argument assumes that the survival of habits is a matter beyond human agency—that we will often inherit habits, in other words, which we would rather be without. Thus Lamarckianism, although considered by many Victorian social theorists to celebrate the capacity of organisms to adapt themselves to changing circumstances, seemed to entail an unwelcome element of fatalism. '[D]espite the appeal of Lamarckism for [Victorian] social evolutionists,' Den Otter remarks, 'other theorists who were . . . determined to retain a place for human agency . . . adhered to arguments drawn from natural selection. To these critics, Lamarckism threatened to lock societies into a rigid hereditary path.' Sandra M. Den Otter, *British Idealism and Social Explanation: A Study in Late Victorian Thought* (Oxford: Clarendon Press, 1996), 90.

[49] Collini, above n.46, 34. [50] Ibid.

[51] *OLOD* 94, 242. For a more general effort by Pollock to connect habit and restraint, see his review of Henri Marion, *De la Solidarité morale* (1882) 7 *Mind* 142–6 at 144 ('[T]he power of habit is not confined to particular classes of actions. Moral self-control, aided by the self-approval which is its immediate result, itself becomes a habit if it is practised with success, especially at the critical stages of life. The character is disciplined for future conflicts, and the conflict when it comes is easier').

things, history reveals common law peoples' love of precedent, law-abidingness, and the rule of law,[52] their distrust of idealism ('[m]en will not suddenly barter their inherited maxims of right and wrong for philosophic ideals'[53]), their belief in the power of reason,[54] their instinct for justice,[55] and their 'deep and peculiar repugnance to the . . . method of dealing with ethical questions which follows . . . from the assumption that they are to be disposed of . . . by some definite and organized authority.'[56]

Consideration of the notion of habit reveals other English traits. To study the English lawyer's habit of mind, Pollock believed, is to encounter English insularity: 'our laws have been eminently national and positive, and our particular legal habit of mind is perhaps the most insular of our many insular traits.'[57] He was not complaining. The gains of our distance from Europe, he argued, exceed the disadvantages.[58] That we are different is a blessing:

Our old English oak is rugged and weather-beaten; its branches are not symmetrical; some limbs have been spread abroad while others have been stunted; it savours its own soil and knows of none other. But in that soil it is fast rooted, and from the deepest fibres that feed it in the secret places of the earth to the topmost that leap to the air and glance in the sun, it still lives and grows. Our Constitution is popular in that the life of the English people, from the greatest to the least, has gone to make it what it is; and it has at all times combined the tenacity of tradition with a great power of assimilating fresh elements, and of adapting existing organs to new purposes. For some

[52] See *EJE* 213–17.

[53] *EJE* 285. Cf. [John Stuart Mill], 'Letter from an Englishman to a Frenchman, on a Recent Apology in "The Journal des Debats," for the Faults of the English National Character' (June 1834) n.s. 8 *Monthly Repository* 385–95 at 395 ('We *have* the diversities of opinion, the noisy conflicts; we do dispute on morality but we do *not* philosophize on it, simply because we do not philosophize upon any thing—it is not our way; we set no value on systematic thought'); also James Bryce, 'The Influence of National Character and Historical Environment on the Development of the Common Law' (1908) 24 *LQR* 9–25 at 15–16.

[54] See *EJE* 271–2.

[55] See *ECL* 43.

[56] *EJE* 272; cf. *ECL* 111; and see also F. Pollock, 'The History of the English Land Laws' (1882) 46 *Macmillan's Magazine* 356–68 at 368 ('The ideal of commercial policy is every man his own landlord. The ideal of the socialist policy is the State every man's landlord. For Englishmen, with English habits of independent activity, and English traditions of the success of unfettered enterprise, the choice between these does not seem to admit of much doubt').

[57] *OLOD* 25.

[58] 'Our long standing apart from the general movement of European thought has had its draw-backs; but I think it the better opinion that both in jurisprudence and in the not wholly dissimilar case of philosophy the gain has outweighed them. And I mean this to be understood . . . both of science and of practice.' *OLOD* 25. Cf. also [A. L. Goodhart], 'Pollock: Lectures', n.d., in Goodhart papers, MS Eng. c. 2910, ff.87–9 at 87: 'Broadly speaking, whatever is not of England in the forms of modern jurisprudence is of Rome or of Roman mould. In law, as in politics, the severance of Britain by a world's breadth from the world of Rome has fostered a new birth which mankind could ill have spared. And the growth of English politics is more closely connected with the independent growth and strength of English law than has been commonly perceived, or can be gathered from the common accounts of English history.' The passage is taken from what appears to be Goodhart's typed transcription of some of Pollock's Oxford lecture notes (the prose is unmistakably Pollock's). The central theme of the notes is the uniqueness of English legal and political arrangements and institutions.

considerable time our national institutions and our national character have been confirming one another in this habit.[59]

Note the mixture of defiance and glorification in this passage. The English are far from perfect. 'It is one of our national defects to underrate the value of the first impression of things, and to spoil even good deeds by an ill manner of doing them.'[60] But, Pollock appears to be saying, do not underestimate the English disposition; we may be insular, but our insularity is no obstacle to our greatness. 'At first we lived in fear of surprises and usurpations; . . . we were jealously insular and held strangers at arm's length . . . But we held fast to our national genius.'[61] Our fatalism, our penchant for trying to muddle through life's problems rather than devising strategies to combat them, our general suspicion of grand schemes and organizing frameworks (the same suspicion that Pollock himself expressed about so much of the philosophy that he read[62])—all of these characteristics Pollock ascribed to the English, and all of them he considered positive attributes. 'Sometimes it is a gift rather than a defect not to see too far or too wide at once; it may save us from fighting against the gods.'[63] Without irony he wrote of how we tend 'not to think of ourselves as setting an example to the world, . . . but to take up the day's work . . . and handle it as best we may.'[64] Chance, we so often recognize, is not for taming, just as we tend to recognize that our resignation 'is less likely to end in crushing disaster than the far-reaching ambition which lays out new worlds for itself, and thinks to build them by forcing the hand of Providence.'[65]

The manner in which Pollock wrote about the English is reflected in his eulogizing of the common law. That phlegmatic character, that English willingness to deal with each day's problems to the best of one's ability, mirrors 'the spirit of the law and the true lawyer'—the lawyer, that is, who asks 'at every doubtful turn: What will help the business through?'[66] Just as Pollock regarded English insularity as a source of pride, moreover, so too he delighted in the detachment of the common law from other legal systems: '[t]here is no case, I believe, of the Common Law having lost ground in the presence of another system; there are certainly many where it has gained.'[67] With the

[59] *OLOD* 162–3; and cf. *GCL* 8.

[60] *OLOD* 194; though cf. *FBJ* 38–9.

[61] *ECL* 114. While Pollock certainly lauded the English character, it is not clear that there is any basis for claiming, as Mylchreest does, that he 'wanted to distinguish between the stable and orderly democracy of the English peoples and the dogmatic ideology and social disorder of the French'. Ian Bruce Mylchreest, *The Anglo-American Dialogue on Constitutionalism, 1860–1920* (Ph.D. dissertation, Graduate School, Cornell University, 1988), 245.

[62] Generally, for an account of suspicion of high theory and abstractions as an English trait, see Peter Ackroyd, *Albion: The Origins of the English Imagination* (London: Chatto & Windus, 2002), 383–94.

[63] *ECL* 58. [64] *ECL* 59. [65] *ECL* 59. [66] *GCL* 113.

[67] *GCL* 77. Around 1911, writing on the question of whether the common law had by that point received Savigny's 'fiction' theory of corporations, Pollock argued that legal borrowings are not tantamount to legal transplants: '[t]he truth is, I believe, that we have to be careful to distinguish occasional borrowing of exotic phrases for ornament from the serious reception of a doctrine, and still

common law, as with many of our other traditions, we rarely 'take any pains to make our ways easy for strangers who have a mind to learn them.'[68] Furthermore, English anti-hubris is reflected in the common law's evolution, which, like chance, is beyond design. '[L]aw and the machinery of law . . . grow and cannot be made to order'[69]—litigants sometimes come unstuck, Pollock was fond of repeating, because they assume the opposite.[70]

The common law evolves because it needs to evolve: like its country of birth, it is not perfect.[71] Once it was the province 'of commonplace, indifferently learned, and not always upright judges, who were ill enough reported for the most part, but perhaps no worse than they deserved to be.'[72] Even in modern times, there is much about the operation of the common law that is sub-optimal. 'The genius of our law deliberately prefers the risk of some hardship in particular cases',[73] judges can be lamentably anti-theoretical when tackling matters which cry out for a theoretical approach,[74] and—notwithstanding that ordinary citizens 'often require the law to perform impossibilities'[75]—lawyers

more from admission of all its consequences.' *EIL* 151. Although Pollock conceded that the House of Lords' adoption of the fiction theory in *Salomon v Salomon & Co. Ltd* [1897] AC 22 'took many of us by surprise at the time' (see (1915) 31 *LQR* 135; and also (1897) 13 *LQR* 6), he did not consider the decision to indicate the common law's reception of the theory. 'We are glad to know', he remarked in 1911, 'that the Common Law is not bound to the "Fiction Theory."' (1911) 27 *LQR* 2. Cf. also F. Pollock to Arthur W. Machen, n.d. [postmark 13 April 1911], in Pollock correspondence, box 1, folder 52: 'You seem to prefer the realist to the fictionist doctrine [of corporate personality]. . . . My only immediate purpose is to show that the Common Law is not tied to any.' For the same point on record, see Pollock, above n.25, xliv; 'English Private Law, 1870–1920' (1924) 2 *Cambridge L. J.* 19–36 at 24–5. And on Pollock and the fiction theory, see further C. H. S. Fifoot, *Law and History in the Nineteenth Century* (London: Bernard Quaritch, 1956), 15–16. Fifoot regards Pollock as an out-and-out opponent of the theory.

[68] *GCL* 77; cf. also *EIL* 139 ('These things may seem strange. Some of them, possibly, may seem hardly credible to some of our Continental brethren. I can only vouch for their truth'); and Frederick Pollock, 'The Continuity of the Common Law' (1898) 11 *Harvard L. Rev.* 423–33 at 427.

[69] *EJE* 236.

[70] 'Litigation is a game in which the court is umpire. . . . It is for the parties to learn the rules and play the game correctly at their peril.' *ECL* 32. Cf. also *EJE* 77; and Sir Frederick Pollock, 'The Foundations of Justice' (1904) 3 *Canadian L. Rev.* 2–15 at 5 ('Litigation, in fact, is something like a game. The parties are players who must know the rules of the game at their peril'); 'Address by Sir Frederick Pollock' (1904) 1 *Univ. of Cincinnati Record* 18–23 at 21 ('[T]he process of law must have seemed to our ancestors to be something very like a game . . . in which the player must observe the rules entirely at his own risk').

[71] '[A] compulsory smattering of undigested Roman law rules and terminology is worse than worthless. But the original authorities of the Roman system are, compared with our own, compendious; and a moderate amount of systematic application under proper guidance will give a man a range of legal ideas more complete in itself and more conducive to orderly thinking than he is likely to get from any other form of legal study at present practicable. In the Common Law we have outgrown Blackstone's work, and we are not yet ready to replace it.' *OLOD* 104.

[72] *EIL* 163. See also *GCL* 122; though cf. *ECL* 50 (on the wisdom and valour of English judges of the thirteenth and fourteenth centuries).

[73] *ECL* 73.

[74] Pollock felt very much this way about the judicial handling of corporate personality: '[n]o one who is familiar with the English judicial mind will be surprised at the scantiness of positive utterances on a question of this high order of generality.' *EIL* 155; and cf. n.67, above.

[75] *EIL* 258–9.

are as restricted as is anyone else in their capacity to secure ideal outcomes. Montesquieu, for all his perspicacity, 'could not escape the besetting temptation of the eighteenth century to regard men as more rational than they are'.[76] By the same token, Pollock warned, we must not mistakenly assume that lawyers are yet more rational. 'One way or another there is a great deal of ancient human nature about man, and it does not forsake him when he determines to be rational and a lawyer.'[77]

But Pollock was keen not to draw attention to the negatives. 'It would be too much to say that the system of the Common Law secures complete uniformity or consistency. Courts are not only liable to errors of judgment, but may be imperfectly informed. But probably it is more successful in these respects than any other system.'[78] Indeed, we would do much better to accentuate the positives; for the common law, he believed, as much as the English disposition, is marked by genius. '[T]he system which we have inherited is unique alike in its history and in its destiny.'[79] It is a thing of romance and great intrigue, which 'grows by what it feeds on';[80] 'underlying all the confusion of detail' there is 'a real organic energy of growth'.[81] Rather than being 'a museum of antiquities,' the common law is 'a living and active law,' a system within which 'doctrines get settled either by a process of semi-conscious consent worked out in the solution of particular cases, or by the development, in the same manner, of conflicting tendencies in professional and judicial opinion until at last a decisive practical choice is called for.'[82] In the courts, 'no sooner is an adventure accomplished than a fresh one is disclosed or arises out of that very achievement.'[83]

Common law principles may never have been committed to what Pollock, as we saw above, called an 'authentic form of words', but the words which have been used to articulate those principles 'it has taken generations of strenuous thought and discussion to bring to their full significance'.[84] 'The legal machinery by which this is done', he observed in 1883 on the subject of strict settlements, 'is little more than two centuries old, and, though refined and improved in details by the ingenuity of generations of conveyancers, has not been much altered in substance since its first invention.'[85] His point was not

[76] *IHSP* 87. [77] *EIL* 221. [78] *FBJ* 324.

[79] *OLOD* 46; see also *ECL* 15. [80] *GCL* 77.

[81] *ECL* 30; and cf. *EIL* 10–11; *GCL* 87 ('The Genius of the Common Law has somehow contrived to extract from all the theoretical confusion a body of law which is quite well understood by those who handle it, and quite sufficient for everyday needs, and has the reputation of being, on the whole, just and merciful').

[82] *GCL* 110; *EIL* 152. See also *ECL* 81.

[83] *GCL* 112–13. See also *ECL* 19 ('. . . the power of taking up fresh material is still alive').

[84] *OLOD* 3; and see also *EIL* 199, 201–2.

[85] *LL* 9. The strict settlement appears to have been first devised by conveyancers and judges in the mid-seventeenth century. For the history, see A. W. B. Simpson, *A History of the Land Law*, 2nd edn. (Oxford: Clarendon Press, 1986), 229–31.

that it was time for an overhaul of the system—as, in fact, it was—but that the system was essentially sound.[86] Small wonder, he believed, that other countries—located, one assumes, in that world to which we do not think of ourselves as setting an example—'have derived their law from England, or come under the influence of English judicial habits', and that 'everywhere under the British flag . . . our forensic and judicial habits have prevailed'.[87] How can we do other than worship the 'masterful potency' of this system?[88] 'So venerable, so majestic, is this living temple of justice, this immemorial and yet freshly growing fabric of the Common Law, that the least of us is happy who hereafter may point to so much as one stone thereof and say, The work of my hands is there.'[89]

We noted in the previous chapter Pollock's fondness for the stirring conclusion. Unsurprisingly, the last quotation appears at the end of one of his Oxford lectures. Look to the final paragraphs of many of Pollock's lectures, indeed, and a style soon emerges. Thus, the conclusion to his North American law school lectures of 1903:

> Remember that our lady the Common law is not a task-mistress but a bountiful sovereign whose service is freedom. The destinies of the English-speaking world are bound up with her fortune and her migrations, and its conquests are justified by her works. . . . The empire of the Common Law is in your hands.[90]

[86] '[Pollock's] *Land Laws* . . . proved exceedingly popular with students until the legislation of 1925 made most of it out of date.' A. L. Goodhart, 'Introduction', in *JLE* ix–xlviii at xii. Strict settlements were subjected to considerable criticism during the late nineteenth century: see W. R. Cornish and G. de N. Clark, *Law and Society in England 1750–1950* (London: Sweet & Maxwell, 1989), 166–72. For all that Pollock was happy to state with pride in all three editions of *The Land Laws* that the strict settlement 'owes nothing to legislation, except by accident' (*LL* 9; *LL(3)* 10), one of the objectives of early twentieth-century land law reform was to refine the operation of the strict settlement through legislation (specifically, through the Settled Land Act 1925): see J. Stuart Anderson, *Lawyers and the Making of English Land Law 1832–1940* (Oxford: Clarendon Press, 1992), 265–6, 290–302. The result of the refining initiative was not especially impressive: during the twentieth century the strict settlement was generally displaced by the trust for sale of land, and in 1985 the Law Commission declared the strict settlement to be 'excessively complex and no longer necessary'. Law Commission, *Trusts of Land* (Law Com. Working Paper No. 94, September 1985), para. 17.1. Since 1996, it has not been possible to create new strict settlements under the Settled Land Act 1925: see Trusts of Land and Appointment of Trustees Act 1996, s. 2(1).

[87] *FBJ* 227; *GCL* 91–2. Sometimes, in Pollock's view, these other countries would fail to come up to scratch: see, e.g., *FBJ* 39. Criminal and constitutional law, he believed, were English law's most notable exports: see *GCL* 85, 89. For Pollock on England generally, see, e.g., *EJE* 63 ('a country second to none in power and resources of every kind').

[88] See *GCL* 2, 93, 125. Cf. Pollock to Holmes, 3 October 1902, in *PHL* i. 107 ('How should the lay gentry, or even the average lawyer, understand the development of the common law, or the work that men such as you . . . put into it?').

[89] *OLOD* 111.

[90] *ECL* 137–8; also Sir Frederick Pollock, 'The Law of Reason' (1903) 2 *Michigan L. Rev.* 159–79 at 179 (same).

Likewise the conclusion to his Carpentier Lectures of 1911:

> There is no more arduous enterprise for lawful men, and none more noble, than the perpetual quest of justice laid upon all of us who are pledged to serve our lady the Common Law.[91]

We also noted in the previous chapter that one could quite easily construct from such concluding passages a portrait of Pollock as a jurist committed to hyperbole and uninterested in nuance. 'Down the ages the works of legal authors have proclaimed the justice, the adaptability, the impartiality and the wisdom of the common law of England', one barrister declared in 1957, and 'it is saddening that' Pollock—'in this century the prime exponent and unchallenged high priest of the cult'—'should have allowed himself to indulge in this sort of idolatry.'[92] '[O]ur lady the Common Law', this commentator adds, 'never existed except in the imagination of Pollock', who might have been well advised to 'go and see a good man in Harley Street' about his delusion.[93] Certainly, as the passages above suggest and as we have already noted (see chapter 2), Pollock seemed to take the view that the image of his lady was resistant to over-use—rather strange for a man who generally eschewed repetition and used imagery with restraint. Yet despite the irksome over-reliance on an image in these passages, let alone the outmoded grandiloquence of the passages themselves, they contain an assertion which, although fairly mundane, deserves our attention: being a dutiful servant to the common law is hard, yet fulfilling and noble, work. Pollock's notion of duty to the common law was touched upon in chapter 2. It is appropriate, at this point, to consider that notion in more detail.

Integral to Englishness, Langford argues, is 'the habitual recognition of *duty*. The determination to do that which ought to be done, simply *because* it ought to be done, is a motive of action which has been shown to be almost peculiar to Englishmen—a motive which most other nations cannot understand.'[94] Leaving aside the question of just how peculiarly English is this manner of behaviour, one might assume Langford to be claiming that, for the English, behaving dutifully is simply a reflex action. Such an assumption, however, would appear to simplify his argument, which in fact seems to be that failure to behave dutifully is commonly considered by the English to be dishonourable. Dutiful behaviour, on this account, is a mark of good character.[95]

[91] *GCL* 125.

[92] C. P. Harvey, *The Advocate's Devil* (London: Stevens & Sons, 1958), 75–6. The preface to the book indicates that it was completed in August 1957.

[93] Ibid. 80, 84.

[94] Paul Langford, *Englishness Identified: Manners and Character 1650–1850* (Oxford: Oxford UP, 2000), 314.

[95] On the Victorian connection between duty and character, see Ian Bradley, *The Optimists: Themes and Personalities in Victorian Liberalism* (London: Faber and Faber, 1980), 182–4; and Stefan Collini, *Public Moralists: Political Thought and Public Life in Britain 1850–1930* (Oxford: Clarendon Press, 1991), 100, 102–3.

Pollock did not assume that the English act dutifully on instinct. What he did believe is that a certain type, indeed class, of Englishman recognizes the ignobility of shirking one's duties. Of course, there are those who recognize no such thing: the 'habitually criminal class', for example, 'holds together in a crooked bond of its own, and makes law within itself against the law. The thief is . . . but a man of perverted conscience'.[96] In claiming as much, Pollock was aligning himself with those Victorians who fretted about the corrosive power of habit, who, as Collini elaborates, tended to understand morality 'very much as a system of obligations' and to regard individual acceptance of duty as the 'moral effort' required to resist weakness of will.[97] As with his use of the notion of habit, nevertheless, when resorting to the idea of duty Pollock generally peddled a more positive message: acceptance of one's duties was, as he put it, 'the nobler way'.[98] Whatever our individual instincts might be on the question of Home Rule for Ireland, he wrote in 1888, the government cannot simply relinquish its duties. 'The cry is, "You cannot, or you will not, perform the office of rulers in Ireland. . . . A just and high-minded nation, a nation that has achieved what England has achieved in the most various undertakings of government, will not be so abject as to give way to such a cry. We cannot in honour abandon our office.'[99] Just as Pollock presents the recognition of honour in duty as a national characteristic—certainly as a characteristic of the English governing class—so too he makes his familiar move of identifying the same characteristic within the English common law, the servants of which ought to understand the principle of *noblesse oblige*: 'a profession, above all a learned profession, is not an affair of bargaining and bread-winning, but the undertaking of a high duty to mankind.'[100]

The basic purpose of this section has been to show how Pollock identified the common law with certain qualities—English qualities, we might say. Like Burke, Pollock considered the principal characteristics of the English to be reflected in the common law. Burke, of course, lauded many English characteristics: the people of England readily discern artifice, he wrote, and 'will shew to the haughty potentates of the world . . . that [England] will not suffer the insolence of wealth and titles, or any other species of proud pretension'.[101] By 1782, as we noted in chapter 2, Burke was convinced that English character shapes English law, that much of what we discover in our political and legal arrangements basically reflects English attitudes, outlooks, and predispositions. 'I give you opinions', he wrote in 1790, 'which . . . are so worked into my mind, that I am unable to distinguish what I have learned from others from the results of my own meditation. It is on some such principles that the majority of the people of England . . . hardly think it lawful to be without.'[102] Many of the principles embedded in the minds of the English people are also

[96] *EJE* 312. [97] Collini, above n.95, 100.
[98] *OLOD* 215. [99] *OLOD* 215. [100] *OLOD* 93.
[101] Burke, above n.22, 202; and, on discernment of artifice, see also ibid. 203–4 ('[t]he ears of the people in England are distinguishing'). [102] Ibid. 197.

at the core of their legal system: so it is that 'the science of jurisprudence . . . is the collected reason of ages, combining the principles of original justice with the infinite variety of human concerns'.[103]

Pollock had little but praise for Burke. In Pollock's eyes, Burke was a thinker 'too great for his generation'[104] and a man whom we 'cannot honour too much'.[105] 'A light of great wisdom shines in almost everything of Burke's making. . . . Shallow or false he could not be.'[106] Although Pollock echoed Burke in connecting the qualities of the common law with the qualities of the English, one might reasonably question whether Pollock's thoughts about this connection even remotely approached the meditative depth that he credited to Burke. Pollock's only obvious objective in exploring the connection, after all, was to formulate effusive conclusions about the genius of the common law. Even the most ardent anglophile is likely to resolve sooner or later that such an exercise lacks substance. Our next task is to move beyond Pollock's rhetoric and encomia and determine whether, in fact, there is much of substance to be discovered in his discourses on the common law. Undertaking this task requires that we continue to draw on all of Pollock's work; nevertheless, two of his books, *The Expansion of the Common Law* and *The Genius of the Common Law*, share a thematic orientation which makes them central to our inquiry.

iii. Reason, common sense, and principle

'For myself I find it difficult to believe that the universe is reasonable,' Pollock wrote to Holmes in 1919, 'but impossible to believe that it is not.'[107] While the place of reason in the universe may have troubled Pollock, the place of reason in the common law gave him no cause for doubt. As we have seen already in this study, Pollock regarded the common law as a wonderful embodiment of human reason. 'Laymen may still be found to say . . . that law is what the judges will; and we are still ready to reply . . . "No: law is reason." Reason, let it be, the best that we can discover in our day.'[108] Pollock, as we saw in chapter 3, considered St German, writing in the sixteenth century, to deserve credit for recognizing that 'where the canonist or civilian would speak of the Law of Nature, the common lawyer speaks of reason'.[109] Understanding the connection between reason and the common law requires, however, that we venture back beyond St German, for 'the Law of Nature, as accepted throughout the Middle Ages, was derived from Greek theories of ethics.'[110] 'Our founders of the thirteenth century, Raleigh, and Pateshull, and Henry of Bratton', followed Roman jurists in drawing inspiration from 'the Greek philosophy of natural justice'.[111]

[103] Burke, above n.22, 193. [104] *IHSP* 97. [105] *OLOD* 42. [106] *IHSP* 90, 96.
[107] Pollock to Holmes, 6 August 1919, in *PHL* ii. 21. [108] *GCL* 2.
[109] *EIL* 58. [110] *ECL* 110. [111] *ECL* 112.

Yet these thirteenth-century publicists made no reference to the Law of Nature. Why not? '[T]he answer is that at no time after, at latest, the Papal interference in the English politics of the first half of the thirteenth century, was the citation of Roman canonical authority acceptable in our country, save so far as it was necessary for strictly technical purposes.'[112] Hence, the common law devised its own nomenclature: the language of reason and reasonableness. '[P]ractical judgment, as Aristotle saw long ago, must measure itself by the imagined judgment of the reasonable man.'[113] 'One of the most characteristic and important features of the modern Common Law is the manner in which we fix the measure of legal duties . . . by reference to a reasonable man's caution,' applying 'the principle of Aristotle' and assuming 'that to be reasonable which appears so to competent persons.'[114] In applying this principle, the common law is simply borrowing an idea and expressing it in its own language: 'the appeal to the test of reasonableness is . . . really the same thing' as 'a reference to the Law of Nature'.[115]

What, however, do 'reason' and 'reasonableness' mean? Pollock approached this question from two different, but not unconnected, angles. First, he associated reason with common sense. The notion of common sense, Postema has observed, often operates within the common law tradition as an 'unspoken test of reasonableness'.[116] Pollock was uninhibited in conceiving of common sense thus. Within the common law tradition, reasonableness is often 'ascertained in the first instance by the common sense of juries, and gradually consolidated into judicial rules of law'.[117] The Holmesian idea, furthermore,

[112] *ECL* 113. [113] *EJE* 271. [114] *EIL* 69, 63.

[115] *EIL* 78. Cf. Arthur L. Goodhart, *English Contributions to the Philosophy of Law: The Seventh Annual Benjamin N. Cardozo Lecture Delivered before the Association of the Bar of the City of New York, 25 May 1948* (New York: Oxford UP, 1948), 35–6 ('Pollock . . . explains that . . . where the canonist or civilian would speak of the Law of Nature, the common lawyer speaks of reason. . . . I doubt whether this is a complete explanation. Is not the difference between "The Law of Nature" and "the law of reason" similar to the difference between a system based on a code and one based on precedent? The common law establishes its general principles by considering how a reasonable man would act in particular circumstances while the natural law method is to state general principles and then to assume that the reasonable man would act in accordance with them. The conclusions at which they arrive are substantially identical, but the methods by which they are reached are different'). The argument that Pollock lacked a firm grasp of what is meant by 'law of nature' is also developed by D. P. Heatley, 'Pollock and Lorimer' (1944) 56 *Juridical Rev.* 6–26 at 9–15. Note that appeals to reasonableness, in Pollock's view, are not always admirable. Consider, he wrote to Holmes, popular journalistic appeals 'to our friend the reasonable man, who in the flesh is a Philistine pig'. Pollock to Holmes, 3 October 1902, in *PHL* i. 107.

[116] Postema, above n.33, 76. One study produced in the United States has shown that the notion of common sense is regularly resorted to in judicial argument: '[t]he words and phrases "common sense," "commonsensical," and "sensible," used as an argument . . . appear upwards of 70,000 times in Westlaw'—an observation which most likely 'understates the reliance on common sense as an argument,' given that the concept is often invoked through the use of less obvious terminology. See Ronald J. Allen and Ross M. Rosenberg, 'Legal Phenomena, Knowledge, and Theory: A Cautionary Tale of Hedgehogs and Foxes' (2002) 77 *Chicago-Kent L. Rev.* 683–734 at 691.

[117] *EIL* 69, and cf. 76, and also Lord Mansfield's dictum that commercial negotiations 'ought not to depend upon Subtleties and Niceties, but upon Rules, easily learned and easily retained, because they are the Dictates of Common Sense, drawn from the Truth of the Case'. *Hamilton v Mendes* (1761) 2 Burrow 1198, 1214.

of an 'external standard of reasonableness'—an idea which, we saw in the last chapter, Pollock approved of and adapted—'enables the law to keep in close touch with the moral and practical sense of mankind in the affairs of life'.[118] Common sense, like reason, he regarded to be synonymous with the notion of natural justice.[119]

But this was not just any old common sense. Pollock certainly respected everyday common sense—much rather that than what he considered to be the uncommon sense of moral philosophers.[120] The common sense which he admired most, however, was that of the common lawyer. Lay common sense is often lamentably short sighted.[121] Juries, for all that they are often repositories of common sense,[122] sometimes produce regrettable verdicts because they become spellbound by legal technicalities ('every lawyer who has sat on committees knows', Pollock maintained, 'that untrained amateur pedantry can be both more absurd and more unjust than any professional bias'[123]). Unfortunate verdicts are often, of course, attributable to a jury having been poorly directed or entrusted to determine an issue of inordinate legal complexity. But—and this is Pollock's point—such verdicts sometimes come about because jurors simply cannot maintain a common-sense perspective on the relevant law.[124]

It should not be inferred from this that the common sense of lawyers and judges is, in Pollock's view, always beyond reproach: notwithstanding his belief that reason, common sense, and natural justice can generally be treated as synonyms, he would occasionally criticize a legal decision on the ground that, while it was well reasoned, the result was 'repugnant to common sense'.[125] By and large, however, he celebrated the capacity of the common law to embody

[118] *ECL* 108. Consider also Pollock's typically commonsensical observation that 'nineteen times out of twenty the best way to determine what is reasonable expectation in the case in hand is to look to the terms on which the parties have agreed.' Frederick Pollock, 'A Plea for Historical Interpretation' (1923) 39 *LQR* 163–9 at 166.

[119] See *ECL* 106 ('common sense, reason, or natural justice—. . . we may use any of these . . . terms at will'). For an historical commentary—very much in line with the position that Pollock takes—on the relationship between common sense and natural justice, see Frits van Holthoon, 'Common Sense and Natural Law: From Thomas Aquinas to Thomas Reid', in *Common Sense: The Foundations for Social Science*, eds. F. van Holthoon and D. R. Olson (Lanham, MD: University Press of America, 1987), 99–114.

[120] 'For my own part, I would in a case of conscience rather consult a right-minded and sensible friend than any moral philosopher in the world.' *IHSP* 3; and cf. *EJE* 286; also Frederick Pollock, 'The Lawyer as a Citizen of the World' (1932) 48 *LQR* 37–42 at 40 ('Common sense is of much more importance than extensive reading of text-writers').

[121] See *ECL* 59 ('lay common sense . . . may be apt to think that we are making a great fuss over nothing . . .'), and cf. also 101.

[122] See, e.g., (1889) 5 *LQR* 104 ('the safeguard in such a case is the common sense of a jury').

[123] *GCL* 25.

[124] See (1891) 7 *LQR* 202–3; (1914) 30 *LQR* 6; (1917) 33 *LQR* 206–7; (1919) 35 *LQR* 4. In Pollock's day, of course, English juries regularly sat on civil as well as on criminal cases.

[125] (1890) 6 *LQR* 121; see also (1888) 4 *LQR* 234; and *EJE* 73. Others have followed him in conceiving of the common law thus: see, e.g., W. T. S. Stallybrass, 'Law in the Universities' (1948) n.s. 1 *Jnl. of the Society of Public Teachers of Law* 157–69 at 162.

'the common sense of reasonable men'.[126] While 'the standard of the Common Law itself is in many respects higher than what commonly passes muster among men of good business repute,' Pollock wrote apropos of the Judicature Acts 1873–5, 'the conscience of the court, if it is still to be an effective power, must not run away from the common sense of mankind.'[127] Not that he believed there was much reason to worry. 'English judges . . . have, as a rule, been men of strong common sense, anxious to do substantial justice, and to give intelligible reasons for it.'[128] '[D]octrines of equity'—about which, we saw in chapter 2, Pollock was never particularly complimentary or enthusiastic—tended to function so much better, he believed, once the mid-nineteenth century Court of Appeal began 'to bring equity more into accordance with common sense'.[129] When, during this period, 'Baron Parke . . . was transferred to the House of Lords as Lord Wensleydale', he came to be lauded precisely because 'no man could handle matters of principle with greater clearness or broader common sense.'[130] 'The common sense of the Common Law', Pollock wrote to Holmes, 'goes much deeper than most nineteenth century judges knew.'[131]

For Pollock, then, the common law is reasonable because, among other things, it is generally commonsensical. The meaning of this claim, he seemed to assume, is self-evident—who, after all, cannot identify common sense? Within late nineteenth- and early twentieth-century jurisprudence, the assumption that the notion of common sense requires no explanation was by no means unique to Pollock. His successor at Oxford, Paul Vinogradoff, wrote a book, *Common-sense in Law*, which, aside from the title, makes no reference at all to common sense; for the most part, the book describes the common law system rather as might an anthropologist, or an alien writing home. 'We have discovered by this time', Vinogradoff remarked of these curious common law earthlings, 'how large a part in the formulation of the law is played by judicial declarations of right in the process of interpretation of statutes as well as in the formation of custom and of case law. But there is a fourth legal source in which the creative power of the Courts is even more conspicuous. . . . This is *Equity*, or fairness.'[132] That Vinogradoff should have written about the common law in this manner is hardly surprising. He was a Russian by birth, having moved to England not long before his fiftieth birthday. His perspective was almost bound to have an anthropological tinge to it.

[126] *EJE* 116. See also Frederick Pollock, 'Judicial Caution and Valour' (1929) 45 *LQR* 293–306 at 294–5.

[127] *ECL* 116. [128] *EJE* 65. [129] *EJE* 74.

[130] *GCL* 28. [131] Pollock to Holmes, 14 August 1921, in *PHL* ii. 74.

[132] Sir Paul Vinogradoff, *Common-sense in Law* (London: Oxford UP, 1913), 208. Thomas Paine's classic, disdainful farewell to Great Britain is another example of a book which, despite its title, does not discuss common sense but simply proceeds as if it embodied the phenomenon. At least Paine, unlike Vinogradoff, bothered to refer to common sense after placing the phrase in his title: Paine, *Common Sense*, iii. 1, iii. 6, iv. 13.

While anthropological detachment is present in *Common-sense in Law*, however, anthropological inquisitiveness is not. Vinogradoff's use of the notion of common sense is, like Pollock's use of the same, entirely unreflective. In more recent times, genuine anthropological inquiry has tended to treat common sense as a problem rather than as a given. '[I]t is an inherent characteristic of common-sense thought', Geertz observes,

to affirm that its tenets are immediate deliverances of experience. . . . Knowing that rain wets and that one ought to come out of it, or that fire burns and one ought not to play with it . . . are conflated into comprising one large realm of the given and undeniable. . . . Yet this is clearly not so. No one, or no one functioning very well, doubts that rain wets; but there may be some people around who question the proposition that one ought to come in out of it, holding that it is good for one's character to brave the elements—hatlessness is next to godliness. And the attractions of playing with fire often, with some people usually, override the full recognition of the pain that will result. Religion rests its case on revelation, science on method, ideology on moral passion; but common sense rests on its assertion that it is not a case at all, just life in a nutshell. The world is its authority.[133]

What Geertz criticizes Pollock believed. Within Pollock's work, that is, the notion of common sense is presented 'as rather commonsensical: what anyone with common sense knows'.[134] 'An air of "of-courseness," a sense of "it figures" is cast over things.'[135] Common sense is 'the general property of at least . . . all solid citizens'.[136] 'There is no esoteric knowledge, no special technique or peculiar giftedness.'[137] It is simply 'what remains of reason when its more sophisticated achievements are all set aside'[138]—what Bertrand Russell was apparently fond of ridiculing as 'the metaphysics of savages'.[139] That the notion of common sense might be, as Geertz puts it, 'problematical'—that it might be 'not what the mind cleared of cant spontaneously apprehends but what the mind filled with presuppositions . . . concludes'[140] —seems never to have occured to Pollock. Everyone blessed with common sense, he apparently believed, is likely to regard not only the attribute, but also the idea of its being an integral feature of the common law, to be uncontroversial.

Pitching Geertz against Pollock makes for an easy line of critique. Geertz can readily be made to play the part of standard-bearer for a modern, enlightened, critical world, despairing of old complacencies that writers like Pollock never saw fit to challenge. To fail to offer such an obvious line of critique

[133] Clifford Geertz, *Local Knowledge: Further Essays in Interpretive Anthropology* (New York: Basic Books, 1983), 75.

[134] Ibid. 77. [135] Ibid. 85. [136] Ibid. 91. [137] Ibid.

[138] Ibid. 92. Cf. Melvin Aron Eisenberg, *The Nature of the Common Law* (Cambridge, Mass.: Harvard UP, 1988), 21.

[139] See Ray Monk, 'Russell' (1999) 74 *Philosophy* 105–17 at 111.

[140] Geertz, above n.133, 77, 84.

would be odd. But the critique itself needs to be assessed critically. Examining the past according to the predilections of the present is an exercise which ought, more often than not, to arouse suspicion. Adopting a presentist—what Hacking calls a 'pen pal'[141]—approach to historical figures and ideas often leads us to distort earlier intellectual inquiries: the past can end up represented not on its own terms, but in accordance with current concerns. Pollock himself, we saw in chapter 3, despaired over those who approach history all too eager to condemn as lacking in modern, intellectual sophistication serious jurists who are no longer around to defend what they had to say. Certainly he did not treat the notion of common sense as problematic. And with hindsight we can easily criticize him for failing to do so. But then he belonged to a generation that was far less prone to rendering ideas problematic than it was to making those ideas, as with so much else, somehow better—a generation of optimists, dedicated by and large to securing improvements, finding consensus, and expanding the collective stock of human rationality, a generation generally committed to the belief that much of the social world is perfectible even if it is not presently perfect.[142] We should concede—and indeed, to some extent, be critical of—Pollock's failure to share the modern academic taste for showing a concept to be essentially contestable. To dwell on this criticism, however, is to risk distorting history. Nineteenth-century jurists did not think like twentieth-century anthropologists, and it would be a bizarre historical study that proceeded on the assumption that they ought to have done.

Pollock's second approach to the question of what is meant by reason and reasonableness comes with a similar warning. The presentist or 'pen pals' perspective on the past is often uncharitable, the perspective of those intent on producing winners' history. Slightly different from that perspective is what Hacking terms the 'doing-and-sharing' attitude towards history. Whereas presentists tend not to be interested in the past unless it reveals something significant about the present, 'doing-and-sharing' is by nature more inclusive: even when earlier thinkers adopted perspectives very different from those which prevail today, they can often be found to be addressing the same 'perennial themes', speaking 'to us directly about matters of joint concern'.[143] The

[141] At the heart of this approach to history is the idea that '[o]ld philosophers are to be studied as pen-friends: one-way discussants across the seas of time. We don't care about them because of their role in *their* day. . . . We care only about the old books that speak to us.' Ian Hacking, *Historical Ontology* (Cambridge, Mass.: Harvard UP, 2002), 55.

[142] See Bradley, above n.95, 74, 200–21; and Walter E. Houghton, *The Victorian Frame of Mind 1830–1870* (New Haven: Yale UP, 1957), 94–6; though cf. Gertrude Himmelfarb, *Victorian Minds* (Chicago: Dee, 1995 [1968]), 300–13. It should be borne in mind too—though there seems no reason to pursue the point here—that some modern psychologists and social scientists are of the view that the concept of common sense has considerable explanatory power: see, e.g., Lynd Forguson, *Common Sense* (London: Routledge, 1989); Siegwart Lindenberg, 'Common Sense and Social Structure: A Sociological View', in *Common Sense*, above n.119, 199–215; and Renée Elio, 'Issues in Commonsense Reasoning and Rationality', in *Common Sense, Reasoning, and Rationality*, ed. R. Elio (New York: Oxford UP, 2002), 3–36.

[143] Hacking, above n.141, 55.

'doing-and-sharing' approach, we might say, puts an emphasis on co-opting earlier thinkers, on making them part of a larger team. Pollock's effort to connect reason with the notion of principle—this being what has been referred to as the second approach—suggests, certainly at first glance, that his work might be enlisted to support a contemporary jurisprudential cause. The accentuation of principle, after all, has been very much an abiding concern of modern legal philosophers. And there is a temptation to argue that Pollock shared this concern, that he offered a late-Victorian perspective on the question of what role principles play within law—a question which has commonly been associated with Anglo-American jurisprudence of the latter half of the twentieth century.[144] This temptation is considerable, for the claim would be that Pollock's reflections on the reasonableness of the common law conceal a viewpoint which, once uncovered, might contribute significantly to our understanding of modern jurisprudence. Coming after the line of argument developed in chapter 3, this would be quite a sting in the tail.

It would be a mistake, however, to succumb to this temptation. Pollock wrote at a time when political philosophy was dominated by a quest for general principles—principles of political economy, of ethics, of jurisprudence, of commerce, and more.[145] One explanation for the dominance of principles during this era is that principled behaviour, like habitual behaviour, was often associated with restraint. The nineteenth-century emphasis on principle, Atiyah remarks,

> is plainly related closely to the idea of self-government in the most literal sense. If Englishmen were to be free, and to be allowed to choose for themselves how to behave, without having a despotic state imposed upon them, then they had to learn how to behave in a social manner. And to do this, it was necessary to learn principles of behaviour of some generality for it was impossible to have guidance on the proper mode of behaviour in every set of circumstances which might arise.[146]

This observation is significant for our purposes because it suggests not just that Pollock's emphasis on principles made sense in the late nineteenth century, but also that we should be wary of trying to emphasize the relevance of his outlook to jurisprudence in the late twentieth century. Pollock's preoccupation with principle, quite simply, had a context of its own. No doubt links with late twentieth-century jurisprudence can be made; but efforts to establish those links are likely to risk turning 'doing-and-sharing' into a variant on presentism. Presently we will encounter Pollock referring, in a fashion somewhat reminiscent of Ronald Dworkin, to the importance of sound principles: in

[144] See generally Neil Duxbury, *Patterns of American Jurisprudence* (Oxford: Clarendon Press, 1995), 205–99.

[145] See P. S. Atiyah, *The Rise and Fall of Freedom of Contract* (Oxford: Clarendon Press, 1979), 345–58.

[146] Ibid. 347.

short, there will be a clear opportunity to present him as a proto-Dworkinian. To take this opportunity, however, would be to risk mischaracterizing Pollock. Notwithstanding their shared preoccupation with the notion of principle, Pollock and Dworkin are jurisprudentially very different. First of all, as is well known, Dworkin believes that nearly all cases permit of right answers: 'no-right-answer cases . . . , if they exist at all, must be extremely rare in the United States and Great Britain. . . . [I]n a complex and comprehensive legal system it is antecedently unlikely that two theories will differ sufficiently to demand different answers in some case and yet provide equally good fit with the relevant legal materials.'[147] Pollock was of a different view: '[t]he assumption that there must be one and only one intrinsically right way of dealing with any practical question is often tacitly made, to the hindrance of rational agreement. . . . [T]he problems of the political sciences, not excluding law, not seldom are more like equations of higher degrees in being capable of two or more solutions.'[148] Secondly, as is equally well known, Dworkin believes that individual rights may operate as 'trumps' over collective goals and the general welfare: '[t]he nerve of a claim of right . . . is that an individual is entitled to protection against the majority even at the cost of the general interest.'[149] Pollock, by contrast, was less enamoured either of individuals ('[r]espect for persons is incompatible with justice', he declares bluntly in his *First Book of Jurisprudence*[150]) or of their rights, insistent as he was that civil liberties are suspended in times of national emergency.[151] Anyone wishing to take Pollock's observations on the subject of principles and present them in a Dworkinian cast would probably have very little difficulty doing so. That such an exercise should prove easy, however, is no guarantee of its intellectual soundness.

With this warning out of the way, we can now proceed to our main task of determining just what Pollock had to say about principles. Human beings, he contended, have a preference for reasoned decisions: '[o]ther things being equal,' we tend to prefer 'that conclusion . . . which has been arrived at upon the fullest discussion and ripest consideration.'[152] Especial tribute must be paid in this context to Lord Mansfield, 'a Scotsman by birth', who 'took up the rationalizing movement' in the second half of the eighteenth century and

[147] Ronald Dworkin, *A Matter of Principle* (Oxford: Clarendon Press, 1986), 144–5.

[148] *EIL* 267. Pollock's position on the right-answer question appears to be closer to Hart's than it is to Dworkin's: cf. H. L. A. Hart, *The Concept of Law*, 2nd edn. (Oxford: Clarendon Press, 1994; 1st edn. publ. 1961), 132 ('In these cases [of indeterminacy] it is clear that the rule-making authority must exercise a discretion, and there is no possibility of treating the question raised by the various cases as if there were one uniquely correct answer to be found, as distinct from an answer which is a reasonable compromise between many conflicting interests'). On other jurisprudential issues, however, Pollock and Hart clearly diverged: see, e.g., H. L. A. Hart, 'Bentham on Legal Rights', in *Oxford Essays in Jurisprudence*, above n.23, 171–201 at 175.

[149] Ronald Dworkin, *Taking Rights Seriously*, rev. edn. (London: Duckworth, 1978), 146.

[150] *FBJ* 37. He had made the same point a year earlier in Frederick Pollock, 'Justice According to Law' (1895) 9 *Harvard L. Rev.* 295–308 at 299.

[151] See chapter 2, 55–6; though cf. *OLOD* 207 (in 'the framing of a good constitution . . . minorities have to be thought of').

[152] *EJE* 52.

ensured that 'it left permanent marks on more than one branch of English law'.[153] The persuasiveness of Mansfield's own judicial opinions had much to do with the fact that he did not neglect the human preference for the decision grounded, as Pollock put it, in 'principles of reason'.[154] Indeed, in Pollock's eyes, Mansfield considered human beings, because of their taste for reasoned decisions, to be attracted to principles. That reason and principle are connected, and that we value both highly, Pollock accepted without question. His primary objective was to explain how the notion of principle ought to be understood in a common law context.

Within the English legal tradition, Pollock argued, 'the interpretation of the law' is the peculiar responsibility of a judiciary which enjoys 'complete . . . detachment . . . from the legislative function.'[155] That '[j]udicial interpretation of the law is the only authentic interpretation' is evident from history: 'in the time of Henry III', for example, '[t]he King's judges, and they alone, had power to lay down what . . . the Common Law . . . must be taken to be.'[156] But can anything prevent the courts, when they interpret the law, from usurping the legislative function? Cannot courts interpret the law more or less however they like? What frustrates unfettered judicial discretion, Pollock argued, is the constraining power of principles. 'Laymen sometimes talk of judge-made law as if judges were legislators and could lay down any rule they chose'; but while '[j]udges are indeed bound to find some rule for deciding every case that comes before them, . . . they must do it without contradicting established principles, and in conformity with the reasons on which previous decisions were founded.'[157] The development of principles is itself the responsibility of the courts, or certainly the upper courts: 'the law is not made by casual and hasty decisions in courts of first instance. Its guiding principles and the harmony of its controlling ideas must be sought in the considered judgments of the higher tribunals which command universal respect.'[158] Although 'principles, even the most certain, are capable of infinite application,'[159] their evolution is rarely haphazard, for the appellate courts invariably seek out 'sound principle[s] of justice'.[160]

It is at this point that the opportunity to present Pollock as a proto-Dworkinian surfaces clearly. Integrity in adjudication, Dworkin argues, 'requires our judges, so far as this is possible, to treat our present system of public standards as expressing and respecting a coherent set of principles' and to seek out 'the principles that provide the best justification available for the doctrines and devices of law as a whole'.[161] For Pollock, '[t]he sound method

153 *EIL* 68, 60. 154 *EIL* 67. 155 *ECL* 79–80.
156 *ECL* 47–8. 157 *ECL* 49. 158 *GCL* 114. 159 *GCL* 112.
160 *GCL* 71. Cf. also *GCL* 115 and *OLOD* 187.
161 Ronald Dworkin, *Law's Empire* (London: Fontana, 1986), 217, 400; and cf. Dworkin, above n.149, 167 ('If a theory of law is to provide a basis for judicial duty, then the principles it sets out must try to *justify* the settled rules by identifying the political and moral concerns and traditions of the community which, in the opinion of the lawyer whose theory it is, do in fact support the rules').

. . . assumes the existence . . . of a larger reason which informs the spirit of the law, and must, in the last resort, be the justification of the controlling rules themselves.'[162] 'In hundreds of cases', he elaborates,

> it is possible to suggest several rules of which, at first sight, any one would serve as well as another; and if we are asked why we have chosen one and rejected the others the answer is that the one we have preferred is deducible from our larger established principles, or at least consistent with and analogous to them, and the others are not.[163]

For at least two reasons, the affinities between the argument advanced by Dworkin and that put forward by Pollock should be treated as superficial. First, there is the question of why principles are significant. Dworkin emphasizes the moral quality of legal principles: 'a "principle" [is] a standard that is to be observed . . . because it is a requirement of justice or fairness or some other dimension of morality.'[164] While it is unlikely that Pollock would have been blind to the fact that legal principles have moral qualities, he accorded that fact no special significance. Secondly, Dworkin constructs his argument about integrity in adjudication in idealistic terms. 'No actual judge could compose anything approaching a full interpretation of all his community's law at once.'[165] Real judges, nevertheless, are likely to produce better judicial decisions if they aspire to the ideal, if they try to 'imitate' judicial perfection 'in a limited way'.[166] Pollock, by contrast, was concerned not so much with what judges ought to do as with what they actually do. Certainly his position is not completely lacking in normativity. One of his more memorable juristic '[d]reams' involves the establishment of a transatlantic Supreme Court in which English and American judges 'assist one another' in deciding 'great and dubious case[s] touching fundamental principles'.[167] By and large, however, he was interested in the real as opposed to the ideal.[168]

The responsibility for developing legal principles, Pollock argued, rests not only with the appeal courts. '[T]he law of England', he wrote in the early 1880s, is 'in sore need of a systematic expounder', a jurist prepared to accept the task of assisting the courts in articulating and explaining the principles of the common law.[169] For the next half century and beyond, Pollock accepted that task as his own. Judicial explanation and development of principles does not always run smoothly,[170] and so assistance from jurists may prove valuable. Thus it is that we regularly find Pollock endeavouring 'to make the principles

[162] *ECL* 108. [163] *ECL* 107. [164] Dworkin, above n.149, 22.
[165] Dworkin, above n.161, 245. [166] Ibid. 245, and cf. also 264–5. [167] *ECL* 22, 20.
[168] For a more general depiction of Pollock's juristic milieu as basically anti-hortatory, see Calvin Woodard, 'History, Legal History and Legal Education' (1967) 53 *Virginia L. Rev.* 89–121 at 104–8, 114–15.
[169] *EJE* 6.
[170] See, e.g., *FBJ* 158 ('It has been found a matter of no small difficulty, both in principle and in the application of the principles to particular cases as they occur, to determine how far a man shall be held answerable for the less obvious and direct consequences of his acts').

and leading features of . . . English law . . . intelligible' to anyone who might be interested.[171] '[T]he doctrine of Possession in the Common Law,' he observed in his Carpentier Lectures, 'can be accounted for by a few comprehensive principles. . . . [F]or the honour of our lady the Common Law I will state these principles in their simplest form.'[172] It was not only the judiciary that jurists could help with principles. The best a jurist can do for the student of law, he told an Oxford audience in 1886, is 'help him to fix in his mind that there are such things as general principles of law'; that is, 'we can give him a clear vision and a firm grasp of elementary principles which, being called to mind as occasion requires, will save him from being oppressed and confused by the multitude of particulars.'[173]

Of course, waxing lyrical about the exposition of principles is not the same as actually engaging in exposition. But in this instance there is substance behind the rhetoric. In the next chapter, we will see that Pollock adopted a fundamentally principle-oriented approach to the law of contract and torts. In his notes in the *Law Quarterly Review*, furthermore, he was more often than not concerned with identifying and explaining the principle at stake in particular cases. 'An English Court of Bankruptcy has no jurisdiction to adjudge bankrupt any "debtor" who is not in strictness a "debtor subject to the English Bankruptcy Act." This is the principle . . . to be deduced from *In re Pearson*.'[174] The decision of the Court of Appeal in '*The Leeds Building Society* v. *Mallandaine* . . . carries somewhat further the principle . . . that interest is chargeable as such to income tax, and is probably a legitimate extension of that principle'.[175] 'There is . . . rather more difficulty than the Court [of Appeal] seems to have realized [in *Machado* v. *Fontes*] in showing that the judgment is consistent with the fundamental principles of private international law. The most obvious and well established of these is that . . . English Courts recognize and enforce, subject to exceptions . . . , rights acquired under the law of any foreign country.'[176] Examples of Pollock using the case notes section of the *LQR* as a place to furrow around for principles are easily multipliable.[177] Among other things, he used his notes to warn barristers 'of the expense and delay which may be caused in a simple case by a disregard of elementary principles',[178] to commend courts when they clarified obscure legal principles or applied principles soundly,[179] to criticize those courts where they failed to identify relevant

[171] *LL(3)* vii. In the same vein, see *EIL* 278; and, for illustrations of Pollock expounding common law principles, see *EJE* 76, 126.

[172] *GCL* 119–20. [173] *OLOD* 94, 102. [174] (1900) 16 *LQR* 219.

[175] (1898) 14 *LQR* 5–6. [176] (1897) 13 *LQR* 334–5.

[177] See, e.g., (1887) 3 *LQR* 252, 360; (1888) 4 *LQR* 115; (1891) 7 *LQR* 308; (1892) 8 *LQR* 10–11, 185; (1893) 9 *LQR* 102–3, 107, 308; (1894) 10 *LQR* 101, 108; (1897) 13 *LQR* 333–7; (1898) 14 *LQR* 3, 114, 224, 335; (1900) 16 *LQR* 109–10; (1901) 17 *LQR* 120, 347–8; (1902) 18 *LQR* 342; (1903) 19 *LQR* 251, 363–4; (1909) 25 *LQR* 7; (1912) 28 *LQR* 339–40; (1914) 30 *LQR* 135–6; (1915) 31 *LQR* 369–70.

[178] (1891) 7 *LQR* 304.

[179] See, e.g., (1886) 2 *LQR* 530; (1887) 3 *LQR* 107, 250; (1890) 6 *LQR* 463; (1901) 17 *LQR* 114; (1907) 23 *LQR* 6–7; (1912) 28 *LQR* 2.

principles or extended principles beyond their natural scope,[180] to note how particular principles of law had evolved,[181] and to argue that 'principles of immense public import' ought to be ratified by the House of Lords.[182] There is hardly any wonder that his son considered him to be in the 'habit of viewing everything from the standpoint of principle'.[183] '[T]he work done for Reason', Pollock asserted, 'is done for eternity.'[184] Since legal principles are, he believed, principles of reason, to dedicate oneself to their excavation and elaboration is to serve the common law for now and forever.

iv. The lady's servants

Jurists, then, so long as they treat their obligations seriously, can make a noble contribution to the advancement of the common law. We saw in chapter 2 that Pollock regarded Langdell as a modern exemplar: '[n]o man has been more ready than Mr Langdell to protest against the treatment of conclusions of law as something to be settled by mere enumeration of decided points. For the law is not a collection of propositions, but a system founded on principles.'[185] Langdell was, in Pollock's eyes, a good example of a jurist whose work and methods had an impact upon the operation of the law—the sort of jurist who thwarted the efforts of those 'who sneer at what they call "academical" learning'[186] and believe that legal scholarship has nothing of significance to offer legal practice. '[T]he continued divorce of the academical from the practical study of law in the old country', he observed in his lecture honouring Langdell's silver jubilee at Harvard, 'is not, in my opinion, a good thing.'[187]

180 See, e.g., (1891) 7 *LQR* 3; (1913) 29 *LQR* 123. 181 See, e.g., (1888) 4 *LQR* 119, 234.
182 (1890) 6 *LQR* 460. 183 Sir John Pollock, 'Introduction', in *PHL* i. xiii–xxiii at xiv.
184 *SHLP* 288.
185 *ECL* 7. One might be inclined to assume from this that Pollock wanted to show that Langdell was, contrary to a fairly common portrait of the man, no unsophisticated legal formalist. (For the common portrait see, e.g., Grant Gilmore, *The Ages of American Law* (New Haven: Yale UP, 1977), 42–8.) It is more likely, however, that Pollock would have considered the concept of legal formalism, rather than Langdell, to be the principal victim of caricature. The persistence of legal formalism, Pollock maintained, permits of a rational and an irrational explanation. 'The rational ground is the need for a hard and fast rule to make it clear the law is the same for all men. . . . The irrational ground goes back to . . . the prehistoric belief in symbolic magic. It is assumed that words in themselves have an operative virtue which is lost if substituted for any other.' *GCL* 14. Pollock's point is that whether or not one approves of the formalist legal mindset, the fact that it has prevailed should not be considered particularly surprising. For his own part, Pollock was not wholly opposed to formalism in law, believing that 'the evils due to formalism' are 'not always due to lawyers' (*GCL* 63) and that bad legal formality is nevertheless preferable to capriciousness (see *GCL* 21). Historically, furthermore, the common law had no problem with formalism, Pollock implied, since it recognized the value of formalism to the pursuit of justice: 'antiquarian lawyers could, almost down to our own time, believe trial by jury to be immemorial' because 'our lady the Common Law never had much trouble with the forms of archaic proof. . . . The ancient rigid formalism . . . still walks' (*GCL* 22).
186 *EIL* 149.
187 *ECL* 8. Cf. *GCL* 111 ('one day your client's interest may well depend on your ability to expose an inaccurate translation from a Year Book'); and *EJE*, 265, 287–97.

Pollock insisted, none the less, that while juristic speculation may inform legal practice and decision-making, it can never itself be a source of law. The declaratory theory of law, Montesquieu observed, holds that 'judges are no more than the mouth that pronounces the words of the law, mere passive beings, incapable of moderating either its force or rigor.'[188] Austin disparaged the theory as 'the childish fiction employed by our judges, that judiciary or common law is not made by them, but is a miraculous something made by nobody, existing, I suppose, from eternity and merely *declared* from time to time by the judges.'[189] As if wishing to provide a basis for Austin's disparagement, Lord Esher proclaimed in 1892 that '[t]here is in fact no such thing as judge-made law, for the judges do not make the law, though they frequently have to apply existing law to circumstances as to which it has not previously been authoritatively laid down that such law is applicable.'[190] The significance of the declaratory theory for our purposes is that it precludes the possibility of juristic speculation having any authoritative legal status: judges cannot make law but can only apply it, and jurists cannot do even that—at best, they are helpful expositors of the law.

This last point was not lost on Pollock. Early in his career, he expressed doubts about the declaratory theory. 'It is constantly said that judges are not to decide what ought to be the law,' he observed in *Essays in Jurisprudence and Ethics*, 'but it is constantly found that they do so decide when positive law, so far as already ascertained, is silent or ambiguous.'[191] By the time of the publication of *A First Book of Jurisprudence*, his scepticism about the theory was, at the very least, not so forthright: 'although declarations of legal principles . . . by courts of justice may well be said to form part of the law, . . . we cannot say of any such declaration or interpretation that it is "a law".'[192] Thus we find Pollock claiming, rather as would a well-drilled declaratory theorist, that judges cannot create law but can only interpret it—indeed he came to argue, as we have seen already in this chapter, that judicial interpretations of the law are the only authentic interpretations.[193] If this is the case, what status are we to accord juristic interpretations of the law? Even early on in his career,

[188] Charles Louis Montesquieu, *The Spirit of the Laws*, trans. T. Nugent (New York: Hafner, 1949 [1748]), 159.

[189] John Austin, *Lectures on Jurisprudence or the Philosophy of Positive Law*, 2 vols., 5th edn. R. Campbell (London: Murray, 1885), ii. 634.

[190] *Willis v Baddeley* [1892] 2 QB 324, 326 (CA). In a similar vein, see *Baylis v Bishop of London* [1913] 1 Ch. 127, 137 (*per* Farwell L. J.); and *Harnett v Fisher* [1927] 1 KB 402, 424 (*per* Scrutton L. J.).

[191] *EJE* 283; and cf. *PCLE* 255 ('In theory the common law does not vary. In fact we know it does vary . . . , but the fact of the variation is no argument for an unlimited power of judicial legislation').

[192] *FBJ* 15.

[193] Note that it is not claimed here that Pollock was a declaratory theorist. Ever careful to stand clear of obvious schools and perspectives, Pollock avoided aligning himself thus. Typically finding something to commend in and something incorrect about the declaratory theory, he argued that 'it is idle to ask in general terms whether our courts do or do not make law; the only answer is that they develop and mould it as interpreters, but do not create it as legislators.' Pollock, 'Judicial Caution and Valour', above n.126, 293.

when the declaratory theory was causing him some serious doubts, Pollock recognized a blunt truth about what jurists do: 'in the case of a text-book, or digest, or abridgement, however carefully it may be compiled, and whoever the author may be, his words are not the law of the land; they are only the statement of his opinion as to what is the result of the authorities.'[194] Indeed, even if a judge writes a law book, 'however much better it may be than another man's book, it is equally powerless to make a binding rule for future decisions'.[195]

None of this should be taken to indicate what Pollock actually believed about the contribution of jurists to the development of the common law. He clearly recognized that the work of jurists can influence judicial interpretations of the law—'[t]he influence of theorists on the judicial development of English law', he wrote in 1891, 'is far greater than is generally supposed'[196]—and when, in 1897, he found his own words adopted by Lindley L. J. in the Court of Appeal he not only felt honoured but would have been happy for other judges to follow suit.[197] By the same token, he felt that the works of some jurists—'with all their pedantry and occasional perversity of intellect'—could, if taken seriously by the courts, have a deleterious effect on the interpretation of the law.[198] But the main point to emphasize about Pollock's reflections on the place of the jurist within the common law tradition is that he purports to offer not an argument but a fact: the writings of jurists, be their calibre high or low, are never legal authority but at best 'may help towards the formation of authority'.[199] Jurists, whether we like it or not, are at the periphery of common law development.

The point would be all well and good, but for one crucial and rather ironic detail: if, over the past two centuries, there has been one jurist who did not remain consigned to the periphery of common law development, it was Pollock. 'His writings', according to one modern commentator, 'were cited in court probably more than any other writings in their authors' lifetime. They could claim . . . a place in the category of our unwritten law.'[200] In chapters 5 and 6, we will examine the substance behind this observation. So far in this chapter, we have considered how Pollock conceived of the common law; for the remainder of the chapter we will examine how this conception informed his thoughts about certain other matters.

v. Legislation

'Pollock's veneration for the common law,' according to Hedley, 'is obvious enough in his writings. But he had curiously little to say on why the common

[194] *EJE* 99. [195] *EJE* 60. [196] (1891) 7 *LQR* 309.
[197] See *EIL* 152; and cf. (1893) 9 *LQR* 9. [198] See *LL(3)* 110–11. [199] *FBJ* 236.
[200] O. Hood Phillips, 'Legal Authors Since 1800', in *Then and Now, 1799–1974: Commemorating 175 years of Law Bookselling and Publishing* (London: Sweet & Maxwell, 1974), 3–30 at 23.

law was a good thing, if it was. And he was no opponent of legislation either.'[201] To understand why Pollock considered the common law to be a 'good thing', we would do well to examine what he has to say about legislation. The statement that he was 'no opponent of legislation' is every bit as troublesome as the counter-claim: just as Pollock dithered over the question of just how much benefit there is to be had from codifying specific areas of law—a matter which we addressed in chapter 2—so too he avoided adopting a consistent line on the general utility of legislation. More often than not, legislation was something to which he did seem opposed—resolutely opposed—though it is easy to see why Hedley should believe otherwise. In Pollock's view, according to Lord Wright, one of the fundamental shortcomings of the common law is that 'it has not fully satisfied the demands of a modern social conscience which has been compelled to call in the act of parliament' on occasions in order to put right what the courts have neglected.[202] '[T]he difficulties of legal title . . . were brought to the attention of Parliament within the present century,' Pollock remarked in his third edition of *The Land Laws* in 1896, and it was Parliament that 'had to bring the law round again to the popular view'.[203] He certainly appreciated that legislation has its uses.[204]

But those uses he regarded as limited. If the legislative reform of land law was to be effective, Pollock continued, the reformers ought to 'consider whether there is any way . . . of . . . going back, in principle though not in form, to the ancient ways of the fathers of the Common Law'.[205] The proposed land law reforms, he believed, were inordinately complex in comparison with the old common law rules.[206] While '[r]eforms of this kind are most useful for their time, and their promoters deserve all honour', they 'add to the complications of a system already too complex; and the day seems to be at hand when the system will no longer bear this process'.[207] His message seemed to be that we should generally be wary of legislative intervention. Besides being prone to excessive complexity, legislators often draft to unacceptably low standards[208]—many statutes, he quipped in the *LQR*, 'do not err on the side

[201] Steve Hedley, 'Sir Frederick Pollock and the Teaching of English Law', in *Learning the Law: Teaching and the Transmission of Law in England 1150–1900*, eds. J. A. Bush and A. Wijffels (London: Hambledon Press, 1999), 407–17 at 408.

[202] Lord Wright, 'Pollock, Sir Frederick, Third Baronet 1845–1937', in *DNB* (*1931–1940*), 711–13 at 712. See also *GCL* 73 ('Both judges and practitioners have often lacked either the wit to know or the will to try how much could be done without legislation').

[203] *LL(3)* 39–40.

[204] See further *OLOD* 12–13; and, for Pollock commending particular legislative initiatives, (1891) 7 *LQR* 6, 12–13, 205; (1892) 8 *LQR* 107, 272; (1893) 9 *LQR* 17–18; (1905) 21 *LQR* 212.

[205] *LL(3)* 138. Cf. also Frederick Pollock, 'Early Landholding and Modern Land-Transfer' (1890) 61 *Macmillan's Magazine* 414–22 at 417.

[206] See *LL(3)* 164–96.

[207] *LL(3)* 194.

[208] See *FBJ* 333–4 ('Rapid increase in the bulk of legislation is a conspicuous feature of the eighteenth century, but . . . the quality of the work becomes worse rather than better as the quantity turned out is greater').

1. Sir Frederick Pollock, by Harry Furniss. (*National Portrait Gallery, London*)

2. Great Court, Trinity College Cambridge, 1860s. (Adv. Alb. 23, p. 8, *courtesy of the Masters and Fellows of Trinity College Cambridge*)

3. Bronze bust of F. W. Maitland. (*Courtesy of Professor Sir John Baker*)

4. Interior of Lincoln's Inn Library, 1917. (*Courtesy of the Treasurer and Masters of the Bench of Lincoln's Inn*)

5. James Shaw Willes. (*Courtesy of the Treasurer and Masters of the Bench of Lincoln's Inn*)

6. Nathaniel Lindley. (*Courtesy of the Treasurer and Masters of the Bench of Lincoln's Inn*)

7. Oliver Wendell Holmes, Jr, 1909. (*Courtesy of Art and Visual Materials, Special Collections Department, Harvard Law School Library*)

8. Sir Courtenay Peregrine Ilbert, by Sydney Prior Hall. (*National Portrait Gallery, London*)

9. Corpus Christi College, Oxford, *c.*1900. (GA Oxon. 6. 18. p. 19, *Bodleian Library, University of Oxford*)

10. Frederick Pollock at work. (*Courtesy of the Treasurer and Masters of the Bench of Lincoln's Inn*)

of lucidity'[209]—so that the result would be 'notoriously ineffectual, or, if not ineffectual, apt to create new troubles greater than any which it cures'.[210] Complaints about statutory ambiguity, and the failure of legislation to secure its objectives, would be far less common occurrences, he believed, were legislators to grasp that the simple legal rule is usually the best rule.[211]

To acquire a sense of Pollock's attitude towards legislation, it is worth splitting his writing on the subject into two categories. In his books and essays, first of all, Pollock's line on legislation was superficially measured but basically hostile. While 'some of our classical authorities exhibit a tendency to regard legislation as the enemy of the law', he observed in his Carpentier lectures, it would be 'too rash to affirm in general . . . that legislation is more likely to be foolish than wise'. Then again, it 'would be more than rash to affirm that, among the well meant statutory reforms of our law, . . . any great proportion have achieved complete success'.[212] The more one reads Pollock's books and essays, the more one finds his antipathy towards legislative initiatives smothering his apparent sense of proportion. Whether it be 'statutory tinkering' or 'the violent remedies' of over-ambitious reformers, legislation is more often than not the work of 'well-meaning and otherwise well-informed men' whose 'improvements of the law . . . are either superfluous or inappropriate', informed by some 'vague feeling that something must be done, somebody indemnified, or somebody else made answerable'.[213] 'It rather pleases me to dream of some planet', he commented in *The Genius of the Common Law*, 'where . . . judicial discretion doing its best to be impartial is not hampered at every turn by the meddling of partisan statutes with their crude remedies of contrary excess.'[214]

If one turns from Pollock's books and essays to his case notes in the *LQR*, one finds this antipathy expressed with even more forthrightness. It is tempting simply to claim that Pollock could afford to be more forthright because most of these case notes were anonymous. But this claim needs to be formulated carefully. The obvious implication of the claim is that, since readers would not be able to identify Pollock as the author of case notes, he could be more or less as critical or outspoken as he wanted to be. But in fact the majority of those who read the *LQR* during Pollock's tenure as Editor would have

[209] (1914) 30 *LQR* 385. For further condemnations of bad draftsmanship, see (1887) 3 *LQR* 362; (1892) 8 *LQR* 105, 107–8; (1893) 9 *LQR* 17; (1896) 12 *LQR* 106–7; (1900) 16 *LQR* 217; (1904) 20 *LQR* 4; (1905) 21 *LQR* 214; (1911) 27 *LQR* 144; (1913) 29 *LQR* 6–7; (1922) 38 *LQR* 401.

[210] *FBJ* 54.

[211] See, e.g., (1885) 1 *LQR* 278; (1888) 4 *LQR* 119, 366–7, 490; (1889) 5 *LQR* 100–1; (1895) 11 *LQR* 312, 320; (1900) 16 *LQR* 116; (1902) 18 *LQR* 107; (1903) 19 *LQR* 363; (1914) 30 *LQR* 147–8, 263.

[212] *GCL* 49. In a similar vein, see also *EJE* 242.

[213] *EJE* 97, 245, 79. See also *FL* 47 ('A law-maker who thinks and speaks as if he were dealing with a nation of fools will never make good laws; a passion for formulas is the mark not of an exact but of a petty mind, and is capable of becoming the ruin of legislation and politics').

[214] *GCL* 66, and see also 118–19.

been able to infer that unsigned notes came from the Editor's pen, not least because a signature was attached to almost everything that did not.[215] The ability to write notes without his name attached to them might, nevertheless, have given Pollock some degree of courage. Before *The Times* and its *Literary Supplement* jettisoned their general policy of anonymous reviewing, May observes, both 'were decidedly not regarded as assemblages of individual opinions, but as organs of a collective judgment that gave them their authority—and also imbued them with a certain mystique'.[216] The *LQR* of Pollock's era might be regarded similarly. Its readers may generally have been able to identify the anonymous notes as the work of Pollock. But this was not just Pollock: it was Sir Frederick Pollock, Bart., the Editor of *The Law Quarterly Review*. Writing as nobody, Pollock was somebody: anonymity gave him a special, authoritative voice—this was the *LQR* speaking. To put the speculation simply: Pollock's boldness as a case note writer may have been due to the peculiar sense of authority (as opposed to the false sense of courage) which sometimes comes with the convention of anonymity.

Even if this speculation is completely wrongheaded, the fact is that Pollock's case notes were usually more candid on the subject of legislation than were his books and essays. 'The reckless drafting of Acts of Parliament, contrasted with the patient and careful analysis bestowed on their interpretation by the Judges,' he noted, 'is a sight which might well make the angels weep.'[217] While 'parliamentary legislation . . . is apt to produce an unsatisfactory kind of law',[218] judicial legislation 'has created at least two-thirds of what is best in the law of England'.[219] Statutes, Pollock claimed in *The Expansion of the Common Law*, tend 'to choke the life out of principles under a weight of dead matter which posterity may think no better than a rubbish-heap'.[220] In his *LQR* case notes, he emphasized how the courts had triumphed with principles where legislators had failed. 'The best and by far the most logical portions of the law of England are the creation of the judges'[221] precisely because these judges

[215] On the drawing of inferences by readers of Victorian journals, see Collini, above n.95, 56. Note that not all anonymous notes contributed to the *LQR* during its first forty years appear to have been written by Pollock. Many of the anonymous notes on conflicts of laws, for example, appear from their style and content to be the work of Dicey: see, e.g., (1892) 8 *LQR* 103–4; (1893) 9 *LQR* 200, 297; (1896) 12 *LQR* 93–4, 96; (1905) 21 *LQR* 2. In this study, *LQR* notes are attributed to Pollock on the basis of internal evidence—his general prose style, idiosyncracies discernible throughout his writings, his tendency to identify himself by citing books by Pollock as the work of 'the present author', and so on. But it almost goes without saying that this method of attribution has its hazards. See, generally, Mary Ruth Hiller, 'The Use and Misuse of Internal Evidence in Authorship Attributions' (1979) 12 *Victorian Periodicals Rev.* 95–101.

[216] Derwent May, *Critical Times: The History of the Times Literary Supplement* (London: HarperCollins, 2001), 415. On the advantages, disadvantages, and politics of anonymity in Victorian periodical literature, see also Laurel Brake, 'Literary Criticism and the Victorian Periodicals' (1986) 16 *Yearbook of English Studies* 92–116 at 97–8; and Oscar Maurer, Jr., 'Anonymity vs. Signature in Victorian Reviewing' (1948) 27 *Univ. Texas Studies in English* 1–27.

[217] (1890) 6 *LQR* 350. [218] (1893) 9 *LQR* 106.

[219] (1902) 18 *LQR* 106. See also (1888) 4 *LQR* 230, 304; (1890) 6 *LQR* 118.

[220] *ECL* 8. [221] (1898) 14 *LQR* 331.

'have always shown, and still show, a really marvellous capacity for developing the principles of the unwritten law, and applying them to the solution of questions raised by novel circumstances'.[222]

It is from Pollock's gloomy reflections on legislation, then, that we can begin to acquire a sense of what he venerated about the common law. His perspective on legislation is that of the classic Burkean Whig: although 'forced to acknowledge the necessity of legislation, for him the common law—that cautious, organic, accretion of slow-won judicial wisdom—remains the true bedrock of English law.'[223] The common law is a good thing because it fosters common sense where legislation tends to frustrate it. It is a good thing because it nourishes principles where legislation is more likely to stifle them. It is also a good thing because, unlike legislation, it is more likely to promote and protect rather than impede and neglect the liberties of citizens. Pollock may not have demonstrated Dworkinian attentiveness to the protection of individual freedoms, but he believed that those freedoms which do exist are best protected by the courts. '[I]f there is any virtue in the Common Law . . . it is that Freedom is her sister, and in the spirit of freedom her greatest work has ever been done.'[224] Legislators, by contrast, are too often inattentive to the costs of the obligations and rights that they seek to establish. When new statutory duties are imposed on landlords, Pollock argued, at least some of the costs of those duties are likely to be transferred to tenants.[225] Likewise with mortgages: when the law—and it is usually, Pollock believed, statute law—makes it easier for mortgagors successfully to contest the terms of mortgages, 'the risk run by the mortgagee [in providing mortgages] only issues in harder terms for the mortgagor.'[226] Too often, in short, legislators impose duties on individuals and groups—landlords, mortgagees, whomever—without realizing that the initiative may diminish the liberty of those whose liberty is supposed to be protected. '[M]ost of the grievances of particular individuals or groups can be removed only by measures which create new grievances elsewhere.'[227] The words are Hayek's, but they might easily have been Pollock's.

The comparison with Hayek should be treated with circumspection: we have already noted the dangers of misrepresentation through reliance on presentist perspectives, and the intimation that Pollock was a Hayekian *avant la lettre* courts those very dangers. The comparison is certainly worth noting, however, because Pollock claimed that the common law lacks a political credo. '[N]ot being tied to dogmas', he wrote to Lytton Strachey, the common law

222 (1893) 9 *LQR* 106.

223 Roderick Munday, 'The Common Lawyer's Philosophy of Legislation' (1983) 14 *Rechtstheorie* 191–203 at 193. See also J. W. Burrow, *A Liberal Descent: Victorian Historians and the English Past* (Cambridge: Cambridge UP, 1981), 138, also 105 (on 'the Burkean Whig's conception' of the common law as 'the slow, anonymous sedimentation of immemorial custom').

224 *GCL* 124.

225 See (1896) 12 *LQR* 9.

226 (1899) 15 *LQR* 3.

227 F. A. Hayek, *Law, Legislation and Liberty: A New Statement of the Liberal Principles of Justice and Political Economy. Vol. i: Rules and Order. Vol. ii: The Mirage of Social Justice. Vol. iii: The Political Order of a Free People* (London: Routledge & Kegan Paul, 1982), i. 144.

'has only two fundamental principles, the publicity of justice and the supremacy of the courts in expounding the law—the rest is variable detail.'[228] Indeed, he had observed six years earlier, '[t]here seems to be no ground for affirming that the Common Law is especially attached to any one form of government.'[229]

Pollock certainly conceded that the common law might be considered to embody a political perspective in that it generally favours *laissez faire* and private ordering over paternalism. 'The Common Law favours competition wherever free competition is practicable,' preferring regulation only when a 'combination of private interests' seeks to impede freedom by exerting a stranglehold over a market.[230] But he did not consider the common law to embody only the one political perspective. The fact that the common law prefers regulation where private interests combine in an effort to control markets might be taken to indicate that it embodies the philosophy of socialism as well as that of *laissez faire*, even if the latter philosophy is more in evidence than the former. 'The element of truth in Socialism', Pollock wrote to Holmes, 'is to my mind something the Common Law knew long before any modern socialists were born: Monopolies are in principle odious, and when they are necessary they must be under public control.'[231] The common law may be political, in other words, but its politics are not consistently of one persuasion.

vi. Politics

So much for the question of whether the common law exhibits a distinct political perspective. What about Pollock himself? Prevarications notwithstanding, Pollock clearly preferred the common law to legislation. Could this preference in any way be said to be political? The most appropriate simple answer—'yes'—is a little too simple. Pollock's preference for the common law over legislation did indeed seem to betray a political perspective, but, as is nearly always the case with Pollock, examination of his perspective reveals it to be rather complicated.

[228] Frederick Pollock to G. L. Strachey, 15 June 1918, in Strachey papers, Add. 60691 f.71. On Pollock's belief in the political neutrality of the common law, see also Cosgrove, above n.14, 153.

[229] *GCL* 57. Pollock's argument about the non-partisan nature of the common law perhaps explains why he approved of Justice Holmes's dissent in *Lochner v New York*, 198 U.S. 45 (1905). Although Holmes's dissent is sometimes interpreted specifically as a reaction against reading Social Darwinist economic philosophy into the U.S. Constitution, Holmes's objection was in fact more general: 'a constitution is not intended to embody a particular economic theory, whether of paternalism and the organic relation of the citizen to the state or of *laissez-faire*.' See ibid. 75–6; and for Pollock's approval of Holmes's dissent, cf. (1905) 21 *LQR* 211–13.

[230] *GCL* 95.

[231] Pollock to Holmes, 3 August 1925, in *PHL* ii. 165. In a similar vein, see also Pollock to Holmes, 1 March 1913, in *PHL* i. 206 ('So far I go with the Socialists as to think it a pretty general rule that, where monopoly is necessary, it is better in public hands. (And so, I think, is the spirit of the Common Law.)').

The late Victorians, Watson argues, were fairly successful in holding socialism at bay as an organized political force.[232] But they never convincingly refuted the ideas behind socialism. When faced with socialist arguments, Victorian intellectuals often seemed unsure of how to react. 'A grand critique of socialism would be a subject for the historian of the twentieth century. Victorian intellectuals, being only vaguely and imperfectly aware of what total state power could inflict upon mankind, were more often hesitant, puzzled and even tolerant of a doctrine that seemed to arise, disturbingly and yet naturally, in the wake of democracy.'[233] In his lectures on *Law and Public Opinion in England*, Dicey noted the rise of socialism but seemed at a loss for a conclusion. '[S]ocialism,' the 'practical tendencies' of which 'are best exemplified in our labour laws,' 'favours the intervention of the State, even at some sacrifice of individual freedom, for the purpose of conferring benefit upon the mass of the people.'[234] Its influence 'is still . . . not apparently on the decline,' and indeed is very much in evidence 'in the Workmen's Compensation Acts, 1897 and 1900, which (to put the matter broadly) makes [*sic*] an employer the insurer of his workmen against any damage incurred in the course of their employment.'[235] Did this mean that socialism was to be welcomed or reviled?

Dicey would in all likelihood have considered revulsion to be the better response, though we cannot be sure. One of his principal objectives in *Law and Public Opinion* was to disapprove of trade unions, and, in particular, to pour scorn on the Trade Disputes Act 1906 (a subject which caused him nearly as much distress as Home Rule).[236] How can anybody, he wrote incredulously to Pollock in 1912, 'believe that peaceful picketing does not require to be severely checked'?[237] Indeed, on the subjects of trade unions and industrial action, he found in Pollock a soul mate of sorts. Dicey noted approvingly that Pollock, 'an impartial jurist',[238] had concluded in the eighth edition of *The Law of Torts* that the Trade Disputes Act was a 'violent empirical operation on the body politic'.[239] Pollock was hardly impartial. Trade unions irked him, and the Labour party seemed incapable of exhausting his contempt.[240] But Pollock's

[232] See George Watson, *The English Ideology: Studies in the Language of Victorian Politics* (London: Allen Lane, 1973), 222.

[233] Ibid. 236.

[234] A. V. Dicey, *Lectures on the Relation between Law and Public Opinion in England during the Nineteenth Century*, 2nd edn. (London: Macmillan, 1914), 64–5.

[235] Ibid. 66, 68–9; and cf. *GCL* 106–7.

[236] See Richard A. Cosgrove, *The Rule of Law: Albert Venn Dicey, Victorian Jurist* (Chapel Hill: University of North Carolina Press, 1980), 207–10.

[237] A. V. Dicey to Frederick Pollock, 18 March 1912, in Pollock correspondence, box 1, folder 19.

[238] Dicey, above n.234, xlviii.

[239] *TLT(8)* v. Pollock was similarly disparaging about the Workmen's Compensation Acts (or certainly what he considered to be the largely pointless litigation that they generated): see, e.g., (1915) 31 *LQR* 136, 365; and cf. also *EJE* 114–43 esp. at 126.

[240] For Pollock's disparagement of trade unions see, e.g., Pollock to Holmes, 25 March 1903, in *PHL* i. 112. For Pollock on the Labour party, see Frederick Pollock to J. R. M. Butler, 16 October 1924, in Butler papers, JRMB 11, 4/3 ('Co-operation between the Liberals and the Labour party seems to me a remote and pious wish: the Liberals have already tried and found it impossible, Ramsay

supposed impartiality is really neither here nor there. The more important point is that Dicey saw him as an ally. What, however, might they have been allied against? Union-friendly legislation? Socialism? The Trade Disputes Act clearly annoyed Dicey, but about socialism in general he was not so outspoken. Pollock likewise disliked the legislation. But where did he stand on socialism?

He was, of course, no socialist. When, in 1903, his son was 'going in for a socialist phase', he confessed to being relieved—'better than the hard-shelled and philosophically unsound individualism of the old utilitarian school'.[241] But it is a phase to which Pollock himself would never have succumbed. Indeed, unlike Dicey, when writing about socialism he saw no need to play his cards close to his chest. The 'Socialist Utopia[]', he observed privately, would inevitably degenerate into a 'despotic oligarchy, none the better for a disguise of philanthropic formulas'.[242] Similar sentiments he expressed publicly. Once the 'working man understand[s] that our new social reformers will confiscate his well-earned cottage neither more nor less than the squire's mansion and the manufacturer's mill . . . I think he will prefer his risks of poverty. . . . We may be permitted to trust . . . that the terrible fascination of revolution may remain, as it yet is, alien and impotent among our people.'[243] Unlike Aristotle, Pollock argued, socialists fail to recognize that it is more important 'to equalize men's wants than their substance'.[244] Following Aristotle, and anticipating a key theme of twentieth-century political and economic thought, he added that private ownership is generally preferable to public ownership because individuals normally place a higher value on that which is exclusively their own as compared with that which is owned communally. As he elaborated: '[c]arefulness is least in that which is common to most: for men take thought

Macdonald [*sic*] being at the mercy of his extremists—or believing himself so—whenever it comes to a decision. And whenever the Labour party finds a dictator he may be an extremist as like as not'). As regards Pollock's broader politics, it is perhaps worth noting that he declared himself 'well pleased' with the Conservative victory of October 1924. Pollock to Holmes, 6 November 1924, in *PHL* ii. 147. His pleasure was probably intensified by the resignation in November of Ramsay MacDonald as the head of the Labour Cabinet. Pollock had misgivings about MacDonald even before he had become Prime Minister in December 1923 (see Pollock to Holmes, 15 November 1923, in *PHL* ii. 124). As leader of the Liberals, David Lloyd George had, in Pollock's eyes, been a sorry sight—'wholly lacking in judgment and very ill informed,' with 'an inveterate habit of taking advice anywhere except in the right quarters'. Pollock to Holmes, 29 October 1931, ibid. 297; and, in a similarly vituperative vein, see Pollock to Holmes, 12 January 1923, ibid. 110. (Curiously, Lloyd George is reputed to have been similarly dismissive of Pollock, supposedly having once asked what it is that Pollock had ever achieved, given that he was never a judge, an eminent barrister, or a politician: see Harold J. Laski to O. W. Holmes, 6 September 1925, in *Holmes–Laski Letters: The Correspondence of Mr Justice Holmes and Harold J. Laski, 1916–1935*, 2 vols., ed. M. DeWolfe Howe (London: Cumberlege, 1953), i. 784.) Compared with Lloyd George, however, MacDonald was a far worse proposition—a 'contemptible worm', 'a shifty knave'; 'I don't trust Ramsay Macdonald', Pollock declared to Holmes, 'further than I can see him'. See Pollock to Holmes, 16 April [May?] 1926, in *PHL* ii. 182; 6 November 1924, ibid. 148; and 11 February 1924, ibid. 127.

241 Pollock to Holmes, 17 January 1903, in *PHL* i. 111.

242 Pollock to Holmes, 3 August 1925, in *PHL* ii. 165.

243 *LL(3)* 195–6.

244 *IHSP* 24.

in the chief place for their own, and less for the common stock. . . . Moreover, the pleasure we take in anything is increased beyond expression when we esteem it our own.'[245] This line of argument, he believed, tends to be neglected by those who place their faith in socialism.[246]

It tends not to be neglected, however, by those who place their faith in the common law. According to Atiyah, 'the separation of law and economics' was something that Pollock generally considered 'no bad thing'.[247] To claim that Pollock considered law and economics to be separate, however, is potentially misleading. Efforts to read particular economic perspectives into the law could certainly leave him exasperated. Presumably recalling the work of Charles Beard, he wrote to Holmes that '[t]he "economic" view of your Constitution has always seemed to me a special kind of pedantry and I am glad to hear it is discredited.'[248] '[J]udges ought to be very careful about committing themselves to fashionable economic theories', Pollock believed, not only because fashions can be ephemeral but also because judges 'are quite likely to misunderstand or misapply' the theories and, having erred, will probably be bailed out by legislators (whose remedies are 'almost sure to be unsatisfactory').[249] But he also believed that certain economic 'philosophies' have evolved naturally within the common law tradition. '[T]he Common Law', he explained,

> has passed or is passing through at least three distinct stages of economic assumption in its dealings with industrial affairs and the relations of capital and labour. There was the medieval stage in which every man was supposed to have his proper state of life, and the law had to see that he was kept in it. . . . Next came the reign of utilitarian individualism. . . . Then . . . it became a tolerated, indeed a probable or plausible, opinion, that the State was abdicating its functions by remaining passive, and should . . . give active assistance in suppressing unfavourable external conditions and equalizing opportunities.[250]

This last perspective—the idea that a non-interventionist State, which fails to remedy imbalances and improve the general welfare, must be in dereliction

[245] *IHSP* 22. Pollock provides as his source for the last sentence of the quotation *Politics* ii. 5, 5–8. The first part of the quotation appears to be a version of *Politics* ii. 3, 33–4 ('that which is common to the greatest number has the least care bestowed upon it. Every one thinks chiefly of his own, hardly at all of the common interest'), though Aristotle made the point in a variety of ways (see also, e.g., *Politics* ii. 5, 15–29). During the second half of the twentieth century, this general line of argument became central to both political theory and neoclassical economics: see, e.g., Garret Hardin, 'The Tragedy of the Commons' (1968) 162 *Science* 1243–8; and Harold Demsetz, 'Toward a Theory of Property Rights' (1967) 57 *Papers and Proceedings of the American Econ. Rev.* 347–59. Articulating the argument in neoclassical-economic terms, Demsetz observes that the 'primary function of property rights is that of guiding incentives to achieve a greater internalization of externalities' (ibid. 348).

[246] *IHSP* 22.

[247] Atiyah, above n.145, 668. Hedley accords Atiyah's claim a presentist dimension when he interprets it to be indicative of Pollock's 'rejection of law-and-economics'. Hedley, above n.201, 412 n.9.

[248] Pollock to Holmes, 29 November 1928, in *PHL* ii. 232; and cf. Charles A. Beard, *An Economic Interpretation of the Constitution of the United States* (New York: Macmillan, 1913).

[249] *GCL* 108. [250] *GCL* 107–8.

of its duty—represented, Pollock claimed in 1911, the spirit of the present generation of English lawyers.[251] This spirit, he believed, was closer to that of socialism than to that of the common law tradition—however much a 'courageous endeavour' socialism might be, after all, 'the one thing in which all socialist plans agree is in requiring not less legal compulsion than is imposed by existing civilized governments, but a great deal more'.[252] The fact that this attitude is at all discernible within the modern common law tradition indicates, according to Pollock, that it is not entirely antithetical to socialism. 'It seems rather idle to ask whether the Common Law is individualist or socialist: it is both and neither.'[253] The common law has always sought to redress inequalities of rights, although, having 'seen too many failures to be over-sanguine about putting the whole world straight', it disclaims 'any power to secure equality of conditions'.[254] In a letter to the Editor of *The Spectator*, published in October 1925, he summarized what he understood to be the politics of the common law thus:

There has always been a strong popular dislike of monopolies and trade rings in this country, and this dislike has found utterance in our law from the thirteenth century onwards. . . . In such cases our law, both judicial and legislative, has acted . . . on the principle that monopoly, where it is unavoidable, must be controlled by public authority acting for the common welfare. . . . But our law has never dogmatized on the questions whether the public control of monopoly shall be central or local. . . . These and other incidental doubts are left to be dealt with on grounds of economic expediency and on the special facts of each case or class of cases.

Here the common law parts company with our modern Socialists who think that they can reduce all such problems to universal formulas, paying very little regard to the lessons of actual experience, and none at all to the dangers of red-tape despotism. . . . Our Lady the Common Law has never had to deal with the enormous delusion that lies at the root of much Socialist and all Communist talk, namely, the assumption that there is somewhere an un-limited store of unused wealth which would make everyone happy and virtuous if only the State could exploit it. . . . I think I know what she would have to say, if the occasion called for it, to the unexplored treasures of Socialist imagining.[255]

251 See *GCL* 108. 252 *GCL* 106, 51. 253 *GCL* 54. 254 *GCL* 54.

255 Frederick Pollock, 'Socialism and the Common Law', *The Spectator*, 24 October 1925, 694–5. The Editor replied: '[i]t is a particular pleasure to us who reverence the Common Law of England to publish this eulogy of its amazing good sense by one of the most distinguished jurists of our time. Readers of recent leading articles in the *Spectator* will know how heartily we agree with the spirit in which Sir Frederick Pollock approaches the problems of to-day. . . . The Common Law of England gloriously sets an example and prescribes an attitude.' Ibid. 695. Cf. F. P., 'Home Politics' (October 1870) 2 *Fraser's Magazine* 404–13. The *Wellesley Index to Victorian Periodicals* suggests that 'F. P.' is probably Pollock. Certainly the prose-style of the piece supports this suggestion. The thesis of the piece, however, is not so easy to identify with Pollock. Addressing the question of how to ensure that the nation is fed, the author claims that it would be 'unsound' to treat the matter simply as one of

The passage is worth quoting at length because it shows Pollock with his guard down. In neither *The Genius of the Common Law* nor any of his other legal writings do we find him addressing the subject of socialism quite so stridently. Although the passage begins with Pollock's familiar claim that the common law might, at one level, be described as socialist because of its traditional distrust of monopolies and cartels, its general tenor is that only deluded fools (and his Lady, he cannot resist reminding us, is no fool) embrace 'Socialist imagining'. Note that Pollock dismissed modern socialism in much the same way as, around the same time, he dismissed certain elements of modern jurisprudence: the socialists, like Wesley Newomb Hohfeld (see chapter 3), apparently wanted to reduce life's complexity to something that could be chalked up on a blackboard. Pollock's principal reason for writing to *The Spectator* seems to have been to try to discourage the advances of various anti-socialist groups that would regularly invite him to join their ranks. He was not open to offers, he pointed out in exasperation, 'partly because I am too old to join new societies . . . , partly because some anti-Socialists appear to require assent to the extreme individualist economic doctrine which dominated our official life during the greater part of the nineteenth century, an assent which I am not prepared to give.'[256] Given his sentiments, none the less, these groups could hardly have been blamed for trying.

For Pollock, to ask how the common law protects equality, or to try to determine whether it is compatible with or antithetical to socialism, is to risk losing sight of the common law's primary purpose: to 'secure the essentials of justice and freedom'.[257] The fundamental problem with the Trade Disputes Act, in Pollock's view, was that it created 'partial anomalies in the narrowest spirit of class hostility and with no regard to legal and very little to natural justice'.[258] The reason that the common law is hostile to monopoly, furthermore, is that monopoly is an abuse of freedom.[259] Of course, the consequences of freedom will not always be welcomed—'[a] man cannot complain if a more skilful or

private duty, and offers a number of 'considerations in favour of State aid'—notwithstanding that there apparently existed 'little immediate hope from the . . . Government in any matter of State aid' (ibid. 409–10, 412). Since Pollock never declared himself an unequivocal anti-interventionist, it is not impossible that he would have held these views and that this piece is his work—especially given that he would have written it in his mid-twenties.

256 Pollock, 'Socialism and the Common Law', above n.255, 694.

257 *GCL* 94.

258 *GCL* 102. Cf. Frederick Pollock, 'The Contact of Public and Private Law' (1923) 1 *Cambridge L. J.* 255–60 at 259 ('A period of reaction from the old doctrines not only of Tory legislators but of Radical economists culminated in the Trade Disputes Act of 1906, a barefaced piece of class legislation due to pressure astutely exerted by the trade unions at the time of the preceding general election. . . . Those who framed or rather those who dictated the Act were evidently thinking of anything rather than the public good or the maintenance of the equality of citizens before the law'); and Pollock manuscripts, MS Eng. c. 3113, ff.13–32 at 28–9 (same).

259 See *GCL* 96–7; cf. also ibid. 67 ('our lady the Common Law smiles a little at those who wonder that she favours economic competition and dislikes monopoly. "How should I not approve competition," she whispers to her more discreet apprentices, "when I owe so much of my resources to the competition of my servants for fees?" ').

fortunate competitor diminishes his profit'[260]—and this may well be why the common law has never committed itself to the view that such consequences 'do not concern the State at all'.[261] But the common law has tended to recognize the restriction of freedom as a greater peril than freedom itself. By promoting economic freedom, the common law on 'agreements in restraint of trade has in our own time effected a change of front that has brought it completely into line with modern business conditions'.[262] '[W]hen once the State intervenes in the management of trade', by contrast, 'there arises an impossibility of putting limits to the State's intervention.'[263] Without doubt, the common law has made economic blunders.[264] Nevertheless, by developing 'solutions acceptable to men of business as just, and to lawyers as workmanlike and scientific', it has kept its 'general methods up to the mark of business requirements'.[265]

In keeping with his era—in keeping with his own character, indeed—Pollock rejected socialism as a political movement while never quite dismissing it as an intellectual proposition.[266] The reality of the matter is that socialism was never anything more than a prop to him, something to be relied upon when discussing the potential excesses of legislative intervention. Neither socialism nor any other political credo could distract him from his devotion to something that, as he saw it, defies systematization, shuns ideology, discards all that is foolish, and preserves much of what is wise; something that stands for reason, freedom, justice, and more or less everything else that could be taken to epitomize English virtue. The common law, on Pollock's account, may sometimes produce doctrines and outcomes that accord with one or another political perspective, but this does not mean that it is committed to any particular perspective; indeed, any effort to show that the common law is so committed will most likely fail to capture it in its full splendour. By both nature and inclination, Pollock would never have risked such failure.

vii. Conclusion

We noted earlier what Geertz termed that 'air of "of-courseness"' which tends to be cast over matters by arguments from common sense. Pollock's argument

260 *GCL* 98.
261 *GCL* 99. 262 *GCL* 98. 263 (1898) 14 *LQR* 229.
264 Though the source of the blunders, Pollock maintained, is usually legislation: see *GCL* 101–2.
265 *GCL* 109, 108.
266 In his *History of the Science of Politics*, Pollock omitted socialism from his survey on the ground that it 'is the political application of economic tenets and not a theory of politics at all'. *IHSP* 133; and cf. Stefan Collini, Donald Winch, and John Burrow, *That Noble Science of Politics: A Study in Nineteenth-century Intellectual History* (Cambridge: Cambridge UP, 1983), 373–4. Given that Pollock felt no need to discuss socialism in relation to political theory, it almost goes without saying that he felt similarly about raising such a discussion in the context of academic law: see F[rederick] P[ollock], review of *Property, its duties and rights historically, philosophically and religiously regarded* (1914) 30 *LQR* 111–12 at 112 ('Probably many good

about the common sense of the common law, being itself resolutely commonsensical, has that very air about it: how could anyone, Pollock seems to be saying, seriously think contrary to *this*? But the fact is that, even in Pollock's day, some jurists did entertain thoughts contrary to his. 'It is fashionable', Roscoe Pound declared in 1908, 'to preach the superiority of judge-made law', 'to point out the deficiencies of legislation and to declare that there are things that legislators cannot do try how they will'; yet 'while bench and bar are never weary of pointing out the deficiencies of legislation, to others the deficiencies of judge-made law are no less apparent.'[267] That Pound should have considered arguments about the superiority of common law over legislation rather outmoded is not surprising: he wrote, after all, at that time when American lawyers were beginning to place a great deal of faith in the remedial powers of statutes.[268] English lawyers of the early twentieth century never embraced statutes with the same enthusiasm as did their American counterparts; the growth of legislation in England was slower and less dramatic, and, even once the reach of statute law had expanded significantly, English lawyers still tended to operate on the assumption that legislative remedies were the exception and common law remedies the rule.[269] And so it is not surprising to find Pollock conceiving of the English common law as he did. For him, the common law was like the British Empire: a formidable power which would probably have been abused and suffered degeneration were it not for the soundness of the principles upon which it was founded and the quality of the people entrusted with its operation. It was after his lifetime that the core of common law doctrine began, like the Empire itself, significantly to shrink.[270]

But then, change did occur. Even if Pollock's perspective on the common law is understandable in context, the law itself outgrew it. Aside from the fact that legislation came increasingly to dominate English law during the twentieth century, common law and statute law became ever more intertwined. Common law interpretative techniques continued to prevail, indeed the common law itself continued to develop, in an era ever more reliant upon

people will classify the book as socialist. Nothing can be said of this, in a legal review not committed to any particular social theories, but that people may label it as they please, and no label will make the wine either better or worse').

[267] Roscoe Pound, 'Common Law and Legislation' (1908) 21 *Harvard L. Rev.* 383–407 at 383–4.

[268] See Guido Calabresi, *A Common Law for the Age of Statutes* (Cambridge, Mass.: Harvard UP, 1982), 1–7.

[269] See Wolfgang Friedmann, *Legal Theory*, 5th edn. (London: Stevens & Sons, 1967), 452 ('The English lawyer . . . does administer and interpret an increasing number of statutes; but, psychologically, if not statistically, these still appear as exceptions rather than as rule, and the theory of statutory interpretation is, accordingly, rather undetermined').

[270] On the shrinking of common law doctrine, see Jack Beatson, *Has the Common Law a Future?* (Cambridge: Cambridge UP, 1996), 16–19. Although Pollock noted the growth of legislation, he did not—certainly at the end of the nineteenth century—believe that such growth led to a concomitant shrinking in the core of common law doctrine. See Pollock, 'The Continuity of the Common Law', above n.68, 433 ('Legislation has grown upon us, but with it and even because of it the reign of judicial law has grown too').

statutes; 'the relationship between common law and statute law must be seen as the relationship between two developing and moving bodies of law', Atiyah declared in 1985, 'and the way in which they interact on each other becomes a matter of no little importance.'[271] Leaving aside this interaction, it should be remembered also that, during the twentieth century, the role of the courts in the lawmaking process changed somewhat. Although Pollock may have found himself increasingly less hostile to the declaratory theory as the years progressed, the twentieth century saw the theory not received but discredited.[272] There are those who would point also to the changing role of the jurist. When Pollock died in 1937, Birks remarks, 'things were not as they are now'.[273] Not only has the convention, which we noted earlier, against citing living authors in court all but faded from view, but English appellate judges today are increasingly willing to make explicit and constructive use of academic commentary. '[T]he work of the judges has become more and more influenced by the teaching and writing of jurists', one commentator remarked in 1983.[274] 'For hundreds of years it was the judges alone who expounded the principles of the common law'; today, 'the search for principle is a task which judge and jurist share together'.[275] These words would be significant enough were the commentator an academic; that they were written by a senior judge makes them resonate all the more.

This last observation needs to be handled with care. Various contemporary judges have been more willing than were their predecessors to acknowledge juristic influence upon judicial decision-making. While such influence has become easier to detect, however, it is not necessarily a modern phenomenon. Recall the observation that concludes section iv of this chapter: few jurists can claim to have been as influential upon the development of the common law as was Pollock. Why should this have been the case? Part of the answer to this question runs throughout this chapter. To understand Pollock's juristic ambitions, we do best not to connect him with one or another modern jurisprudential tradition but to see him as a throwback to an even earlier generation of jurists, a generation that wrote unashamedly about the reasonableness and, indeed, the glory of the common law. Pollock seemed neither comfortable with, nor able to write confidently about, legal philosophy. With the common law, quite the opposite was the case. Much of what he had to say about the common law tradition may well, to modern ears, sound old-fashioned, reactionary even; but to those of his era who would have defended that tradition—to more or less everyone connected to Bar and bench, in other words—his voice must have epitomized clarity, good sense, and defiance.

[271] P. S. Atiyah, 'Common Law and Statute Law' (1985) 48 *Mod. L. Rev.* 1–28 at 1.

[272] See Rupert Cross and J. W. Harris, *Precedent in English Law*, 4th edn. (Oxford: Clarendon Press, 1991), 27–36; and cf. also Beatson, above n.270, 10–13.

[273] Peter Birks, 'The Academic and the Practitioner' (1998) 18 *Legal Studiesw* 397–414 at 398.

[274] Robert Goff, 'The Search for Principle' (1983) 69 *Proc. Brit. Acad.* 169–87 at 182.

[275] Ibid. 171, 187.

But are we not speculating? It should be clear by now that Pollock venerated the common law tradition. But it does not necessarily follow from this that what he had to say about the common law should have been inspirational. Where is the proof? Our next task is to find that proof. We will see that the proof comes in two basic forms. On the one hand, there is what we might crudely term Pollock's editorial contribution to the development of modern law. This will be the subject of chapter 6. On the other, there is his more conventional juristic contribution. Being of the view that the treatises of living authors cannot be authoritative sources of law, Pollock nevertheless produced two common law treatises that were as close to being sources of law as juristic commentary is ever likely to come. It is to the lives of these treatises that we turn next.

5

JURISTS' LAW

The role of jurist resists a standard job specification. Besides being scholars and teachers, academic lawyers will sometimes serve as law reformers, as advisers to the legal profession, as members of public committees concerned with matters of legal policy, and as social commentators—journalists, for example—offering opinions on significant legal issues. English jurists, like their colleagues in continental Europe and the United States, quite regularly perform these ancillary roles. Yet academic commentary often creates the impression that only on the continent and in North America does the work of jurists make any significant mark beyond the confines of the university. In England, according to van Caenegem, 'the role of professors of law and of theoretical study—"legal science"—has in the course of the centuries been marginal. No contrast could be greater than between this English development and its continental counterpart, for there the impact of "professors' law" has been of the greatest importance.'[1] English jurisprudence students are often surprised to learn that Hans Kelsen's Pure Theory of Law—something that generally strikes them as ethereal, abstruse, and completely irrelevant to law—was not only the work of a continental jurist whose ideas sometimes found their way into courtrooms and constitutions, but was also considered, in the context in which it was devised, to have some practical-legal significance.[2] Nor

[1] R. C. van Caenegem, *Judges, Legislators and Professors: Chapters in European Legal History* (Cambridge: Cambridge UP, 1987), 53. See also John Henry Merryman, *The Civil Law Tradition: An Introduction to the Legal Systems of Western Europe and Latin America*, 2nd edn. (Stanford, CA: Stanford University Press, 1985), 56–7 ('The teacher-scholar is the real protagonist of the civil law tradition. The civil law is a law of the professors. . . . The tradition of the scholar as an important force in the development of the common law is very recent and still, comparatively, very weak. The common law is still a law of the judges'); and Ian Fletcher, 'An English Tragedy: The Academic Lawyer as Jurist', in *Lawyers and Laymen: Studies in the History of Law presented to Professor Dafydd Jenkins on his seventy-fifth birthday, Gŵyl Ddewi 1986* (Cardiff: University of Wales Press, 1986), 316–35 at 318, 321 (arguing that whereas, historically, the role of the continental jurist 'assumed a pre-eminence which transcended any purely academic context in which legal learning might happen to be centred, and recaptured that influence upon the living practice and administration of the law which had been such a remarkable feature of the Roman classical period', the doctors of law at the English universities up until the nineteenth century 'did not see fit to devote themselves to the scholarly investigation of the law as actually practised within the courts of the country in which they were living').

[2] 'Kelsen's use of norms in order to explicate rules of law may have derived in part from confusions that affected Habsburg law. . . . There existed so many levels of jurisdiction . . . that endless con-

is it only a difference between England and the continent. 'It is perhaps not surprising, in view of the historical role of the jurist in Roman law, that academics still play a major role in modern civil law systems', Atiyah has remarked; '[b]ut even in modern America, which of course has almost no civil law antecedents, the academic plays a far higher role than he does in England.'[3] Indeed, he adds elsewhere, '[t]he leading American law schools have had a great influence on the American legal order', whereas 'English law schools have a negligible influence on the English legal order.'[4]

There is no need here to subject to detailed scrutiny the belief that jurists are more influential and respected elsewhere. Certainly there is some evidence that, during the second half of the twentieth century, English academic lawyers contributed significantly to the development of law, and to the understanding of law, outside the universities.[5] More importantly for the purposes of this study, much the same observation might credibly be made about jurists of the second half of the nineteenth century also. Indeed, the basic purpose of this chapter and the next one is to show that Pollock's initiatives as treatise writer and editor bear out this last claim. But before we set about trying to demonstrate as much, before we consider further, that is, just what sort of jurist Pollock was, we might do well to consider just what sort of jurist he was not.

While, on occasions, English jurists of the twentieth century were influential voices in legal affairs, few of them could accurately have been described as public intellectuals. Given that the twentieth century is generally considered not to have been a vintage one for the public intellectual in any event, it is perhaps not surprising that a nation and a legal system both of which have been more wary than welcoming of intellectualization should have proved generally resistant to this figure.[6] Yet this resistance had not always been

flicts ensued. To disentangle levels and accretions, it was essential to propound ideal types. As a further debt to Austria, Kelsen's jurisprudence, shorn of social science and ideology, flourished as a corrective in a nation where professors of law could implement their theories. Desire to expunge extraneous influence was less likely among Anglo-Americans, where judges, not professors, fashion laws.' William M. Johnston, *The Austrian Mind: An Intellectual and Social History, 1848–1938* (Berkeley: University of California Press, 1972), 97. For Kelsen's influence on law (among other things, he drafted the Austrian Constitution of 1920 and in the following year was appointed to the Austrian Constitutional Court), see Rudolf Aladár Métall, *Hans Kelsen. Leben und Werk* (Vienna: Deuticke, 1969), 28–57, 106–8.

[3] P. S. Atiyah, *Pragmatism and Theory in English Law* (London: Stevens & Sons, 1987), 38–9.

[4] P. S. Atiyah and Robert S. Summers, *Form and Substance in Anglo-American Law: A Comparative Study of Legal Reasoning, Legal Theory, and Legal Institutions* (Oxford: Clarendon Press, 1987), 403–4. With regard to the United States more generally, cf. Martin Amis's observation that '[t]he life of the American intellectual is qualitatively different from its British equivalent. In America, intellectuals are public figures (whereas over here they are taken rather less seriously than ordinary citizens—at most, they are licensed loudmouths).' Martin Amis, *The Moronic Inferno and Other Visits to America* (Harmondsworth: Penguin, 1986), 54.

[5] For fragments of this evidence, see Neil Duxbury, *Jurists and Judges: An Essay on Influence* (Oxford: Hart, 2001), 101–15.

[6] It should not be assumed that twentieth-century Britain was completely devoid of public-intellectual culture. The philosopher, C. E. M. Joad, and other academics who, from the beginning of the 1940s, regularly appeared as panelists on BBC Radio's *The Brains Trust* very much fitted within the public intellectual mould. Likewise, the BBC's Third Programme provided something of a platform

present. The last quarter of the nineteenth century, according to Stapleton, represented the high-water mark for the British public intellectual. 'In this period intellectuals perceived themselves as scholars whose first duty was to educate the newly literate and political classes of late Victorian Britain. They framed their interests and activities accordingly. On the one hand, they were polymaths who straddled across the disciplinary barriers of the humanities with comparative ease; on the other, they engaged fully in the wider activities of public life, performing a variety of work which their scholarship both informed and was stimulated by in turn.'[7] Collini has a specific designation for these intellectuals: public moralists. Public moralists emphasized 'failings of character as the chief source of civic as well as private woe' and sought 'to persuade their contemporaries to live up to their [the public moralists'] professed ideals'.[8] To be persuasive, public moralists needed—herein lies the significance of the word 'public'—to capture the minds of an audience. Seeking 'to remind their more self-interested contemporaries of the strenuous commitments entailed by the moral values embedded in . . . public discourse', public moralists demonstrated a capacity to persuade which was largely attributable to the fact that they were fundamentally confident '—confident of having the ear of the important audience, confident of addressing concerns and invoking values which were largely shared with that audience, confident of an easy, intimate, even conversable, relationship with both Reason and History.'[9]

Just as the public moralist might be considered a distinctive species of Victorian public intellectual, the Victorian jurist might, in many instances, be considered a distinctive type of public moralist. '[A]ny discussion of the "voices" available to the public moralist in this period,' Collini observes, 'needs to be able to accommodate the particular kind of authority laid claim to by the writer who draws upon a legal or jurisprudential idiom.'[10] Maine, Fitzjames Stephen, and Dicey all epitomized the jurist as public moralist: '[a]ll three belonged . . . to that well-connected intellectual-cum-political stratum which . . . staffed the overlapping worlds of law, administration, and the higher

for public intellectuals before the beginnings of its dismemberment in the late 1950s. Generally, on the deteriorating significance of public intellectuals, see Richard A. Posner, *Public Intellectuals: A Study of Decline* (Cambridge, Mass.: Harvard UP, 2001); Thomas Bender, *Intellect and Public Life: Essays on the Social History of Academic Intellectuals in the United States* (Baltimore: Johns Hopkins UP, 1993); and Michael Ignatieff, 'The Decline and Fall of the Public Intellectual' (1997) 104 *Queen's Quarterly* 395–403. Posner and Bender, concerned, as they are, primarily with the United States, believe that the best of the public intellectual tradition may well be reprised; Ignatieff, reflecting on Europe, is signally less sanguine.

[7] Julia Stapleton, *Political Intellectuals and Public Identities in Britain since 1850* (Manchester: Manchester UP, 2001), 17.

[8] Stefan Collini, *Public Moralists: Political Thought and Public Life in Britain 1850–1930* (Oxford: Clarendon Press, 1991), 2.

[9] Ibid. 58. The confidence was in evidence, Collini remarks, notwithstanding that 'many of these figures'—Herbert Spencer and Leslie Stephen would be apt examples—'were aware that they held views which were regarded with some suspicion in the best circles.' Ibid. 17.

[10] Ibid. 255.

reaches of education and journalism.'[11] But not all Victorian jurists conformed to the type. For example, 'Maitland's writings are not those of a "public moralist", and his professional "voice" did not easily lend itself to direct participation in political debate'.[12] '[F]or the jurist of this period, . . . the desire to shape public discussion could pull in a different direction from the desire to contribute to the progress of one's "discipline".'[13] Maitland wished more than anything else to engage in careful historical research, an ambition distinctly removed from that of influencing public opinion.

Of course, the more pertinent question for the purposes of this study concerns Pollock. Did he conform to the type? It is significant that Collini does not characterize him thus. This is not to say that Pollock failed to exhibit any of what Collini considers to be the public moralist's primary characteristics. Pollock did many of the things that any public moralist worth his salt was supposed to do. As has been observed already in this study, furthermore, his initiatives as a votary for the League of Nations showed that, when the mood took him, he could adopt a public moralist's voice. But Pollock the early twentieth-century elder statesman, speaking up for the League of Nations, was a rather different creature than Pollock the late-Victorian jurist. In this latter capacity, he rather resisted the appellation of public moralist. As a jurist, that is, his principal concern was not to shape public consciousness but to make a lasting contribution to legal science. So far, this study has considered his general contribution to that science. Our attention now shifts primarily to two of his more specific contributions to legal science—his efforts to explicate the foundational principles, and thereby capture the doctrinal elegance, of the law of contract and torts.

In the eyes of many lawyers of Pollock's generation, Pollock's two greatest works were *Principles of Contract at Law and in Equity*, first published in 1876, and *The Law or Torts*, which first appeared in 1887. Assessments of these works tend to be of one voice: indeed, it seems most appropriate to examine them over one lengthy chapter rather than two comparatively short ones because, as is commonly acknowledged, both works share the same basic objective, highlight the same general juristic issues, and marked a new and distinctive era in English legal thought. The late nineteenth century heralded the beginning of the modern English legal treatise-writing tradition, the principal distinguishing characteristic of which was that treatises were ever more regularly being written by lawyers with academic aspirations (and, eventually, careers). The tradition appears to have begun with Pollock and William Anson—both men produced treatises on contracts in the 1870s and were elected to posts at Oxford in the early 1880s.[14] The treatises of Pollock and Anson exemplify

[11] Ibid. 270. [12] Ibid. 303–4. [13] Ibid. 269.

[14] See A. W. B. Simpson, 'The Rise and Fall of the Legal Treatise: Legal Principles and the Forms of Legal Literature' (1981) 48 *Univ. Chicago L. Rev.* 632–79 at 664. Simpson notes that both *Principles of Contract* and *The Law of Torts* 'were written while Pollock was Corpus Professor of Jurisprudence at

another distinctive characteristic of this tradition: a preoccupation with discovering and setting out in a coherent fashion the principles underlying what would often be a vast mass of relevant case law. It was observed in chapter 4 that Pollock not only extolled the principled nature of the common law, but, as primary case note writer for the *Law Quarterly Review*, worked hard to highlight legal principles in action. This preoccupation with principle becomes yet more apparent in his treatises.

That Pollock's treatises are shrines to legal principle is hardly a neglected fact. In the standard accounts of the man, the observation is about as common as stories of his reticence. 'His books on Contract and Tort', according to Holdsworth, 'were the first books in which the principles of these branches of law were treated in a manner which was both scientific and literary'.[15] For Hazeltine, they 'inaugurated a new era in the history of our modern Common Law' by exposing 'the fundamental principles of obligation arising *ex contractu* and *ex delicto* as found in the cases'.[16] Likewise Lord Wright: *Principles of Contract* and *The Law of Torts* marked 'a new period of English legal study', both books being 'expositions of the principles of English law, illuminated by accurate history, combining the philosophy of law with its practical aspects, wedding realism to speculation.'[17] If this chapter simply put flesh on the bones of this observation—for these quotations amount to but one observation—then the reality of the matter would be that it would have little point at all. The purpose of this chapter is to look behind the basic claim that Pollock spearheaded a new tradition of principle-oriented treatise writing and determine what he actually did with the notion of principle. What did he argue? And how were his arguments received?

This last question opens up two further lines of inquiry. The first concerns the reception of Pollock's treatises on contract and torts by other jurists. Certain of Pollock's arguments on these subjects, we will see, featured within and to some degree inspired significant juristic debates. Secondly, there is the matter of how Pollock's arguments were received by English judges. Sir William Holdsworth must be adjudged to have done sterling work in raising the profile of jurists among bench and Bar, W. T. S. Stallybrass noted on Holdsworth's death in 1944, so long as it is recognized that this is an area in which Pollock stands nonpareil.[18] To be eclipsed by Pollock in this respect appears to have been no cause for shame. 'The writings of a lawyer like Pollock,' the Master of the Rolls observed in 1937, 'constantly cited in the

Oxford' (ibid. 664 n.233). While this is true of the latter text, it is not true of *Principles of Contract*: the book first appeared in 1876 and Pollock became Corpus Professor in 1883.

[15] Sir William Holdsworth, *Some Makers of English Law: The Tagore Lectures, 1937–38* (Cambridge: Cambridge UP, 1938), 285.

[16] H. D. Hazeltine, 'Sir Frederick Pollock, Bart., 1845–1937' (1949) 35 *Proc. Brit. Acad.* 233–56 at 245.

[17] Lord Wright, 'In Memoriam: Right Hon. Sir Frederick Pollock, Bart., K.C., D.C.L. 1845–1937' (1937) 53 *LQR* 151–67 at 154. In a similar vein, see also C. H. S. Fifoot, *English Law and its Background* (London: Bell, 1932), 185–6.

[18] W. T. S. Stallybrass (1944) 60 *LQR* 147–53 at 152.

Courts and quoted by the judges, are entitled to claim a place under his category of unwritten law, even in a system like ours which does not normally seek its law from institutional writers.'[19] A later Master of the Rolls would, in the early 1950s, offer much the same observation.[20] 'Equally at home in the Inns of Court and in the Universities,' Fifoot remarks, Pollock 'was for sixty years at the heart of the law.'[21] While he may not have been the most convincing of public moralists, it would be a mistake to believe that Pollock's influence failed to extend beyond the universities. This much we noted in the previous chapter. An objective of this chapter is to try to provide some insight into just how much influence Pollock had, particularly over the English courts. What unfolds here is by no means a comprehensive account of Pollock's influence—providing such an account is probably impossible—but rather an account centred primarily upon the works by Pollock to which the English courts have been most consistently indebted.

i. Contract

Some of the great jurists of history have produced, early in their careers, works of such authority and maturity that it is difficult not to believe that they were written after a lifetime's research and reflection. Savigny's great treatise on the law of possession, for example, was first published when he was but 24 years old.[22] Hersch Lauterpacht had completed his classic monograph on the centrality of analogy to the international legal order by the time that he was 27.[23] Pollock himself was no slouch. He was 32 when his 600-page *Principles of Contract* first appeared. Almost a decade earlier, Stephen Leake had produced a contracts treatise which would eventually have much the same title.[24] Whereas

[19] Wright, above n.17, 152.

[20] See Lord Justice Denning, 'The Universities and Law Reform' (1951) n.s. 1 *Jnl. of the Society of Public Teachers of Law* 258–69 at 263 ('The writings of Sir Frederick Pollock and other great professors of law have had a greater influence on the law than the judgments of many of our judges. By studying the cases and extracting from them principles of general application they have made clear the path for future decisions').

[21] C. H. S. Fifoot, *Judge and Jurist in the Reign of Victoria* (London: Stevens & Sons, 1959), 136. See also Alan Harding, *A Social History of English Law* (Gloucester, Mass.: Smith, 1973 [1966]), 349 ('Pollock . . . was a new type of figure in English law—a jurist whose opinion was constantly sought by government and judges').

[22] Friedrich Carl von Savigny, *Das Recht des Besitzes. Eine civilistische Abhandlung* (Giessen: Bey Heyer, 1803).

[23] Hersch Lauterpacht, *Private Law Sources and Analogies of International Law (with Special Reference to International Arbitration)* (London: Longmans & Co., 1927). The book grew out of Lauterpacht's Ph.D. dissertation, submitted at the London School of Economics in 1925. On the book as evidence of Lauterpacht's precocious talent, see Alfred P. Rubin, *Ethics and Authority in International Law* (Cambridge: Cambridge UP, 1997), 141 n.19.

[24] Stephen Martin Leake, *The Elements of the Law of Contracts* (London: Stevens & Sons, 1867). By its third edition, the book had become *A Digest of Principles of the Law of Contracts* (London: Stevens & Sons, 1892), and, by its fourth edition (under A. E. Randall's editorship), it had simply become *Principles of the Law of Contracts* (London: Stevens & Sons, 1902). Among lawyers it is, according to convention,

'Leake's book was for practitioners,' however, 'Pollock's book was for students of principles and legal thinkers.'[25] Intended 'to supplement rather than to compete with existing works', *Principles of Contract* was not a compilation of cases for the convenience of the busy practitioner but 'a Treatise on the general principles which determine the validity and effect of Contracts in their inception.'[26]

To obtain a basic understanding of Pollock's approach to the law of contract, the best place to start, one might expect, would be the introduction to his treatise on the subject. In fact, one of the most notable and instructive of his general observations on contract is to be found around one-third of the way through his main book on Spinoza. 'Most of the definitions found in our law books,' he states in that study,

> and not least the definitions of Contract, are loose and unsatisfying. They are vague, insufficient, and redundant; they assume knowledge of other matters that have never been explained; they fail, in Spinoza's language, to expound the thing defined in terms of its *causa proxima*. But Savigny goes to the root of the matter and gives us a clear statement of the simple elements that make up the legal idea. His definition is accurate and exhaustive, and therefore fruitful.[27]

There are two points to note about this passage. First, it leaves us in suspense: how did Savigny define contract? In *Spinoza*, rather bizarrely, Pollock does not tell us. For his account of this definition, it is necessary to look to the first chapter of *Principles of Contract*. Secondly, although Pollock leaves us in suspense over what the definition might be, he does tell us why it is to his liking. Savigny's definition of contract is to be commended because it is clear, simple, accurate, and exhaustive—an impressive synthesis, in other words, of the many elements that make up what Pollock calls this 'special and complex conception'.[28] The notion of synthesis is important here. In *Principles of Contract*, Pollock seems to be under the spell not only of Savigny's definition of contract, but of Savigny himself ('a man of true scientific genius', in Pollock's estimation).[29] But as Fifoot points out, it is the influence 'of Savigny the syn-

known and referred to more simply still, as Leake on *Contracts*. On Leake, see Thomas Glyn Watkin's entry in *Biographical Dictionary of the Common Law*, ed. A. W. B. Simpson (London: Butterworths, 1984), 308–9; Simpson, above n.14, 664; and Fifoot, above n.21, 27.

[25] Wright, above n.17, 154.

[26] *PCLE* v. See also P. S. Atiyah, *The Rise and Fall of Freedom of Contract* (Oxford: Clarendon Press, 1979), 682–3.

[27] *SHLP* 139. This passage is taken from the second edition of the book, published in 1899. In this edition, at the end of the opening sentence of the quotation, Pollock inserted a footnote stating that '[s]ince the first [i.e., 1880] edition was written there has been a great improvement in the method and form of our text-books.' An equally uninformative variant on the quotation appears in Frederick Pollock, 'The Scientific Character of Spinoza's Philosophy' (May 1873) n.s. 13 *Fortnightly Rev.* 567–85 at 574.

[28] *PCLE* 1.

[29] *PCLE* 2 n.*b*. On Savigny's influence upon nineteenth-century Anglo-American juristic thought generally, see Michael H. Hoeflich, 'Savigny and his Anglo-American Disciples' (1989) 37 *American Jnl. of Comparative Law* 17–37.

thesist not of Savigny the historian' that is primarily in evidence here.[30] *Principles of Contract* is very much an historical work—Pollock can be found constantly tracing legal principles back to their earliest authorities. History, however, is simply the means of rooting out principles. The articulation of those principles once they have been excavated is, for Pollock, the key to successful synthesis. To synthesize—to take a vast quarry of case law and render it less formidable by organizing it, so far as is possible, in accordance with governing legal principles—is, in his view, the best service that a legal treatise can provide. But it must always be remembered that synthesis is dependent upon principle.

This section begins with an examination of how Pollock, following Savigny, defined contract. Having set out this definition, we then proceed to consider Pollock's conception of contract within a broader framework, focusing in particular upon his fairly complex and sometimes misrepresented perspectives on the will theory, consideration, and good faith. Through an analysis of Pollock's perspectives on these themes it should become clear that the articulation and elaboration of principles was, so far as he was concerned, not only a prerequisite to effective summary and synthesis but also an exercise in legal critique. Indeed, an examination of Pollock's general endeavours as a treatise writer reveals how jurists, when they dedicate themselves seriously to determining principles of law, will almost inevitably discover instances where those principles are ambiguous, incoherent, insufficiently developed, or even absent.

a. *Conceptualizing contract*

'It is somewhat curious', Pollock observed at the outset of the first edition of *Principles of Contract*, 'that no such thing as a satisfactory definition of Contract is to be found in any of our books.'[31] Perhaps the reason for this, he continued, is that 'not one definition but a series of definitions is required'.[32] Any such definition must surely incorporate the notion of consent—this, after all, is 'the main thing that goes to make a contract'.[33] But the notion has limited explanatory value in this context, for while '[e]very contract involves consent . . . many legal transactions involve consent without being contracts.'[34] Savigny, Pollock observed, began with an analysis of the general idea of a legal agreement—*der Vertrag*—and worked inwards towards the specific idea of a contractual relationship. For Savigny, and for Pollock, there are at least five elements integral to the consent that makes a legal agreement. First, the agreement must involve at least two persons. Secondly, 'these persons have a distinct intention, and the intention of both or all of them is the same.'[35] Thirdly, 'they must be aware that that their intentions agree and . . . must

[30] C. H. S. Fifoot, *Law and History in the Nineteenth Century* (London: Quaritch, 1956), 7.
[31] *PCLE* 1. [32] *PCLE* 1. [33] *PCLE* 1. [34] *PCLE* 1. [35] *PCLE* 2.

communicate them to one another'.[36] Fourthly, '[t]he intention of the parties must . . . be an intention directed to legal consequences; and, finally, those consequences must be such as to confer rights or impose duties on the parties themselves.'[37] 'The central part of this group of ideas is that the parties *concur in expressing a common intention*', this intention being communicated by 'proposal and acceptance'.[38]

How might the notion of contract be distinguished from this general idea of legal agreement? '[I]n the case of a contract something remains to be done by one or each of the parties, which the other has or will have a right to call upon him to do.'[39] A contract, in other words, generates obligation, and 'the common intention expressed by the parties . . . contemplates a future performance' which will extinguish this obligation.[40] 'On the side of the party so bound' by the obligation, 'this intention is' expressed as 'a promise. This is the specific mark of Contract . . . which distinguishes it from the genus Agreement.'[41]

In the first edition of *Principles of Contract*, this is all that Pollock had to say about contract as a concept before he began to explore its many legal dimensions. 'The leading ideas' have been 'worked out', he declared early in the first chapter; the remainder of the treatise he devoted to the exposition and elaboration of legal principles.[42] While, on the face of it, his conceptual analysis seems as unremarkable as it is brief, it has a fair amount of historical significance. During the nineteenth century, the so-called 'will theory' of contract began to take hold in English legal thought.[43] According to this theory, it is the will of the parties to a contract that explains why the contract binds. Given that willing is, as Savigny put it, an 'invisible event',[44] it is of course necessary that the will of the parties be declared for a contract to be binding. And it is necessary, too, that there is, between the parties, a meeting of minds which renders meaningful the notion of a singular 'will'. Thus it is that Savigny refers to a contract as 'a union of several wills to a single, whole and undivided will'.[45] Liabilities, according to the will theory, arise from this union of will.

The will theory did not originate with Savigny. Robert Joseph Pothier had championed the theory in his *Traité des Obligations*, first published in the early 1760s.[46] Not only was Pothier's treaty influential in France—portions of it

[36] *PCLE* 2. [37] *PCLE* 2. [38] *PCLE* 3–4. [39] *PCLE* 5. [40] *PCLE* 5.

[41] *PCLE* 5. Cf. also Frederick Pollock, 'Contracts in Early English Law' (1893) 6 *Harvard L. Rev.* 389–404. Leake had argued along similar lines some nine years earlier in the first edition of his *Elements of the Law of Contracts*, above n.24, 11–12. According to Jackson, however, as compared with Leake's work, 'Pollock's . . . may have done more to make this learning generally accepted.' R. M. Jackson, 'The Scope of the Term "Contract"' (1937) 53 *LQR* 525–36 at 533.

[42] *PCLE* 6.

[43] See Atiyah, above n.26, 407.

[44] Friedrich Carl von Savigny, *System des heutigen römischen Rechts*, 9 vols. (Berlin: Veit, 1840–51), iii. 258.

[45] Ibid. iii. 309.

[46] Robert Joseph Pothier, *Traité des Obligations, selon les règles tant du for de la conscience que du for extérieur*, 2nd edn. (Paris: Orléans, 1768; 1st edn. publ. 1761).

found their way more or less directly into the Civil Code[47]—but, particularly after its appearance in translation in 1806,[48] it also had a significant impact on English understandings of contract.[49] Pothier is almost as much of a presence throughout the first edition of *Principles of Contract* as is Savigny, and his influence on contract theory in England generally was probably greater than was Savigny's.[50] A serious study of the will theory would trace its roots well beyond Pothier, through Aquinas and back to Aristotle.[51] But that exercise is not necessary here. What matters for our purposes is the popularity of the theory in nineteenth-century England. 'No man has entered into an agreement or contract to do, or not to do, some particular thing', Kindersley V. C. observed in *Haynes v Haynes* in 1861,

> unless he has willed that the thing should be done or forborne, and also has communicated that will to the other party by some act engaging to carry it into effect; when both parties will the same thing, and each communicates his will to the other, with a mutual engagement to carry it into effect, then (and not till then) an agreement or contract, between the two is constituted. Now this is not a mere theoretical disquisition, but a statement of sound practical principles of universal law, and of the law of England in particular.[52]

'This idea has proved so tenacious in English law', Atiyah remarks, 'that even the modern lawyer, accustomed as he is to the many derogations from freedom of contract today, still takes it for granted that contractual obligations are created by the will or the intention of the parties.'[53] The opening pages

[47] See, e.g., *Code Civil*, arts. 1101 (general statement of contract), 1131–3 (contractual cause), and 1150–1 (damages).

[48] M. [Robert Joseph] Pothier, *A Treatise on the Law of Obligations, or Contracts*, 2 vols., trans. W. D. Evans (London: Butterworths, 1806).

[49] See generally C. Malecki, 'L'Erreur sur la personne en droit anglais et en droit français des contrats: De l'influence déterminante de Pothier sur la Common Law?' (1995) 72 *Revue de Droit international et de Droit comparé* 347–83; and David Ibbetson, *A Historical Introduction to the Law of Obligations* (Oxford: Oxford UP, 1999), 220–44; though cf. A. L. Goodhart, 'Mistake as to Identity in the Law of Contract' (1941) 57 *LQR* 228–44 at 235–8.

[50] See Atiyah, above n.26, 399–400, 682–3; and A. W. B. Simpson, 'Innovation in Nineteenth Century Contract Law' (1975) 91 *LQR* 247–78 at 254–5; though cf. Roscoe Pound, 'The Influence of Civil Law in America' (1938) 1 *Louisiana L. Rev.* 1–16 at 7 ('[In English law during the second half of the nineteenth century], Savigny had quite as much influence on the later texts on Contracts as Pothier had had on the earlier decisions').

[51] For such a study, see James Gordley, 'Natural Law Origins of the Common Law of Contract', in *Towards a General Law of Contract*, ed. J. Barton (Berlin: Duncker & Humblot, 1990), 367–465. See also James Gordley, *The Philosophical Origins of Modern Contract Doctrine* (Oxford: Clarendon Press, 1991), 10–29, 161–4; and Ibbetson, above n.49, 215–23.

[52] *Haynes v Haynes* (1861) 1 Drewry & Smale 426, 433. See also *Pole v Leask* (1863) 33 L.J. Ch. 155, 161 ('No one can become the agent of another person except by the will of that other person'); *Dickinson v Dodds* (1876) 2 Ch.D. 463, 472, CA ('It must, to constitute a contract, appear that the two minds were at one, at the same moment of time, that is, there was an offer continuing up to the time of the acceptance'); and *Cundy v Lindsay* (1878) 3 App. Cas. 459, 465–6, HL (*per* Lord Cairns, LC).

[53] Atiyah, above n.26, 406.

of Pollock's *Principles*, or certainly of its first edition, epitomize the nineteenth-century English belief that communion of will is the basis of contractual liability.[54]

But there was something not quite right about the will theory. The fact that parties agree is, according to the theory, enough to bind them. But what if, for one reason or another, one of the parties claims that there was not really a meeting of minds? Proof of the parties' intentions, not assertions that those intentions corresponded, is far more important to the courts. And so although, during the nineteenth century, English judges did not turn their backs on the will theory—while the theory continued, as Atiyah observes, to have 'a profound effect on the very functions of contract law, as perceived by the Courts'[55]—those judges increasingly looked not to what parties had said, but to what had been done (or had not been done), in order to determine whether there existed a valid and enforceable contract.[56] Objective manifestations of intent, rather than verbal formulations of an apparent *consensus ad idem*, gradually became the more significant test of contractual liability.

The nineteenth-century English courts largely accepted the will theory, but, having done so, found that the theory could only serve their purposes convincingly if invested with an objective, evidentiary dimension. Pollock likewise found himself backing away from the subjective logic of the will theory after having initially embraced it. In the third edition of *Principles of Contract*, published in 1881, Savigny's influence is not quite so strong. Rather than emphasizing equation of intentions as the basis of liability, Pollock was by this point arguing that the promisor's obligation derives from his having so expressed himself as to entitle the other party to rely on his acting in a certain way.[57] Almost forty years later, rather puzzlingly, he wrote to Holmes of how this change of emphasis reflected his discovery of 'reasonable expectation as the real fundamental conception in contract', even though what Pollock had actually highlighted was the more general notion of reliance.[58] But this is a minor point. More significant is the fact that Pollock had apparently decided it was inappropriate to determine liability simply by trying to ascertain whether the parties had willed the same thing.

In the introduction to a collection of Pollock's essays, published in 1961, Arthur Goodhart presented Pollock as a jurist who never accepted the will theory. In *Principles of Contract*, Goodhart claimed, we find Pollock 'departing

[54] For further illustrations of nineteenth-century juristic support for the will theory, see Atiyah, above n.26, 684–5.

[55] Ibid. 408.

[56] See ibid. 407–8. For the determination of validity by reference to an omission rather than to an act, see *Byrne & Co. v Leon van Tienhoven & Co.* (1880) L.R. 5 C.P.D. 344, 347, *per* Lindley J. (contending, *pace* Pothier, that an uncommunicated revocation of an offer ought to be regarded as 'no revocation at all' and, therefore, incapable of overriding consent between contracting parties).

[57] See *PCLE(3)* xx–xxi; also *PCLE(4)* v.

[58] Pollock to Holmes, 10 August 1920, in *PHL* ii. 48; and see also Atiyah, above n.26, 408.

from the stock definition of a contract as an agreement based on a meeting of the minds of the contracting parties. . . . The function of the law of contract, [Pollock] held, was to establish a positive sanction for the enforcement of good faith; there was, therefore, no necessity to prove that there had been a meeting of the minds.'[59] The Pollock with whom Goodhart presents us is the one who considered the law of contract to be fundamentally concerned with reasonable expectation. There seems to be a simple explanation for Goodhart's interpretation of Pollock: although he purports to represent Pollock's views as expressed in the first edition of *Principles*, his footnotes suggest that he was according variorum status to the edition that he apparently had at hand—the eleventh edition, published five years after Pollock's death and edited by Percy Winfield.[60]

By presenting Pollock straightforwardly as an opponent of the will theory, Goodhart is able to offer a fairly attractive picture of Pollock—Pollock, that is, as a critic of conventional thinking about contracts. Not for Pollock the route of Samuel Williston, Arthur Corbin, the American Law Institute, and others who had 'substantially accepted'[61] the will theory, Goodhart contends. But this comparison of Pollock's position with an apparent contracts orthodoxy in the United States seems shaky, to say the least. The claim that Corbin had substantially accepted the will theory is certainly contestable.[62] While Pollock's thinking about contract evolved in the late nineteenth century, furthermore, the major works on contracts by Williston, Corbin, and the American Law Institute did not appear until the early 1920s.[63] During the early years of the twentieth century, we will see, Pollock was to cross swords with Williston—but it was consideration, not the will theory, that fuelled their disagreement.

Pollock, in fact, was not a jurist who diverged from early twentieth-century American contracts scholars by rejecting the will theory, but one who, having lost his initial enthusiasm for that theory, adopted an outlook not a million miles away from the most noted American contracts scholar of the late nineteenth century, Christopher Columbus Langdell. In his *Summary of the Law of Contracts*, published one year before the third edition of Pollock's *Principles*, Langdell made his dissatisfaction with the will theory quite plain: '[i]n truth,

59 A. L. Goodhart, 'Introduction', in *JLE* ix–xlviii at x–xi.

60 See ibid. x n.4.

61 Ibid. x.

62 For a presentation of Corbin as an out-and-out opponent of the will theory, see Morton J. Horwitz, *The Transformation of American Law, 1870–1960: The Crisis of Legal Orthodoxy* (New York: Oxford UP, 1992), 35–6, 49–51.

63 See Samuel Williston, *The Law of Contracts*, 4 vols. (New York: Baker, Voorhis, 1920–2); Arthur L. Corbin, *Cases on the Law of Contracts: Selected from Decisions of English and American Courts* (St Paul, Minn.: West, 1921). The American Law Institute was established in 1923, and its earliest work in restating the law of contract was mainly attributable to Williston and Corbin: see, e.g., *Restatement of the Law of Contracts: Preliminary Draft No. 1–68*, prepared by Samuel Williston and Arthur L. Corbin (Philadelphia: American Law Institute Publishers, 1924–32).

mental acts or acts of the will,' he wrote, 'are not the materials out of which promises are made; a physical act on the part of the promisor is indispensable.'[64] Pollock, of course, purported to emphasize the reasonable expectation of the promisee, rather than the behaviour of the promisor, as the fundamental feature of contract. But then, as he recognized, a reasonable expectation must derive from what Langdell termed a physical act. From the fourth edition of *Principles* onwards, Pollock articulated this point particularly vividly: '[i]f A . . . so bears himself towards B that a reasonable man in B's place would naturally understand A to make a promise, . . . no further question can be made about what was passing in A's mind.'[65] For B's reasonable expectation to arise, A must have acted towards him.

Goodhart's presentation of Pollock as an opponent of the will theory and a challenger of orthodoxy makes for good reading but questionable history. If it is accepted that Pollock was not always opposed to the will theory, but that his attitude towards it cooled, an obvious question arises: why did his perspective change? Perhaps the best answer to this question is the simplest: his perspective changed because he recognized, as did so many other nineteenth-century English lawyers, that the will theory had a tendency to fly in the face of common sense—and we know from chapter 4 just how highly Pollock prized common sense.[66] It seems just as likely, however, that Pollock backed away from the will theory because it could not explain what he himself discovered about contract law.

The first edition of *Principles* alone reveals contract law to be a formidable construction, full of nooks and crannies into which something as basic as the will theory cannot always cast much light. *Principles* went through ten editions during Pollock's lifetime. Working through these editions, one finds him doing something akin to what reviewers of law textbooks regularly complain about: introducing the general topic with a few pages of theory, but quickly jettisoning the theory in favour of chapter upon chapter of black letter law. In fact, throughout Pollock's editions of his *Principles*, doctrine is not so much divorced from theory as in tension with it. As his exposition of principles became, from one edition to the next, increasingly nuanced, the contract theory upon which he relied struggled all the more to accommodate and explain what he found. The doctrinal fabric of contract law became ever more complex—a fact which

[64] C. C. Langdell, *A Summary of the Law of Contracts*, 2nd edn. (Boston: Little, Brown & Co., 1880), 244. This work first appeared in 1879 as part of his *Cases on Contracts*.

[65] *PCLE(4)* 4.

[66] On the capacity of the will theory to confound common sense, see W. R. Cornish and G. de N. Clark, *Law and Society in England 1750–1950* (London: Sweet & Maxwell, 1989), 200–6. Nineteenth-century mistake-as-to-agreement cases—*Raffles v Wichelhaus* (1864) 2 H. & C. 906 being the classic example—may also have contributed to Pollock's change of perspective: in such cases, after all, there was rarely any discernible meeting of minds. To make this connection with any confidence would be difficult, however, since Pollock, as Simpson has demonstrated, analysed *Raffles v Wichelhaus* in terms of mistake in order to show that the decision supports the will theory: see A. W. Brian Simpson, *Leading Cases in the Common Law* (Oxford: Clarendon Press, 1995), 159–60; and cf. Ibbetson, above n.49, 228–9 (using, instead of *Raffles v Wichelhaus*, the example of Pollock on *Couturier v Hastie* (1856) 5 HLC 673).

sometimes caused Pollock to despair in his correspondence with Holmes[67]—and, as it did so, theoretical models emphasizing will, reliance, or whatever else, began to seem inordinately simple.

This disjunction between theory and doctrine is apparent even in the first edition of *Principles*, when Pollock was still enthusiastic about the will theory. Having set out his stall in accordance with this theory, he proceeded to elaborate various doctrinal problems which, though Pollock did not use them to demonstrate the theory's limitations, effectively do just that. Much of his discussion is premised on the insight that a meeting of minds does not guarantee a valid contract. We may agree, yet, unbeknownst to us or not, what we agree upon may be unlawful.[68] We may agree, but our agreement may be physically or legally impossible to perform.[69] Pollock seemed especially troubled by those scenarios in which, although we appear to have agreed, the assumption of agreement is founded on mistake.[70] 'Error is the greatest defect that can occur in a contract,' Pothier observed in his *Traité des Obligations*, 'for agreements can only be formed by the consent of the parties, and there can be no consent when the parties are in error respecting the object of their agreement.'[71] Pollock did not accept this view.[72] 'It is quite wrong,' he insisted, 'to say that a consent determined by mistake . . . is *no* consent', for '[i]f it were so the agreement would be absolutely void in all cases.'[73] Not only are many mistakes insufficiently serious to invalidate a contract, but even serious mistakes will often, rather than rendering a contract void, be treated by the courts as the responsibility of the party in error.[74] 'The general rule', indeed, 'is that mistake *as such* has no legal effects at all.'[75] A court might uphold the validity of a contract in the face of mistake by resorting to the notion of presumed intention: 'courts of law as well as courts of equity have assumed a power to put a restricted construction on general words when it appears on the face of the instrument that it cannot have been the real intention of the parties that they should be taken in their apparent general sense.'[76] Furthermore, a court might do the same by looking to the 'conduct or position' of the parties rather than their apparent intentions.[77] Although, in the first edition of *Principles*, Pollock did not develop this last claim into an argument about either reliance or reasonable expectation, the fact that he made it is evidence enough that, at

[67] See, e.g., Pollock to Holmes, 10 August 1920, in *PHL* ii. 48; 11 November 1920, ibid. 57.

[68] See *PCLE* 218–321.

[69] See *PCLE* 322–54.

[70] See *PCLE* 355–443.

[71] Pothier, above n.48, i. 12.

[72] It is worth noting that it is not absolutely clear that Pothier did either! See J. C. Smith and J. A. C. Thomas, 'Pothier and the Three Dots' (1957) 20 *Mod. L. Rev.* 38–43.

[73] *PCLE* 356 n.*a*.

[74] See *PCLE* 358–67; although cf. Gordley, *Philosophical Origins of Modern Contract Doctrine*, above n.51, 198, who shows that Pollock, following Savigny, was at times keen to emphasize the vitiating potential of mistake.

[75] *PCLE* 358.

[76] *PCLE* 414. In equity, he added, it is sufficient that evidence of such intention be found external to, and not necessarily within, the instrument for a court to assume this power. Ibid.

[77] *PCLE* 356.

the time of that edition, he believed that contract doctrine presented problems of liability too complex to be resolved by the will theory.

The key point here is not that Pollock outgrew the will theory in particular, but that all contractual theories seemed ultimately to leave him with a sense of unease. Although he made use of the notion of presumed intention to try to fill in some of the gaps left by the will theory, for example, he soon found that the notion pointed to fresh doctrinal problems as it resolved others. Pollock's wariness about the doctrine of frustration illustrates this point. Frustration makes no appearance in the first edition of *Principles of Contract*—not surprisingly, for the doctrine did not properly evolve until the early twentieth century.[78] Yet when frustration did begin to evolve as a doctrine, the courts tended to conceive of it as being bound up (rather problematically, it has to be said) with the notion of presumed intention: according to this theory—the so-called 'implied condition' theory—of frustration, the parties to a contract will be discharged from their liabilities where it is fair to assume that they would never have agreed to the contract had they envisaged what eventually transpired. '[N]o Court has an absolving power' when dealing with contracts, Lord Loreburn explained in 1916, 'but it can infer from the nature of the contract and the surrounding circumstances that a condition which is not expressed was a foundation on which the parties contracted.'[79] If what has transpired, he continued, is something about which the parties, 'as sensible men', would at the outset have said, 'if that happens, of course, it is all over between us', then the contract ought to be treated as having come to an end.[80] The artificiality of this particular theory is largely attributable to the fact that a condition is implied on the basis of something that the contracting parties did not foresee: it is difficult to understand how those parties could be taken, impliedly or otherwise, to have provided for something which did not occur to them—or, for that matter (as Lord Wright added in the 1940s), why they would have agreed that the contract should come to an end had this thing occurred to them.[81]

Pollock had certainly glimpsed the problem by 1910. Near the end of that year, he remarked in the eighth edition of *Principles* on how so little of the law had changed in the eight years since the previous edition. What little had changed, he added, 'strengthen[s] my belief that "Impossible Agreements" is not really a legal category at all'.[82] The words were not accompanied by any

[78] See Simpson, above n.50, 269–73. 'Before 1863', according to Beatson, 'it was a general rule of the law of contract that a person was absolutely bound to perform any obligation which had to be undertaken, and could not claim to be excused by the mere fact that performance had subsequently become impossible.' J. Beatson, *Anson's Law of Contract*, 28th edn. (Oxford: Oxford UP, 2002), 531.

[79] *F. A. Tamplin Steamship Co. Ltd v Anglo-Mexican Petroleum Products Co. Ltd* [1916] 2 AC 397, 404 (HL).

[80] Ibid.

[81] 'It is not possible, to my mind, to say that, if they had thought of it, they would have said: "Well, if that happens, all is over between us". On the contrary, they would almost certainly on the one side or the other have sought to introduce reservations or qualifications or compensations.' *Denny, Mott & Dickson Ltd v James B. Fraser & Co. Ltd* [1944] AC 265, 275 (HL).

[82] *PCLE(8)* ix.

deed: the chapter on impossible agreements in the eighth edition of *Principles* is basically the chapter that we find in the seventh.[83] For the ninth edition, however, Pollock squared up to the task. 'I finished a new chapter for my old book of *Contract*', he wrote to Holmes in August 1920, 'entitled "Conditions and herein of Frustration".' This new chapter replaced what, in the first eight editions of the book, had been the chapter on 'Impossible Agreements'—a subject which, Pollock continued, 'I now think was never a rational category'.[84] That he had become disenchanted with the notion of impossible agreements certainly did not mean that he was wholly enamoured of what he had put in its place. 'I am revising the old book on Contract, rather drastically in parts', he had written to Holmes in March:

> some of it seems to me but callow stuff now. I have in my mind somewhat large rearrangement, such as a new head of Conditional Contracts with 'frustration of adventure' prominent, but have not made up my mind whether it is worth the pains. After all, is not the implied condition in those cases something of a fiction to screen rules of policy imposed on the parties and becoming, like equity of redemption, a real part of the contract only after that pressure has been applied?[85]

Pollock decided—as his August letter indicates—that the effort was worth the pain, and the drastic revision was undertaken for the ninth edition of *Principles*. The volume appeared in 1921, with a 'new chapter which tries to give an orderly statement of the new doctrine about "frustration"'.[86] But although Pollock wanted—as any good treatise writer would—to make sense of the doctrine, the exercise seemed to hold little appeal for him. The reason he considered the exercise necessary was that the First World War had generated a fairly large body of case law concerning contracts which had become impossible to perform.[87] In *Metropolitan Water Board v Dick, Kerr & Co.*, for example, war-time restrictions had imposed an indefinite delay on the performance of a contract to build a reservoir. Although the contract contained a delay clause, the House of Lords held that this clause was only intended to apply to temporary difficulties (such as labour shortages), and that the contract was frustrated because the interruption not only was beyond the contemplation of the parties but also because it 'vitally and fundamentally change[d] the conditions of the contract'.[88] Pollock dutifully ran through the war-time frustration cases in the ninth edition of *Principles*,[89] though it is clear from the Preface that he considered them a great deal of fuss over nothing. Contracts the conditions

[83] Cf. *PCLE(7)* 398–437 with *PCLE(8)* 418–62.

[84] Pollock to Holmes, 10 August 1920, in *PHL* ii. 48.

[85] Pollock to Holmes, 14 March 1920, in *PHL* ii. 38–9. Cf. also Pollock to Holmes, 11 November 1920, ibid. 57.

[86] Pollock to Holmes, 2 May 1921, ibid. 67.

[87] See *PCLE(9)* viii.

[88] *Metropolitan Water Board v Dick, Kerr & Co.* [1918] AC 119, 126 (*per* Lord Finlay, L.C.).

[89] *PCLE(9)* 331–4.

of which have fundamentally changed plainly should not be treated as enforceable, he asserted, because 'in all contracts the promisee's rights and remedies are founded on and measured by his reasonable expectation, and the purpose of the law is to protect and forward reasonable men's business.'[90] Rules for excluding the possibility of the legitimate enforcement of such contracts 'may have to be formulated for the sake of visible completeness,' he added, 'but search for the neatest way' of establishing this exclusion 'is a matter of merely speculative interest.'[91]

Although the doctrine of frustration seemed to bore Pollock, he appreciated all the same that it needs explaining in a contracts treatise. His attitude towards frustration might be contrasted with that which he adopted towards quasi-contracts. In a wonderfully laconic case note in the first volume of the *Law Quarterly Review*, Pollock observed that a recent decision of the Court of Appeal had been 'noteworthy' because it illustrated 'a tendency which appears to be very marked among modern judges, to extend rights of indemnity, or in general terms to increase the number of obligations *quasi ex contractu* known to the law of England'.[92] Given that the note consists of little more than this one sentence, it is difficult to know whether Pollock approved or disapproved of the tendency. What does seem clear, however, is that he saw no reason to treat quasi-contracts as part of the law of contract. Pollock noted in the first edition of *Principles* that in instances where one person receives some benefit from another, and where the person in receipt would be unjustly enriched were he or she not required to provide some sort of restoration or payment for that benefit, it may be 'just and expedient' for the law to impose upon the receiver 'an obligation analogous to contract'.[93] But this, he believed, is not so much the law of contract as the law of fictitious contracts: 'quasi-contracts . . . are dealt with by the fiction of an implied previous request, which often has to be supplemented . . . by an equally fictitious promise.'[94] For all that he was concerned in *Principles* with contracts both at law and in equity, he saw no need to accord anything more than cursory attention to quasi-contracts. During the second half of the twentieth century, many academic lawyers thought along lines similar to Pollock's. Gradually, the notion of quasi-contracts was jettisoned;[95] and as jurists, along with the courts, became increasingly preoccupied with principles of liability arising out of unjust enrichment (and there came to be born that subject which we now know of as the law of restitution[96]), matters of quasi-contractual—what we would now call restitutionary—

[90] *PCLE(9)* viii. [91] *PCLE(9)* viii. [92] (1885) 1 *LQR* 392. [93] *PCLE* 29.

[94] *PCLE* 29; and cf. William A. Keener, *A Treatise on the Law of Quasi-Contracts* (New York: Baker, Voorhis, & Co., 1893), who, somewhat ironically, declared that in using the term 'quasi-contract' he simply 'followed the lead of Sir Frederick Pollock and Sir William Anson' (v).

[95] The term 'quasi-contract', Birks recently observed, is one of those 'obscure and sometimes fictionalizing formulae from the past'. Peter Birks, 'Preface', in *Breach of Trust*, eds. P. Birks and A. Pretto (Oxford: Hart, 2002), vii–xiv at vii.

[96] In England the birth of the subject was, in effect, announced by Robert Goff and Gareth Jones, *The Law of Restitution* (London: Sweet & Maxwell, 1966). For key texts which show how the subject has

obligation were increasingly identified as belonging to a category of their own, a category founded largely on equitable principles and generally resistant to being subsumed under the heading of 'contract law'.[97]

b. Offer, acceptance, and consideration

We have seen in this study that Pollock never seemed to take to jurisprudence—notwithstanding that he wrote a book on the subject—because his appreciation of the complexity and nuance contained within so much legal doctrine made it difficult for him to subscribe to abstract or highly generalized propositions. This reluctance to embrace generalizations is very much evident in his writings about contract. A contract, he was happy to concede, is a species of promise. 'Every promise enforceable by law is a contract,' he observed in 1897, 'and all contracts are regarded in the modern Common Law as founded on promises express or implied, that is to say, either framed in words or inferred from the promisor's acts or conduct.'[98] But if a contract is to be binding, must the promise that it entails be accepted by the promisee? Generally, Pollock believed, we can safely answer this question in the affirmative. 'When a promise has been accepted as binding by the person to whom it is made, there is an agreement.'[99] Without such acceptance, 'there is no agreement, and therefore the [promisor] cannot be bound to do anything.'[100]

Or rather, in such circumstances, a promisor cannot *usually* be bound to do anything. Although the 'main principle' of contract law is that 'a contract is constituted by the acceptance of a proposal', Pollock remarked in the first edition of *Principles*, 'considerable difficulties arise' when that principle is applied to 'particular instances'.[101] In the first edition, Pollock developed this point in a fairly half-hearted fashion, offering but a handful of instances in which the principle 'must be cautiously applied' because the acceptance in question was conditional or ambiguous.[102] From the third edition of *Principles* onwards, however, he became more forthright in asserting that not all enforceable contracts demand that an offer be accepted. Although, 'in practice', offer

grown, see, e.g., Peter Birks, *An Introduction to the Law of Restitution*, rev. edn. (Oxford: Clarendon Press, 1989; orig. publ. 1985); Peter Jaffey, *The Nature and Scope of Restitution: Vitiated Transfers, Imputed Contracts and Disgorgement* (Oxford: Hart, 2000); and Andrew Burrows, *The Law Of Restitution* (London: Butterworths, 2001). See generally D. J. Ibbetson, 'Unjust Enrichment in English Law', in *Unjust Enrichment and the Law of Contract*, ed. E. J. H. Schrage (Dordrecht: Kluwer, 2001), 33–52; Ibbetson, above n.49, 277–93.

[97] See generally Jaffey, above n.96, 30–75. Jaffey, in fact, is less willing than are many other restitution lawyers to draw lines between matters of restitutionary and contractual obligation; nevertheless, he does a good job of revealing the grain in his effort to rub against it.

[98] [Frederick Pollock], 'Contract', in *Encyclopaedia of the Laws of England, being a New Abridgement by the Most Eminent Legal Authorities*, 12 vols., ed. A. W. Renton (London: Sweet & Maxwell, 1897), iii. 335–51 at 335.

[99] Ibid. [100] *PCLE(4)* 23. [101] *PCLE* 8. [102] *PCLE* 23–4.

and acceptance 'are the normal and most important elements' of a contract, he remarked in the fourth edition, there are 'difficulties' in treating these elements together as 'parts of the general conception of contract' because sometimes an offer might be treated as irrevocable in the absence of acceptance.[103] For Pollock, the common law rule regarding promises in deeds—such promises being binding irrespective of the promisee's acceptance—illustrates the point.[104] It was a point lost on Anson, who, in the second edition of his own contracts treatise, stuck rigidly to the view that, in contract law, offer and acceptance accompany one another like blackboards and chalk. Although 'Pollock in the third edition of his "Principles of Contract" suggests that there are modes of forming agreement otherwise than by question and answer', Anson noted, 'I still think that question and answer, in however elliptical a form, are the inevitable mode of coming to agreement.'[105] The point of highlighting this difference of opinion is not to try to determine which perspective is the soundest, but to emphasize that, for Pollock, the proposition that all contracts must entail offer and acceptance was too much of a generalization.

For Pollock, then, all contracts involve an offer, and most contracts require an acceptance. What status did he accord consideration? In modern English law, consideration—the provision of something with legally recognizable value in exchange for a promise, so as to make the promise legally enforceable—is regarded as essential to the formation of nearly all contracts.[106] But it has not always been treated thus.[107] During his thirty-two years as Chief Justice of the King's Bench, for example, Lord Mansfield—whose vision of the common law, we noted in the previous chapter, was very much an inspiration to Pollock—mounted three lines of assault on the doctrine of consideration. First, Mansfield is often considered to have introduced into English law the argument that the existence of prior moral obligations between contracting parties may suffice to make binding their express (albeit gratuitous) promises to one another.[108] This argument can be seen not so much as a rejection of

[103] *PCLE(4)* 9. Cf. Gordley, *Philosophical Origins of Modern Contract Doctrine*, above n.51, 176–7, who concludes (mistakenly, I think) that Pollock was, in effect, undermining his own position rather than merely detecting exceptions to a general principle. See further Pollock's discussion of acceptance of terms annexed to contracts by way of reference: Frederick Pollock, 'Acceptance of Offer with Conditions Annexed by Reference' (1934) 50 *LQR* 29–32.

[104] See *PCLE(4)* 6–7. For the common law rule, see *Hall v Palmer* (1844) 3 Hare 532. Though a promise made by deed is binding, the promisee cannot be compelled to accept the benefit conferred: *Townson v Tickel* (1819) 3 B. & Ald. 31. See also Ibbetson, above n.49, 245–7.

[105] Sir William R. Anson, *Principles of the English Law of Contract and of Agency in its Relation to Contract*, 2nd edn. (Oxford: Clarendon Press, 1882), 15 n.1.

[106] '[I]t must be admitted that in modern law the presence of consideration is a necessary condition for the enforceability of a promise'. P. S. Atiyah, *Essays on Contract* (Oxford: Clarendon Press, 1986), 182.

[107] For a memorable modern rejection of consideration, see Charles Fried, *Contract as Promise: A Theory of Contractual Obligation* (Cambridge, Mass.: Harvard UP, 1981), 28–39.

[108] See C. H. S. Fifoot, *Lord Mansfield* (Oxford: Clarendon Press, 1936), 242–4; James Oldham, *The Mansfield Manuscripts and the Growth of English Law in the Eighteenth Century*, 2 vols. (Chapel Hill: Univer-

consideration as an appeal for a more relaxed conception of the doctrine—a conception along the lines of the Roman and civilian *causa promissionis*—whereby a pre-existing moral obligation is treated as the reason for the making of, and therefore as consideration for, a promise. Secondly, even if a stricter conception of consideration is an important ingredient for establishing contractual enforceability, Mansfield contended in 1763, that conception should not constitute the sole test by which to create contractual obligations, for consideration is only one of several methods of providing evidence of the promisor's intention to be bound.[109] Thirdly, and perhaps most controversially, Mansfield argued in 1765 that although consideration may be necessary for evidentiary purposes in the case of oral commercial contracts, there is no such need with respect to commercial transactions in writing: generally, '[i]n commercial cases amongst merchants, the want of consideration is *not* an objection'[110] since the custom prevailing among them is sufficient to make written promises binding. In the short term, Mansfield's distinction between oral and written contracts—notwithstanding that there was little if any sound authority to support it[111]—was received with a degree of enthusiasm both in the English courts and in juristic literature.[112] In the longer term, however, the distinction was rejected, as was his more general argument that the existence of a prior moral obligation may be sufficient to guarantee the enforceability of an express, if gratuitous, promise.[113]

While Pollock would normally dismiss unsound legal arguments, he viewed Mansfield's ill-judged effort to diminish the significance of consideration as the noblest of failures.[114] This sentiment is perhaps primarily indicative of his intense respect for Mansfield. But it indicates also that, like Mansfield, he regarded consideration as a doctrine that deserved to have its wings clipped.[115]

sity of North Carolina Press, 1992), i. 224–5, 240–4; and, for relevant case law, *Atkins v Hill* (1775) 1 Cowp. 284; *Trueman v Fenton* (1777) 1 Cowp. 544; and *Hawkes v Saunders* (1782) 1 Cowp. 289.

[109] *Mayor of Yarmouth v Eaton* (1763) 3 Burr. 1402.

[110] *Pillans and Rose v Van Mierop and Hopkins* (1765) 3 Burr. 1663, 1669. It appears that Mansfield was attempting to introduce a Scottish rule into English law: see The Rt. Hon. Lord Denning, *Borrowing From Scotland* (Glasgow: Jackson, Son & Co. (Murray Foundation Lecture no. 26), 1963), 13–14.

[111] See Fifoot, above n.108, 133–4.

[112] For judicial reception, see Fifoot, ibid. 134–5. For juristic reception, see David Liebermann, *The Province of Legislation Determined: Legal Theory in Eighteenth-Century Britain* (Cambridge: Cambridge UP, 1989), 110–11. For both, see J. H. Baker, *An Introduction to English Legal History*, 4th edn. (London: Butterworths, 2002), 352–3.

[113] See *Rann v Hughes* (1778) 4 Brown P. C. 27 (report of pleadings and arguments); 7 Term Rep. 350 n. (report of judges' opinions); and *Eastwood v Kenyon* (1840) 11 A. & E. 438. See further A. W. B. Simpson, *A History of the Common Law of Contract: The Rise of the Action of Assumpsit* (Oxford: Clarendon Press, 1975), 617–19; also Anson, above n.105, 43–4; Simpson, above n.50, 262–3; Ibbetson, above n.49, 205–6; and cf. Lord Wright, 'Ought the Doctrine of Consideration to be Abolished from the Common Law?' (1936) 49 *Harvard L. Rev.* 1225–53 at 1243 ('. . . Lord Mansfield has been vindicated to some extent, though the logical view is not to say that there is moral consideration, but that there is no consideration').

[114] See *ECL* 118–19 ('The adoption of the Law Merchant, under the directing genius of Lord Mansfield . . .').

[115] Although my argument here is that Pollock's attitude towards consideration was probably very much inspired by Mansfield, it should be noted also that Pollock's attitude may owe something to his

'He sympathized with Mansfield's attempt to qualify' the doctrine, Lord Wright noted in his obituary on Pollock; 'the attempt, [Pollock] said, came too late.'[116] Less than a year before the need for this obituary had arisen, Wright had produced an article in which he concluded that there appeared to be 'no practical objections to the abolition of the doctrine' of consideration from the common law.[117] '[T]here is a dead weight of legal conservatism to be overcome', Wright insisted, which means 'that there is little prospect in the near future of the English law being changed in so vital a respect'.[118] But this conservatism cannot hide the truth: the doctrine of consideration 'should be abolished'.[119] Many of Wright's arguments in this article—particularly his emphasis on the fact that various legal systems are able to cope without the doctrine of consideration,[120] and his lament that Mansfield's efforts to resist the doctrine were not received more sympathetically[121]—are ones with which Pollock would have readily concurred. Indeed, he concurred with Wright's conclusion. 'Lord Wright has sent me his attack on the doctrine of consideration appearing in the June Harvard Law Rev.—mighty good', he wrote to Goodhart in 1936. 'I see no defence for the doctrine as it stands. . . . Sooner or later Consideration should go to New Jersey to keep company with replications *de injuria* and the other oddities that survive there. The doctrine might have worked out rationally but for the rule—of obscure origin—that there must be a definite moment when the promise is exchanged for consideration.'[122]

But Pollock avoided trampling on consideration in public. As a treatise writer, his job—certainly as he saw it—was to explain the principles of the law of contract rather than campaign to have some of them abolished. Perhaps he was right and Wright was wrong: after all, was it really appropri-

grounding in continental will theory, which accorded no significance to consideration: see Ibbetson, above n.49, 236–7; and Vernon V. Palmer, *The Paths to Privity: A History of Third Party Beneficiary Contracts at English Law* (San Francisco: Austin & Winfield, 1992), 186–9.

[116] Wright, above n.17, 159. Lord Goddard also attributed this view to Pollock—and agreed with him—in *Terrell v Secretary of State for the Colonies* [1953] 2 QB 482, 498. See further *PCLE* 153; Pollock to Holmes, 16 October 1908, in *PHL* i. 145–6.

[117] Wright, above n.113, 1253.

[118] Ibid. Just how heavily this conservatism weighed is apparent from the Law Revision Committee's *Sixth Interim Report (Statute of Frauds and the Doctrine of Consideration)*, Cmd. 5449 (London: HMSO, 1937). 'Many of us would like to see the doctrine [of consideration] abolished root and branch', the Committee reported, '[b]ut a recommendation to this effect would probably be unwise. It is so deeply entrenched in our law that any measure which proposed to do away with it altogether would almost certainly arouse suspicion and hostility' (ibid. para. 27). The Committee was chaired by Wright.

[119] Wright, above n.113, 1253.

[120] See ibid. 1226, 1236–7, 1246 ('I wonder how things would have gone if the common lawyers had extended their outlook beyond the English cases to a system of law such as the Roman Dutch or had broken loose from their close adherence to tradition and precedent, or had ever considered scientific theories of contract').

[121] See ibid. 1241–6.

[122] Frederick Pollock to A. L. Goodhart, 16 June 1936, in Goodhart papers, MS Eng. c. 2889 f.11. Goodhart was a member of the Law Revision Committee which produced the *Sixth Interim Report* (above n.118).

ate for a senior judge, let alone an eminent expositor of doctrine, to write so negatively about one of the key components of English contract law? But then Pollock approved of what Wright had to say. The significant difference between the two men was that Pollock avoided expressing this approval publicly (though to be fair, considering that he had but six months to live after the appearance of Wright's article, there was little time left for him to make a stand). Rather than strike at the heart of the doctrine of consideration, Pollock only ever found it in himself to prod and poke. Like Wright, he noted that the absence of the doctrine seems not to stop systems of contract from functioning: ancient conceptions of contract, he stressed, had no need for consideration. 'The doctrine of Consideration in its present general form is of comparatively modern origin even if we look to the history of English law alone. . . . The most we can affirm is that the general idea was formed somewhere in the latter part of the fifteenth century.'[123] Consideration, he speculated, had probably grown out of *causa promissionis* and associated Roman and civilian notions (such as *causa meritoria* and *causa reciproca*). Even if it is the case that 'the English Consideration' is 'directly descended from the Roman Causa', nevertheless, the former concept is more expansive than is the latter:

> [t]he Roman theory whether in its classical or in its modern shape falls short of the completeness and common sense of our own; but only one step seems wanting. If the Roman lawyers or the civilians in modern times had ever fairly asked themselves what were the common elements in the various sets of facts which under the name of *causa* made various kinds of contracts actionable, they could scarcely have failed to extract something equivalent to our Consideration.[124]

In due course, Pollock would change his mind about the relationship between *causa* and consideration: since the *causa* necessary to validate the Roman *pact* was not the same as the consideration required in English law, he came to argue, it is better to emphasize the differences rather than the similarities between the two concepts. 'The Romanist spook of *causa*', he wrote

[123] *PCLE* 116, 149. Pollock probably found consideration emerging a little sooner than it actually did in English law: cf. J. H. Baker, 'Origins of the "Doctrine" of Consideration, 1535–1585', in *On the Laws and Customs of England: Essays in Honor of Samuel E. Thorne*, eds. M. S. Arnold, T. A. Green, S. A. Scully, and S. D. White (Chapel Hill: University of North Carolina Press, 1981), 336–58 at 337 ('We have never known quite when or how "consideration" appeared in the *assumpsit* declaration. . . . With reasonable confidence, however, we can reduce our concentration to the half century from 1535 to 1585. By the 1580s the reports are full of discussions about consideration. . . . A mere fifty years earlier there was no trace of "consideration" in *assumpsit* declarations or in the few reported discussions related to such actions'); David J. Ibbetson, 'Consideration and the Theory of Contract in Sixteenth Century Common Law', in *Towards a General Law of Contract*, above n.51, 67–123; and also James Barr Ames, 'Two Theories of Consideration: I. Unilateral Contracts' (1899) 12 *Harvard L. Rev.* 515–31 at 521–4 (repr. in James Barr Ames, *Lectures on Legal History and Miscellaneous Legal Essays* (Cambridge, Mass.: Harvard UP, 1913), 323–40 at 329–32).

[124] *PCLE* 149.

to James Barr Ames in 1888, 'may now be dismissed, I think, as a finally exorcised, played out, and discredited spook. On the whole I believe more and more in the indigenous character of the Common Law.'[125] More intriguing is the question of whether Pollock changed his mind about the significance of consideration itself. In the first edition of *Principles*, he quickly moved from noting the non-essential nature of consideration to treating it as a distinctive achievement of the common law: whatever the many varieties of *causa*,[126] collectively they could not add up to 'our Consideration'. Although we know that, at the end of his life, he was willing privately to agree with Wright that, ideally, consideration ought to be banished from the common law, throughout the ten editions of *Principles* that he produced during his lifetime he not only accorded the doctrine the textbook writer's customary respect but also suggested that it was something of which common lawyers could be proud. Consideration, rather than being an irrational mistake, is, in *Principles of Contract*, one of the common law's great mysteries, a doctrine difficult to pin down either historically or analytically.

In the first two editions of *Principles*, Pollock seemed to be overawed by this mystery, intimidated by the difficulties the doctrine presents. While, in both editions, he was not shy of setting out how others have defined consideration, he neither committed himself to any one of these definitions nor offered a definition of his own. Instead of trying to define the concept, he paid close attention to the history of consideration and to its associated principles (that the law will not inquire into the adequacy of consideration, that mutual promises may be tantamount to consideration, and so on).[127] Consideration itself remained as a black hole. Not until the third edition of *Principles* did he attempt to remedy this defect. Declaring in that edition that 'an author should be his own severest critic', Pollock claimed that '[m]ost of the topics of general importance discussed in the book have been reconsidered with regard not only to the bearing of the latest authorities on them, but to the fitting treatment and disposition of them on principle.'[128] In comparison with various other topics, consideration escaped lightly—indeed, the main difference between the third and the previous editions is that the notion is defined. For Pollock, A provides consideration when he does something, or he abstains from doing something (he pays B a fee, for example, or he raises no objection to B's cattle grazing on his land), or he promises to do or to abstain from doing something,

[125] Frederick Pollock to James Barr Ames, 23 June 1888, in Ames correspondence, box 1, folder 32.

[126] On *causa* in its various forms, see Wright, above n.113, 1235.

[127] See *PCLE* 147–65. The second edition of *Principles* is not significantly different from the first: 'there is always the temptation', Pollock remarked somewhat unpromisingly in the preface to the second edition, to insert new materials crudely—for example, by 'merely adding a new reference in a footnote'—thereby evading 'the duty of considering' how those materials bear upon 'the points they deal with. . . . I have striven to withstand the temptation, but I cannot be sure that I have always withstood it.' *PCLE(2)* ix.

[128] *PCLE(3)* v.

in order to get B to agree to his wishes. 'An act or forbearance of the one party, present or promised, is the price for which the promise of the other is bought.'[129]

Although this is hardly the most memorable of definitions—Pollock would try to improve the wording in subsequent editions of *Principles*—it made a notable impact upon English case law. In *Dunlop v Selfridge*—the House of Lords decision of 1915 in which it was held that 'only a person who is a party to a contract can sue on it'[130]—Lord Dunedin declared himself 'content to adopt' the definition of consideration as worded in the eighth edition ('a work', he added 'to which I have often been under obligation').[131] Four years later, in *Balfour v Balfour*, Lord Atkin likewise adopted Pollock's definition—although, unlike Dunedin, Atkin felt no need to reveal his source.[132] Indeed, since *Dunlop v Selfridge* Pollock's definition—with its emphasis on the idea that consideration may come from the promise to act and not necessarily from the act itself—has often been treated as if it were woven into the fabric of English case law.[133] Certainly we do not find judges disagreeing with the definition—*Principles of Contract* has generally been well received in the English courts[134]—and often we find them conceiving of consideration much as Pollock would have done.[135]

[129] *PCLE(3)* 179.

[130] *Dunlop Pneumatic Tyre Co. Ltd v Selfridge Ltd* [1915] AC 847, 853. The principle is now modified by the Contracts (Rights of Third Parties) Act 1999, s. 1, though there are criteria which must be satisfied before the statute will apply (see s. 1(1)(b), (2), and (3)).

[131] *Dunlop v Selfridge*, above n.130, 855, citing *PCLE(8)* 175 ('An act or forbearance of one party, or the promise thereof, is the price for which the promise of the other is bought, and the promise thus given for value is enforceable').

[132] See *Balfour v Balfour* [1919] 2 KB 571, 578 ('The consideration, as we know, may consist either in some right, interest, profit or benefit accruing to one party, or some forbearance, detriment, loss or responsibility given, suffered or undertaken by the other. That is a well-known definition'). That Atkin is borrowing from Pollock is evident from his comment, earlier in the same paragraph, that 'there are agreements between parties which do not result in contracts within the meaning of that term in our law. The ordinary example is where two parties agree to take a walk together' (ibid.). Cf. *PCLE(7)* 3–4: '[a]n appointment between two friends to go out for a walk . . . is not an agreement in the legal sense: for it is not meant to produce, nor does it produce, any new legal duty or right, or any change in existing ones.' Pollock himself, as we noted above, was relying here on Savigny's discussion of *Vertrag*: see further Simpson, above n.66, 281. On the long-term implications of Atkin's reliance on Pollock, see B. A. Hepple, 'Intention to Create Legal Relations' (1970) 28 *Cambridge L. J.* 122–37 at 127–37.

[133] See B. J. Reiter, 'Courts, Consideration, and Common Sense' (1977) 27 *Univ. Toronto L. J.* 439–512 at 440–1; Atiyah, above n.26, 690; [Stephen A. Smith], 'Case 1: Promises of Gifts. England', in *The Enforceability of Promises in European Contract Law*, ed. J. Gordley (Cambridge: Cambridge UP, 2001), 51–8 at 53; Robert Upex, *Davies on Contract*, 8th edn. (London: Sweet & Maxwell, 1999), 29–30.

[134] See, e.g., *Hedley Byrne & Co. Ltd v Heller & Partners Ltd* [1964] AC 465, 528; *Widnes Foundry (1925) Ltd v Cellulose Acetate Silk Co. Ltd* [1931] 2 KB 393, 414; *Rose & Frank Co. v J. R. Crompton and Bros. Ltd* [1923] 2 KB 261, 277. (Lindley J. refers in *Byrne v van Tienhoven.*, above n.56, to Pollock's 'excellent work on Principles of Contract' (ibid. 347)—perhaps the only conclusion he could have reached, given that Pollock had dedicated the book to him.) Not that the arguments that Pollock advanced in *Principles* have always been accepted in court: cf. *Phillips v Brooks Ltd* [1919] 2 KB 243, 245 (*arguendo*); *A. N. Satterthwaite & Co. Ltd v New Zealand Shipping Co. Ltd (The 'Eurymedon')* [1971] 2 Lloyd's Rep. 399, 406.

[135] Lord Denning, for example, tended to conceive of consideration in Pollockian terms: see *Williams v Williams* [1957] 1 WLR 148, 151; *Ward v Byham* [1956] 1 WLR 496, 498. More recently, see *Williams v Roffey Bros. & Nicholls (Contractors) Ltd* [1991] QB 1.

But this is not to claim that his definition has been welcomed in all quarters. Many have resisted it. Those who have resisted it, however, have tended to be jurists rather than judges.

c. *Mutual promises*

What explains this resistance? To answer this question, we must first try to unravel Pollock's definition of consideration. The definition has at least three noteworthy features. First, it does not require that something be transferred between promisee and promisor: consideration consists of the promisee's doing or not doing something, or of promising the same. Secondly, although there need not be any transfer, there must be an exchange of values. A's performance or promise must be undertaken in exchange for—it is the price that A pays to buy—B's promise. Thirdly, A's action or inaction, or promise of the same, need not be valuable to anyone other than B. '[T]he leading and characteristic point of the modern learning of Consideration' is that its value to B is 'the value he has himself chosen to put upon it.'[136] Consideration which is, objectively speaking, nominal or negligible is still consideration.

Pollock's understanding of consideration certainly appealed to Holmes. The law of contract was a matter on which Pollock and Holmes often failed to see eye to eye. 'Holmes's theory that there is no such thing as a duty to perform a contract,' but only to perform or to pay damages at the promisor's option, has generally been regarded by English contract lawyers 'as a brilliant but wholly unsound paradox'.[137] Pollock objected to this theory more than have most. If the duty to perform a contract 'is, as you maintain, only alternative', he asked Holmes in 1897, why does the history of assumpsit suggest otherwise?[138] Forty years later, close friendship was not going to stop Pollock from being yet more brutal: '[i]f the promise in a contract were held to be in the alternative—perform *or* pay damages—then (1) there could be no decrees for

[136] *PCLE* 150–1.

[137] Atiyah, above n.106, 59. For Holmes's theory, see O. W. Holmes, Jr., *The Common Law* (Boston: Little, Brown & Co., 1881), 301 ('The only universal consequence of a legally binding promise is, that the law makes the promisor pay damages if the promised event does not come to pass. In every case it leaves him free from interference until the time for fulfilment has gone by, and therefore free to break his contract if he chooses'); also Holmes, 'The Path of the Law' (1897) 10 *Harvard L. Rev.* 457–78 at 462 ('The duty to keep a contract at common law means a prediction that you must pay damages if you do not keep it,—and nothing else'). A modern variant on this theory is the doctrine of 'efficient breach'. According to this doctrine, it is permissible for A to renege on a contract to supply goods to B and to sell those goods to C at a higher price so long as A compensates B fully with damages for injuries caused by the breach or for loss of expectation. A may wish to breach and compensate if to do so will leave him or her better off and B no worse off. The doctrine, although it has met with a good deal of academic criticism, has not been shunned entirely by the courts: see Stephen Waddams, *Dimensions of Private Law: Categories and Concepts in Anglo-American Legal Reasoning* (Cambridge: Cambridge UP, 2003), 143–5.

[138] Pollock to Holmes, 17 September 1897, in *PHL* i. 79–80.

specific performance: (2) there would be no reason for allowing any implied exception of frustration or the like: (3) (and chiefly) it would not answer reasonable expectations of promisees. . . . No doubt it might be the law in some other planet.'[139] Throughout their many years of correspondence, neither Pollock nor Holmes seemed to give any ground on this matter.[140] On the subject of consideration, however, they were at one from the start. Pollock sent Holmes a copy of the first edition of *Principles* and Holmes was apparently very much impressed by what he read.[141] 'I am . . . struck anew with the value of your book', he wrote to Pollock apropos of the second edition, and 'I referred to your account of Consideration in one of my articles as the best which I had seen.'[142] The conception of consideration advanced by Holmes in *The Common Law*, although somewhat different in terms of terminology from the definition formulated by Pollock, similarly treats consideration as the way in which the promisee buys the promise of the promisor:

> it is the essence of a consideration, that, by the terms of the agreement, it is given and accepted as the motive or inducement of the promise. Conversely, the promise must be made and accepted as the conventional motive or inducement for furnishing the consideration. The root of the whole matter is the relation of reciprocal conventional inducement, each for the other, between consideration and promise.[143]

Just as Holmes echoed Pollock on the subject of consideration, Pollock himself echoed Langdell. In his *A Summary of the Law of Contracts*, Langdell defined consideration straightforwardly as 'the thing done by the promisee in exchange for the promise'.[144] Like Pollock, furthermore, Langdell saw no reason to make a fuss about any disparity in the exchange of values between promisee and promisor: 'the smallest consideration would in most cases support the largest promise . . . because the law shuts its eyes to the inequality between them'; and where the 'inequality' is so serious 'that the law

[139] Pollock to Holmes, 13 June 1927, in *PHL* ii. 201.

[140] See, e.g., Holmes to Pollock, 11 December 1928, in *PHL* ii. 233–4; and Pollock to Holmes, 24 December 1928, ibid. 234–5. 'In all the long years of their correspondence,' Atiyah remarks, 'neither of them budged an inch' (above n.106, 59 n.2).

[141] See James R. Gordley, review of G. Gilmore, *The Death of Contract* (1975) 89 *Harvard L. Rev.* 452–67 at 464; also Gordley, *Philosophical Origins of Modern Contract Doctrine*, above n.51, 173.

[142] Holmes to Pollock, 17 June 1880, in *PHL* i. 15.

[143] Holmes, *The Common Law*, above n.137, 293–4. Alschuler suggests that Holmes may be guilty of 'borrowing his concept of consideration from Pollock without attribution'. Albert W. Alschuler, *Law Without Values: The Life, Work, and Legacy of Justice Holmes* (Chicago: University of Chicago Press, 2000), 123. The suggestion seems harsh. Although Holmes's conception of consideration has affinities with Pollock's, it is articulated very much in Holmes's own language and does not contain all of the elements that Pollock's notion of consideration embraces; furthermore, when Holmes is clearly indebted to Pollock—as is the case when he analyses the nature of promising—he accords appropriate credit: see *The Common Law*, ibid. 297–8.

[144] Langdell, above n.64, 58. Pollock claimed that Langdell's definition 'may be justified out of St German'. See Frederick Pollock, 'Holdsworth's History of English Law' [1925] *Jnl. of the Society of the Public Teachers of Law* 30–3 at 31.

cannot shut its eyes', it will prove 'fatal to the validity of the promise'.[145] Pollock's position was much the same: it is irrelevant whether the promisor, in accepting the consideration, appears to benefit; '[h]is acceptance shows that he has set some value on it',[146] and that is all that matters. For Pollock, Hobbes crystallized the issue: '[t]he value of all things contracted for is measured by the appetite of the contractors, and therefore the just value is that which they be contented to give.'[147]

Others, however, did not see value of consideration quite so straightforwardly. In due course, furthermore, neither would Pollock. The basic problem for various jurists, Pollock included, concerned whether consideration must be a fresh detriment, as it were, or whether it can come from a pre-existing duty.[148] If the value of whatever the promisor bargains for is irrelevant, in other words, might it be sufficient consideration for the promisee to do (or promise to do) what he is already bound to do? '[S]ince the promisee has given nothing which he was not already bound to give,' Samuel Williston answered in 1894, the answer must be no: 'neither performance nor promise of performance of what one is already bound to perform is a valid consideration.'[149] Pollock agreed: 'neither the promise to do a thing nor the actual doing of it will be a good consideration if it is a thing which the party is already bound to do . . . by a subsisting contract with the other party.'[150]

But what if the promisee is already bound to do this thing not for the promisor, but for a third party? In this instance, Pollock claimed in the first edition of *Principles*, 'there seems to be no solid reason why the promise should not be good in itself, and therefore a consideration. It creates a new and distinct right, which must always be of some value in law, and may be of appreciable value in fact.'[151] His words echoed those used by Wilde B. in *Scotson v Pegg* (they were also cited approvingly by James J. in *Merrick v Giddings*, a decision of the Supreme Court of the District of Columbia).[152] Pollock, however, considered the reasoning in *Scotson v Pegg* to be muddled from beginning to end.[153] By the time of the fourth edition of *Principles*, more importantly, he was

[145] Langdell, above n.64, 70–1. See also E[dward] Q. K[easbey], 'The Origin and Nature of Consideration in the Law of Contract' (1883) 6 *New Jersey L. J.* 296–301, 324–35 at 325–8.

[146] F[rederick] Po[llock], 'Contract', in *Encyclopaedia Britannica*, 11th edn. (1910), vii. 35–40 at 37.

[147] Hobbes, *Leviathan*, I. xv. 102, cited in *PCLE* 154. More generally, on the relevance of Hobbesian thought to the common law model of contract, see Atiyah, above n.26, 41–4; and Ibbetson, above n.49, 215–17.

[148] For a detailed account of the problem, see N. E. Simmonds, 'Bluntness and Bricolage', in *Jurisprudence: Cambridge Essays*, eds. H. Gross and R. Harrison (Oxford: Clarendon Press, 1992), 1–28 at 12–18.

[149] Samuel Williston, 'Successive Promises of the Same Performance' (1894) 8 *Harvard L. Rev.* 27–38 at 33, 38.

[150] *PCLE* 157.

[151] *PCLE* 158.

[152] See *Scotson v Pegg* (1861) 6 H. & N. 295, 300 (*per* Wilde B). ('[I]f a person chooses to promise to pay a sum of money in order to induce another to perform that which he has already contracted with a person to do, I confess I cannot see why such a promise should not be binding'); and *Merrick v Giddings*, 1 Mackey (D.C.) 394, 409–11 (1882).

[153] See F[rederick] P[ollock], 'Preface to Vol. CXXIII' (1911) 123 *Revised Reports* v–viii at v–vi. *Shadwell v Shadwell* (1860) 9 C.B. (N.S.) 159, which also dealt with the question of whether considera-

questioning the soundness of his own original claim.[154] As the years progressed, Pollock became more forthright in declaring that a promisee's performance of, or promise to perform, something he or she is already obliged to do for a third party cannot, in fact, be good consideration moving to the promisor. 'Performance of what one is already bound to perform by a contract with A [the third party]', he argued in 1897, 'cannot on principle, for want of any new detriment, be any consideration for a new promise to Z [the promisor], a stranger to the contract.'[155] In the sixth edition of *Principles*, published three years earlier, his language had (much as in the fourth edition) been more guarded: the most he was prepared to say was that it is difficult to follow the reasoning of those who find consideration for Z in the promisee's performance of, or promise to perform, a pre-existing duty to A.[156] In the seventh edition, however, we find him somewhat bolder:

> It seems . . . that if a promise is given in exchange merely for the performance of the promisee's duty under an existing contract with a third person, it is not binding. Authority, however, is the other way so far as it goes. . . . Not that I am at all desirous of upholding the authority of the cases in question. I venture to submit, on the contrary, that they were wrongly decided, or at any rate not on right grounds.[157]

The long and short of all of this is that Pollock's opinion changed. What he saw as good consideration in the first edition of *Principles* he no longer believed to be such by the time of the fourth edition. Williston welcomed Pollock's volte-face.[158] James Barr Ames, by contrast, believed that Pollock had moved from being right to being wrong.[159] The general question of whether a promise becomes enforceable because of the performance of, or the promise to perform, a pre-existing duty—be it a duty to the promisor or to a third party—is not technically, Ames maintained, a problem about consideration.[160] But even if the problem is conceived thus, he added, the answer is still that such a performance or promise generates good consideration, since 'consideration is any act or forbearance by one person given in exchange for the promise of another'.[161] Ames's definition of consideration—differing, as it does, only slightly from Pollock's—is sufficiently wide to allow a promise to be

tion can be derived from promises to third parties, Pollock considered to be just as unsatisfactory: see F[rederick] P[ollock], 'Preface to Vol. CXXVII' (1911) 127 *Revised Reports* v–vii at vi.

[154] See *PCLE(4)* 178–9. [155] Pollock, above n.98, iii. 341. [156] See *PCLE(6)* 174–7.

[157] *PCLE(7)* 186–9. The passage can also be found in Frederick Pollock, 'Afterthoughts on Consideration' (1901) 17 *LQR* 415–22 at 419–22.

[158] Williston, above n.149, 34–5.

[159] James Barr Ames, 'Two Theories of Consideration: II. Bilateral Contracts' (1899) 13 *Harvard L. Rev.* 29–42 at 30 n.4 (repr. in Ames, *Lectures on Legal History*, above n.123, 340–53 at 341). For an umpireal assessment of the disagreement between Williston and Ames, see Joseph H. Beale, Jr., 'Notes on Consideration' (1903) 17 *Harvard L. Rev.* 71–82.

[160] Ames, above n.123, 521 (repr. 329). [161] Ibid. 519 (repr. 327).

consideration for another promise: we have a binding contract, on this definition, if I promise you X and, in return, you promise me Y. It matters not that neither of us has performed anything: consideration arises when the mutual promises are made, not when they are executed. Ames had no problem at all with this state of affairs: '[s]ince a promise is an act, one who defines consideration as any act or forbearance given in exchange for a promise, will necessarily find a consideration in every case of mutual promises. This, it is submitted, is the correct view upon principle.'[162]

Not everybody was convinced that it was the correct view upon logic. A promise is only of value if binding. But how do mutual promises become binding? To say that a promise is binding because it was given in consideration of another promise might be considered to create a vicious circle, from which the only escape is to suppose that the reciprocal promises breathe life into one another at the same instant. Anson had noted this apparent circularity problem in the first edition of his *Principles of the English Law of Contract.*[163] The first edition of Pollock's *Principles*, by contrast, offers a simple statement of principle: '[r]eciprocal promises may be and in practice constantly are the consideration for one another, and so constitute a binding contract.'[164] In the United States, various professors of contract law were of the view that Anson's point deserved serious attention. In 1914, Williston attempted to show the logical absurdity of treating mutual promises as consideration for one another, and in so doing relied on (among other things) the arguments of Henry Ballantine, a law professor at the University of Wisconsin.[165] Nobody, Ballantine had observed, has successfully shown 'how it is that reciprocal promises can support each other, like two men mutually holding each other above the ground. . . . The solution of this question tests to the uttermost one's theory of consideration.'[166] But Ballantine was not claiming that the question is insoluble. 'I do not find that reciprocity which furnishes the consideration or source of obligation in the actual performance', he remarked,

> but in the *promised* performances, the reciprocity of undertakings in the terms of the bargain. . . . The reason the law regards the agreement as binding is that it is a non-gratuitous transaction involving some degree of reciprocity or mutuality from the standpoint of the parties, not because there is an exchange of present values.[167]

[162] Ames, above n.159, 29 (repr. 340).

[163] See Sir William Reynell Anson, *Principles of the English Law of Contract* (Oxford: Clarendon Press, 1879), 80.

[164] *PCLE* 156. This statement survives up until, and including, the sixth edition.

[165] Samuel Williston, 'Consideration in Bilateral Contracts' (1914) 27 *Harvard L. Rev.* 503–29.

[166] Henry Winthrop Ballantine, 'Is the Doctrine of Consideration Senseless and Illogical?' (1913) 11 *Michigan L. Rev.* 423–34 at 427.

[167] Henry Winthrop Ballantine, 'Mutuality and Consideration' (1914) 28 *Harvard L. Rev.* 121–34 at 126–7.

Williston had cited Ballantine as his ally, in other words, when they were really in disagreement. In fact, at one or another level, everybody in this debate over mutual promises seemed to be in disagreement. Of the views of all the relevant protagonists, those of Pollock and Langdell were perhaps the closest. Even they, however, were not playing from quite the same script. Langdell argued tenaciously that, as a matter of logic, mutual promises are consideration for each other: neither he nor Pollock, he believed, had defended mutual promises in a circular or question-begging fashion; 'if we have,' he added, 'the only consequence is that we have not proved the proposition which we were supporting,—not that the proposition itself is untrue.'[168] Pollock clearly regarded Langdell's 'masterly' defence of the mutual-promises-as-consideration thesis to be preferable to any of the competing arguments advanced by Williston and Ames.[169] But whereas Langdell sought to defend mutual promises on the basis of logic, Pollock defended them on grounds of practicality. 'Have you ever found any *logical* reason', he wrote to Holmes in 1908, 'why mutual promises are sufficient consideration for one another (like the two lean horses of a Calcutta hack who can only just stand together)? I have not.'[170] The explanation for why the exchange of promises alone makes them enforceable, he observed six years later, 'is one of the secret paradoxes of the Common Law.'[171]

The claim that the enforceability of mutual promises cannot be defended on grounds of logic still surfaces now and again in modern contracts jurisprudence.[172] It is not clear, however, that the claim can be sustained. In the case of mutual promises, it is not necessary for the bindingness of either promise to precede the bindingness of the other if that other is itself to be binding. Although the bindingness of each is the condition for the bindingness of the other, that is, it is not a precondition. The two promises become binding, and thus valuable, simultaneously. Each promise, to be enforceable, requires only the bindingness of the other promise; and so, if the two promises become

[168] C. C. Langdell, 'Mutual Promises as a Consideration for Each Other' (1901) 14 *Harvard L. Rev.* 496–508 at 498. For the argument that the Langdellian position is not a question-begging one, see Clarence D. Ashley, 'What is a Promise in Law?' (1903) 16 *Harvard L. Rev.* 319–28 at 320–1.

[169] *PCLE(7)* 189 n *z*. See further Richard Bronaugh, 'A Secret Paradox of the Common Law' (1983) 2 *Law and Philosophy* 193–232 at 204. Bronaugh's article, though its emphases and conclusions generally differ from those to be found here, sets out carefully the positions of the various protagonists in this debate.

[170] Pollock to Holmes, 16 October 1908, in *PHL* i. 146. Cf. Holmes to Pollock, 12 March 1911, ibid. 177.

[171] [Frederick Pollock], review of J. G. Pease and A. M. Latter, *The Student's Summary of the Law of Contract*, 2nd edn. (1914) 30 *LQR* 128–9 at 129. See also *PCLE(8)* 191.

[172] See, e.g., Richard A. Epstein, 'Contracts Small and Contract Large: Contract Law through the Lens of Laissez-Faire', in *The Fall and Rise of Freedom of Contract*, ed. F. H. Buckley (Durham, NC: Duke UP, 1999), 25–61 at 44 ('The logical circularity lies in the fact that one has to assume that A's promise is enforceable (for it to be a detriment) in order for B's promise to be enforceable. But A's promise is not enforceable unless by parity of reasoning B's promise is enforceable as well. So the enforcement of each promise is said to presume the validity of the other; hence the validity of neither is established').

binding simultaneously, every condition for the bindingness of each will have been met. The circularity problem identified by Williston and others only emerges if one mistakes conditions for preconditions. Not that any argument about the logic of mutual promises doctrine has much import here. Paradoxical or not, illogical or not, the doctrine of mutual promises was one with which Pollock was happy to live. 'What logical justification is there', he asked in 1912, 'for holding mutual promises good consideration for each other? None, it is submitted.'[173] Both Ballantine and Williston—who were at least united in believing that Langdell's defence of the doctrine of mutual promises was wrongheaded—were quick to cite this statement as evidence that Langdell's closest ally had in fact undergone a change of heart, much as he had changed his mind about whether performance of a pre-existing duty for a third party could be good consideration.[174] Yet both were ripping Pollock's words out of context. Although there may be no logical justification for holding mutual promises to be good consideration for one another, he continued, 'the contrary doctrine would only have led to cumbrous fictions, and our seventeenth-century ancestors rightly took the illogical course and said very little about it.'[175] The doctrine of mutual promises was the least infelicitous fiction, the kind of scaffolding (as Pollock was apparently wont to put it[176]) that the common law would assemble from time to time in order to make sense out of nonsense. The differences of opinion among Langdell, Williston, Ames, and Ballantine—the debate over whether or not logic supported the doctrine of mutual promises—seemed, for Pollock, unnecessarily earnest. 'Learned Americans', he observed in 1921,

> are still engaged from time to time in valiant efforts to reduce the common-law rules of contract, and the doctrine of consideration in particular, to strict logical consistency. That quest is, in my humble judgment, misconceived. Legal rules exist not for their own sake, but to further justice and convenience in the business of human life; dialectic is the servant of their purpose, not their master. Reasonableness, no doubt, is the ideal of the Common Law; and the words "reason" and "logic" go back to Latin and Greek words of like or nearly like original import; nevertheless the field of reason, as we understand it in English, includes many things outside strict logical deduction. One could say more of this, but it would be superfluous for the greater part of English readers.[177]

[173] F[rederick] P[ollock], review of C. D. Ashley, *The Law of Contracts* (1912) 28 *LQR* 100–1 at 101.

[174] See Ballantine, above n.166, 426; Williston, above n.165, 508.

[175] Pollock, above n.173, 101. On the efforts of the seventeenth-century English courts to make the doctrine of mutual promises workable, see S. J. Stoljar, *A History of Contract at Common Law* (Canberra: Australian National UP, 1975), 147–63.

[176] '[H]e had a sympathy with fictions. Some even of the more bizarre appealed to him, partly perhaps because of his historical or antiquarian sense, partly perhaps because of some humorous vein. He saw that they were useful to help the judges in their task of extending rules from case to case, by a sort of analogy, an "as if". They were to him, as he said, a kind of scaffolding.' Wright, above n.17, 159.

[177] *PCLE(9)* x-xi. See also F[rederick] P[ollock], review of T. Baty, *Vicarious Liability* (1916) 32 *LQR* 226–7 at 227.

These observations were somewhat off the pace. By 1921, Langdell and Ames had been dead for over a decade and mutual promises were no longer a hot topic among American contract law professors. Whereas Pollock depicted these professors as preoccupied with developing competing brands of formalism—with a debate which ran its course within the first fifteen years of the twentieth century—American contracts scholarship (indeed, American legal scholarship generally) was moving into an era during which all brands of formalism were treated with a marked degree of suspicion.[178] If formalist approaches to contract were coming into fashion anywhere, it was, ironically, in England.[179] 'In England with its comparatively stabilized civilization,' Arthur Goodhart wrote in 1929, 'the desire for logic and consistency is paramount', whereas in the United States 'it has been found necessary for the Courts to be more venturesome in adapting the materials with which they must work.'[180] The true extent to which England and the United States were diverging is difficult to determine.[181] But for our purpose this matters little. Pollock may have assumed that the debate over mutual promises enjoyed greater longevity than was the case, just as, by the early 1920s, he seemed to be somewhat out of touch with the drift of Anglo-American contracts theorizing; nevertheless, his perspective on mutual promises was not only clear but also consistent with his general approach to the doctrine of consideration. With mutual promises specifically as with consideration generally, he felt, it is very easy to exaggerate the significance of the difficulties.[182] Legal doctrine, he insisted, may operate reasonably and justly even while defying logic; and if doctrine does operate so, assertions about its illogicality will make for a rather pointless line of critique.

d. Good faith

Pollock, then, found little reason to get worked up about the doctrine of consideration and its various quirks. Whereas twentieth-century American contracts scholars seemed to think that the world might stop turning unless they formulated a theory of consideration which could account for the enforcement of mutual promises, Pollock was happy to attribute the enforce-

[178] See, e.g., Arthur L. Corbin, 'Contracts for the Benefit of Third Persons' (1930) 46 *LQR* 12–45; Corbin, 'Recent Developments in the Law of Contracts' (1937) 50 *Harvard L. Rev.* 449–75; Karl N. Llewellyn, 'What Price Contract?—An Essay in Perspective' (1931) 40 *Yale L. J.* 704–51; and cf. William M. Wiecek, *The Lost World of Classical Legal Thought: Law and Ideology in America, 1886–1937* (Oxford: Oxford UP, 1998), 183–4, who seems to push a little too hard when he interprets Pollock's observations as indicating that he 'had espied the future'—viz., the growth of American legal realism.

[179] See Atiyah, above n 26, 662.

[180] Arthur L. Goodhart, 'The New York Court of Appeals and the House of Lords' (1929), in his *Essays in Jurisprudence and the Common Law* (Cambridge: Cambridge UP, 1931), 268–81 at 280–1.

[181] In response to Goodhart's observation the American legal realist, Thurman Arnold, could not resist a wisecrack remark: 'England must have been an interesting place to live during the industrial revolution when the future was not so cut and dried as it is in the year 1931.' Thurman W. Arnold, review of A. L. Goodhart, *Essays in Jurisprudence and the Common Law* (1931) 41 *Yale L. J.* 318–20 at 319.

[182] See also Atiyah, above n.26, 688.

ability of such promises to the perverse genius of his lady the common law, and to leave the matter there. But what explains this rather relaxed approach to issues of consideration? The somewhat crude answer to this question seems to be that Pollock believed the law of contract to be founded on something bigger than consideration.

According to McKendrick, Pollock never 'sought to articulate a principle of good faith and fair dealing'.[183] The index to the first edition of *Principles* makes no reference to good faith—a surprising omission, McKendrick adds, 'given Pollock's declared aim of incorporating the rules of equity into his book (where one might have expected to discover some role for good faith) and his willingness to draw on the experience of civilian jurisdictions.'[184] A basic difficulty with all of Pollock's treatises is that one usually has to look very closely indeed to discover his own thoughts on an issue. Sometimes, one will not discover those thoughts no matter how closely one looks. The primary purpose of these treatises, after all, is not to offer speculation or ideas but to try to provide a coherent account of extant legal principles. Their indices generally illustrate that objective: while one is directed to legal categories—such as consideration, misrepresentation, and mistake (to offer examples from the first edition of *Principles*[185])—rarely if ever is one directed to theories or arguments. That 'good faith' is absent from the index to the first edition of *Principles* is perhaps no more surprising than the absence of 'freedom of contract', 'will theory', or 'bargaining power'. To put the matter bluntly, the indices to the various editions of *Principles* are only helpful if one is searching for cases, categories, rules, and statements of principle.

If one starts at the front rather than at the back of any of these editions, one is unlikely to conclude that Pollock never articulated a principle of good faith. The principle on which he tends to focus is perhaps not best described as one of 'good faith and fair dealing'—while he does connect good faith with contractual bargaining, it would be misleading to suggest that his primary concern was to articulate a theory of good faith in contractual negotiations. He did clearly contend, nevertheless, that good faith is signally relevant to the performance of contracts.

We have already observed how, in the Preface to the ninth edition of *Principles*, Pollock claimed that the purpose of the law of contract is to support the reasonable expectations of reasonable men as they go about their business.[186] Some thirty-six years earlier, in the Preface to the fourth edition, he had explicitly formulated this claim in terms of good faith:

[183] Ewan McKendrick, 'Good Faith: A Matter of Principle?', in *Good Faith in Contract and Property*, ed. A. D. M. Forte (Oxford: Hart, 1999), 39–62 at 47.

[184] Ibid. 47 n.43.

[185] When the indexing of any of Pollock's works was undertaken by others, Pollock would customarily acknowledge as much. That the Preface to the first edition of *Principles* contains no such acknowledgement suggests that he produced its index.

[186] See *PCLE(9)* viii.

The law of Contract may be described as the endeavour of the State . . . to establish a positive sanction for the expectation of good faith which has grown in the mutual dealings of men of average right-mindedness. Accordingly the most popular description of a contract that can be given is also the most exact one, namely that it is a promise or set of promises which the law will enforce. . . . He who has given the promise is bound to him who accepts it, not merely because he had or expressed a certain intention, but because he so expressed himself as to entitle the other party to rely on his acting in a certain way.[187]

This passage, with its emphasis on what in due course came to be known as the 'reliance interest' in contractual matters, has, notwithstanding the obviously nineteenth-century English language, a twentieth-century American resonance to it. Most of the law of contract might be considered to stem from the 'fundamental premise that only those contracts that have been relied on will be enforced', Fuller and Perdue contended in their classic American law review article of 1936, and 'a rationalization of contract' in accordance with this premise might well 'have advantages over the more customary modes of thought which tend to relegate the reliance interest to the field of not-quite contract law'.[188] In arguing that the purpose of the law of contract is to establish a positive sanction for the enforcement of good faith, Pollock was certainly not trying to do anything as ground-breaking as were Fuller and Perdue. Nevertheless, it is important to appreciate that he was doing more than just grumbling about the will theory. As was noted earlier, Pollock never found it in himself to go so far as to reject the will theory—a point captured in the passage above, which makes it clear that he considered a meeting of minds to be part, but only part, of the explanation for why a contract is enforceable. It is obvious also, however, that Pollock considered the notion of good faith to support an argument somewhat more ambitious than the claim that there is a limit to the utility of the will theory. For he maintained that the reason for looking not only to agreements between, but also to the reasonable expectations of, contracting parties is to ensure, besides enforceability, that whatever protections those parties are afforded are just.

Enforcement of good faith in matters of bargain and promise is among the most important functions of legal justice. It might not be too much to say that, next after keeping the peace and securing property against violence and fraud so that business may be possible, it is the most important.[189]

[187] *PCLE(4)* 9.

[188] See Lon L. Fuller and William Perdue, Jr., 'The Reliance Interest in Contract Damages' (1936–7) 46 *Yale L. J.* 52–96, 373–420 at 370–1.

[189] Pollock, above n.146, 35.

So it is that good faith—in matters of bargain as well as of promise—comes across loud and clear as a fundamental principle in Pollock's contracts jurisprudence. But what should we make of his enthusiasm for this principle? The first, perhaps elementary, answer is that this enthusiasm may be the key to understanding his attitude towards the doctrine of consideration. Where a contract exists between A and B, and A acts in breach of good faith thereby confounding the reasonable expectations of B, the law, Pollock appeared to believe, ought to enforce A's promise to B irrespective of whether B provided consideration for it. The very first case note of Pollock's to appear in the *Law Quarterly Review* concerned *Foakes v Beer*, in which the House of Lords held that payment by a debtor of less than is owed to the creditor cannot discharge the original debt even if the creditor promised that the payment would have this effect. The creditor in *Foakes v Beer* may hardly have demonstrated good faith in reneging on her promise not to sue the debtor, but this was of no real consequence because the promise was not provided in exchange for consideration. 'If the question be . . . whether consideration is, or is not, given in a case of this kind,' the Earl of Selborne maintained, 'I cannot say that I think consideration is given.'[190] In his case note in the *LQR*, Pollock seemed to welcome the decision: '[i]t absolutely determines a principle of law which has for more than two centuries and a half been the subject of doubt and criticism, namely that an agreement not under seal made by a creditor to accept a smaller sum in lieu of an ascertained debt is *nudum pactum* and therefore void.'[191] In the fourth edition of *Principles*, published in the same year, however, his assessment of the case was noticeably less enthusiastic: *Foakes v Beer*, he declared, is one of those cases in which '[t]he doctrine of Consideration has been extended with not very happy results beyond its proper scope'; indeed, it is 'the strictly logical result of carrying out a general principle beyond the bounds within which it is reasonably applicable.'[192] The latter of the two assessments—that which is to be found in *Principles* rather than in the *LQR*—was probably the one to which Pollock was committed: certainly he continued to repeat it in the six further editions of *Principles* that appeared during his lifetime. Of course, even if it was the case that he disapproved of *Foakes v Beer*, it is also the case that this disapproval was not expressly formulated as an argument about good faith. Yet it would be odd to regard Pollock's disapproval as having nothing to do with his belief that the enforcement of good faith in matters of bargain and promise is integral to legal justice. Given his understanding of good faith, and given what he had to say about *Foakes v Beer*, it seems likely that he would have preferred to see the House of Lords decide the case with this principle, rather than with the doctrine of consideration, in mind.

[190] *Foakes v Beer* (1884) 9 App. Cas. 605, 613. [191] (1885) 1 *LQR* 134.

[192] *PCLE(4)* 242. Pollock appreciated that the outcome in *Foakes v Beer* seemed to be largely due to the peculiarities of pleading: see *PCLE(5)* 179–80; and, more generally, Merton L. Ferson, 'The Rule in *Foakes v Beer*' (1921) 31 *Yale L. J.* 15–23; and cf. Joseph Gold, 'The Present Status of the Rule in Pinnel's Case' (1941) 30 *Kentucky L. J.* 72–100, 187–204 at 195–7.

The question of whether Pollock's enthusiasm for the notion of good faith explains his attitude towards the doctrine of consideration is perhaps rather less intriguing than the fact that he should have demonstrated this enthusiasm in the first place. Pollock's style as a contracts scholar was, after all, nearly always expository. When setting out the principles of the law of contract he was not only willing to acknowledge those instances in which the principles were coherent and had been developed by the courts with wisdom and care, but was usually merciless in drawing attention to those cases in which the development of principle had been accorded too little attention.[193] Whether supportive or critical of particular rules of contract, however, the fact is that he was almost exclusively concerned with the law itself, either as it stood or as it had evolved. Although keen to hold up a mirror to the law of contract, Pollock never seemed particularly interested in visions of a better system.

His espousal of the notion of good faith provides, however, an exception to this generalization. By the end of the twentieth century, good faith had become a significant concept in English contract law—particularly in the law of consumer contracts, where European consumer protection principles have had a marked influence on judicial decision-making.[194] Although some academic commentators regard good faith with considerable suspicion—a concept which 'could well work practical mischief if ruthlessly implanted in our system of law,' as one of their number put it[195]—others argue strongly that the adoption of a good faith criterion in English contract law would bring benefits.[196] The crucial point for our purposes is that it is still the case, just as it was in Pollock's day, that there exists no explicit general doctrine in English law that imposes a positive duty of good faith on contracting parties. 'In many civil law systems, and perhaps in most legal systems outside the common law world,' Lord Justice Bingham observed in 1989, 'the law of obligations recognises and enforces an overriding principle that in making and carrying out contracts parties should act in good faith. . . . English law has,

[193] See, e.g., *PCLE* 73, 76–7, 189, 357, 467.

[194] See generally Jack Beatson and Daniel Friedmann, 'Introduction: From "Classical" to Modern Contract', in *Good Faith and Fault in Contract Law*, eds. J. Beatson and D. Friedmann (Oxford: Clarendon Press, 1995), 3–21 at 14–15; and Gunther Teubner, 'Legal Irritants: Good Faith in British Law or How Unifying Law Ends Up in New Divergences' (1998) 61 *Mod. L. Rev.* 11–32.

[195] Michael G. Bridge, 'Does Anglo-Canadian Law Need a Doctrine of Good Faith?' (1984) 9 *Canadian Business Law Jnl.* 385–426 at 426. It is quite often observed that the notion of good faith has received a much better press among contracts scholars in the United States as compared with in England—see, generally, E. Allan Farnsworth, 'Good Faith in Contract Performance', in *Good Faith and Fault in Contract Law*, above n.194, 153–70—although even in the United States the idea has often been approached with caution and scepticism: see, e.g., Clayton P. Gillette, 'Limitations on the Obligation of Good Faith' [1981] *Duke L. J.* 619–65.

[196] A major obstacle to the adoption of a criterion of good faith in English law is posed by the fact that there seems to be little agreement on what such a standard should embody. '[W]e in England find it difficult to adopt a general concept of good faith', Goode has remarked, because 'we do not quite know what it means'. Roy Goode, 'The Concept of "Good Faith" in English Law', *Saggi, Conferenze e Seminari* (Roma: Centro di studi e ricerche di diritto comparato e straniero, 1992), ii. 3–10 at 3, available at http://w3.uniroma1.it/idc/centro/publications/02goode.pdf (last visited 5 April 2004).

characteristically, committed itself to no such overriding principle but has developed piecemeal solutions in response to demonstrated problems of unfairness.'[197] When Pollock maintained that the purpose of the law of contract is to uphold the enforcement of good faith so as to protect the reasonable expectations of promisees, he was, rather unusually, stating a preference rather than a legal position.

Why would he have done this? It is impossible to know for sure, but at least three answers suggest themselves. The first, and certainly the least convincing answer is that Pollock may have been inspired by Roman and civilian conceptions of good faith. In Roman law, for example, breach of contract was considered to be a matter of bad faith and remedies for such breaches were required to be consonant with good faith.[198] Although Pollock appears never explicitly to discuss this requirement, it is hardly likely that he would have been unaware of it. But even if he was aware of Roman and civilian understandings of good faith, and even if he found those understandings to be agreeable, none of this explains why he should have concluded that the establishment of a positive sanction for the enforcement of good faith bargaining should be the basic purpose of English contract law. At best—though even this conclusion seems to require unwarranted speculation—we might surmise that Pollock's statements about good faith being at the heart of contract law could derive from his understanding of the Roman and civilian traditions.

A somewhat more promising answer to the question of why Pollock should have exhibited such enthusiasm for the doctrine of good faith is that Lord Mansfield had already made a strong case for it. Insurance law has traditionally been underpinned by a doctrine of *uberrima fides* or utmost good faith: contracts of insurance more than most other contracts, so the argument goes, require that the contracting parties be under a duty to disclose material facts to one another where to omit to do so is likely to put the withholding party at an unfair advantage. This argument—with which, not surprisingly, Pollock

[197] *Interfoto Picture Library Ltd v Stiletto Visual Programmes Ltd* [1989] QB 433, 439, CA. See also The Hon. Steyn J., 'The Role of Good Faith and Fair Dealing in Contract Law: A Hair-Shirt Philosophy?' [1991] *Denning L. J.* 131–41.

[198] For specific instances of this duty in the *Digest*, see, e.g., Paul D. 17. 1. 22. 4; Gai. D. 17. 1 27. 4; Paul D. 18. 1. 57. 3; Ulp. D. 19. 1. 1. 1 ('anything done contrary to good faith falls within the action on purchase'); Pomp. D. 19. 1. 6. 9; Ulp. D. 19. 1. 11 pr 1 ('The buyer has the action on purchase. . . . [I]ncluded in this action is only what the parties agreed to be held responsible for. This is an action of good faith, and nothing conforms better to good faith than that the parties to the contract be held responsible for what they agreed'). On good faith in Roman law, see generally Marijan Horvat, 'Osservazioni sulla "bona fides" nel diritto romano obbligatorio', in *Studi in onore di Vincenzo Arangio-Ruiz nel XLV anno del suo insegnamento*, ed. M. Lauria et al. (Naples: Jovene, 1953), 423–43; also Roscoe Pound, *An Introduction to the Philosophy of Law* (New Haven: Yale UP, 1922), 170, 188–9. On the same in civil law, see Friedrich Kessler and Edith Fine, '*Culpa in Contrahendo*, Bargaining in Good Faith, and Freedom of Contract: A Comparative Study' (1964) 77 *Harvard L. Rev.* 401–49; and Reinhard Zimmermann, *The Law of Obligations: Roman Foundations of the Civilian Tradition* (Oxford: Oxford UPress, 1996 [1990]), 674–6.

was familiar[199]—is often traced back to Mansfield.[200] 'Good faith forbids either party', Mansfield observed in *Carter v Boehm*, 'by concealing what he privately knows, to draw the other into a bargain. . . . The reason of the rule which obliges parties to disclose, is to prevent fraud, and to encourage good faith.'[201] In fact, Mansfield did not consider the principle of good faith to be limited to insurance contracts. In *Bexwell v Christie*, decided ten years after *Carter v Boehm*, he declared fraudulent the action of a person who advertised his property for auction to the highest bidder but who surreptitiously employed a bidder of his own to try to inflate the price. 'The basis of all dealings ought to be good faith; . . . that could never be the case, if the owner might secretly and privately enhance the price, by a person employed for that purpose.'[202]

The third answer is that Pollock's attraction to the idea of good faith may be attributable to his understanding of duty as a general virtue. It was observed in chapter 2 that Pollock belonged to that late-Victorian generation which emphasized qualities such as trustworthiness, integrity, altruism, and public spirit as integral to good character. Those who demonstrate good character, he believed, ought to be protected by the law: hence his claims that contract law should support and enforce the reasonable expectations of reasonable businessmen, and that the law generally ought to uphold what he referred to as 'the moral judgment of an average right-minded man'.[203]

Whatever might explain Pollock's expression of preference for the enforcement of good faith, it is important to emphasize that his understanding of this idea was very much of his era. Conceptions of good faith proliferated during the twentieth century. Variously, good faith has been explained as 'accept[ing] the fact and necessity of a major role for custom and convention in contract',[204] 'as an "excluder"' which 'functions to rule out many different forms of bad faith',[205] as 'a standard that has honesty and fairness at its core',[206] and 'as the cornerstone of a systematic co-operative ethic in contract'.[207] Any

[199] See *PCLE* 449; *PCLE(8)* 564.

[200] See, e.g., R. A. Hasson, 'The Doctrine of *Uberrima Fides* in Insurance Law—A Critical Evaluation' (1969) 32 *Mod. L. Rev.* 615–37; Eric M. Holmes, 'A Contextual Study of Commercial Good Faith: Good-Faith Disclosure in Contract Formation' (1978) 39 *Univ. Pittsburgh L. Rev.* 381–452; and Kessler and Fine, above n.198, 441–2.

[201] *Carter v Boehm* (1766) 3 Burr. 1905, 1910–11.

[202] *Bexwell v Christie* (1776) 1 Cowp. 395, 396.

[203] *PCLE(9)* viii; *EJE* 270. We first encountered this man in section ii(c) of chapter 3.

[204] B. J. Reiter, 'Good Faith in Contracts' (1983) 17 *Valparaiso Univ. L. Rev.* 705–34 at 730.

[205] Robert S. Summers, '"Good Faith" in General Contract Law and the Sales Provisions of the Uniform Commercial Code' (1968) 54 *Virginia L. Rev.* 195–267 at 196, 262. See also Robert S. Summers, 'The General Duty of Good Faith—Its Recognition and Conceptualization' (1982) 67 *Cornell L. Rev.* 810–40 at 818–21.

[206] E. Allan Farnsworth, 'On Trying to Keep One's Promises: The Duty of Best Efforts in Contract Law' (1984) 46 *Univ. Pittsburgh L. Rev.* 1–20 at 8.

[207] Roger Brownsword, 'Positive, Negative, Neutral: The Reception of Good Faith in English Contract Law', in *Good Faith in Contract*, eds. R. Brownsword, N. J. Hird, and G. Howells (Dartmouth: Ashgate, 1999), 13–40 at 39.

contracts scholar knows how easy it would be to expand this list of examples. Many of these modern notions of good faith are complex, and some of them are fairly abstract. But Pollock wanted to cut through complexity and abstraction. 'The whole topic is surrounded with a great deal of confusion in our books'[208] was his classic lament as a contracts scholar. For Pollock, there would be no point in resorting to an idea such as good faith unless it very obviously served to clarify something about contract law. The purpose of uncovering and articulating principles, was after all, to make it easier to grasp legal doctrine. Any principle—and especially one without much in the way of legal standing—which served to muddle rather than to simplify was hardly deserving of emphasis.

So it is that Pollock's articulation of the idea of good faith is very much an exercise in eschewing abstraction and keeping to what he would have considered to be the real and the true. For the purpose of capturing his understanding of good faith, it is worth briefly considering two well-known English essays on good faith in the law of contract. In his *Current Legal Problems* lecture of 1956, Raphael Powell, according to Roger Brownsword, 'invited his audience to entertain the radical thought that the common law of England might be improved if it were to adopt an explicit doctrine of good faith in contracts'.[209] The reader who blinks will miss any radical propositions that might be sheltering in Powell's lecture. Very much an exercise in erudition and scholarly caution, the lecture attempts to determine the status of good faith within various legal systems: thus, the Romans very clearly had a doctrine of good faith ('[t]hough there is very little in the texts to suggest that the Roman lawyers were avowedly concerned with ethical principles in their treatment of good faith'[210]), English contract law 'abounds with illustrations of the rule of good faith'[211] (though 'there is no overriding general positive duty of good faith'[212]), and 'German law has adopted the Roman rule that it is part of the judge's function to determine whether performance has been in accordance with good faith'[213] (though in the German context the principle 'does require a certain amount of give and take'[214]). Certainly it is possible to infer from Powell's lecture that he believed the English courts would probably handle some matters of contractual liability better were they to embrace good faith in the manner of the German courts.[215] But it is not clear that his normative or reformist ambition extended to recommending the adoption of an explicit doctrine of good faith.

What is clear, as Brownsword points out, is that Powell was averse 'to lawyers dabbling in morality', and that he believed 'that good faith doctrines seem to

[208] *PCLE* 357.
[209] Roger Brownsword, '"Good Faith in Contracts" Revisited' (1996) 49 *Current Legal Problems* 111–57 at 111.
[210] Raphael Powell, 'Good Faith in Contracts' (1956) 9 *Current Legal Problems* 16–38 at 20.
[211] Ibid. 23. [212] Ibid. 25. [213] Ibid. 32. [214] Ibid. 37.
[215] See ibid. 36–7; cf. also Brownsword, above n.209, 115–16.

be more effective where they are based on custom and common opinion rather than on abstract moral theory'.[216] 'I believe', Powell confessed, 'in the fundamental decency of the common man', and '[w]hen I read of a lawyer trying to tread daintily in the china-shops of ethics, I wish that someone would lead him back to the streets where walk all manner of men.'[217] Brownsword, by contrast, in his own *Current Legal Problems* lecture, emphasizes good faith as a moral imperative. Contrasting '"a good faith requirement" . . . that contractors should perform and enforce their contracts in line with the spirit of the agreement' with 'the adoption of a "good faith regime" . . . in which . . . the traditional "adversarial" ethic of contract is *systematically* replaced by an ethic of "co-operation",' Brownsword argues 'that it would be rational for English law to move from having no doctrine of good faith to having a good faith requirement' and 'even more rational to adopt a good faith regime.'[218] 'A good faith regime,' he elaborates, 'systematically endeavours to encourage a disposition to co-operate and to shield contractors who are so disposed against exploitation and opportunism.'[219] 'Once we move on to a good faith regime, . . . co-operation becomes the guiding standard.'[220]

The point of contrasting Powell's and Brownsword's conceptions of good faith is not to express a preference for either. Brownsword seems unable to locate the impetus for the move to a good faith regime. If we have not felt inspired to create such a regime already, why should our feelings change in the future? Powell, in turn, offers an account of good faith which, by modern standards, seems quaint and somewhat complacent. In short, both conceptions might be faulted. The significant point for our purposes is that Pollock's understanding of good faith is broadly identifiable with Powell's, and light years away from Brownsword's. Whereas Brownsword emphasizes a so-called ethic of co-operation, Pollock, as we saw in the previous chapter, firmly believed that the common law should facilitate competition: while he would not have expected the law to allow one party knowingly to take advantage of another party's failure to appreciate the extent of his or her contractual rights, he would have had no problem with one party exploiting his or her superior knowledge of the market in order to gain an economic advantage over that other party.[221] More importantly, Pollock would have sided with Powell over the matter of moral theory and its relevance to good faith. 'I do not see that

[216] Brownsword, above n.209, 117, 116.

[217] Powell, above n.210, 17, 38.

[218] Brownsword, above n.209, 113–14.

[219] Ibid. 139.

[220] Ibid. 150.

[221] Cf. ibid. 135: 'the idea of contract as an institution dedicated to the facilitation of mutually beneficial transactions is both vulnerable and rather vague. . . . If, however, we locate this conception of contract in a community in which autonomy is valued, then we can begin to repair these deficiencies. For we can suppose that members of such a community would judge it rational to choose an institution of contract that is designed to facilitate the making of mutually advantageous transactions rather than an institution that is designed to facilitate one-sided advantage-taking, and that they would conceive of a good faith regime as an attempt to translate this choice into the details of contract doctrine.'

a jurist is bound to be a moral philosopher more than other men', Pollock wrote.[222] 'We [jurists] may take the morality of men living together in settled societies as an existing and sufficiently ascertained fact', but '[i]t is for the moralist and the metaphysician to analyse it if they can; enough for us that it is there.'[223]

Pollock treated the notion of good faith much as he treated the notion of common sense: as something in need of no elaboration. 'Where a promisor seeks to renege on contractual obligations, thereby defeating the reasonable expectations of the promisee, then the law ought to support fair and honest dealing by upholding those reasonable expectations'—this would seem to be the long and short of what he meant by good faith. His apparent disinclination to adopt anything resembling a theoretical approach to the notion was, of course, but a specific illustration of his decidedly cautious attitude towards theoretical approaches to law in general (see chapter 3). The fact that he seemed to have no inclination to approach the idea of good faith theoretically also serves as a reminder about the dangers of presentism (see chapter 4): just as Pollock's use of the notion of principle does not make him a harbinger of modern jurisprudential debates about right answers, integrity, and the like, so too his enthusiasm for the doctrine of good faith does not make him a significant forerunner to the various modern theoretical justifications of this doctrine. Good faith, in his hands, has a distinctly old-fashioned look about it.

ii. Torts

Pollock was not eight months dead before Isaac Briggs's *Notes on Pollock's 'Contracts'* was published. The book—a 'nutshell' text if ever there was—was of a type that seemed to drive Pollock to despair during his lifetime. 'As a matter of scientific and literary principle,' he wrote to one of his publishers in 1891, 'the whole tribe of analysers and abridgers is an abomination to me.'[224] Briggs was very clearly a member of that tribe, and the opening words of his *Notes* set the tone for the rest of the book: '[a] small analysis is here offered of Sir Frederick Pollock's "Principles of Contract". . . . Many students have no doubt felt the need of an analysis of standard works like "Pollock," which on a first perusal may tend to confuse, by reason of their breadth of

[222] *EJE* 23.

[223] *EJE* 25–6. See also Gordley, *Philosophical Origins of Modern Contract Doctrine*, above n.51, 216–17.

[224] Frederick Pollock to John Murray, 29 March 1891, in Pollock correspondence (Murray). Cf. Frederick Pollock, 'English Law Studies' (1894) 28 *Irish Law Times* 245–6 at 245 ('As for abridgments [*sic*] and epitomes of leading cases, which do not give the actual text of the subject, they may possibly be of some use for examination purposes, though I should doubt even that, if the examiners know their business. The best that can be said for cases treated in this way is that they may by accident have notes of some value hung upon them. But the man who is lawyer enough to write valuable notes is not usually the man capable of treating the authorities in that fashion').

range and their novelty.'[225] However depressing Briggs's book might seem, nevertheless, it also stands as testament to the fact that *Principles* was a core contracts text. Besides being an important source—or at least an important source of a source—for law students, the book also made an impact at higher legal levels. We have observed already, for example, that the definition of consideration which Pollock put forward in *Principles* was explicitly adopted by the House of Lords in *Dunlop v Selfridge*. It is worth noting also that in the United States, where the book underwent numerous special American editions[226] and where there is a long tradition of footnoting and use of citations in judicial opinions, the courts have quite often relied on *Principles* as secondary authority for one or another legal proposition.[227] All in all, as law books go, *Principles* has enjoyed a fairly long and happy shelf life.

Yet *Principles* is not generally considered to be either the most important or the most influential of Pollock's legal treatises. 'Pollock on Contract', Lawson remarks, 'was by no means so important a book as Pollock on Torts'.[228] Why should *The Law of Torts* have been considered the worthier of the two books? The standard answer to this question is that whereas Pollock's contracts treatise was essentially a study of the principles underlying an established body of law, his treatise on torts was both a study of principles and an effort to establish a body of law—to show, that is, that there really is a unified Law of Torts rather than just a haphazard collection of rules about different kinds of torts. This unifying initiative came at just the right time: the increase, during the nineteenth century, of industrial and particularly railway accidents meant that

[225] I. G. Briggs, *Notes on Pollock's 'Contracts'* (London: Stevens & Sons, 1937), v. *TLT* was subjected to a similar treatment: see J. K. Mannooch, *An Analysis of Sir Frederick Pollock's Law of Torts for Students* (London: Stevens & Sons, 1911). Notwithstanding Pollock's professed distaste for abridgements, Mannooch's book was published with his permission: see ibid. v.

[226] Beginning with Gustavus H. Wald's 1881 adaptation of *PCLE(2)* (Cincinnati: Clarke & Co., 1881).

[227] See, e.g., *Ward v Sherman*, 192 U.S. 168, 175–6 (1904) (and cf. *Hart v Adair*, 9 Cir., 244 F. 897, 901 (1917)); *Miller v Ammon*, 145 U.S. 421, 426 (1892) ('Pol. Cont. pp.253 to 260'); *Swift & Co. v United States*, 111 U.S. 22, 30 (1884); *Chapman v County of Douglas*, 107 U.S. 348, 356 (1883); *Cundick v Broadbent*, 383 F. 2d 157, 160 (10th Cir, 1967); *Ham v Blankenship*, 194 F. 2d 430, 433 (5th Cir, 1952); *Vincennes Bridge Co. v Board of County Comm'rs*, 8 Cir., 248 F. 93, 105 (1917); *Truman v Berlanti and Hartford*, 14 A.D. 2d 514, 516 (1961); *Gastonia Personnel Corp'n v Rogers*, 276 N.C. 279, 289–90 (1970); *Kern County Land Co. v Lake County*, 232 Or. 405, 411 (1962); *Hill County v Shaw & Borden Co.*, 9 Cir., 225 F. 475, 478–9 (1915); *Clarke v Rogers*, (C.C.A. 1st Cir.) 183 F. 518, 523 (1910); *Danvers Savings Bank v National Surety Co.*, (C.C.A.) 166 F. 671, 674 (1909); *Baltimore & O. R. Co. v Hamburger*, (E. D. Va. Cir. Ct.) 155 F. 849, 852 (1907); *Johnson & Johnson v Herold*, (N. J. Cir. Ct.) 161 F. 593, 600 (1907); *Ingersoll v Coram*, (Mass. Circ. Ct.) 127 F. 418, 434 (1903); *Batchelder & Lincoln Co. v Whitmore*, (C.C.A. 1st Cir.) 122 F. 355, 361 (1903); *Wilson v Clonbrock*, (E. D. Pa. Cir. Ct.) 105 F. 846, 848 (1901); *Nevada Co. v Farnsworth*, (Utah Cir. Ct.) 89 F. 164, 167 (1898); *Loewer v Harris*, (C.C.A. 2nd Cir.) 57 F. 368, 373 (1893); *Lack v Borsum*, 44 F. Supp. 47 (W. D. La. 1942); *Virginia Shipbuilding Corp. v U.S. Shipping Board Emergency Fleet*, 292 F. 440, 454 (E. D. Va. 1923); *In re International Mineral Co.*, 222 F. 415, 427 (D. Conn. 1915); *In re Watmough*, 210 F. 539, 541 (N. D. Ohio 1913); and *Vanderbilt v Schreyer*, 91 N.Y. 392, 401 (1883).

[228] F. H. Lawson, 'Doctrinal Writing: A Foreign Element in English Law?', in *'Ius Privatum Gentium'. Festschrift für Max Rheinstein zum 70. Geburtstag*, 2 vols., eds. E. von Caemmerer, S. Mentschikoff, and K. Zweigert (Tübingen: Mohr, 1969), i. 191–210 at 199. Much the same remark has been made by others: see, e.g., Wright, above n.17, 154 ('There followed in 1882 the book on Torts, in some respects more brilliant than his Principles of Contract'); also cf. ibid. 163–4.

legislators and judges had to categorize and determine how to deal with an ever proliferating number and variety of liability claims.[229] Although Pollock's book was not the first English torts treatise—that honour properly goes to Charles Addison's work of 1860[230]—it was the first to take what was a fast-evolving and essentially undefined body of doctrine and attempt to establish it as a core legal category. While *Principles* was a noble effort at synthesis, so the common contention goes, *Torts* was also path-breaking.[231]

This contention is not disputed here. Indeed, it seems correct: unifying the law of torts was certainly one of Pollock's ambitions.[232] Not disputing the contention, however, is not the same as relying upon it. Understanding Pollock's contribution to the development of tort law requires not that we simply reiterate his own conviction that *Torts* 'is a book of principles if it is anything',[233] but that we acquire some sense of the theoretical backdrop to his inquiries, of just what he was reacting to, and of what he was trying to achieve in the name of principle. This section begins with an account of the natural law foundations of English tort law, and then moves to an examination of how Pollock endeavoured to forge a unitary law of torts out of a fairly disparate body of wrongs. To a large degree, this unifying exercise was one of compartmentalization. We will see, however, that Pollock wanted not only to compartmentalize the law of torts, but also to demonstrate that the subject was generally amenable to being explained in terms of principles. These principles are not always clear, precise, or even well-established—indeed, many a paragraph in *Torts* begins with a statement of a principle followed by an explanation of how

[229] On the impact upon the law of the nineteenth-century growth of industry and the railways, see, e.g., P. W. J. Bartrip and S. B. Burman, *The Wounded Soldiers of Industry: Industrial Compensation Policy 1833–1897* (Oxford: Clarendon Press, 1983); R. W. Kostal, *Law and English Railway Capitalism 1825–1875* (Oxford: Clarendon Press, 1994).

[230] C. G. Addison, *Wrongs and their Remedies: being a Treatise on the Law of Torts* (London: V. & R. Stevens, 1860). On the unsystematic nature of Addison's treatise, see Thomas C. Grey, 'Accidental Torts' (2001) 54 *Vanderbilt L. Rev.* 1225–84 at 1230–1. Addison's treatise was not, strictly speaking, the first English torts text, an anonymous study of the *Law of Actions on the Case for Torts and Wrongs* having appeared some time around 1720: see Percy H. Winfield, *The Province of the Law of Tort* (Cambridge: Cambridge UP, 1931), 8. For Pollock's disparaging view of this anonymous work, see *TLT* vi.

[231] 'The book's just claim to fame is that it is the first English textbook to attempt to uncover the underlying principles of the subject and to present a *Law of Torts*.' Michael Taggart, *Private Property and Abuse of Rights in Victorian England: The Story of Edward Pickles and the Bradford Water Supply* (Oxford: Oxford UP, 2002), 167–8. See also Anon., review of *TLT(5)* (1897–8) 1 *Literature* 24–5 at 25; A. T. Denning, review of P. H. Winfield, *A Text-Book of the Law of Tort* (1947) 68 *LQR* 516–18. Although Denning was happy to say some nice (along with some critical) things about the book under review, he was eager to emphasize that both Winfield and John Salmond—torts scholars who had produced treatises 'so useful in the Courts' because 'they are not digests of cases but repositories of principles' (ibid. 516)—were simply following in Pollock's footsteps.

[232] '[T]he purpose of this book is to show that there really is a Law of Torts, not merely a number of rules of law about various kinds or torts—that this is a true living branch of the Common Law, not a collection of heterogeneous instances.' *TLT* vi. Cf. Frederick Pollock, 'Judicial Caution and Valour' (1929) 45 *LQR* 293–306 at 296 ('the pedestrian timidity that shrinks from hazarding any general conclusion will only land us in a still less desirable state, that of having no principle at all, but a heap of unrelated instances which those who come after may or may not find to be consistent with one another').

[233] *TLT* viii.

the courts have so far grappled unsuccessfully with it. The quest to uncover principles is more or less constantly in evidence in that treatise, all the same. Although the focus on principles served the cause of unification, it also enabled Pollock to reveal his preferences for particular visions of torts doctrine—indeed, we will see in this section that he was far more ready to take a prescriptive approach to torts than he was to the law of contract. Having considered some of Pollock's preferences, we then examine the positions that he took on the establishment of a general principle of negligence liability and on the question of the degree to which liability should be imposed for intentional wrongdoing. Both of these positions require fairly complex presentations, and both turn out to be innovative and historically significant.

a. The natural law backdrop

Pollock's contracts scholarship, indeed nineteenth-century English contracts jurisprudence generally, evolved very much with an eye to the ideas of the great continental will theorists. In English tort law scholarship during this period, by contrast, there was nobody comparable with Savigny or Pothier lurking in the background. Whereas any late nineteenth-century commentator on contracts had a fairly formidable body of antecedent theory to grapple with, the torts specialist was dealing with a subject which was largely an indigenous development from its eighteenth-century natural law foundations.[234]

These foundations require at least a brief explanation. One way of setting out the foundations is to begin with the general action of trespass during the middle ages—an immensely complex subject which, thankfully, we need do no more than touch upon here. During the thirteenth century it became established that writs of trespass could, almost without exception, be issued with respect only to wrongs committed with 'force and arms' (*vi et armis*) and 'against the King's peace' (*contra pacem Regis*).[235] Liability for trespass was nominally strict,[236] though considerations of fault gradually crept into the medieval actions.[237] As the centuries progressed—to summarize a great deal—fault came increasingly to play a role in relation to trespassory liability, but that role

[234] See Ibbetson, above n.49, 153–4.

[235] See Robert C. Palmer, *English Law in the Age of the Black Death: A Transformation of Governance and Law* (Chapel Hill, NC: University of North Carolina Press, 1993), 152–70; George E. Woodbine, 'The Origins of the Action of Trespass' (1924) 33 *Yale L. J.* 799–816; (1925) 34 *Yale L. J.* 343–70 at part ii, 358–64. A writ of trespass could also be issued where there had been an infringement of a royal franchise: see S. F. C. Milsom, 'Trespass from Henry III to Edward III' (1958) 74 *LQR* 195–224, 407–36, 561–90 at 417–28; also Baker, above n.112, 60–1; and, on the King's peace, *OLOD* 65–90.

[236] See Robert J. Kaczorowski, 'The Common-Law Background of Nineteenth-Century Tort Law' (1990) 51 *Ohio State L. J.* 1127–99 at 1169; Wex S. Malone, 'Ruminations on the Role of Fault in the History of the Common Law of Torts' (1970) 31 *Louisiana L. Rev.* 1–44 at 9–14; and cf. Morris S. Arnold, 'Accident, Mistake, and Rules of Liability in the Fourteenth-Century Law of Torts' (1979) 128 *Univ. Pennsylvania L. Rev.* 361–78 at 361–4.

[237] Various factors, such as reliance on juries and (from the fourteenth century onwards) the development of the inevitable accident defence, appear to have ensured that liability for trespass was only

was far from well defined.[238] Roman law offered a perspective from which fault could be treated less equivocally: not only had the Romans posited a basic distinction between contract and torts—legal obligations *ex contractu* and *ex delicto*—but within the Roman law tradition the relevance of fault (*culpa*) to liability for wrongs was fairly precise and well-established.[239] It is well known and documented that English jurists of the seventeenth and eighteenth centuries looked to this tradition for inspiration in seeking to produce orderly accounts of the common law.[240] During this same period, representatives of the northern natural law school also drew upon the Romanist tradition in endeavouring to articulate moral precepts and responsibilities. 'The natural lawyers', Stein observes, 'reduced the various kinds of delict in Roman law to the general principle that one was liable for all loss caused to another by one's wilfulness or fault.'[241] Again summarizing a great deal, the gradual recognition of the role of fault in trespass was partially attributable to seventeenth- and eighteenth-century receptiveness not only to Roman law ideas but also to natural law adaptations of those ideas.

To account for the development of a fault-based approach to trespass, in other words, is to tell part of a broader story about how English legal thought came to be influenced by a combination of Roman law and natural law. The general story is well summarized by Simmonds:

> The theories of natural law that developed in the seventeenth and eighteenth centuries exerted a powerful influence on legal thinking. Lawyers already possessed, in the Roman *Corpus Iuris*, an impressive *model* of systematic legal thinking, but the intellectual perspectives needed as the basis for doctrinal science were provided by natural law. . . . Earlier forms of legal writing had tended to present a rag-bag of actions or remedies, or comments on individual laws. It was under the influence of natural law theory that these legal materials came to be regarded as deriving their coherence from an underlying structure of individual rights and duties.[242]

nominally strict: on the impact of juror deliberation, see S. F. C. Milsom, *Historical Foundations of the Common Law*, 2nd edn. (London: Butterworths, 1981), 296–7; on the impact of the inevitable accident defence, see Stephen G. Gilles, 'Inevitable Accident in Classical English Tort Law' (1994) 43 *Emory L. J.* 575–646.

[238] See generally Ibbetson, above n.49, 57–70; also S. F. C. Milsom, 'Not Doing is No Trespass: A View of the Boundaries of Case' [1954] *Cambridge L. J.* 105–17 at 107–8.

[239] See, e.g., J. Inst. 4. 3–4; Gai. D. 17. 2. 72; Gai. D. 44. 7. 1. 4. For analysis of the passages from the *Digest*, see David Ibbetson, '"The Law of Business Rome": Foundations of the Anglo-American Tort of Negligence' (1999) 52 *Current Legal Problems* 74–109 at 81–2.

[240] See, e.g., Simpson, above n.14, 655–8; Helmut Coing, 'Das Schrifttum der englischen Civilians und die kontinentale Rechtsliteratur in der Zeit zwischen 1550 und 1800' (1975) 5 *Ius Commune* 1–55 at 17–33; Alan Watson, '*Justinian's Institutes* and Some English Counterparts', in *Studies in Justinian's Institutes: In Memory of J. A. C. Thomas*, eds. P. Stein and A. D. Lewis (London: Sweet & Maxwell, 1983), 181–6.

[241] Peter Stein, *Roman Law in European History* (Cambridge: Cambridge UP, 1999), 109.

[242] N. E. Simmonds, *The Decline of Juridical Reason: Doctrine and Theory in the Legal Order* (Manchester: Manchester UP, 1984), 50–1.

Note the two overlapping ways in which the ideas of the natural lawyers proved useful to jurists. First, natural law provided for English jurists the impetus to try to show that the seemingly haphazard miscellany that was common law doctrine did in fact conform to a coherent framework. Secondly, the natural law tradition actually suggested a framework: the framework of rights and duties. Since natural law thinking could aid systematization through the provision of a framework of rights and duties, it possessed value for anyone in the eighteenth century seeking to determine the nature and boundaries of, say, trespassory liability.[243] Our concern is not with the eighteenth century and liability for trespass but with the nineteenth century and Pollock's work on torts. Although we are currently a little distance from that work, it is worth elaborating briefly on the natural law foundations of English torts jurisprudence from the eighteenth century onwards so as to set the context for Pollock's own torts scholarship.

Consider, first of all, the idea that natural law of the seventeenth and eighteenth centuries provided the impetus for English jurists to engage in systematization. In the law of contract, natural law bore its influence as a systematizing force indirectly—mainly through Pothier's version of the will theory.[244] The influence of natural law ideas upon juristic speculation about torts was, perhaps inevitably, rather different from the influence of natural law upon writing about contracts. Two years after the publication of the first volume of Blackstone's *Commentaries on the Laws of England*, and over one-and-a-half centuries before Lord Atkin's landmark speech in *Donoghue v Stevenson*,[245] Francis Buller, in his *Introduction to the Law Relative to Trials at Nisi Prius*, contended that liability arises through neglect of one's duty to take reasonable care not to injure one's neighbour.[246] The contention had its roots both in Roman law and in the writings of natural lawyers, particularly Samuel Pufendorf.[247] Not that Pufendorf and other natural lawyers had been concerned with legal questions about liability for wrongs. Their concern, rather, had been with the 'general duties of humanity'—with the expectations to be attributed to human beings for the purpose of determining what constitutes sociable behaviour.[248] The natural lawyer's concern with wrongs, Ibbetson

[243] See Ibbetson, above n.49, 158. [244] See ibid. 219–20.

[245] *Donoghue v Stevenson* [1932] AC 562, HL.

[246] See Sir Francis Buller, *An Introduction to the Law Relative to Trials at Nisi Prius. By a Learned Judge* (Dublin: Watts, 1767), 24. The figure of the neighbour as a guide to determining duty of care precedes *Donoghue v Stevenson* in English case law, too: see Baker, above n.112, 415. While the invocation of this figure in Buller's *Nisi Prius* might be regarded as the anticipation of the modern reasonable care standard, furthermore, the similarity can be overstressed: see Gilles, above n.237, 643–4.

[247] See especially Pufendorf, *De Jure Naturae et Gentium*, 3. 1. 6. On the general influence of Book III of Pufendorf's *De Jure Naturae et Gentium* on the development of the law of obligations in Europe, see Berthold Kupisch, 'La responsabilità da atto illecito nel diritto naturale', in *La responsabilità civile da atto illecito nella prospettiva storico-comparatistica*, ed. L. Vacca (Turin: Giappichelli Editore, 1995), 123–43 at 125–38; also Franz Wieacker, *A History of Private Law in Europe, with Particular Reference to Germany*, trans. T. Weir (Oxford: Clarendon Press, 1995), 246–8.

[248] Stephen Buckle, *Natural Law and the Theory of Property: Grotius to Hume* (Oxford: Clarendon Press, 1991), 72–3.

explains, was the concern of the moral philosopher: within the natural law tradition, 'emphasis fell on the individual's duty, with the obligation to compensate for breach of duty as a purely secondary matter'.[249] None the less, the key point for our purposes is that duty as a juristic theme—in particular, the early version of the duty of care concept which we encounter in Buller's *Nisi Prius*—has roots in the natural law notion of duty.

Anyone seeking to demonstrate a link between torts jurisprudence and natural law thinking is served well by Buller's *Nisi Prius*. If we look instead to Buller's better-known contemporary, Blackstone, we can still find this link—though it is by no means as obvious as it is in the work of Buller. Blackstone's natural law sympathies are readily discernible from the *Commentaries*, even if, as various commentators have shown,[250] the manner of his reliance on natural law ideas is subtle. In the Introduction to the *Commentaries*, the reliance in fact seems anything but subtle: '[m]an . . . must necessarily be subject to the laws of his Creator. . . . [A]s man depends absolutely upon his Maker, . . . it is necessary that he should . . . conform to his Maker's will. This will of his Maker is called the law of nature. . . . This law of nature, being . . . dictated by God himself, is of course superior in obligation to any other. . . . [N]o human laws are of any validity, if contrary to this.'[251] The subtlety of Blackstone's reliance rests not in the way in which he aligns himself with natural law thought, but in the way in which he connects natural law ideas with common law doctrine.

Blackstone's method of classifying and explaining the principles of English law, although apparently not indebted to any particular natural law writer, is very much derived from seventeenth- and eighteenth-century natural law tenets.[252] While his explanation of the significance of the law of nature in the Introduction to the *Commentaries* is to some degree drawn from the Swiss jurist, Jean-Jacques Burlamaqui,[253] it is to Hugo Grotius and to Pufendorf (whose ideas Burlamaqui popularized) that Blackstone refers most often. Krieger posits the link between Blackstone and Pufendorf unequivocally: 'Blackstone not only took his prefatory exposition of general natural-law principles primarily from Pufendorf but supported his explanation of particular personal and property rights and torts with references from the same authority.'[254] The

[249] Ibbetson, above n.49, 166; in a similar vein, see also Ibbetson, above n.239, 86.

[250] See, e.g., H. L. A. Hart, 'Blackstone's Use of the Law of Nature' (1956) 3 *Butterworths S. African L. Rev.* 169–74; J. M. Finnis, 'Blackstone's Theoretical Intentions' (1967) 12 *Natural Law Forum* 163–83; Nigel E. Simmonds, 'Reason, History and Privilege: Blackstone's Debt to Natural Law' (1988) 105 *Zeitschrift der Savigny-Stiftung (Germ. Abt.)* 200–13.

[251] Blackstone, *Commentaries*, 1. 39–41. Although no human law should be permitted which contradicts the law of nature, he continues, '[t]here are . . . a great number of indifferent points in which both the divine law and the natural leave a man at his own liberty'. Ibid. 42. For the significance of this qualification, see Hart, above n.250, 171.

[252] See Simmonds, above n.250, 206–9.

[253] See Hart, above n.250, 170 ('Blackstone's express statements about the law of nature in the Introduction' are largely 'a translation from Burlamaqui'); though cf. Finnis, above n.250, 171, who makes it clear that Blackstone's reliance on Burlamaqui is actually quite limited.

[254] Leonard Krieger, *The Politics of Discretion: Pufendorf and the Acceptance of Natural Law* (Chicago: University of Chicago Press, 1965), 257. See also ibid. 261–2; and cf. Peter Birks, 'Negligence in the

reference to torts in this passage serves to reinforce the point about subtlety. It is in Book III of the *Commentaries* that Blackstone discusses various 'private wrongs'—trespass, nuisance, waste, and so on—that roughly correspond to some of the main categories of modern tort law. Yet, as Krieger appears to recognize, Book III contains almost no discussion of or reference to natural law theory.[255] 'Book III was an exposition of precisely the material that could not be easily fitted into the natural law framework.'[256] (Indeed when, as a Justice of the Court of Common Pleas, Blackstone was required to offer an opinion on the distinction between trespass and case—between, that is, immediate and consequential injury in torts—he resorted in his reasoning not to natural law but to Newtonian physics.[257]) In short, it seems that Blackstone made good use of natural law theory apart from when writing about private wrongs or torts.

In fact, however, as Kennedy has attempted to show, Book I of the *Commentaries* ('Of the Rights of Persons') is heavily laden not only with natural law ideas but also, implicitly, with the concept of tort. 'The "absolute" rights of personal liberty, bodily security, and private property discussed in the first part of Book I,' he argues, 'are the foundations of modern tort law.'[258] Not only, for Blackstone, are '[t]he absolute rights of every Englishman . . . founded on nature and reason',[259] but those rights also necessitate the categories of private and public wrongs;[260] and some of these wrongs—though, admittedly, not all of them[261]—may, by virtue of the fact that they 'exist parasitically on the system of rights',[262] be taken to have their foundations in natural law. Although Blackstone may not have fitted private wrongs explicitly into his natural law framework, natural law and the notion of tort are nevertheless connected within his scheme.

Eighteenth Century Common Law', in *Negligence: The Comparative Legal History of the Law of Torts*, ed. E. J. H. Schrage (Berlin: Duncker & Humblot, 2001), 173–227 at 212–13, where a similar argument is presented but with an emphasis on Grotius rather than Pufendorf.

[255] See Krieger, above n.254, 301 n.9.

[256] Simmonds, above n.250, 205.

[257] *Scott v Shepherd* (1773) 2 Wm Bla. 892, 894–6. For an intriguing study of this opinion, see Noel M. Swerdlow, 'Blackstone's "Newtonian" Dissent', in *The Natural Sciences and the Social Sciences: Some Critical and Historical Perspectives*, ed. I. B. Cohen (Dordrecht: Kluwer, 1994), 205–34. Not that Blackstone considered Newtonian physics and natural law to be incompatible: see *Commentaries*, I. 38.

[258] Duncan Kennedy, 'The Structure of Blackstone's Commentaries' (1979) 28 *Buffalo L. Rev.* 205–382 at 325. As is fairly well known, Kennedy has been criticized for assuming that Blackstone must have chosen his organizational scheme for the *Commentaries* with a view to legitimating the eighteenth-century English legal system. See John W. Cairns, 'Blackstone, An English Institutist: Legal Literature and the Rise of the Nation State' (1984) 4 *Oxf. Jnl. Leg. Studs* 318–60 at 350–2. Our concern here is not with this particular interpretive question but with the oblique connection that Blackstone makes between natural law and private wrongs—a connection which Kennedy captures well.

[259] Blackstone, *Commentaries*, I. 127. [260] See ibid. I. 53, 122.

[261] See ibid. I. 55: 'But, with regard to things in themselves indifferent [q.v. above n.251], the case is entirely altered. These become either right or wrong, just or unjust, duties or misdemeanors, according as the municipal legislator sees proper, for promoting the welfare of society, and more effectually carrying on the purposes of civil life.'

[262] Simmonds, above n.250, 205. See further Kennedy, above n.258, 241–4.

There would be no value in trying to elaborate this last argument here. Introducing Blackstone into our picture is important, nevertheless, for the purpose of understanding Pollock's torts jurisprudence. Although, in Pollock's eyes, Blackstone was by no means as lamentable a scholar as was Coke,[263] the *Commentaries* had to be approached with circumspection: 'much good history is in fact to be found in [the] *Commentaries*. But there are also several more or less ingenious but wholly groundless conjectures, and . . . not a few downright errors.'[264] Significantly, however, Pollock appreciated Blackstone as a political thinker.[265] This is not entirely surprising. As we have already seen in this study, Pollock regularly adopted a discernibly Blackstonian voice when he extolled the common law as the embodiment of the law of nature or reason.[266] As a treatise writer, Pollock was not as forthcoming as was Blackstone in trying to ground legal principles in natural law (though in his more general legal writing, as we have noted already in this study, he regularly insisted upon the connection of principle and reason); but what Pollock the treatise writer did share with Blackstone was that classic legal-scientific urge to bring coherence to a body of law. Out of this common ground there emerges a crucial difference between the two jurists. 'Blackstone's basic task', Simmonds explains, 'was to present the shapeless assemblage of forms of action as a body of substantive principles, founded in natural law. Yet he was in no position to simply abandon the traditional modes of legal thought and fundamentally revise the accepted framework in the way that became possible for the Victorian treatise writers.'[267] The forms of action, to put the point very simply, bore more heavily on Blackstone than they did on Pollock.

b. The forms of action

If the common assessment is correct, and Pollock's *Torts* is indeed a more accomplished effort at synthesis than is Pollock's *Principles*, it may well be because the nineteenth-century law of torts was less theoretically encumbered than was the nineteenth-century law of contract. Less baggage does, after all, usually make for an easier ride. As compared with contract, however, torts

[263] See, e.g., *FBJ* 250 ('Coke enounced this opinion with his usual vehemence and even more than his usual inaccuracy or disingenuousness in reading his own particular opinion into the authorities on which he professed to rely').

[264] *EIL* 9. Cf. also [Frederick Pollock], 'Nasmith's Institutes of English Private Law', *Saturday Rev.*, 8 January 1876, 54–5 at 54 ('The defects of Blackstone's arrangement entailed not only logical confusion, but also large substantive omissions').

[265] See *IHSP* 84–5.

[266] The voice referred to here was, we have seen, more attributable to Mansfield than to Blackstone. But then Blackstone, like Pollock, was very much in thrall to Mansfield: see Paul O. Carrese, *The Cloaking of Power: Montesquieu, Blackstone, and the Rise of Judicial Activism* (Chicago: University of Chicago Press, 2003), 162–9.

[267] Simmonds, above n.250, 204.

did not so much carry less baggage as different baggage. The subject of torts generated more than its fair share of problems for nineteenth-century treatise writers not only because it had not previously been theorized to the extent that the law of contract had, but also because it posed particularly difficult questions about legal history and doctrine. Pollock's generation, unlike earlier English jurists, had the opportunity to tackle these questions with a view to drawing a line under some of them, to establishing that their relevance to tort law from then onwards would be essentially historical. Not that very much was consigned to the past quite so easily.

At the time that Pollock embarked on his career as a jurist, the medieval forms of action were on their way to being buried. The burial process had begun in the 1830s, when most of the forms of action were abolished for procedural purposes and replaced by a uniform-writ system (the formalities of which were relaxed in the 1850s and 1870s).[268] Yet, as Maitland appreciated, the forms of action were not easily discarded: '[t]he forms of action we have buried,' he remarked in his posthumously published lectures on the subject, 'but they still rule us from their graves.'[269] Pollock recognized much the same. In the first edition of *Torts*, he outlined the standard story of the forms of action:

> The original theory of the common law seems to have been that there were a certain number of definite and mutually exclusive causes of action, expressed in appropriate forms. The test for ascertaining the existence or non-existence of a legal remedy in a given case was to see whether the facts could be brought under one of these forms. Not only this, but the party seeking legal redress had to discover and use the right form at his peril.[270]

Legal historians of more recent times have emphasized that this standard story—which, in the least sensitive of hands, can turn the formalities of the forms of action into something reminiscent of Kafka—needs to be approached warily.[271] Pollock's concern was neither to reiterate nor to question

[268] Uniformity of Process Act 1832, 2 & 3 Will. IV c. 39; Real Property Limitation Act 1833, 3 & 4 Will. IV c. 27, s. 36; Common Law Procedure Act 1852, 15 & 16 Vict. c. 76, ss. 2–3; Judicature Act 1873, 36 & 37 Vict. c. 66. For Pollock's assessment (and approval) of these changes, see Frederick Pollock, 'The Law of England I–L Victoriae' (1887) 3 *LQR* 343–7 at 345–6.

[269] F. W. Maitland, *The Forms of Action at Common Law: A Course of Lectures*, eds. A. H. Chaytor and W. J. Whittaker (Cambridge: Cambridge UP, 1936; orig. publ. 1909), 1.

[270] *TLT* 429.

[271] According to Milsom, the history of the English common law has often been distorted 'by excessive deference to the formal aspect of the forms of action. Of course, the existence of boundaries between actions made a difference to the problem of change, which presented itself as a matter of rival forms. But it did not necessarily make change more difficult, because the old rule could be left untouched, harmlessly in force.' S. F. C. Milsom, 'Reason in the Development of the Common Law' (1965) 81 *LQR* 496–517 at 499. As regards the literary analogy, see Franz Kafka, *Der Prozeß. Roman* (Frankfurt: Fischer, 1979 [1925]), 106 ('. . . but it sometimes happened that the case headed where the Advocate could no longer follow it. . . . The case had simply reached the stage where further assistance was ruled out, it had disappeared into remote, inaccessible courts where even the accused was

the story but to connect the legacy of the forms of action with the development of modern tort law. Originally, tort was understood not as a set of 'authentic general principles' but as 'a mere enumeration of actionable injuries'.[272] 'Thus in the Anglo-Saxon laws we find minute assessments of the compensation due for hurts to every member of the human body, but there is no general prohibition of personal violence'; furthermore, '[w]hatever agreements [were] outside the specified forms were incapable of enforcement'.[273] The forms of action, in other words, had militated against abstraction to principle.

In torts, the classic illustration of this was the emergence of actions on the case from the fourteenth century onwards. The 'action upon the case'—or 'case', to use the common abbreviation—evolved as 'a residuary title including a great number of miscellaneous cases on what would now be called nuisance or negligence'.[274] 'Wherever general trespass did not lie Case might be employed, subject to mediaeval limitations to the effect that it must not be used where another writ . . . could be used.'[275] The basic problem with writs of trespass *vi et armis* was that they lacked elasticity: successfully to bring an action of trespass, a plaintiff had to plead that the defendant had forcibly caused his injury. Case provided the plaintiff with the opportunity to plead special circumstances, such as negligence, which trespass *vi et armis* and other forms of action did not permit.[276] The classic special circumstance in English law was the liability of the master for the actions of his servant.[277] To sue the servant was in all likelihood pointless; but since the servant's actions were the immediate cause of the injury, the plaintiff would have found it difficult if not impossible to bring trespass *vi et armis* against the master. The advantage of case in this context was that it accommodated the doctrine of *respondeat superior*, enabling the plaintiff to sue the master for the servant's negligence.[278]

But while the flexibility of case—its miscellaneous, ad hoc qualities—sometimes proved a godsend to plaintiffs, this same flexibility created headaches for anyone seeking to explain trespass and case in a coherent and principled fashion. As Pollock appreciated, new causes of action did not always fit neatly into the old forms of pleading: 'the old system of the common law,' he

beyond an Advocate's reach. One might then come home one day and find on the table all the countless pleas relating to one's case, which one had drawn up with such pains and vain hopes, returned because at the new stage of the process they were not admissible, they were mere waste paper').

[272] *TLT* 21–2. [273] *TLT* 21–2.

[274] Percy H. Winfield, 'The Foundation of Liability in Tort' (1927) 27 *Columbia L. Rev.* 1–11 at 5.

[275] A. K. Kiralfy, *The Action on the Case* (London: Sweet & Maxwell, 1951), 44. Kiralfy's and Winfield's studies of case are now dated—particularly in light of the ground-breaking work by Milsom (above nn. 235, 237, and 238)—and so have to be used with circumspection. The quotations provided here are sufficiently general to be uncontroversial.

[276] On the link between case and the emergence of the tort of negligence, see Percy H. Winfield, 'The History of Negligence in the Law of Torts' (1926) 42 *LQR* 184–201 at 191–7.

[277] See John H. Wigmore, 'Responsibility for Tortious Acts: Its History' (1894) 7 *Harvard L. Rev.* 315–37, 383–405 at 330–7, 383–405.

[278] See Kaczorowski, above n.236, 1175.

observed, produced 'distinct kinds of wrong' with their 'distinct and appropriate remedies. But a strict observance of these distinctions in practice would have led to intolerable results, and a working margin was given by beneficent fictions which . . . extended the usefulness of the law at the cost of making it intricate and difficult to understand.'[279] The problem was not simply that these fictions had often proved difficult to translate into a substantive law of torts. Equally troublesome was the fact that trespass and case evolved so as to permit of no obvious principled distinction. Some forms of case, for example, had the appearance of trespass, since they involved direct harm.[280] In 1833 it was established that where the relevant harm was not wilfully inflicted, the plaintiff might elect to sue in either trespass or case.[281] Not two decades had passed before it became possible to join trespass and case in the same suit.[282] The lines between the writs, in short, had sometimes become blurred.

The fundamental problem for the nineteenth-century torts systematizer was that it was not only the forms of action that had retained much of their vitality—so too had the jurisprudential problems they had generated. Pollock captured the problem in the first edition of *Torts*. 'The ancient common law', he observes, 'knew nothing of large classifications. There were forms of action' which 'fell, in a manner, into natural classes or groups. But no attempt was made to discover or apply any general principle of arrangement.'[283] Later in the treatise he remarks that although the forms of action 'are now abolished in England', in order 'to maintain an action there must still be some cause of action known to law.'[284] And although, '[w]here there is an apparent alternative' form of action, 'we are no longer bound to choose at our peril,' it is nevertheless the case that 'we must have at least one definite ground.'[285] So it is that, on occasions, 'we have to go back to the old forms and see what the appropriate action would have been.'[286] The past was not to be shaken off easily.

c. *A law of torts*

But then the point of *Torts* was not so much to shake off the past as to incorporate what had survived of that past into a comprehensive account of tort law as it stood in Pollock's day. Since the thirteenth century, the law of torts had expanded far beyond the general action of trespass. Not only had the intervening period seen the growth of various types of action on the case (the principal being nuisance, conversion, and defamation) but there was also an

[279] *TLT* 278. [280] See Kiralfy, above n.275, 44.

[281] *Williams v Holland* (1833) 10 Bing. 112. See generally M. J. Prichard, 'Trespass, Case and the Rule in *Williams* v. *Holland*' [1964] *Cambridge L. J.* 234–53.

[282] Common Law Procedure Act 1852, 15 & 16 Vict. c. 76. s. 41.

[283] *TLT* 2. [284] *TLT* 431, and cf. Maitland's conclusion to Appendix A of the book at 474.

[285] *TLT* 431. [286] *TLT* 279.

ever expanding residuary body of precedents establishing unique torts or 'torticles'—instances, that is, in which a claimant had convinced a court that some specific loss ought to be compensated.[287] Even an analysis focusing solely on trespass would have to acknowledge that, since matters of liability were generally left to juries, little resembling legal principles existed in this field before the nineteenth century. Notwithstanding the mid-nineteenth century efforts to do away with the forms of action, in short, the substantive law of torts was basically as jumbled and unprincipled during this period as it had ever been. Any lawyer who, during the last half of that century, felt the urge to tidy up torts had a good deal of work on his hands.

Pollock set about this task with what certainly looks like a threefold plan. First of all, he felt it necessary 'to fix the contents and boundaries of the subject'.[288] Secondly, he wished to show that 'the law of torts is a body of law capable of being expressed in a systematic form and under appropriate general principles'.[289] Finally, it is clear, although he never offered any specific statement of intent to this effect, that he wanted to show that at the heart of modern tort law there rests a principle of utmost generality—namely, an overarching principle of liability. All three of these objectives need to be elaborated if we are to appreciate just how Pollock contributed to the shaping of modern tort law.

1. Compartmentalization

While fixing the boundaries of contract is difficult enough, Pollock maintained, we at least 'have this much to start from, that there are two parties, of whom one agrees to terms offered by the other. . . . In the law of torts we have no such starting-point, nothing (as it appears at first sight) but a heap of miscellaneous instances.'[290] What, after all, are the defining characteristics of a tort? We can certainly say what a tort is not: '[a] tort is an act or omission giving rise . . . to a civil remedy which is not an action of contract.'[291] The more significant challenge, however, is that of formulating a definition of tort 'beyond the restrictive and negative one'; for on this matter 'our books, ransack them as we will, refuse to utter any certain sound whatsoever'.[292] If the mish-mash of rules that make up the law of torts truly is 'founded on any general principles of duty and liability, those principles have nowhere been stated with authority'.[293] It would be easy, Pollock recognized, for the modern jurist to

[287] See Bernard Rudden, 'Torticles' (1991–2) 6/7 *Tulane Civil Law Forum* 105–29.

[288] *TLT* 1. [289] *TLT* 5. [290] *TLT* 1–2.

[291] *TLT* 4. This negative definition may have been influenced by the County Courts Act 1846, 9 & 10 Vict. c. 95, s. 129. In the Court of Appeal, the definition has been found wanting: see *Dubai Aluminium Co. Ltd v Salaam* [2001] QB 113, 132 (*per* Evans LJ).

[292] *TLT* 4.

[293] *TLT* 5. See also [Frederick Pollock], 'Torts', in *Encyclopaedia of the Laws of England*, above n.98, xii. 189–95 at 189 ('Any systematic treatment of the subject as a whole is so modern that questions

remain resigned to this state of uncertainty and to conclude that rationalizing the law of torts—with its many 'excrescences, defects, and anomalies'[294]—is very likely an impossible task. The desire to rationalize torts may even be misplaced: after all, the genius of the common law is sometimes evident from its ability—this being Pollock's argument about mutual promises—to make a virtue out of irrationality. Rather than seek to achieve what may well be impossible, Pollock believed, it is probably better to pursue the less ambitious but feasible task of compartmentalizing the different types of civil wrongs so as to impose upon the bulk of the law of torts a broad organizational structure.

Pollock's approach to the compartmentalization of torts was not wholly novel. The various 'species of torts' he organized into three groups: 'Personal Wrongs' affecting safety and freedom, personal relations, reputation, and general matters of estate; 'Wrongs to Property' (trespass being the principal of these, though this is not to overlook interference with 'franchises, patents, copyrights', and other 'rights analogous to property'); and 'Wrongs to Person, Estate, and Property generally' (being nuisance, negligence, and '[b]reach of absolute duties').[295] This organizational scheme is partly reminiscent of that to be found in Thomas Cooley's American torts treatise of 1880, which in turn brings to mind some of the structure of Book III of Blackstone's *Commentaries*.[296] Both works were clearly in Pollock's thoughts during the preparation of the first edition of *Torts*.[297]

Pollock's organization of *Torts* should not be regarded, however, simply as an adaptation of the schemes devised by Blackstone and Cooley. Behind his system there are two other sources of inspiration. In the letter of dedication which opens *Torts*, Pollock proclaims his effort 'to turn to practical account the lessons of what I saw and heard' at 'Harvard and its Law School' in 1884, 'this present book [being] in some measure the outcome of that endeavour.'[298] But it was not so much the Harvard Law School that inspired *Torts* as that most fleeting and famous member of its Faculty, Oliver Wendell Holmes, Jr., the man to whom Pollock's letter of dedication was addressed. 'You will recognize in my armoury some weapons of your own forging,' Pollock declared

going to the foundation of its legal principles are still unsettled, or so recently decided that the consequences of the decisions are not yet worked out').

[294] *TLT* 6. [295] *TLT* 7.

[296] Thomas M. Cooley, *A Treatise on the Law of Torts, or, the Wrongs Which Arise Independent of Contract* (Chicago: Callaghan & Co., 1880). That Cooley should have been influenced by Blackstone's organizational scheme is perhaps not surprising: a decade before the appearance of *A Treatise on the Law of Torts*, Cooley had compiled an American edition of the *Commentaries* (Chicago: Callaghan & Co., 1871; 2nd edn. 1872).

[297] For the presence of Cooley's work in *Torts*, see, e.g., *TLT* 61 n.*z*, 91 n.*m*, 101 n.*f*, 107 n.*z*, 121 n.*g*, 133 n.*q*, 155 n.*c*, 187 n.*x*, 244 n.*u*, 286 n.*k*, 310 n.*t*, 409 n.*d*. For the presence of Book III of the *Commentaries*, see, e.g., *TLT* 13–14 nn.*m*–*o*, 148 n.*d*, 156 n.*d*, 183 n.*b*, 189 n.*z*, 196 n.*a*, 198 n.*f*, 279 n.*k*, 282 n.*s*, 285 n.*f*, 329 n.*p*, 339 n.*o*, 343 n.*b*, 343 n.*d*, 405 n.*l*.

[298] *TLT* vi. Pollock had visited the Harvard Law School during 1884 while on a canoeing trip to Quebec: see F. Pollock, 'A Canadian Holiday' (Feb. 1885) 51 *Macmillan's Magazine* 259–65 at 264; *FMG* 193–4, 202.

to Holmes in this letter.[299] In another letter to Holmes, written two years earlier, he had professed to be largely sympathetic to the 'classification of Wrongs' that Holmes had attempted in his article, 'The Theory of Torts', first published in 1873.[300] Since the article was, in part, a broadside against Austin—specifically, against Austin's claims that culpability is a prerequisite for liability and that negligence can be 'analyzed . . . as the state of the party's mind'[301]—it is perhaps hardly surprising that Pollock should have found it to his liking. But what Pollock took from Holmes was not his criticisms of Austin—he had more than enough such criticisms of his own—but the suggestion that torts can be broadly organized under the headings of strict liability, intentional wrongs, and negligence. 'At one end . . . of the liabilities discussed in a treatise on torts,' Holmes suggested,

> we should find . . . cases . . . in which the cause of action is determined by certain overt acts or events alone, irrespective of culpability. . . . At the other extreme . . . are found those liabilities in which culpability is in general an essential element. . . . Half-way between the two groups . . . lie the great mass of cases in which negligence has become an essential averment.[302]

This notional treatise seems to be very much along the lines of the one that Pollock decided to write. Having to some extent followed Blackstone and Cooley in classifying torts in terms of personal wrongs, wrongs to property, and general wrongs, he proceeded to laminate upon this threefold scheme another one—the scheme suggested by Holmes.[303] The three groups of wrongs appear, Pollock maintained, 'to have certain distinctive characters with reference to the nature of the act or omission itself'.[304] With personal wrongs, 'generally speaking, the wrong is wilful or wanton'[305]—in other words, personal wrongs are more often than not intentional torts. Whereas, in the case of personal wrongs 'the legal wrongs are such as to be also the object of strong moral

[299] *TLT* vi.

[300] Pollock to Holmes, 3 July 1874, in *PHL* i. 4. See [O. W. Holmes, Jr.], 'The Theory of Torts' (1873) 7 *American L. Rev.* 652–63; repr. in Felix Frankfurter, 'The Early Writings of O. W. Holmes, Jr.' (1931) 44 *Harvard L. Rev.* 717–827 at 773–85.

[301] Holmes, above n.300, 652, 653 (repr. 773, 775). Cf. John Austin, *Lectures on Jurisprudence or the Philosophy of Positive Law*, 2 vols., 5th edn. R. Campbell (London: Murray, 1885), i. 476–80.

[302] Holmes, above n.300, 653 (repr. 774). Two years earlier, Holmes had suggested that 'Torts is not a proper subject for a law book'—a sentiment which makes Pollock's letter of dedication in *TLT* seem almost ironic. As is perhaps clear from the passage quoted here, however, by the time 'The Theory of Torts' was published Holmes seemed no longer to hold to this view. See [Oliver Wendell Holmes], review of C. G. Addison, *The Law of Torts* (1871) 5 *American L. Rev.* 340–1 at 341; also cf. Warren A. Seavey, 'Principles of Torts' (1942) 56 *Harvard L. Rev.* 72–98 at 72; Grey, above n.230, 1232; and John C. P. Goldberg, 'Unloved: Tort in the Modern Legal Academy' (2002) 55 *Vanderbilt L. Rev.* 1501–19 at 1505–6.

[303] See Kenneth J. Vandevelde, 'A History of Prima Facie Tort: The Origins of a General Theory of Intentional Tort' (1990) 19 *Hofstra L. Rev.* 447–97 at 462–3.

[304] *TLT* 8. [305] *TLT* 8.

condemnation', as regards wrongs to property 'this element is at first sight absent, or at any rate indifferent', so that '[t]he law . . . is stricter, on the face of things, than morality.'[306] Indeed, in this instance 'the law expects me at my peril to know what is my neighbour's in every case', and the duty which it imposes upon me 'is an absolute duty not to meddle without lawful authority with land or goods that belong to others.'[307] According to Pollock, in other words, wrongs to property are likely to be governed by strict liability. With respect to general wrongs, 'the acts or omissions complained of have a kind of intermediate character. They are not as a rule wilfully or wantonly harmful; but neither are they morally indifferent, save in a few extreme cases'.[308] These are instances in which '[t]he party has . . . done acts . . . which a prudent man in his place would know to be attended with certain risks.'[309] Having failed to guard 'against risk to others . . . which a man of common sense and competence would in his place foresee', this party faces '[l]egal liability for negligence'.[310] Thus it is that Pollock achieved an amalgamation of Blackstone, Cooley, and Holmes: personal wrongs are usually intentional torts, wrongs to property tend to be governed by strict liability, and liability for general wrongs is normally based on negligence.

Given that this amalgamation was the work of Pollock, it is perhaps inevitable that it was not straightforward. Not only did he invest it with his characteristic quota of qualifying words and phrases, but also he interpreted Holmes's scheme somewhat differently than did Holmes himself. Intentional torts, in particular, Pollock conceived more expansively than did Holmes, including under this heading not only Holmes's torts of deceit, malicious prosecution, conspiracy, and slander and libel, but also 'seduction' and the 'enticing away of servants'.[311] Pollock's approach to intentional torts warrants examination, and we will turn to it in due course. At this point, rather than dwell further on whom and what may have inspired his method of compartmentalizing torts, it is more important to consider just how he set about the exercise. For Pollock's effort at compartmentalization, as opposed to his compartmentalizing scheme, reveals a side to his legal personality that is not easily explained.

It was noted in chapter 4 that, to Pollock's mind, there are much worse things in the world than to be a legal formalist.[312] But this does not mean that he put himself forward as a formalist. The idea of being identified with a specific school or perspective was, we saw in chapter 3, anathema to him. Yet his approach to the law of torts brings him about as close to the stereotypical formalist as a jurist is ever likely to get. In *Torts*, Pollock's greatest desire seems to be to put, and to keep, everything in its proper place. Messiness must not be tolerated. Holmes might again be summoned to bear some of the

[306] *TLT* 9–10. [307] *TLT* 10. [308] *TLT* 10. [309] *TLT* 10. [310] *TLT* 11.

[311] *TLT* 7. See also Vandevelde, above n.303, 463. On the common law attitude towards the enticing away of servants, see Gareth H. Jones, 'Per Quod Servitum Amisit' (1958) 74 *LQR* 39–58.

[312] See, in particular, chapter 4, n.185.

responsibility for the outlook. 'The business of the law of torts is to fix the dividing lines between those cases in which a man is liable for harm which he has done, and those in which he is not', Holmes declared tersely in *The Common Law*.[313] While finding and maintaining bright lines is not really possible—while '[l]egal, like natural divisions, however clear in their general outline, will be found on exact scrutiny to end in a penumbra'—'the tendency of the law must' nevertheless 'always be to narrow the field of uncertainty'.[314] Holmes had a taste for tidiness as did Pollock, and to share this taste could, in Pollock's eyes, only be a virtue.[315] But to attribute Pollock's fastidious conceptualism to his admiration for Holmes would be to overlook the crucial differences between the two men. Holmes uttered his fair share of formalist sentiments—indeed, the notion of Holmesian formalism is not oxymoronic[316]—but he was not, first and foremost, a legal formalist. Having made his case in *The Common Law* for fixing the lines that assist in establishing liability, for example, Holmes turned from vague formalist into unequivocal pragmatist:

> the next question is how to determine the circumstances necessary to be known in any given case in order to make a man liable for the consequences of his act. . . . How is it decided what those circumstances are? The answer must be, by experience. . . . [E]xperience is the test by which it is decided whether the degree of danger attending given conduct under certain known circumstances is sufficient to throw risk upon the party pursuing it.[317]

Pollock understood Holmes's outlook. In his review of *The Common Law* he referred to Holmes as a purveyor of 'systematic legal criticism'—a distinctively 'American school of legal criticism distinguishable from anything that has yet taken root here'.[318] Holmes, Pollock appreciated, was both systematic and judgemental. But while *Torts* reveals Pollock's indebtedness to Holmes the systematizer—and it is crucial to emphasize that this argument concerns *Torts* specifically as opposed to Pollock's work generally—the book owes little to Holmes the pragmatist or proto-realist. And even though it would be fair to say that, at one level or another, Pollock and Holmes were both systematizers, they were very different examples of the same species. Whereas Holmes's taste for tidiness was tempered by pragmatic considerations, Pollock's taste for tidiness—certainly as exhibited in *Torts*—bordered on the obsessive. Throughout

313 Holmes, above n.137, 79. 314 Ibid. 127.

315 Hence Pollock's assessment of *The Common Law*: 'Holmes shows us how dimly felt grounds of expediency . . . have issued in the establishment of principles which are now capable of being expressed in a rational form for the most part. . . . Holmes's book will be a most valuable—we should almost say an indispensable—companion to the scientific student of legal history.' [Frederick Pollock], 'Holmes on the Common Law', 51 *Saturday Rev.*, 11 June 1881, 758–9. Cf. Pollock to Holmes, 9 October 1908, in *PHL* i. 142 ('Your outlook on things in general is much after my own heart . . .').

316 See Grant Gilmore, *The Ages of American Law* (New Haven: Yale UP, 1977), 48–56.

317 Holmes, above n.137, 147–9.

318 Pollock, 'Holmes on the Common Law', above n.315, 758.

the book, he seems extremely reluctant to countenance the possibility that the law is in a state of uncertainty. On one of the few occasions when he concedes that it is uncertain—addressing the question of whether or not inevitable accident is a ground of liability[319]—he is conspicuously irritated at being unable to straighten out 'a topic not so much obscure in itself as obscured by the indirect and vacillating treatment of it in our authorities'.[320] What look like problems invariably turn out not to be: hence, although 'the term "immediate cause" is not capable of perfect or general definition', this should cause lawyers no alarm since, 'for the purpose of civil liability, . . . consequences . . . deemed "immediate"' are those which 'a person of average competence and knowledge . . . might be expected to foresee'.[321] If it can be proved that a consequence was not 'intended or foreseen by the actor', then 'whether the consequence was "immediate" or not does not matter'.[322] Problem solved. 'This may look a mess', Pollock often seems to be saying, 'but just watch me take care of it.'

In *Torts*, there are three specific ways in which this attitude surfaces. First, there is Pollock's insistence on line-drawing. Mid-way through the first edition of *Torts*, he declares that the overlap between contract and torts—in particular, the capacity for contractual and tortious liability to co-exist—'gives rise to troublesome questions which we are not yet ready to discuss'.[323] When, in the final chapter of the book, he confronts these questions, his basic point is that although 'we have torts which are not in any natural sense independent of contract',[324] the liability issues that arise in contract and in torts can generally be delineated.[325] Indeed, for one reason or another, contract and torts are best kept separate.[326] Pollock makes much the same argument, though somewhat more forcefully, when discussing the relationship between the law of torts and the law of property. Commenting on obstruction of light as a 'species of nuisance', he worries about 'the risk of digressing from the law of Torts into the law of Easements'.[327] When writing about trespass, he inevitably cannot avoid the subject of possession.[328] Yet although 'the common law has a theory of possession, and a highly elaborated one'[329]—indeed, Pollock and R. S. Wright contributed to the elaboration of this theory in their book on possession in the common law, which appeared the year after the first edition of *Torts*—'[f]urther details on the subject would not be appropriate here. They belong rather to the law of Real Property.'[330] Everything is

[319] See *TLT* 115–29.

[320] *TLT* 129. On the ambiguity surrounding inevitable accident as a defence in English tort law, see David Kretzmer, 'Transformation of Tort Liability in the Nineteenth Century: The Visible Hand' (1984) 4 *Oxf. Jnl. Leg. Studs.* 46–87 at 74–6.

[321] *TLT* 28. [322] *TLT* 28. [323] *TLT* 354. [324] *TLT* 432. [325] See *TLT* 429–66.

[326] See, e.g., *TLT* 46 ('In the law of contract various grounds of personal disability have to be considered with some care. . . . In the law of tort it is otherwise'), 237–8 ('. . . the law of tort is here much complicated with the law of contract. . . . The grounds and results . . . of liability are largely similar, but cannot be assumed to be identical').

[327] *TLT* 336. [328] See, e.g., *TLT* 310–13. [329] *TLT* 276. [330] *TLT* 287–8.

kept neat and tidy: in *Torts*, everything other than the law of torts is swept under the carpet.

Secondly, when writing about torts, Pollock wanted simplicity as well as neatness. Like Holmes, he insisted that the exercise of establishing negligence must not involve analysing the party's state of mind.[331] 'Jurisprudence is not psychology, and law disregards many psychological distinctions not because lawyers are ignorant of their existence, but because for legal purposes it is impracticable or useless to regard them.'[332] As Pollock elaborates this point, one senses his exasperation: '[n]egligence is the contrary of diligence, and no one describes diligence as a state of mind. The question for judges and juries is not what a man was thinking or not thinking about, expecting or not expecting, but whether his behaviour was or was not such as we demand of a prudent man under the given circumstances.'[333] Nowhere is Pollock's reluctance to bring psychology into tort law more obvious than in his treatment of what lawyers of his generation, and of the following generation, commonly called 'nervous shock'.[334] The question of whether a person can be liable for causing nervous shock is not addressed in the first edition of *Torts*, for the simple reason that the courts had up until that point been given no reason to accord the question any specific attention. Soon after the appearance of *Torts*, however, the Privy Council held in *Victorian Railways Commissioners v Coultas* that illness caused by shock arising from fright could not give rise to a cause of action: the action which caused the fright could not be said to have caused immediate physical harm, and so the subsequent illness was too remote a consequence of that action.[335] Upholding the defendant's appeal, Sir Richard Couch explained that:

[d]amages arising from mere sudden terror unaccompanied by any actual physical injury, but occasioning a nervous or mental shock, cannot . . . be considered a consequence which, in the ordinary course of things, would flow from the negligen[t action]. If it were held that they can, . . . it would be extending the liability for negligence much beyond what that liability has hitherto been held to be. . . . [I]n every case where an

[331] See *TLT* 355. [332] *TLT* 355–6. [333] *TLT* 356.

[334] Today, lawyers are more likely to refer to psychiatric injury, damage, or harm rather than to nervous shock. One senior judge observed not too long ago that we need to dispense with 'the label "nervous shock,"' since it 'is not only misleading and inaccurate but, with its echoes of frail Victorian heroines, tends to disguise the very serious damage which is, in many cases, under discussion'. See the Foreword by the Rt. Hon. Sir Thomas Bingham in Nicholas J. Mullany and Peter R. Handford, *Tort Liability for Psychiatric Damage: The Law of 'Nervous Shock'* (Sydney: Law Book Co., 1993), vii. Other judges have made much the same point: see, e.g., *McLoughlin v O'Brian* [1983] 1 AC 410, 432 (*per* Lord Bridge). Nevertheless, the term is still sometimes used: see David W. Robertson, 'Liability in Negligence for Nervous Shock' (1994) 57 *Mod. L. Rev.* 649–63 at 652 n.16.

[335] *Victorian Railways Commissioners v Coultas* (1888) 13 App. Cas. 222. The plaintiffs, a man and a woman, had to cross a railway level crossing. The gates at the crossing were closed, and so the gatekeeper opened them. As the plaintiffs crossed, a train approached at rapid speed, nearly hitting the woman. The medical evidence indicated that she suffered severe nervous shock from the fright. The lower court had awarded damages, finding that the opening of the gates to the level crossing was an act of negligence.

accident caused by negligence had given a person a serious nervous shock, there might be a claim for damages on account of mental injury. . . . [T]heir Lordships decline to establish such a precedent.[336]

Victorian Railways Commissioners v Coultas is commonly cited as a good example of the 'pull-yourself-together' attitude of the late nineteenth- and early twentieth-century courts towards claims based on nervous shock. The decision, according to one commentator, 'reflected prevalent attitudes extolling the virtues of self-reliance, laced with mistrust of the fledgling discipline of psychiatry and fears of opening the floodgates'.[337] Pollock dealt with the decision in the second edition of *Torts*. '[I]t is submitted that the decision is not satisfactory',[338] he declared; but his dissatisfaction had nothing to do with the Privy Council's restrictive attitude towards the notion of nervous shock. Of course, 'the passion of fear . . . cannot in itself be regarded as measurable temporal damage; . . . the judgment appealed from, if and so far as it purported to allow any distinct damages for "mental injuries", was erroneous.'[339] What disappointed Pollock was the court's assumption that 'physical illness caused by reasonable fear' is, as a ground of action, no more plausible than is the claim of psychiatric injury.[340] *Victorian Railways Commissioners v Coultas* was accorded some authority in the United States,[341] but, to Pollock's delight, the English courts gradually came around to the view that he held.[342]

They did not stick with that view for very long, however. In the later editions of *Torts* Pollock can be found insisting, much as he had in the second

[336] *Victorian Railways Commissioners v Coultas*, ibid. 225–6.

[337] H. Teff, 'Liability for Negligently Inflicted Psychiatric Harm: Justifications and Boundaries' (1998) 57 *Cambridge L. J.* 91–122 at 92. Cf. W. G. Earengey, 'The Legal Consequences of Shock' (1992) 60 *Medico-Legal Jnl.* 83–109 at 85: 'it would be unfair to the judges of a past generation to criticize their rulings in the light of modern knowledge. . . . Even doctors in those days took little interest in what was described as "the vapours," and often refrained from giving treatment for many forms of mental disturbance which they rather contemptuously called "nerves".' Earengey's paper was originally read before the May 1933 meeting of the Medico-Legal Society and published that year in the first volume of the *Medico-Legal and Criminological Review*. For broader historical analysis of nervous shock as a legal concept, see Barbara Young Welke, *Recasting American Liberty: Gender, Race, Law, and the Railroad Revolution 1865–1920* (Cambridge: Cambridge UP, 2001), 139–234.

[338] *TLT(2)* 46. [339] *TLT(2)* 46. [340] *TLT(2)* 46–7.

[341] See, e.g., *Mitchell v Rochester Railway Co.*, 151 N.Y. 107, 45 N.E. 354 (1896); and also, generally, Archibald H. Throckmorton, 'Damages For Fright' (1921) 34 *Harvard L. Rev.* 260–81.

[342] See, e.g., *Pugh v London, Brighton and South Coast Railway Co.* [1896] 2 QB 248 (noted approvingly by Pollock at (1896) 12 *LQR* 303); *Wilkinson v Downton* [1897] 2 QB 57 (noted approvingly by Pollock at (1897) 13 *LQR* 239); *Dulieu v White & Sons* [1901] 2 KB 669 (noted approvingly by Pollock at (1901) 17 *LQR* 350); *Janvier v Sweeney* [1919] 2 KB 316 (noted approvingly by Pollock at (1919) 35 *LQR* 287–8). In *Dulieu v White*, Pollock himself, or rather his position on nervous shock, is noted approvingly (by Kennedy J. at 672). Cf. Lord Denning's unwillingness to embrace Pollock's position in the later case of *King v Phillips* [1953] 1 QB 429, 440–1. In New Zealand, where legislative reforms during the early 1990s encouraged a restrictive approach to damages claims for mental trauma, Pollock's position met with some late twentieth-century—having already received some early twentieth-century—judicial approval: see *Bradley v Wingnut Films Ltd* [1994] EMLR 195, 205–6 (NZ High Ct); also *Stevenson v Basham* (1922) 41 NZLR 225, 229–30 (NZ Sup. Ct).

edition, that '[t]he fallacy' of the courts in many nervous shock cases 'consists in supposing the fear or distress itself to be relied upon as the gist of the action.'[343] Assuming the shock and the illness to be direct consequences of the negligent act or omission, it is 'the illness, not the shock' that 'furnishes the measurable damage'.[344] Within but two years of Pollock's death, the English appeal courts had started on the path towards the modern understanding of nervous shock or psychiatric injury as a harm in itself rather than as part of the process by which harm is caused.[345] Pollock, despite his criticisms of *Victorian Railways*, came to represent a view no less old-fashioned than that exemplified by the case itself: like the Privy Council, he not only disagreed with allowing damages for any injury other than the physical kind, but he also seemed suspicious of the idea that an injury could be of anything other than the physical kind.[346] 'Psychiatric injury' would probably never, for him, have been a phrase suitable for use without scare-quotes.

The final way in which there surfaces in *Torts* a fastidious attitude towards the general subject matter is actually illustrated by Pollock's position on nervous shock. For the purposes of ascertaining negligence, he believed, fear of harm must be distinguished from physical injury ensuing from such fear, assuming this fear to be reasonably held and attributable to the defendant's act or omission. Matters of tort law, he emphasized, involve many a careful distinction, and it would be a poor lawyer who did not approach torts analytically. This is not to claim that tort law is an exercise in logic. '[T]he rule of "natural and probable consequences"', for example, 'is not a logical definition, but only a guide to the exercise of common sense', and so the lawyer does well not 'to adventure himself with philosophers in the logical and metaphysical controversies that beset the idea of cause.'[347] But a refined understanding of the law of torts does require an ability to appreciate that 'the consequence [of an act] may be more than was intended, or different',[348] and that justification is conceptually distinct from excuse[349] (even if it is not clear 'that the precise distinction is always possible to observe, or that anything turns on it'![350]), along with various other subtle conceptual differences.[351] That Pollock should have placed a premium on analytical skill is hardly surprising: we saw in chapter 3 that his co-authored book on possession was largely an

343 *TLT(13)* 52. 344 *TLT(13)* 51.

345 For an overview of how the case law has developed, see Teff, above n.337, 95–120.

346 Cf. the distinctly modern view of Lord Steyn in *White v Chief Constable of South Yorkshire Police* [1999] 2 AC 455, 492 (HL): 'Courts of law must act on the best medical insight of the day. Nowadays courts accept that there is no rigid distinction between body and mind. Courts accept that a recognisable psychiatric illness results from an impact on the central nervous system. In this sense therefore there is no qualitative difference between physical harm and psychiatric harm. And psychiatric harm may be far more debilitating than physical harm.' It would be wrong, however, to assume that Pollock's restrictive approach to nervous shock would find no supporters today. For one modern commentator very much on Pollock's wavelength, see Jane Stapleton, 'In Restraint of Tort', in *The Frontiers of Liability*, 2 vols, ed. P. B. H. Birks (Oxford: Oxford UP, 1994), ii. 83–102 at 95–6.

347 *TLT* 33. 348 *TLT* 29. 349 *TLT* 319. 350 *TLT* 93 n.*a*.

351 See, e.g., *TLT* 118 (on inevitable accident), 277 (on possession and detention).

exercise in analytical jurisprudence, and that he was himself a very good analytical jurist.

It was also observed in that chapter that Pollock was, in a very specific sense, somewhat behind the times. Notwithstanding his analytical skills, he generally declared his allegiance to a jurisprudential tradition which, by the late nineteenth century, was being consigned to the past. This observation might profitably be developed at this point. The idea of jurists' law can be understood in at least two ways: on the one hand, there are the legal explanations that jurists provide primarily for the benefit of those—mainly other jurists—who seek to understand law as an intellectual discipline; and on the other hand, there are the explanations that jurists provide for the assistance of those—mainly practitioners and students—who want to know which laws will apply where, and how those laws will work. *Torts* is primarily jurists' law in the latter sense, though it is not wholly divorced from academic concerns. At the risk of exaggerating the distinction, we might say that whereas a book such as Pollock's *Oxford Lectures* was clearly written with a university audience in mind, *Torts* reads as if meant to be read—or certainly consulted—by the likes of his colleagues at Lincoln's Inn.

It was argued in chapter 3 that analytical jurisprudence thrived because it was congenial to the knowledge requirements of the late nineteenth-century universities. Although, in *Torts*, Pollock made good use of his own analytical skills, he did so primarily for practical as opposed to intellectual purposes. His analytical approach to the law of torts was, as indicated above, part of a more broadly formalist approach to the subject. Not only did he consider the systematization of torts necessary, but he was frankly bewildered by those who approached the task in a defeatist fashion. 'I live in wonder', he wrote, why 'the learned friends who see nothing but shreds and patches in the law of civil wrongs do not go in mourning for the good old days when there was . . . only a list of compensations due for specified kinds of bodily harm.'[352] Adopting a formalist approach to torts was, for him, a good means of imposing a system and clearing up clutter.

And there was a considerable amount of clutter that needed attention. The modern substantive law of torts was difficult territory to which the old maps provided little guidance. Whereas the law of contract was blessed with towering path-breakers like Pothier and Savigny, furthermore, the law of torts had been rather unconvincingly hacked at by a number of English and American treatise writers who were mediocre at best.[353] Pollock would probably not have felt safe relying very much—he certainly avoided relying very much—on these

[352] F[rederick] P[ollock], review of P. H. Winfield, *The Province of the Law of Tort* (1931) 47 *LQR* 588–9 at 589.

[353] The likes of 'the late Mr Addison,' as Pollock wrote in 1931, 'for whose judgment nobody now cares a farthing'. Pollock, above n.352, 589. Pollock's broader point was that Addison probably deserved better treatment at the hands of history; but it is clear also that he regarded Addison—'his book on Torts was only less bad than his book on Contracts' (ibid.)—basically as a journeyman jurist.

treatises.[354] But where else could he look for guidance? Blackstone's organization and account of private wrongs was useful, but, like all his historical work, it had to be treated with a good deal of caution. Holmes was more valuable still, and Pollock, as we will see further, did not hesitate to follow his example. Holmes was not really a guide, however, but a contemporary fellow traveller taking much the same set of first steps into tort law as was Pollock himself. For someone who was seeking, without much in the way of reliable guides or earlier examples, to explain the modern law of torts in a coherent and principled fashion, it made good sense to adopt a conceptually strict, highly compartmentalized, indeed essentially formalist approach to the task. Pollock, we might say, was adopting the most obviously risk-free strategy available.

That he should have done so gives rise to an irony of sorts. By the late nineteenth century, it was fair to say that the systematic and theoretical treatment of the English law of contracts had been very much the work of jurists. In so far as there had been any comparable treatment of the law of torts, however, it was attributable in the main to the initiatives of the courts. 'Torts . . . is altogether modern', Pollock wrote in 1886, and '[t]he really scientific treatment of its principles begins only with the decisions of the last fifty years.'[355] Pollock wanted to continue, indeed he did continue, what the courts had begun: his goal was to make a crucial juristic contribution to the science of tort law. Had he been an American rather than an English jurist, his work on the law of torts would probably have ensured his place among the vanguard of the late nineteenth- and early twentieth-century legal scientists. 'The contribution of the scientists to tort law' in the United States, after all, 'was to isolate Torts as a distinct field of study, to supply that field with an overarching theoretical perspective, and to transform its existing rules and maxims into doctrines consistent, where possible, with that perspective.'[356] The American contribution was, in essence, Pollock's contribution.

Yet we saw in chapter 3 that Pollock the legal scientist was more of the old guard than of the vanguard. We know the reason for this: his academically oriented work drew upon a tradition of legal science which, by the late nineteenth century, was looking jaded. But his work as a treatise writer was, oddly enough, methodologically more attuned to the university culture of that period. Pollock was a more convincing legal scientist when he turned his attention to black letter law than when he turned his attention to jurisprudence.

Of course, jurisprudence was very much what defined him as a university professor. At Oxford, he taught mainly jurisprudence and legal history.[357]

[354] See *TLT* xxxiv. Cooley's *Treatise on the Law of Torts* was, we noted above (see nn.296–7), something of an exception here.

[355] *TLT* vi–vii.

[356] G. Edward White, *Tort Law in America: An Intellectual History*, rev. edn. (New York: Oxford UP, 2003), 38.

[357] See, e.g., Pollock notebooks, Misc. 795, 1–42 ('Oxford Lectures: October Term 1883, "Forms and Authorities of Law"'), 43–63 ('January 1884: "The Arrangement of Private Law"'), 137–75 ('Hilary

Certainly some of his lectures there covered the law of obligations,[358] but most of his teaching on contract and torts took place at the Inns of Court during the 1880s.[359] His Oxford colleagues may have thought of him as many things, but it is doubtful that they would have thought of him first and foremost as an expositor of the law of torts or contract. This is more likely to have been an identity (though, given his editorial work, certainly not the only identity) accorded to him by his colleagues in London.[360] The American legal scientists, according to White, 'were expected to "expound" upon and "systematize" their fields as well as inculcate their students in the scientific method'.[361] So far as the law of torts was concerned, Pollock certainly did his fair share of expounding and systematizing. Away from the Inns of Court, however, it is not at all obvious that he did much in the way of inculcating the method. Had he been an American law professor—a scenario which requires that we imagine Pollock with a different personality as well as a different homeland—he would in all likelihood have been caught up in what White calls 'the knowledge revolution', promoting the idea 'that knowledge, although infinite, was capable of being reduced to discernible units'.[362] As a non-resident Oxford law professor, however, he was unlikely to have become caught up in any such revolution—even if England had witnessed one.

And of course it is crucial to stress that, in England, it really would be overemphatic to claim that anything tantamount to a knowledge revolution did occur. Within the universities there were certainly epistemic shifts; most notably, there was that 'hardening of knowledge' which was discussed in chapter 3 and which seems to be part of the explanation for the flourishing of analytical jurisprudence. It is because this hardening occurred that Pollock's own incursions into jurisprudence came to have a rather wilted look to them. But this hardening process did not similarly affect Pollock's treatise writing. That it ever could have seems almost inconceivable, for his treatises, particularly his many editions of *Torts*, were as carefully compartmentalized and analytical as any late-Victorian scientific thinker might have wished for. The

Term 1889—"Analytical Jurisprudence"'), Misc. 798, 1–35 ('Oxford 1898–1901. Theory of the State in English Publicists. History of Courts and Procedure in England').

358 See Pollock notebooks, Misc. 795, 64–77 ('January 1885: "Theory of Civil Liability"'), also 102–19 ('Michaelmas Term 1886: "Possession"' [these lectures were repeated, Pollock states (ibid. 137) in the October terms of 1888 and 1890]).

359 See, e.g., Pollock notebooks, Misc. 797, 1–75 (1884 October Term and Michaelmas Term lecture notes on the 'Principles of the Law of Torts'), 104–22 (1885 Hilary Term notes on 'Possession and Trespass'), 124–32 (notes for the 1886 Easter and Trinity terms on 'The Relations of Contract and Tort'), 133–8 (1886 Michaelmas Term notes on 'The Law of Contract—with special reference to Finch's Select Cases'), 139–48 (1887 Hilary Term (untitled) notes on contracts), Misc. 798, 1–88 (various sets of Inns of Court lectures on torts and, mainly, contract). See also Frederick Pollock, 'Liability for the Torts of Agents and Servants' (1885) 1 *LQR* 207–24 at 207 n.1.

360 Both *Principles* and *Torts* were recommended reading for those studying for the Bar in the late nineteenth century: see W. W. Rouse Ball, *The Student's Guide to the Bar*, 4th edn. (London: Macmillan, 1887), 62–3. Interestingly, Rouse Ball lists *Torts* as necessary reading and *Principles* as 'desirable' reading.

361 White, above n.356, 39.

362 Ibid. 26, 25.

irony is that while this body of work was widely admired by legal instructors and practitioners, it was jurists' law in the second rather than in the first of the senses that we have outlined—it was not the work that defined him as a university jurist. In this latter capacity, Pollock was as if fated half-heartedly to promote a legal-scientific notion which seemed, by the time that he succeeded Maine, to be sinking in quicksand.

2. *A family of principles*

Writers on tort law have been fond of pointing out that, beyond the fact that it is a French word for wrong, 'tort' eludes a satisfactory simple definition. '[T]he term "tort" cannot be defined in language not itself needing definition', Pollock's friend, Melville Bigelow observed. 'The difficulty grows out of the fact that there is no such thing as a typical example, an actual tort, that is to say, which contains all the elements entering into every other.'[363] Pollock saw no reason to adopt a different line. 'It is hardly possible', he wrote, 'to frame a definition of a tort that will satisfy all the meanings in which the term has been used by persons and in documents of more or less authority in our law, and will at the same time not be wider than any of the authorities warrant.'[364] The fact that it is impossible to find a comprehensive definition of a tort does not mean, nevertheless, that it is impossible 'to sum up the normal idea of tort'.[365] According to Pollock, when a person suffers a harm which arises from 'an act or omission' (which is not 'merely the breach of duty arising out of a personal relation, or undertaken by contract'), a tort exists. The act or omission may give rise to the tort in four ways: the act may have been intended to cause the harm complained of; it may not only have caused harm but also be contrary to law or 'an omission of specific legal duty'; it may have caused harm which was unintentional but which should have been foreseen and prevented; or it may be that the defendant failed to avoid or prevent harm which he or she was under a duty to avoid or prevent.[366] Liability for the tort does not necessarily rest only with the person who acts or omits to act, for 'running through the whole' of tort law is 'the rule that a master is answerable for the acts and defaults of his servants in the course of their employment.'[367]

[363] Melville M. Bigelow, *Elements of the Law of Torts: A Text Book for Students* (Cambridge: Cambridge UP, 1889), 3. In much the same vein, see, e.g., P. H. Winfield, *A Text-Book of the Law of Tort* (London: Sweet & Maxwell, 1937), 1 ('[I]t is perhaps impossible to give an exact definition of "a tort", . . . and . . . it is certainly impossible to give a definition which will satisfy every theorist who has taken any interest in the topic'); Thomas Atkins Street, *The Foundations of Legal Liability: A Presentation of the Theory and Development of the Common Law*, 3 vols. (Northport, NY: Thompson, 1906), i. xxv ('No definition of tort at once logical and precise can be given. . . . [T]here is no typical tort, and in the nature of things it is impossible that a specification of the circumstances under which delictual liability is imposed should have finality'). Any torts lawyer will know how easily these examples could be multiplied.

[364] *TLT* 18–19. [365] *TLT* 19. [366] *TLT* 19.

[367] *TLT* 19–20, also 63 ('Whoever commits a wrong is liable for it himself. It is no excuse that he was acting, as an agent or servant, on behalf of and for the benefit of another. But that other may well also be liable').

In describing tort thus, Pollock, by his own concession, had not provided a definition of the term. 'This is indication [of 'general principles'] rather than definition', he wrote.[368] '[B]ut to have guiding principles indicated is something.'[369] The key to advancing the science of tort law is to explain, elaborate, connect, and distinguish these principles—to move beyond 'a mere enumeration of actionable injuries'[370] and to produce instead a 'continuous view'[371] of the subject. Not surprisingly, most of *Torts* is devoted to this general task. Like Pollock's contracts treatise, it is crammed full with statements of principle: '[n]o man can authorize a thing and at the same time affect to disavow its consequences'; 'an officer is not protected from the ordinary consequence of unwarranted acts which it rested with himself to avoid'; '[t]he law does not and cannot undertake to make men render active service to their neighbours at all times when a good and brave man would do so'[372]—examples such as these can be found by selecting almost any page of *Torts* at random. More often than not, Pollock was trying to highlight and clarify principles where, in the case law, 'the true principle is indicated but not made prominent'.[373] At other junctures he wished to tackle what he termed 'real difficulties of principle',[374] and, in particular, to dispel questionable or false notions of principle: hence, the 'proposition' that there is a 'principle . . . that "a man is presumed to intend the natural consequences of his acts" . . . is acceptable, but . . . ambiguous'; furthermore, contrary to the principle stated in 'some books', there 'is no such general rule of law' that 'a man cannot sue for injury suffered by him at the time when he is himself the wrong-doer.'[375]

Odd though it may seem, it is because *Torts* is so unswervingly focused upon principles that it has little legal relevance today: the law of torts has changed so much that most of Pollock's discussion of principles is out of date, and even those parts of his discussion which remain valid have been superseded by more modern presentations. From the perspectives of jurisprudence and legal history, none the less, there are facets of Pollock's project that are intriguing. Consider, first of all, a jurisprudential observation. It was noted in chapter 4 that although it is hardly likely that Pollock would have failed to see that legal principles have a moral dimension, he accorded this moral dimension no special significance. The manner in which he dealt with the principles of tort law provides a clue as to why this should have been the case. The illustrations of Pollock's statements of principle selected in the paragraph above indicate that he did not consider all legal principles to be of the same kind. Stating the legal principle sometimes meant providing the reason for the existence of a legal rule. But more often than not, when Pollock stated a legal principle what he was actually doing was setting out the legal rule itself. This, indeed, is why much of his discussion of the law of torts bears so little relevance to the law

[368] *TLT* 19–20. [369] *TLT* 20. [370] *TLT* 22.

[371] *TLT* 177. The language is reminiscent of Holmes, above n.137, 131 ('. . . whether . . . fraudulent, malicious, intentional, and negligent wrongs can be brought into a philosophically continuous series').

[372] *TLT* 73, 102, 352. [373] *TLT* 384. [374] *TLT* 438. [375] *TLT* 30, 150.

as it stands today. Usually, for Pollock, to state the principle is simply to state the law.

This last observation takes us back to an argument which was elaborated in chapter 4, and which might usefully be developed here. It would be an overstatement to claim that the distinguishing of principles and rules was a late twentieth-century jurisprudential development. Certainly Ronald Dworkin has done much to elevate the notion of principle within modern jurisprudence, so that, in his writings and in the writings of like-minded legal philosophers, principles are very obviously more than just legal rules. But it is too often assumed that because Dworkin and other modern legal philosophers have emphasized the notion of principle thus, their forerunners must have been wholly neglectful of what principles stand for. As the twentieth century drew to a close, various legal philosophers began to argue—and argue convincingly—that there is something fundamentally wrongheaded about the supposition that Dworkinian legal philosophy must be somehow more sophisticated than modern legal positivism.[376] The most famous representative of modern positivist jurisprudence set out clearly and modestly what, for our purposes, is the most significant facet of this argument. In his Postscript to *The Concept of Law*, H. L. A. Hart commented that notwithstanding his original failure to accord sufficient consideration to 'arguments from what my critics call legal principles',[377] the Dworkinian contrast between rules and principles is none the less too sharp.[378] Not only, Hart added, have those critics tended to neglect what he himself considered to be his understated acknowledgement of the operation of principles within adjudication and legal reasoning,[379] but they have also failed to appreciate that 'there is . . . no incompatibility . . . between the admission of principles as part of the law and the doctrine of a rule of recognition'.[380] Hart's basic reaction to those who considered him to have neglected the legal significance of principles was one of bewilderment: 'what precisely is it that I am charged with ignoring? What are legal principles, and how do they differ from legal rules? As used by legal writers "principles" often include a vast array of theoretical and practical con-

[376] The best exposition of this argument so far is that of Matthew H. Kramer, *In Defense of Legal Positivism: Law without Trimmings* (Oxford: Oxford UP, 1999), 128–92. For a challenging response to Kramer, see David Dyzenhaus, 'Positivism's Stagnant Research Programme' (2000) 20 *Oxf. Jnl. Leg. Studs.* 703–22; and for a rejoinder that lives up to the challenge, see Matthew H. Kramer, 'Dogmas and Distortions: Legal Positivism Defended—A Reply to David Dyzenhaus' (2001) 21 *Oxf. Jnl. Leg. Studs.* 673–701. For yet further interventions, see David Dyzenhaus, 'Caveat Reviewer: A Reply to Matthew Kramer' (2001) 21 *Oxf. Jnl. Leg. Studs.* 703–4; and James Allan, 'A Modest Proposal' (2003) 23 *Oxf. Jnl. Leg. Studs.* 197–210.

[377] H. L. A. Hart, *The Concept of Law*, 2nd edn. (Oxford: Clarendon Press, 1994), 259.

[378] See ibid. 259–63.

[379] As Hart himself noted, the failure of his critics to appreciate his acknowledgement of the role of principles is probably attributable to the fact that he tended not to refer to principles explicitly: see ibid. 263, 132–3 (on the use in law of 'common judgments of what is "reasonable"' or of 'variable standard[s]'—sc., principles—such as 'the use of the standard of due care in cases of negligence'); for explicit resort to the notion of principle, cf. ibid. 159.

[380] Ibid. 266.

siderations only some of which Dworkin meant to raise.'[381] Like Pollock, Hart spent his pupillage at Lincoln's Inn,[382] and both men seem to have adopted what we might call a Chancery barrister's commonsensical view of principles: neither wanted to play down the role of principles within the law, but both were insistent that there is no point in treating principles as if they were not part of the fabric of the law. For lawyers, according to this view, principles are useful, indeed indispensable, but there is no need to aggrandize them.

In so far as *Torts* holds any interest for us today, it is because there are legal-historical as opposed to jurisprudential lessons to be learned from Pollock's treatment of principles. Pollock presents the principles of tort law as if they made up one big family—this is the secret to his exposition of a unitary Law of Torts—and it is perhaps not surprising to discover that he had his family favourites. Critical commentary is as thin on the ground in *Torts* as it is in *Principles of Contract*—the typical Pollockian criticism is that 'it would be a pity if the principle were not reconsidered by a higher court'.[383] But *Torts* differs from *Principles* in one significant respect. When, in *Principles*, Pollock made a case for the principle of good faith in contractual negotiations, he was advancing an argument which, being normative, was conspicuously different from the general tenor of analysis in that treatise. But in *Torts* the resort to normative commentary is not quite so unusual. This is probably because, as compared with the law of contract, the subject of torts was more up-in-the-air. Whatever the reason, it is clear that Pollock was willing to express his preference for certain principles over others, and to argue that some principles ought to be treated as law even when the courts were not committed to treating them thus.

There is no need to examine every instance in *Torts* where Pollock shows a preference for a particular principle. In at least four instances, nevertheless, his preferences make for interesting reading in light of how English tort law developed or because of how his work on torts has been interpreted. The first of these instances concerns remoteness of damage. In the modern history of English law, two competing principles have been used to determine the scope of liability in negligence. The first of these principles has it that negligent wrongdoers should be held liable for all direct consequences of their, or their agent's, actions, even if those consequences were not reasonably foreseeable. This is the principle upon which the Court of Appeal eventually settled in

[381] Ibid. 259–60.

[382] Whereas Pollock was a nonentity as a practising barrister, Hart was a success. 'He read for the Bar examinations and was called to the Bar in 1932. For the next eight years he practised as a Chancery barrister establishing a successful junior practice in such complicated matters as trusts, family settlements and succession, and related questions of taxation.' Neil MacCormick, *H. L. A. Hart* (London: Arnold, 1981), 2. A detailed account of Hart's period at Lincoln's Inn appears in chapter 3 of Nicola Lacey's *A Life of H. L. A. Hart: The Nightmare and the Noble Dream* (Oxford: Oxford UP, forthcoming 2004).

[383] See, e.g., *TLT* 56 ('*Osborn v Gillett* stands in the book, and we cannot actually say it is not law; but one would like to see the point reconsidered by the Court of Appeal').

1921 in *Re Polemis*.[384] The second principle has it that consequences are too remote, and so do not give rise to liability, if a reasonable man would not have foreseen them. This principle had been somewhat hesitantly propounded in 1850 by Pollock C. B.,[385] and was stated more confidently by his grandson in *Torts*. Confidence aside, however, Frederick Pollock knew that in putting forth this principle he was not stating the law but making an argument for what the law should be. '[F]or the purpose of civil liability,' he wrote, 'consequences . . . deemed "immediate," "proximate," or . . . "natural and probable"' are those 'which a person of average competence and knowledge . . . might be expected to foresee.'[386] In stating as much, however, he was outlining not the position in law but '[t]he view which I shall endeavour to justify'.[387] Support for his view, leaving aside his grandfather's remarks, could be found in only one nineteenth-century English decision;[388] even in the first half of the twentieth century, furthermore, judicial alliance with what might be termed the Pollock line only took the form of dicta.[389]

But this line did become law. It was noted above that, in stressing that tort law is not a matter of logic, Pollock argued in *Torts* that the rule of 'natural and probable consequences' must be treated as a guide to the exercise of common sense rather than as a logical definition. Bankes L. J., delivering the leading judgment in *Re Polemis*, drew attention to what he considered to be the wisdom of Pollock's argument.[390] Pollock, however, was in no mind to repay the compliment. 'The Lords Justices [in *Re Polemis*] quote the opinions on which they rely, and say nothing of . . . ones which are hardly consistent with their view', he wrote; worse still, their judgments are unnecessarily abstruse:

> The judgments touch more or less on the questions of terminology which beset the adjectives 'natural,' 'probable,' and 'proximate.' But, with great respect, the question accepted as correct when and so far as the existence of liability is wholly in dispute—namely: Is the damage such as the defendant could reasonably be expected to anticipate?—avoids all these niceties of words. It says nothing about nature or probability,

[384] *Re Polemis* [1921] 3 KB 560. Although this decision established the principle, its establishment had probably been a long time coming: see Ibbetson, above n.49, 176.

[385] See *Rigby v Hewitt* (1850) 5 Ex. 240, 243; *Greenland v Chaplin* (1850) 5 Ex. 243, 248 (dissenting on point).

[386] *TLT* 28.

[387] *TLT* 28. Over a decade before the appearance of *Torts*, the American torts jurist, Francis Wharton, had offered qualified support for Pollock C. B.'s principle. See Francis Wharton, *A Treatise on the Law of Negligence* (Philadelphia: Kay, 1874), § 78. As compared with Wharton's analysis of the principle, that to be found in *Torts* is casually formulated. For the argument that Pollock's formulation is 'thoroughly muddled', see Abraham Harari, *The Place of Negligence in the Law of Torts* (Sydney: Law Book Co. of Australasia, 1962), 94 n.33.

[388] *Sharp v Powell* (1872) L.R. 7 C.P. 253. See also *TLT* 43 ('the rule . . . laid down [in *Sharp v Powell*] . . . , it is submitted, is the right one').

[389] See *Cory v France, Fenwick & Co.* [1911] 1 KB 114, 122; *Bournhill v Young* [1943] AC 93, 101; *Woods v Duncan* [1946] AC 401, 442.

[390] *Re Polemis*, above n.384, 569–70, citing *TLT(11)* 35–6.

and steers clear of the philosophers' controversies on the relation of cause and effect. It is a question intelligible to plain men, even if they do not always agree in their answers in the particular case.[391]

Pollock did not make any further significant progress with his assault on the principle supported in *Re Polemis*—although, on more than one occasion during his lifetime, the English courts were prepared explicitly to endorse his understanding of remoteness and causation.[392] Responsibility for advancing the campaign fell, rather, to his successor at the helm of the *Law Quarterly Review*. Between the 1920s and the 1960s, Arthur Goodhart used the pages of the *LQR* relentlessly to promote and elaborate Pollock's position on liability for consequences.[393] His support for that position by no means convinced everybody.[394] Nevertheless, his efforts made a critical impression on some senior members of the judiciary.[395] When, in 1961, the Judicial Committee of the Privy Council basically endorsed Goodhart's campaign, concluding that 'a man should be responsible for the natural or necessary or probable consequences of his act' where 'it is judged by the standard of the reasonable man that he ought to have foreseen them',[396] his work in this context—and Pollock's work—was done.[397]

Our second example of Pollock's choice of a principle is by no means as significant as the first, and can be dealt with comparatively briefly. It is a choice which evolves out of the question whether inevitable accident is a plausible defence to an action for trespass. Pollock, it was noted earlier, was

[391] Frederick Pollock, 'Liability for Consequences' (1922) 38 *LQR* 165–7 at 166–7. See further *TLT(12)* vii ('It may be presumptuous to be dissatisfied with the unanimous judgment of a strong Court, but I cannot help thinking that too much stress was laid on recent dicta of eminent judges which were not strictly necessary for arriving at the results, and too little on the general current of nineteenth-century authorities'); and ibid. 35–51; also *TLT(13)* 37–9.

[392] See *Adelaide Steamship Company v The Crown* (1922) 10 Lloyd's L. Rep. 288, 292, KBD (*per* McCardie J.); *Haynes v Harwood* [1935] 1 KB 146, 163, CA (*per* Maugham L. J.). In the latter case, counsel for the respondent were stopped after citing the very passage from *TLT* upon which Maugham L. J. relied: see ibid. 149–50. Maugham himself was not citing Pollock directly, but was quoting a passage from the decision of the King's Bench Division in which Finlay J. had cited the passage from *TLT*: see *Haynes v Harwood* [1934] 2 KB 240, 248. This possibly explains why counsel felt safe to cite the passage themselves. Cf. also *Matthews v MacLaren* [1969] 1 Lloyd's Rep. 374, 381 (Can. Sup. Ct of Ontario).

[393] See, e.g., A. L. Goodhart, 'The Imaginary Necktie and the Rule in *Re Polemis*' (1952) 68 *LQR* 514–35; 'Liability and Compensation' (1960) 76 *LQR* 567–88 at 568; and his case notes at (1928) 44 *LQR* 142 and (1954) 70 *LQR* 306. Goodhart pursued his mission mainly, but not exclusively, in the *LQR*: see also Goodhart, 'Liability for the Consequences of a "Negligent Act"', in *Cambridge Legal Essays: Written in Honour of and Presented to Doctor Bond, Professor Buckland and Professor Kenny*, eds. P. H. Winfield and A. D. McNair (Cambridge: Heffer & Sons, 1926), 101–21 (repr. in Goodhart, *Essays in Jurisprudence and the Common Law*, above n.180, 110–28).

[394] See, in particular, H. L. A. Hart and Tony Honoré, *Causation in the Law*, 2nd edn. (Oxford: Clarendon Press, 1985), 254–75. Hart and Honoré had their own detractors: see, e.g., Glanville Williams, 'The Risk Principle' (1961) 77 *LQR* 179–212.

[395] See Duxbury, above n.5, 93–8.

[396] *Overseas Tankship (U.K.) Ltd v Morts Dock and Engineering Co. Ltd (The Wagon Mound)* [1961] AC 388, 423 (*per* Viscount Simonds).

[397] See A. L. Goodhart, 'Obituary: Re Polemis' (1961) 77 *LQR* 175–8 at 175–6; *Hughes v Lord Advocate* [1963] 2 WLR 779, HL Sc. (affirming Privy Council decision); and Goodhart (1964) 80 *LQR* 1–4.

conspicuously exasperated by the lack of legal certainty on this matter. But he did not let the problem defeat him: throughout successive editions of *Torts* he amassed doctrinal support for the principle that inevitable accident is a satisfactory defence, so long as the accident results from a lawful act executed in a reasonable and careful manner.[398] A defendant might escape liability for trespass, in other words, if he or she could prove that the accident occurred despite the exercise of reasonable care. The apparent simplicity of this principle certainly appealed to some judges and barristers during the middle part of the twentieth century.[399] Thanks to Pollock the principle became 'so well recognized', Lord Denning wrote in 1951, 'that the action for trespass to the person is comparatively rare'.[400] But if Pollock's preference for a principle did have any consequence in this instance, the consequence was short-lived. In 1959, in *Fowler v Lanning*, Diplock J. held that the burden of proving negligence in actions for unintentional trespass to the person lay upon the claimant rather than the defendant.[401] Subsequently, this ruling was upheld by the Court of Appeal.[402] In cases of trespass, therefore, inevitable accident today has no place as a defence because it is for the claimant to establish the defendant's negligence.[403] At the risk of appearing to lurch from trespass to nuisance, it might be noted that if, as in the landmark case of *Rylands v Fletcher*,[404] a defendant is liable notwithstanding that he has taken reasonable care, it can hardly benefit him to prove inevitable accident.[405] The principle which Denning once considered so well recognized is now not recognized at all.[406]

More interesting—to move to our third illustration—is Pollock's interpretation of *Rylands v Fletcher* itself. In essence, we noted earlier, Pollock accepted Holmes's general branching of torts into strict liability, intentional wrongs, and negligence. We also noted that Pollock considered strict liability to apply in the main to wrongs to property. Indeed, *Rylands v Fletcher* was another of those instances that drew out his formalist streak: '[t]he detailed illustration of the rule in *Rylands v Fletcher*', he declared in *Torts*, 'belongs to the law of property rather than to the subject of this work.'[407] All the same, Pollock dedicated over twenty pages of his book to the case and, apparently keen to ensure that they

[398] See, e.g., *TLT(3)* 121–35; *TLT(6)* 131–45.

[399] See, e.g., *Read v J. Lyons & Co.* [1945] KB 216, 244–5, CA (*per* du Parcq L. J.); *National Coal Board v J. E. Evans & Co.* [1951] 2 KB 861, 864, CA (*arguendo*); *The Paludina* [1927] AC 16, 18, HL (*arguendo*). Cf. *Fowler v Lanning* [1959] 1 QB 426, 430–1, QBD (*per* Diplock J.).

[400] Denning, above n.20, 263.

[401] See *Fowler v Lanning*, above n.399.

[402] *Letang v Cooper* [1965] 1 QB 232. In fact, the ruling had been presaged over a decade before the appearance of *TLT*: see *Holmes v Mather* (1875) L.R. 10 Ex. 261, which Pollock struggled with at *TLT* 127–9.

[403] This is not to discount the possibility of *res ipsa loquitur*, i.e. the fact of the accident may raise an inference of negligence which, if not rebutted, is sufficient to impose liability on the defendant.

[404] *Rylands and Horrocks v Fletcher* (1865) 3 H. & C. 774 (Court of Exchequer); (1866) L.R. 1 Ex. 265 (Court of Exchequer Chamber); (1868) L.R. 3 H.L. 330 (House of Lords).

[405] Cf. *TLT* 128.

[406] See further W. V. H. Rogers, *Winfield & Jolowicz on Tort*, 16th edn. (London: Sweet & Maxwell, 2002), 868–9.

[407] *TLT* 397–8.

would not go unnoticed, published them separately as an article in the *Law Quarterly Review*.[408] That the case should have occupied him so is not surprising. Although *Rylands v Fletcher* essentially restated older strands of authority in the form of a general principle,[409] that principle seemed, for Pollock and for others, to run counter to one which had begun to emerge in the English law of torts during the nineteenth century: the principle, that is, that liability should be imposed only for negligent conduct.[410] In *Rylands v Fletcher*, as students of English law know, the House of Lords (affirming the decision of the Court of Exchequer Chamber) held that a person who brings onto his land something likely to do damage if it escapes will—in the event that it does escape[411]—be liable, irrespective of fault, for any consequential damage. Although the decision was to be reined in by a number of defences—consent of the claimant, act of a stranger, act of God, and so on[412]—it established, in essence, that where something dangerous escapes from a person's land, the law will impose strict liability rather than apply a general standard of reasonable care. Holmes, who by no means believed that nineteenth-century tort law was reducible to negligence, saw wisdom in *Rylands v Fletcher*: 'the safest way to secure care', he maintained, 'is to throw risk upon the person who decides what precautions shall be taken.'[413] Pollock put forward a similar point: according to the rule in *Rylands v Fletcher*, 'certain things are a source of extraordinary risk, and a man who exposes his neighbour to such risk is held, although

[408] Frederick Pollock, 'Duties of Insuring Safety: The Rule in *Rylands v Fletcher*' (1886) 2 *LQR* 52–65.

[409] See F. H. Newark, 'The Boundaries of Nuisance' (1949) 65 *LQR* 480–90 at 487 ('*Rylands v Fletcher* . . . is generally regarded as an important landmark—indeed, a turning point—in the law of tort; but an examination of the judgments shows that those who decided it were quite unconscious of any revolutionary or reactionary principles implicit in the decision. They thought of it as calling for no more than a restatement of settled principles. . . . And in fact the main principle involved was extremely simple, being no more than the principle that negligence is not an element in the tort of nuisance').

[410] See Frederick Pollock, review of J. C. Miles, *A Digest of English Civil Law* (1910) 26 *LQR* 420–2 at 421 ('In our judgment the Common Law is coming, if it has not already come, to hold that a man who wilfully or negligently causes temporal damage of any kind is liable unless he can show justification or excuse'); Simpson, above n.66, 197–8; also Roscoe Pound, 'Natural Natural Law and Positive Natural Law' (1960) 5 *Natural Law Forum* 70–82 at 73 ('Pollock was convinced that liability without fault was a survival from the primitive household organization of society and was on the way to disappear from the law'); and, more generally, A. H. Manchester, *A Modern Legal History of England and Wales 1750–1950* (London: Butterworths, 1980), 297–301.

[411] And if that person's use of the land was 'non-natural'. Blackburn J. made no mention of this proviso in his crucial judgment in Exchequer Chamber; rather, it was introduced by Lord Cairns in the House of Lords: see (1868) L.R. 3 H.L. 330, 337–40; and, for a doctrinally-situated analysis of 'non-natural', see F. H. Newark, 'Non-Natural User and *Rylands v Fletcher*' (1961) 24 *Mod. L. Rev.* 557–71.

[412] See, e.g., *Gill v Edouin* (1894) 71 L.T. 762; 72 L.T. 579; *Box v Jubb* (1879) 4 Ex. D. 76; *Nichols v Marsland* (1876) 2 Ex. D. 1.

[413] Holmes, above n.137, 117. For a critical analysis of the argument that Holmes advocated the establishment of negligence as the universal rule in tort law, see David Rosenberg, *The Hidden Holmes: His Theory of Torts in History* (Cambridge, Mass.: Harvard UP, 1995). Rosenberg endeavours to show that Holmes consistently argued in favour of strict liability. See also Grey, above n.230, 1275–6; and cf. Holmes to Pollock, 22 March 1891, in *PHL* i. 35–6 ('The general criterion of liability in tort . . . is the tendency of an act under the circumstances known to the actor—according to common experience. If the probability of harm is very great and manifest the act is called malicious or intentional. . . . If less but still sufficient to impose liability it is called negligent').

his act is not itself wrongful, to insure his neighbour against any consequent harm'.[414] But whereas Holmes was saying why, in his opinion, the decision made good sense, Pollock was simply setting out what he considered to be the rationale behind it. The differences of approach are significant. Holmes struggled to square *Rylands v Fletcher* with his theory of external standards, but nevertheless appeared to like the decision.[415] Pollock struggled with the decision and disliked it.

Ironically, Pollock disliked *Rylands v Fletcher* largely because he liked what Holmes had to say about liability. '[T]he standards of the law are external standards,' Holmes wrote in *The Common Law*.[416]

> [A] certain average of conduct . . . is necessary to the general welfare. If, for instance, a man is born hasty and awkward, is always having accidents and hurting himself or his neighbors, no doubt his congenital defects will be allowed for in the courts of Heaven, but his slips are no less troublesome to his neighbors than if they sprang from guilty neglect. His neighbors accordingly require him, at his proper peril, to come up to their standard, and the courts which they establish decline to take his personal equation into account.[417]

Pollock took this idea of external standards to heart and attempted to use it as a foundation-stone within his own jurisprudence. That effort, we saw in chapter 3, met with little success—largely because it never became clear that Pollock actually had a jurisprudential perspective of his own. When writing about torts, however, he resorted to the notion of external standards with considerably more confidence. The notion shows how *Rylands v Fletcher* could have been decided on the basis of negligence, he contended, as opposed to strict liability: '[t]he law', that is, 'might have been content with applying the general standard of reasonable care, in the sense that a reasonable man dealing with a dangerous thing . . . will exercise a keener foresight and use more anxious precaution than if it were an object unlikely to cause harm.'[418] 'A rule casting the responsibility of an insurer on innocent persons is a hard rule,' he continued, and 'one does not see why the policy of the law might not have been

[414] *TLT* 394. See also Rosenberg, above n.413, 156, where a similar parallel is drawn.

[415] See Holmes, above n.137, 156–8; also Fifoot, above n.21, 51–2; Simpson, above n.66, 197; and, more generally, Nathan Isaacs, 'Fault and Liability' (1918) 31 *Harvard L. Rev.* 954–79. Much as Holmes's position on *Rylands v Fletcher* was not Pollock's own, Pollock nevertheless appreciated it and did not misrepresent it: see Rosenberg, above n.413, 154.

[416] Holmes, above n.137, 110. Cf. James Barr Ames, 'Law and Morals' (1908) 22 *Harvard L. Rev.* 97–113 at 106 (repr. in Ames, *Lectures on Legal History*, above n.123, 435–52 at 439–40); Tony Honoré, *Responsibility and Fault* (Oxford: Hart, 1999), 24–5.

[417] Holmes, above n.137, 108.

[418] *TLT* 393. See further Rosenberg, above n.413, 152. The argument that *Rylands v Fletcher* would have been better decided on the basis of negligence instead of strict liability now holds good in Australia: see *Burnie Port Authority v General Jones Pty Ltd* (1994) 120 ALR 42 (removing the rule in *Rylands v Fletcher* from Australian law on the basis that adequate protection is afforded by a 'non-delegable duty' in negligence).

satisfied by requiring the defendant to insure diligence in proportion to the manifest risk.'[419] Of course, his indicated preference of principle could not change anything: the rule in *Rylands v Fletcher* may well have struck Pollock 'as at once historically unwarranted and ethically unsound',[420] Fifoot has observed, but he 'could only accept and deplore a *res judicata*'.[421] The question, for Pollock, seemed to be whether he could limit the damage inflicted by *Rylands v Fletcher*.

Pollock believed that this was possible. 'The authority of *Rylands v Fletcher* is unquestioned, but . . .'[422]—this short phrase captures his attitude towards the decision: while it had to be accepted, at least two lines of argument could be developed to try to ensure that its application was restricted. First, there were those defences against the rule—consent of the claimant, act of a stranger, act of God, and the like—some of which had been adverted to in the judgment of Blackburn J. in *Rylands v Fletcher* in the Exchequer Chamber.[423] That judgment, Pollock noted, 'carefully prepared as it evidently was,' did not offer a principle 'clear enough for universal acceptance'.[424] Secondly, the strictness of strict liability inevitably produced some anomalous consequences. Imagine, Pollock hypothesized, that a railway company failed to maintain an embankment over which its tracks ran, so that a train is derailed and its passengers are injured. Imagine also that the collapse of the embankment 'throws water, or earth, or both, upon a neighbour's land so as to do damage there. The result of applying the rule in *Rylands v Fletcher* will be that the duty of the railway company as landowner to the adjacent landowner is higher than its duty as carrier to persons whom it has contracted to carry safely; or property is more highly regarded than life and limb.'[425] Thus it was that Pollock chipped away at the rule in *Rylands v Fletcher*. As is so often the case with Pollock, he occupied a middle ground of sorts, clearly unhappy with the rule and yet resigned to the necessity of a residuary body of strict liability in tort law.[426] It is not possible to determine whether he was successful in his efforts to limit the application of the rule. But it is clear that the rule was rarely applied in the twentieth century and that its scope was restricted by the courts.[427] Whatever Pollock's influence on the reception of *Rylands v Fletcher*, it is unlikely that its fate would have troubled him.

Our final example of Pollock demonstrating significant support for a particular principle centres upon his efforts to grapple with another form of liability. 'Vicarious liability'—liability incurred by one party for the torts committed by someone else—is a phrase that Pollock purported to have

[419] *TLT* 398–9. [420] Fifoot, above n.30, 10. [421] Fifoot, above n.21, 54.
[422] *TLT* 401. [423] See *TLT* 400–3. [424] *TLT* 398. [425] *TLT* 404.
[426] See J. L. Barton, 'Liability for Things in the Nineteenth Century' [1984] *Law & Social Change* 145–55 at 152.
[427] On the rarity of *Rylands v Fletcher* liability claims, see, e.g., *Atiyah's Accidents, Compensation and the Law*, 5th edn. P. Cane (London: Butterworths, 1993), 85. On the restrictive approach of the courts, see, e.g., *Read v J. Lyons & Co. Ltd* [1947] AC 156, HL; *Cambridge Water Co. v Eastern Counties Leather plc* [1994] 2 AC 264, HL.

coined.[428] This type of liability, according to Fifoot, he disliked more than he did strict liability.[429] Pollock's position, however, was subtler than this assessment suggests. When, in 1916, Thomas Baty produced a book forthrightly denouncing the doctrine of vicarious liability, Pollock chided what he clearly considered to be a callow critique: Baty's 'real weakness, it seems to us, is in assuming that a proposition is necessarily wrong because some one has expressed it in terms open to exception or given a bad reason for it. If that were so, the elements not only of law but of geometry would be in danger.'[430] While '[r]eally learned writers may be allowed to take some liberties,' Pollock added with a twist of the knife, 'young ones had better . . . remember that scoring points off the verbal laxities of an argument is not the same thing as refuting the substance.'[431] Declaring open season on vicarious liability was not, for Pollock, an appropriate course of action. Where, then, did he stand on the doctrine? Wherever he stood, furthermore, why might his position not have been obvious to Fifoot?

As with *Rylands v Fletcher*, Pollock dedicated a significant chunk of *Torts* to vicarious liability.[432] Hardly surprisingly, he began with the basic legal principles. 'Whoever commits a wrong is liable for it himself. It is no excuse that he was acting, as an agent or servant, on behalf of and for the benefit of another. But that other may well be also liable.'[433] For example, according to Willes J. in an Exchequer Chamber decision of 1867, 'the master is answerable for every such wrong of the servant or agent as is committed in the course of the service and for the master's benefit, though no express command or privity of the master be proved.'[434] Willes J. offered this statement as a 'general rule',[435] and Pollock, in *Torts*, was prepared to treat the statement as 'classical authority'.[436] But he had a problem with Willes's proposition: '[n]o reason for the rule, at any rate no satisfying one, is commonly given in our books.'[437] Pollock considered, and considered unsatisfactory, the various reasons that had been offered from Blackstone onwards for holding a master liable for acts of his servant.[438] Summarizing the law, he lamented the 'singularly intricate and clumsy state of things' and professed to find it 'incredible that such a state of

[428] See Pollock to Holmes, March 1916, in *PHL* i. 233. For an informative and succinct discussion of vicarious liability, see Tony Weir, *Tort Law* (Oxford: Oxford UP, 2002), 95–106.

[429] Fifoot, above n.21, 54–6.

[430] Pollock, review of Baty, *Vicarious Liability*, above n.177, 227.

[431] Ibid. 226. See also Pollock to Holmes, March 1916, in *PHL* i. 233–4. (Holmes replied to this incompletely dated letter on 24 March: see ibid. 234).

[432] *TLT* 63–91. Again, he published the section separately in the *LQR*: Frederick Pollock, 'Liability for the Torts of Agents and Servants' (1885) 1 *LQR* 207–24.

[433] *TLT* 63. [434] *Barwick v English Joint Stock Bank* (1867) L.R. 2 Ex. 259, 265. [435] Ibid.

[436] *TLT* 66. The assumption at the heart of Willes J.'s opinion in *Barwick v English Joint Stock Bank* is that vicarious liability could arise only if some benefit accrued to the master from the servant's wrong. In due course, the House of Lords established that an employer could be liable even though the employee intended only to benefit himself: *Lloyd v Grace, Smith & Co.* [1912] AC 716, commented on by Pollock at *TLT(10)* 80–1.

[437] *TLT* 66–7. [438] See *TLT* 67–8.

things should nowadays be permanently accepted either in substance or in form.'[439]

Pollock's problem, however, was not so much with the law as it stood as with the quality of the reasons that had been provided to explain the law as it stood. While, in *Torts*, he was content to summarize the law and note its lack of rationale, he had argued in the early 1880s that 'the rule of vicarious liability', although 'not easy to justify on any rational grounds', does in fact permit of a persuasive reasoned explanation.[440] The starting point for this explanation, according to Pollock, is the insight that vicarious liability and strict liability share a 'common feature': both impose 'liability on men beyond their own acts or defaults'.[441] At this point, rather startlingly, Pollock seemed to be making no distinction between taking on a servant and, as in *Rylands v Fletcher*, bringing something dangerous onto one's land: in both instances, 'a man has for his own convenience brought about or maintained some state of things which in the ordinary course of nature may work mischief to his neighbours.'[442] Does this mean, then, that masters should be strictly liable for the acts of their servants? Sometimes, Pollock concluded, they should be: '[i]f the [employee's] business be extra hazardous . . . , we should expect to find strict liability.'[443] But only rarely, for 'in the great majority of cases the risk is ordinary,' and '[i]n these cases . . . reasonable care is sufficient for safety and is the measure of the employer's duty.'[444]

So it is that Pollock claimed 'to have arrived at something like a rational foundation of an employer's liability to the public for the acts of his servants'.[445] Leaving aside those rare instances when it is appropriate to impose strict liability on an employer, '[h]e is answerable, not for his servants as agents, or because they are his agents, but for the conduct of his undertaking with due caution.'[446] To understand the rationale behind vicarious liability, in other words, it is important to look not to the fact of agency, but to the personal standards and behaviour of the principal. In 1839, Lord Brougham had suggested that the rule of vicarious liability could be explained essentially in terms of cost-benefit. 'The rule of liability, and its reason, I take to be this: I am liable for what is done, for me and under my orders by the man I employ, . . . and the reason that I am liable is . . . that by employing him I set the whole thing in motion, and what he does, being done for my benefit and under my direction, I am responsible for.'[447] But Pollock paid no attention to this explanation, preferring instead one which was offered three years later by Chief Justice Shaw of the Supreme Judicial Court of Massachusetts: '[t]his rule is obviously founded on the great principle of social duty, that every man, in the management of his own affairs, whether by himself or by his agents or

[439] *TLT* 90–1. [440] *EJE* 116. [441] *EJE* 120, 119. [442] *EJE* 122.
[443] *EJE* 124. [444] *EJE* 125. [445] *EJE* 126. [446] *EJE* 126.
[447] *Duncan v Findlater* (1839) 6 Cl. & F. 894, 909–10 (HL). See also Cornish and Clark, above n.66, 489–90; and John W. Salmond, *Essays in Jurisprudence and Legal History* (London: Stevens and Haynes, 1891), 161–3.

servants, shall so conduct them as not to injure another; and if he does not, and another thereby sustains damage, he shall answer for it.'[448] Given Pollock's own preoccupation with personal duty—a matter which we considered in chapters 2 and 4—it is not particularly surprising that he should have seized upon and lauded Shaw's statement.[449] Masters should shoulder responsibilities for the faults of their servants for no reason other than that this is what we should expect of masters as a matter of duty: 'I am answerable for the wrongs of my servant . . . because . . . I am bound to see that my affairs are conducted with due regard to the safety of others.'[450]

For Pollock, then, the rule of vicarious liability appeared to derive naturally 'from elementary principles'.[451] That English judges and jurists had usually tried to justify vicarious liability by reference to the wrong principles caused him to despair—and it might be that Fifoot assumed this despair to be indicative of Pollock's fundamental dissatisfaction with the rule of vicarious liability itself. But Fifoot was probably making a different assumption. Although Pollock believed that the rule of vicarious liability could be defended on principle, he also believed that the legal development of the rule made this defence difficult to sustain. While social duty may necessitate vicarious liability, Pollock contended, such liability must still be limited.[452] For example, 'it does not seem quite reasonable that the owner of the undertaking should be bound to persons who are inside it . . . in the same way as those who are outside', namely, 'the public at large, who have nothing to do with the undertaking.'[453] '[T]he servant or workman who is in the undertaking,' after all, 'has entered into it of his own free will. . . . [T]he master's duty to the servant . . . might justly be fixed at this point.'[454] In due course, some judges would embrace

[448] *Farwell v Boston & Worcester Railroad Corp.*, 45 Mass. 49, 55–6 (1842). See also *TLT* 67; *EJE* 127. On Shaw's contribution to the development of tort liability in the United States, see Charles O. Gregory, 'Trespass to Negligence to Absolute Liability' (1951) 37 *Virginia L. Rev.* 359–97. Gregory suggests that Shaw may have wanted the increasingly risky activities of a developing industrial economy to be less vulnerable to liability than they had been under earlier common law rules. The suggestion is questioned by E. F. Roberts, 'Negligence: Blackstone to Shaw to ?—An Intellectual Escapade in a Tory Vein' (1965) 50 *Cornell L. Q.* 191–216 at 201–13. Cf. also Cornelius J. Peck, 'Negligence and Liability without Fault in Tort Law' (1971) 46 *Washington L. Rev.* 225–43 at 229.

[449] '. . . a more lucid statement than I have been able to find in any English book.' *EJE* 127. Pollock also considered the link between vicarious liability and social duty to be evident in a book by Charles Sainctelette, a Belgian government official of the 1880s: Charles Sainctelette, *De la Responsabilité et de la garantie. Accidents de transport et de travail* (Brussells: Bruylant-Christophe, 1884). 'La responsabilité du fait d'autrui', Sainctelette wrote, 'n'est pas une fiction inventé par la loi positive. C'est une exigence de l'ordre social' (ibid. 124). Cf. *TLT* 67 n.*r*.

[450] *TLT* 68. [451] *EJE* 131.

[452] Cf. Rosenberg, above n.413, 132 where Pollock is presented as a reformer dedicated to the expansion of vicarious liability. Rosenberg's Pollock also expressed 'frank and notorious opposition to *Rylands*' and so found himself 'out on something of a weak limb in a professional milieu that required deference to precedent' (ibid. 264 n.63).

[453] *EJE* 131–2.

[454] *EJE* 132. It is hardly surprising to discover, given this line of reasoning, that Pollock was generally sympathetic to the doctrine of common employment: see *EJE* 141 ('when a servant suffers by the negligence of a fellow servant it is so likely to be in some considerable degree by his own fault that it would be unjust to hold the master liable'), 142–3.

Pollock's argument—particularly those who believed that *volenti non fit injuria* ought to limit or even negate vicarious liability.[455] During the 1880s, however, Pollock seemed to be pushing against the wind: while the argument which he had advanced 'is in fact, or very nearly so, the rule of the English common law', he noted, 'as the law [now] stands it is otherwise' because of 'the changes in the common law made by the [Employers' Liability] Act of 1880.'[456] This Act ensured that the employer's duty to the servant was not fixed in the way Pollock felt it ought to be: 'a "workman" within the meaning of the Act is put as against his employer in approximately . . . the same position as an outsider as regards the safe and fit condition of the material instruments . . . of the master's business.'[457] Pollock had little problem in principle with the concept of vicarious liability. What irked him was legislation which took no account of the distinction between the 'outsider' who is injured by a principal's undertaking and the agent who is injured by that undertaking but who has consented to be involved in it. Fifoot very possibly took Pollock's dissatisfaction with the legislation to be dissatisfaction with the basic concept.

It is noticeable that Pollock's views on remoteness, inevitable accident, and strict and vicarious liability—irrespective of their particular strengths and weaknesses—featured at one point or another in the English courts. A more extensive study of Pollock's preferred principles of tort law would reveal that English judges have regularly accorded significance to his views.[458] Rather than

[455] See *Hayward v Drury Lane Theatre Ltd* [1917] 2 KB 899, 911 CA (*per* Scrutton L. J.); *Performing Right Society Ltd v Mitchell and Booker (Palais de Danse) Ltd* [1924] 1 KB 762, 767–8 KBD (*per* McCardie J.); and cf. *Holdman v Hamlyn* [1943] KB 664, 667 CA (*per* Du Parcq L. J.).

[456] *EJE* 132, 134, 135. [457] *TLT* 90.

[458] See, e.g., *Peek v Derry* (1888) L.R. 37 Ch.D. 541, 581 (*per* Sir J. Hannen); *Derry v Peek* (1889) 14 App. Cas. 337, 375 (*per* Lord Herschell); *Marney v Scott* [1899] 1 QB 986, 991–2 (*per* Bigham J.); *Howard v Furness-Houlder Argentine Lines Ltd* (1936) 55 Lloyd's. L. Rep. 121, 129 (*per* Lewis J.); *Hurst v Picture Theatres Ltd* [1915] 1 KB 1, 15 (*per* Kennedy L. J.), 18–19 (*per* Phillimore L. J.); *The Amerika* [1914] P. 167, 187 (*per* Buckley L. J.); *Horton v London Graving Dock Company Ltd* (1949–50) 83 Lloyd's L. Rep. 207, 213 (*per* Tucker L. J.); *Wilkinson v Rea Ltd* (1941) 69 Lloyd's L. Rep. 147, 155 (*per* Luxmoore L. J.); *Sedleigh-Denfield v O'Callaghan* [1940] AC 880, 918 (*per* Lord Porter); *Liddle v Yorkshire (North Riding) County Council* [1934] 2 KB 101, 111 (*per* Scrutton L. J.); *Cassell & Co. Ltd v Broome* [1972] AC 1027, 1099 (*per* Lord Morris); *Compania Mexicana de Petroleo El Aguila S.A. v Essex Transport & Trading Co. Ltd* (1928) 32 Lloyd's L. Rep. 182, 194 (*per* Bateson J.); *Oram v Hutt* [1914] 1 Ch. 98, 107 (*per* Lord Sumner); *Addis v Gramophone Co. Ltd* [1909] AC 488, 498, 500 (*per* Lord Collins). One judge in particular, McCardie J., rarely missed an opportunity to cite, and praise, *TLT*: see, e.g., *Buckland v The King* [1933] 1 KB 329, 343 ('It will suffice to refer to Sir Frederick Pollock's admirable book on the Law of Torts . . .'); *Pratt v British Medical Association* [1919] 1 KB 244, 259 ('. . . his luminous work on the Law of Torts'); *Fisher v Oldham Corporation* [1930] 2 KB 364, 375 ('. . . his masterly treatise on Torts'); *Gayler and Pope Ltd v B. Davies and Son Ltd* [1924] 2 KB 75, 77–9, 83–4; *Performing Right Society Ltd v Mitchell and Booker (Palais de Danse) Ltd* [1924] 1 KB 762, 767–8; *Phillips v Britannia Hygienic Laundry Co. Ltd* [1923] 1 KB 539, 544, 548, 551, 553–4; though note McCardie's criticism of *TLT(10)* 530–8 in *Maclenan v Segar* [1917] 2 KB 325, 330. (Having McCardie J. as an admirer was probably a mixed blessing: a believer in flogging and the sterilization of persons with mental defects, while also holding to various liberal values, he is one of the most controversial and intriguing judges throughout the history of English law. Possibly the eeriest judicial essay ever published is his epilogue to a book of essays celebrating contempt for others: see Henry A. McCardie, 'Epilogue', in *Red Rags: Essays of Hate from Oxford With an Epilogue by Mr Justice McCardie*, ed. R. C. Carr (London: Chapman & Hall, 1933), 285–91. 'Science has supplied us with much,' he wrote, 'but it has not yet found a formula for happiness' (ibid. 290). Six months after writing these words, he had taken

try to make anything of this observation now, it may be best to wait until the conclusion of the chapter, when we will be a in a position to say something about Pollock's treatise-writing achievements generally. Before reaching that point, there are two other investigations that need to be undertaken. The second of these concerns Pollock's views on intentional harm—views which were welcomed more in the American than in the English courts. The first concerns his more traditional, but nevertheless intriguing, conception of negligence.

3. At the head of the family

Pollock, we know, was eager to uncover and present a family of tortious principles because he wanted to demonstrate that Torts is a unified body of law rather than a set of miscellaneous rules. But it would be wrong straightforwardly to assume that he was wholly successful in his endeavour. By the end of the nineteenth century, the law of torts remained highly fragmented.[459] Even at the end of the twentieth century, academic lawyers were still grappling with the question of whether torts had been successfully unified under a general principle of liability[460]—not least because there still existed a body of ad hoc 'torticles' which often proved difficult to categorize by reference to general doctrines.[461] The tort of negligence was a different matter: during the twentieth century, specific duties of care were replaced by an overarching duty of care, so that negligence became largely organized under a general liability principle.[462] Although the twentieth-century crystallization of negligence is a story somewhat peripheral to our objectives here, it makes sense briefly to examine the background to that story. For there, in the background, we discover Pollock.

Before the emergence of an independent tort of negligence during the nineteenth century, the term 'duty' had no technical overtones in English tort law.[463] With the development of negligence, however, the situation was bound to change: the failure to exercise care—this being the essence of negligence—

his own life.) Inevitably, some judges have cited *TLT* in order to disagree with it: see, e.g., *Wilchick v Marks* [1934] 2 KB 56, 65 (*per* Goddard J.); *Jackson v Watson & Sons* [1909] 2 KB 193, 200 (*per* Vaughan Williams L. J., though cf. Kennedy L. J. ibid. 206). And some judges appear to have stopped counsel from citing Pollock while he was alive: see *Parr v Lancashire and Cheshire Miners' Federation* [1913] 1 Ch. 366, 372 (*per* Neville J); also *Haynes v Harwood*, above n.392, 149–50.

[459] See Ibbetson, above n.49, 178–87.

[460] See, e.g., Peter Cane, *The Anatomy of Tort Law* (Oxford: Hart, 1997), 21–2.

[461] See Rudden, above n.287, *passim*.

[462] See Bob Hepple, 'Negligence: The Search for Coherence' (1997) 50 *Current Legal Problems* 69–94. Although Hepple acknowledges the dominance of the 'duty of care' principle, his argument is that a more coherent framework of negligence will only be achieved once that principle has been replaced by a broad principle of fault.

[463] See Percy H. Winfield, 'Duty in Tortious Negligence' (1934) 34 *Columbia L. Rev.* 41–66; also M. J. Prichard, Scott *v.* Shepherd *(1773) and the Emergence of the Tort of Negligence* (London: Selden Society, 1976), 30–3.

can only be a legal wrong if the law imposes a duty to exercise that care. Negligence liability, as it developed in the nineteenth century, appeared to require three basic ingredients: an antecedent duty to take care owed by the defendant to the plaintiff; a breach of this duty by the defendant; and consequential loss to the plaintiff.[464] As Ibbetson has explained, the nineteenth-century equation of negligence with the failure to observe a specific duty to take care provided Pollock and others with a means of distinguishing those situations in which liability would be imposed from those in which it would not.[465] In *Torts*, Pollock defines negligent liability by citing the words of Alderson B.—'[n]egligence is the omission to do something which a reasonable man . . . would do, or doing something which a prudent and reasonable man would not do'[466]—and then immediately qualifies the definition: negligence is thus, 'provided, of course, that the party whose conduct is in question is already in a situation that brings him under the duty of taking care'.[467] In other words, 'not every person injured by a negligent act would necessarily be entitled to compensation; liability would arise if and only if a duty were owed *to that person*.'[468] Yet again, Pollock seemed keen to highlight the limited applicability of a legal concept: the duty of care was not a universal duty of care.

Even in the first edition of *Torts*, however, Pollock struggled with the question of just how extensive this duty of care could be. Over the next four decades, as *Torts* went through another dozen editions and the courts moved towards a more generalized notion of a duty of care, this struggle intensified. It is clear from the first edition that the establishment of a general principle of duty—to sit at the head of the family of principles, as it were—appealed to Pollock. Four years before this edition, in *Heaven v Pender*, Brett M. R. had attempted to formulate such a principle: when a person is 'placed in such a position with regard to another that every one of ordinary sense' would recognize that not to 'use ordinary care and skill' would 'cause danger of injury to the person or property of the other, a duty arises to use ordinary care and skill to avoid such danger.'[469] Even though, in *Heaven v Pender*, two members of the court were unwilling to accept such a broad proposition,[470] for Pollock the decision amounted to a 'general rule that every one is bound to exercise due care towards his neighbours in his acts and conduct, or rather omits or falls short of it at his peril'.[471] Since Brett M. R.'s dictum complemented that of Alderson B.—both regarded 'the reasonable man' as the appropriate standard for the determination of negligence liability—it is perhaps not surprising that

[464] See Winfield, above n.463, 41; W. W. Buckland, 'The Duty to Take Care' (1935) 51 *LQR* 637–49 at 637–9; R. W. M. Dias, 'The Breach Problem and the Duty of Care' (1956) 30 *Tulane L. Rev.* 377–408 at 400; and D. J. Ibbetson, 'The Tort of Negligence in the Common Law in the Nineteenth and Twentieth Centuries', in *Negligence*, above n.254, 229–71 at 234.

[465] Ibbetson, above n.49, 170–1.

[466] *Blyth v Birmingham Waterworks Co.* (1856) 11 Ex. 781, 784.

[467] *TLT* 355.

[468] Ibbetson, above n.49, 171. See also Warren A. Seavey, 'Principles of Torts' (1942) 56 *Harvard L. Rev.* 72–98 at 76–7.

[469] *Heaven v Pender* (1883) 11 QBD 503, 509.

[470] See ibid. 516.

[471] *TLT* 353.

Pollock should have approved of it. '[T]he standard of duty' in cases of negligence, he observed, 'is . . . the foresight and caution of . . . the average prudent man. This idea . . . pervades the mass of our authorities.'[472] Yet Pollock drew from Brett M. R.'s words no lessons about standards of reasonableness or prudence—for such lessons, he believed, one does better to look to Aristotle[473]—but found, rather, an indication of to whom a duty of care is owed. We owe a duty of care, in short, to our neighbours. Is there a single 'moral idea'[474] underlying the law of torts in its entirety? To such a sweeping question one would expect, from Pollock, a guarded answer. His response, however, was unequivocal:

> 'Thou shalt do no hurt to thy neighbour.' Our law of torts, with all its irregularities, has for its main purpose nothing else than the development of this precept.[475]

Of course, Pollock was not the first English jurist to express this sentiment: we have encountered it already in Buller's *Nisi Prius*. For his own part, Pollock traced the sentiment back not to Buller but to one of the best-known sentences from the *Institutes* ('[t]he precepts of the law are these: to live honestly, to injure nobody, and to give every man his due') and to the Catechism of the Anglican Church ('[m]y duty towards my Neighbour is to love him as myself, and to do to all men as I would they should do unto me').[476] By Pollock's standards, his willingness to embrace these highly general propositions without any provisos is akin to a rush of blood to the head. Buckland, after quoting Pollock's summary and endorsement of the 'general rule' in *Heaven v Pender*, seemed bewildered by the absence of any caveat: '[t]his [sc., Pollock's endorsement] looks rational, but there is nothing in it about duty to one person and not to another.'[477] Buckland's puzzlement was attributable both to his own inattentive reading of *Torts*, and to Pollock's own rather inattentive editing of the text. In the thirteenth edition (upon which Buckland relied), Pollock's

[472] *TLT* 357.

[473] See *TLT* 357 n.*k*, possibly a reference to *Nicomachean Ethics* vi. 10–13.

[474] *TLT* 12.

[475] *TLT* 12. See also Pollock, 'Torts', above n.293, 190: 'it seems the simpler and more rational way to consider the modern law of torts as enforcing so much of the moral duty "to hurt nobody by word nor deed" as positive law can conveniently enforce in an individualist and competitive scheme of society.'

[476] See *TLT* 12, esp. n.*i*; and cf. ibid. 129–30 ('In short, life could not go on if we did not, as the price of our own freedom, abide some measure of inconvenience from the equal freedom of our neighbours'); also Frederick Pollock, 'Spinoza as a Moral Philosopher' (1888) 18 *Time* 416–19 at 416–17 ('Morality in the civilised world at any rate is, like civilised law, fixed in its main lines though capable of development. Indeed, the fundamentals of both, in their simplest terms, coincide; Ulpian's sum of the commandments of the law, *honeste vivere, alterum non laedere, suum cuique tribuere*, is very like part of the duties to one's neighbour set forth in the Church Catechism, which indeed may have been taken from Ulpian through Justinian's Institutes').

[477] Buckland, above n.464, 641. See also Goodhart, above n.59, xii ('Pollock was the last man . . . to believe that there were vague general duties . . .').

assessment of *Heaven v Pender* remained unchanged from the first edition. Yet, from the sixth edition onwards, Pollock had inserted a passage at the very beginning of the treatise which made it clear that he no longer believed that there was an unqualified rule that everyone must exercise due care towards his neighbours. 'All members of a civilized commonwealth', he wrote,

> are under a general duty towards their neighbours to do them no hurt without lawful cause or excuse.

This, of course, was the sentiment which he had purported to draw from the *Institutes* and the Catechism. But this new passage came with a typically Pollockian note of caution:

> [t]he precise extent of the duty, as well as the nature and extent of the recognized exceptions, varies according to the nature of the case.[478]

This note of caution takes us back to Pollock's tempering of Alderson B.'s words in *Blyth v Birmingham Waterworks*—another assessment which remained substantially unchanged throughout all of the editions of *Torts* with which Pollock was involved.[479] In that treatise—and this seems to encapsulate the struggle to which we referred a moment ago—we are confronted with a jurist who balked at generalizations but who wanted to see established a general principle of tortious liability. As the editions progressed, Pollock became ever more confident about stating that negligence liability in particular was moving towards the fundamental principle that it is wrongful to cause harm to others in the absence of some specific ground of justification or excuse.[480] His willingness to state as much and his juristic renown meant that, for many early twentieth-century torts scholars, he was a convenient foil for separating two schools of thought about negligence.[481] On the one hand, there were those who, like Pollock, believed that negligence was gradually settling upon, if it had not already settled upon, a general principle of liability (though their

[478] *TLT(6)* 1.

[479] See, for the last illustration, *TLT(14)* 350. Although *TLT(14)* was published two years after Pollock's death, Pollock had collected detailed notes for the edition, many of which notes were incorporated into the treatise by his posthumous editor, Philip Landon: see *TLT(14)* v-vi; also *Wringe v Cohen* [1940] 1 KB 229, 239 (*per* Atkinson J.); and cf. Wright, above n.17, 164.

[480] See, e.g., *TLT(11)* 21 ('The whole modern law of negligence, with its many developments, enforces the duty of fellow-citizens to observe in varying circumstances an appropriate measure of prudence to avoid causing harm to one another. The situations in which we are under no such duty appear at this day not as normal but as exceptional').

[481] See A. L. Goodhart, 'The Foundation of Tortious Liability' (1938) 2 *Mod. L. Rev.* 1–13; Glanville L. Williams, 'The Foundation of Tortious Liability' (1939) 7 *Cambridge L. J.* 111–32. On the matter of whether there exists a general principle of negligence liability, Goodhart uncharacteristically took the opposite view to Pollock (see below). Williams sided with neither Pollock nor his detractors, but forged a characteristically ingenious middle-route.

understanding of this principle was rarely if ever the same as Pollock's).[482] On the other hand, there were those who could identify no general principle of negligence liability but only a number of specific rules prohibiting certain kinds of harmful activity.[483] For our purposes, neither the shortcomings nor the strengths of Pollock's position matter all that much as compared with the timeliness of his intervention. For, during the first half of the twentieth century, jurists were not the only ones grappling with the idea of a singular negligence principle.

In his speech in *Donoghue v Stevenson*, Lord Atkin did as Pollock had done before him and used the figure of the neighbour to illustrate the notion of a duty of care. It will suffice here to quote just a small part of a famous passage from that speech:

> In English law there must be, and is, some general conception of relations giving rise to a duty of care, of which the particular cases found in the books are instances. . . . You must take reasonable care to avoid acts or omissions which you can reasonably foresee would be likely to injure your neighbour. Who, then, in law is my neighbour? The answer seems to be—persons who are so closely and directly affected by my act that I ought reasonably to have them in contemplation as being so affected when I am directing my mind to the acts or omissions which are called in question.[484]

Pollock was clearly flattered that Lord Macmillan saw fit to rely on *Torts* when preparing his speech—perhaps the most carefully conceived speech of all—in *Donoghue v Stevenson*.[485] Nevertheless it is Lord Atkin's speech, and particularly his articulation of the so-called 'neighbour principle', that casts the most interesting light on Pollock's understanding of negligence liability. Pollock welcomed the decision in *Donoghue v Stevenson* for at least four reasons. First, it determined that establishing a duty of care did not demand privity between the parties: students must now 'clear their minds', Pollock observed, 'of the entanglement with purely contractual notions that has so much hampered this branch of the law.'[486] Secondly, he applauded the fact that the deci-

[482] The best representative of this position was probably Percy Winfield: see, e.g., P. H. Winfield, 'The Law of Tort' (1935) 51 *LQR* 249–62; Winfield, above n.274, 10; above n.276, 195–9; and, generally, Sir P. H. Winfield, *Select Legal Essays* (London: Sweet & Maxwell, 1952), 3–131.

[483] The best representative of this position was probably John Salmond: see, e.g., John W. Salmond, *The Law of Torts: A Treatise on the English Law of Liability for Civil Injuries* (London: Stevens and Haynes, 1907), 20–4. It almost goes without saying that Pollock preferred Winfield's position, though Pollock himself felt it was worth indicating this preference: see F[rederick] P[ollock] (1927) 43 *LQR* 149.

[484] *Donoghue v Stevenson*, above n.245, 580.

[485] See ibid. 610 (citing *TLT(13)* 570), 613. The citation to *TLT(13)* 570 had originally been provided by counsel for the respondent: see *Donoghue v Stevenson*, above n.245, 566. For Pollock's reaction to Lord Macmillan's use of *Torts*, see Frederick Pollock, 'The Snail in the Bottle, and Thereafter' (1933) 49 *LQR* 22–6 at 25. On Lord Macmillan's speech generally, see Alan Rodger, 'Lord Macmillan's Speech in *Donoghue v Stevenson*' (1992) 108 *LQR* 236–59.

[486] Pollock, above n.485, 24. See also Wright, above n.17, 164. The privity association appears to be traceable to *Winterbottom v Wright* (1842) 10 M. & W. 109.

sion marked the way forward for the growth of negligence as an independent tort.[487] Thirdly, he approved of Lord Atkin's precise formulation of the neighbour principle—and, in particular, his (and Lord Macmillan's) imposition of a clear requirement of reasonable foreseeability in order for a duty of care to exist.[488] Do not assume, Pollock warned his readers, that 'the effect of the decision' is to create 'a multifarious duty towards every person who may possibly become a consumer.'[489] Finally, *Donoghue v Stevenson* was very clearly an instance of what Pollock called judicial valour.[490] Lords Buckmaster and Tomlin, dissenting, were reproved by Pollock for their 'timidity. . . . Parts of their opinions read as if they had forgotten that they were judging in a Court of last resort.'[491] Lords Atkin, Thankerton, and Macmillan, by contrast, '[w]e have to thank . . . for overriding the scruples of . . . colleagues who could not emancipate themselves from the pressure of a supposed current of authority in English courts.'[492] This last point is especially significant. Pollock not only believed in the notion of a general duty towards one's neighbour, but also, in the later editions of *Torts*, appeared to believe that it was only a matter of time before the notion made its way into the law. *Donoghue v Stevenson*, one current Law Lord has observed,

> was the case for which much of the English legal profession had been waiting for some time. . . . [T]he confused state of [the law of negligence liability] . . . [w]e can see . . . for ourselves if we open a contemporary edition of Sir Frederick Pollock's book on *Torts*. . . . A test case was bound to come sooner or later. *Donoghue* was the test case and Lord Atkin was clearly determined . . . to write himself into the history books.[493]

From the preceding discussion it should not be inferred that Lord Atkin's 'neighbour principle' must have been inspired by Pollock. That he influenced Lord Atkin is certainly conceivable—not least because it is possible to discern other juristic influences on Lord Atkin's speech.[494] But there appears to be no direct evidence that Pollock was influential in this instance. Pollock did, nevertheless, anticipate the emergence of the neighbour principle. For this, it

[487] See Pollock, above n.485, 24, esp. Pollock's approval of Lord Macmillan's claim that 'the categories of negligence are never closed' (*Donoghue v Stevenson*, above n.245, 619).

[488] See R. F. V. Heuston, '*Donoghue v Stevenson* in Retrospect' (1957) 20 *Mod. L. Rev.* 1–24 at 16, esp. n.74.

[489] Pollock, above n.485, 23. Much the same warning was issued by American jurists in light of Cardozo J.'s landmark opinion in *MacPherson v Buick Motor Co.*, 111 N.E. 1050 (N.Y. 1916). See John C. P. Goldberg and Benjamin C. Zipursky, 'The Moral of *MacPherson*' (1998) 146 *Univ. Pennsylvania L. Rev.* 1733–847 at 1750–77.

[490] See Pollock, 'Judicial Caution and Valour', above n.232, 294–7.

[491] Pollock, above n.485, 22.

[492] Ibid. Cf. Geoffrey Lewis, *Lord Atkin* (Oxford: Hart, 1999), 65–6.

[493] Rodger, above n.485, 246.

[494] See ibid. 243–5 (on Francis Bohlen and Arthur Goodhart as possible influences).

might be argued, he deserves little credit. After all, the seeds of the principle had been sewn (albeit too widely for Lord Atkin's liking,[495] and without the explicit invocation of the neighbour motif) in *Heaven v Pender*, four years before the first appearance of *Torts*. Those with a mind to probe deeper and wider might also point out that the principle is a feature of the natural law backdrop to English tort law: the idea that everyone ought to take reasonable care not to injure his neighbour had been in the air long before either *Donoghue v Stevenson* or *Torts*.[496]

From two other perspectives, however, it might be argued that Pollock's own formulation of the neighbour principle was genuinely prescient and intriguing. First of all, it is notable that Arthur Goodhart was highly critical of what might be termed Pollock's case for a neighbour principle. Given that we have seen in this study how Goodhart was prone to taking Pollock's side in juristic debates, it is worth considering why, in this instance, he felt unable to do so. For Goodhart, the problem with Pollock's case for a neighbour principle was simple: it was wishful thinking, without any secure foundation in law. Having noted Pollock's view that 'as a general proposition of English law' it is wrong to harm one's neighbour without justification or excuse,[497] Goodhart observed that Pollock 'cites no case which is specifically based on this fundamental principle of English law, but is content to refer to three dicta'.[498] That Pollock could find only meagre authority for this principle, Goodhart added, 'leaves us with an impressive sounding formula which on analysis seems to have virtually no content'.[499] But how could a jurist as meticulous as Pollock have ended up defending a principle in so flimsy a fashion? The clue to the answer lies in Goodhart's summary of his critique: 'having first stated as a proposition of general jurisprudence what a civilized law of tort ought to contain, [Pollock] was anxious to prove that this could be found in the modern common law.'[500] It is difficult to know whether Pollock really was anxious in the way that Goodhart describes. But what is clear is that he was making a normative argument about the law of torts: just as was the case when he discussed various other tortious principles, and when he discussed the notion of good faith in contractual negotiations, his case for a neighbour principle was, in essence, a prescriptive exercise. Throughout all of the editions of *Torts*, and especially from the sixth edition onwards, Pollock made it clear that some version of the neighbour principle—he was never

[495] *Donoghue v Stevenson*, above n.245, 580 ('To seek a complete logical definition of the general principle is probably to go beyond the function of the judge, for the more general the definition the more likely it is to omit essentials or to introduce non-essentials. The attempt was made by Brett M. R. in *Heaven* v. *Pender*. . . . As framed, it was demonstrably too wide, though it appears to me, if properly limited, to be capable of affording a valuable practical guide').

[496] See Ibbetson, above n.49, 196; above n.464, 269; and also Landon's comment at *TLT(14)* 43 that 'Pollock would not have claimed to be a pioneer in the effort to discover a general basis of tortious liability.'

[497] *TLT(13)* 20.

[498] Goodhart, above n.481, 3.

[499] Ibid.

[500] Ibid. 4.

entirely clear about how widely or narrowly the principle should be construed—should form the basis of tortious liability. Rather than simply state the law, he stated the principle upon which he believed the law ought to be premised.

This is another instance in which the law evolved in a manner very much congenial to Pollock's wishes. The second reason his case for a neighbour principle might be considered innovative is that, at the time he was making it, many other lawyers were wary of the initiative. The thirteenth edition of *Torts*—the final one to appear in Pollock's lifetime—was published three years before *Donoghue v Stevenson*. When the fourteenth edition appeared in 1939 its new editor attempted to turn back the clock. 'We are . . . justified in assuming,' he wrote, 'notwithstanding the dicta in *Donoghue v Stevenson*, that the existence of the duty to take care cannot be referred to any single principle of liability. . . . Pollock did not adopt this method of exposition, and it is respectfully submitted that some confusion is the result.'[501] In the years immediately following *Donoghue v Stevenson*, various judges shared this reluctance to treat the case as establishing a general principle.[502] But this reluctance did not prevail in the long term. Inevitably, during the second half of the twentieth century, the English courts struggled with Lord Atkin's neighbour principle. It is important to emphasize, nevertheless, that the courts were generally having difficulty not with the principle itself but with the question of where it ought to be applied.[503] Differing perspectives on the applicability of the principle lead to different conclusions about where the boundaries of negligence ought to be fixed, and Pollock, like Lord Macmillan, would certainly have expected such differences to be an ever-present feature of the law of torts. But what Pollock—certainly the Pollock who produced the early editions of *Torts*—might not have expected was the acceptance of the neighbour principle itself. His case for such a principle was not made with the greatest consistency, and, as Goodhart appreciated, he had a crafty knack for slipping his own perspectives into his doctrinal expositions and passing them off as if they were law. But it is crucial to stress that he allied himself with this principle when it was almost radical, and certainly unfashionable, to do so. In this instance, it seems hardly extravagant to conclude that Pollock, like Francis Buller and Lord Esher, was somewhat ahead of his time.

[501] *TLT(14)* 346. See also P. A. Landon (1941) 57 *LQR* 179–83; and Ibbetson, above n.464, 261–2.

[502] See, e.g., *Farr v Butters Bros & Co.* [1932] 2 KB 606, 613–14 (*per* Scrutton L. J.); also Ibbetson, above n.49, 191 ('Judges . . . , although less hide-bound by previous precedents, did not expand the law into a whole new range of situations simply on the grounds that the defendant had carelessly caused foreseeable harm to the plaintiff').

[503] See, e.g., *Candler v Crane, Christmas & Co.* [1951] 2 KB 164, CA; *Hedley, Byrne & Co. Ltd v Heller & Partners Ltd* [1964] AC 465, HL; *Home Office v Dorset Yacht Co. Ltd* [1970] AC 1004, HL; *Anns v Merton London Borough* [1978] AC 728, HL; *Caparo Industries plc v Dickman* [1990] 2 AC 605, HL; *Page v Smith* [1996] AC 155, HL.

d. Torts of intention

There is one other way in which Pollock contributed to the shaping of modern tort law. We have seen that, in his effort to compartmentalize the law of torts, Pollock borrowed and adapted Holmes's tripartite arrangement of torts under the headings of strict liability, negligence, and intentional wrongs. Our analysis of *Torts* has led us to consider Pollock's views on strict liability and negligence. But we have had no reason, so far, to examine his analysis of the intentional torts. Since this analysis has sometimes been treated as the most noteworthy contribution that Pollock made to torts jurisprudence, it deserves our attention.

Five years before the appearance of the first edition of *Torts*, Pollock was invited by the Government of India to draft an Indian Civil Wrongs Bill. The purpose of the Bill—the first draft of which was completed in 1886—was to establish in India a codified, if slightly simplified, version of English tort law. It seems clear that Pollock was disappointed that the Bill was never enacted.[504] He included it in *Torts*, almost as if out of defiance, from the second edition through to the thirteenth—by which point, nearly half a century old, it bore little relevance to anything.[505] If the Bill retains any significance at all, it is in so far as it provides some insight into Pollock's early thinking on the place of malice in the law of torts. While, Pollock decreed, '[e]very one commits a wrong who harms another . . . by an act intended to cause harm', a 'person is not wronged who suffers harm or loss in consequence of any act done for a lawful purpose and in a lawful manner in the exercise of ordinary rights.'[506] Hence, if 'A digs a deep well on his land to obtain a water supply for agricultural purposes', thereby intercepting and drying up the water supply to B's land, 'A has not wronged B'.[507]

In the Civil Wrongs Bill as it stood in 1886, Pollock had nothing more to say about common rights to percolating water than what is set out in the last paragraph. By the time that he came to prepare the 1890 edition of *Torts*, however, he felt that his illustration needed complicating. What if 'B digs a still deeper well on his own land, and thereby intentionally cuts off the supply of water to A's well'? 'Here', according to Pollock, 'B has wronged A, for he has used his own land not for any lawful purpose, but only for the unlawful purpose of doing wilful harm to A.'[508] Were Pollock stating the law as it then stood in the United States, he would have been entirely correct.[509] But, as he

[504] See the comments of Lord Rodger in *Standard Chartered Bank v Pakistan National Shipping Corp. (No. 2)* [2003] 1 Lloyd's Rep. 227, 237, HL.

[505] For the first appearance of the Bill in *Torts*, see *TLT(2)* 517–83. 'Had I been left to my own judgment, I should have hesitated to reprint once more the draft of a code prepared for the Government of India many years ago', he wrote in the Advertisement to the tenth edition, 'but I am assured on excellent Indian authority that magistrates and practitioners . . . have not ceased to find it useful as a compendious manual of principles.' *TLT(10)* viii.

[506] *TLT(2)* 522, 535.

[507] *TLT(2)* 536.

[508] *TLT(2)* 536, and cf. 517.

[509] *Greenleaf v Francis*, 18 Pick. 117 (1836) (distinguishing reasonable and malicious collection of percolating water). See generally Ernest W. Huffcut, 'Percolating Waters: The Rule of Reasonable User' (1904) 13 *Yale L. J.* 222–7.

conceded, his statement was 'commonly supposed not to be the law of England'.[510] Not that this fact fazed him: while his assertion of B's wrongfulness was generally presumed not to be the correct statement of English law, he continued, 'I know of no distinct authority that it is not so . . . and I submit that on principle it ought to be so.'[511] Although Pollock insisted that B ought, as a matter of principle, to be adjudged a wrongdoer, he omitted to stipulate the principle on which this judgment should be based. When, later in the Civil Wrongs Bill, the issue of malicious wrongdoing arose again, he was clearly in no mind to elaborate on what he had said already: the law relating to those 'miscellaneous wrongs which may be generally described as malicious interference with rights', he claimed, 'is neither settled enough to make immediate codification prudent, nor of sufficient practical importance to make it probable that delay will do any harm.'[512] The treatment of intentional torts in the Civil Wrongs Bill reads very much like a story without an ending, and with part of the plot missing.

In chapter 2 of *Torts*, Pollock set about subjecting intentional torts to a more substantial treatment. His opening sentence is not exactly confidence-inspiring: '[t]here is no express authority that I know of for stating as a general proposition of English law that it is a wrong to do wilful harm to one's neighbour without lawful justification or excuse.'[513] We noted near the end of the last section that Goodhart likewise recognized no authority that substantiated this proposition, and that he took Pollock to task for assuming the proposition to be correct. Goodhart objected to Pollock's assertion not only because he considered it to be unsupported by proper legal authority—a point which was noted earlier—but also because the assertion was confined to wilful harm. '[I]nstances in which harm is inflicted merely for the purpose of harming must be exceedingly rare', Goodhart remarked, and so Pollock's definition of tortious liability in terms of wilful harm to one's neighbour must be considered extremely narrow.[514] As we saw in the previous section, Pollock did not define tortious liability as narrowly as Goodhart suggested he did. Goodhart's mistake in this instance was to fix upon Pollock's use of the neighbour motif in relation to intentional torts and treat it as an attempt to formulate a basic test of liability. Pollock's general remarks on tortious liability appear in chapter 1 of *Torts*, his discussion of liability for negligence in chapter 11 (chapter 12 in

[510] *TLT(2)* 536 n.*f.* The law as it then stood in England was that B, in Pollock's scenario, could not have wronged A since B is the absolute owner not only of his land but also of all that lies beneath it, and so he may dig therein and apply all that it contains to his own purposes. *Chasemore v Richards* (1859) 7 HLC 349.

[511] *TLT(2)* 536 n.*f.* See also Williams, above n.481, 126–7 n.63.

[512] *TLT(2)* 558. The unsettled nature of the law was illustrated, Pollock believed, by the case of *Lumley v Gye* (1853) 2 E. & B. 216, in which the Queen's Bench had recognized the common law tort of inducing breach of contract. For Pollock, this case showed that the mid-nineteenth-century courts were at best grappling towards, and were certainly some way off settling upon, a general principle regarding intentional harm. See *TLT* 454–5; *TLT(2)* 558; and, more generally, Waddams, above n.137, 23–39.

[513] *TLT* 21.

[514] Goodhart, above n.481, 2–3.

the later editions). In chapter 2, throughout all of the editions, he very pointedly confined his opening observation to liability for wilful harm.

Nevertheless, Pollock conceded what bothered Goodhart most: that there is no express authority for the proposition that intentionally inflicting harm on another, without lawful justification or excuse, is a tort. Pollock's next move was possibly the most audacious that he ever made as a jurist. Not only did he make light of the concession—there is no 'express authority for the general proposition that men must perform their contracts' either, he asserted, but this does not mean that they need not do so[515]—but he argued that good moral sense demands that the proposition be accepted. 'If there exists . . . a positive duty to avoid harm, much more must there exist, whether it be so expressed in the books or not, the negative duty of not doing wilful harm; subject, as all general duties must be subject, to the necessary exceptions.'[516] Although various commentators have described this as an argument premised on the need for symmetry of doctrine,[517] Pollock's use of the words 'much more' (instead of, say, the word 'equally') suggests that he considered the negative duty to be more pressing than its positive counterpart. Certainly he appreciated that this negative duty, even if it is more pressing, cannot be an absolute one. An obvious exception to the duty is the principle—which Pollock filed under *damnum sine injuria*[518]– that commonplace and desirable activities which cause loss should not occasion liability: '[c]ompetition in business . . . is the most obvious example. . . . To say that a man shall not seek profit in business at the expense of others is to say that he shall not do business at all.'[519] What needs to be emphasized, nevertheless, is the fact that Pollock insisted that a duty not to do wilful harm ought to be legally recognized. Indeed, his position was uncharacteristically dogmatic: in the absence of lawful justification or excuse, a person should not be permitted to injure another without incurring any legal liability.

Holmes similarly argued that 'the intentional infliction of temporal damage, or the doing of an act manifestly likely to inflict such damage and inflicting it, is actionable if done without just cause.'[520] In this instance, however, it was

[515] *TLT* 21. [516] *TLT* 22.

[517] See, e.g., Taggart, above n.231, 168; Kenneth J. Vandevelde, 'The Modern Prima Facie Tort Doctrine' (1990–1) 79 *Kentucky L. J.* 519–55 at 547–8.

[518] Damage without wrongful act. The Latin clearly irked Pollock: see *TLT* 130; also (1886) 2 *LQR* 117 ('"Damnum sine iniuria" standing alone as a sort of compound noun, seems hardly good Latin. English lawyers, however, have so used it since the fifteenth century at the latest').

[519] *TLT* 129. For similar reasoning and illustrations to Pollock's, see Oliver Wendell Holmes, Jr., 'Privilege, Malice, and Intent' (1894) 8 *Harvard L. Rev.* 1–14 at 3–4. Cf. also F. A. Hayek, *Law, Legislation and Liberty: A New Statement of the Liberal Principles of Justice and Political Economy. Vol. i: Rules and Order. Vol. ii: The Mirage of Social Justice. Vol. iii: The Political Order of a Free People* (London: Routledge & Kegan Paul, 1982), i. 102 ('[S]ome harm knowingly caused to others is even essential for the preservation of a spontaneous order: the law does not prevent the setting up of a new business even if this is done in the expectation that it will lead to the failure of another. . . . The harm that one does to another which the law aims to prevent is thus not all harm but only the disappointment of such expectations as the law designates as legitimate').

[520] Holmes, above n.519, 3.

Holmes who was following Pollock rather than Pollock who was following Holmes. One of the two cases upon which Holmes relied to substantiate his claim that his argument was a 'commonplace'[521] was the Court of Appeal decision in *Mogul Steamship Co. v McGregor*. In the course of that decision, Lord Justice Bowen, one of the greatest judges Pollock claimed ever to have known, lent his support to the intentional torts doctrine in language that departed little from Pollock's own: 'intentionally to do that which is calculated in the ordinary course of events to damage, and which does, in fact, damage another in that other person's property or trade, is actionable if done without just cause or excuse'.[522] Bowen L. J.'s 'masterly judgment', Pollock wrote in the *LQR*, had established a 'broad principle' the importance of which 'admits of no denial'.[523] It was probably Pollock, however, who deserved the plaudits. In this instance, as various commentators have recognized, it was he who marked out the path.[524]

[521] Ibid. 2–3.

[522] *Mogul Steamship Co. Ltd v McGregor, Gow, & Co.* (1889) 23 QBD 598, 613. See also Bowen L. J.'s opinions in *Ratcliffe v Evans* [1892] 2 QB 524, CA; and *Skinner & Co. v Shew & Co.* [1893] 1 Ch. 413, CA. For Pollock on Bowen L. J., see *FMG* 172–3; and cf. also R. F. V. Heuston, 'Judicial Prosopography' (1986) 102 *LQR* 90–113 at 103.

[523] (1890) 6 *LQR* 113. Cf. also Frederick Pollock, 'The Merger Case and Restraint of Trade' (1904) 17 *Harvard L. Rev.* 151–5 at 151–2. Pollock, it might be noted, was not uncritical of the Court of Appeal's decision in *Mogul*, or of Bowen L. J.'s judgment. He urged that the case 'be considered by the House of Lords', adding that: '[t]he notion that acts, e.g. of competition, which would be lawful if done for the sake of defeating A as a trader, become unlawful if done from ill-will to A, a notion which appears to be countenanced by Lord Justice Bowen, introduces into the law a subtle, and possibly perilous, refinement.' (1890) 6 *LQR* 113. The decision was in due course affirmed on appeal to the House of Lords: [1892] AC 25. See further Taggart, above n.231, 210–11. The subsequent development of the English law on intentional torts made it clear that the courts generally considered Bowen L. J.'s judgment to go too far: see G. H. L. Fridman, 'Malice in the Law of Torts' (1958) 21 *Mod. L. Rev.* 484–500 at 496.

[524] See, e.g., Vandevelde, above n.303, 471 ('The first treatise writer to posit a general theory of intentional tort appears to have been Pollock, who in that respect anticipated Holmes by about seven years'); Taggart, above n.231, 167–71; Morris D. Forkosch, 'An Analysis of the "Prima Facie Tort" Cause of Action' (1957) 42 *Cornell L. Q.* 465–82 at 469–71; and Joseph W. Ginn III, 'Prima Facie Tort' (1980) 11 *Cumberland L. Rev.* 113–32 at 114–15. See also *Morrison v National Broadcasting Co.*, 266 N.Y.S. 2d 406, 410–12 (1965); and the memorandum of the Hon. Eduardo C. Robreno in *Charles Shaid of Pennsylvania Inc. v George Hyman Const. Co.*, 947 F. Supp. 844, 847–8 (E.D. Pa. 1996) ('The prima facie tort doctrine carries an honorable pedigree. Its roots can be traced back at least to the late nineteenth century and the seminal pronouncements of Sir Frederick Pollock . . .'). It is worth noting more generally that *Torts*, like *Principles*, has been relied upon regularly in the U.S. courts: see, e.g., *King v Patterson*, 9 A. 705, 710 (N. J. Err. & App. 1887); *Morgan v Andrews*, 64 N. W. 869, 871 (Mich. 1895); *Warax v Cincinnati, N. O. & T. P. Ry. Co.*, 72 F. 637, 643 (C. C. Ky. 1896); *Louisville & N. R. Co. v Spinks*, 30 S. E. 968, 969 (Ga. 1898); *Tuttle v Buck*, 119 N. W. 946, 947–8 (Minn. 1909); *Southern Ry. Co. v Carter*, 51 So. 147, 149 (Ala. 1909); *Martin v Schwertley*, 136 N. W. 218, 220 (Iowa 1912); *Going v Southern Ry. Co.*, 69 So. 73, 75 (Ala. 1915); *Currie v Malloy*, 116 S. E. 564, 567 (N. C. 1923); *Elmore v Atlantic Coast Line Ry. Co.*, 131 S. E. 633, 635 (N.C. 1926); *Adams v F. W. Woolworth Co.*, 257 N.Y.S. 776, 780 (N.Y. Sup. 1932); *Dallas v Wagner*, 168 S.E. 838, 840 (N.C. 1933); *Southern Ry. Co. v Harpe*, 58 N.E. 2d 346, 348 (Ind. 1944); *State ex rel. Bumgarner v Sims*, 79 S.E. 2d 277, 290 (W. Va. 1953); *Rau v Commissioner of Internal Revenue*, 301 F. 2d 51, 57 (9th Cir. 1962); *McDaniel v Bullard*, 216 N.E. 2d 140, 144 (Ill. 1966); *Murphy v Godwin*, 303 A. 2d 668, 674 (Del. Super. 1973); *Alexander v Unification Church of America*, 634 F. 2d 673, 678 (C.A.N.Y. 1980); *Pacific Mutual Life Ins. Co. v Haslip*, 499 U.S. 1, 61 (1991) (O'Connor, J. dissenting).

Not only would the English courts not keep to that path, however, but it was not always clear just what Pollock thought when they departed from it. In 1897, in *Allen v Flood*, the majority of the House of Lords held that a person is free to cause deliberate economic harm to another so long as the means that he employs in doing so are not unlawful in themselves.[525] While Pollock had contended that the causing of wilful harm must, in the absence of lawful justification or excuse, occasion liability, *Allen v Flood* basically established that a particular type of wilful harm—intentionally inflicted economic harm—is, unless unlawfully procured, permissible. Did the decision not fly directly in the face of Pollock's argument? Pollock himself seemed unsure. Whereas the House of Lords in *Allen v Flood* adopted an abstentionist approach to intentionally inflicted economic harm, the Court of Appeal (in *Flood v Jackson*) had appeared to adopt an interventionist approach. This latter approach was well summarized in the Court of Appeal by Lord Esher M. R.:

> [o]ne person has a perfect right to advise another not to make a particular contract, and that other is at perfect liberty to follow that advice. But if the first person uses that persuasion with intent to injure the other, or to injure the person with whom he is going to make the contract, then the act is malicious, and the malice makes that unlawful which would otherwise be lawful.[526]

This interventionist, motive-focused approach, whereby intentional injury causing loss is considered *prima facie* actionable unless the harm can be shown to be justifiable, was the one which was generally adopted in the United States during the late nineteenth and early twentieth centuries.[527] Indeed, it is the approach which Pollock, ahead of Holmes and Bowen, has been credited for inspiring. Yet by 1895, the year in which *Flood v Jackson* was decided, Pollock could be seen to be struggling with that approach. During that year, the House of Lords decided the well-documented case of *Bradford v Pickles*.[528] In *Pickles*, it was held that the lawful use of property does not become illegal because it is prompted by selfish or malicious motives. For Pollock, *Pickles* and *Flood v Jackson* sat uncomfortably alongside one another: whereas the first case established that 'malicious use which has regard to property is not itself an abuse and illegal', the second indicated that 'the malicious use of a right which has not reference to property is, or may be, an abuse, and is, or may be, illegal. As regards the exercise of the one class of rights, motive is irrelevant; as regards the exercise

525 *Allen v Flood* [1898] AC 1. The House of Lords reached its decision in December 1897. On the historical significance of the case, see Tony Weir, *Economic Torts* (Oxford: Clarendon Press, 1997), 21–43.

526 *Flood v Jackson* [1895] 2 QB 21, 38.

527 See Hazel Carty, *An Analysis of the Economic Torts* (Oxford: Oxford UP, 2001), 6–7; also Christian Witting, 'Of Principle and Prima Facie Tort' (1999) 25 *Monash Univ. L. Rev.* 295–316 at 296–302.

528 *Bradford (Mayor of) v Pickles* [1895] AC 587. On this case, see generally Taggart, above n.231, *passim*; and also A. W. B. Simpson, *Victorian Law and the Industrial Spirit* (London: Selden Society, 1995).

of the other class of rights, motive is, or may be, material.'[529] It seemed that something had to give, and, since *Pickles* had already gone to the House of Lords, the appeal of *Flood v Jackson* offered the most obvious solution.

Although Pollock was happy that *Flood v Jackson* was appealed, it is not easy to determine what he thought of *Allen v Flood.* The opening page to his short article published hot on the heels of the decision suggests that he welcomed it. 'When the House of Lords, after the fullest consideration, has spoken the last word, it is hardly needful for those who are satisfied to add to its reasons. As regards the immediate result, we shall only say that a contrary decision would, in our humble opinion, have let loose a disastrous flood of speculative actions.'[530] By the conclusion of that article, however, Pollock was bemoaning their Lordships' failure to produce 'more compact' and 'more satisfying' opinions akin to Holmes's famous dissenting judgment in *Vegelahn v Guntner.*[531] To Holmes himself he wrote frankly of how *Allen v Flood* was composed of '80 or 90 pages of judges' opinions, mostly wrong'.[532] His judgement, however, seems to have been that those in the majority were often verbose and analytically lax rather than wrong. Although there are 'many things the dicta in *Allen v Flood* have unsettled', he claimed in a follow-up letter, 'that decision I think is the only safe one for a world of people who mostly get muddled over subtle distinctions and think them unjust whenever they can't understand'.[533] The conclusion of the majority, after all, was in line with Holmes's dissent.[534] And Holmes's dissent was based upon the argument which he and Pollock had likewise developed with respect to intentional harm: that such harm should give rise to liability in the absence of lawful excuse. In a roundabout way, therefore, it is possible to see that *Allen v Flood* did not fly in the face of Pollock's argument regarding wilful harm. The basic difference between his position and that of the majority of the House of Lords seemed to be one of emphasis: *Allen v Flood* laid stress upon the general permissibility of a particular type of intentional harm, whereas Pollock argued that one should generally be liable for intentionally injuring another. Both positions allowed for a middle ground.[535]

[529] (1896) 12 *LQR* 5. See also Pollock to Holmes, 29 December 1896, in *PHL* i. 72.

[530] Frederick Pollock, '*Allen* v *Flood*' (1898) 14 *LQR* 129–32 at 129.

[531] Ibid. 132. [532] Pollock to Holmes, 28 December 1897, in *PHL* i. 81.

[533] Pollock to Holmes, 30 March 1898, in *PHL* i. 84–5. On analytical laxity in *Allen v Flood*, see John Finnis, 'Intention in Tort Law', in *Philosophical Foundations of Tort Law*, ed. D. G. Owen (Oxford: Clarendon Press, 1995), 229–47 at 237–42.

[534] Cf. Holmes J. in *Vegelahn v Guntner*, 167 Mass. 92, 108–9 (1896) with Lord Watson in *Allen v Flood*, above n.525, 107; and see *TLT(6)* 317 n.g ('. . . the dissenting judgment of Holmes J. seems to be in accordance with our own latest authorities').

[535] Cf. J. B. Ames, 'How Far An Act May be a Tort Because of the Wrongful Motive of the Actor' (1905) 18 *Harvard L. Rev.* 411–22 at 422 (repr. in Ames, *Lectures on Legal History*, above n.123, 399–411 at 410–11), concluding that Lord Watson's remark in *Allen v Flood* (above n.525, 92) that 'the law of England does not . . . take into account motive as constituting an element of civil wrong' is 'as far from the truth as would be the statement that malevolently to damage another is always a tort. The truth lies

If *Allen v Flood* posed a genuine difficulty for Pollock, it was that of showing how the decision was a legitimate exception to a more general principle. This difficulty seemed to be preying on his mind in the sixth edition of *Torts*.[536] Just how far-reaching an exception was *Allen v Flood* to his proposition that there exists a general 'negative duty' not to do wilful harm? 'The only thing that seems fairly certain' in light of the decision, Pollock remarked,

> is that whatever may be the extent of liability [for procuring breach of contract] . . . , the decisive element of liability is not malice. Apparently, the cause of action (if it is to be allowed) must be simply the wilful procurement of the breach of a legal duty, and the exceptions (for exceptions there must be) stand on some other ground than absence of ill-will towards the plaintiff.[537]

For Pollock, this was not certain enough. In the United States, he claimed, the scope of liability for wilful procurement of breach of legal duty had been formulated more precisely.[538] Although *Allen v Flood* established that lawful conduct intended to harm is not rendered unlawful because of that intent, the precise range of circumstances in which liability *would* arise as a result of intentional harm was far from obvious. '[I]n England, . . . only the authority of the House of Lords can finally dispose of the doubts which still surround this topic. For the present they are rather increased than diminished.'[539]

The sixth edition of *Torts* appeared just too late for the inclusion of *Quinn v Leathem*, which came for hearing before the House of Lords in May 1901.[540] The decision, James Barr Ames asserted in 1905, rendered *Allen v Flood* 'harmless'.[541] In the seventh edition of *Torts*, Pollock, not surprisingly, was not prepared to say anything quite so forceful: *Allen v Flood*, he declared in the Preface, had 'been largely modified by the decision of the House of Lords in *Quinn v Leathem*'.[542] Whereas *Allen v Flood* established that intentionally inflicted economic harm would only be actionable if some unlawful act could be demon-

in the middle. In certain cases, in spite of the wrongful motive of the actor, malevolently to damage another is lawful, either because the act is merely the exercise of an absolute legal right, or because it is justified by paramount considerations of public policy. Except in such cases, however, wilfully to damage another by a positive act and from a spirit of malevolence is a tort, even though the same act, if induced by a rightful motive, would be lawful.' See also Pollock, 'Torts', above n.293, 191–3; and (1906) 22 *LQR* 118.

536 See *TLT(6)* v; also H. L. Wilgus, 'The Authority of *Allen v Flood*' (1902) 1 *Michigan L. Rev.* 28–57 at 28–9.

537 *TLT(6)* 318. 538 See *TLT* 319. 539 *TLT(6)* 319.

540 *Quinn v Leathem* [1901] AC 495. The case, or rather Lord Lindley's judgment in the case, is subjected to an interesting jurisprudential analysis by N. E. Simmonds, 'Rights at the Cutting Edge', in Matthew H. Kramer, N. E. Simmonds, and Hillel Steiner, *A Debate over Rights: Philosophical Enquiries* (Oxford: Clarendon Press, 1998), 113–232 at 168–76; cf. also N. E. Simmonds, *Central Issues in Jurisprudence: Justice, Law and Rights*, 2nd edn. (London: Sweet & Maxwell, 2002), 273–4.

541 Ames, above n.535, 411 (repr. 399).

542 *TLT(7)* v. On the House of Lords' move from *Allen v Flood* to *Quinn v Leathem*, see Heuston, above n.522, 92–5.

strated, *Quinn v Leathem* established that lawful conduct by two or more might be actionable when conduct by one is not: the principle that lawful conduct intended to harm does not become unlawful because intentional, in other words, had to be considered in light of the tort of conspiracy. Did this proviso to *Allen v Flood* dispose of those doubts to which Pollock had adverted in the sixth edition of *Torts*? The answer to this question is more or less obvious from the Preface to the seventh edition. One of the clearest clues to indignation on Pollock's part is often his resort to the language of personal duty. 'It has been my duty to make an attempt towards summing up the results [of *Quinn v Leathem*] in a form which, so far as possible, may be consistent in itself and not contradict any binding authority.'[543] Making sense of *Quinn v Leathem* was difficult—notwithstanding the obligation to try—not least because the emphasis placed upon the tort of conspiracy was unnecessary: 'the cause of action was, in effect, ruining the plaintiff's business by coercing his customers not to deal with him'[544]—it was the presence of threats, in other words, rather than the fact of combination, that distinguished *Quinn v Leathem* from *Allen v Flood.* The doubts, Pollock concluded, remained: still '[t]here is a class of cases . . . where the exceptions are not yet adequately refined. . . . We do not need the House of Lords to tell us that whoever unlawfully interferes with his neighbour commits an unlawful act; we desire to have it made clear what kind of conduct is unlawful and what is not.'[545]

In *Rookes v Barnard*, Lord Reid, elaborating on his oft-quoted observation that '[i]t is exceedingly difficult to determine just what was decided in *Quinn v Leathem*', referred approvingly to Pollock's assessment of the decision.[546] Perhaps it is indicative of Pollock's juristic status that, sixty years after his having criticized the House of Lords for its failure to determine the circumstances in which wilful harm is unlawful harm, a Law Lord should have considered his criticism to be worthy of a compliment. To emphasize this point, however, would be to risk distorting the significance of Pollock's ideas in this particular context. For, as Pollock's successor as the editor of *Torts* was to state candidly, Pollock's argument about wilful harm was not accepted in the English courts.[547] Pollock himself, rather than adopt an obviously oppositional stance, tried to manoeuvre his own perspective so that it did not seem wholly out of line with the decisions of the House of Lords. Of course, this did not stop him from sniping at dicta and detail, and indeed it is difficult, when setting out Pollock's views on a decision like *Allen v Flood*, to determine precisely what he believed. Pollock had an opinion, but he knew that his opinion was not widely shared among the senior judiciary; and so he sought to be enthusias-

543 *TLT(7)* v. 544 *TLT(7)* 318–19.

545 *TLT(7)* 320. See also (1925) 41 *LQR* 369 (on *Sorrell v Smith* [1925] AC 700).

546 *Rookes v Barnard* [1964] 1 Lloyd's Rep. 28, 35–6.

547 See *TLT(14)* 44–5; also Forkosch, above n.524, 470 n.30; and Jack E. Brown, 'The Rise and Threatened Demise of the Prima Facie Tort Principle' (1959) 54 *Northwestern Univ. L. Rev.* 563–74 at 566–7.

tic about judicial efforts to develop points of principle but also struggled to resist attacking those efforts which he simply could not square with his own argument about the wrongfulness of intentional harm. It was a sizeable feat to perform.

In one instance, the feat seemed all but beyond him. We saw earlier that Pollock, in the notes to his Civil Wrongs Bill, claimed that if B intentionally digs a deep well on his land in order to do harm to A, then B, having used his land 'for the unlawful purpose of doing wilful harm to A', ought 'on principle' to be held liable for his conduct. In *Bradford v Pickles*, the House of Lords held that B could not be liable in these circumstances because, contrary to the implication in Pollock's assertion, the fact that B's use of his property was maliciously motivated did not render that use unlawful: indeed, the motive which prompts the use is immaterial. How would Pollock deal with the House of Lords' clear refusal to adopt his own perspective? According to Landon, 'Pollock . . . refused to alter his exposition. There was a stubborn texture in him which made him unwilling to admit that his theories were erroneous, whatever the House of Lords might say.'[548]

But Pollock did alter his exposition. When 'a learned contributor' produced for the *LQR* a note contending that, as between *Flood v Jackson* and *Bradford v Pickles*, the former was the preferable decision, Pollock, adopting his Editor's voice, added immediately that '[w]e are unable to agree to this'.[549] Of course, this was not tantamount to support for what the House of Lords had done. But he clearly recognized resistance to be pointless. In the early editions of *Torts*, Pollock had asserted that there was 'on principle . . . much to recommend' those 'recognized authorities in the law of Scotland who say that an owner using his own land must act "not in mere spite or malice, *in aemulationem vicini*" '.[550] Unfortunately, he added, 'there is really no positive English authority on the matter.'[551] In *Pickles*, Lord Watson dealt with the matter directly: 'I am aware', he noted, 'that the phrase "*in aemulationem vicini*" was at one time frequently, and is even now occasionally, very loosely used by Scottish lawyers. But I know of no case in which the act of a proprietor has been found to be illegal . . . where it was not attended with offence or injury to the legal rights of his neighbour.' In essence, he continued, the law of Scotland corresponds in this context 'with the law of England. No use of property, which would be legal if due to a proper motive, can become illegal because it is prompted by a motive which is improper or even malicious.'[552] In the fifth edition of *Torts*, the first to appear after *Pickles*, Pollock removed his earlier observations concerning the appropriately principled nature of the Scottish position and accepted that, as regards malicious use of one's land, there now was a positive English authority on the matter.[553] Having himself 'supposed . . . that the

548 *TLT(14)* 45. 549 (1896) 12 *LQR* 6. 550 *TLT* 137. 551 *TLT* 138.
552 *Bradford v Pickles*, above n.528, 598.
553 See *TLT(5)* 139–40; also Taggart, above n.231, 177.

law of Scotland does recognize inquiry into . . . motive or disposition', he now appreciated 'that no such difference between the English and the Scottish systems really exists', that in neither system was malice relevant to civil liability.[554] Whatever Pollock thought of the decision in *Pickles*—and it is not clear just what he did think of it—he appreciated that it was conclusive: indeed, he very pointedly did not subject the decision to the type of damage-limitation exercise that he had undertaken in relation to *Rylands v Fletcher*. In this instance, there really was a *res judicata*; so far as Pollock was concerned, after *Pickles*, '[t]he vacuum in English authority had been filled, and that was an end to the matter.'[555]

iii. Conclusion

As a treatise writer Pollock, it should be remembered, produced not only *Principles of Contract* and *The Law of Torts* but also *A Digest of the Law of Partnership*, which we briefly considered in chapter 2. It might be argued that the *Digest* was his most influential legal text, considering that it evolved into the Partnership Act of 1890.[556] But Pollock himself did not regard it that way. For him, one of the principal reasons for the introduction of a Partnership Act was to enable the authorization, and to regulate the formation, of limited liability partnerships.[557] This particular reform initiative had met with no success throughout the mid-nineteenth century and fared no better in Pollock's hands: in 1882, the limited liability partnership proposal was dropped from the Partnership Bill, and it was not until 1907 that such partnerships were recognized by English law.[558] Pollock's apparent air of indifference upon seeing his *Digest* transformed into a statute seems attributable not to the fact that one of his principal proposals was stymied, but to the fact that he considered legislation to be ancillary to the real business of law. Upon the passing of the Act, he wrote desultorily of how he 'doubted whether [it] will add much to the knowledge of the law possessed by practising members of the Chancery Bar', and that even if 'members of the Common Law Bar, and probably students . . . , will be thankful for the Act', it must be borne in mind that '[c]odes are not meant to dispense lawyers from being learned'.[559] The fact is, he believed, that good legislation will often do nothing more than schematize that which good

[554] (1896) 12 *LQR* 7. See also Pollock's editorial postscript to Melius de Villiers, 'Nuisances in Roman Law' (1897) 13 *LQR* 387–94 at 394.

[555] Taggart, above n.231, 177.

[556] For Pollock's own account of how the text became law, see *DLP(5)* v–vi.

[557] See *EJE* 99–106; also *DLP* 20–36.

[558] See *EJE* 102 ('many attempts to introduce the [limited liability partnership] system have been made in this country, and thus far none have been successful'). On the rejection of limited liability partnership throughout the history of English law, see Ron Harris, *Industrializing English Law: Entrepreneurship and Business Organization, 1720–1844* (Cambridge: Cambridge UP, 2000), 29–31, 273–4. For its eventual recognition, see the Limited Partnerships Act 1907, 7 Edw. VII c. 24.

[559] *DLP(5)* vi–viii.

lawyers already know: '[t]he right kind of consolidating legislation is that which makes the law more accessible without altering its principles or its methods.'[560] What genuinely interested Pollock were these principles and methods: legal principles and methods, particularly legal principles, were, for him, the engine of the law. In the many editions of his treatises on contract and torts, we find him charting the life and the pedigree of the various principles that compose these bodies of doctrine. The study of different types and manifestations of principle was not only an activity he loved, but also the most valuable work he believed a jurist could undertake. If chapter 4 was essentially an essay on his devotion to the intricacies, blemishes, obscurities, and perversities of the English common law, this chapter has been dedicated to his effort to demonstrate that devotion.

The length of this chapter alone should make it obvious that his effort was anything but half-hearted. Having travelled this distance, any reader is entitled to ask what has been established here, other than that Pollock loved law. In essence, there are six basic insights to be drawn from this chapter, and it probably makes sense, by way of conclusion, to try to collect these insights together.

The first, and perhaps the most obvious observation to offer is that Pollock contributed crucially to the modern English legal treatise-writing tradition. During the nineteenth century, English legal treatise writing was the province of practitioners rather than academics. Matters could hardly have been otherwise. There existed at this time no English academic-legal profession to speak of—indeed even Pollock, we know, was not primarily a university lawyer. But he signalled the beginning of a change from one juristic era to another. '[T]he old fashioned English lawyer's idea of a satisfactory body of law', Thomas Erskine Holland remarked in 1869, 'was a chaos with a full index',[561] and English legal treatise writers before Pollock were basically contributing to the effort to index this chaos.[562] Pollock was one of the most energetic and successful of a number of late-Victorian treatise writers who were trying to do something different, who were out to demonstrate that 'in the beginning there were principles, and that in the end those principles were found to cover a large multitude of cases deducible from them.'[563] We should resist trying to

[560] *DLP(5)* viii.

[561] Thomas Erskine Holland, 'The Classification of the Statutes' (1869), in his *Essays Upon the Form of the Law* (London: Butterworths, 1870), 161–72 at 171.

[562] See Simpson, above n.14, 636–62. For an abridged account of the same, see A. W. B. Simpson, 'The Legal Treatise and Legal Theory', in *Law, Litigants and the Legal Profession*, eds. E. W. Ives and A. H. Manchester (London: Royal Historical Society, 1983), 11–29 at 13–24. Cf. Frederick Pollock, 'Our Jubilee' (1935) 51 *LQR* 5–10 at 5 ('At the date of my call to the Bar text-books were for the most part either works of authors already classical, encumbered rather than refitted with the confused annotations of editors, or mere repertories of decisions compiled with little sound learning and no literary skill. Some editors, indeed, were really learned, but few had the gift of orderly method, and of their style the less said the better').

[563] T. F. T. Plucknett, *Early English Legal Literature* (Cambridge: Cambridge UP, 1958), 19. Even Pollock—who as a treatise writer, we have seen, could adopt a decidedly formalist approach to the

hold up Pollock as a fine example of the Victorian legal scientist as public moralist. But he was a perfect example of the legal scientist as successful treatise writer.

The second point to note is that Pollock was, indeed, a great treatise writer. Many English treatise writers failed to succeed at the Bar, and so even if barristers had considered it permissible to cite the works of these writers in court it is unlikely that they would have felt inclined to do so. Although Pollock was no practising barrister, he was a valued adviser to the legal profession.[564] This may have been due in part to the fact that the Pollock name was, as various commentators have noted, equated within the profession with sound legal skills and judgment.[565] But the name was not everything. Pollock, as other lawyers have appreciated, was genuinely a skilled expositor of legal principles. '[T]here is not the least evidence', Simpson has remarked, 'that Dean Langdell, the Continental Pandectists, or even the great Savigny had any effect on the nineteenth-century common law of tort, either in England, the United States, or anywhere else.'[566] But Pollock seems to have been a different case. Not only were his works frequently cited in the English courts while he was alive—a point which was noted in the previous chapter—but those citations often did seem to be indicative of his influence upon the arguments of counsel and judges in relation to both contract and torts.[567]

The third point to note is that Pollock cannot straightforwardly be presented as a legal formalist or as an arch-rationalizer of legal doctrine. 'The common law frame of mind', Sugarman argues,

> assumes that although the law may appear to be irrational, chaotic and particularistic, if one digs deep enough and knows what one is looking for, then it will soon become evident that the law is an internally coherent and unified body of rules. This coherence and unity stem from the fact that law is grounded in, and logically derived from,

presentation of doctrine—considered it futile to try to produce treatises which essentially serve as legal indices. 'Ambitious writers have sometimes gone to work', he wrote, 'as if it were possible to reduce the whole contents of a legal system to a sort of classified catalogue where there would be no repetitions or cross references, and the classification would explain itself. Ambition on that scale is destined to disappointment by the nature of things.' Frederick Pollock, 'Divisions of Law' (1894) 8 *Harvard L. Rev.* 187–99 at 187–8. See also *FBJ* 80; and Waddams, above n.137, 230–1.

[564] See Fifoot, above n.21, 136 ('A brooding presence near the Bench . . .').

[565] See, e.g., John Smith, 'Dons and Judges: Friend or Foe?' (1998) 5 *Judicial Studies Board Jnl.* 2–5 at 2.

[566] A. W. Brian Simpson, 'The Elusive Truth About Holmes' (1997) 95 *Michigan L. Rev.* 2027–43 at 2032.

[567] See Lord Tomlin, 'The Law Quarterly Review' (1935), as reported (presumably by A. L. Goodhart) at (1935) 51 *LQR* 568–71, 570 ('What the influence of those two books [sc., *Principles* and *Torts*] has been in all the lands which own the sway of the Common Law is something beyond measurement'). Since Tomlin's address was an after-dinner tribute to Pollock, he could hardly have said anything negative. Indeed, some of his other remarks in this tribute—e.g., '[t]here is none to stand beside' Pollock 'in the world of the law. . . . There is none other of like stature with him'—are overblown. None the less, Tomlin's assessment of the influence of *Principles* and *Torts* seems to have been widely shared among lawyers and judges of the period and ought not to be discounted simply because it was offered as part of a general exercise in flattery.

a handful of general principles; and that whole subject-areas such as contracts and torts are distinguished by some common principles or elements which fix the boundaries of the subject.[568]

There is no doubt that Pollock liked legal subject-areas to have boundaries: this much is evident from his effort to compartmentalize the law of torts. But he did not believe—for all that he exhibited the classic common law mindset—that bodies of doctrine are necessarily internally coherent, or logically derived from principles. For Pollock, one fascinating aspect of the common law, one part of its genius, is its capacity to lack coherence or defy logic and yet still be reasonable. Only by appreciating this insight, he believed, can we understand how common law systems can uphold mutual promises as consideration for one another. To claim, as Pollock did, that the common law is founded on reason is not the same as claiming that it is rational, or even potentially rational. His treatises, in short, were not rationalizing exercises.

This last point can be developed into a more general one concerning historical as opposed to juristic argument. Rarely are there any absolutes with Pollock. We have seen in this chapter how he would inspire an idea and then back away from it, formulate a powerful argument and then qualify it, provide an arresting definition of a concept and then basically dismiss the concept itself: dead-ends abound, and they can be frustrating. But it is important not to make out that Pollock was bolder than he really was. Aggrandizing his accomplishments might make for better stories; but the result will be poorer history. To provide an account of Pollock's work on contract and torts is to show how we cannot judge the quality or predict the impact of a legal idea by reference to the forcefulness of its expression. Pollock was no great defender of consideration, yet his definition of the doctrine proved a success in the courts. He ultimately laid to rest his own argument about liability for intentional wrongdoing; yet that argument, for all that it was rejected by the House of Lords, was very well received in the United States. In these ways and others, Pollock's work demonstrates that the impact of juristic speculation is subtle, and that legal historians may well make serious errors of judgement where they constantly accord most significance to the loudest voices. Even the strongest arguments, indeed, will not always be the most historically significant ones.

The fifth general point to draw from this chapter is that Pollock's treatises were not wholly lacking in normative arguments. 'Pollock was not a juristic speculator', Landon declared in the fourteenth edition of *Torts*. 'He was little interested in what the law ought to be.'[569] It is perfectly understandable that

[568] David Sugarman, 'Legal Theory, the Common Law Mind and the Making of the Textbook Tradition', in *Legal Theory and the Common Law*, ed. W. Twining (Oxford: Blackwell, 1986), 26–61 at 26.

[569] *TLT(14)* 43. Cf. Fifoot, above n.21, 55 ('even [Pollock's] tough mind was enervated by the contemporary itch to moralise').

Landon should have described Pollock, certainly Pollock the treatise writer, thus: as was noted earlier in this chapter, one has to look very closely indeed at *Principles* and *Torts* to discover Pollock's thoughts on particular issues. But we have seen that close inspection does, sometimes, reveal those thoughts, and that Pollock did use his treatises to advance arguments about, for example, contractual good faith, remoteness of damage, and liability for intentional harm. We have seen, furthermore, that although these arguments were often presented *sotto voce*, counsel and judges by no means always failed to heed them.

It may well have been precisely because his arguments were subtle and understated that they sometimes proved influential. Another reason for their influence may have been Pollock's persistence. Our final general observation is that it is often the diligent and the unspectacular that makes the deepest long-term impact on the development of the law. We have noted already in this book that Pollock was no Holmes. He was, rather, Holmes's worker-bee, wallflower sister. But for all the dryness of *Principles* and *Torts*, they were highly valuable to the legal profession. Indeed, for English lawyers and judges they contained all the right ingredients: trustworthy, carefully-compartmentalized, regularly updated accounts of the case law; analyses rooted in, and often appealing to, common sense; explanations of doctrine by reference to broader principles; indications of where the legal rules seemed unsatisfactory; and a modicum of decidedly muted argument. Juristic pyrotechnics were not what the legal profession wanted. Prosaic reliability—Pollock—was a far more valuable commodity.

Treatise writing was not Pollock's only great juristic skill. We now turn away from his treatises and examine his initiatives with the Law Reports and the *Law Quarterly Review*. As we have seen in this chapter, the work that he put into the *LQR* sometimes complemented that which he put into his treatises. The purpose of the next chapter, however, is to consider Pollock not so much as a legal writer as a legal editor. For it is through editing—editing the words of judges, and serving as the editor of England's first academic-legal journal—that he made his other significant contribution to the development of modern English legal thought.

6

EDITORSHIPS

> But to whom was he, Tom Towers, responsible? No one could insult him; no one could inquire into him. He could speak out withering words, and no one could answer him: ministers courted him, though perhaps they knew not his name; bishops feared him; judges doubted their own verdicts unless he confirmed them; and generals, in their councils of war, did not consider more deeply what the enemy would do, than what *The Jupiter* would say.[1]

It would be wrong to think that the average Victorian editor bore much resemblance to Tom Towers, Trollope's editor of *The Jupiter*. John T. Delane, one of the more notoriously autocratic editors of *The Times*, is reputedly the inspiration for the character,[2] but few nineteenth-century editors—and certainly none apart from newspaper editors—had anything approaching the power of Delane. The nineteenth century was the age of the editor, all the same. Not only is the editor 'essentially a nineteenth-century creation',[3] it has been claimed, but '[e]diting is at the core of the Victorian experience'; indeed, 'the editor was situated at the nucleus of the Victorian world'.[4]

The Victorians, being of an era during which print was popularized, and before the arrival of competition in the form of the electronic media, perhaps not surprisingly felt an intense affection for words in print. Many nineteenth-century newspapers filled page after page by reporting the business of magistrates' courts—not only trials but examinations and committals as well—because their readers seemed never to tire of such material.[5] 'No one familiar with the Victorian press will have failed to wonder at the tremendous appetite of its readers for extensive verbatim reporting of parliamentary, judicial, and other forms of proceedings.'[6] By the late nineteenth century, this

[1] Anthony Trollope, *The Warden* (London: Penguin, 1994 [1855]), 135.

[2] See Christopher Kent, 'Higher Journalism and the Mid-Victorian Clerisy' (1969) 13 *Victorian Studies* 181–98 at 191.

[3] Christopher Kent, 'The Editor and the Law', in *Innovators and Preachers: The Role of the Editor in Victorian England*, ed. J. H. Wiener (Westport, Conn.: Greenwood Press, 1985), 99–119 at 99.

[4] Joel H. Wiener, 'Introduction', in *Innovators and Preachers*, above n.3, xi–xix at xii–xiii.

[5] See Marjorie Jones, *Justice and Journalism: A Study of the Influence of Newspaper Reporting upon the Administration of Justice by Magistrates* (Chichester: Barry Rose, 1974), 7–31.

[6] Kent, above n.3, 106.

appetite—indeed, the general appetite for print—was easy to satisfy. The development during the nineteenth century of mechanized typesetting and powered printing, along with decreasing paper costs, meant that printed material could be produced more cheaply and quickly than ever before.[7] And as print proliferated, it became increasingly obvious that the printed page could often benefit from, indeed was regularly in need of, editorial intervention.

While such intervention probably occurred only superficially in those publications which were in the business of straightforwardly reporting the day-to-day affairs of, say, courts and Parliament, the editor could serve as a crucial mediator between authors and audience when the purpose of the publication—be it a newspaper, a periodical, or whatever—was to exercise and encourage discrimination. Studies of the editorial initiatives of figures such as Leslie Stephen and John Stuart Mill—to offer just two examples—show how the Victorian editor tended to play a crucial role in determining the identity and the voice of a 'serious' journal.[8] Editors make choices—about whom to commission, what to accept and reject, what to excise, insert, or rewrite, where to place contributions, and so on—and the ability to make those choices means that the editor often has considerable power.[9] Before Francis Jeffrey, the creator of the *Edinburgh Review*, Walter Bagehot wrote in 1855, 'an editor was a bookseller's drudge; he is now a distinguished functionary'.[10] The founder of the *Nineteenth Century*, James Knowles, Pollock remarked, was not so much an editor as 'a literary showman. His peculiar gift was a discerning eye for the contributors whose names would make the most attractive contents list for the next few months'.[11] While Victorian editors only rarely made fortunes or found themselves named in the Honours List, it has been observed, many of them were powerful movers and shakers in nineteenth-century intellectual life.[12]

But this was not power without accountability. The better quality Victorian periodicals were, to borrow Sir Walter Besant's description of the *Saturday*

[7] See generally Simon Eliot, *Some Patterns and Trends in British Publishing, 1800–1919. Occasional Papers of the Bibliographical Society, vol. viii* (London: The Bibliographical Society, 1994); Alexis Weedon, *Victorian Publishing: The Economics of Book Production for a Mass Market, 1836–1916* (Aldershot: Ashgate, 2003). Paper costs decreased significantly when the stamp tax was abolished in the mid-1850s: see Stamp Act 1854, 17 & 18 Vict. c. 83, s. 1 (stamp duties repealed 'in respect of . . . several Instruments, Matters, and Things . . . , or upon and in respect of the Vellum, Parchment, or Paper upon which any of them respectively shall be written').

[8] See Barbara Quinn Schmidt, 'In the Shadow of Thackeray: Leslie Stephen as the Editor of the *Cornhill Magazine*', in *Innovators and Preachers*, above n.3, 77–96; and Ann P. Robson and John M. Robson, 'Private and Public Goals: John Stuart Mill and the *London and Westminster*', ibid. 231–57.

[9] For a succinct analysis of the various dimensions of editorial power (though in a context very different from the one being considered here), see Nicholas Spadaccini and Jenaro Talens, 'Introduction: Textual Editing, the Writing of Literature, and Literary History', in *The Politics of Editing*, eds. N. Spadaccini and J. Talens (Minneapolis: University of Minnesota Press, 1992), ix–xxii.

[10] Walter Bagehot, 'The First Edinburgh Reviewers' (1855), in *The Collected Works of Walter Bagehot. Vol. i: The Literary Essays (in two volumes)*, ed. N. St John Stevas (London: The Economist, 1965), 309–41 at 332.

[11] *FMG* 93.

[12] See Hartley S. Spratt, 'The Aesthetics of Editorship: Creating Taste in the Victorian Art World', in *Innovators and Preachers*, above n.3, 43–60 at 43.

Review, seeking to engage with 'the educated mind of the country'.[13] The readers of these periodicals were invariably intelligent, discriminating, and opinionated. Few of them would have struggled to detect an inappropriate or incompetent editor.[14] Many of them could express dismay and disgruntlement in the same 'tone of acidic gentlemanliness'[15] that ran throughout most of the journals that they read. Contributors to and readers of these journals were often quick to tell editors just what they thought about the handling of their articles or the contents of particular issues,[16] and perceived editorial weaknesses would often attract criticism.[17] To earn and maintain the respect of those who wrote for and read his periodical, therefore, the late nineteenth-century editor would usually have to take a decidedly professional approach to his role. Pollock, in his memoirs, remarked on just how many late nineteenth-century editors seemed successfully to adopt such an approach.[18] Whereas 'gentlemanly amateurism' had been very much the style of the early nineteenth-century journal editors, the editors of the second half of the century were generally attentive to intellectual developments within the evolving university system.[19] Indeed, editing served the ambitions of that system: during the late nineteenth century, some members of the emerging academic profession came to regard editing—the editing of books as well as of journals—as a career opportunity.[20] Academics were unlikely to secure the editorships of any of the major Victorian monthly, fortnightly, or weekly magazines—those posts were invariably landed by metropolitan men of

[13] Sir Walter Besant, *Autobiography of Sir Walter Besant* (London: Hutchinson & Co., 1902), 93. As was noted in chapter 2, the *Saturday Review* was for many years edited by Pollock's brother. For every *Saturday Review*, *Edinburgh Review*, and *Nineteenth Century* there was many a lower-grade, less discriminating quarterly whose editor was in a position associated not so much with power and respect as with frequent desperation. See Joanne Shattock, 'Spreading it Thinly: Some Victorian Reviewers at Work' (1976) 9 *Victorian Periodicals Newsletter* 84–7. 'An authoritative article in one of the major quarterlies', Shattock notes, 'was not uncommonly the product of months of effort. . . . But when one begins to examine the affairs of a not so august organ of opinion, it is clear that the editor was frequently forced to settle for something a bit more slapdash, and often second-hand' (ibid. 84). Indeed, those with a mind to be cynical about modern academics boosting *vitae* by recycling their work, or about lowered scholarly standards in a world where journals struggling for copy cannot be too choosy, should note that the Victorians were hardly more commendable. Some Victorian essayists, Shattock shows, devised various methods that 'made a little go a very long way' (ibid. 86).

[14] See Kent, above n.2, 193–4; and Alvar Ellegård, 'The Readership of the Periodical Press in Mid-Victorian Britain' (1957) 63 *Göteborgs Universitets Årsskrift* 1–41 at 10–11, 22–8.

[15] Kent, above n.2, 185.

[16] See Robson and Robson, above n.8, 242–4.

[17] See Edwin Mallard Everett, *The Party of Humanity: The Fortnightly Review and Its Contributors 1865–1874* (Chapel Hill: University of North Carolina Press, 1939), 14–15, 19–20.

[18] See *FMG* 89–93.

[19] Joanne Shattock, 'Showman, Lion-Hunter, or Hack: The Quarterly Editor at Mid-Century' (1983) 16 *Victorian Periodicals Rev.* 89–103 at 92. Shattock observes that whereas the Editorship of the *Quarterly Review* was regarded in 1825 as the sort of post that no person with serious professional ambitions would accept, by the 1850s it was considered to be a respectable scholarly position (ibid. 98). See also Stefan Collini, *English Pasts: Essays in History and Culture* (Oxford: Oxford UP, 1999), 308–9; and, on gentlemanly amateurism as a lamentable nineteenth-century English trait, George C. Brodrick, 'A Nation of Amateurs' (1900) 48 *Nineteenth Century* 521–35.

[20] See Rosemary Jann, *The Art and Science of Victorian History* (Columbus: Ohio State UP, 1985), 216–17.

letters.[21] During the last four decades of the nineteenth century, nevertheless, a number of new periodicals were established which, being both scholarly and specialist, required editors with academic ability and credentials. *Nature*, founded in 1869, led the way; *Mind* was established in 1876, the *English Historical Review* in 1886, the *Classical Review* and the *Proceedings of the Aristotelian Society* in 1887, and the *Economic Journal* in 1891. The *Law Quarterly Review*, a somewhat unconventional member of this family, was founded in 1884.

Editing was very clearly part of Pollock's professional identity. He may have spent twenty years as a non-resident Oxford professor, but he was the Editor of the *Law Quarterly Review* for thirty-five years and Editor-in-Chief of the Law Reports for forty. Whereas the role of professor never seemed fully to engage him, his professional attitude towards and his remarkable stamina for editing suggested that he was trying to emulate those editors whom he so admired at the helm of the great late-Victorian periodicals. As Editor-in-Chief of the Law Reports he was responsible for the reporting of important English case law, and as Editor of the *LQR* it was his task to secure as well as to produce a continuous body of legal commentary—much of it on the cases he had included in the Law Reports. Both editorships involved making judgements that could affect the development of the law. With the Law Reports these judgements mainly concerned which cases to report, and how to report them. Determinations about inclusion—what to cover, accept, solicit, and so on—obviously had to be made with respect to the *LQR* as well. Pollock's influence upon the law as Editor of the *LQR* is ascribable not so much to the way in which he edited, however, as to the way in which he would use the journal's pages to mount campaigns and advance causes.

The principal purpose of this chapter is to consider Pollock's achievements and influence as editor of these two publications. With both there is a difficulty in that certain pieces of information that would have proved valuable for assessing his editorial work appear not to be available. Shortly after Pollock's retirement as Editor-in-Chief of the Law Reports, the Incorporated Council of Law Reporting moved its administrative office from Montague Street to Serjeants' Inn. In May 1941, Serjeants' Inn was destroyed by a German air raid, and the Council's Minute Book number 5, covering the period 1909–40, was lost.[22] Furthermore, it appears that Pollock kept very little correspondence at his chambers relating to either the Law Reports or the *LQR*.[23] As regards the *LQR* specifically, it is worth noting that the journal does

[21] See Stefan Collini, *Public Moralists: Political Thought and Public Life in Britain 1850–1930* (Oxford: Clarendon Press, 1991), 40–1.

[22] The Incorporated Council of Law Reporting Minute Book no. 6 (covering the period 1941–51) contains a note providing the following statement: 'Book no. 5 destroyed by enemy action in May 1941 in the War 1939–1945.'

[23] Paul Baker, letter to author, 17 October 2002: 'Pollock's chambers were on the second floor north of 13 Old Square [Lincoln's Inn]. After his death they were taken over by Professor A. L. Goodhart who had been sharing them since he became editor of the Law Quarterly Review in 1926. Shortly after I became Editor of the Review in 1971, Goodhart gave up the chambers and I assisted him in

not maintain an archive, and that its publishers hold no material relating to Pollock's editorship. In short, there are gaps in the original sources which may explain why, in this chapter, accounts of certain of Pollock's editorial initiatives are not as detailed as one might have liked them to be.

Enough information is available, none the less, to make it possible to advance one specific line of argument. Not only was editing at the very least as much a part of Pollock's professional identity as was being a jurist, but it may well be that his work as an editor had a greater influence upon the development of the law than did his more conventional juristic pursuits. To be more assertive in setting forth this argument would be rash: it is impossible, after all, precisely to measure Pollock's influence as an editor against his influence as a jurist. But it should become clear as this chapter unfolds that Pollock the editor seems to be at least as significant a figure in the history of English law as was Pollock the treatise writer. And there would appear to be no controversy at all in claiming that Pollock the editor was far more influential a figure than was Pollock the professor of jurisprudence.

Before we turn to the Law Reports and the *LQR*, it is worth trying to explain why editing was so much a feature of Pollock's professional identity. Part of the explanation is that he clearly enjoyed editing, even if aspects of the job would sometimes exasperate him. There is also the fact that editing was, for Pollock as for many other Victorian intellectuals, a major source of income.[24] He appears not to have needed the money.[25] None the less, his attitude towards royalties, which was touched upon in chapter 2, shows that money mattered to him; and although it would be wrong to suggest that money was always a determining factor in the professional choices that he made, there seems no doubt that his taste for particular tasks was swayed to a large degree by the amount of remuneration that those tasks attracted. In the next section we will see that, for Pollock, editing was one of the tasks that generated the best financial returns. More specifically, and perhaps most significantly, his work within the university system appears never to have proved as reliably lucrative as did some of his work as an editor.

clearing them. There were a considerable number of Pollock's books, but very little correspondence.' Pollock may well have thrown away much of his correspondence. There is certainly an indication that he was inclined to dispose of material for which he no longer had use. Lincoln's Inn Library possesses a catalogue of Pollock's personal books (MS Misc. 1047), handwritten by Pollock himself and dated October 1888, in which Pollock notes (at 1): '[b]ooks struck out and marked T were given to the Toronto University Library, July 1890'.

[24] On editing as a source of income in the late nineteenth century, see Collini, above n.21, 41–2.

[25] Pollock's will (obtainable from the York Probate Registry) is dated 23 May 1935, and in it he left all of his property to his son. The net value of his estate amounted to £20,154.88. (See also *The Times*, 25 February 1937, 10, col. F.) In 2002, this sum would have had the purchasing power of approximately £1,087,000. (Throughout this section, comparative valuations have been arrived at using the Economic History Services online inflation calculator: *http://eh.net/hmit/ppowerbp/*.)

i. Money

The last chapter provided a fair amount of detail about Pollock's two great treatises, yet failed to answer a simple question: how well did they sell? Although there is no reason to assume that either sold poorly—the fact that there were regularly new editions of each seems to rebut such an assumption—it is impossible to say anything precise because the sales figures for *Principles* and *Torts* are not available. Both books were published by Stevens & Sons. In 1950, Stevens & Sons officially merged with Sweet & Maxwell, though affiliations between the two law publishers date back to the 1820s. A considerable amount of information relating to royalties for Stevens and Sweet & Maxwell titles was either destroyed or lost as a consequence of the IRA's bombing of the Canary Wharf office tower in February 1996 and the publisher's subsequent relocation.[26] Only one piece of information about payments to Pollock has survived. A company ledger detailing royalty arrangements for various Stevens and Sweet & Maxwell publications indicates that, from the inception of the *Revised Reports* in 1891, no more than five volumes were to be published in any one year, that the General Editor 'Sir F. Pollock receives £131.5 when [a] vol. is ready for press and £131.5 on publication', and that '[f]rom vol. 29 author [i.e., Pollock] has received £270 per volume.' The ledger continues: '[f]or vols. 100 to 109 editors' fee to be £230. From vols 110 to end of series [i.e., volume 149, published in 1917] editors' fee to be £220 (provided falling off of subscribers does not increase to make publication absolute loss to publishers)'.[27]

It has not been possible to determine if subscriptions to the *Revised Reports* did decline, but it seems likely that they did—not only because that last parenthetical remark suggests subscriptions were falling off from at least volume 110 onwards, but also because the *English Reports*, established in 1900, were a more comprehensive and popular competitor.[28] Declining subscriptions or not, however, the fact is that Pollock was receiving no small fee for his editing of the *Revised Reports*; £263 in 1891 is roughly equivalent to £16,300 in

[26] Lucy White (Library & Information Manager, TLR Europe), email to author, 24 January 2003.

[27] Undated and unpaginated company ledger held at Thomson University Library, 100 Avenue Road, London. Pollock edited the first 54 volumes of the *Revised Reports* with the assistance of R. Campbell and O. A. Saunders; volumes 55–63 with the assistance of O. A. Saunders and A. B. Cane; volumes 64–93 with the assistance of O. A. Saunders, J. G. Pease, and A. B. Cane; volumes 94–5 with the assistance of O. A. Saunders, J. G. Pease, A. B. Cane, and William Bowstead; and volumes 96–149 with the assistance of O. A. Saunders, J. G. Pease, and William Bowstead. The plural possessives in the quoted passage seem to indicate that Pollock shared the payments.

[28] For a rather tetchy defence of—essentially an advertisement for—the *Revised Reports* in the face of the competition, see A. E. Randall, 'The Revised Reports' (1912) 28 *LQR* 276–82. 'A general charge has been brought against the Revised Reports that they omit important cases', Randall noted. 'Like all general charges it is somewhat difficult to meet. . . . The publication of the Revised Reports has led to one result for which the profession has every reason to be thankful, and that is that a sufficient law library can be purchased for a reasonable sum of money' (ibid. 276, 280). Randall was Pollock's successor as Editor of the *LQR*, though he was killed in an accident only five years after assuming this role: see (1925) 41 *LQR* 125, 243–4.

2002. This comparison of figures should not be taken too seriously: translating late nineteenth-century sums into early twenty-first-century values is a rough-and-ready and not necessarily revealing exercise, since, even if there were an agreed index of inflation as between past and present, it would still be difficult to take account of the varying components of the cost of living, or of the different social significance to be attached to apparently similar levels of income and expenditure.[29] Even with this warning in mind, however, and even assuming that Pollock was passing a percentage of his fees for editing the *Revised Reports* on to his assistants, the sum that he was being paid—up to five times a year—was clearly considerable. '[F]or a man who lived forty weeks in London,' Rouse Ball remarked in 1887, '£250 a year' would probably be enough to enable him 'to live very comfortably' without 'indulg[ing] in any extravagances.'[30] Pollock, it appears, received somewhere in the region of that amount for his editing of each of the 149 volumes of the *Revised Reports*. And of course, in any given year between 1891 and 1917, the editing of these reports would have been, for Pollock, just one of numerous sources of income.

Considering how much Pollock would have earned just from editing the *Revised Reports*, it is worth trying to ascertain roughly how much income certain of his other activities would have generated. First of all, however, recall one piece of information that has already been revealed about his earnings. For serving as the Professor of Jurisprudence at University College London in 1882–3, it was noted in chapter 2, Pollock was paid just over £57. Even in 1883 this was something of a pittance; indeed, the dismal remuneration was very likely a primary reason for his eagerness to quit the post. It is interesting, at this point, to contrast Pollock's professorship at UCL with that which he held at the Inns of Court from 1884 to 1890. We saw in chapter 2 that Pollock did not want this latter post to come to an end. Indeed, for all that he had little positive to say about the system of education at the Inns of Court, he was decidedly disgruntled when his tenure was not renewed for a third term. If money goes a long way to explaining why he wanted out of UCL, it goes just as far in explaining why he wished to keep his professorship at the Inns of Court. In July 1875, the salaries for the four Inns of Court professorships had been set at 1,000 guineas per annum.[31] Compared with the salaries of High Court judges of this period—which had been set at £5,000[32]—this figure may have seemed quite humble. For a professorship, however, the salary was considered, certainly at Lincoln's Inn, to be excessively high. A report of a Committee of the Inn pointedly noted in December 1889 that the professors

[29] See Collini, above n.21, 35.

[30] W. W. Rouse Ball, *The Student's Guide to the Bar*, 4th edn. (London: Macmillan & Co., 1887), 59.

[31] *The Records of the Honorable Society of Lincoln's Inn. The Black Books: Vol. v, 1845–1914*, ed. R. Roxburgh (London: Lincoln's Inn, 1968), 198.

[32] Supreme Court of Judicature Act 1873, 36 & 37 Vict. c. 66, s. 13. Not until the 1950s did this figure change: Judges' Remuneration Act 1954, 2 & 3 Eliz. II c. 27 (increasing salaries of High Court judges to £8,000). More generally, see Brian Abel-Smith and Robert Stevens, *Lawyers and the Courts: A Sociological Study of the English Legal System, 1750–1965* (London: Heinemann, 1967), 38, 290–3.

were still being paid 'the very large sum of 1,000 guineas'.[33] By May 1891, the system of tuition at the Inns had been overhauled and the professors replaced with readers appointed on the more modest salary of £500 per annum.[34] Pollock had enjoyed the last of the golden years of professorial remuneration: it seems hardly surprising that he should have wanted to retain his post.

Pollock is remembered as a professor at neither UCL nor the Inns of Court, of course, but at Oxford. What was his salary there? The University statute in force at the beginning of his two decades at Oxford decreed that the Corpus Professor of Jurisprudence was to be paid by the College rather than the University.[35] College records reveal that Pollock was paid £500 per annum, £300 being his stipend as a non-resident Professor, the remaining £200 being his entitlement as an Official Fellow.[36] Had he been resident, he would have been paid £900[37]—a figure very close to the $4,500 that was the standard salary of law professors at Harvard during the early 1880s.[38] It would be rash to conclude that his salary as a non-resident professor was meagre: considering that he would have received meals and college accommodation free of charge, and that his teaching obligations were very light, it might even be regarded as reasonable. None the less, he probably earned as much each year from editing the *Revised Reports* as he did from his Oxford professorship, and

[33] *Records of the Honorable Society of Lincoln's Inn*, above n.31, 263. [34] See ibid. 289–90.

[35] *Statuta Universitatis Oxoniensis* (Oxford: Clarendon Press, 1883 edn.), 36.

[36] College ledger (Corpus Christi), ref. F/1/5/2–5. Payments to Pollock ceased 22 November 1887 to 24 February 1888 inclusive. This presumably reflects the fact that he was re-elected Professor on 25 February 1888 and thereby also readmitted as a Fellow. In 1893 he was only paid £300 for the year. He was also paid £50 for serving as College vice-president from February 1890 to January 1891 (ibid). I am grateful to Dr Simon Bailey at the Bodleian Library and Dr Michael Stansfield at Corpus Christi College, Oxford, for help in locating this information.

[37] According to the statutes of Corpus Christi College of 1882, the Professor of Jurisprudence 'shall receive from the College a stipend, if he is resident, of 700 [pounds] per annum, and if not, of 300 [pounds] per annum'. *Statutes made for the University of Oxford, and for the Colleges and Halls therein, by the University of Oxford Commissioners, acting in pursuance of the Universities of Oxford and Cambridge Act, 1877* (Oxford: Clarendon Press, 1883), 243.

[38] On 31 December 1882 the U.S. dollar closed at 4.85 against the British pound, as it did on the same date in 1881, 1884, and 1886: see file _GBP_D.csv, downloadable at http://www.globalfindata.com (last visited 6 April 2004); also Lawrence H. Officer, 'Integration in the American Foreign-Exchange Market, 1791–1900' (1985) 45 *Jnl. of Economic History* 557–85 at 575. In the 1880s, the standard Harvard Law School salary appears to have been a source of some discontent there. See O. W. Holmes to Charles W. Eliot, 1 November 1881, President's papers, box 70, folder 1881, F-W: 'My salary, as I understand, would be that of the other law professors, viz.: $4,500. . . . As the taking of this place will involve a pecuniary sacrifice which . . . would probably be considerable, I think I should ask that as soon as any law professor's salary is raised mine should be. Without repeating, I think what was understood with Prof. [James B.] Thayer as to raising the salary to $5,000 should be understood with me'. For a critical overview of late nineteenth-century law school salaries, particularly in the United States, see Charles Noble Gregory, 'The Wage of Law Teachers' (1898) 14 *LQR* 34–42. Gregory, a professor of law at the University of Wisconsin, observed that the salary structure at the Harvard Law School at the end of the nineteenth century had hardly changed since Holmes was on the Faculty. Pollock added in an editorial intervention that the salaries at Harvard were more or less commensurate with those of English academic lawyers (ibid. 36). According to Gregory, the highest law teacher's salary at Cambridge, England, in the late 1890s was £800 per annum, whereas 'at Oxford . . . the professors are paid from £500 to £1,200, the readers £300 to £400, [and] the lecturers £150 to £400' (ibid. 38).

certainly earned more than double his Oxford salary from teaching at the Inns of Court.

The point to be emphasized here is that Pollock appears not to have been especially dependent on his Oxford salary. Indeed, if his Inns of Court professorship is not treated as a university post, it seems correct to claim that, as compared with other ventures, university work accounted for relatively little of his income. Although it is impossible to offer a complete account of Pollock's earnings from royalties, it is evident that throughout his career a steady stream of income came from his books. During his lifetime, 13,500 copies of his *First Book of Jurisprudence* were printed. It sold at six shillings (the price was increased to seven shillings and six pence in 1923), and Pollock received a royalty of one-sixth of the retail price in Britain and the dominions and one-tenth of the English published price in the United States.[39] Although figures are unavailable, it seems inconceivable that the many editions of his textbooks on contract and torts (and possibly also his *Digest of the Law of Partnership*) would not have generated considerably higher royalties than did the *First Book of Jurisprudence*. Between August 1890 and April 1935, the total print run of his *Introduction to the History of the Science of Politics* was 25,000 copies. The book was priced at two shillings and six pence, and Pollock received one-sixth of the retail price in England and one-twelfth of the retail price in the United States.[40] The same royalty arrangement applied to his *Oxford Lectures*, published in 1890 at a price of nine shillings with a print run of 1,000 copies.[41] After deduction of production and publication expenses, Pollock received a 50 per cent royalty for *Essays in the Law* (priced at two shillings and six pence with a print run of 2,000 copies),[42] and he and R. S. Wright received 60 per cent of the net profits from their *Possession in the Common Law*.[43] Pollock also received 60 per cent royalties for his editions of Maine's *Ancient Law*—though by 1906, when Pollock's first edition of *Ancient Law* appeared, demand for the text was on the wane.[44] Pollock's notes to his editions of *Ancient Law*, which were originally published as a separatum,

[39] Robert Machesney (Macmillan Archive, Basingstoke), email to author, 2 July 2002.

[40] Ibid. [41] Ibid. [42] Ibid.

[43] 'Terms with Profr. F. Pollock & Mr R. S. Wright. For the printing and publication of a work entitled "Possession in English Law" [*sic*]', Oxford UP Archive, CON 3/478. I am grateful to the Oxford UP Archivist, Dr Martin Maw, for supplying me with a copy of this document.

[44] Hence, the relevant company ledger at the John Murray Archive, 50 Albemarle St., London, shows that Pollock received numerous small royalty payments on this text: e.g., £30 11s 1d paid in April 1911; £33 08d in April 1914; and £44 16s 14d in March 1920 (by which point the price of *Ancient Law* had been raised from 5/– to 7/6). Ledger N 411–12, Murray Archive. Much to Pollock's consternation, Murray had advertised *Ancient Law* as being under his editorship before he had taken on the task. See Frederick Pollock to John Murray, 11 April 1905, in Pollock correspondence (Murray): 'I have just seen a copy of "Ancient Law", apparently the issue of 1901, with a new title page describing it as edited by myself, but no new matter of any kind. I must really protest against this, as the volume contains no work of mine at all, and the statement that it does is very like a fraud on the public. An advertisement might be inserted to justify the title page by explaining that a commentary uniform with the text is to follow. . . . [I]n any case I cannot allow my name to be used in a misleading manner, though I should be extremely sorry to be driven to a public protest.'

generated similarly modest sums.[45] For his short book on *The Land Laws* he agreed to a flat fee of £100 plus further payments of £25 for new editions in 1887 and 1896.[46] And for his memoirs, published four years before his death, he received two royalty payments amounting to just under £47.[47]

Although some of these royalty payments look meagre at first glance, they seem far more substantial when one takes account of inflation: £47 in 1934, to take the last example, had roughly the same purchasing power as did £2,500 in 2002. It is important to keep in mind, furthermore, that there were many books for which Pollock would have received royalties about which it has not been possible to obtain information.[48] Given how many books, and how many editions of books, Pollock produced, royalty payments would have been, for him, a regular occurrence. And the royalties, even though many of them may look negligible in isolation, would have mounted up considerably. Alongside the book royalties there were also payments for various forms of public service, such as drafting the Partnership Bill (for which Pollock was paid £100 in the late 1870s[49]) and for chairing the Royal Commission on Public Records.[50] It was noted in chapter 2 that Pollock eventually stopped seeking re-election to the Corpus Chair because, he claimed, twenty years was a sufficiently long time for anyone to hold such a post. That reason may well be genuine; but it is likely also that when Pollock did eventually leave Oxford, he had held the

[45] Pollock received a royalty cheque of £49 10s on the first print run of his *Introduction and Notes to Maine's 'Ancient Law'* (Ledger N 319, Murray Archive). Subsequent royalty cheques, mainly for sales during the War years, were for comparatively paltry sums (Ledgers N 309–10, P 409, Murray Archive). Pollock took 50 per cent royalties on all sales.

[46] Machesney, above n.39.

[47] For *FMG* Pollock was to receive royalties of 10 per cent on the first 1,000 sales, 15 per cent on sales 1,001–4,000, and 20 per cent thereafter (with royalties of 15 per cent on U.S. sales throughout). There was an initial print run of 1,500, and Pollock received royalty cheques for £30 15s 4d in December 1933 and £16 2s 4d in June 1934. Ledger H-1, f.321, Murray Archive. For *S*, published two years after *FMG*, Pollock received royalties of 10 per cent on both domestic and overseas sales. The book sold for 2/– and the print run is not ascertainable. Deborah Blake (Editorial Director, Duckworth), email to author, 8 July 2002.

[48] Duckworth, for example, holds no records for their publications before 1935 because of a fire that year (Deborah Blake, email to author, 5 July 2002), and so it has not been possible to obtain royalty information about the two editions of *SHLP*. In some instances, information relating to Pollock's books is incomplete: e.g., 2,500 copies of his *LCDE* were printed between 1876 and 1892 and the volume was priced at 3/6, but details of royalty terms and payments are not available. Machesney, above n.39.

[49] See Alan Rodger, 'The Codification of Commercial Law in Victorian Britain' (1992) 108 *LQR* 570–90 at 578.

[50] It has not been possible to trace details of payments to Pollock for his chairing of the Royal Commission on Public Records. But it is known that the Secretary of the Commission, Hubert Hall, was paid a salary of £250 per annum. When the Commission proved dilatory in producing its final report—a detail which was noted in chapter 2—the Treasury withheld Hall's salary: Hubert Hall to Frederick Pollock, 1 December 1917, PRO: T1/12391; W. Niemeyer to Frederick Pollock, 3 January 1918, PRO: T1/12391 ('If . . . you will be so good as to give the Treasury a definite assurance that the [Third and Final] Report will be completed by the 31st March next . . . , we will . . . think it fair that the salary of Mr Hall, the Secretary, should be revived at the rate of £250 a year from 1st December, 1917, up to the date of signing'). Hall's salary was reinstated: Frederick Pollock to Malcolm Ramsay, 8 January 1918, PRO: T1/12391 ('I note with satisfaction that the Treasury is prepared to pay Mr Hall's salary . . .').

Corpus Chair long enough to have acquired all the prestige-value that the title could bestow upon him. It is equally likely that he would not have envisaged being faced with a shortage of profitable ways in which to fill up his newly acquired free time.

ii. The Law Reports

'I don't precisely know why F. P. made room at Oxford,' Maitland wrote to Henry Jackson in 1904, 'but he is very well paid as editor of the Law Reports.'[51] The Council of Law Reporting—it was incorporated by Royal Charter in 1870—was established in 1865 and began issuing the first numbers of the Law Reports at the end of that year.[52] Three different series of reports were created at the outset—appellate, chancery, and common law—and separate editors were appointed for each series.[53] The editors were each to be paid £600 per annum—a figure which some members of the Bar considered extravagant.[54] In 1894, the Council resolved to appoint Pollock as Editor-in-Chief of the Law Reports. The appointment was initially for twelve months, commencing 1 February 1895, and the salary remained at £600.[55] The job, however, was significantly expanded: from now on, there would not be different editors for the separate series of reports; rather, all of the reports would come under Pollock's general editorship.[56]

Pollock appears to have had little to do with the Incorporated Council of Law Reporting. Soon after he began as Editor-in-Chief of the Law Reports, the Council determined that he should attend its meetings when it was deemed appropriate by the Chairman or Vice Chairman.[57] But he appears only rarely to have attended meetings, and never to have spoken when he did.[58] It is far

[51] F. W. Maitland to Henry Jackson, 10 January 1904, in *The Letters of Frederic William Maitland*, ed. C. H. S. Fifoot (London: Selden Society, 1965), 372.

[52] See W. T. S. Daniel, *The History and the Origin of the Law Reports* (London: Clowes, 1884), 247–8; Edward Jenks, *A Short History of English Law: From the Earliest Times to the End of the Year 1927*, 4th edn. (London: Methuen, 1928), 195–7; Sir William Holdsworth, *A History of English Law*, 16 vols., eds. A. L. Goodhart and H. G. Hanbury (London: Methuen, 1965), xv. 254; Nathaniel Lindley, 'The History of the Law Reports' (1885) 1 *LQR* 137–49 at 141–2; *FBJ* 293–4; and Alan Harding, *A Social History of English Law* (Gloucester, Mass.: Smith, 1973 [1966]), 356–7.

[53] See Daniel, above n.52, 255–6; Holdsworth, above n.52, 256; and John William Wallace, *The Reporters, Arranged and Characterized with Incidental Remarks*, 4th edn. (Boston: Soule & Bugbee, 1882), 538–41.

[54] See Daniel, above n.52, 152; also the remarks of W. M. Best reported at ibid. 166, 205.

[55] Incorporated Council of Law Reporting Minute Book no. 3: minutes of Council meeting of 15 November 1894.

[56] See Holdsworth, above n.52, 256; A. L. Goodhart (1936) 52 *LQR* 1.

[57] Incorporated Council of Law Reporting Minute Book no. 3: minutes of Council meeting of 19 March 1895.

[58] Pollock was present by invitation, but apparently did not speak, at Council meetings on 11 December 1895, 20 May 1896 (Minute Book no. 3), 21 March 1899, and 18 December 1900 (Minute Book no. 4).

from obvious that the Council was especially enthusiastic about his initial appointment; indeed, before he took office one of its members proposed 'that the question of the appointment of the Editor be postponed with a reference to a Committee to consider whether the vacancy should not be advertised'.[59] If, in fact, there was an attitude of suspicion towards Pollock on the part of the Council, it would have been entirely understandable. 'Until 1895,' Winfield claimed in the 1920s,

> the Law Reports were not manifestly better than the reports published by various legal journals, nor did they completely satisfy the needs of the profession. They were a commercial success, and that seemed to be sufficient to their proprietors. The cases were occasionally prefaced by head-notes which were little better than huddled abridgements of the facts followed by a bald statement of the result of the litigation.[60]

Before 1895, this last observation was regularly being put forward in the *LQR*. 'A principle stated in six lines of a head-note is one thing', one commentator observed acidly in 1893, 'a conglomeration of facts with copious extracts from documents, and possibly fifteen or twenty letters of the alphabet representing persons or places, is another.'[61] That Pollock was providing a platform for this sentiment might alone have been irksome; it was probably far more troubling to some members of the Incorporated Council of Law Reporting, however, that nobody used the pages of the *LQR* to express this sentiment more intensely than did Pollock himself.

Only the legacy of John Austin took more flak from Pollock than did the pre-1895 Law Reports. No turn was left unstoned: he complained about the failure of the Law Reports to appear on time,[62] the reporting of too many cases (which he often took to be the reason for late publication),[63] the introduction of inaccuracies into judgments,[64] tardiness in reporting decisions,[65] sloppy editing of judicial opinions,[66] various editorial indulgences and embellishments,[67] and the failure to report some cases of legal significance.[68] 'The

[59] Incorporated Council of Law Reporting Minute Book no. 3: minutes of Council meeting of 15 November 1894. The proposal was not seconded. No significance should be read into the fact that Pollock was appointed for only one year, as all appointments to Law Reports editorships had to that point been made on an annual basis; indeed, throughout Pollock's tenure as Editor-in-Chief he continued to be re-appointed annually: see *FMG* 188.

[60] Percy H. Winfield, *The Chief Sources of English Legal History* (Cambridge, Mass.: Harvard UP, 1925), 192.

[61] John Mews, 'The Present System of Law Reporting' (1893) 9 *LQR* 179–87 at 182. Cf. the far more complimentary post-1895 piece by Showell Rogers, 'On the Study of Law Reports' (1897) 13 *LQR* 250–69 esp. at 254. In the nineteenth century, the quality of head-notes was a similarly vexatious subject in the United States: see the account of Alden I. Rosbrook, 'The Art of Judicial Reporting' (1925) 10 *Cornell L. Q.* 103–34 at 114–19.

[62] See, e.g., (1887) 3 *LQR* 248.

[63] See (1889) 5 *LQR* 107; also (1892) 8 *LQR* 191.

[64] See, e.g., (1888) 4 *LQR* 115; (1892) 8 *LQR* 108.

[65] See, e.g., (1888) 4 *LQR* 115.

[66] See, e.g., (1891) 7 *LQR* 300; (1893) 9 *LQR* 12; (1894) 10 *LQR* 104.

[67] See, e.g., (1890) 6 *LQR* 357; (1892) 8 *LQR* 192.

[68] See, e.g., (1894) 10 *LQR* 12.

general management of the Law Reports has been anything but satisfactory for some years past, and we see no signs of mending', he complained in the early 1890s.[69] 'In our opinion the Council of Law Reporting would have done much better to keep the guinea taken off from the subscription a few years ago, and use it in improving the quality of their work and the punctuality of its production.'[70] Nothing offended him more than the notorious head-notes. 'A head-note is or should be the key to the case, the clue of legal principle which we can follow as we progress through the intricacies of the report.'[71] It should provide 'the "legal pith" of a case and the legal pith only'.[72] The pre-1895 head-notes, however, were consistently slipshod and often practically useless. 'In *Dashwood* v. *Magniac* . . . The Law Reports head-note states everything except what was the point decided'; 'the head-note to *Seagrove* v. *Parks* . . . is expressed with great ingenuity, so as to conceal from attention the only point of the case worth notice'; 'the Law Reports head-note [in *Tilbury* v. *Silva*] is misleading'; '[i]n *Levy* v. *Walker*, . . . the Law Reports head-note is long and clumsy, as usual'; the head-note in *Nordenfelt v Nordenfelt* makes one ask whether 'it would not have been very hard for the reporter . . . to help the reader a little more.'[73] 'The inaccuracy of the head-notes of the Law Reports' was, he concluded in 1891, 'a scandal without any apparent remedy.'[74]

Pollock himself was, of course, to be the remedy. The fact that the pre-1895 Law Reports were not under the control of a single editor meant that the different series varied as to quality of publication and efficiency of production. Certainly at least one of the pre-1895 editors recognized that there was a need for some general reforms.[75] Faced with so much criticism of the Law Reports, the Incorporated Council of Law Reporting decided to impose 'unity of command' by 'setting a poacher'—Pollock—'to be gamekeeper'.[76] No documentation has surfaced which indicates why Pollock was chosen to be Editor-in-Chief, but it is not difficult to think of possible reasons for the choice. The prospect of vengeance was probably in the minds of some Council members. Had Pollock proved an inept editor, he would have looked particularly foolish. Indeed, his outspokenness about the Law Reports before 1895

[69] (1891) 7 *LQR* 1. [70] (1890) 6 *LQR* 232. [71] (1890) 6 *LQR* 470.

[72] (1892) 8 *LQR* 191. Interestingly, once Pollock had become Editor-in-Chief, he felt able to excuse the occasional lengthy head-note: see (1898) 14 *LQR* 108.

[73] (1892) 8 *LQR* 8; (1891) 7 *LQR* 201, 2, 3; (1893) 9 *LQR* 201. There is, of course, much more in the same vein: see, e.g., (1892) 8 *LQR* 109; (1893) 9 *LQR* 12.

[74] (1891) 7 *LQR* 297. See also (1894) 10 *LQR* 290.

[75] See G. W. Hemming, 'The Law Reports' (1885) 1 *LQR* 287–97. Hemming was at this point the Editor of the Chancery series and apparently 'direct[ed] the labours of about one-half of the Staff' of the Law Reports (ibid. 287). His article is a response to criticisms of the Law Reports put forward by Lindley (above n.52), and although he was endeavouring 'to relieve [my staff of reporters] from an imputation of negligence which I do not think they deserve' (Hemming, ibid. 294), much of his article (see, e.g., ibid. 287–8, 291–4) makes it clear that the Law Reports at that time were in need of some improvement. Cf. also *FMG* 186–7.

[76] *FMG* 187. See also Sir William Holdsworth, *Some Makers of English Law: The Tagore Lectures 1937–38* (Cambridge: Cambridge UP, 1938), 289; Holdsworth (1937) 53 *LQR* 181.

may have provided him with an especial motivation to take the job very seriously. Not only would failure in the post surely silence him, but it would furthermore very likely silence anyone else minded to carp about the quality of editing.

This is not to suggest that Pollock would have been appointed purely in the hope that he would have fallen flat on his face. By 1895, he had already spent a decade running a tight ship with the *LQR*—a different proposition from editing the Law Reports, certainly, but one which similarly required the abilities of working to production schedules and getting the best out of what could sometimes be rough-hewn material.[77] By this time, furthermore, he had been working from Lincoln's Inn—close to the judges and the reporters who produce what it is that goes into the Law Reports—for nearly a quarter of a century. He was little use in court—that much would have been well known among his peers—but he was a serious journal editor and the author of many insightful legal articles and treatises, a diligent if dour workhorse with a particular talent for types of endeavour that, certainly in his day, the best legal minds tended to eschew in favour of practice. In short, Pollock, like James Kent in the early nineteenth-century United States, seemed to have a temperament and an aptitude that suited him to the task of distilling and clarifying what came out of the courtroom.[78] It seems most likely that he was appointed to the general editorship of the Law Reports because most Council members, even if they were wary of him owing to his outspokenness about the efforts of his predecessors, would have been confident that the duties assigned to him would be carried out efficiently and satisfactorily.

Whatever the Council's reasons for settling on Pollock, there seems little doubt that he turned out to be what its members had desired. Pollock was Editor-in-Chief of the Law Reports from 1895 until virtually the end of his life.[79] Not only did he assume responsibility for the Law Reports of England and Wales, but he was also throughout this period the Editor of the Indian

[77] Pollock conceded that he occasionally published 'barely passable' material in the *LQR* 'out of compassion for writers', though he added in retrospect that he considered he had been wrong to do so: Frederick Pollock, 'Our Jubilee' (1935) 51 *LQR* 5–10 at 9.

[78] On Kent's contribution to law reporting in the United States, see John H. Langbein, 'Chancellor Kent and the History of English Legal Literature' (1993) 93 *Columbia L. Rev.* 547–94 at 571–84. Pollock and Kent were comparable in many ways: essentially reserved with a tendency towards the laconic, immensely learned, serious about money, suspicious of legislation and more disposed to the common law, blessed with long and happy marriages, multilingual, enthusiasts for legal principle, and quick to uphold the importance of legal science. For these qualities in Kent, see Langbein, ibid. 554–5; G. Edward White, 'The Chancellor's Ghost' (1998) 74 *Chicago-Kent L. Rev.* 229–62 at 229, 236–7, 242–5; Donald M. Roper, 'The Elite of the New York Bar as Seen from the Bench: James Kent's Necrologies' (1972) 56 *New York Historical Society Quarterly* 199–237 at 200–4; Carl F. Stychin, 'The Commentaries of Chancellor James Kent and the Development of American Common Law' (1993) 37 *Am. J. Leg. Hist.* 440–63 at 446, 461–2; and David W. Raack, '"To Preserve the Best Fruits": The Legal Thought of Chancellor James Kent' (1989) 33 *Am. J. Leg. Hist.* 320–66 at 330–1, 352–5, 359, 362–5. For Pollock on Kent's *Commentaries*, see Sir Frederick Pollock, 'English Law Studies' (1894) 28 *Irish Law Times* 245–6 at 245.

[79] Although he ceased to be Editor-in-Chief in 1935, he served as a co-editor in 1936 with Alfred Topham, who became sole editor in 1937.

Appeals series of the Law Reports, which was composed of Privy Council cases heard on appeal from the East Indies.[80] Before 1895, this series had been in an even more lamentable state than had the Law Reports of England and Wales.[81] In light of this fact, and considering also what Pollock had to say about the abilities of Indian law reporters,[82] it seems likely that editing the Indian Appeals series would have required considerable effort on his part. None of the work seemed to daunt him. While Pollock cut a rather lackadaisical figure as a professor, he edited the Law Reports with notable gusto. Before officially assuming office, he persuaded the Incorporated Council of Law Reporting to change the formal abbreviation of the Law Reports from 'Law Rep.' to 'LR'.[83] Once in office, he immediately introduced a uniform printing style throughout the various Law Reports, thereby reducing the printer's bill.[84] Small matters, certainly, but very much the initiatives of a new broom; displays of keenness which were invariably absent from his university career.

Simply to portray Pollock as an enthusiastic editor of the Law Reports would be misleading. In this role, he had both a sense of purpose and a sense of belonging. The two attributes tended to merge in his testaments to the collective endeavours of his team. 'We are all comrades working together for the benefit of our common profession and learning,' he wrote in 1909.[85] The benefit was, for Pollock, obvious: since 'the authority of decisions tends to increase wherever they are systematically reported,'[86] diligence in law reporting would reduce the number of instances in which the common law led to ambiguous conclusions. The work was without doubt, he insisted in 1903, fundamentally important:

> we, the staff of the Law Reports, consider ourselves as exercising an office of trust on behalf of the legal profession not only in England, but in every jurisdiction where the common law is received or its authorities quoted. . . . [W]e are about a work the English-speaking world cannot do without. In our modest and ministerial field of

[80] The Indian Appeals series of the Law Reports began in 1872. The first volume to be edited by Pollock appeared in 1896, and from 1896 to 1916 he worked with an assistant editor, Arthur Stone, though he was sole editor from 1917 to 1935 (whereupon he was succeeded by Alfred Topham). The series ran until 1950.

[81] For a candid assessment of the state of the Indian Appeals series (and other Indian law reports) before 1895, see J. J., 'The Art of Law-Reporting' (1898) 8 *Madras L. J.* 455–64; and also, on the difficulties facing the Privy Council in determining what the law was in this context, Frederick Pollock, 'The Jurisdiction of the Privy Council' (1906) 7 *Jnl. of the Society of Comparative Legislation* 330–2 at 331–2.

[82] See chapter 2, 77; also Pollock to Holmes, 3 March 1930, in *PHL* ii. 259; 5 May 1930, ibid. 263; and 25 May 1930, ibid. 266.

[83] Incorporated Council of Law Reporting Minute Book no. 3 (index): editorial arrangements.

[84] See *FMG* 186.

[85] Frederick Pollock, 'Government by Committees in England' (1909) 25 *LQR* 53–69 at 69 (repr. *EIL* 110–40 at 138).

[86] Frederick Pollock, 'The Continuity of the Common Law' (1898) 11 *Harvard L. Rev.* 423–33 at 427 n.1.

operation we are helping to maintain a national and more than national heritage, the ancient and still vital growth of the common law.[87]

The work was fundamentally fulfilling as well. '[E]diting the Law Reports', he claimed, 'has been of the greatest value in keeping me in touch with the practising leaders of the profession.'[88] He and his team of reporters, when dealing with judges and barristers, would adhere to 'customary and unwritten understandings'[89]—indeed, the day-to-day process of editing the Law Reports seemed to involve little in the way of formalities. 'We confer freely and confidentially, as occasion requires, with the judges and with the counsel engaged in cases to be reported and with one another. . . . What rules we have . . . are mostly unwritten. . . . I . . . give my colleagues as free a hand as possible and never . . . write a formal letter when I can help it.'[90] The semi-official status of the Law Reports—the Incorporated Council has no monopoly over reporting, and the Law Reports enjoy no privilege of exclusive citation—seemed to appeal to Pollock.[91] The state of near-unaccountability that came with this status, he believed, was something of which he and his team had to make a virtue.

Disciplined co-operation is . . . a necessity. . . . [O]ur bond is more like that of a college crew than that of a Government office. . . . We are answerable to the council who appoint us, and to the council alone; and in the most improbable case of an attempt at formal interference from any other quarter, I should have no hesitation in telling the intermeddler, however exalted his professional or official position might be, to mind his own business.[92]

Intermeddlers within the organization would no doubt have been treated likewise. Uninhibited informal interchange among the staff of the Law Reports might have been a virtue in Pollock's eyes, but there is no doubt that he generally wanted matters resolved his way.[93] When his Assistant Editor,

[87] *EIL* 241–2, 257. The essay from which this quotation is taken ('English Law Reporting') was first published at (1903) 19 *LQR* 451–60.

[88] *FMG* 189.

[89] *EIL* 246.

[90] *EIL* 245. See also Frank Evans, 'Law Reporting: A Reporter's View' (1904) 20 *LQR* 88–93 at 89. 'On the Day of Judgment', Pollock is reported to have said, 'one of my credit notes will be the amount of red tape I have *not* put into the Law Reports.' Sir John Pollock, *Time's Chariot* (London: Murray, 1950), 69.

[91] See *EIL* 242–5. Cf. also Eldon R. James, 'The Future of Judicial Reporting' (1938) 23 *Massachusetts L. Q.* 25–7 at 26. While Pollock saw no need for the Law Reports to be granted the privilege of exclusive citation in court, he did not welcome 'the enormous and uncontrolled multiplication of law reports'. Pollock, above n.77, 10.

[92] *EIL* 244–5. See also Pollock to Holmes, 17 July 1929, in *PHL* ii. 245–6.

[93] See, e.g., Pollock to Holmes, 30 January 1919, in *PHL* ii. 5 ('The *Law Reports* have changed their printers and I am striving to teach the new people divers things they ought to know—such as not meddling with punctuation out of their own heads'); 14 March 1920, ibid. 39 ('In the *Law Reports* I fight with wild beasts in the shape of grossly incompetent printers' readers'); 3 June 1920, ibid. 45 ('If the

Arthur Stone, retired in 1916 he was delighted: 'I shall get the whole thing under my direct control', he wrote to Holmes. 'I think a nominal increase of work will on the whole be more than made up for by abolishing friction and circuity.'[94] Given Pollock's character, what is perhaps most remarkable about his involvement in the Law Reports is not that he professed to enjoy much of the interchange that came with his position but that his role seemed well suited to him. Here was a notoriously difficult and taciturn man working at the heart of a talkative profession. That someone so famed for his reticence should have professed to enjoy the dialogue necessitated by editing is by no means beyond comprehension—Pollock, we know, appeared not to recognize his own uncommunicativeness. It does seem odd, none the less, that he should actually have proved adept in an occupation which involved a good deal of informal interchange with others. How is this aptitude to be explained?

It is tempting to answer that whatever talent he may have lacked as a communicator he compensated for as a manuscript editor. In this context, however, it would be wrong to conclude that Pollock did lack appropriate communicative skills. Given that his approach to life was generally to avoid ever saying anything more than was really necessary, he seems to have been well cut out for dealing with judges and their opinions. Indeed, although Pollock probably said very little to judges, reporters, and counsel, it is clear that he listened to them. It seems that he would solicit opinions from judges and counsel about particular cases and their suitability for inclusion in the Law Reports—he certainly received, and took on board, plenty of their advice.[95] Furthermore, he followed the custom of sending judges the edited reports of their unwritten judgments for approval and correction, and his reactions to their responses tended to be sufficiently accommodating and laconic to avert protracted squabbles.[96]

There were certainly opportunities for such squabbles. Most judges' suggested emendations to draft reports were minor—and the suggestions, unless

printers of the *Law Reports* go on as they are doing there will be manslaughter'); 3 March 1930, ibid. 260; 16 July 1931, ibid. 291.

[94] Pollock to Holmes, 30 January 1916, in *PHL* i. 230. See also H. D. Hazeltine, 'Sir Frederick Pollock, Bart., 1845–1937' (1949) 35 *Proc. Brit. Acad.* 233–56 at 241 ('[H]e was in reality the chief of the reporters. The Law Reports which appeared during the many years of his editorship might well be described, with fairness to all who helped him, as "Pollock's Reports", on the analogy of Coke's Reports and Plowden's Reports').

[95] See, e.g., Ernest Murray Pollock to Frederick Pollock, 14 March 1930, in Pollock correspondence, box 1, folder 63 ('*Garland* v. *Archer-Shee*. The judgment in this case cannot claim a place in the Law Reports. Such is my opinion.' The case was not reported until it reached the House of Lords: *Archer-Shee v Garland* [1931] AC 212); W. Warrington to Frederick Pollock, 26 April 1909, in Pollock correspondence, box 1, folder 57 ('I agree with Cook that [Ralston's Patent] is not a case to report. It involved questions of fact only.' The case was not reported); Matthew I. Joyce to Frederick Pollock, 28 February 1914, in Pollock correspondence, box 1, folder 40 ('*Barry* v. *Guest*—I agree to the reporting of this case being dropped').

[96] See *EIL* 255–6 ('[T]he obligation of the reporters and the profession to the learned judges for the time and care they bestow, purely as a matter of grace, on the revision of their reported judgments . . . is far greater than any one could guess who does not see the work done').

they introduced inaccuracies, were followed[97]—though occasionally a judge could prove difficult. In November 1901, Joyce J. complained that one of his judgments had not arrived in time for him to correct the transcript. Moreover, the transcript did not meet with his approval. 'I do not like the judgment as proposed by [Pollock's assistant, G. W.] Hemming but would prefer that you should adopt the MS. herewith that is made up from the Report in the Law Journal.'[98] It is difficult to imagine that Pollock would have been at all happy to be told that he should rely upon material taken from what he considered to be the Law Reports' 'chief competitor'.[99] Nevertheless, he saw no reason to counter Joyce, and he immediately instructed Hemming to use Joyce's version of the judgment.[100] 'Any suggestion from the judges is,' he wrote in 1903, 'most respectfully considered, and observations from the profession at large, whether constructive or critical, are welcome.'[101] It is evident from the manner of most judges' communications with Pollock over the Law Reports that they took it for granted that he would accede to their wishes.[102] This does not mean, however, that they took him for granted. 'I think your draft [of *Lynn v Bamber*] is excellent', McCardie J. wrote to Pollock in 1930. 'I would, however, *omit* the *semble*'—Pollock duly did—as '[i]t seems unnecessary. I greatly appreciate your care and thought.'[103] The judiciary was no different from Pollock himself in appreciating the value of suitably edited law reports, and judges appear by and large to have respected him for the job that he did.

[97] See, e.g., Charles Clauson to Frederick Pollock, 13 January 1931, in Pollock correspondence, box 1, folder 15: 'LR, January Chancery number: 1931, 1 Ch. 143 line 14; erratum: for sheriff read bailiff' (the change was made: *Re Harris* [1931] 1 Ch. 138, 143); Walter Phillimore to Frederick Pollock, 23 October 1909, in Pollock correspondence, box 1, folder 57 (correcting minor error at [1909] 2 KB 391).

[98] Matthew I. Joyce to Frederick Pollock, 11 November 1901, in Pollock correspondence, box 1, folder 40. The following year, Joyce asked to see a second set of proofs for a report that he had apparently amended in detail: Matthew I. Joyce to Frederick Pollock, 13 November 1902, in Pollock correspondence, box 1, folder 40.

[99] *EIL* 250.

[100] Frederick Pollock to G. W. Hemming, 12 November 1901, in Pollock correspondence, box 1, folder 40 ('Please see the judge's note on the other leaf, and his new version of the judgment. . . . It is obviously impossible for anyone who did not hear the case to say whether his criticism is justified or not'). On judges' revisions of judgments, see C. F. Parker, 'Law Reporting and the Revision of Judgments' (1955) 18 *Mod. L. Rev.* 496–7 esp. at 497 ('[W]e ought to acknowledge openly that the *Law Reports* may not in fact contain the most accurate version of the judgment which was delivered, although it may be the version of which the judge finally approved . . .').

[101] *EIL* 245. Cf. S. P. J. Merlin to Frederick Pollock, 5 August 1931, in Pollock correspondence, box 1, folder 56 (request from a rent-assessor that a correction be published to the head-note in *Hudd v Matthews* [1930] 2 KB 197. It appears that Pollock did not accede to the request.)

[102] See, e.g., R. J. Parker to Frederick Pollock, 10 January 1909, in Pollock correspondence, box 1, folder 57 ('I don't like the head note in the case and have altered it as I think it should go'); though cf. Lord Tomlin to Frederick Pollock, 26 April 1931, in Pollock correspondence, box 1, folder 72 ('*Homes* v. *Newman*. Your decision as to reporting this case must of course prevail.' The case is reported at [1931] 2 Ch. 112).

[103] Henry McCardie to Frederick Pollock, 5 June 1930, in Pollock correspondence, box 1, folder 55. McCardie, as we know from chapter 5, was very much an admirer of Pollock. The word *semble* appears nowhere in *Lynn v Bamber* [1930] 2 KB 72.

Pollock did not always get it right. We will see later in this chapter that one particularly important decision of the House of Lords suffered badly under his editorship. Furthermore, although it is by and large not too difficult to portray positively Pollock's accomplishments as Editor-in-Chief of the Law Reports, such a portrait provides little or no insight into what he actually stood for and achieved in this role. Did he have any editorial philosophy or policies? There were certainly two, and just possibly there were three, objectives that Pollock pursued.

First of all, and perhaps most predictably, he wanted inelegant language banished from the Law Reports. 'Laying down the law is in the hands of the King's judges,' he wrote to his team of reporters in 1935, 'but it is our business to see that their decisions and the facts and arguments on which they are delivered are presented to the profession in clear and intelligible form and in good English.'[104] In matters of clarity, judges nearly always needed a helping hand. Naturally, 'some judges are more careful and more concise in their language than others. But the cases are rare indeed in which a mere verbatim note of anything said extempore, however good it may have been to hear, can be accepted as readable English.'[105] Privately, he would express this sentiment in sharper terms. 'Keeping bad English out of the Law Reports does not become easier', he wrote to Holmes in 1919. 'In the lump, between ourselves, we are an illiterate profession.'[106] Five years later, he professed that he was beginning to wonder 'how long I ought to keep on with the *Law Reports*. . . . If only I could have a successor warranted to correct bad English as rigorously as I do. Why judicial language (in unwritten judgments) runs to a kind of journalistic jargon which no human being speaks and only second-rate newspaper men write—that is one of the mysteries of iniquity.'[107] Although Pollock no doubt did sometimes become exasperated with the Law Reports, he generally seems to have derived dour satisfaction from judging—and, of course, correcting—the judges. He was certainly unremitting as an editor of bad judicial prose. Although 'some weeds are very hard to grub up finally', he noted, 'I do my best to wage a war of extermination.'[108] Thus we find him altering Court of Appeal judgments containing '*such* as a mere demonstrative, *prior to* as an indiscriminate substitute for *before*, *as to whether*, hardly ever required and seldom tolerable, and the like',[109] 'rewrit[ing] sentences purporting to represent a technical French original, which had come out little better than nonsense',[110] editing 'considerably' the 'offhand judgment' of 'the one weak judge of our Chancery Division . . . to make a decent show of it',[111]

[104] (1937) 53 *LQR* 201. [105] *EIL* 252.

[106] Pollock to Holmes, 24 November 1919, in *PHL* ii. 30.

[107] Pollock to Holmes, 14 August 1924, in *PHL* ii. 145.

[108] *EIL* 252–3. See also *FMG* 188–9.

[109] Pollock to Holmes, 17 July 1929, in *PHL* ii. 246. See also 16 August 1929, ibid. 251.

[110] Frederick Pollock, 'The Lawyer as a Citizen of the World' (1932) 48 *LQR* 37–42 at 39. In the same vein, see *EIL* 253–4.

[111] Pollock to Holmes, 12 June 1926, in *PHL* ii. 182. The judge in question was Sir John Meir Astbury (1860–1939), Judge of the High Court of Justice, Chancery Division, 1913–29.

and '[a]lmost every month . . . restor[ing] one or more sentences in unwritten judgments to grammar or sense or both.'[112]

The war that Pollock waged was against verbosity and excess as well as bad language. In the late nineteenth century, according to one modern commentator, judgments in the various law reports began to increase in length.[113] Yet if this was the case Pollock could hardly have contributed to the trend, for he tried to ensure that little other than cases that needed to be reported found their way into the Law Reports, and that those cases were reported as economically as possible. Before 1895, he had lamented that 'the bulk of our current series of authorized Law Reports is at least double what it ought to be. Much stricter control ought to be exercised both by the general editor and by the judges.'[114] He noted with pride that under his editorship, 'with few and accidental exceptions,' if a case did not appear in the Law Reports then it was 'not worth reporting'.[115] On occasions, it seems, the decisions that did appear in the Law Reports would be substantially pruned.[116] 'He deprecated profuse judgments and, unless necessary for the understanding of the case, long statements of facts', one of his sub-editors recalled. 'In the case of one eminent judge, who had given permission for his judgments to be edited freely, the judgments were undoubtedly much improved by the judicious use of the Editor's blue pencil.'[117] Mastery of legal doctrine, Langdell advised American law students in the 1870s, requires, among other things, an appreciation that 'the cases which are useful and necessary . . . bear an exceedingly small proportion to all that have been reported. The vast majority are useless, and worse than useless, for any purpose of systematic study.'[118] Pollock's work as Editor-in-Chief of the Law Reports at least ensured that anyone engaged in

[112] Pollock to Holmes, 15 October 1928, in *PHL* ii. 232.

[113] See Steve Hedley, 'Words, Words, Words: Making Sense of Legal Judgments, 1875–1940', in *Law Reporting in Britain*, ed. C. Stebbings (London: The Hambledon Press, 1995), 169–86.

[114] *EJE* 243. See also (1894) 10 *LQR* 14.

[115] *EIL* 250. The exceptions do exist. Pollock himself added that he had once sanctioned the reporting of a Court of Appeal decision, 'though it did not add anything to what we already knew at home for settled law, because I happened to know that the case and the points involved in it had excited a good deal of interest in the West Indies' (ibid.). See also A. E. Randall (1921) 37 *LQR* 265 ('We venture to think that *Lucas-Tooth* v. *Lucas-Tooth* . . . might have been omitted without any serious loss to the profession'); and cf. Pollock to Holmes, 19 July 1923, in *PHL* ii. 119 ('I groan over the amount of merely ephemeral stuff . . . we have to print in the *Law Reports*').

[116] On occasions, Pollock would publish a condensed report of a decision and then supplement the report with a note in the *LQR* providing some of the detail that had been omitted from the Law Reports: see, e.g., (1906) 22 *LQR* 356. During the First World War, he was apparently keener than usual to excise superfluity from the Law Reports owing to the paper shortage and mounting production costs: Pollock to Holmes, 14 May 1917, in *PHL* i. 244; 18 April 1918, ibid. 263; and 30 May 1918, ibid. 265.

[117] Edward Potton (1937) 53 *LQR* 200. Cf. Lord Maugham (1937) 53 *LQR* 173 ('I . . . recall the great care with which he perused the judgments. . . . I remember a case in which I had had occasion to refer by way of illustration to some Anglo-Saxon law. . . . Alas! my learning . . . was a little out of date according to the learned editor, and a passage over which I had taken some pains was (with my consent) rightly suppressed').

[118] Christopher Columbus Langdell, *A Selection of Cases on the Law of Contracts* (Boston: Little, Brown & Co., 1871), viii.

the systematic study of modern English law would not have to wade through page upon page of insignificant cases.[119]

Addressing an American audience in April 1929, Arthur Goodhart used this last point as the basis for praising the manner in which Pollock edited the Law Reports:

> Perhaps the reason why the English lawyer is not dissatisfied with the present system is that the 'myriad' precedents do not exist. . . . Only a small proportion of decided cases are reported each year; unless a case deals with a novel point of law—and novelty is strictly construed—it will rarely find its way into the *Reports*. . . . It is hardly surprising that the English lawyer has no difficulty in digesting the annual reports, and that he does not, therefore, demand a change in the established system.[120]

At the time that Goodhart made this observation, he was a visiting professor at the Yale Law School. At least one of his colleagues there was decidedly less enthusiastic about Pollock's editorial style: 'one wonders how many inconvenient cases are taken out and buried under the process which [Goodhart] describes.'[121] Did Pollock, besides seeking to abolish inelegance and excess from the Law Reports, also endeavour to suppress cases? Anyone searching for an answer to this question will most likely end up frustrated. There seem to be plenty of after-dinner anecdotes about Pollock refusing to report important cases; but these stories are rarely in print, and even when they are in print they are difficult if not impossible to substantiate. Pollock was happy to admit that there were numerous instances where he deferred reporting what was obviously an important case because it was to be the subject of an appeal. But this, he insisted, was 'quite a different matter' from suppressing a case. 'I cannot remember ever having done such a thing', he claimed. Indeed, there was a simple reason for not doing such a thing: where there is some feeling within the profession that a decision should be reported, 'it is safer to report . . . than to leave it aside'.[122]

It is worth mentioning that Pollock offered these observations in 1903. All instances in which he is alleged to have tried to suppress cases seem to arise in the later years of his editorship. *May & Butcher v The King* came before the House of Lords in 1929. Their Lordships' decision, H. C. Gutteridge

[119] In the eyes of one commentator, 'he edited the judges' prose ruthlessly and, more important still, published only select cases on appeal and very few at first instance', thereby doing 'more effectively for English law what Langdell originally had hoped for as a goal of his system.' Robert Stevens, *Law School: Legal Education in America from the 1850s to the 1980s* (Chapel Hill: University of North Carolina Press, 1983), 143 n.7.

[120] Arthur L. Goodhart, 'Case Law in England and America' (1930) 15 *Cornell L. Q.* 173–93 at 179; repr. in Arthur L. Goodhart, *Essays in Jurisprudence and the Common Law* (Cambridge: Cambridge UP, 1931), 50–74 at 57.

[121] Thurman W. Arnold, review of Goodhart, *Essays in Jurisprudence and the Common Law* (1931) 41 *Yale L. J.* 318–20 at 320.

[122] *EIL* 251.

remarked in 1932, 'appears to constitute a serious inroad on principles which have hitherto been regarded as axiomatic in mercantile law'.[123] But he could not be sure that this assessment was correct: it is 'unfortunate', he noted, that, although *May & Butcher* ... will, in all probability, become a leading case on the question of the validity of agreements to enter into contracts', the 'speeches of the three members of the House of Lords who dealt with the matter are not accessible' and the *ratio decidendi* of the case is 'only ascertainable by reference to the judgments in another case.'[124] It was 'somewhat disconcerting', furthermore, that the case to which one had to look for the *ratio* to *May & Butcher*, the decision of the Court of Appeal in *Hillas & Co. v Arcos Ltd*,[125] had similarly 'been ignored by all the various series of law reports, with the exception of the "Commercial Cases" and "Lloyd's List Reports"'.[126] When *Hillas v Arcos* was decided by the House of Lords in July 1932, *May & Butcher* was again cited—by two Law Lords—as unreported authority.[127] In the same month, the *LQR*—by this point under Goodhart's editorship—carried a rather bashful case note which sought both to play down the significance of the failure to report *May & Butcher* and to compensate for this failure by providing 'the true facts' of the case based on the original transcripts of the judgments.[128] It was not the *LQR* but the Law Reports that really ought to have been making amends. Another two years would pass, nevertheless, before Pollock reported *May & Butcher*.[129] Its late appearance in the Law Reports was, according to Goodhart, 'striking ... but ... not exceptional'.[130] Pollock similarly appeared reluctant, and was certainly slow, to report *Tart v Chitty*[131] and *Baker v Longhurst*.[132] The highly unpopular decision in *L'Estrange v Graucob*[133]—one of the classic harsh exemption clause cases—is another such instance.

[123] H. C. G[utteridge] (1932) 48 *LQR* 4–6 at 5.

[124] Ibid. 5–6.

[125] *Hillas & Co. v Arcos Ltd* (1931) 36 Com. Cas. 534; (1931) 40 Lloyd's L. Rep. 307, CA.

[126] Gutteridge, above n.123, 4.

[127] *Hillas & Co. Ltd v Arcos Ltd* (1932) 43 Lloyd's L. Rep. 359, 365 (*per* Lord Tomlin), 371 (*per* Lord Wright).

[128] F. W. McC[ombe], 'Contract to Make a Contract' (1932) 48 *LQR* 310–16 at 311. McCombe was a barrister of the Middle Temple. His note continues: '[i]n the opinion of the House of Lords, ... the result of [*May & Butcher*], so far from making any serious inroad on principles which had hitherto been regarded as axiomatic in mercantile law, as the learned author of the note in *Hillas's Case* suggests, followed inevitably from the application of, and rested upon, general principles of contract' (ibid. 312). Cf. A. L. Goodhart, 'Precedent in English and Continental Law' (1934) 50 *LQR* 40–65 at 55.

[129] [1934] 2 KB 17. See A. L. Goodhart, 'Reporting the Law' (1939) 55 *LQR* 29–34 at 31.

[130] Goodhart, ibid.

[131] *Tart v G. W. Chitty & Co. Ltd* [1933] 2 KB 453, KBD (decided June 1931). Cf. *EIL* 255 ('About two months ... is the more usual lapse of time between the date of a decision and that of its appearance in the *Law Reports*').

[132] *Baker v E. Longhurst & Sons Ltd* [1933] 2 KB 461, CA. In this last instance, dissatisfaction with reporting appeared not to be confined to the case itself. Scrutton L. J. noted that '[t]his Court had said three times, but unfortunately no one had reported those cases, that if the driver of a vehicle proceeded at such a speed that he could not pull up within the limits of his vision he was in the wrong. If a driver could not see where he was going he must stop. That principle had been applied three times by this Court' (ibid. 465 n.10). On *Tart v Chitty* and *Baker v Longhurst*, see Goodhart, above n.129, 33.

[133] Eventually reported late in 1934 at [1934] 2 KB 394. The case was decided in February of that year.

Alfred Denning—who, as a judge, had no time for decisions upholding inordinately wide exemption clauses[134]—ought to have been opposed once and for all to *L'Estrange v Graucob*. But he recalled in 1979 that, during his years at the Bar, the decision, and especially the fact that it was not quickly reported, served him well:

[i]n those days I wasn't concerned so much with the rightness of the cause. I was concerned only, as a member of the Bar, to win it if I could. But, the Reporter was wise. He didn't think much of it [i.e., *L'Estrange v Graucob*]. He didn't record it in the Law Reports. But my Company had it privately printed: and I went round the County Courts of England winning case after case most unrighteously for this Company.[135]

We should not be quick to condemn Pollock's actions in this context. It is hardly surprising that a man who edited the Law Reports into his nineties should have occasionally been dilatory.[136] We might even question how much significance should be accorded to the claim that cases were suppressed. When one commentator writes of *Blacker v Lake & Elliott Ltd*[137] that it was a case which 'Pollock refused to admit to the Law Reports',[138] it seems important to add that this means nothing more than that *Blacker v Lake* is just one of the many cases that Pollock did not report. There appears to be no evidence that he actively sought to suppress this case. The likelihood is that far more cases were refused than were granted admission to the Law Reports, and so it seems almost inevitable that judges, counsel, and even reporters would occasionally express surprise that particular cases remained unreported. Of course cases were suppressed, if suppression is taken to mean not published. Suppression, in this sense, was a crucial part of Pollock's job.

This is not to insist that, throughout Pollock's tenure as Editor-in-Chief, all was well in the world of the Law Reports. Not long after Pollock's death the Lord Chancellor, Frederick Maugham, appointed a committee to review the existing arrangements for recording case law. The committee suggested, among other things, that the Law Reports should appear more speedily and that more cases should be reported.[139] Although the committee offered nothing

[134] See P. S. Atiyah, 'Contract and Tort', in *Lord Denning: The Judge and the Law*, eds. J. L. Lowell and J. P. W. B. McAuslan (London: Sweet & Maxwell, 1984), 29–77 at 40–5.

[135] The Rt. Hon. Lord Denning, MR, *This is My Life* (London: Council of Legal Education (Child & Co. Lecture), 1979), 5. The passage also appears in his *The Family Story* (London: Butterworths, 1981), 99.

[136] Pollock clearly became self-conscious about his age during the later years of his editorship. In 1924, the year before his eightieth birthday, he claimed that he did not expect to edit the Law Reports beyond the age of eighty and expressed concern that an octogenarian editor would be considered too old. See Pollock to Holmes, 24 March 1924 in *PHL* ii. 130; 14 August 1924, ibid. 145.

[137] (1912) 106 LT 533.

[138] J. L. Barton, 'Liability for Things in the Nineteenth Century' [1984] *Law & Social Change* 145–55 at 154.

[139] Lord Chancellor's Department, *Report of the Law Reporting Committee. March, 1940* (London: HMSO, 1940), 6, 14, 19, 21 ('we have little doubt that the Reports in the Law Reports can and ought

in the way of proposals for reform, it did recognize that unreported cases posed a jurisprudential problem. C. K. Allen identified the gist of the problem not long before the committee produced its report: '[i]f the Judge is to be bound by precedents, he should have all the relevant authorities at his command. But he cannot carry them all in his head, nor is it always easy to find them.'[140] The problem perhaps had more practical resonance for barristers: unreported cases are still considered binding, and so (before the advent of electronic transcripts) a barrister could be put at a disadvantage in the courtroom because opposing counsel cited as authority what was effectively a secret weapon—the unpublished decision that he or an associate happened to remember and then locate in the form of, say, a stenographer's transcript.[141] By the end of the 1930s, to put the matter simply, there was a considerable amount of concern over the fact that, despite the many series of law reports, no guarantee existed that an important case would be reported. The committee appointed to investigate the state of law reporting was in no doubt that Pollock had not helped matters: 'we think that no one would deny that . . . during the long period of Pollock's editorship of the Law Reports, numerous cases were omitted from the Law Reports and reported in other Reports which have been of importance in the development of the law.'[142]

The problem of the unreported but important case was not the only one identified by the committee on law reporting. The repetition among the law reports, discrepancies and inaccuracies in reporting, the expense of the reports, and the library space required—these were all recognized as problems, too.[143] But it is the committee's handling of the problem of incomplete reporting that is most significant for our purposes. One member of the committee proposed that more cases could be reported, and purely oral judgments abolished, by appointing official shorthand writers to transcribe all opinions delivered in courts. The transcripts would then be promptly reviewed by the relevant judges, filed in the courts' records, and made available to the various series of law reports for publication. In effect, the bulk of the editorial process would be completed before the transcripts had left the courts, thereby reducing the likelihood of discrepancies in reporting, facilitating speedier publication, expanding the choice of cases available to the law reports, and making it necessary for lawyers to consult only one source.[144] The majority of the

to be speeded up'), 22 ('[t]he "Law Reports" might, we think, take a more generous view of what is reportable, particularly in the range of cases which exemplify the application of a legal principle').

[140] Carleton Kemp Allen, *Law in the Making*, 3rd edn. (Oxford: Clarendon Press, 1939), 269. Cf. also Frederick Pollock, 'Judicial Caution and Valour' (1929) 45 *LQR* 293–306 at 306.

[141] On these 'unexploded land mines, ready to do damage', see John P. Dawson, *The Oracles of the Law* (Buffalo, NY: Hein, 1986 [1968]), 84. See also Carleton Kemp Allen, 'Case Law: An Unwarrantable Intervention' (1935) 51 *LQR* 333–46 at 341–2; *Report of the Law Reporting Committee*, above n.139, 24–5; G. W. Keeton, *The Elementary Principles of Jurisprudence*, 2nd edn. (London: Pitman & Sons, 1949), 104; and O. M. Stone, 'Knowing the Law' (1961) 24 *Mod. L. Rev.* 475–80.

[142] *Report of the Law Reporting Committee*, above n.139, 16.

[143] See ibid. 2. [144] See ibid. 23–30 (dissentient report).

committee rejected the proposal: it would involve 'a charge on the public funds' and would also probably lead to the reporting of too many cases—there seemed to be no need to produce 'a rubbish heap in which a jewel will rarely, if ever, be discovered'.[145]

The Law Reports might have been reporting too few cases for the committee's liking, in other words, but that did not mean that there must be an advantage to having a permanent record of all judgments. Precisely what the committee did regard as appropriate coverage in the Law Reports, however, was anyone's guess. 'We fear that the sum of this somewhat long Report is negative', the committee concluded. 'That there are inconveniences, to say the least, in the present state of affairs, we are not prepared to deny. But we cannot recommend any cure for them which would not bring greater evils in its train.'[146] The 'recommendation of the minority report is logical and courageous', one commentator concluded, but from the majority of the committee 'one expected more'.[147]

Who was the author of this 'logical and courageous' dissent? It was none other than Arthur Goodhart. Within the space of a decade he had radically changed his tune—gone was the vote of confidence for economical Law Reports. Between the beginning and the end of the 1930s, the time during which this change took place, matters appear to have proceeded as normal with the Law Reports, with one exception: in the middle of the decade, the Editor-in-Chief of the past forty years retired and, soon afterwards, died.[148] The basic feeling of satisfaction that Goodhart had claimed English lawyers shared with respect to the Law Reports during Pollock's lifetime was certainly not shared by Goodhart himself—or at least not after Pollock's death. 'It is our belief', he observed in 1939, with no reference to what he had said a decade earlier,

> that the major error of the past has been the attempt to limit the number of cases reported. . . . It is frequently said that cases which deal with questions of fact and not with questions of law should be omitted from the reports, but this distinction is a misleading and an illusory one. . . . It is more inconvenient to find that one leading case is not reported than to have twenty unimportant cases in the books. With a proper system of indexing it is possible for a reader to skip those cases which he does not

[145] See, above n.139, 20.

[146] Ibid. 21–2; and see also 17 ('we do not think any large measure of reform of Law Reporting feasible').

[147] Richard O' Sullivan, 'On Law Reporting' (1940) 4 *Mod. L. Rev.* 104–10 at 104–5.

[148] Goodhart marks Pollock's retirement as Editor-in-Chief of the Law Reports in a short note at (1936) 52 *LQR* 1, concluding that 'of Sir Frederick Pollock it may well be said that he has never done a piece of slipshod work in the course of his full and very distinguished life'. The remark might be considered to have the scent of hypocrisy about it, though in truth that would be a harsh assessment: although it seems likely that Goodhart felt, or came to feel, that Pollock was a somewhat disappointing Editor-in-Chief it would, of course, have been thoroughly unbecoming of the Editor of the *LQR* to note Pollock's retirement with anything other than praise.

need, but there is no way in which he can conveniently consult an important case which has been omitted.[149]

The question of what prompted Goodhart's volte-face can only be answered by speculation, and there is no obvious need for that on this occasion. For our purposes, it is more important to consider what his change of mind signified. By the 1940s, there was no shortage of soul-searching in the English legal periodicals—and even, occasionally, on the bench—about how the system of law reporting ought to operate.[150] Observers recognized that although the Editor-in-Chief of the Law Reports occupied a position of considerable power, he was barely accountable in exercising that power.[151] Having for the best part of a half-century been in the hands of one man, the Law Reports were, by 1940, operating in as unregulated a manner as they had been in 1903, when Pollock had declared that 'there is no fixed rule for deciding which cases are to be published'[152] and had expressed great pride in how he was able to perform his role casually and without any interference from others. For those who shuddered at the informality of the system, the bad news was that there was no major reform on the horizon.[153] The development of the Law Reports onwards from the 1940s is not, however, relevant here. The crucial point is that, by the middle part of the twentieth century, it became clear that some senior lawyers and judges were not comfortable with the fact that the editing of those Reports had for so long been left to the discretion of one man.

iii. The Law Quarterly Review

While there may have existed some discomfort over Pollock's single-handed editing of the Law Reports, the similar control that he exerted over the *Law*

[149] Goodhart, above n.129, 32–3. A decade later, he felt even more intensely about the matter: see A. L. Goodhart (1949) 65 *LQR* 154–7 esp. at 156 ('We have had "thrillers" entitled "*The Lost Lady*", "*The Lost Diamond*", and "*The Lost Will*": perhaps some member of the Bar will write one on "*The Lost Judgment*". He would not have far to seek for adequate material').

[150] See, e.g., Roland Burrows, 'Law Reporting' (1942) 58 *LQR* 96–106; C. G. Moran, 'Law Reporting: What Cases Should be Reported?' (19 October 1946) 202 *Law Times* 181–3; C. G. Moran, 'Law Reporting: Control' (2 November 1946) 202 *Law Times* 208–10; *Re Haynes' Will Trusts* [1949] 1 Ch. 5, 10 (*per* Roxburgh J.); *Gibson* v. *South American Stores Ltd* [1949] 2 All ER 985, 995 (*per* Sir Raymond Evershed, MR). Burrows was the first Consulting Editor of the All England Law Reports. Moran was a reporter for the *Law Times*.

[151] See Moran, 'Law Reporting: What Cases Should be Reported?', above n.150, 182; cf. also Burrows, above n.150, 103–5, who refers to reporters but clearly means this to include the role of the editor.

[152] *EIL* 249.

[153] 'In its essentials the system of law reporting remained very much the system which had been criticised so convincingly over the years.' A. H. Manchester, *A Modern Legal History of England and Wales, 1750–1950* (London: Butterworths, 1980), 26. Certainly the conclusion of Pollock's reign over the Law Reports did not bring an end to concerns about major cases going unreported: see Gavin Drewry, 'Reporting the Law' (18 August 1969) 119 *New Law Jnl.* 801–2; and, more generally, C. G. Moran, *The Heralds of the Law: Essays on the Reporting of Law Cases* (London: Stevens & Sons, 1948).

Quarterly Review invariably provoked admiration rather than consternation. In the United States, editing a law review has traditionally been a rite of passage for the smarter law student.[154] The notes which those reviews carry, normally written by student editors, occasionally drove Oliver Wendell Holmes to despair. He had no problem with the activity of law journal editing—he himself was responsible for the *American Law Review* in the early 1870s—but he could not abide jejune editors. To Pollock he confessed a feeling of 'aggravation in seeing' the 'lamentably stupid' and 'cocky notes' of 'the young gentlemen of the *Harvard Law Rev.*'[155] That someone of Pollock's stature was willing to invest so much energy in and devote so many years to editing a legal periodical probably struck him as the height of English eccentricity. In fact—and Holmes would no doubt have expected this to be the case—even in England few other editors have been as intensely committed to a law journal as was Pollock to the *LQR*.

The *LQR* was established in 1884 at All Souls College, Oxford. Although Pollock was a member of the original group that devised the idea of the journal he was not, he insisted, one of the chief founders. The principal credit for founding the *LQR*, he claimed, fell to 'Sir William Markby, Sir William Anson (both excellent men of business), and Sir Thomas Erskine Holland, to whom, if to any one man, the conception of the plan was due.'[156] 'In the course of several meetings . . . of which there is no formal record,' Pollock recalled, 'we agreed upon the adventure of a new periodical aiming at the promotion of legal science without neglect of practice, and devoted chiefly to the Common Law but not disregarding comparative study.'[157] The founding group invited Pollock to be the journal's first editor,[158] and he served in this capacity from 1885, the date of the first volume, to 1919 (and again, briefly, in 1925).[159]

[154] On the history of the student-edited law review in the United States, see Michael I. Swygert and Jon W. Bruce, 'The Historical Origins, Founding, and Early Development of Student-Edited Law Reviews' (1985) 36 *Hastings L. J.* 739–91.

[155] Holmes to Pollock, 13 August 1906, in *PHL* i. 131; 6 September 1906, ibid. 133; 7 March 1909, ibid. 152.

[156] (1926) 42 *LQR* 137. Cf. A. L. Goodhart (1926) 42 *LQR* 1 ('Sir Frederick was its real founder . . .'); also Goodhart (1937) 53 *LQR* 204. Albert Dicey was also a member of the founding syndicate, though, according to Pollock, his contribution to the establishment of the journal was not quite so significant: (1926) 42 *LQR* 137. Markby was apparently 'honorary secretary and treasurer to the *Review* for a number of years.' Lucy Markby, *Memories of Sir William Markby, K.C.I.E. By His Wife* (Oxford: Clarendon Press, 1917), 77. On the founding of the *LQR*, see also Richard A. Cosgrove, *Our Lady the Common Law: An Anglo-American Legal Community, 1870–1930* (New York: New York UP, 1987), 47–48; and F. H. Lawson, *The Oxford Law School, 1850–1965* (Oxford: Clarendon Press, 1968), 73. Although Pollock would have been paid for editing the *LQR*, it has not been possible to ascertain his fee. The sum that he was paid for editing the Law Reports would certainly have been considerably higher.

[157] Pollock, above n.77, 6. On the objectives of the *LQR* during the later decades of the twentieth century, see William Twining, *Blackstone's Tower: The English Law School* (London: Stevens & Sons, 1994), 110–11.

[158] Pollock, above n.77, 6–7.

[159] Pollock served as 'emergency' editor of the *LQR* in 1925 owing to the death of A. E. Randall: see Pollock to Holmes, 16 November 1925, in *PHL* ii. 171. Arthur Goodhart became the editor after the publication of the October 1925 issue: (1925) 41 *LQR* 244.

Although the *LQR* was very much the creation of a group of academic lawyers—or certainly lawyers with academic pretensions—it differed from most other specialist journals which emerged during this period in that it did not define itself by reference to a scholarly society or university.[160] 'Holland', Pollock noted, 'was the only one [of the founders] who could be justly called a typical academic scholar'; and even though the journal was conceived at Oxford, it was settled 'from the outset' that 'the seat of editorial work' would be 'in London'.[161] The *LQR* was, nevertheless, representative of the late nineteenth century move towards discipline-specificity and professional intellectual activity rather than a late illustration of the gentlemanly-amateur ethos of the classic Victorian periodicals. Before the 1880s, English law journals—journals such as the *Law Times*, the *Law Magazine and Review*, and the *Law Journal*—were filled mainly with the work of practitioners and journalists. Their audiences were educated gentlemen interested in the law, the wealthy classes, students preparing for law examinations, and the legal profession. In the main, these journals were filled with unsigned editorials, legal gossip, reports on cases and statutes, lists of recent law books, and articles calling for this or that reform of the law. Only the *Law Magazine and Review* among them exhibited occasional academic pretensions.[162] Before the founding of the *LQR*, Pollock recalled, the English law journals offered 'very little serious [legal] criticism; it was mere chance whether important books received any fitting notice; there was no real editing . . . and no security against the admission not only of poor work but of mere nonsense.'[163] The *LQR* 'was as new a departure in England as it certainly would have been in the United States', a note writer in the *Harvard Law Review* proclaimed in 1893, for '[i]t was the first periodical there, and is still the only one, which has given the scientific, the historical, and the philosophical aspects of law an equal place by the side of those that are more practical.'[164] Although earlier English journals had provided an outlet for the practically-minded legal writer, none before the *LQR* had regularly accommodated scholarship.[165]

So, how was the *LQR* received? Initial reactions were mixed.[166] 'Mr Pollock may be congratulated on the handsome volume formed by the first year of his editorial labours', the reviewer for the *Law Journal* commented in February 1886.[167] Seven years later, the same journal was paying tribute to Pollock's achievement in having established 'the greatest of legal quarterly reviews'.[168]

160 Cf. Collini, above n.21, 213, 269. 161 Pollock, above n.77, 6–7.

162 See generally Richard A. Cosgrove, 'Victorian Legal Periodicals' (1975) 8 *Victorian Periodicals Newsletter* 21–5.

163 Pollock, above n.77, 6. 164 Anon. (1893) 6 *Harvard L. Rev.* 442.

165 See A. W. B. Simpson, 'The Rise and Fall of the Legal Treatise: Legal Principles and the Forms of Legal Literature' (1981) 48 *Univ. Chicago L. Rev.* 632–79 at 662.

166 See Raymond Cocks, *Foundations of the Modern Bar* (London: Sweet & Maxwell, 1983), 188–9.

167 Anon., 'The Law Quarterly' (6 February 1886) 21 *Law Jnl.* 86–7 at 86.

168 Anon., 'The Law Quarterly Review' (8 July 1893) 28 *Law Jnl.* 490. See also Anon., 'The Law Quarterly Review' (23 January 1892) 27 *Law Jnl.* 63 for a similarly complimentary assessment.

Yet, later in that same volume, it is asserted that the *LQR* is not, 'in any sense, an organ of the professional opinion of any body of lawyers', and that 'the editor of the best known of the quarterly legal reviews does not see fit to make it, what its name asserts it to be, a law review.'[169] A similar pattern of compliments followed by reservations appeared in the *Law Times*. According to one reviewer, writing in July 1889, the *LQR* was 'full of interesting matter'.[170] Twelve months later, however, a decidedly less positive verdict was being pronounced: '[i]t is as dry as tinder. . . . If anything, this magazine is too academic to be of interest to the busy lawyer, and students of legal science are becoming fewer every year.'[171] The *LQR*, it seemed, was unlikely to be of interest to real lawyers. 'Very scientific, no doubt, but atrociously dull.'[172]

Such criticisms appear not to have left Pollock dispirited.[173] Given his character, the likelihood is that early negative reactions to the journal would simply have strengthened his resolve to continue editing it. In any event, after a few years it would have been easy for him to ignore these reactions and take comfort instead in the manner of praise that appeared in the *Harvard Law Review* of 1893. A year earlier T. Cyprian Williams, the author of *A Treatise on the Law of Vendor and Purchaser*, had been so enthusiastic about the *LQR* that he rather lost control of his syntax: '[m]ay I say', he wrote to Pollock, 'that the number of times which I have had to refer to the *Law Quarterly Review* for historical information not to [be] found elsewhere shows how admirably the excellent purpose of that magazine has been carried out?'[174] Pollock was probably far happier to receive the laconic praise of Viscount Haldane in 1914: '[t]he Law Quarterly is a great comfort house. I read it and expand my legal mind regularly.'[175] In due course, there would be plenty more compliments of this nature.[176] Although the sincerity of many such compliments could be called into question owing to the fact that they tended to appear within solicited testimonials, most of those who paid tribute to the *LQR* under

[169] Anon., 'The Law Quarterly Review' (7 October 1893) 28 *Law Jnl.* 655.

[170] Anon. (20 July 1889) 87 *Law Times* 222.

[171] Anon. (12 July 1890) 89 *Law Times* 198.

[172] Anon. (1 April 1893) 94 *Law Times* 499. Cf. Anon., 'The Law Quarterly Review' (7 October 1893) 28 *Law Jnl.* 655 ('The notes upon the reported cases of the quarter are duller than usual, many of them being little more than short head-notes garnished with epithets, commendatory or the reverse').

[173] See Pollock, above n.77, 7: 'one or two journalists of the obsolete rule of thumb school did attempt to regard [the *LQR*] as a fad of unpractical Oxford professors. I took a little malicious pleasure in finding an occasion to observe that the Review was edited in Lincoln's Inn and published in Chancery Lane.'

[174] T. Cyprian Williams to Frederick Pollock, [?] July 1892, in Pollock correspondence, box 1, folder 75. Cyprian Williams's son, Orlando, married Pollock's daughter, Alice, in 1912: see *Who Was Who (1961–1970)*, 1208.

[175] Viscount Haldane to Frederick Pollock, 25 June 1914, in Pollock correspondence, box 1, folder 28. Haldane's letter was in response to Pollock's *LQR* case note on *Sinclair v Brougham* [1914] AC 398. In that note, Pollock writes that '[t]he fullest exposition of the doctrine [of tracing] is in Lord Haldane's judgment, which is careful to point out that it does not depend on any fiduciary relation.' (1914) 30 *LQR* 263.

[176] See, e.g., (1935) 1 *LQR* 1 (Lord Haldane); (1935) 1 *LQR* 4 (O. W. Holmes); (1935) 1 *LQR* 568–9 (Lord Tomlin).

Pollock's editorship were not generally noted for lauding institutions for which they had no affection.

There is, in any event, no need to dwell on such testimonials. More important for our purposes is the question of what the *LQR* contained. The earliest volumes of the journal are, in a sense, the most interesting in that they show Pollock's contributors—and perhaps Pollock himself—struggling to embrace the norms of the professional scholarly periodical. No articles were to be anonymous—almost any unsigned contribution could be assumed to be the work of the Editor—so that authors would generally bear responsibility for what they wrote, readers (and bibliographers) could identify the work of particular authors, and the journal could derive proper benefit from attracting highly reputed contributors.[177] Pollock would decide what was to be published—it would be a long time before law journals would begin to utilize peer review—and whatever was accepted for publication would appear, he claimed, 'with as little editorial interference as may be'.[178] This last claim is open to dispute. Pollock would, in fact, quite regularly follow the Victorian convention of attaching editorial notes to articles. Two contributions on subjects close to his heart—torts and Shakespeare—were supplemented with numerous square-bracketed interventions by 'F. P.'[179] Indeed, the essay on *The Merchant of Venice* was published with a reply by Pollock and the author's response.[180] That the *LQR* carried an article on Shakespeare was in itself significant. Some authors, Pollock observed, assumed that the *LQR* would, in the tradition of the classic Victorian periodicals, publish material on more or less any subject. Thus it is that he received requests from 'authors' to publish their translations of Balzac or word-for-word reproductions of passages from old law treatises.[181] Not all would-be contributors grasped the purpose of the journal.

These occasional misunderstandings may have been attributable to the fact that Pollock's *LQR*, while it did not carry just about anything, did contain material on a remarkable array of topics. This breadth of coverage is not especially surprising: after all, we have seen in this study that Pollock was involved in organizations of considerable intellectual diversity and ambition—the Cambridge Apostles is perhaps the most notable of these—and that he did not always think and work with an eye to disciplinary boundaries. Although the *LQR* belonged to an era of increasing intellectual specialization, it was slow to lose that distinctive Victorian polymath quality: anyone looking back to its earliest issues, Pollock remarked in 1935, would 'see at a glance that in some points it was experimental'.[182] Perhaps unsurprisingly, the journal

[177] See Pollock, above n.77, 7–8. The system of indexation that Pollock applied in the *LQR* was adopted from *Mind*: see (1916) 32 *LQR* 18.

[178] Pollock, above n.77, 7.

[179] See Edward Jenks, 'Theories of Tort in Modern Law' (1903) 19 *LQR* 19–36; Julius Hirschfeld, 'Portia's Judgment and German Jurisprudence' (1914) 30 *LQR* 167–74.

[180] Frederick Pollock, 'A Note on *Shylock* v. *Antonio*' (1914) 30 *LQR* 175–7; Julius Hirschfeld, 'A Response' (1914) 30 *LQR* 178.

[181] Pollock, above n.77, 9. [182] Ibid. 7.

displayed its Editor's taste for the cosmopolitan and limited interest in the parochial: it would carry its fair share of articles with titles such as the 'Reform of Company Law', 'Notes on Insurance Law', 'Registration of Title to Land', and 'Powers and the Rule Against Perpetuities'—it was not intended, after all, to give a wide berth to black-letter lawyers—but it also contained plenty of articles on subjects such as the 'Constitutional History of Hungary', 'War and the Law', 'Moslem International Law', 'Indictments for Adultery and Incest Before 1650', and 'Reason and Conscience in Sixteenth-Century Jurisprudence'. Some subjects regularly had essays devoted to them. Public international law, it has been observed, was well represented in the *LQR* throughout the years of Pollock's editorship.[183] During this period, articles would also frequently appear on Roman law, legal history, conflicts of laws, the law of India, and legal education.

While these thematic preferences corresponded with the professed orientation of the journal they were also, more obviously, indicative of the interests of Pollock's contributors. Who were these contributors? Most were jurists, though Pollock would also publish articles by judges and other senior members of the legal profession. The first three volumes of the *LQR* were heavily reliant on contributions from his friends and the journal's founders: Holland, Anson, Dicey, Maitland, Nathaniel Lindley, Paul Vinogradoff, John Salmond, and John Chipman Gray, among others. It is only by volume four that Pollock can be seen to be less dependent on this core group and that the names of the contributors become less predictable. Even though the list of contributors expands, nevertheless, there are, throughout his years as Editor, names that appear volume upon volume. Howard Elphinstone contributed articles regularly from volume 2 through to 33; John Salmond from 3 to 34; A. V. Dicey from 1 to 31; T. E. Holland from 1 to 28; W. R. Anson from 1 to 17; F. W. Maitland from 2 to 17; Paul Vinogradoff from 1 to 30; T. Cyprian Williams from 4 to 31; W. W. Buckland from 6 to 34; Edward Jenks from 9 to 33; and W. S. Holdsworth from 18 to 35, the final full volume that Pollock edited, and beyond. Certain of these authors—Maitland, Dicey, Vinogradoff, and Holdsworth are conspicuous in this respect—would contribute two or even three articles in some years.

None of these authors, however, contributed as frequently as did the Editor. It is open to debate whether Pollock was, as has been claimed, 'the Review's best reviewer',[184] but he was certainly its most prolific: to every issue between 1885 and 1919 he appears to have contributed reviews and notices of books. During that period, he published in the *LQR* twenty-nine of his own arti-

[183] 'Pollock . . . rendered signal services to international law, not least by welcoming into the pages of the *Law Quarterly Review* . . . articles on international law questions at a time when few alternative outlets for such articles were available.' D. H. N. Johnson, 'The English Tradition in International Law' (1962) 11 *Int'l & Compar. L. Q.* 416–45 at 422 n.16.

[184] Edward Potton (1937) 53 *LQR* 199.

cles[185]—a further fourteen were published in the years after his editorship. To focus on the number of articles published is, in this instance as in so many others, to risk distorting the actual achievement. Many of Pollock's pieces were articles only by virtue of their location in the journal. An article by Pollock would often be a case note with a title,[186] a short curiosity piece,[187] a text of a university lecture,[188] or a barely edited reproduction of a section from one of his treatises.[189] This is not to deny that he wrote for the *LQR* some very good essays. Indeed, given that the journal bore his name, it is hardly surprising that he should have placed in it some of his most significant, inspired, and insightful pieces.[190] Even some of his shorter 'articles' are superb illustrations of considered analysis and critique. As often as not, nevertheless, the reader of Pollock's contributions to the *LQR* is likely to come away from them feeling short-changed. More than anything, these essays—taken collectively—generate the impression of an immensely bright and erudite author whose final product might often have been all the better had he enjoyed less of a free rein. None of the articles is superficial, but a fair number of them are somewhat lazy and unambitious, the work of someone who was being neither scrutinized nor pushed. Pollock himself conceded that his position as Editor permitted him the occasional liberty: he admitted, for example, that after the First World War he resolved to use the pages of the *LQR* to voice his support for the League of Nations.[191] Yet the freedom that he granted himself hardly proved profitable: compared with certain of his other essays on the League of Nations, his articles on this subject in the *LQR* were some of his more stodgy and less engaging contributions to post-War debate.[192] All too often, certainly so far as essay writing is concerned, the *LQR* failed to bring out the best in Pollock.

This does not mean, however, that Pollock's contributions to the *LQR* were of little real significance. In one specific way, the journal did bring out the best in him. Pollock could be economical with words on the page as well as in person. One of the reasons that his essays can disappoint, indeed, is that one

[185] Two of these were in two parts, and one was co-authored.

[186] See, e.g., Frederick Pollock, 'The Dog and the Potman: Or "Go It, Bob"' (1909) 25 *LQR* 317–21; '*Abrams* v. *United States* (250 U.S. 616)' (1920) 36 *LQR* 334–8.

[187] See, e.g., Frederick Pollock, 'The Supreme Court of the United States' (1892) 8 *LQR* 162–4; 'The "Renvoi" in New York' (1920) 36 *LQR* 91–2.

[188] See, e.g., Frederick Pollock, 'The Vocation of the Common Law' (1895) 11 *LQR* 323–36 (repr. *ECL* 1–23); 'Judicial Records' (1913) 29 *LQR* 206–16 (repr. *EIL* 222–40).

[189] See, e.g., 'Liability for the Torts of Agents and Servants' (1885) 1 *LQR* 207–24 (repr. *TLT* 63–91); 'The Nature and Meaning of Law' (1894) 10 *LQR* 228–39 (repr. *FBJ* 3–27).

[190] Perhaps the best example—though it appeared some time after Pollock ceased to be Editor—is Pollock's essay on 'Judicial Caution and Valour', above n.140.

[191] See Pollock, above n.77, 9–10.

[192] See Frederick Pollock, 'The Work of the League of Nations' (1919) 35 *LQR* 193–8; 'Methods of International Arbitration' (1919) 35 *LQR* 320–38; and cf. Frederick Pollock, 'Cosmopolitan Custom and International Law' (1916) 29 *Harvard L. Rev.* 565–81; also 'The American Plan for Enforcing Peace' (May 1917) 119 *Atlantic Monthly* 650–5.

would sometimes prefer that he said more. But there is one form of legal analysis to which his style was perfectly suited. Case notes—the commentaries on legal decisions carried by many law journals—tend to benefit from brevity of expression. Most legal academics and practitioners would probably say that a good case note will identify the principle, or principles, at stake in a decision—an epitome of the facts of the case is not always necessary—and then provide a concise and incisive critique of what the court has done. If this is a fair summary of what makes for good case notes then Pollock, as has often been observed, was a past master at producing them.[193]

Case notes appeared in the *LQR* from its inception. Pollock wrote the vast majority of those that were published in the journal before 1912, and continued to contribute regularly to the Notes section for over two decades thereafter.[194] His appointment as Editor-in-Chief of the Law Reports in 1895 meant that, from then onwards, many of his notes would concern cases he had edited.[195] There would obviously be no more complaints about the quality of the reporting: 'the editor of this *Review*', now that he is also Editor-in-Chief of the Law Reports, Pollock wrote in the *LQR* in 1895, 'cannot be expected to criticize in public the work for which he is himself answerable to the profession'.[196] But this hardly left the Notes section at a loose end. The work of the courts, as opposed to the reporting of the work of the courts, provided plenty in the way of subject matter.

Any reader attentive to the footnotes of this study will have deduced already that Pollock liked to pursue campaigns through the case notes section of the *LQR*. The section provided a platform from which he could, among other things, express his dissatisfaction with the state of legal education at the Inns of Court (see chapter 2) and his distrust of ambitious legislative proposals (see chapter 4). Given that the section was primarily concerned with cases, it is perhaps inevitable that he also used it to oppose specific positions taken by the courts.

The stance adopted by the House of Lords in *Derry v Peek*[197] came under particular fire from Pollock. In *Derry v Peek*, the directors of a tramway company assumed that the Board of Trade would award them the right to use steam power and so stated in their prospectus that they had this right before it had been granted. Relying on the prospectus, the respondent bought shares in the company. Subsequently, the Board of Trade refused to award a

[193] See, e.g., A. L. Goodhart (1937) 53 *LQR* 204; Lord Tomlin (1935) 51 *LQR* 1.

[194] From October 1912 onwards, the *LQR* began to include within the Notes section a sub-section of case notes devoted to company law. In the 1913 volume, 'F. E.'—identifiable from later volumes as Frank Evans—is listed as the author of the company law case notes. Evans was a member of the editorial team that worked with Pollock on the Law Reports. The notes on company cases continued until 1920. Evans died in the autumn of 1921: see (1921) 37 *LQR* 411.

[195] See *FMG* 190 ('[As Editor-in-Chief of the Law Reports] I have much readier access to information and learned opinion . . . than I should have outside it'); also, for case notes following cases, see, e.g., (1911) 27 *LQR* 1; (1916) 32 *LQR* 137–8.

[196] (1895) 11 *LQR* 1.

[197] *Derry v Peek* (1889) 14 App. Cas. 337, HL.

right to use steam power to the company and the company was wound up. The Court of Appeal held that the fact that there exist no reasonable grounds for believing a statement to be accurate is sufficient to establish liability for fraud. The House of Lords reversed this decision, holding that negligent misstatements were not of themselves sufficient to give rise to liability for fraud. Most Chancery lawyers considered the decision of the House of Lords to be wrong.[198] Pollock, certainly in this instance, could be counted among their number. When the decision of the Court of Appeal was reversed, he was blunt: 'the decision of the House of Lords has dangerously relaxed the legal conception of honesty.'[199] Subsequently, he used the Notes section of the *LQR* to mount a merciless crusade against the decision.[200] The essence of the crusade is easily captured: '[t]his is the law; whether this ought to be the law is quite another question'[201]—especially considering that 'the result of this law is to encourage practices which may easily go to the very verge of fraud.'[202]

It is not really possible to determine how effective Pollock's campaign against *Derry v Peek* was, though it seems hardly likely that it was ineffective.[203] Certainly the decision was gradually sapped of strength. 'My enemy *Derry v Peek* has not been so much as cited in court here—certainly nothing like a judicial discussion', Pollock wrote from Calcutta in 1893.[204] More important to him, of course, was its reception at home. Parliament quickly expressed dissatisfaction over the decision,[205] but the most significant body blow to *Derry v Peek*—in Pollock's lifetime, at least—did not come until 1914. In that year, in *Nocton v Ashburton*, the House of Lords held that while, as *Derry v Peek* had established, a fiduciary may not be liable to his client in deceit, he may nevertheless be partially liable in equity for loss incurred owing to his innocent misrepresentations.[206] The House, in reaching its decision, was led by the then Lord Chancellor, Viscount Haldane; its decision was reserved on 8 May 1914

[198] See David Ibbetson, *A Historical Introduction to the Law of Obligations* (Oxford: Oxford UP, 1999), 181 n.80; W. R. Cornish and G. de N. Clark, *Law and Society in England, 1750–1950* (London: Sweet & Maxwell, 1989), 221. Cf. also Friedrich Kessler and Edith Fine, '*Culpa in Contrahendo*, Bargaining in Good Faith, and Freedom of Contract: A Comparative Study' (1964) 77 *Harvard L. Rev.* 401–49 at 445–7.

[199] Frederick Pollock, '*Derry* v. *Peek* in the House of Lords' (1889) 5 *LQR* 410–23 at 422.

[200] See, e.g., (1890) 6 *LQR* 112; (1891) 7 *LQR* 5, 107; (1892) 8 *LQR* 7, 113; (1896) 12 *LQR* 205; (1899) 15 *LQR* 236–7; (1900) 16 *LQR* 217; (1907) 23 *LQR* 133; (1911) 27 *LQR* 276. See also Pollock, above n.140, 297–8.

[201] (1891) 7 *LQR* 310.

[202] (1893) 9 *LQR* 202. See also C. H. S. Fifoot, *Law and History in the Nineteenth Century* (London: Quaritch, 1956), 10 ('. . . he hastened . . . to add this case to the index of unhappy if not, alas, forbidden law').

[203] See W. M. C. Gummow, 'Compensation for Breach of Fiduciary Duty', in *Equity, Fiduciaries and Trusts*, ed. T. G. Youdan (Toronto: Carswell, 1989), 57–92 at 57–9; and David Sugarman, 'Legal Theory, the Common Law Mind and the Making of the Textbook Tradition', in *Legal Theory and Common Law*, ed. W. Twining (Oxford: Blackwell, 1986), 26–61 at 47.

[204] Pollock to Holmes, 11 December 1893, in *PHL* i. 49.

[205] See the Directors' Liability Act 1890, 53 & 54 Vict. c. 59, s. 3(1) (imposing a statutory duty of care on those who issue prospectuses).

[206] *Nocton v Lord Ashburton* [1914] AC 932.

and delivered on 19 June[207]—six days before Haldane wrote to Pollock about how the *LQR* was 'a great comfort house' to him. A few days before the decision was reserved, Pollock had been provided the opportunity to witness their Lordships' minds at work:

> Haldane asked me last week to a tobacco talk of *Derry* v *Peek* and the possibility of minimizing its consequences. The Lords are going to hold that it does not apply to the situation created by a positive fiduciary duty such as a solicitor's, in other words, go as near as they dare to saying it was wrong, as all in Lincoln's Inn thought at the time.[208]

Not surprisingly, *Nocton v Ashburton* contains no reference to Pollock's assessment of *Derry v Peek.* It is noted, nevertheless, that *Derry v Peek* 'has been the subject of much comment',[209] that it 'is in some quarters thought to have introduced a far-reaching change into the law',[210] and that it has been accepted 'in certain quarters under protest'.[211] *Nocton v Ashburton* certainly satisfied Pollock. 'Learned friends whom it amuses to read between the lines' of the case, he remarked somewhat mischievously, 'may be of the opinion that Lord Haldane would have liked to get rid of *Derry v Peek* altogether had he been free to do so'.[212]

The story of *Nocton v Ashburton* rather conjures up an image of Pollock working in constructive partnership with senior members of the judiciary. But it ought to be emphasized that, even if he enjoyed such a relationship occasionally and with specific judges, the relationship hardly existed across the board. The *London Tramways* case of 1898, in which the House of Lords declared that it would not review its own decisions (effectively confirming the impossibility of reversing *Derry v Peek*, among other things), might have been an instance in which relations between Pollock and at least one senior judge did not run smoothly.[213] Pollock not only published an error-strewn report of *London Tramways* in the Appeal Cases—a corrigendum slip had to be issued to put right, among other things, the name of the case—but he also produced in the *LQR* a note on the case (with the name still wrong) in which he suggested that Lord Halsbury, the prime architect behind the decision, had little grasp of the history of the rule that the House of Lords had established.[214] One legal historian has claimed—though has provided little evidence—that behind the scenes there was a conflict between Pollock and Halsbury.[215]

207 See Gummow, above n.203, 57–8.
208 Pollock to Holmes, 20 May 1914, in *PHL* i. 215.
209 *Nocton v Ashburton*, above n.206, 946 (*per* Viscount Haldane).
210 Ibid. 969 (*per* Lord Shaw). 211 Ibid. 970 (*per* Lord Shaw).
212 Frederick Pollock, '*Nocton* v. *Lord Ashburton*' (1915) 31 *LQR* 93–5 at 95.
213 *London Tramways v London County Council* [1898] AC 375.
214 (1898) 14 *LQR* 331–2.
215 See David Pugsley, 'London Tramways (1898)' (1996) 17 *Jnl. Leg. Hist.* 172–84 at 175–7. Pugsley demonstrates that counsel for the appellants in *London Tramways* relied heavily for authorities on

Whether or not there was a conflict, the case serves as a reminder that Pollock was, however highly regarded were his abilities and connections, essentially an outsider—an appropriate invitee to the occasional judicial meeting, no doubt, but ultimately a rather unusual and potentially disagreeable figure who could easily turn out to be the judge's nemesis rather than an ally.

The point that deserves emphasis here is that Pollock, as a writer of case notes, was fulfilling the task of a legal critic rather than a lawyer, commending the courts when they performed well and endeavouring to correct them when they erred. The types of criticism that he offered are predictable in light of some of the ground covered already in this study. He was notably keen to stress that courts ought to identify key legal principles when reaching decisions.[216] He would commend judges when they clarified principles,[217] criticize them when they failed to identify applicable principles or extended principles beyond their natural scope,[218] and would urge the House of Lords to ratify 'principles of immense public import'.[219] What

Pollock's *FBJ* ('London Tramways', 174–5). He also notes that Pollock observed in the first edition of that book (1896) that '[a]t present it seems to be the accepted view . . . that the House of Lords . . . should hold itself absolutely bound by its own former decisions' (*FBJ* 310–11). But he then adds that 'it is clear that [Pollock] did not approve of the rule, and he did not approve of the *London Tramways* decision' ('London Tramways', 175). In *FBJ*, Pollock neither explicitly endorses nor disapproves of the rule that a court of last resort should not be able to correct itself—he simply discusses its history, some of the problems associated with the rule, and the conventions of certain other jurisdictions (see *FBJ* 309–20). For Pugsley, the fact that the Law Reports carried an error-strewn report of the *London Tramways* case 'suggests that the editor disapproved of the decision . . . and was trying to minimise its importance' ('London Tramways', 176). It seems highly unlikely that Pollock would have deliberately botched the report of any decision; and it is not obvious why doing such a thing would be indicative of disapproval or be considered a good strategy for diminishing a decision's significance. Following the appearance of the case in the Law Reports, Pugsley adds, there came 'a rather sour case note in the *Law Quarterly Review*, still getting the name of the case wrong' (ibid.). In that note, Pollock writes that 'Lord Halsbury's historical observation about the English principle [regarding the conclusiveness of HL decisions] having "been established now for some centuries" . . . is, so far as we know, not only unproved but against the evidence.' (1898) 14 *LQR* 332. Since Pugsley himself notes that 'Lord Halsbury's statement that the rule had been "established now for some centuries" is odd' ('London Tramways', 177), one assumes that Pollock's articulation of much the same point cannot be the source of sourness. However, the rest of the case note seems anything but sour. The core of it runs thus: '[i]n spite of the obvious objections which may be brought against the judicial immutability of the principles laid down by the final Court of Appeal, there is no reason for serious dissatisfaction. It may be doubted whether at the present day even a reformer such as Bentham might not prefer the coherent legislation of the Courts to the ill-constructed statutes enacted by Parliamentary ignorance and incapacity; and the work of the Courts will be more coherent in proportion as its finality is recognized.' (1898) 14 *LQR* 331. Although Pugsley concludes that '[t]he conflict between Pollock and Halsbury was long-running' ('London Tramways', 177), it is not in fact obvious that there was a conflict. Certainly Pugsley shows that Pollock and Halsbury might have irritated one another—Halsbury failed to take account of Pollock's explanation of precedent in the House of Lords, Pollock made a mess of reporting the *London Tramways* decision—but there appears to be no hard evidence that they crossed swords.

[216] See, e.g., (1887) 3 *LQR* 252, 360; (1888) 4 *LQR* 115; (1891) 7 *LQR* 308; (1892) 8 *LQR* 10–11, 185; (1893) 9 *LQR* 102–3, 107, 308; (1894) 10 *LQR* 101, 108; (1897) 13 *LQR* 333–7; (1898) 14 *LQR* 3, 5–6, 114, 224, 335; (1900) 16 *LQR* 109–10, 219; (1901) 17 *LQR* 120, 347–8; (1902) 18 *LQR* 342; (1903) 19 *LQR* 251, 363–4; (1909) 25 *LQR* 7; (1912) 28 *LQR* 339–40; (1914) 30 *LQR* 135–6; (1915) 31 *LQR* 369–70.

[217] See, e.g., (1886) 2 *LQR* 530.

[218] See, e.g., (1913) 29 *LQR* 123; (1891) 7 *LQR* 3.

[219] (1890) 6 *LQR* 460.

particularly concerned Pollock (again, fairly predictably) was the question of whether a principle applied by a court was sound[220]—soundness being a concept that he never defined in his case notes but which he regularly equated with the idea of commonsensicality.[221] This recurring exercise identifiable within Pollock's notes—uncovering and assessing the soundness of the general principles at the heart of specific cases—was never presented as if it were a distinctive juristic project. Throughout the many volumes of the *LQR* that Pollock edited, nevertheless, one keeps encountering the same questions: what was the legal principle which guided the court to this decision? Are we convinced of the soundness of that principle? Does the principle depart from commonsense expectations of the law? If it does, is this indicative of some legal shortcoming, or of the fact that sometimes too much is expected of the legal machinery?

There is one other question that is regularly posed in Pollock's case notes: what more could have been done? 'It is to be regretted that . . .'—as was intimated at the outset of this book—is a regular refrain in the *LQR* during the years of Pollock's editorship.[222] But what is being regretted? Although, occasionally, the regret is that a court attempted to do too much,[223] the feeling usually runs in the opposite direction. Over and again the reader of Pollock's notes is informed that a court could have done more or performed better. 'The judgment gives a hint that their Lordships were aware of [the problem]', he rather typically remarks in a note of 1902, 'but we should have liked a more distinct exposition.'[224] Similarly, in a note four years earlier: 'one is tempted to wonder whether the House of Lords in its judicial capacity might not have done the work better as well as sooner.'[225] The predominant critical style in the case notes of this period might be termed the 'okay, but' approach: '[w]e are by no means prepared to say that the decision . . . was wrong, but the very short judgment does not adequately show to our mind that it was right'; '[t]he fairness of this decision is obvious. Yet . . .'; '[t]he decision, we doubt not . . . is sound . . . but. . . .'[226] Repeatedly in Pollock's notes we encounter what would, during the twentieth century, become one of the case note writer's favourite lamentations: that the court did not dig deeper or tie up loose ends, that relevant legal sources were not considered, or that reasons adduced for decisions were insufficiently clear, elaborated, or compelling.[227]

[220] See, e.g., (1887) 3 *LQR* 107, 250; (1890) 6 *LQR* 463; (1894) 10 *LQR* 103; (1901) 17 *LQR* 114; (1905) 21 *LQR* 219; (1907) 23 *LQR* 6–7; (1912) 28 *LQR* 2, 4.

[221] See, e.g., (1890) 6 *LQR* 237; (1891) 7 *LQR* 103, 307; (1894) 10 *LQR* 13, 300; (1895) 11 *LQR* 314; (1896) 12 *LQR* 203; (1897) 13 *LQR* 126; (1905) 21 *LQR* 102; (1909) 25 *LQR* 116; (1914) 30 *LQR* 390.

[222] See, e.g., (1890) 6 *LQR* 122; (1892) 8 *LQR* 268; (1901) 17 *LQR* 122; (1902) 18 *LQR* 113; (1903) 19 *LQR* 258; and cf. (1913) 29 *LQR* 243.

[223] See, e.g., (1915) 31 *LQR* 365; and cf. Pollock to Holmes, 30 March 1898, in *PHL* i. 84–5.

[224] (1902) 18 *LQR* 335. [225] (1898) 14 *LQR* 2.

[226] (1898) 14 *LQR* 4; (1899) 15 *LQR* 108; (1903) 19 *LQR* 128.

[227] See, e.g., (1885) 1 *LQR* 393; (1889) 5 *LQR* 99, 442–3; (1890) 6 *LQR* 114; (1893) 9 *LQR* 206; (1895) 11 *LQR* 216, 318; (1897) 13 *LQR* 228, 231, 334–5; (1898) 14 *LQR* 4, 340; (1899) 15 *LQR* 109, 225; (1900)

The language of principle was very much a feature of twentieth-century academic law. It was argued in chapter 4, however, that, although Pollock spoke this language fluently, it would be a mistake to try to make him bear any special responsibility for the manner of its development in modern Anglo-American jurisprudence. We need not be quite so cautious when assessing the significance of his predilection for requesting more from the courts. Certainly Pollock did not invent this style of critique: the pre-*LQR* English legal periodicals are by no means bereft of commentaries taking judges to task for flimsy work. But Pollock was the first jurist to produce such critique relentlessly. During the years when the *LQR* was under his editorship, hardly an issue would pass without it being respectfully submitted that a court might have done more. Opinions about this style are not important here: the key point is that it became popular within twentieth-century academic law. Pollock, as the Editor of the *LQR*, consistently adopted a style of legal commentary that would come to be favoured by many later English legal writers.

There is a temptation to argue that this style came to be favoured because it was Pollock's style. But it is perhaps more accurate to claim that it became popular because, through Pollock's effort, it was the style of the *LQR*. As the Editor, Pollock preferred not to sign his notes. It was argued in chapter 4 that although lawyers of Pollock's era would most likely have known him to be the author of most case notes that appeared in the *LQR*, the fact of anonymity tended to give these notes extra gravitas: they represented not simply Pollock's views but the views of the journal. It is worth remarking that those who contributed signed or initialed notes to the *LQR* during the years of Pollock's editorship would likewise often lament that a court had failed to do more in reaching a decision.[228] There was a distinctive style to virtually all of the case notes carried by the journal, in other words, rather than just those that were written by Pollock. It cannot seriously be envisaged that Pollock would have required other writers to adopt his style; but it may well have been that others adopted the style because they recognized it to be that of an especially well-practised case note writer.

Besides ensuring that his own case note writing style permeated the *LQR*, Pollock also made sure that the Notes section offered distinctly academic perspectives on law. One of the reasons his style endured may well be that he tended to write case notes with academically oriented lawyers in mind. Even though, by the later years of Pollock's editorship, English university lawyers were still fairly few in number, his case notes were regularly devoted to showing how legal problems are not only of interest to, but might be profitably handled

16 *LQR* 1, 7; (1901) 17 *LQR* 116–17, 354; (1902) 18 *LQR* 230; (1906) 22 *LQR* 122, 124–5; (1907) 23 *LQR* 129, 130; (1908) 24 *LQR* 366; (1913) 29 *LQR* 8–9; (1915) 31 *LQR* 256–7; (1919) 35 *LQR* 288; (1921) 37 *LQR* 395.

[228] See, e.g., (1893) 9 *LQR* 6 (John R. Adams), 200 (A. V. Dicey?); (1903) 19 *LQR* 246 (A. V. Dicey); (1914) 30 *LQR* 134–5 (C[harles] S[weet]).

by, academics. 'No part of the law is drier than the rules as to the incidence of stamp duty,' Pollock wrote in 1901,

> yet, oddly enough, no branch of the law more often raises speculative questions of jurisprudence. Is a benefit under a contract 'property'? Is the benefit of a contract to transfer 'suitable land' within certain limits, but otherwise to be determined by the contractor's option, in Roumania, or is the benefit of a contract to cultivate other such land in a certain manner 'property locally situate out of the United Kingdom'? These are inquiries of a kind which delights and perplexes jurists.[229]

Pollock wanted not only to invest practical legal matters with academic significance, but also to show that judges might benefit from taking account of arguments expounded by jurists. The court might have made far less heavy weather of the case, he would argue from time to time, had it been aware of the academic literature on the issue at stake.[230] On the rare occasions that the courts were clearly receptive to juristic opinion, he would tend to respond appreciatively.[231] It seems rather ironic that the case note—a genre of legal writing which has not always been taken seriously by those who are drawn to law as an object of academic inquiry—should have been, for Pollock, a primary medium through which to promote academic conceptions of law. Perhaps it is equally ironic that it was as an editor, possibly more than as a professor, that Pollock conducted some of his most steadfast campaigning for the recognition of law as an academic discipline. To study the Notes section of the *LQR* throughout the years of Pollock's editorship is to witness that discipline coming alive. Certain of Pollock's concerns—his emphasis on principle, his insistence that courts too often leave stones unturned—are no less obvious within academic law today.

iv. Concluding observations

As an editor, Pollock had stamina, dynamism, and power. Both the Law Reports and the *LQR* brought something of the missionary out of him: banish inelegant language, report only what needs to be reported, be obstructive in the face of bad decisions, sanctify principle, invest law with an academic identity—one could hardly say that he was short of goals, or that he had no success in pursuing them. Pollock the editor certainly cuts a rather more determined and successful—and well-remunerated!—figure than the rather atomistic and unfocused jurisprudence professor we studied in chapter 3.

Nevertheless, it is that image of the man as an outsider—properly connected neither to the world of the university nor to the world of the court-

[229] (1901) 17 *LQR* 114. [230] See, e.g., (1892) 8 *LQR* 185; and cf. (1898) 14 *LQR* 333.
[231] See, e.g., (1891) 7 *LQR* 309; (1893) 9 *LQR* 9.

room—which is most likely to linger. 'I remember him well', Lord Denning wrote in 1984. 'He was dry, forbidding, taciturn, bespectacled, with a shaggy moustache. He was wise to give up trying to practise as an advocate. He was doomed to have been an utter failure. But . . . his written word was as clear as his spoken word was obscure.'[232] Although, when considering Pollock's achievements as an editor, it is difficult not to admire him, that admiration is likely to feature as part of a broader and more complex estimation of the man. Whether we consider Pollock as an editor, treatise writer, jurisprudence professor, or general jurist-about-town, the figure in our mind's eye is likely to remain pretty much unchanged: he was an awkward if highly respected individual, lacking in social skills but blessed with an abundance of intellectual stamina; someone who was not only unable to suffer foolishness but who would regularly embark upon crusades to eradicate this quality from the law where he believed that the consequences of its presence were especially regrettable; a renowned scholar who, for all his academic credentials, preferred not Oxford but Lincoln's Inn, who spent most of his professional life, indeed, in the environment of those who were responsible for producing the law which he edited and upon which he commented; a member of an eminent legal family whose connections probably ensured that he was closer than would be any modern academic lawyer to the major affairs of the English legal world; but also a man who, for all that he was based at the heart of that world, never conventionally belonged to it.

[232] Lord Denning (1984) 100 *LQR* 513.

7

EPILOGUE

It is difficult to know whether, for English academic lawyers, things have never been better or have never been worse than they are today. For scholars of a certain generation, there might be an especial temptation to become wistful about a past when the vacations seemed longer and the terms more relaxed, when one could find time to walk to the library for no other reason than to browse the shelves, and when writing an article could take forever and a day and the manuscript would be typed by a secretary. Inordinate sentimentality is not a prerequisite to taking the view that, at some point in the late twentieth century, rain stopped play and the halcyon days of the university lawyer were gone for good. Just a few months before his death in October 1948, W. T. S. Stallybrass delivered his Presidential Address to Society of Public Teachers of Law. He hardly set out to impress: 'I had . . . very stupidly forgotten that the President had to deliver an Address. . . . I am afraid that I never was learned and in the last two years have not had time to make myself learned and I have not had time even to write out what I am going to say. . . . I am afraid that I may be covering ground covered by older Addresses, though I have not had time to re-read them.'[1] Stallybrass's insouciance probably seems remarkable to many a modern legal academic: what in his life could have been so demanding as to prevent him, over a period of two years, from writing out a short lecture? There will also be those, nevertheless, who will consider his attitude not so much startling as enviable: how nice it would be, they will say, to inhabit his world, to be untouched by modern university culture.

In reality, of course, this world would hardly have been free of stress. Although Stallybrass seemed to take a lotus-eater's approach to his Presidential address, he was by no means completely idle: he reputedly took his teaching (and his undergraduates) very seriously, between 1928 and 1945 he edited four editions of *Salmond on Torts*, and for the last year and a half of his life he was the Vice-Chancellor at Oxford.[2] Academic lawyers before the late twen-

[1] W. T. S. Stallybrass, 'Law in the Universities' (1948) n.s. 1 *Jnl. of the Society of Public Teachers of Law* 157–69 at 157.

[2] See F. H. Lawson, *The Oxford Law School, 1850–1965* (Oxford: Clarendon Press, 1968), 129–30; H. F. J[olowicz], 'In Memoriam: W. T. S. Stallybrass' (1948) n.s. 1 *Jnl. of the Society of Public Teachers of*

tieth century would have suffered differently, and in ways not necessarily less intense, than do their modern counterparts. Even if it were possible to recapture the university world that Stallybrass inhabited—do away, first of all, with the personal computers, the central heating, and the smoking restrictions—it would most likely turn out to be somewhere that we would have done better just to remember rather than revisit.

As a jurist, Pollock would probably have coped as well today as he did in the late nineteenth and early twentieth centuries. Although it is unlikely that he would ever have become an especially engaging teacher, he produced more than his fair share of books and articles, was internationally respected, and seemed happy to turn his hand to administrative affairs. His remarkable industriousness and learning would, in any era, compensate significantly for his reserve. Whatever the prospects for a contemporary Pollock, however, it is important to emphasize that he himself was part of a world very different from that of the modern academic lawyer. Understanding his status and significance in the world that he inhabited is difficult. Pollock, we have seen, made a virtue of the notion of character. To try to understand him by emphasizing his own character, however, is to risk simplification. Without doubt, he had defining attributes: he appears always to have been assiduous, always to have loved the law, always to have been dedicated to intellectual self-improvement, always to have lacked a way with the spoken word. But if these attributes represent his character, they are hardly the measure of the man. '[T]he more closely and scrupulously you follow someone's footsteps through the past the more conscious do you become that they never existed wholly in any one place along the recorded path. . . . They are always in motion.'[3] Pollock differed from none of us in presenting more than one persona to the world: he could, for example, be snobbish or miserly or quick to quibble, just as he could be thoughtful or generous or diplomatic. Representing him requires an acknowledgement not only of those predominant personal characteristics that seem to typify his 'character', but also of those fluctuating minor traits that made him complex.

Early in this book we considered a number of Pollock's traits, and it was suggested that he may well have been trusted and admired among his peers because some of his less appealing attributes complemented his more positive ones. His reluctance to engage in frivolity and flattery and his propensity towards candour were perhaps qualities just as valuable to those seeking his advice as was his assiduousness and erudition. To enlist his help was to have seriousness and sagaciousness on one's side. This does not mean that he was ruthlessly objective. While he would often choose his words

Law 170; and Brian Simpson's short entry on Stallybrass in the *Biographical Dictionary of the Common Law*, ed. A. W. B. Simpson (London: Butterworths, 1984), 483.

[3] Richard Holmes, *Footsteps: Adventures of a Romantic Biographer* (London: HarperCollins, 1995), 69. More generally, see Paula R. Backscheider, *Reflections on Biography* (Oxford: Oxford UP, 1999), 90–124.

cautiously, he was not shy of taking sides. Those who sought him out would generally have been aware of his preferences and dislikes, and might well have gone to him knowing full well that his assessment would accord with their own. But they would also have expected any assessment he offered to be robust. His dour diligence and dry erudition, in short, seemed to elicit the sort of trust that is sometimes withheld from more charismatic figures.

There may be a suspicion that this study is a thinly disguised paean to the decidedly uncharismatic figure in the history of English legal thought, that it seeks to put on a pedestal the everyday, diligent plodder who lacks the sparkle or special quality of, say, a Holmes or a Maitland. Certainly a core argument of this book is that it is often mundane, unremitting donkey-work—the successive editions of a treatise, say, or the dripping tap of a case note campaign—that can have as deep an impact on the long-term development of the law as can the insights of any genius. It is more important to emphasize, however, that Pollock was no mediocrity. He was one of that great late nineteenth-century group of legal writers who determined, with very little in the way of indigenous precedent, what inquiry into law from an academic perspective should entail. As compared with any contemporary English academic lawyer, he was remarkably driven, creative, prolific, and bold, his interests strikingly diverse. Within the field of law there can be little he did not turn his hand to; outside of it, there is an astonishing amount to which he did. It is quite often remarked that English academic law after Pollock's era truly did lose its sparkle,[4] and if the purpose of this book were to invoke a lament then there would be a convenient one to hand: what happened to us? Why are we no longer as fascinated and intoxicated by, and eager to intellectualize, the tradition and the operation of the common law? Why have there been so few jurists since Pollock with comparable ambition and breadth?

The lament may be conveniently at hand, but it has no place in this book. Questions such as those set out above presuppose a desirable past and a relatively impoverished present. The truth is that Pollock's era produced its fair share of drones, just as there have come out of the modern English university some of the greatest legal minds. Pollock's intellectual qualities—the depth and breadth of his knowledge, his linguistic skills, his tirelessness as a legal analyst—made him different from most modern legal academics; equally, however, these qualities set him apart from many of his contemporaries. We know, moreover, that Pollock himself was not always intellectually ambitious. The decline of comparative jurisprudence in the late nineteenth century might well have been an inevitability—perhaps nobody, after Maine, could have suc-

[4] See, e.g., Brian Abel-Smith and Robert Stevens, *Lawyers and the Courts: A Sociological Study of the English Legal System, 1750–1965* (London: Heinemann, 1967), 166–8; F. H. Lawson, 'Doctrinal Writing: A Foreign Element in English Law?', in '*Ius Privatum Gentium*'. *Festschrift für Max Rheinstein zum 70. Geburtstag am 5. Juli 1969*, 2 vols., eds. E. von Caemmerer, S. Menstschikoff, and K. Zweigert (Tübingen: Mohr (Seibeck), 1969), i. 191–210 at 200 (on the 'symptoms of a general decline in the quantity and quality of mental activity among lawyers after the brilliant performance of the mid-Victorian age').

cessfully maintained the vitality of the subject—but what is certain is that Pollock achieved so little of note as a comparatist that he could hardly have helped the cause. By no means has this study sought to bemoan the passing of good times or to cast a flattering light on the past. The leading Victorian jurists, Pollock among them, did a great deal to accord law the status of a university discipline and show their successors how to conceive of law as an object of academic inquiry; it would be a mistake, however, to assume that everything the Victorians touched turned to gold.

Intellectual histories that come replete with ticks and crosses tend to arouse suspicion. At various points in this book there have been opportunities to criticize positions that Pollock adopted, or positions assumed by his critics, and occasionally these opportunities have been taken. By and large, however, this study has been more concerned with discovering just what Pollock's beliefs were, and with putting those beliefs in a context, rather than with trying to determine when he was right and when he was wrong. His contribution to jurisprudence was, it has been suggested, rather muddled and lacking in direction. Yet it has also been argued that this contribution has an historical significance which has generally been overlooked. His writings on the common law were, in comparison with his writings on jurisprudence, bold and provocative. But these writings, perhaps because they were essentially nineteenth-century reformulations of insights more commonly associated with the great common lawyers of the seventeenth and eighteenth centuries, add relatively little to the history of English legal thought. Of course, if Pollock's philosophy of the common law counted for nothing, it would not deserve our attention: the fact that he was such an accomplished and passionate defender of the common law tradition is reason enough to accord his philosophy a chapter of this book. Nevertheless, it is in the field of jurisprudence—where, as regards Pollock, there is not much evidence of either accomplishment or passion—that his legacy weighs more heavily.

Pollock's principal legacy belongs to England's juristic as opposed to its jurisprudential tradition. As a treatise writer and an editor, he did a great deal to set the tone, determine the methods, and identify the norms of modern academic-legal inquiry. He wrote treatises, articles, and case notes that—whatever ticks and crosses one might put in their margins—epitomized for many late nineteenth- and twentieth-century jurists the art of elegant and enlightened doctrinal critique. He was not, certainly by modern standards, a model academic lawyer. But as a legal scholar he was exemplary and inspirational—a juristic representative of what Max Weber called the *Rechtshonoratioren*, the eminent lawyers within any legal system who play a crucial role in its development.[5] We find in Pollock's writings no compelling conception of legal science. Those writings illustrate, none the less, that such science need not be

[5] See Max Weber, *Economy and Society: An Outline of Interpretive Sociology*, 2 vols., eds. G. Roth and C. Wittich, trans. E. Fischoff et al. (Berkeley: University of California Press, 1968 [1922]), ii. 788.

committed to the idea that law is fundamentally rational, coherent, and amenable to thorough systematization. Indeed, Pollock appreciated—as many English jurists have appreciated—that the law will sometimes, and to no obvious disadvantage, defy rationality. Neither do we discover within Pollock's writings the affirmation of any particular theory. But we do encounter his commitment to reason, his disposition towards nuance, his unwillingness to make grand claims, his talent for understated prescription, and an intimate, seemingly effortless grasp of legal systems and problems.

Pollock's works are hardly ever read today, and with good reason: his expositions of the law are generally outdated, his manner essentially antiquated. The purpose of this book is to urge not the reinstatement of his writings on reading lists but contemplation of his endeavour. With the law he never seemed ill at ease, never at a loss for words. He loved his subject, and by devoting himself to it he contributed crucially to the vocabulary of modern academic law. Pollock, it might be said, inadvertently did a great deal to define us: he is a fundamental link between the past and the present. While we may, of late, have had rather little use for him, the likelihood is that English legal thought would have unfolded differently without him. His intellectual legacy, for all its blemishes, stands as one of the major accomplishments of the English juristic tradition.

INDEX

Abdication Act 1936 79
academic law 245, 247–8, 326
  Pollock's attitude towards 52, 167
action upon the case 234–5
Addison, Charles 226, 245
Admiralty Court
  Pollock as judge of 30
Advocacy
  Pollock's lack of talent for 31–2
agreement
  as integral to contract 191
  elements of 191–2
  see also contract
Alderson, Edward 263, 265
Allen, Carleton Kemp 307
Allen v. *Flood* 274, 275–7
Alpine Club 15, 23; *see also* mountaineering
American Law Institute 195
American legal realism 80, 115, 215
Ames, James Barr 67, 206, 211–12, 213, 215, 276–7
Amos, Andrew 42
Amos, Sheldon 42–3, 44
Anderson v. *Gorrie* 69
Annan, Noel 17
anonymity 171–2, 313
Anson, William 30, 47, 52, 55, 104, 126, 187, 202, 314
anthropology
  Pollock's attitude towards 87
Aquinas, Thomas 193
Aristotle 92, 157, 176, 193, 264
Astbury, John Meir 302
Athenaeum Club 19, 24
Atiyah, Patrick 162, 177, 181–2, 185, 193, 194
Atkin, James Richard (Lord) 229, 266–9
Austin, John 3, 11, 41–3, 45, 56, 58, 83–4, 97–106, 114, 116, 120, 124, 129, 131–5, 140, 168, 238, 295
  Pollock as critic of 104–5, 117–18, 126, 138
  see also jurisprudence
Austin, John L. 99
Austin, Sarah 43

Bagehot, Walter 285
Ballantine, Henry 212–13, 214
Bankes, John Eldon (Lord) 252
Barker, Ernest 39–40, 116
Baty, Thomas 258
Beard, Charles 177
Bentham, Jeremy 58, 98, 104, 107, 114, 131, 140, 145
Besant, Walter 285
Bexwell v. *Christie* 221
Bigelow, Melville 34, 248
Bingham, Thomas (Lord) 219–20, 242
biography 325
Birkenhead, Lord, *see* Smith, F. E.
Birks, Peter 182
Blackstone, William 9–10, 17, 143, 147, 237–8, 239, 246
  tort law and 229–32
Bluntschli, Johann Caspar 44
Blyth v. *Birmingham Waterworks* 263, 265
Bodin, Jean 104
Bowen, Charles 273, 274
Bradford v. *Pickles* 274, 275, 278–9
Brandeis, Louis 77
Brett, William Balliol (Lord Esher) 168, 263–4, 269, 274
Bridge, Michael 219
Briggs, Isaac 224
British Academy 24
  Pollock as one of first Fellows of 19, 23
Brougham, Henry Peter (Lord) 259
Brownsword, Roger 222–3
Bryce, James 2, 23, 25, 52, 56, 62–3, 104–5, 135
Buckland, William 97–8, 264, 314
Buller, Francis 229–30, 269
Burke, Edmund 39–40, 113, 144, 155, 156
Burlamaqui, Jean-Jacques 230
Burrow, John 90–1, 113, 116–17

Cambridge Conversazione Society, *see* Cambridge University Apostles
Cambridge University
  Apostles 14–15, 21, 24, 47, 121, 313; Pollock's donations to 82
  law school 17–18
  Trinity College 14, 24
Carter v. *Boehm* 221
case law 122–4
case notes 316–22
Castletown, Clare 34
causation 244
Chalmers, Mackenzie Dalzell 27
chance 150
character 7, 37–41, 83, 325
  English 149–50
civil liberties
  Pollock and 55–6
Civil Wrongs Bill (India) 25, 270–1
Clark, E. C. 101
Cliffe Leslie, T. E. 101
Clifford, William Kingdon 17, 62, 95
  predictivism and 121–2
Coke, Edward 25–9, 127, 128, 145–6, 147, 232
Coleridge, John Duke (Lord) 27
Collini, Stefan 39, 90–1, 113, 116–17, 135, 147–8, 155, 186–7
command theory of law 43, 98, 99, 120, 126; *see also* jurisprudence
common employment 260
common law 66–7, 107, 126, 142, 280
  character and 40
  custom and 143–4
  English character and 150–4, 155–6, 206
  legislation and 181–2
  monopoly and 178–9
  nature of 8
  Pollock on economic philosophy of 177–80
  Pollock's philosophy of 8, 40, 152–4, 173–4
  see also common sense; principle
common sense 196, 224, 244, 320
  as contested concept 160
  common law and 158–9
  natural justice and 158
  reason and 157–8
comparative law 111–12
consideration 9
  causa and 205–6
  derived from pre-existing duty, Pollock on 210–11
  mutual promises as 212–14
  Pollock's and Holmes's shared view of 209
  Pollock's and Langdell's shared view of 209–10
  Pollock's attitude towards 203–7
  Pollock's definition of 206–8
  see also contract law; Wright, Robert Alderson
contract
  definition of 190
  as promise 201
  will theory of 192–4;
  see also contract law; Savigny, Friedrich Carl von
contract law 187, 189–224
  acceptance in 201–2
  consideration in 195, 202
  frustration and 198–200
  good faith in, Pollock and 195
  implied conditions and 198–9
  mistake and 196–7
  Pollock and 9
  reliance interest in 194, 197–8, 217
conveyancing
  Pollock's difficulty with 21
Cooley, Thomas 237–8, 239
Corbin, Arthur L. 195
Cory, William 35
Cosgrove, Richard 141
cosmos 86
Couch, Richard 242–3
Council of Law Reporting 294–6
Council of Legal Education 51
Courtenay, W. L. 124
Cranworth Commission 26–7
critical reverence 100–2
custom
  immemorial 146
  see also common law

damnum sine injuria 272
Dartmoor 17
Darwin, Charles 48–9, 113
declaratory theory of law 168
  Pollock's ambivalence over 168–9
Delane, John T. 284
Denning, Alfred (Lord) 139, 189, 254, 306, 323
Derry v. *Peek* 316–18
Dewey, John 100, 107, 112
Dicey, Albert Venn 3, 11, 46, 52, 57, 67, 126, 135
  elected to Vinerian Chair over Pollock 47–8
  Home Rule and 56
  military law and 55
  as public moralist 186
  socialism and 175
  trade unionism and 175–6
disciplinary boundaries
  Pollock's general disinterest in 117
Donoghue v. *Stevenson* 266–7, 269
Dunlop v. *Selfridge* 207, 225
duty 60, 221
  English character and 154
  Pollock's attitude towards 155
duty of care 229, 262–9; *see also* negligence

Dworkin, Ronald 140, 142, 162–3, 250–1
integrity in adjudication and 164–5
principles and, compared with Pollock 162–5

Eastwood, R. A. 101
Edinburgh Review 285, 286
editing
influence and 288
Pollock's enthusiasm for 287–8
in Victorian era 284–7
Eliot, Charles 67
Elphinstone, Howard 21, 314
Englishness 148–51, 154
and common law 155–6
English Reports 289
equity 159
Pollock's attitude towards 20–1
Esher, Lord, *see* Brett, William Balliol
external standards 127, 157–8, 256–7
Pollock's adaptation of Holmes on 119–20, 123–5
see also Holmes, Oliver Wendell, Jr.

fencing 15, 16, 89
Fifoot, Cecil 36, 86–7, 95, 140, 189, 190–1, 258, 260, 261
'Fight for Right' movement 23
Pollock's support for 2
Finch, Henry 143
Flood v. *Jackson* 274, 275, 278
Foakes v. *Beer* 218
foreseeability 251–2
forms of action 232–5
Fortescue, John 147
Fowler, Thomas 55
Fowler v. *Lanning* 254
Frazer, James 87
Freeman, E. A. 55
freemasonry
Pollock and 15
friendships
Pollock and 17–19, 31–7
Froude, J. A. 55
Fuller, Lon L. 217

Geertz, Clifford 160, 180
Gény, François 38
Gifford, Hardinge Stanley (Lord Halsbury) 318–19
Goff, Robert (Lord) 182
good faith 9, 215–24
definitions of 221–2
see also contract law
Goodhart, Arthur L. 4, 36, 40–1, 126, 140, 194–5, 196, 204, 215, 253, 268, 271–2, 304, 305
as Corpus Professor of Jurisprudence 139
on law reporting 308–9

Gorrie, John 68–70
Goudy, Henry 51
Gray, John Chipman 89, 314
Grotius, Hugo 230
Gutteridge, H. C. 304–5

habit 147–50
of mind 126–7, 147–8
Hacking, Ian 161–2
Haldane, Richard Burdon (Viscount) 312, 317–18
Hale, Matthew 40, 143
Halsbury, Lord, *see* Gifford, Hardinge Stanley
Hanbury, Harold G. 55
Hanworth, Lord, *see* Pollock, Ernest Murray
Hardwicke, Lord, *see* Yorke, Philip
Harris, Jose 39
Harrison, Frederic 136, 137
Hart, H. L. A. 98–9, 131, 163, 250–1
Harvard Law Review 67
Harvard Law School 64, 237
Pollock at 32–3, 64–5, 67
Harvey, C. P. 154
Harvie, Christopher 132–3
Hayek, Friedrich 173, 272
Haynes, Edmund Sydney Pollock 31, 35–5
Hazeltine, Harold D. 2, 63, 188
Heaven v. *Pender* 263, 265, 268
Hedley, Steve 169–70, 303
Hedley, Thomas 146
Hemming, G. W. 296, 301
Henry, Alexander 45
Heyck, T. W. 60
Hillas v. *Arcos* 305
historical method 113–14, 118
historical perspective 161–2, 282
historical school 23; *see also* Savigny, Friedrich Carl von
Hobbes, Thomas 58, 96, 104, 105, 210
Hohfeld, Wesley Newcomb 88, 109, 179
Holdsworth, William 35, 141, 188, 314
Holland, Thomas Erskine 28, 43, 52, 101, 105, 126, 129, 280, 310–11, 314
Holmes, Oliver Wendell, Jr. 3, 9–10, 15, 17, 19, 22, 34, 50, 86, 90, 108, 113, 118, 237–8, 239, 240, 254, 272–3, 274, 275, 291, 310, 326
external standards of liability and 119, 256
Pollock and 25–6, 34–5, 38, 81, 208–9
prediction theory and 119–21, 123–4
Home Rule
Pollock's attitude towards 57, 155
Horwitz, Morton 130–1

Ibbetson, David 229–30, 263
Ilbert, Courtenay Peregrine 25–6
income 288
attributable to Pollock 10, 289–94
see also royalties

industrial accidents
and liability claims 225–6
inevitable accident 241, 253–4
Inns of Court
Pollock as professor at 50–1, 247, 290–1
insurance law 220
intentional torts 270–9
Pollock's conception of 239
see also malicious use
international law 96, 128–9
Pollock's conception of 106

Jackson, Henry 294
James, William 86, 108
Jann, Rosemary 60, 62
Jeffrey, Francis 285
Jenks, Edward 314
Jevons, W. S. 136
Jhering, Rudolph von 125
journalism 18
Joyce, Matthew 301
judicial function 164
principle and 165–6
judicial language
Pollock's editing of 302–3
judicial valour 267
jurisprudence 247
analytical 7–8, 99–100, 129, 130–1, 244–5
late Victorian university culture and 90, 131–5
Pollock's view of 58, 89, 102–6, 106–10, 117
censorial 98
Corpus Chair of, Pollock and 7, 49–50, 54–5, 59–60, 88–9, 139–40, 293–4
evolutionary 112–13, 116
expository 98
general 98, 110, 140
historical and comparative 7–8, 48–9, 134–7
late Victorian university culture and 90–1
Pollock's dislike of Roscoe Pound's approach to 114–15
Pollock's endorsement of Maine's approach to 102–3
Pollock's general preference for 109–16
natural law, Pollock and 107
Pollock's general attitude towards 7–8, 44, 88–9, 91, 140, 201
positivist 99
purpose of, according to Pollock 128
juristic elegance 129–30
juristic influence 184–5, 246–7, 261–2, 281, 283, 327–8
Pollock and 188–9
Victorian 186–7
juristic speculation
legal authority and 141, 168–9

jurists
as public intellectuals 185–6
as public moralists 186–7
see also juristic influence

Kafka, Franz 233–4
Kelsen, Hans 184–5
Kennedy, Duncan 231
Kenny, C. S. 54
Kent, James 297
Kipling, Rudyard 19
Knowles, James 285
Knox, John 75
Kramer, Matthew 250
Krieger, Leonard 230–1

Lamarck, Jean-Baptiste 147–8
Lamb, William (Lord Melbourne) 84
Landon, Philip 278, 282–3
Langdell, Christopher Columbus 64–6, 167, 209, 214, 215, 281, 303
mutual promises and 213
will theory of contract and 195–6
see also legal formalism; legal science
Langford, Paul 154
languages
learning, Pollock's skill at 16
Laski, Harold 32, 36–7, 56
Lauterpacht, Hersch 96, 189
law and economics 177
Law Quarterly Review 1, 11, 16, 30, 36, 40, 68, 117, 166–7, 188, 253, 287–8, 295, 309–22
anonymity of case notes in 171–2
early reception of 311–13
Pollock's contributions to 314–16
polymath quality of early volumes of 313–14
Law Reports 6, 10–11, 54, 67, 68, 77, 287–8, 294–309
head notes in 295–6
Indian 77, 297–8
Pollock appointed editor of 296–7
Pollock's criticisms of 295–6
Pollock's editing of 298–306
Pollock retires from 79
problem of unreported cases and 306–8
law reviews
American 310
in Victorian England 311
Lawson, F. H. 32, 53
law teaching
Pollock and 53
League of Nations 23, 187
Pollock's support for 2, 72–5
Leake, Stephen 189, 190
legal authority 144, 145
works of living authors and 144–5
see also juristic influence

legal education
  Pollock's attitude towards 63–4
legal formalism 167, 215, 281–2
  Pollock and 239–46
legal history 128, 129
  Pollock's contribution to 5, 188
legal scholarship
  professionalization of 7, 60–1
  see also scholarship
legal science 246–7
  comparative jurisprudence and 118
  Langdellian 65–6
  Pollock's conception of 61–2, 84, 90, 97, 106, 116–27
legislation 142, 279–80
  Pollock's attitude towards 169–74
L'Estrange v. *Graucob* 305–6
liability
  strict 255–7
  vicarious 257–62
  see also industrial accidents; negligence; tort law
Lincoln's Inn
  Pollock as Treasurer of 78
  Pollock's work at 20–1, 24, 29
Lindley, Nathaniel 21–2, 314
Lloyd George, David 176
Lobban, Michael 97, 125
Locke, John 58
London Tramways v. *London County Council* 318–19
Loreburn, Lord, *see* Reid, Robert
Lyall, Alfred Comyn 26

McCardie, Henry 261–2, 301
MacCormick, Neil 140
MacDonald, Ramsay 131, 175–6
Machiavelli, Niccolò 96
McKendrick, Ewan 216
Macmillan & Co. 82
Macmillan, Hugh Pattison (Lord) 266–7, 269
Macaulay, Thomas Babbington 25
Maine, Henry 3, 7, 8, 15, 18, 23, 26, 48–9, 52, 53–4, 90, 91, 102, 112–13, 116, 118, 134–8, 292, 326
  as jurisprudence professor at Oxford 110–11
  as public moralist 186
  Maitland's reservations about work of 114
  resignation from Corpus Chair 46–7
Maitland, Ella Fuller 34
Maitland, Florence 34
Maitland, Frederic William 3, 11, 15, 19–20, 23, 47, 54, 81–2, 114, 116–17, 125, 187, 233, 294, 326
malicious use 270–1, 274–5
Malthus, Thomas 38
Mansfield, Lord, *see* Murray, William
Markby, William 52, 69, 310
May & Butcher v. *The King* 304–5
Melbourne, Lord, *see* Lamb, William
Meredith, George 32
Metaphysical Club 121
Metaphysical Society 15, 17, 18
Mill, John Stuart 100, 132, 285
Milsom, S. F. C. 133, 233
Milton, John 17
Mogul Steamship Co. v. *McGregor* 273
Monroe Doctrine 71
  Pollock's interpretation of 71–2
Montesquieu, Charles de Secondat, Baron de 113, 152, 168
morality 98, 238–9
  as distinct from law 124–5
Morgan, Edmund M. 33
Mossolov, Alexandre 85
mountaineering 16, 23, 89
Mulla, Dinshah 77
Murray, William (Lord Mansfield) 8–9, 146–7, 163–4, 220–1
  attitude towards consideration 202–4
mutual promises 9, 213–14; *see also* consideration
mysticism
  Pollock and 92–4

natural law 9
  tort law and 228–32
  see also jurisprudence
natural selection
  Pollock's attitude towards 75
negligence 242, 244–5, 256–7, 262–9; *see also* tort law
nervous shock 242–4
Nineteenth Century 285, 286
Nocton v. *Ashburton* 317–18
normativity 165, 219–20, 251–70, 282
nutshells 52, 224–5

Oakeshott, Michael 127
Oko, Adolph 78–9
Oxford University 59
  Corpus Christi College, Pollock at 55, 59, 291
  jurisprudence at 135
  Pollock as jurisprudence professor at 47–50, 52–61, 62–4, 291–2
  Pollock on undergraduates at 53, 63
  Roman law at 23

pantheism 92, 95
Parke, James (Baron) 159
Partnership Act 1890 279
Partnership Bill 279, 293
partnership law 27, 279–80
Pearson, Karl 62
Perdue, William 217
periodicals
  scholarly, growth of in Victorian era 287

philosophy
Pollock's attitude towards 85–7, 89, 109–10
physical fitness
Pollock and 15–16
Pocock, J. G. A. 40
politics 142
Pollock and 57, 174–80
Pollock, Alice 14
Pollock, Ernest Murray (Lord Hanworth) 20, 32, 36
Pollock, Frederick *passim*
Pollock, Georgina 14, 38, 86
death of 78–9
Pollock, John 2, 14, 79
Pollock, Jonathan Frederick 20, 29, 252
Pollock, Walter Herries 18, 286
Pollock, William Frederick 13, 22
possession 109
Postema, Gerald 157
Pothier, Robert Joseph 192–3, 245
Pound, Roscoe 31, 181, 114–15
Powell, F. Y. 55
Powell, Raphael 222–3
pragmatism 108, 240
prediction theory
Pollock's adaptation of 119–25
Pollock's conception of legal science and 120
see also Holmes, Oliver Wendell, Jr.
presentism 161, 224
principle 128, 141–2, 182
common law and 152, 188
contract law and 190
history and 191, 251
debate over, in jurisprudence 250–1
judicial function and 165–6
meanings of, for Pollock 249–50
neighbour 229, 264–9; *see also* duty of care
Pollock as expositor of 165–7, 192, 225–6, 249–70, 280, 320
reason and 167
restraint and 162
soundness and 164–5
tort law and 248–69
see also common sense; judicial function; reason
Principles of Contract 189–202, 204–14, 216–19, 224–5; *see also* contract law
Privy Council
Pollock admitted to 30
property law 241–2
Proust, Marcel 81
public moralism 1–2
Pollock and 187
Victorian jurists and 186–7
public ownership
Pollock on disadvantages of 176–7
Pufendorf, Samuel 229, 230
Pugsley, David 318–19

quasi-contracts 200
Queen Victoria 39
Quinn v. *Leathem* 276

Rabelais Club 15
Raleigh, Thomas 105
rationality 237
reason 93, 95, 142, 156
common law and 145–7
common sense and 157–8
law of nature and 107–8, 156
principle and 157, 167
reasonable expectation 194–5, 197–8, 200, 209, 216–17, 218, 220–1; *see also* contract law; good faith
reasoned elaboration 320–1
rectitude 127–30
Reid, Robert (Lord Loreburn) 198
Renan, Ernest 62
Re Polemis 252–3
restitution 200–1
Revised Reports 289–91
Pollock's editing of 68
rights 231
Pollock and 88, 16–17, 163
Dworkin and 163
Roman law 9, 205, 220, 222, 228, 264
Pollock as student of 22–3, 251
see also Oxford University
Romanticism 92
Rookes v. *Barnard* 277
Round, J. H. 136–7
Rouse Ball, W. W. 290
Rousseau, Jean-Jacques 86
Royal Commission on Labour
Pollock as member of 68
Royal Commission on Public Records 293
Pollock's chairing of 76
royalties 288
Pollock's attitude towards 81–2
Pollock's, from books 292–3
Russell, Bertrand 86, 160
Rylands v. *Fletcher* 254–7, 258, 279

Sainctelette, Charles 260
St German, Christopher 21, 107, 147, 156
Salmond, John 314
Sankey, John (Lord) 78
Santayana, George 86, 111
Saturday Review 285–6
Savigny, Friedrich Carl von 23, 113, 120, 150–1, 189, 190–1, 245, 281
explanation of will theory 192
Schiller, F. C. S. 55, 108
scholarship 127–30
as craft, Pollock's view of 128–9
professionalization of 132–3

scientific naturalism 62
Scott, Leslie 32
Seeley, J. R. 66
Selden Society
  Pollock's directorship of 76
Shakespeare, William 17, 313
Shaw, George Bernard 19
Shaw, Lemuel 259–60
Sidgwick, Henry 3–4, 133, 136–7
Simmonds, Nigel 228, 232
Simon, John 79
Simpson, Brian 144, 145, 281
Smith, F. E. (Lord Birkenhead) 31
social contract 116
socialism
  Pollock's attitude towards 176–7
  Victorians and 175
  see also Dicey, Albert Venn
Societas Spinoza
  Pollock as curator of 76
  see also Spinoza, Benedict
Soffer, Reba 132
Sorabji, Cornelia 36
Spinoza, Benedict 33, 62, 85, 89, 92–7
Stallybrass, W. T. S. 188, 324
Stapleton, Julia 186
state 126
Stein, Peter 228
Stephen, James Fitzjames 3, 15, 26–8, 100, 113
  as public moralist 186
Stephen, Leslie 17–18, 19, 26, 36, 56, 122
Stevens & Sons 289
Stone, Arthur 299–300
Strachey, Lytton 17, 18, 126, 173
Stubbs, William 55, 113
Sugarman, David 61, 281–2
Sumner, W. G. 87
Sunday Tramps 16, 18, 24
Surrey 17, 19
Sweet & Maxwell 289
synthesis 190–1, 226

Taft, William Howard 73
Thayer, James B. 33
The Law of Torts 225–7, 235–49, 251–2, 254, 256–61, 263–73, 276–9, 282–3; *see also* tort law
theory
  Pollock's aversion to 88, 108, 115, 137
Tomlin, Thomas (Lord) 281
tort law 9–10, 224–79
  Pollock's effort to unify 226–7, 236–48
Trade Disputes Act 1906 175–6, 179
trade unionism 175–6; *see also* Dicey, Albert Venn
treatise writing 245–6, 279–81
  Pollock and 8–9, 67–8, 187–9
  Victorian jurists and 232–3
trespass 227–8, 234–5
Trevelyan, G. M. 32
Trinidad
  Pollock's work in 68–70
Trollope, Anthony 284
Twining, William 85, 140

uberrima fides 220–1
Underhill, Evelyn 92
United States of America 17
  Pollock lecturing in 66
University College London
  Pollock as jurisprudence professor at 41–6, 55, 290
unjust enrichment 200
utilitarianism 114

van Caenegem, R. C. 184
Vegelahn v. *Guntner* 275
Venezuela and Guiana
  boundary dispute between, Pollock and 70–1
Victorian Railways Commissioners v. *Coultas* 242–4
Vinogradoff, Paul 49, 54, 90, 91, 111, 118, 159–60, 314

Wagner, Richard 17
Watson, William (Lord) 278
Weber, Max 327
White, G. Edward 246, 247
Willes, James Shaw 20, 22, 258
Williams, Glanville 134
Williams, T. Cyprian 312, 314
Williston, Samuel 32, 36, 195, 210–14
will theory 9
  difficulties with 194
  Pollock's attitude towards 194–201
  see also contract; contract law; Savigny, Friedrich Carl von
Winch, Donald 90–1, 113, 116–17
Winfield, Percy 141, 195
Wittgenstein, Ludwig 99
Wright, Robert Alderson (Lord) 77, 170, 188–9, 198
  on consideration 204–5, 206
Wright, Robert Samuel 82, 241, 292

Yorke, Philip (Lord Hardwicke) 20
Younghusband, Francis 2, 23

The manufacturer's authorised representative in the EU for product safety is Oxford University Press España S.A. of El Parque Empresarial San Fernando de Henares, Avenida de Castilla, 2 - 28830 Madrid (www.oup.es/en or product.safety@oup.com). OUP España S.A. also acts as importer into Spain of products made by the manufacturer.
Printed and bound by CPI Group (UK) Ltd, Croydon, CR0 4YY
14/09/2026
02216286-0007